MARC JOSEPH

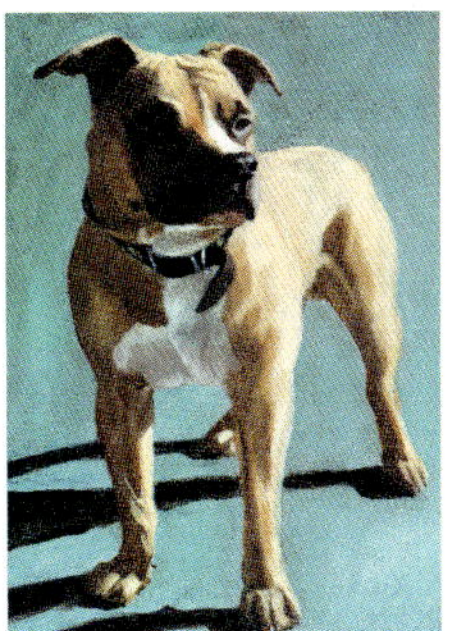

represented by

maverick**artist**
Chelsea Arts Building
134 W. 26th St. Suite 740 NYC 10001
212.367.0977 / info@maverickartist.com

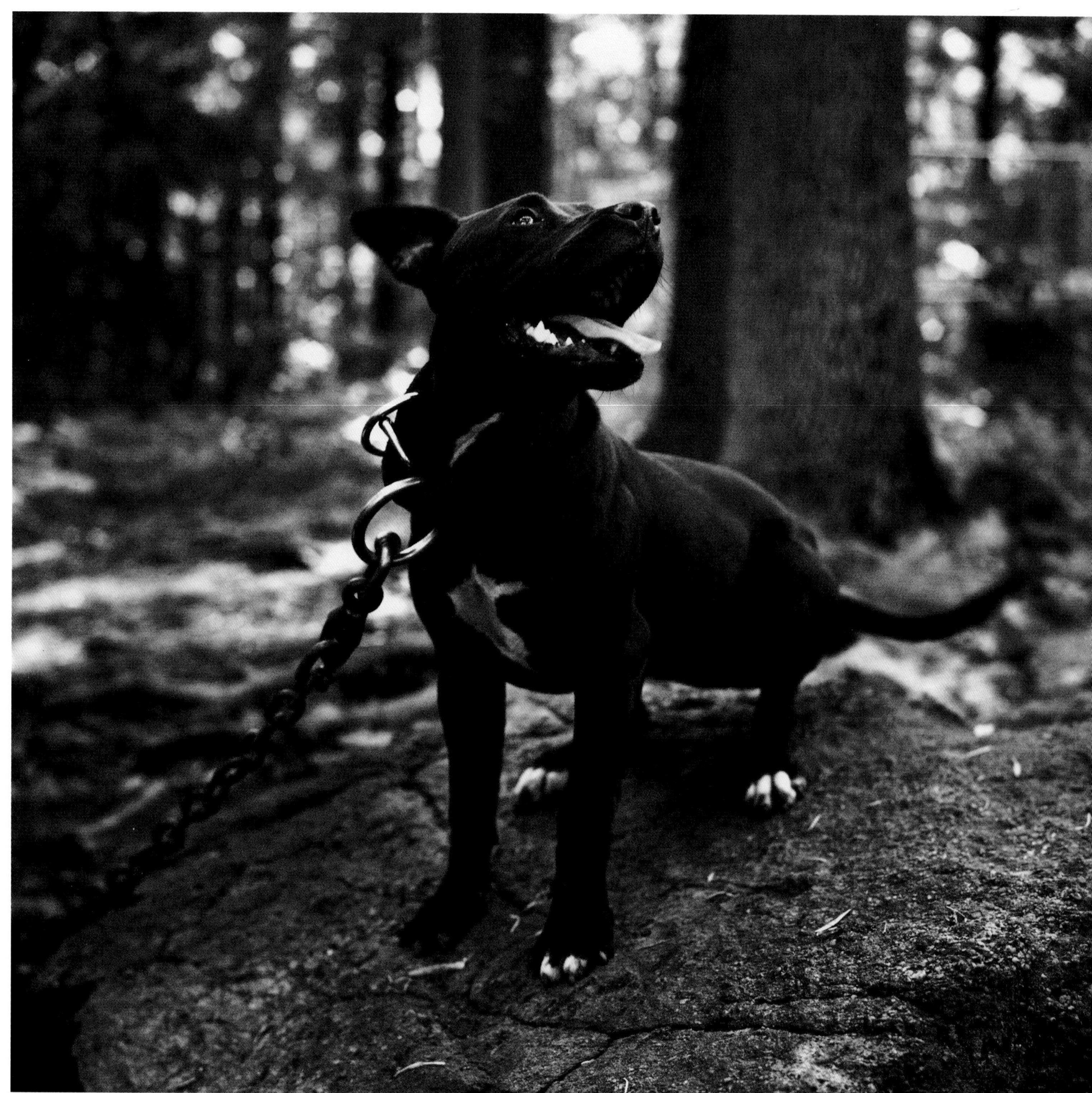

MARC JOSEPH AMERICAN PITBULL

ESSAY: JAMES FREY INTERVIEWS: CORY REYNOLDS

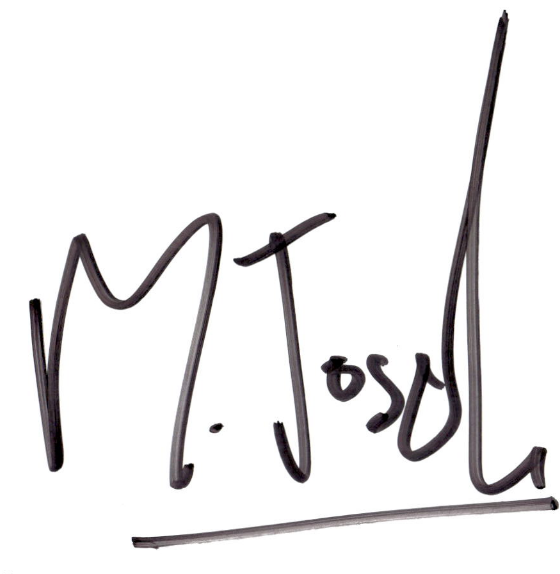

STEIDL

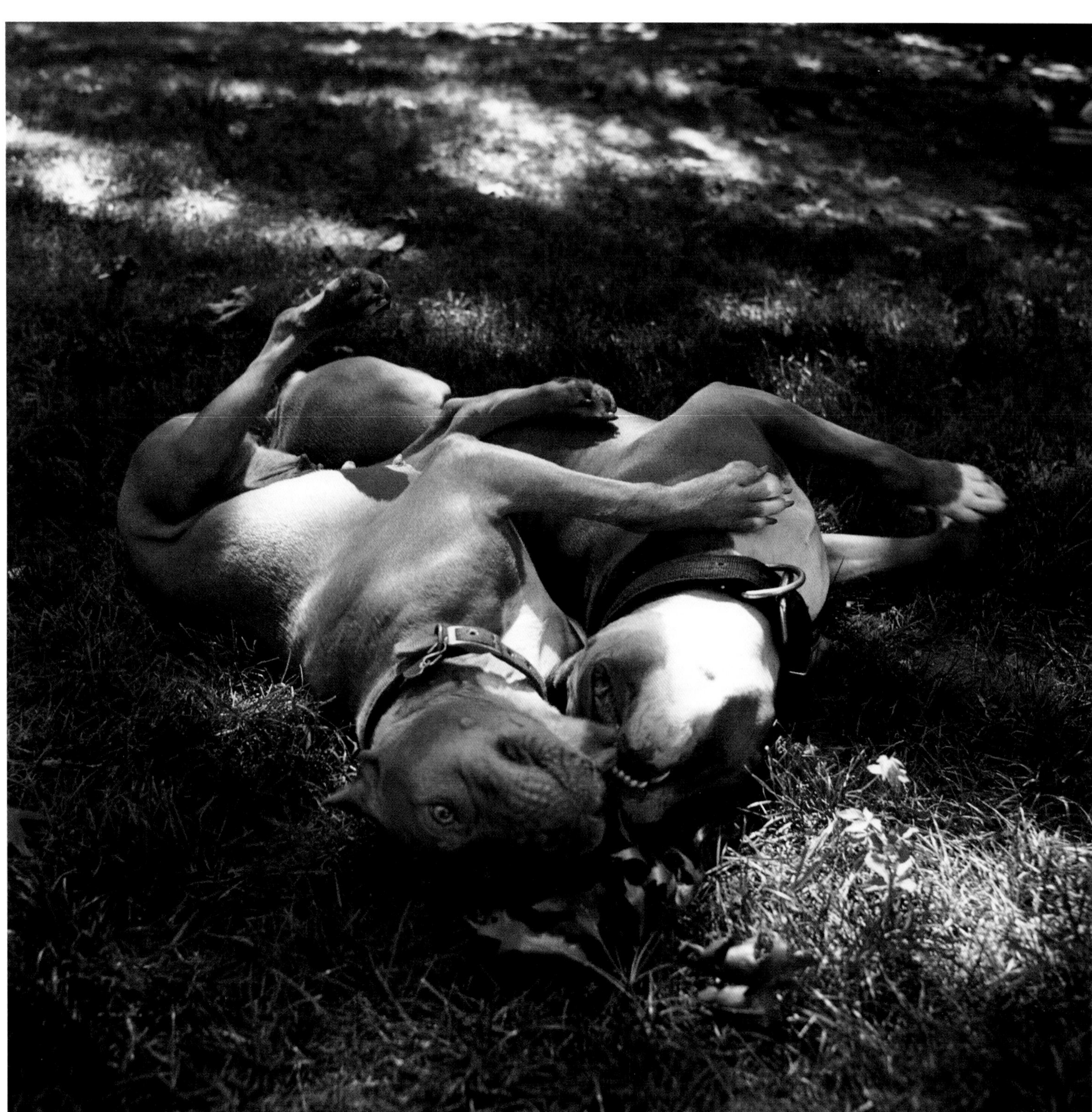

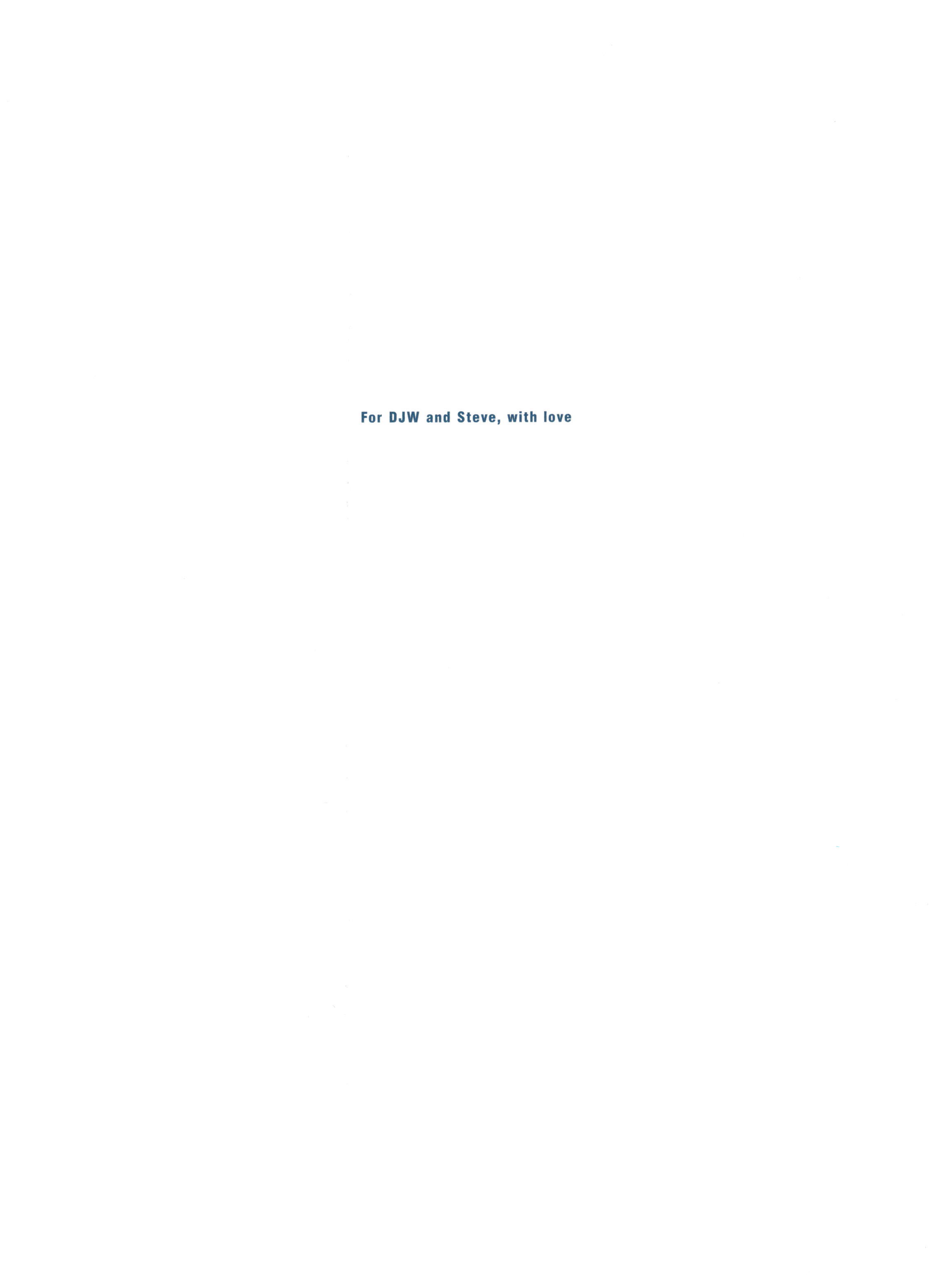

For DJW and Steve, with love

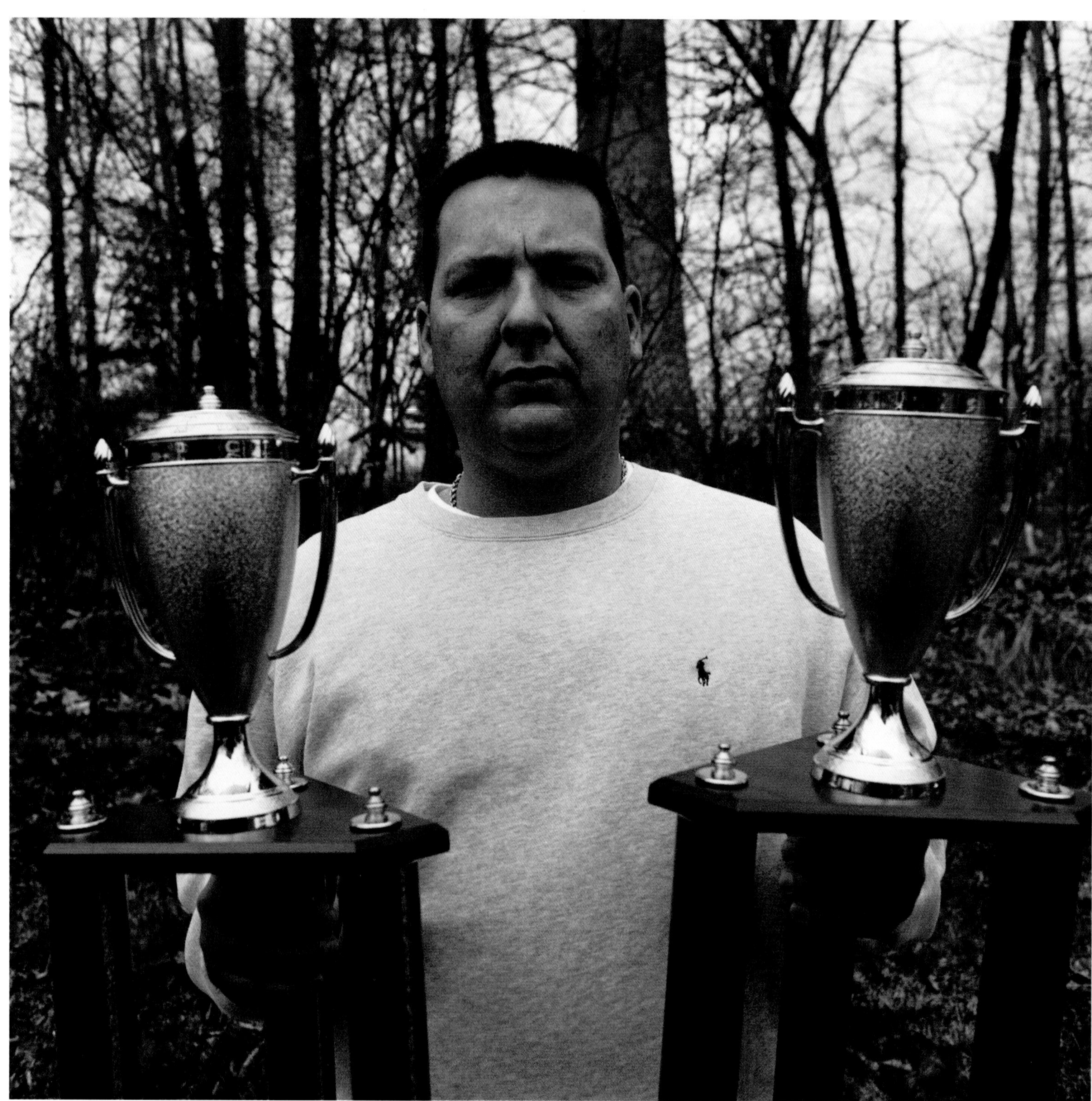

Let's see a show of hands.
I want to know. Who among us—
    man, woman, or beast—
Lives by a code.
Be it of good or evil, it matters not.
But I want to know: who's strong, who's tough.
I want to go back to Homeric days.

NICK TOSCHES from Invocation

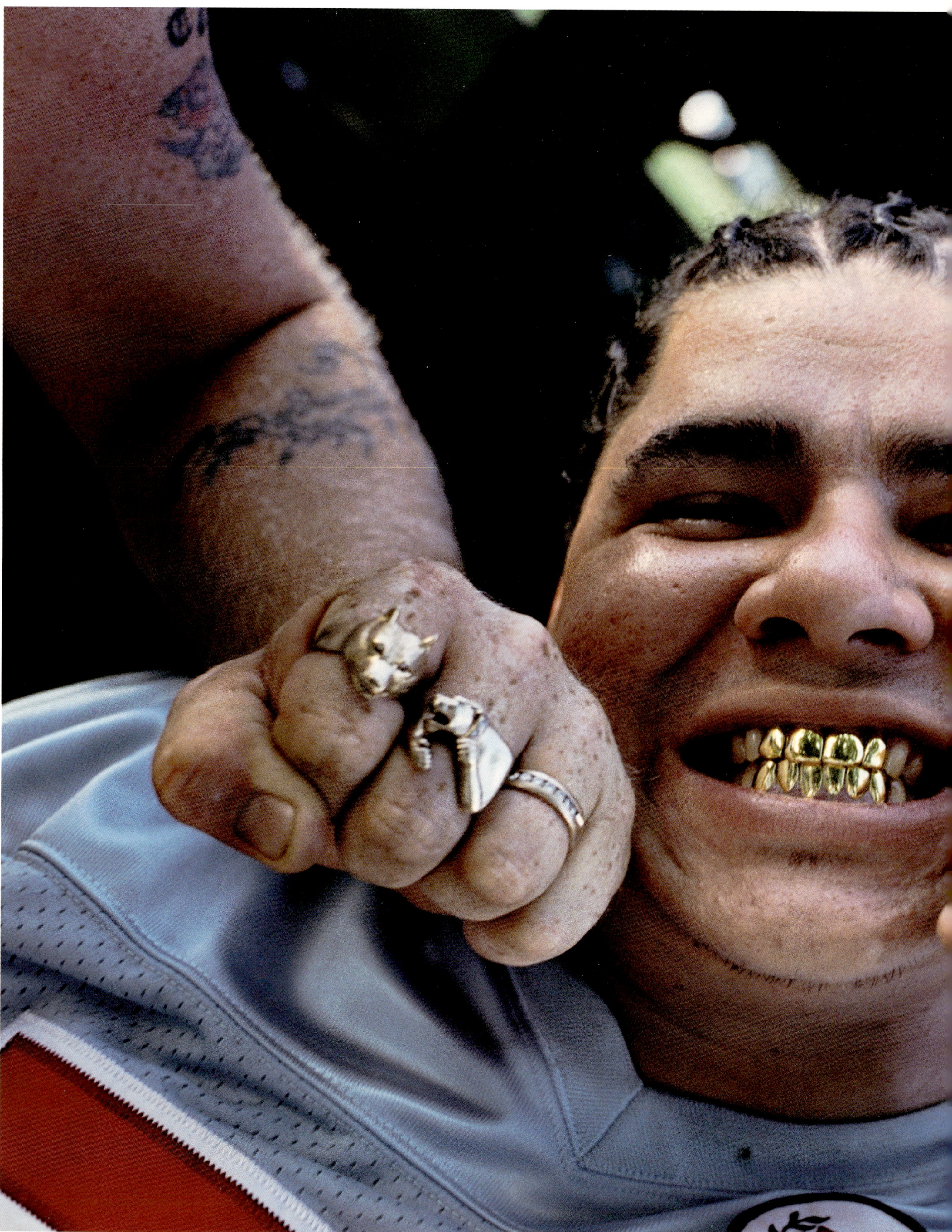

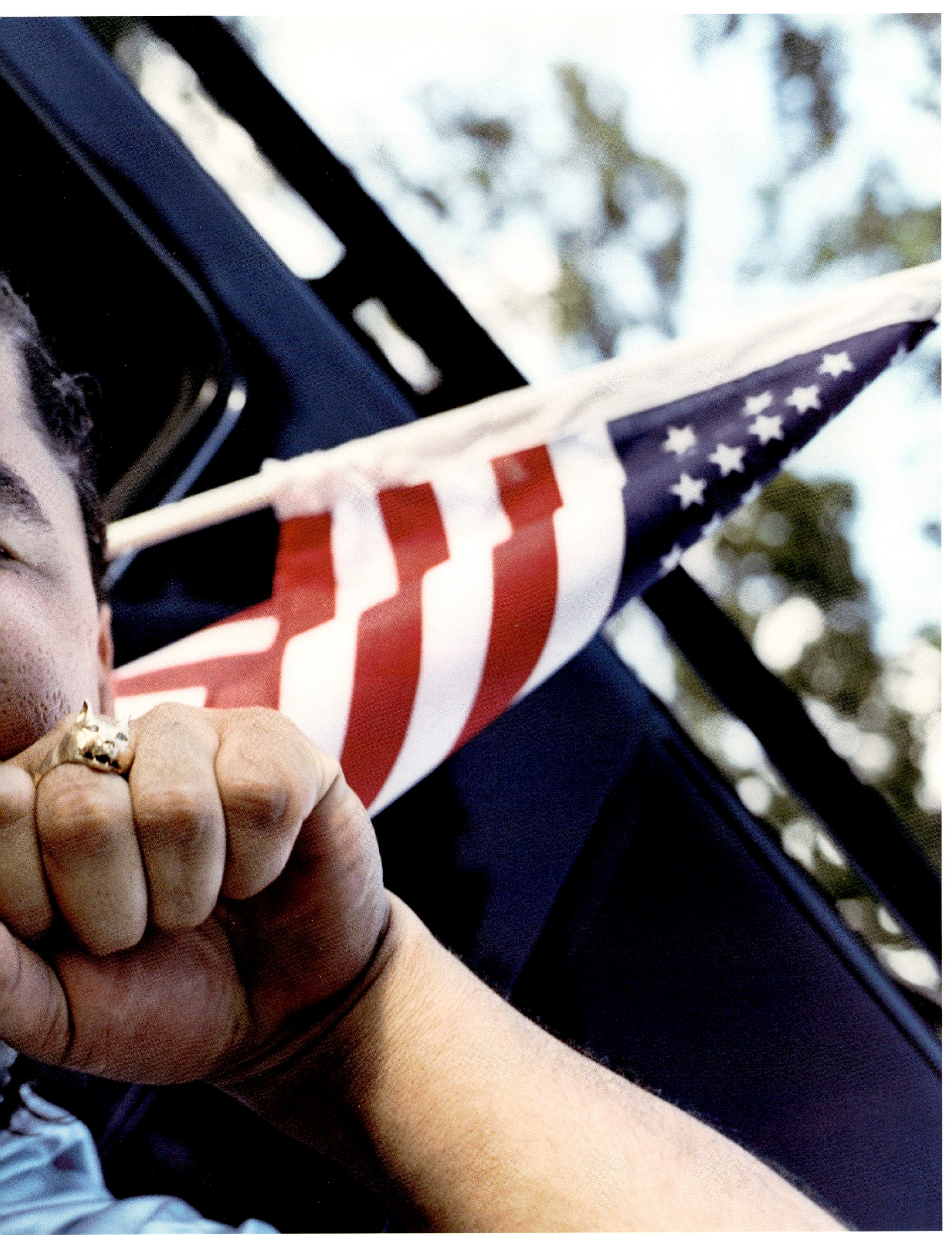

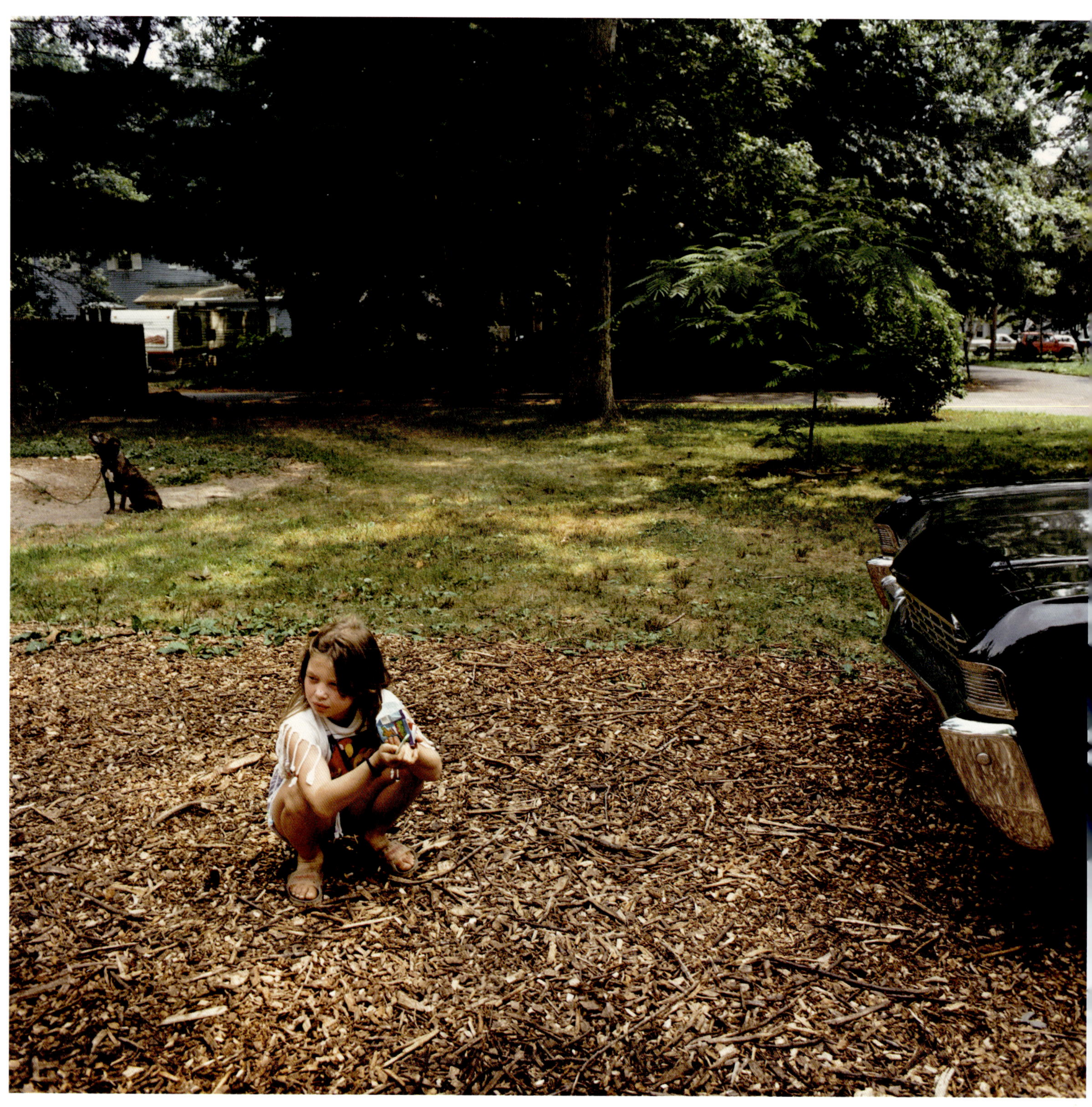

If you love something and others fear the thing you love, do you love it more?
Do you also love their fear?
If the thing you love is hated and reviled by others, do you feel stronger?
Does the hate and fear they feel strengthen you?

Our neighbors on Mott Street knew and loved my Bulldog, Rudy, but some people who didn't know us were actually a little afraid of him, which, on the surface, was so funny—he was such a clumsy, lazy, forty-eight-pound doofus. No fire at all, really, except if some neighborhood dog barked at him like crazy from across the street, or if an off-the-leash dog came up and goosed him from behind—that always pissed us off. Quietly, the hair on his back would stand up, and he'd be on point, ready to go. It never went anywhere, though. He'd usually get distracted by someone coming up to us to give him a pat on the back. His tank-wide chest and big old head were a bit too much for him to negotiate, but he was all muscle and love. Climbing up and down the stairs of the fifth-floor walk-up where we lived was his workout. I lost him after nine-and-a-half years, one month after I started to make these pictures—something called cardiomyopathy. His heart got too big.

I've come to learn just how strongly people can feel about certain things that are an important part of their lives—especially the Bulldogs—and how these things seem to shape almost everything about the way they are, and the way they choose to live (down in the beautiful Big Thicket and everywhere else). Hundreds of rolls of film, over ten thousand miles travelled, and I still could have kept on going. Sometimes it was hard to come home. It was even harder to get my head around the idea of ever finishing. The photographs in this book, taken over the past three years, of my Bulldog friends and their dogs, only begin to express my love for the time I've had and my holy wonder with it all.

MARC JOSEPH September 2003

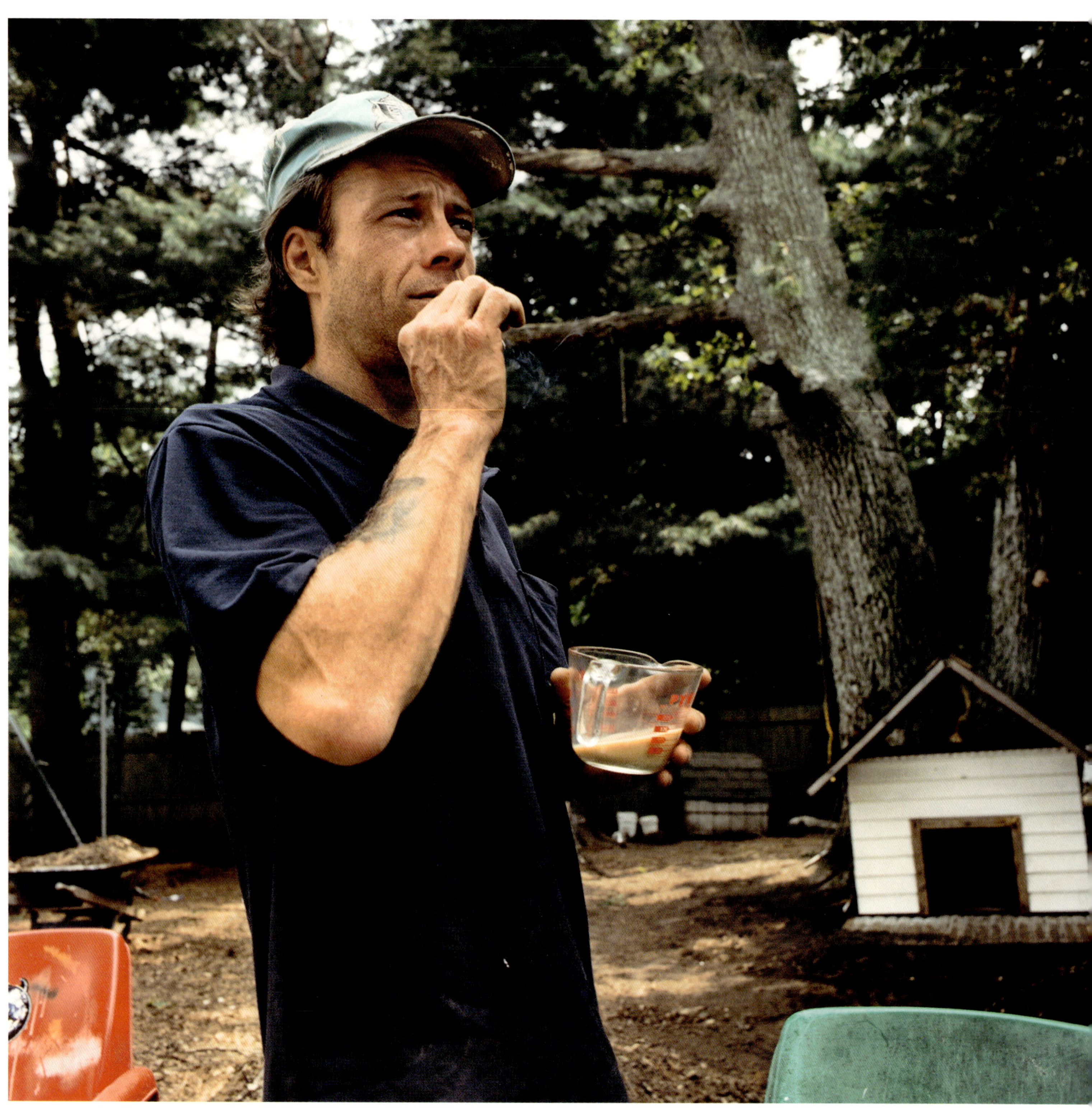

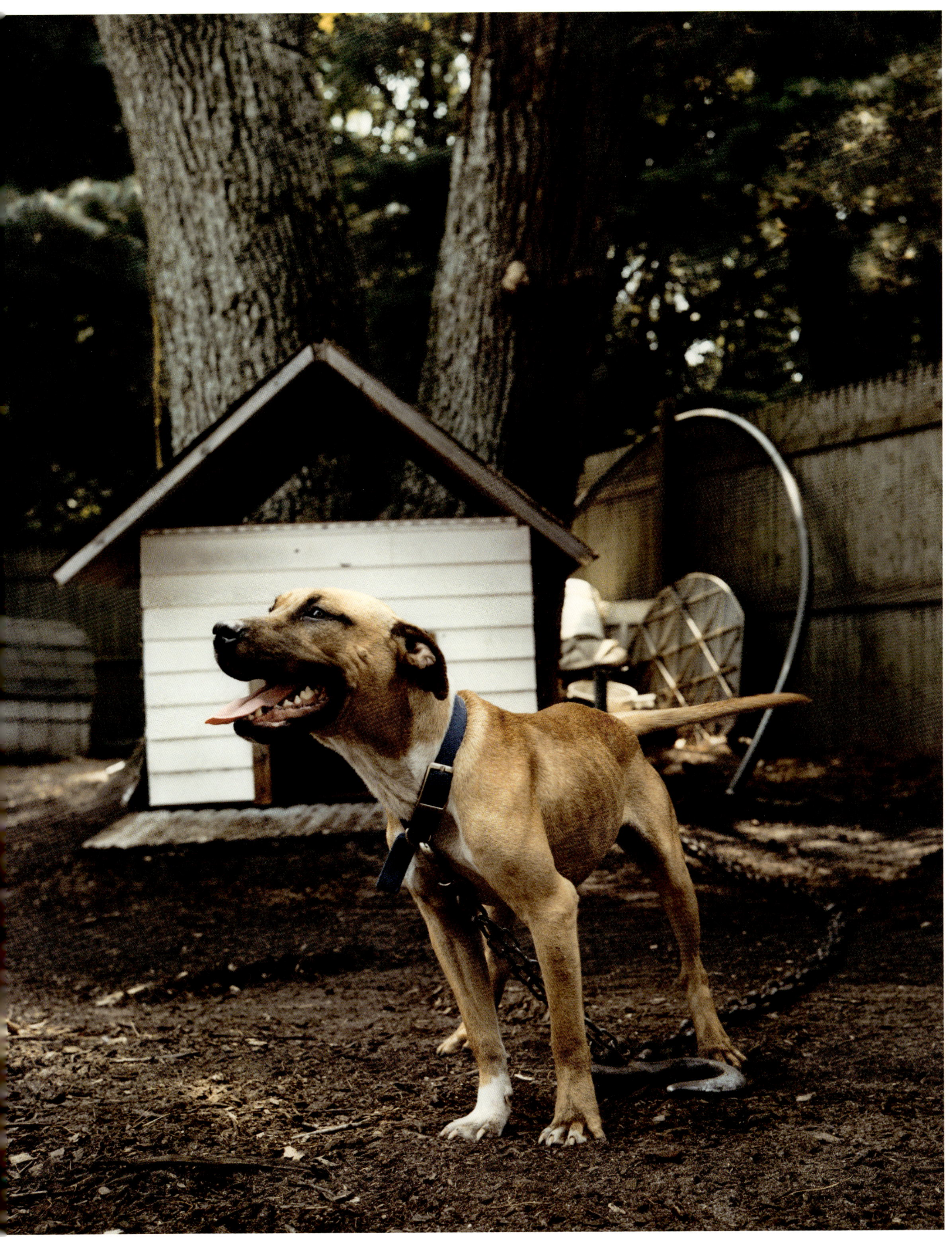

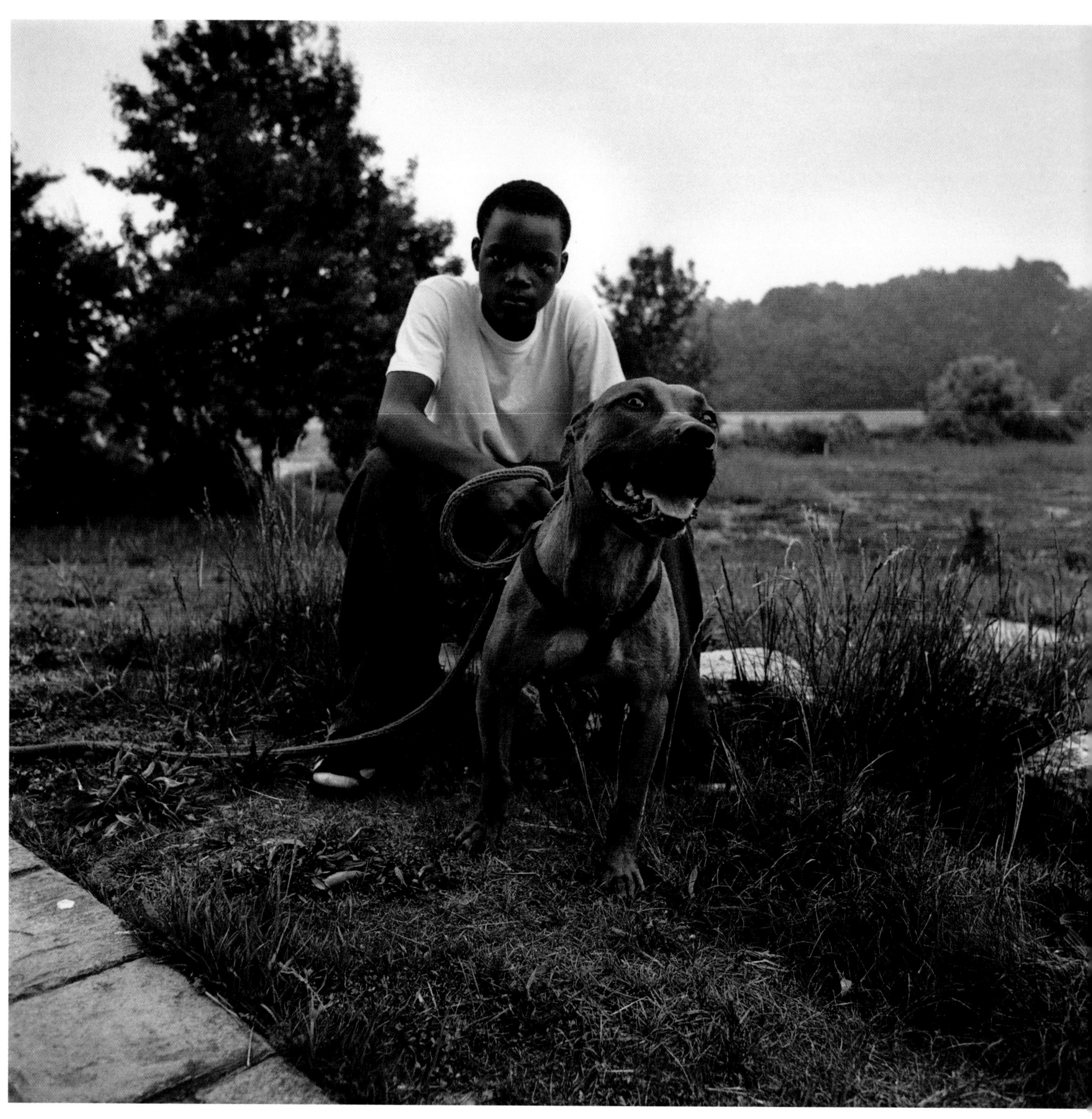

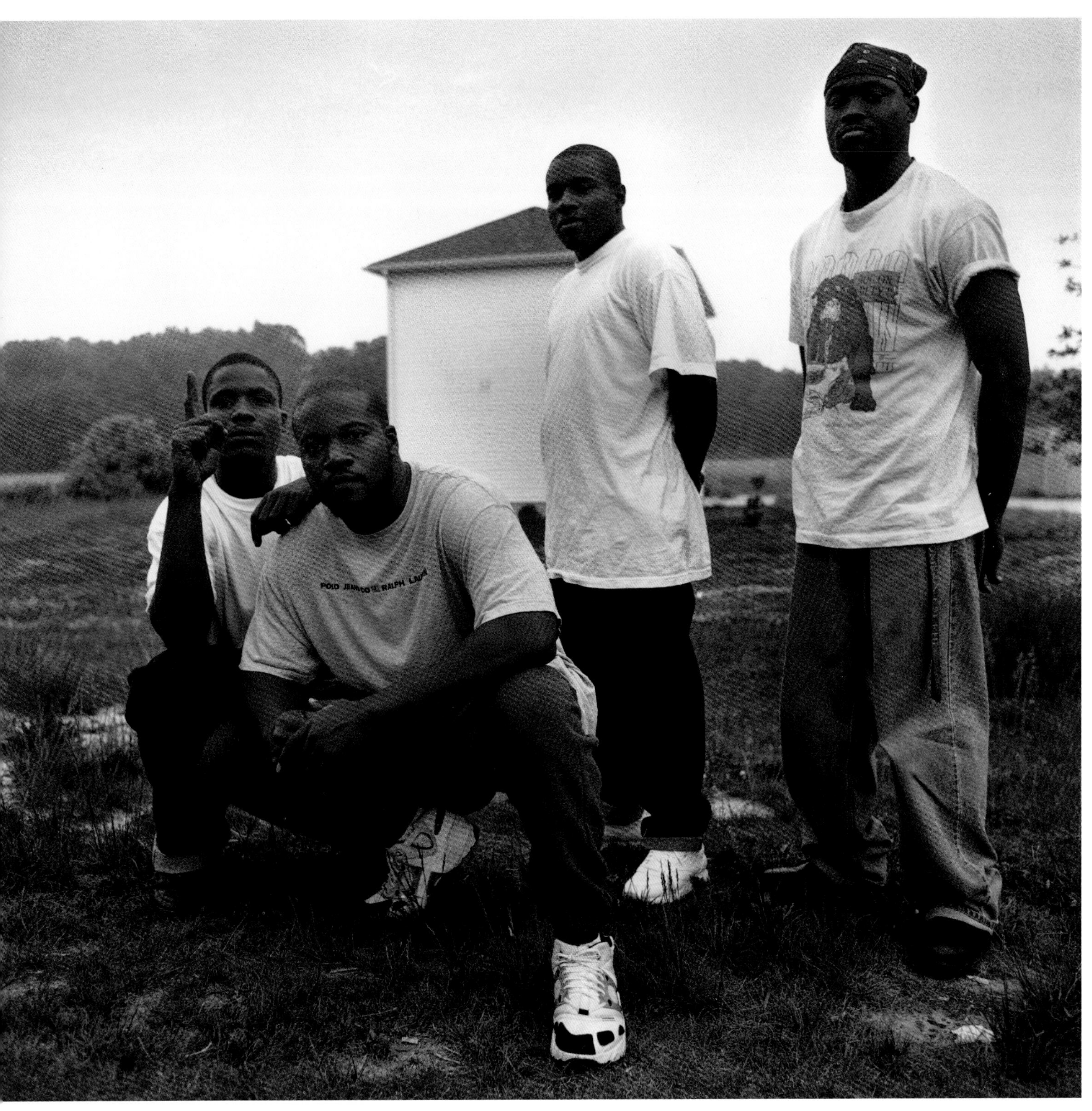

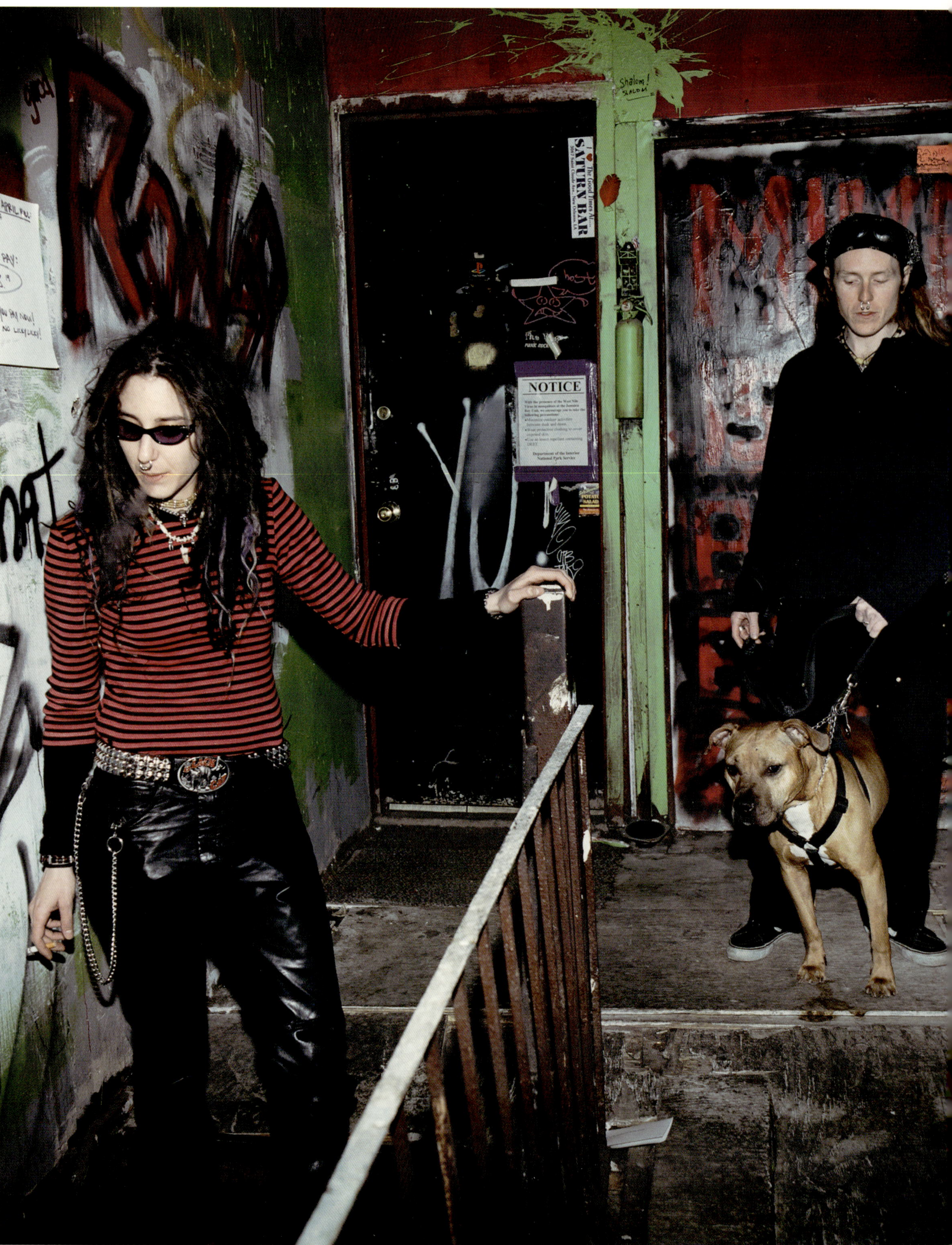
Shalom!
I ♥ The Good Times At...
SATURN BAR
3067 Saint Claude Ave. New Orleans LA
NOTICE
Department of the Interior
National Park Service

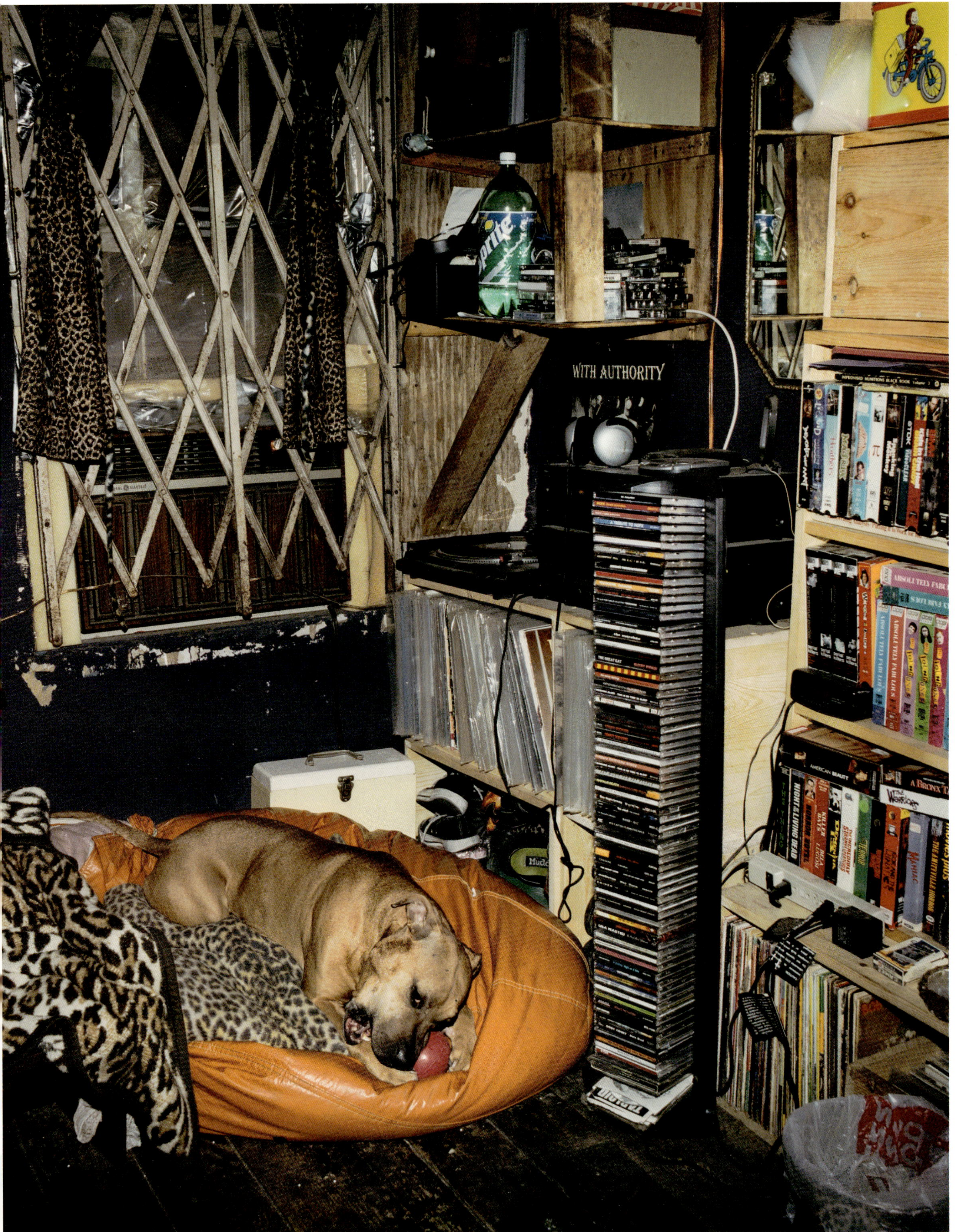
Sprite
WITH AUTHORITY
AMERICAN BEAUTY

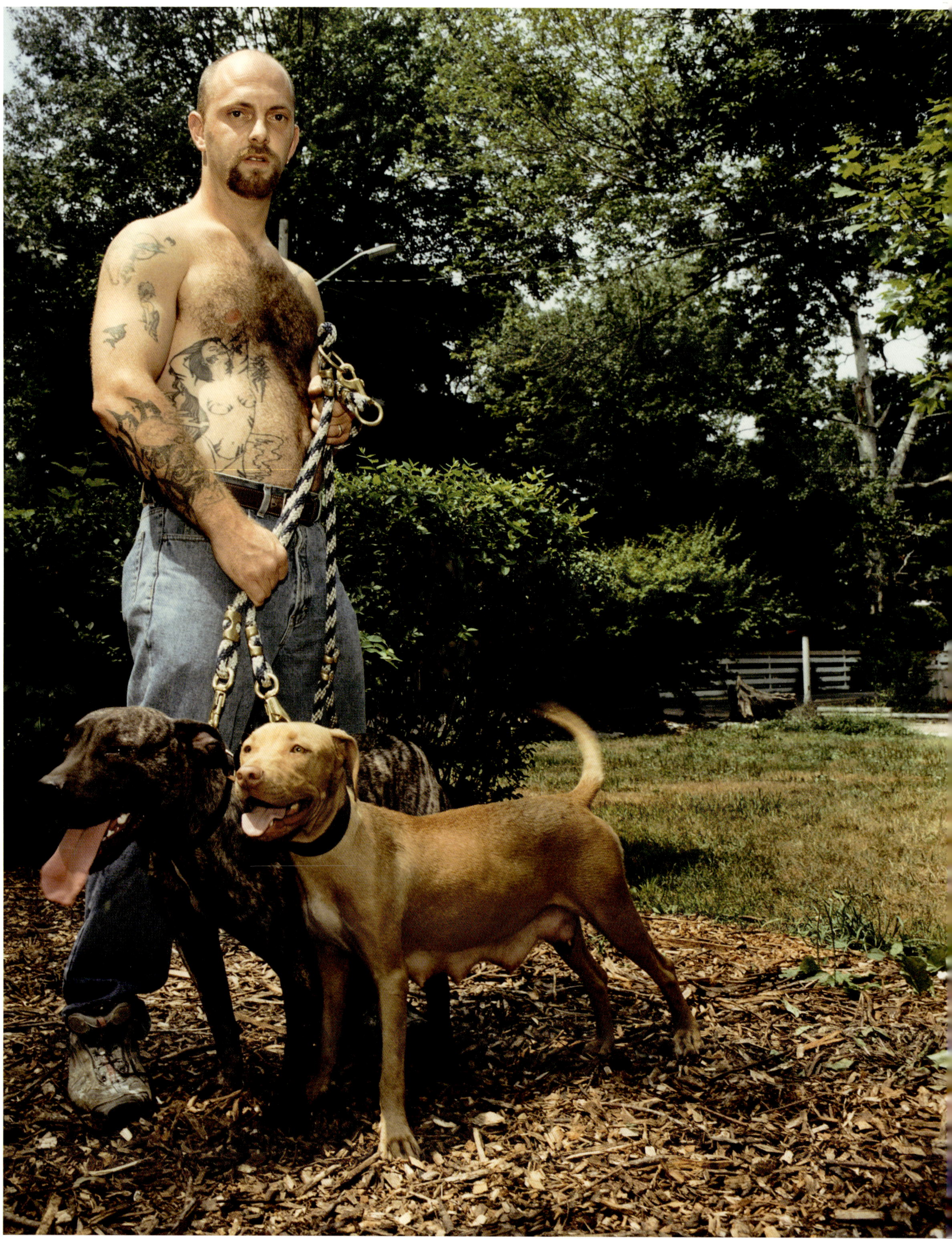

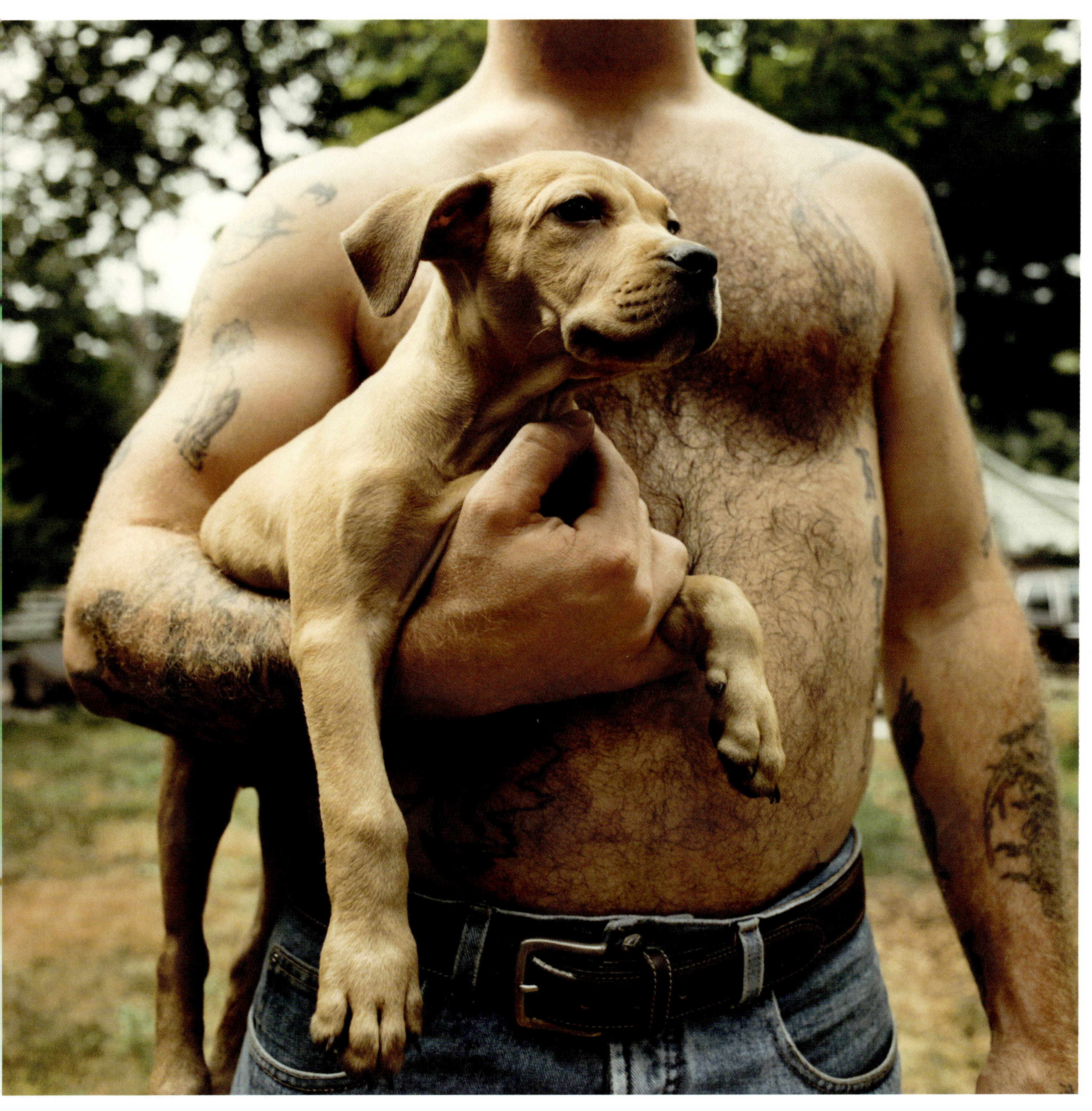

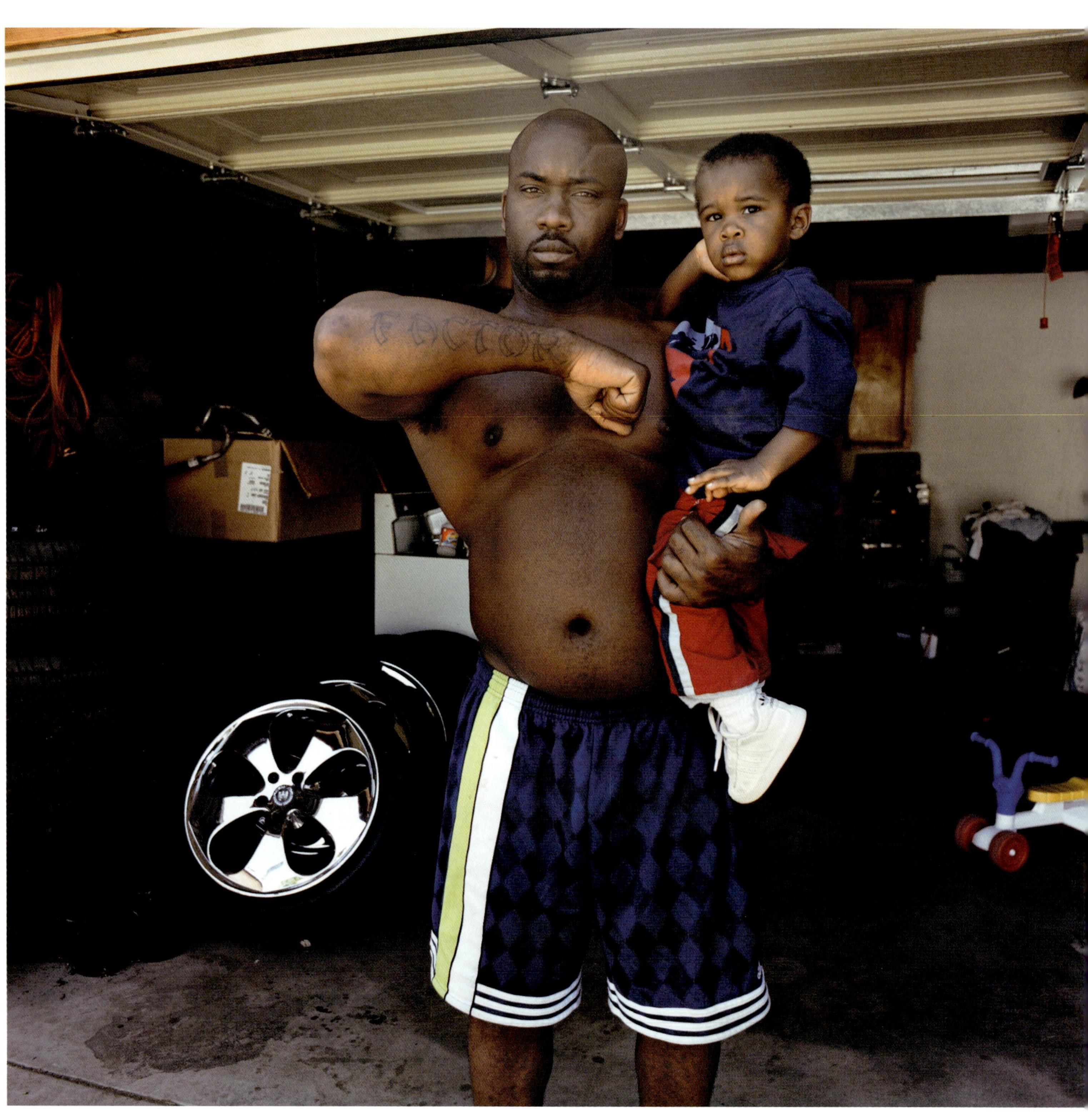

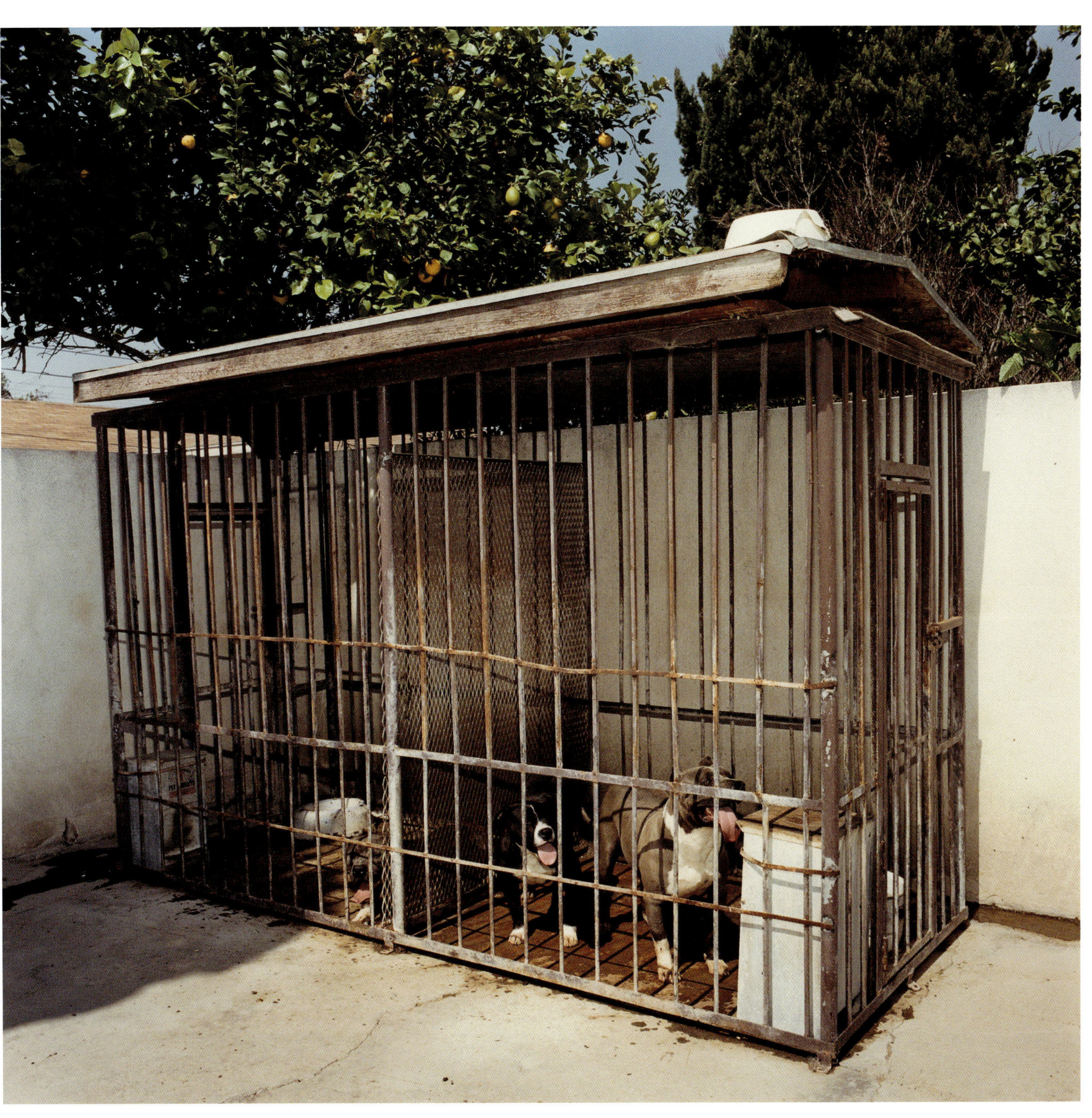

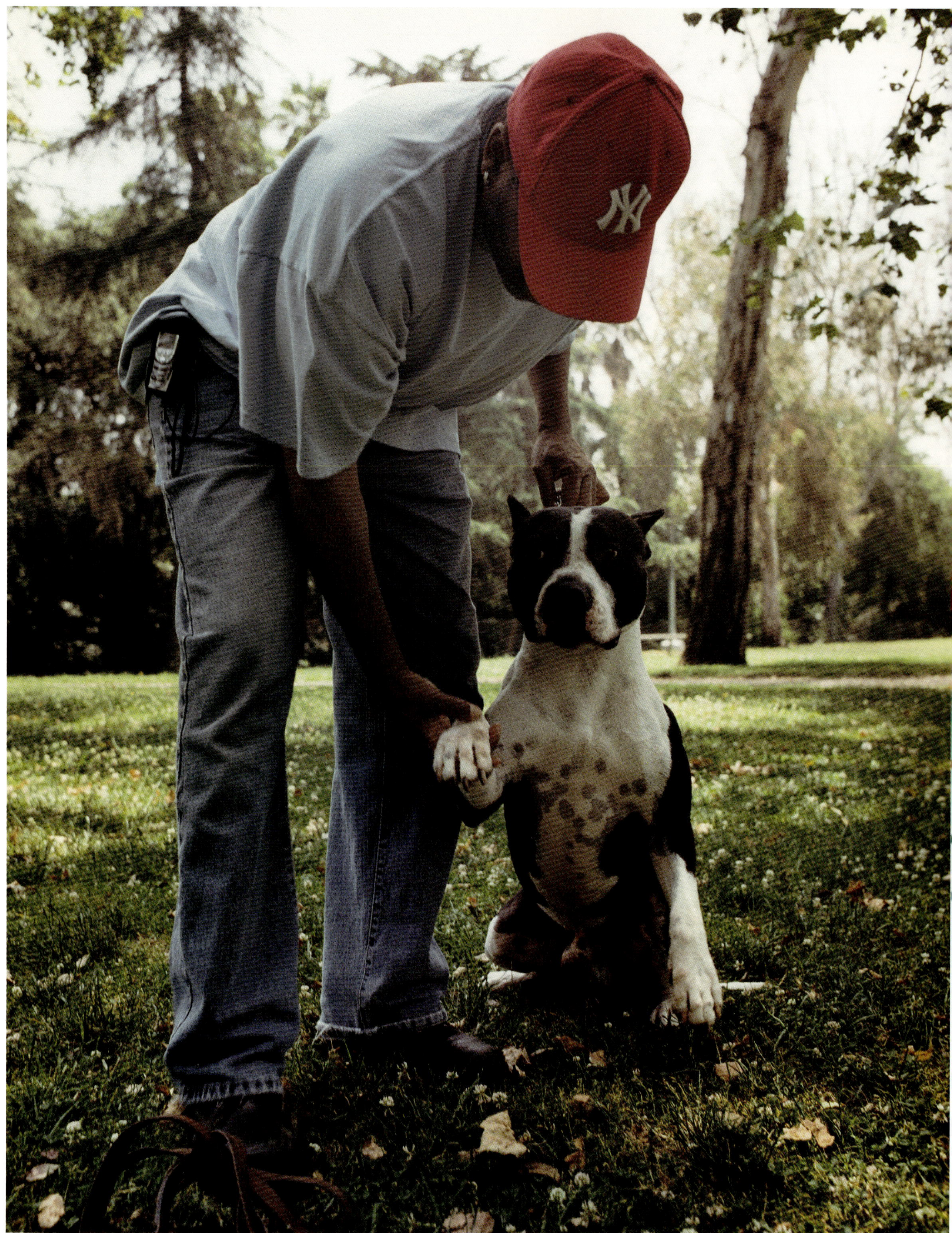
NY

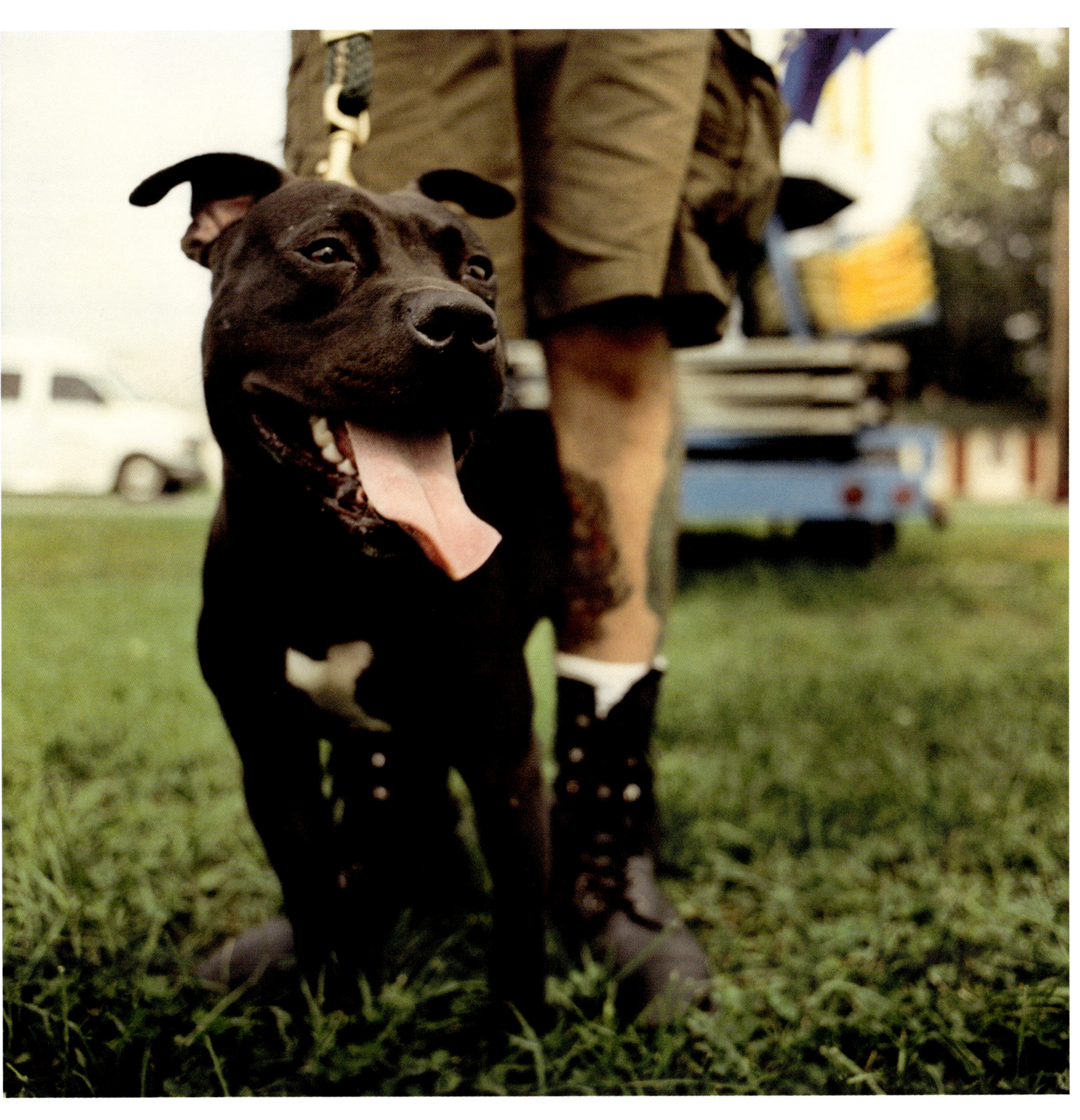

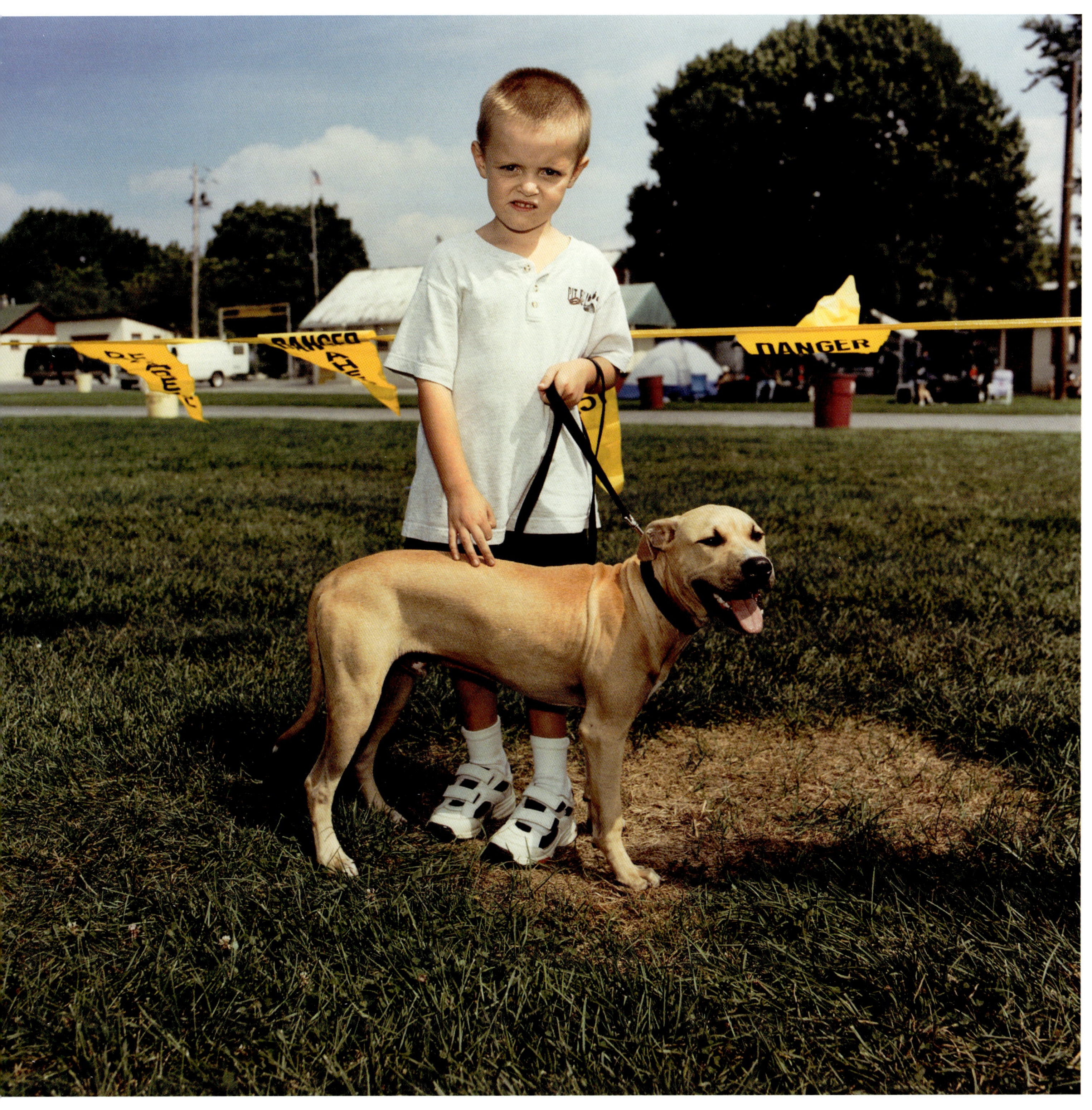
DANGER

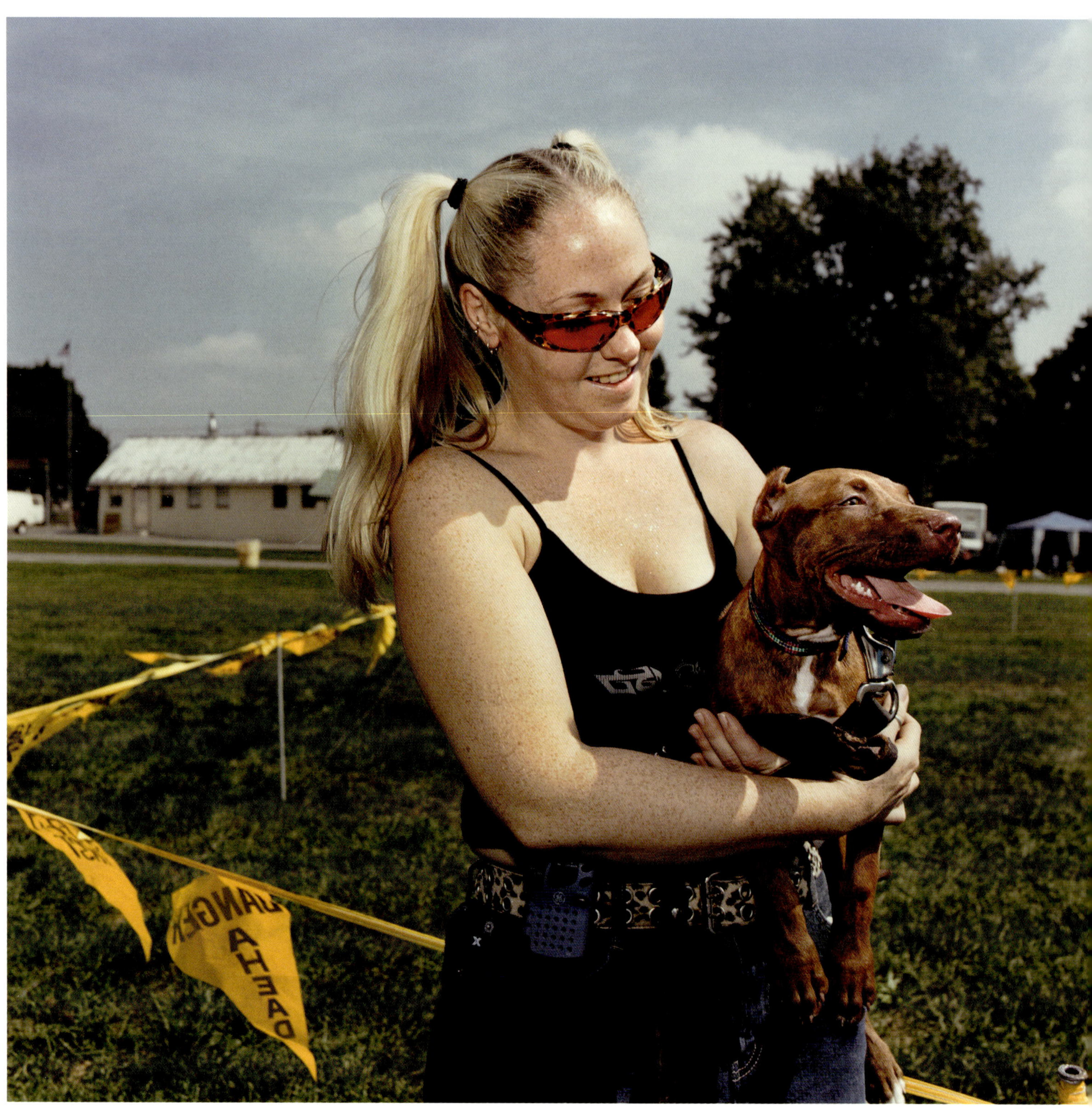

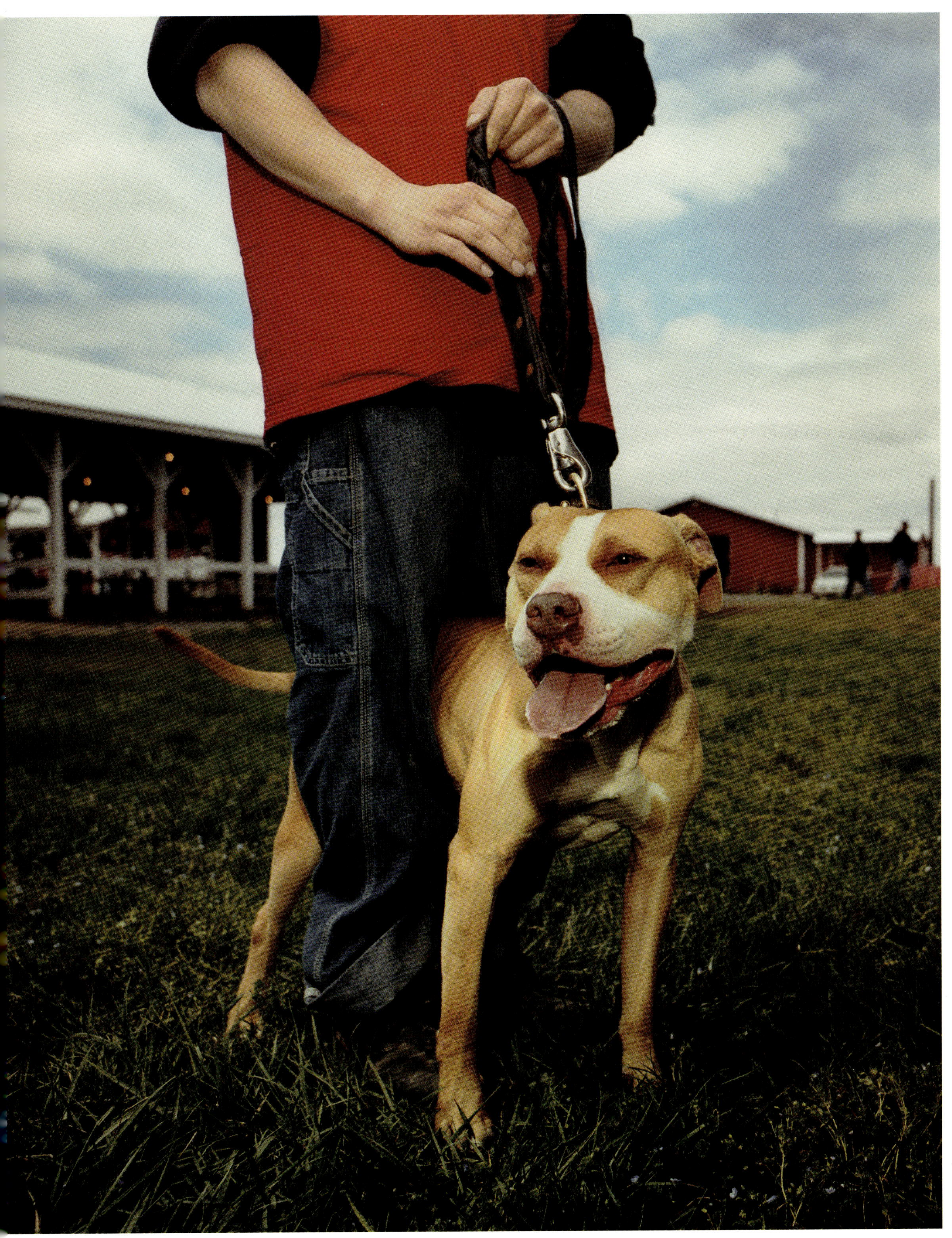

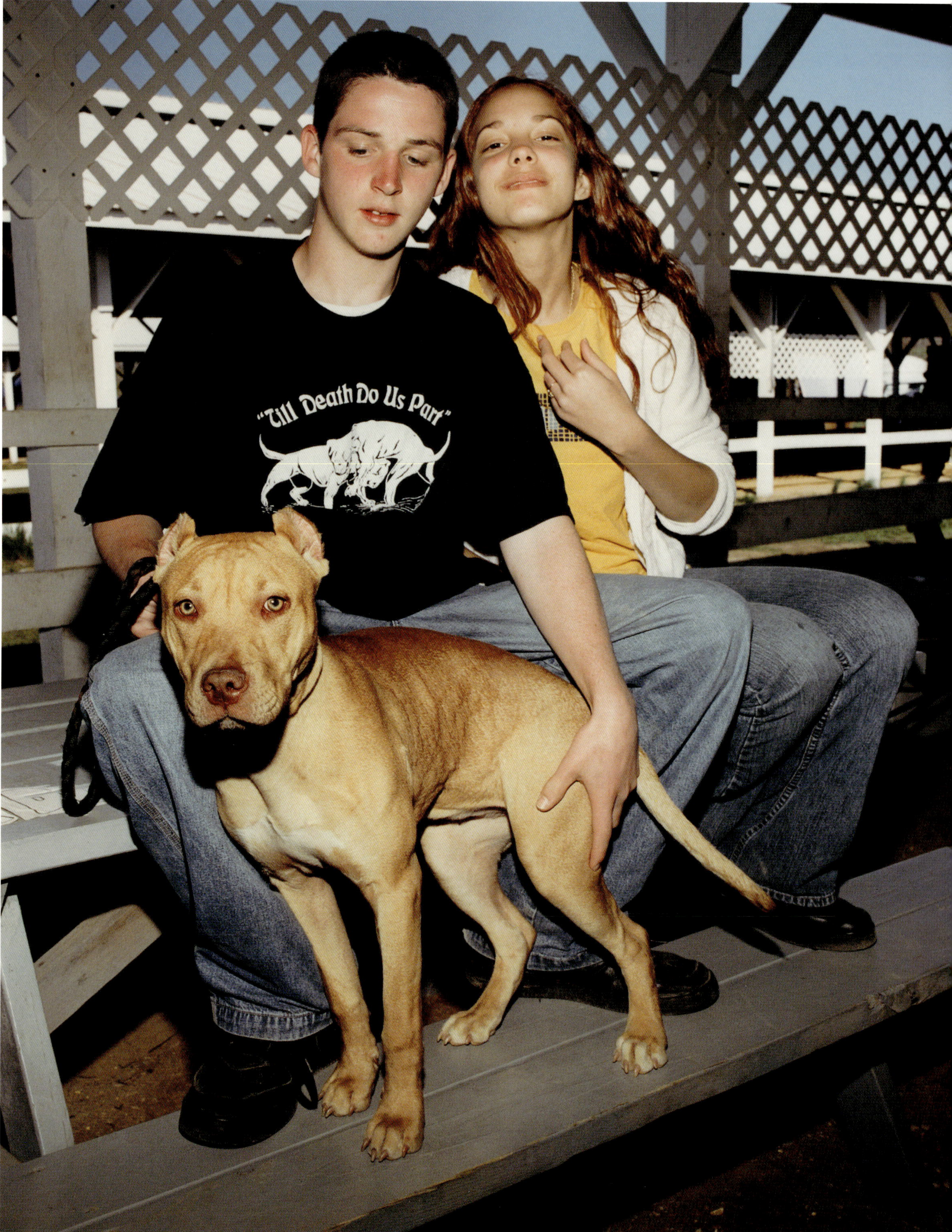
"Till Death Do Us Part"

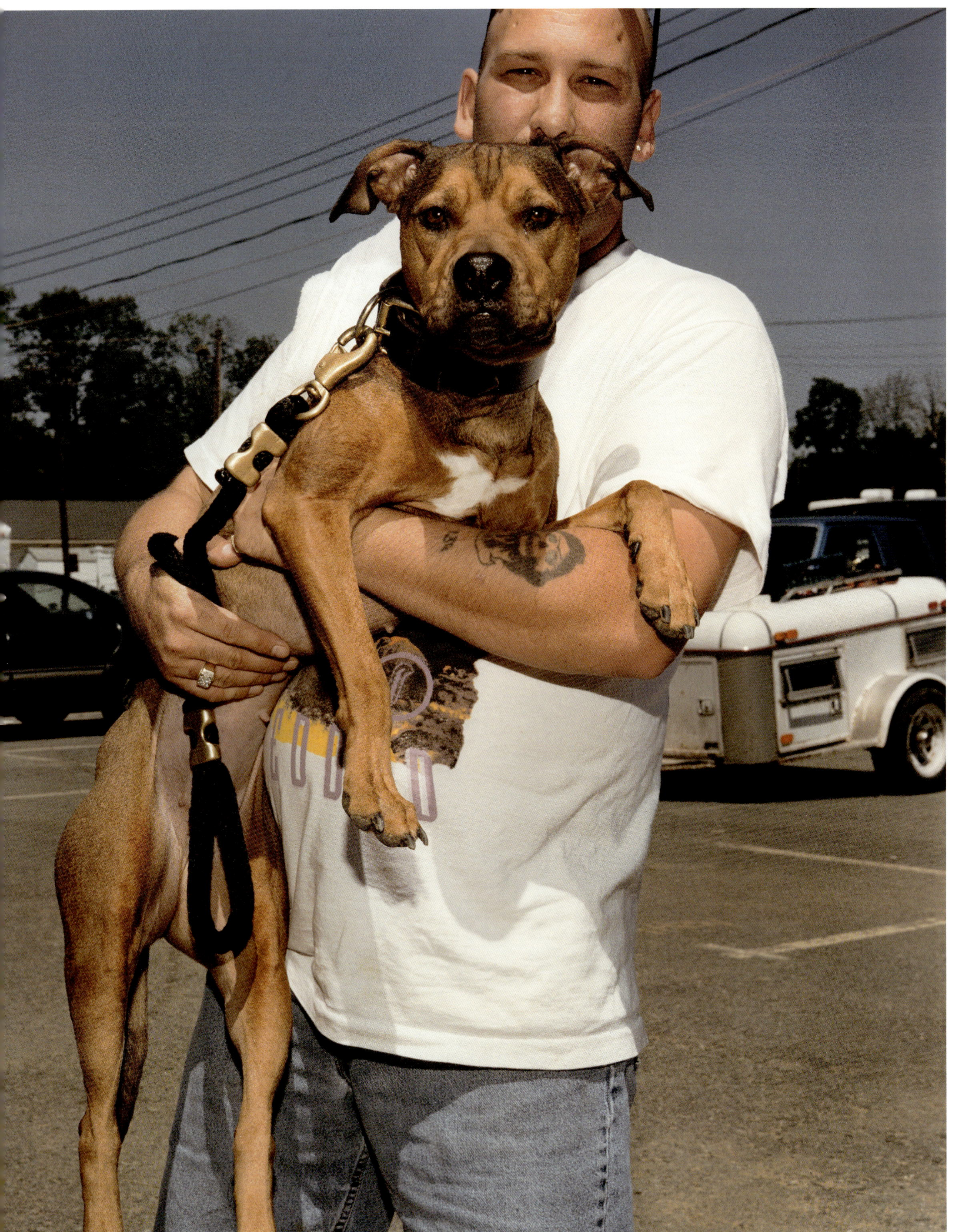

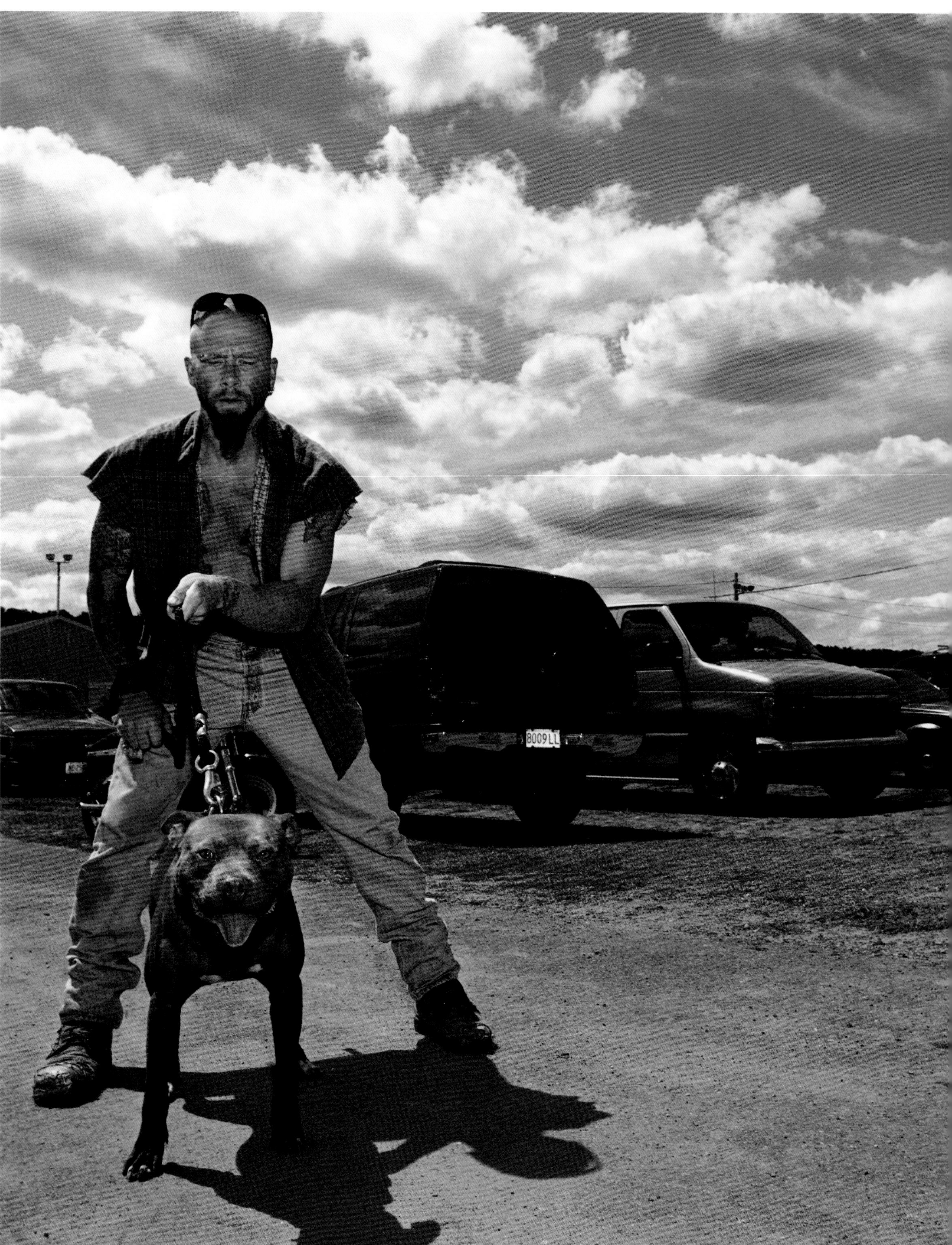
8009LL

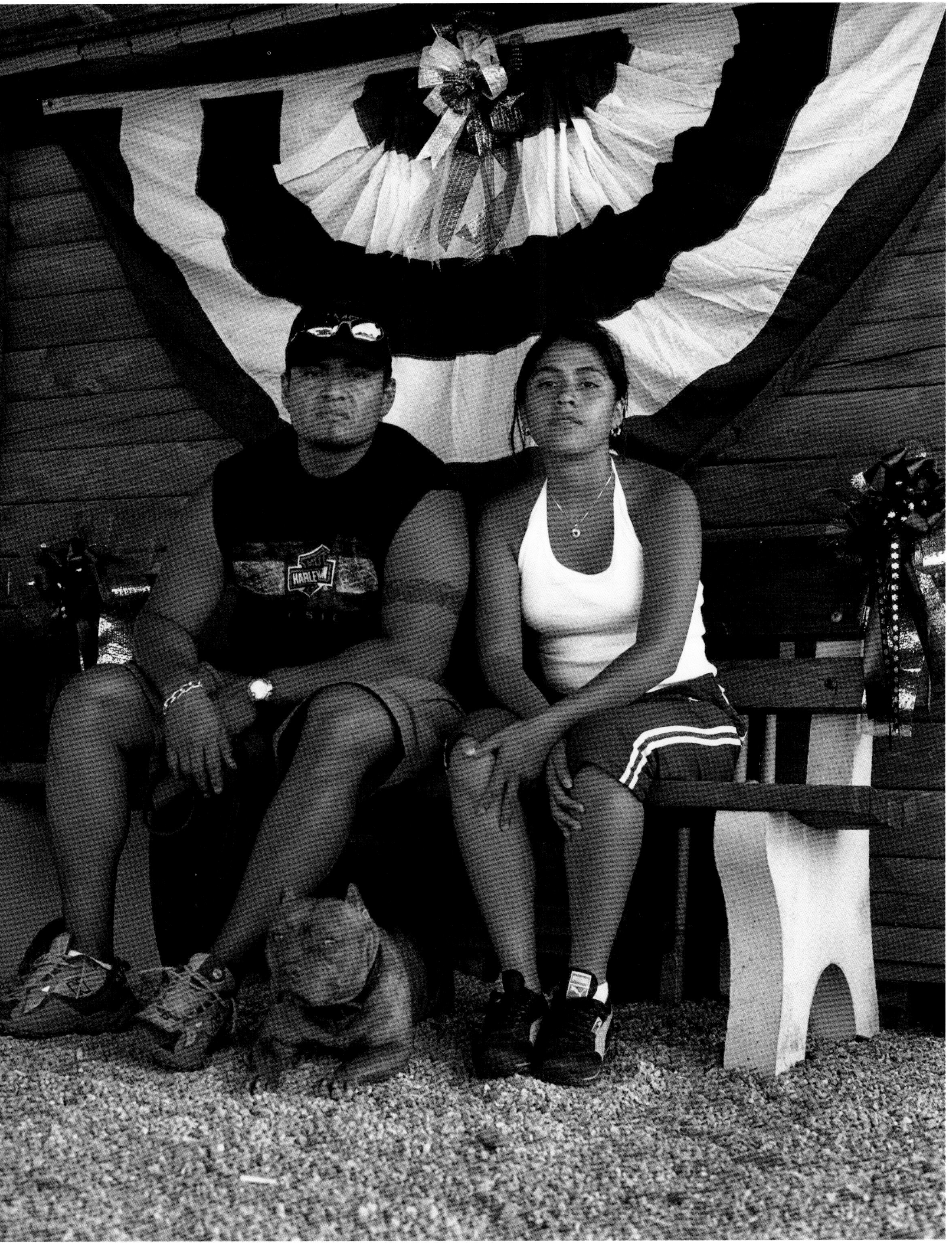
HARLEY

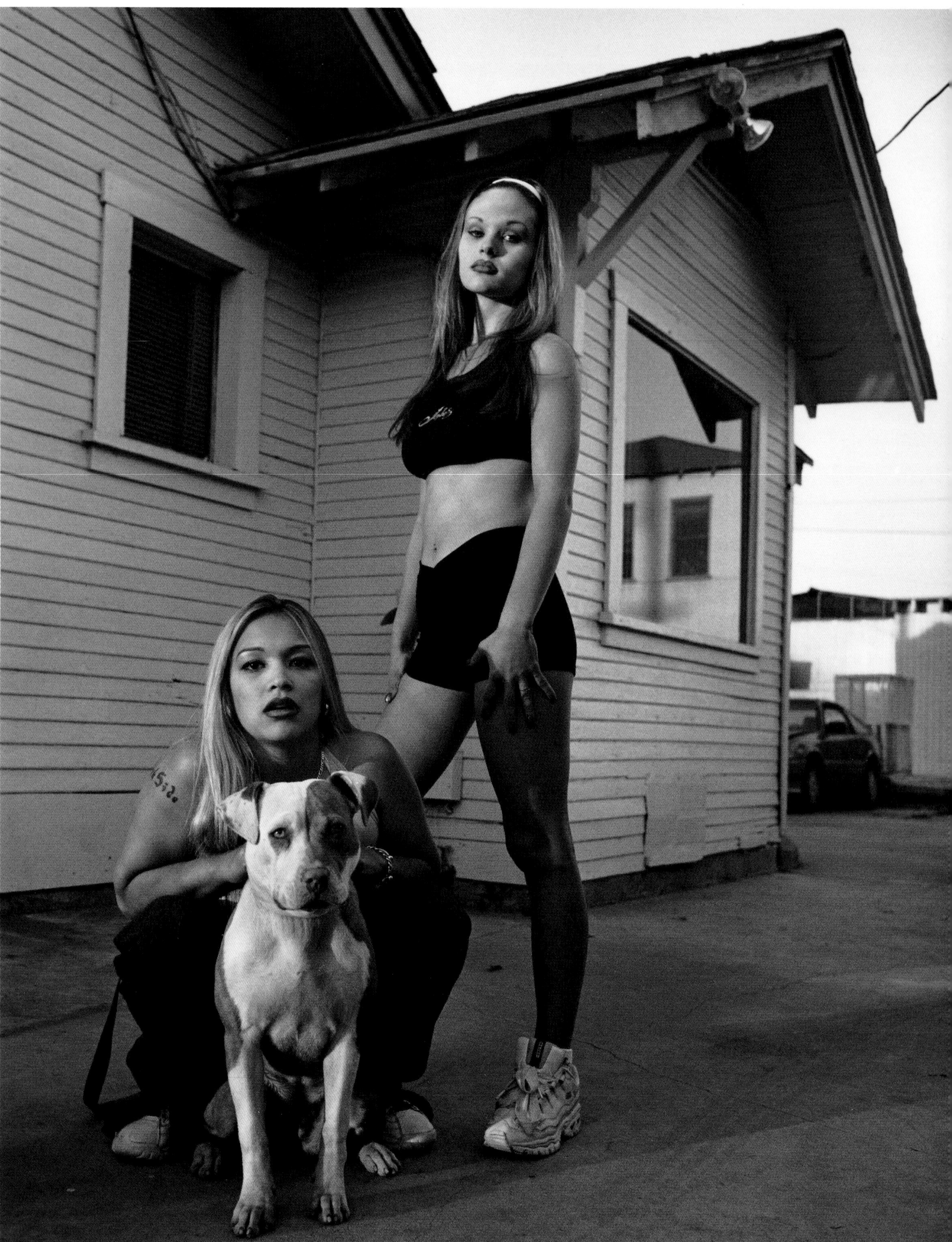

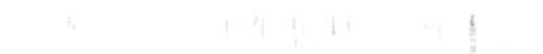

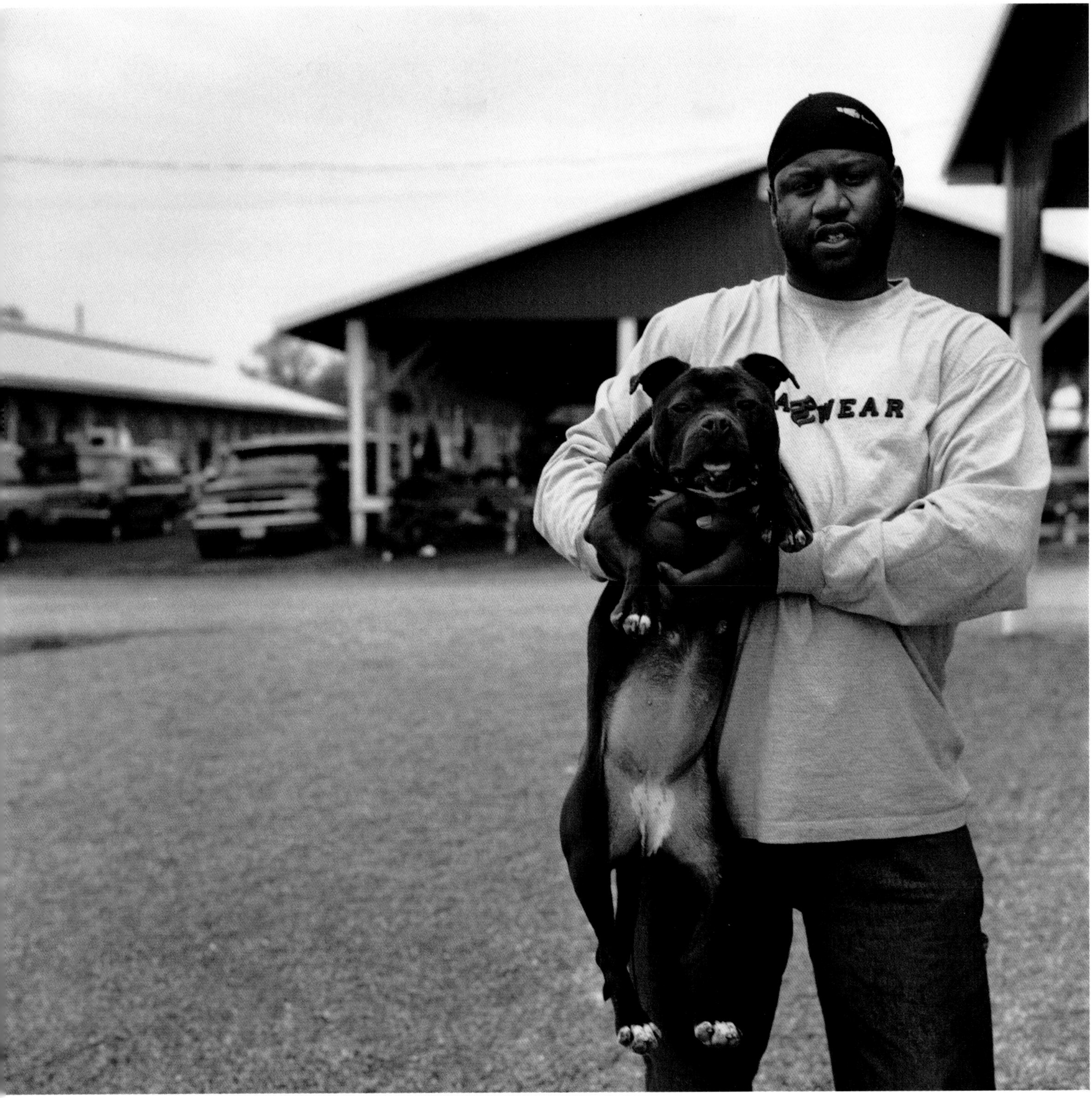

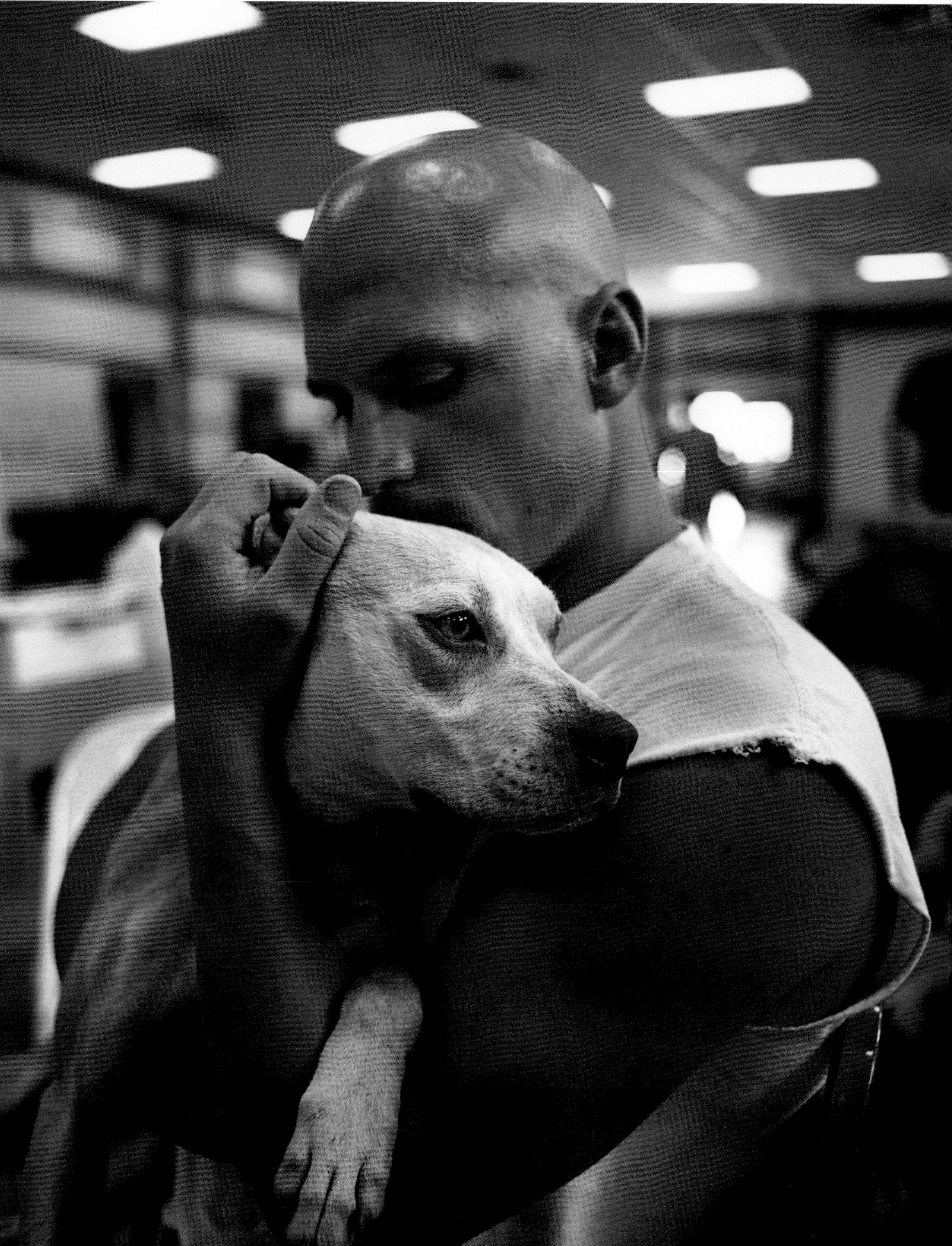

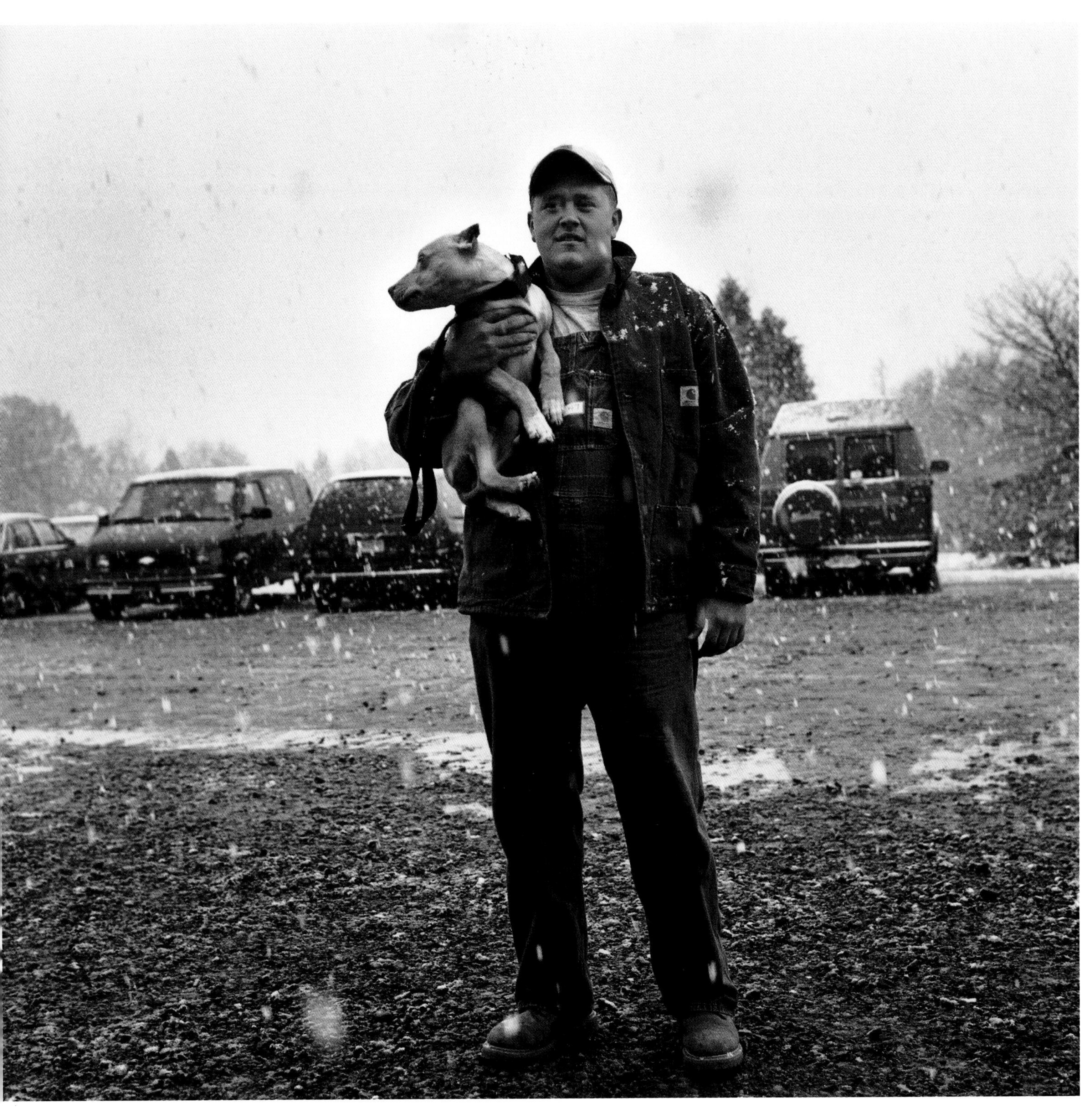

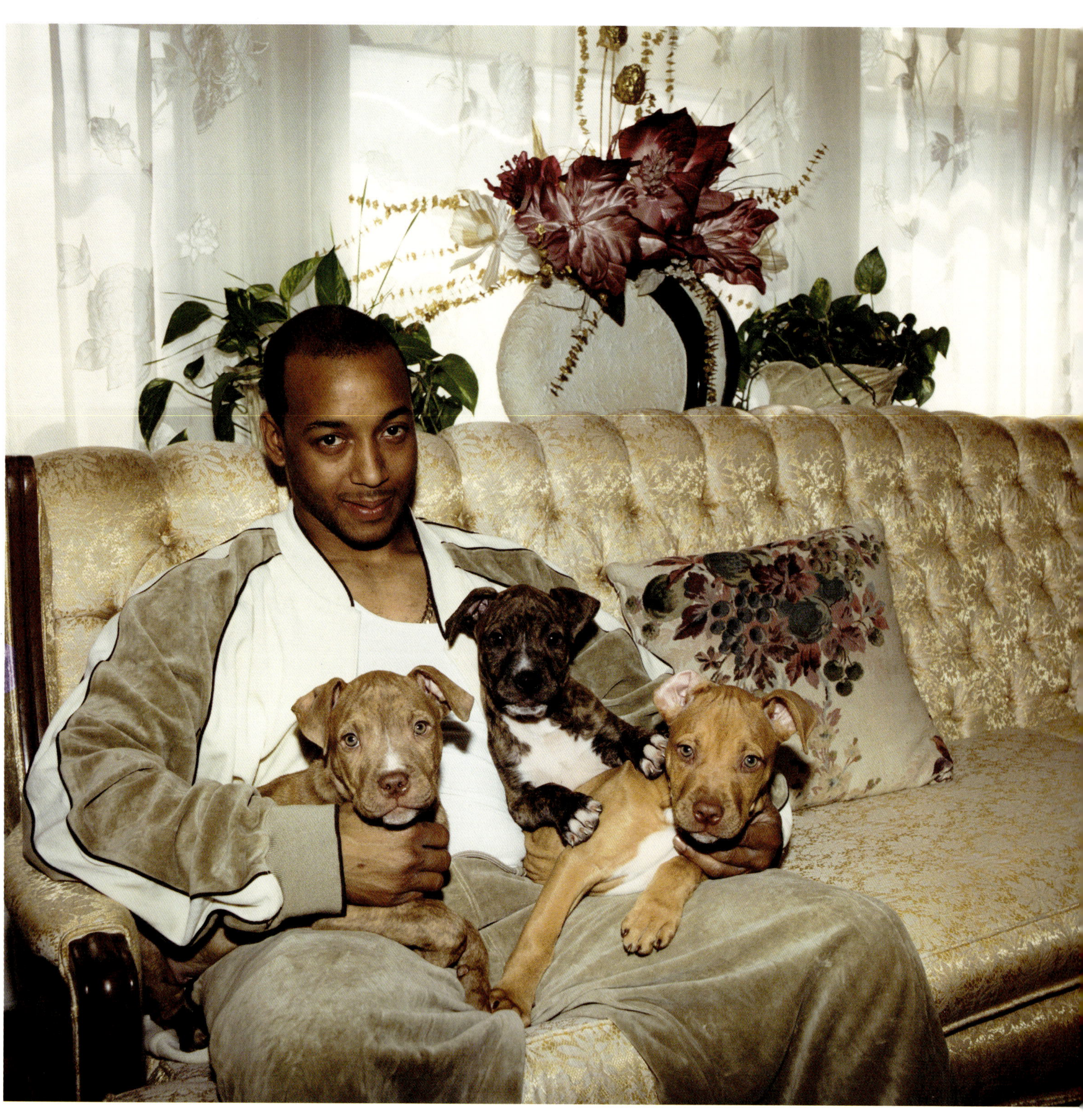

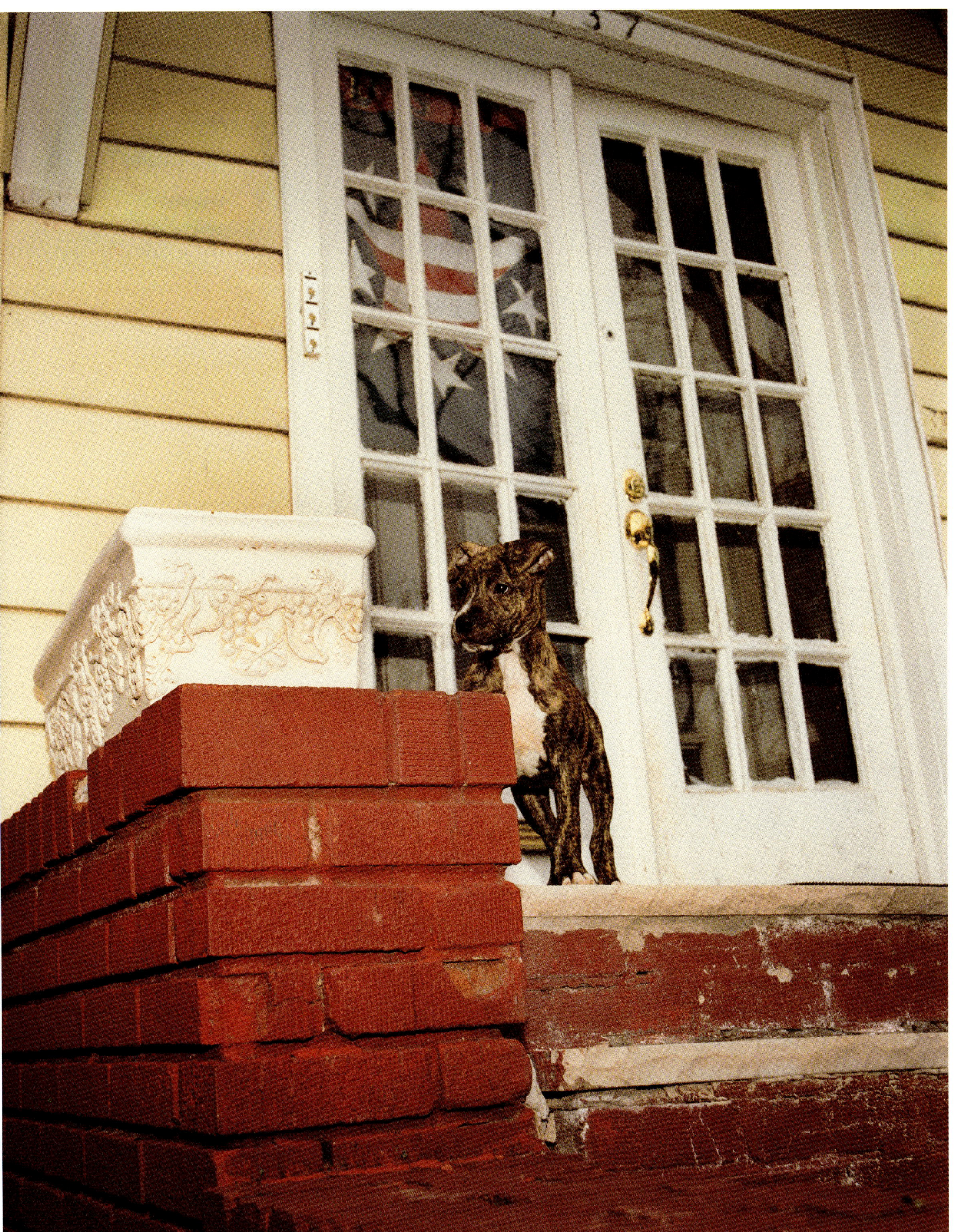

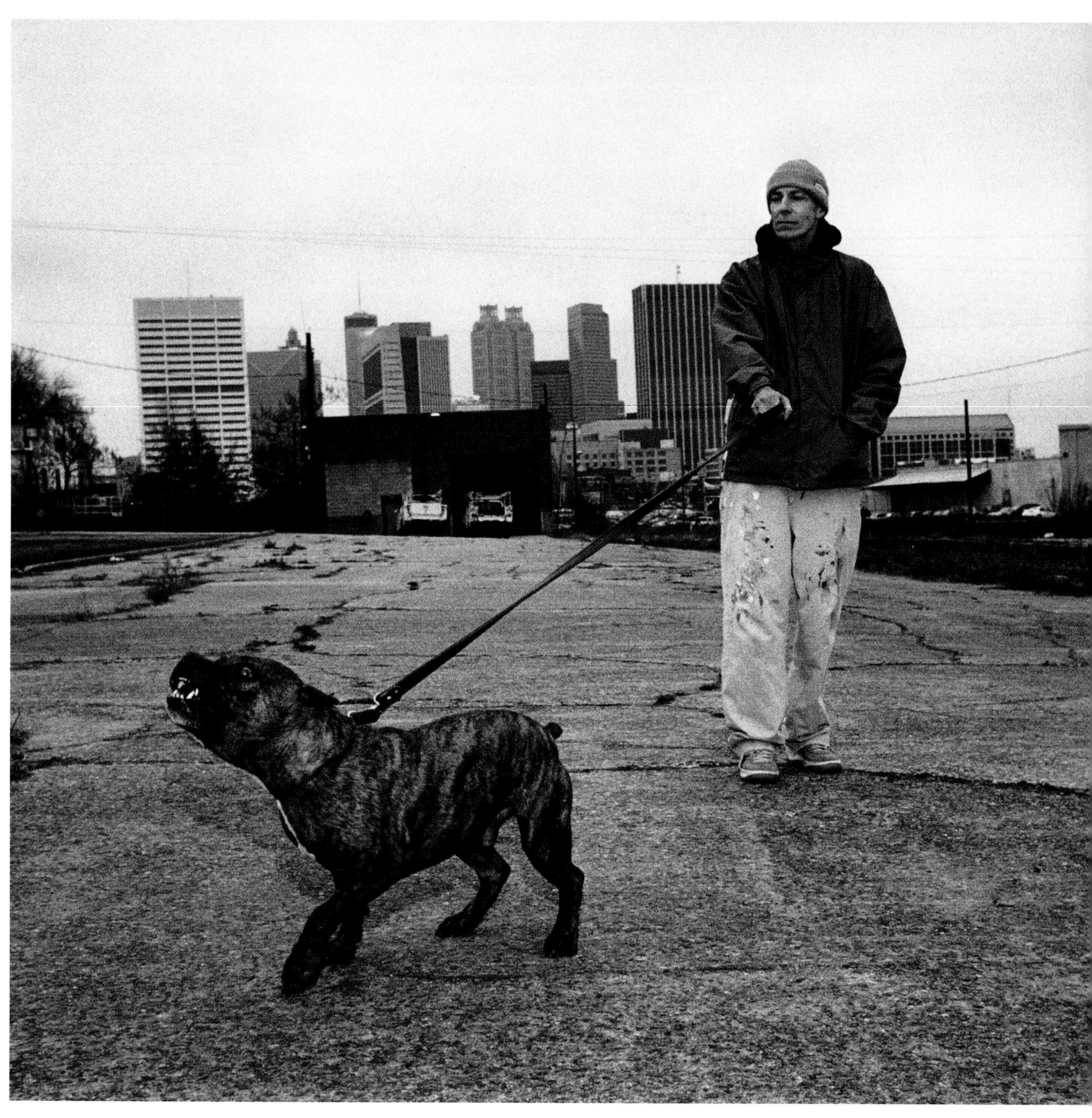

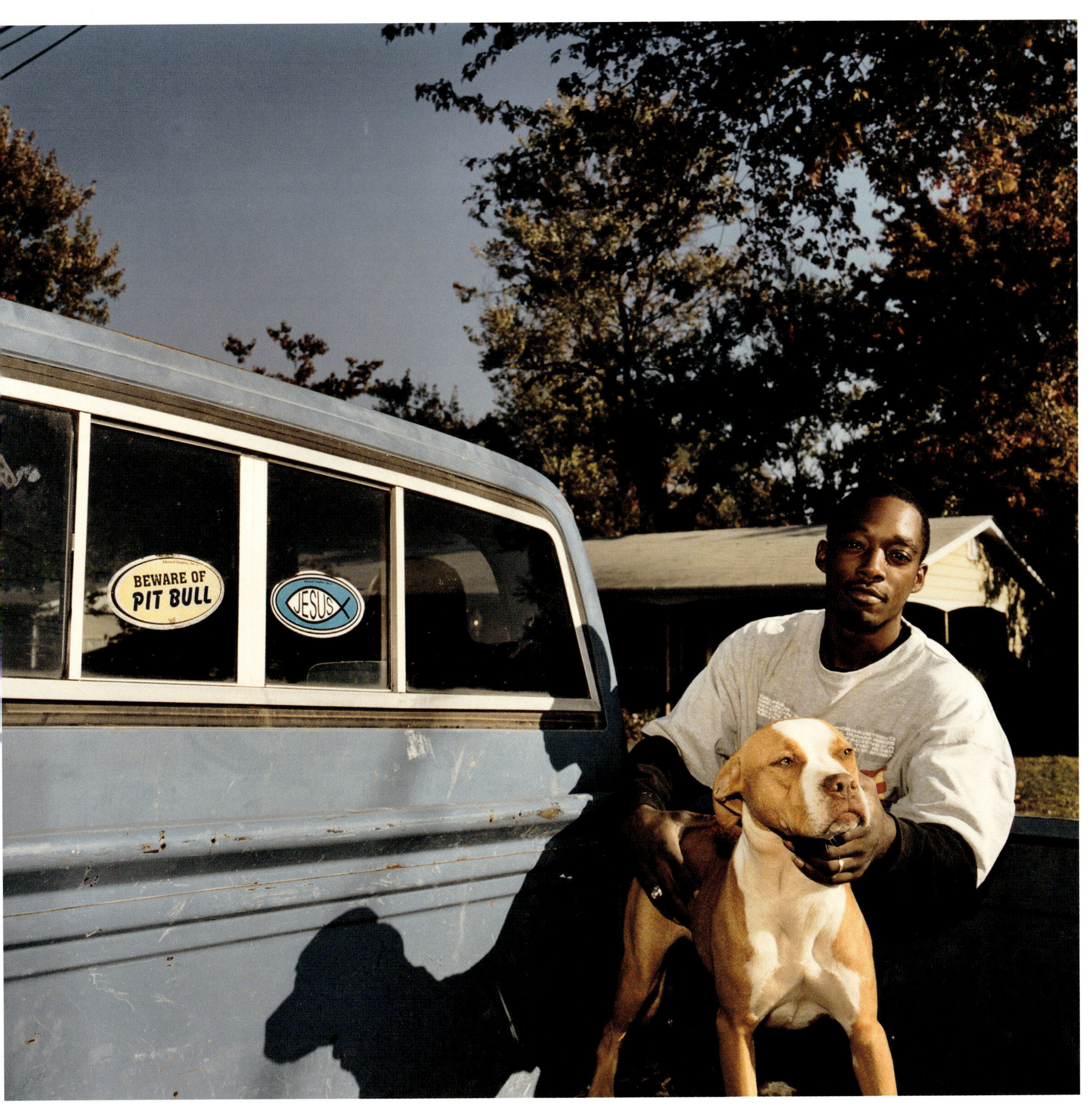
BEWARE OF
PIT BULL
JESUS

Louis B. Colby is a living legend within the breed. A self-proclaimed retired dog-fancier and farmer who raises cattle, game fowl, and rare Belgian Pletnyk doves, he has lived and worked with American Pit Bull Terriers all his life. His father John Pritchard Colby is widely credited with the most significant early development of the breed in the United States—the Colby Strain has been in existence for over one hundred years.

• In my lifetime, I've had a few thousand American Pit Bull Terriers. We currently have fifteen dogs at home. All of my sons have our dogs, as well as some friends that keep dogs for us. There are a total of probably forty dogs in the family now.
• We always have a housedog. Logan is the one at present. In addition, we have a barn/kennel with heated stalls for the New England weather. But most of our dogs stay in chain link pens with individual insulated dog houses. I work my dogs on Colby's Noiseless Treadmills, the first carpet mill. It's been made and sold by three generations of Colbys and is still the world's leading treadmill for all breeds of dogs.
• Dog fighting has never been legal in any state. Back in my youth, and up until about the time of World War II, registration of Pit Bulls was not the norm. However it surely is today, with the ADBA (American Dog Breeders Association) and the UKC (United Kennel Club) now so successful. Many years ago, a breeder's hand-written pedigree was all that was expected. Today, registration papers are mandatory if you're breeding and selling dogs.
• Dime was [a dog who was] special to me, not for one particular reason, but because he was the perfect typical specimen of the breed. In those days—the forties and fifties—the average Pit Bull was smaller than today's. Dime was small, too—thirty-eight pounds on chain, and thirty-one pounds in condition. The preferred color then was brindle with a black nose and an even white blaze. Along with cropped ears, he had all these points.
• Dime was a kennel dog all his life until he was old and feeble. Then my children would bring him into our house and let him on their beds at night. He was naturally housebroken and never soiled the house.
• While Secretariat, the famous racehorse, was spectacular himself, his progeny never approached his stature. Dime, on the other hand, was considered a great producer by leading dog-men of the era such as Al Brown, Maurice Carver, Howard Heinzl, Ed Crenshaw...who all owned a dog or two bred from Dime. Dime sired seventy-eight pups for me from fifteen different breedings.
• No species of animal is as loyal to mankind as a dog—and no breed is as loyal as a Pit Bull Terrier.

LOUIS B. COLBY Newburyport, Massachusetts

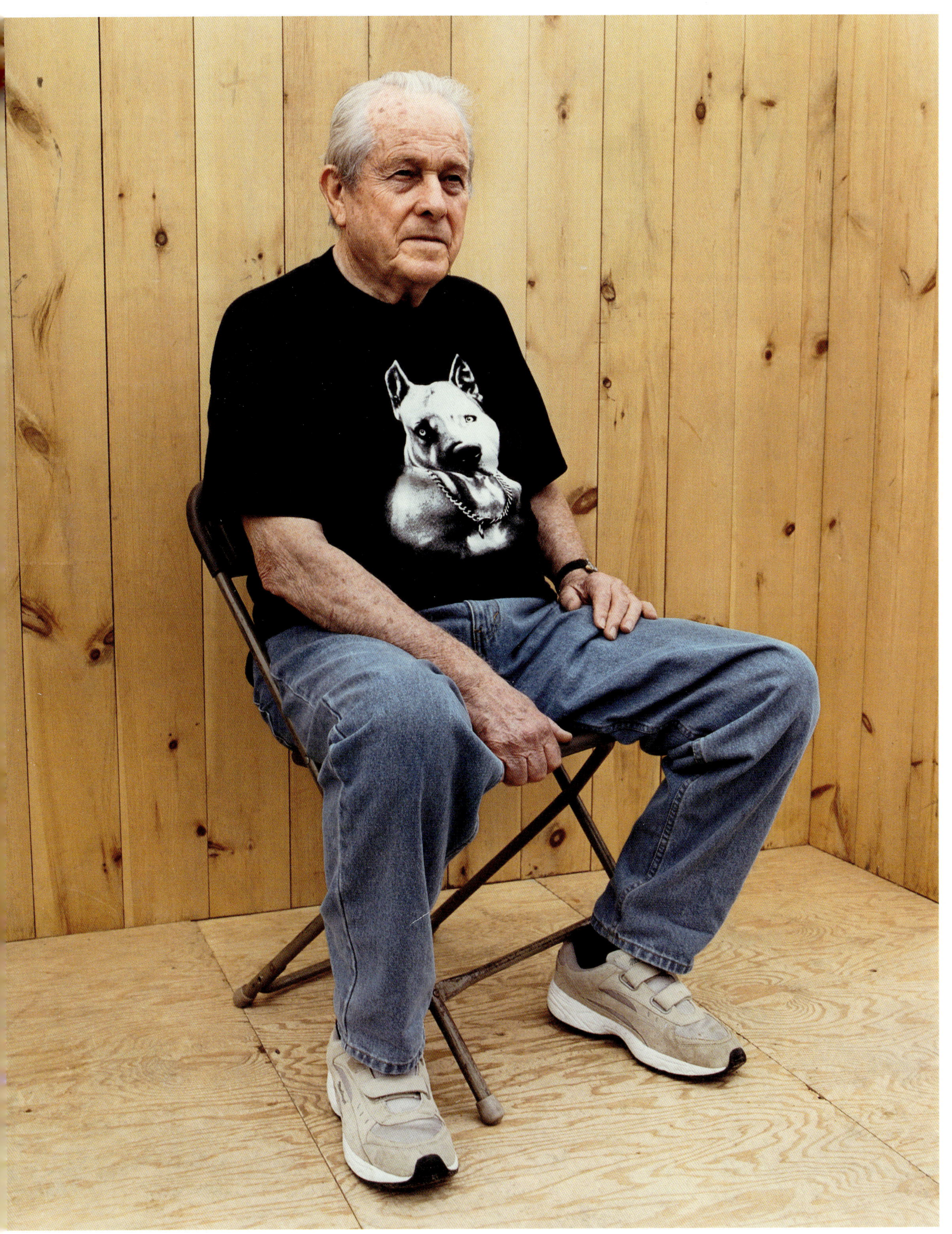

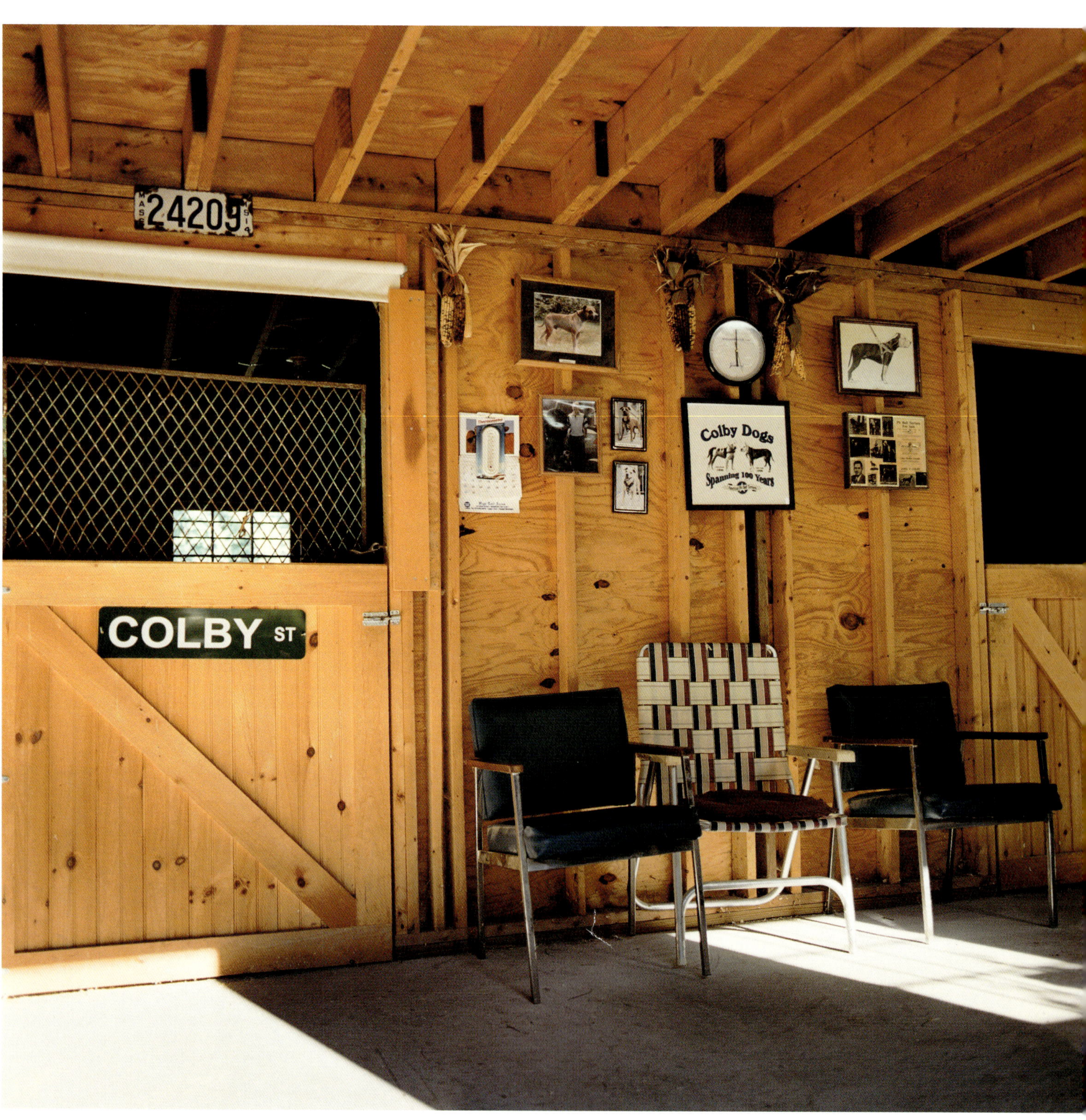
24209
COLBY ST
Colby Dogs
Spanning 100 Years

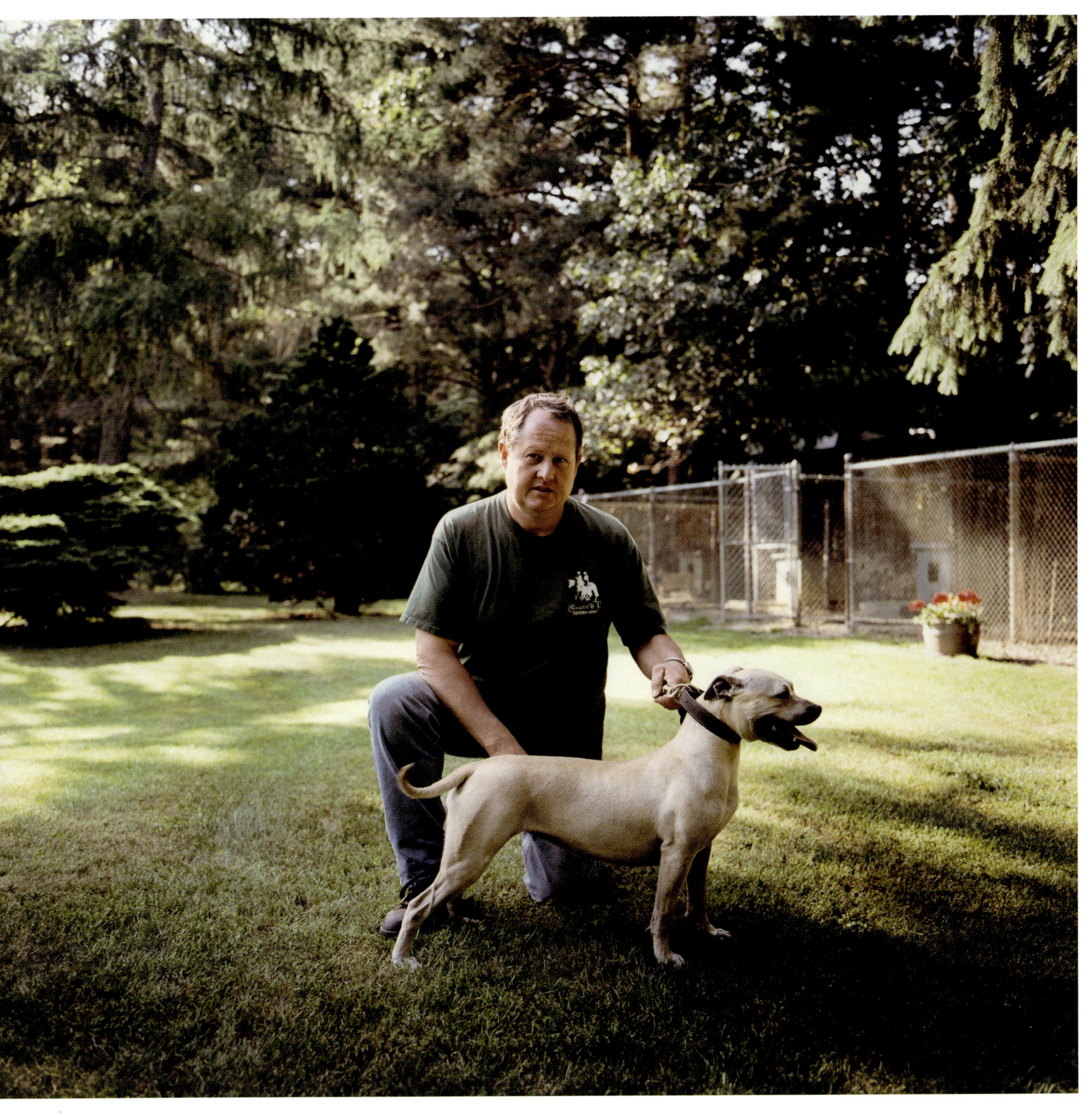

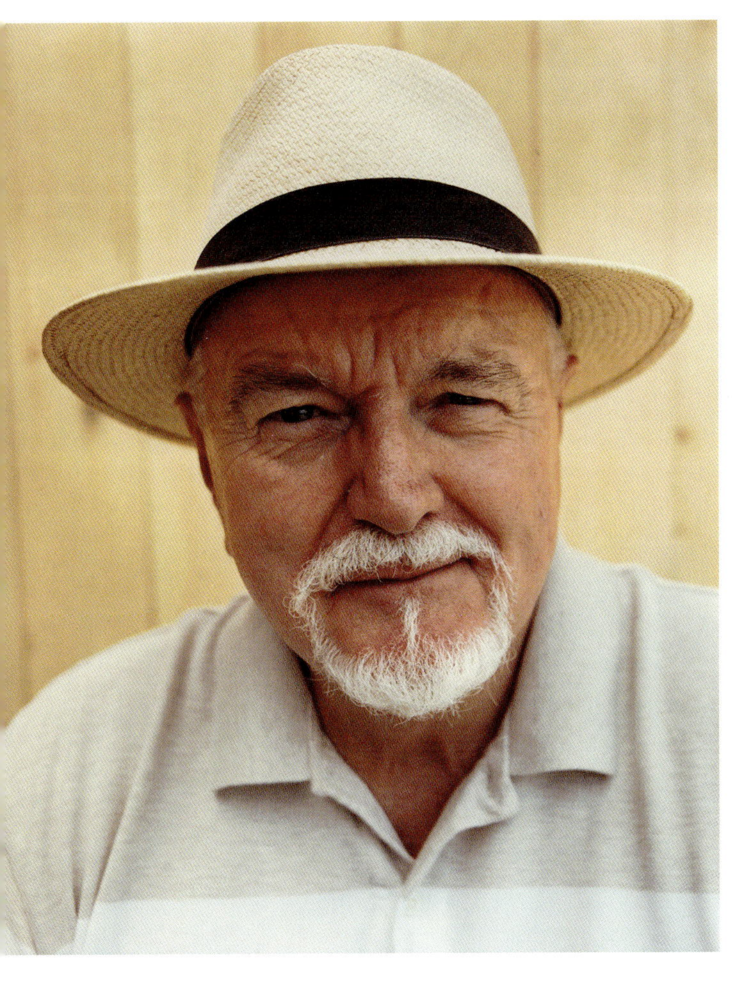

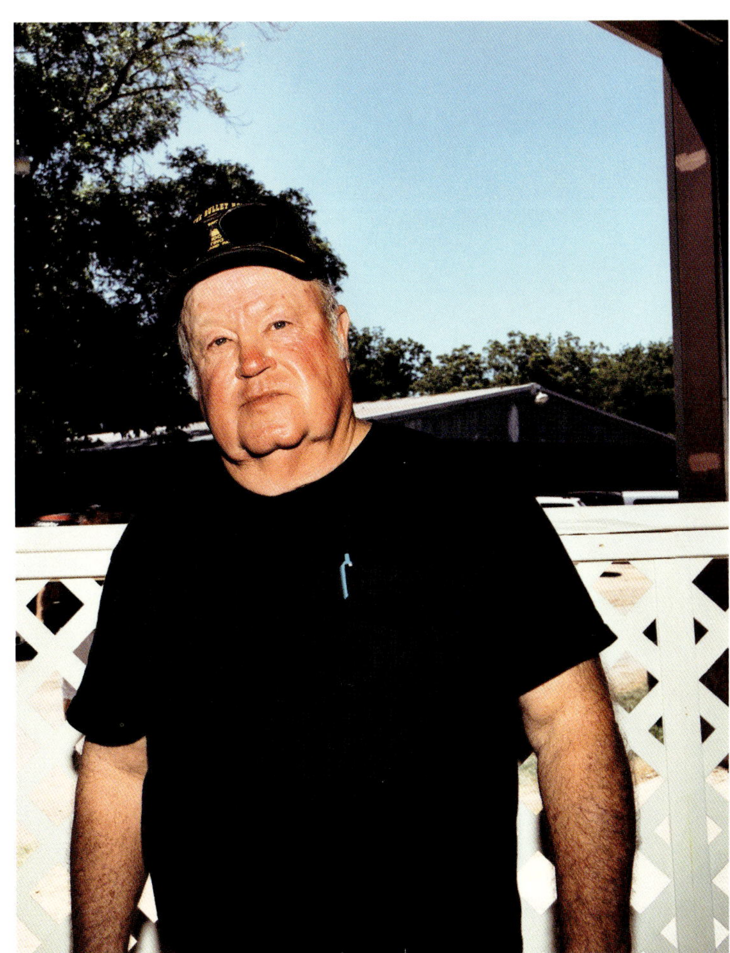

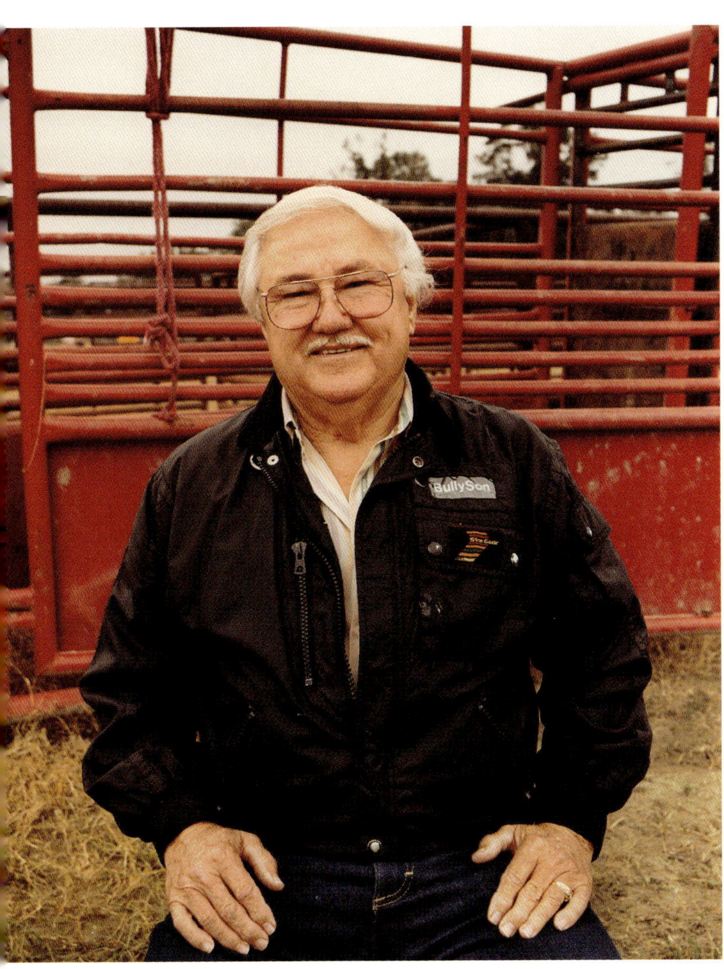
BullySon

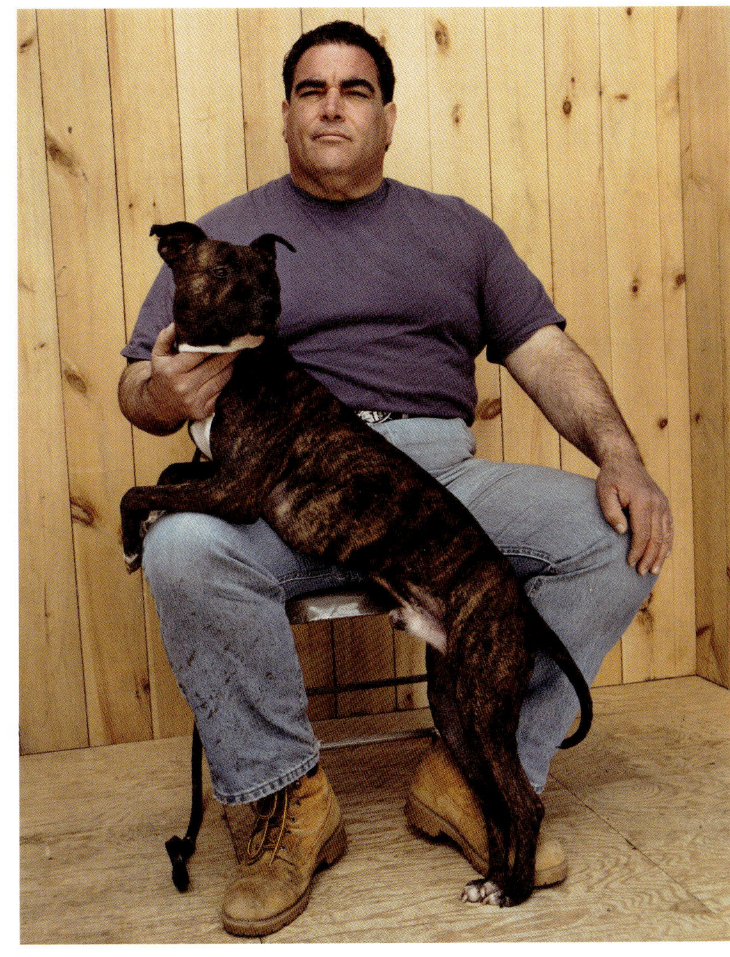

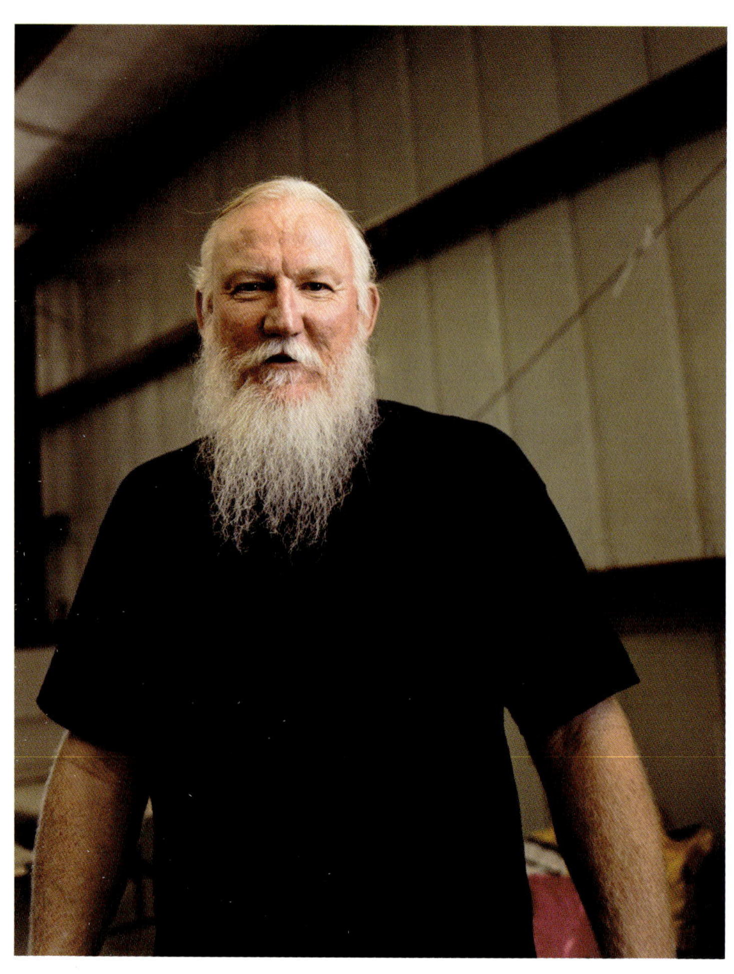

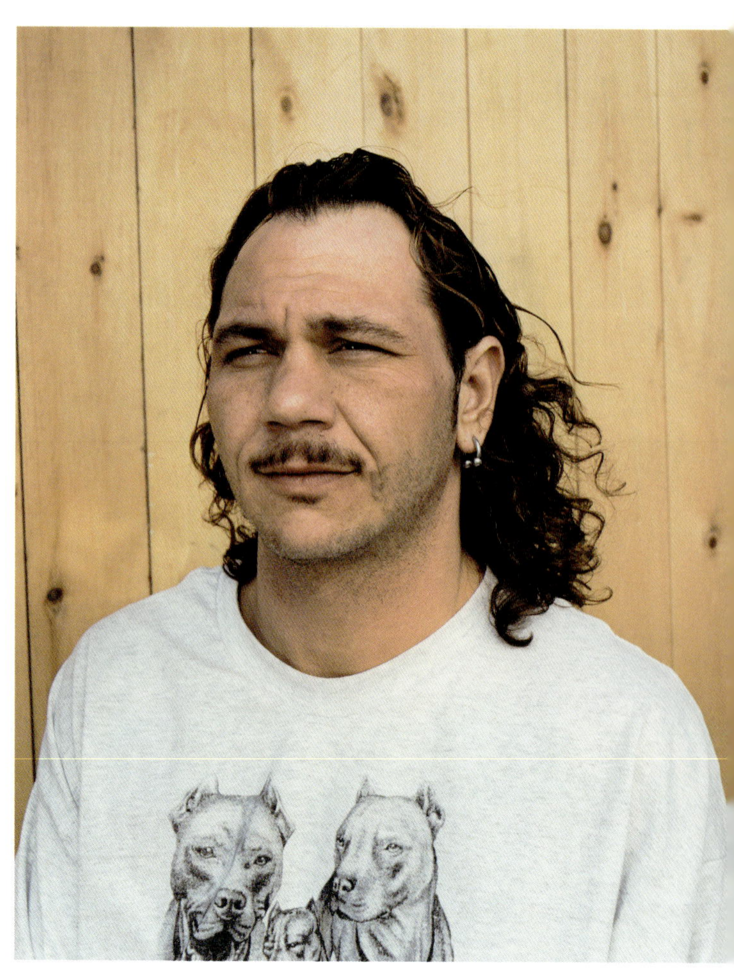

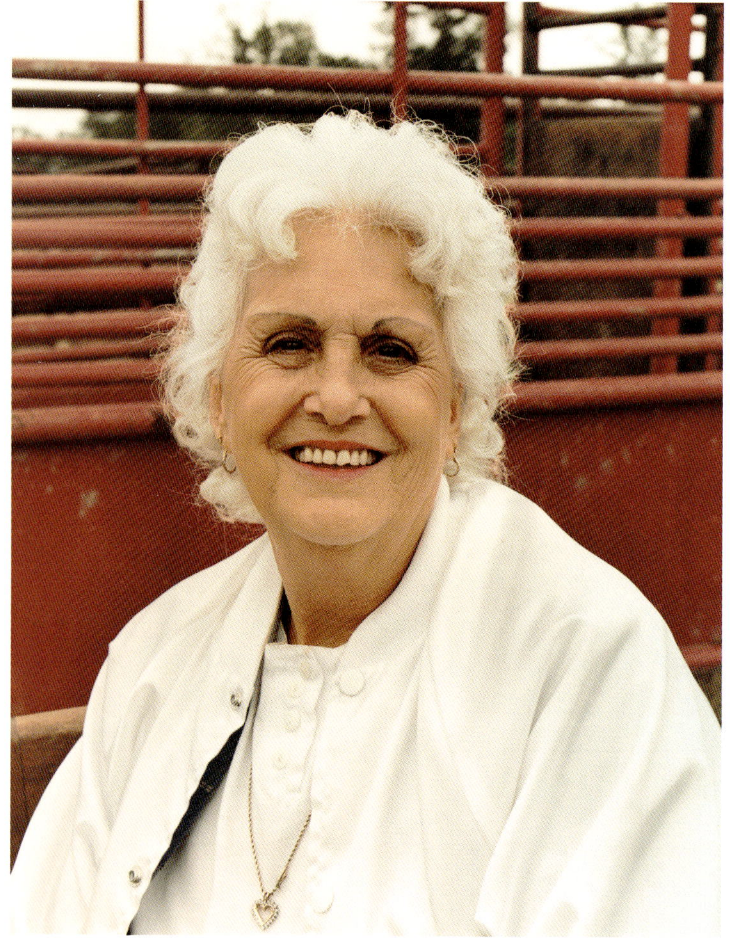

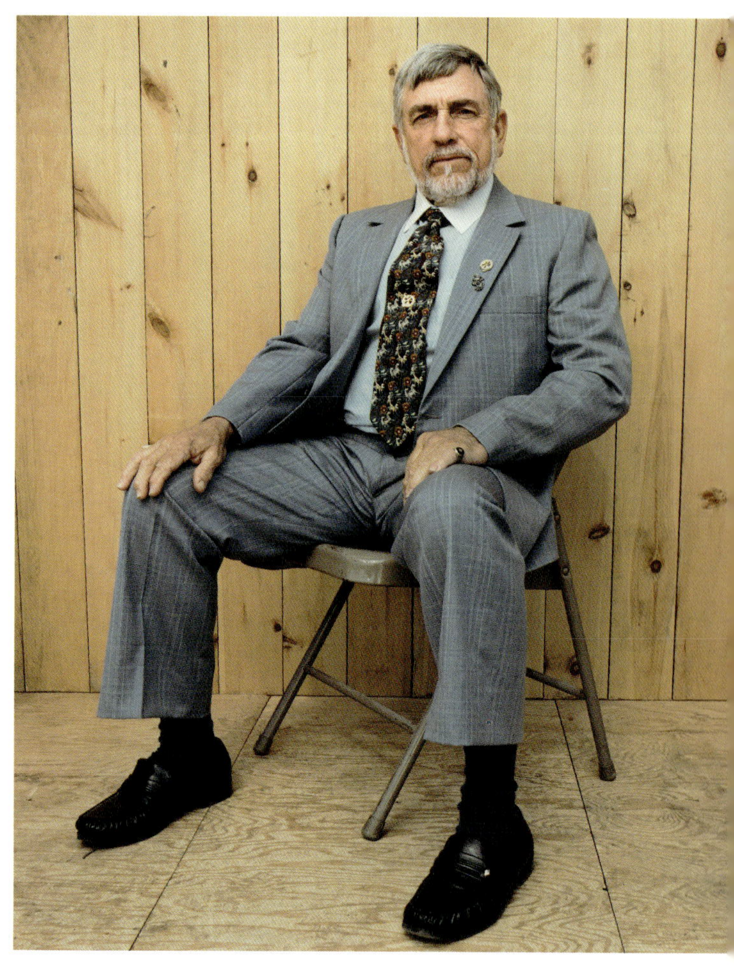

Floyd Boudreaux has been involved with American Pit Bull Terriers from the time of his youth. A perfect southern gentleman and devoted family man, he has been raising dogs from the Boudreaux bloodline that has been his hallmark since the late 1930s.

• I've been working with the breed over half a century. I also have chickens. My dad had 'em before I did, and then I had 'em before I went to grade school. My son too. It's always been a family affair. We do it on a shoestring, keep all the dogs on the same yard. But this is just a hobby. I'm a stone setter by trade, and my son does the same. Custom work is what I do, and I've been at it for a long time. My next birthday I'm going to be seventy.

• I'm located in the "hub city"—Lafayette, Louisiana. It's a bit warm, but I got it fixed pretty nice for the dogs. I have a kennel for them, plus I have what we call a "lean-to" that they can get under when it gets warm or cool or whatever. I don't have many dogs, and I don't breed many either—I don't mass produce. Every now and again, when I need a litter, I just kinda breed one. I'd say I have twenty dogs right now, counting the puppies. I don't have any favorites, I sure don't.

In terms of working with these animals, good old common sense will carry you a long way—I don't think it takes a rocket scientist. 'Course I've been very fortunate to succeed with the dogs and the chickens. And no, they're not ferocious. I wouldn't keep nothing that's ill-tempered in the chickens or the dogs. I got neighbor's kids and grandkids... Hell, they all play here. So I have no use for that. It's not my cup of tea.

• And the dogs don't take as much work as people think. First thing in the morning I'll pick up all the waste and make sure they have water before I ride off for that day. Then I do the same when I get back in the evening. Before we even have any supper, we'll just clean up with the dogs and make sure everything is secured and everybody's got water. The grown dogs, we feed once in the evening. We feed the young ones twice a day. And the little bitty ones, all their kennels and brood pens have self-feeders, so they can eat all they want at any given time.

• With the birds, you show both males and females, but mostly the males. They're just dominant—in all walks of life it's the same. You show the more outgoing animals. 'Course you can get to where they get spoiled, the dogs *and* the birds. My grandkids have one dog that they call by the name of Girlfriend. She's a national champion puller dog, but she's only twenty-nine pounds—and she's a house dog. These dogs sure enjoy the [weight] pulling. They pull on command. In other words, you can't touch them, you can't force them, you can't threaten them. They all do this on their own, and if they choose not to do it they just don't. I would never force an animal to do anything that he wouldn't do on his own.

• When I was a younger fella we had some bird dogs, some champion dogs, sure did. Pointers and Irish Setters. But I wasn't much in the sport of killing birds, so I just stuck to the Bulldogs instead. They're sharp, they're smart, they're loyal... They're the All-American dog.

FLOYD BOUDREAUX Lafayette, Louisiana

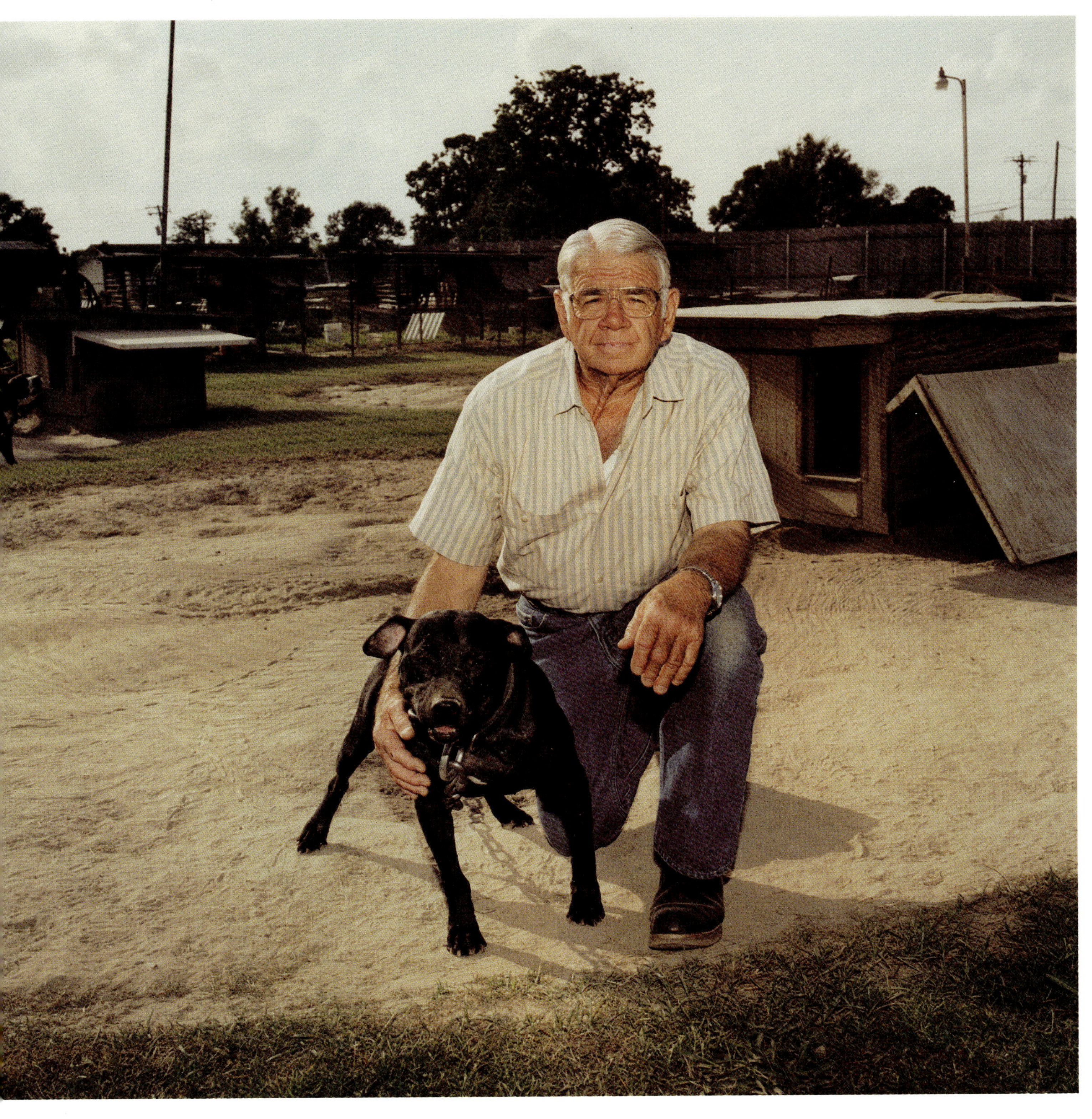

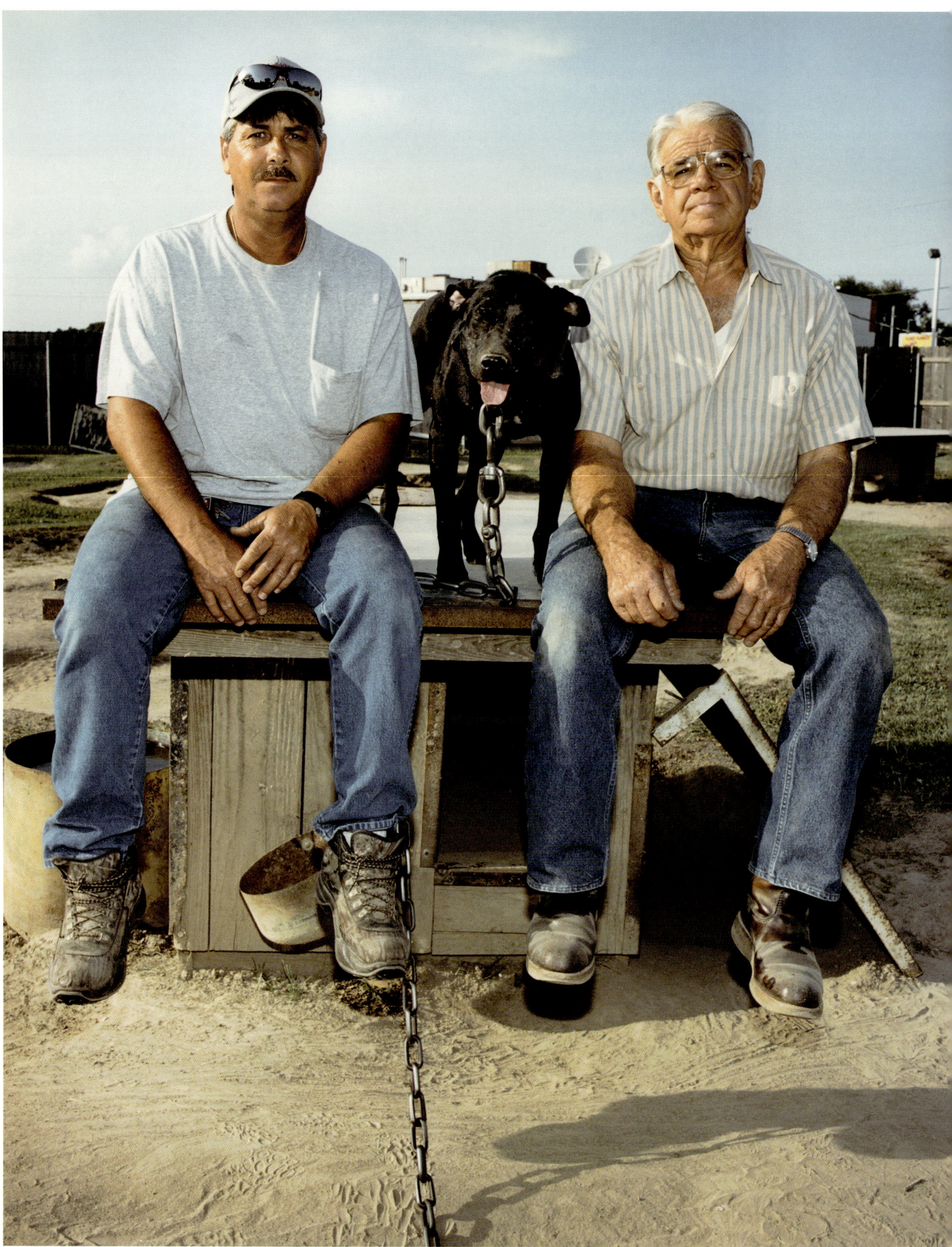

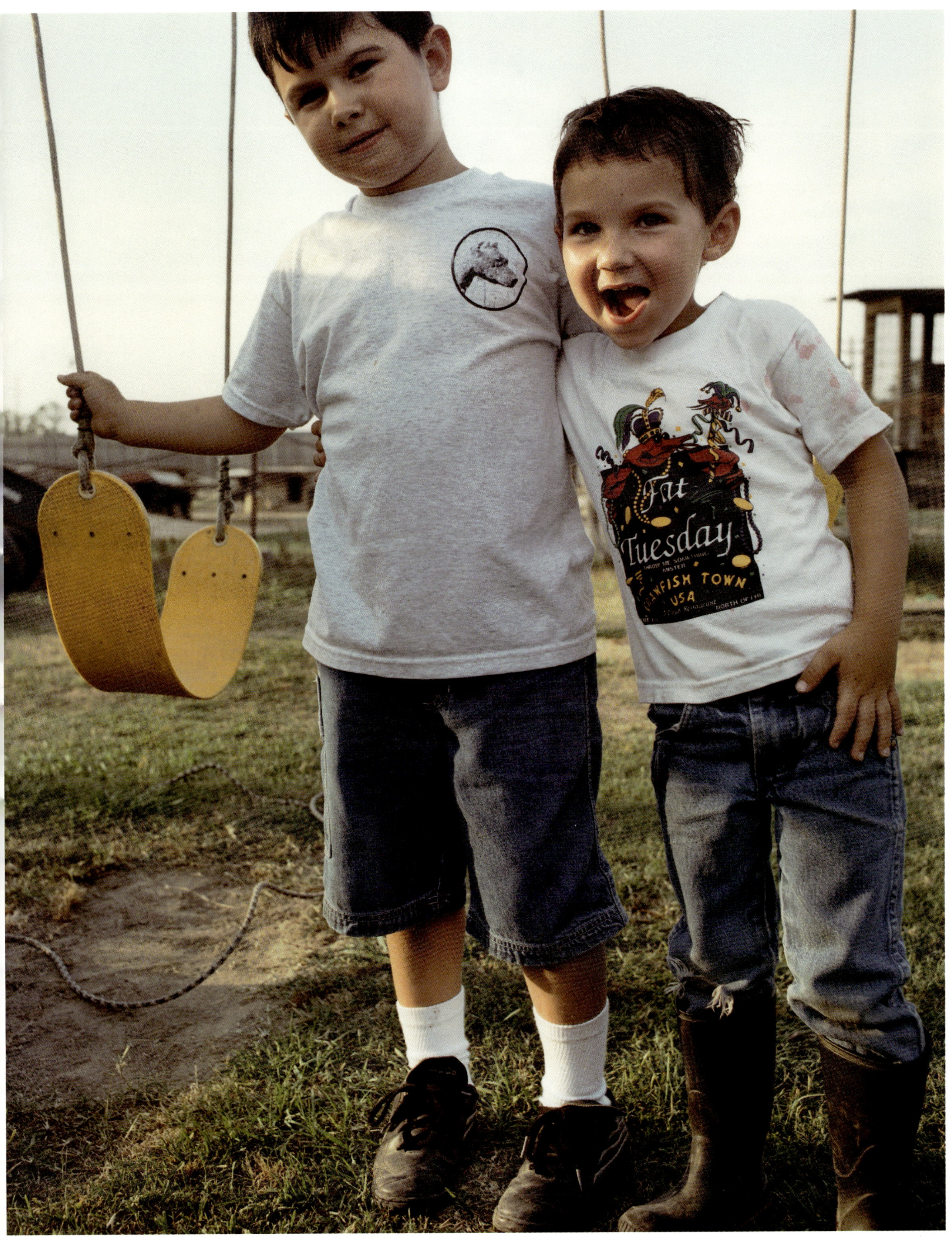
Fat Tuesday
USA

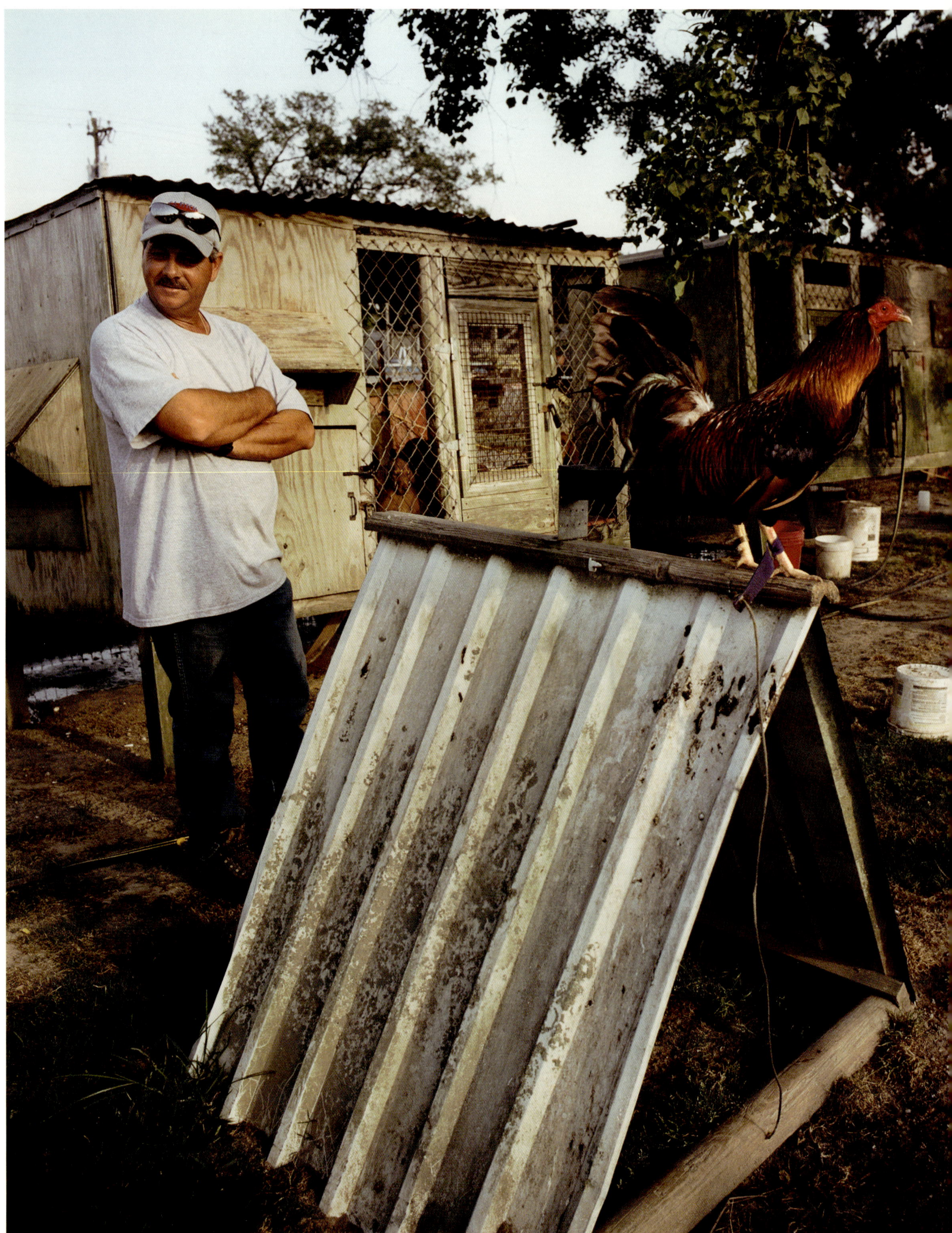

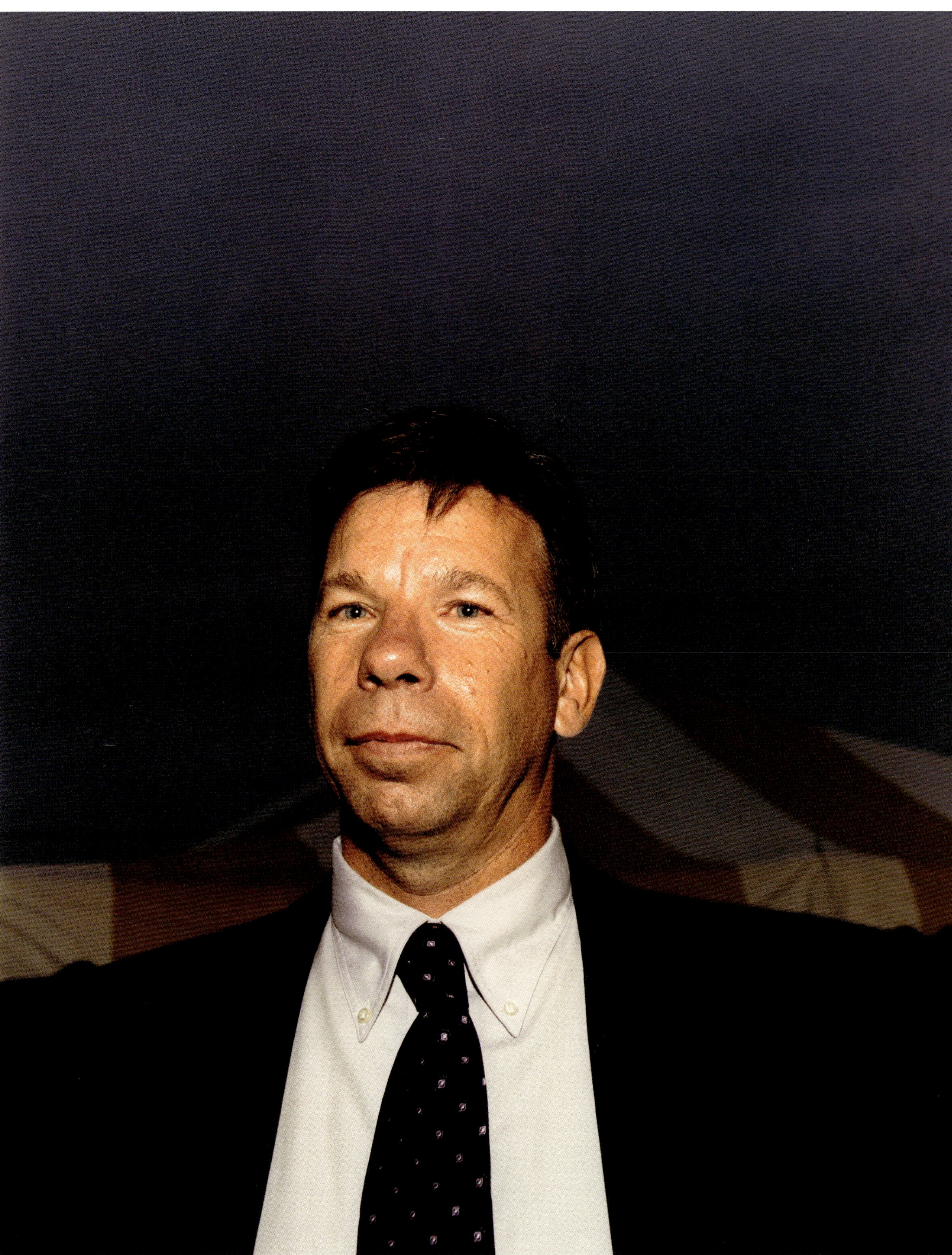

AMERICAN PIT BULL TERRIER
CONFORMATION STANDARD

OVERALL APPEARANCE: 20 POINTS

**Start your judging as the dogs are walking into the ring.
You can judge gait and movement.
You should be able to see from the first, the dogs
you want to work with.
Find the right TYPE first.**

Conforming to type

Type is the essence of the breed. Breed type is that collection of specific characteristics which, when taken together, separate one breed from another.

Athletic–Solid front end, light and springy back end
Sturdy–not racy or frail
Confident, secure, carries its territory with him
Should look like an American Pit Bull Terrier
from across the ring

Balance

Height to weight–(square dog)
Head in proportion to body
Equal angulation of front to back
Length of neck

Overall appeal

Clean and shiny
Alert and outgoing
Presentation

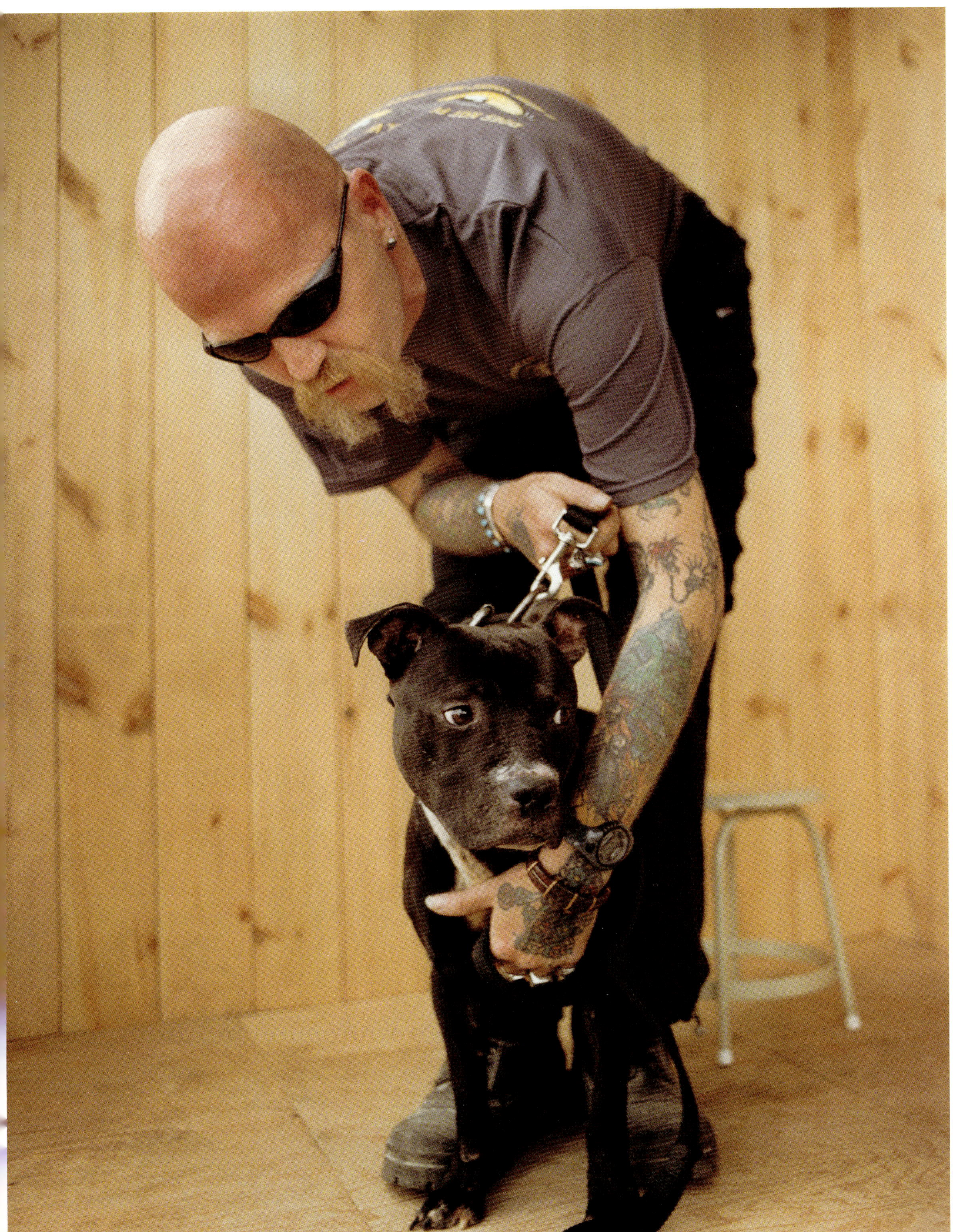

ATTITUDE: 10 POINTS

Should reflect these traits

Proud—non-threatened
Alert and outgoing—friendly to humans
Interested in things around them
In control of their space

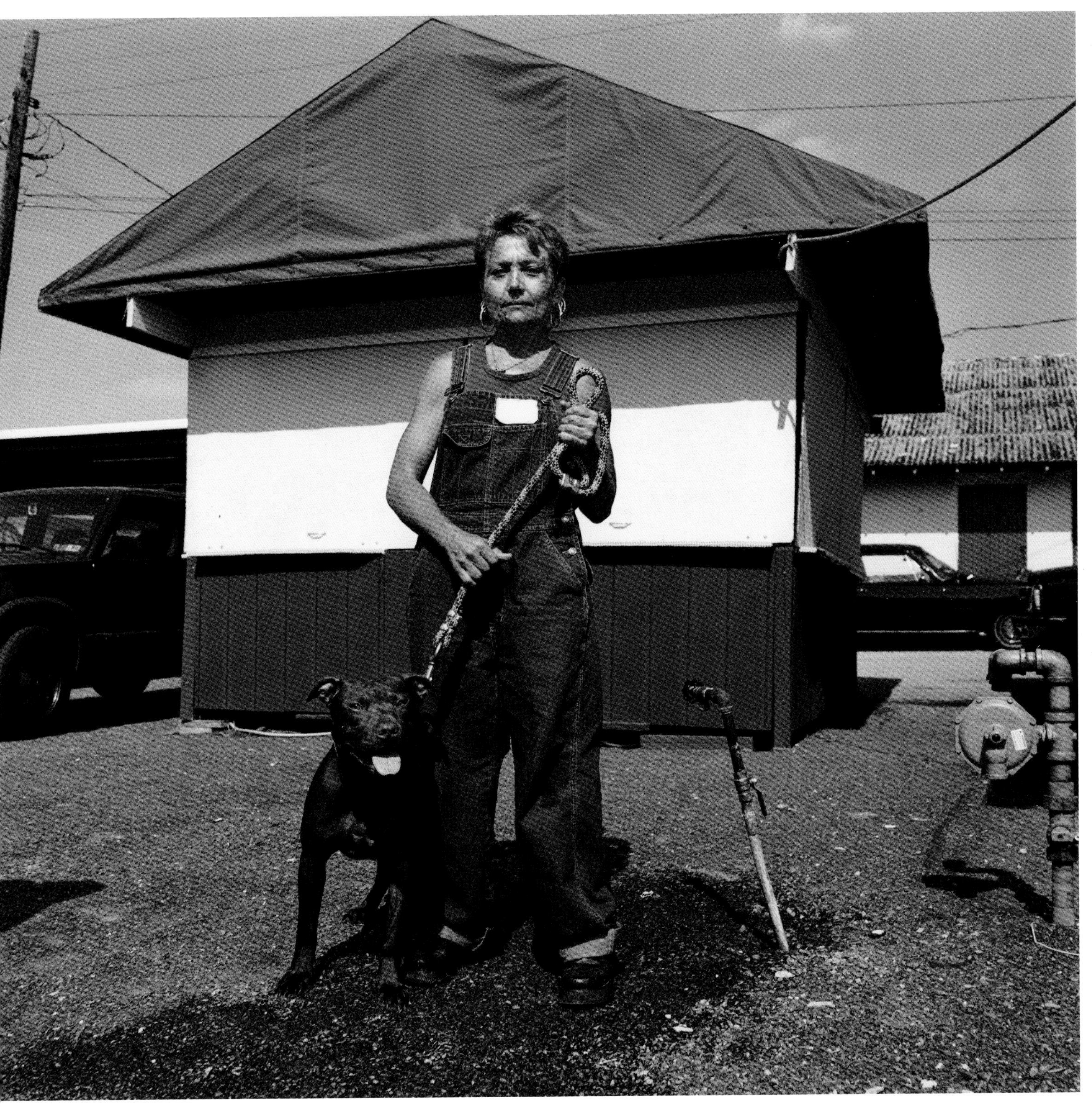

BACK END: 30 POINTS

Hip

Long and sloping—low set tail
Alert and outgoing—friendly to humans

Angulation of back leg

The comparative length of femur, tibia/fibula and metatarsus causes angulation or lack of angulation

Femur—short. Stifle joint in upper one third of the back leg
Tibia / fibula longer
Metatarsals—too long dog becomes cow-hocked.
Ratio between lengths of bone causes a bent stifle, which leads to a bent hock, natural springiness

Muscle attachment—well past the joint

Muscles are to be long and flat, well conditioned

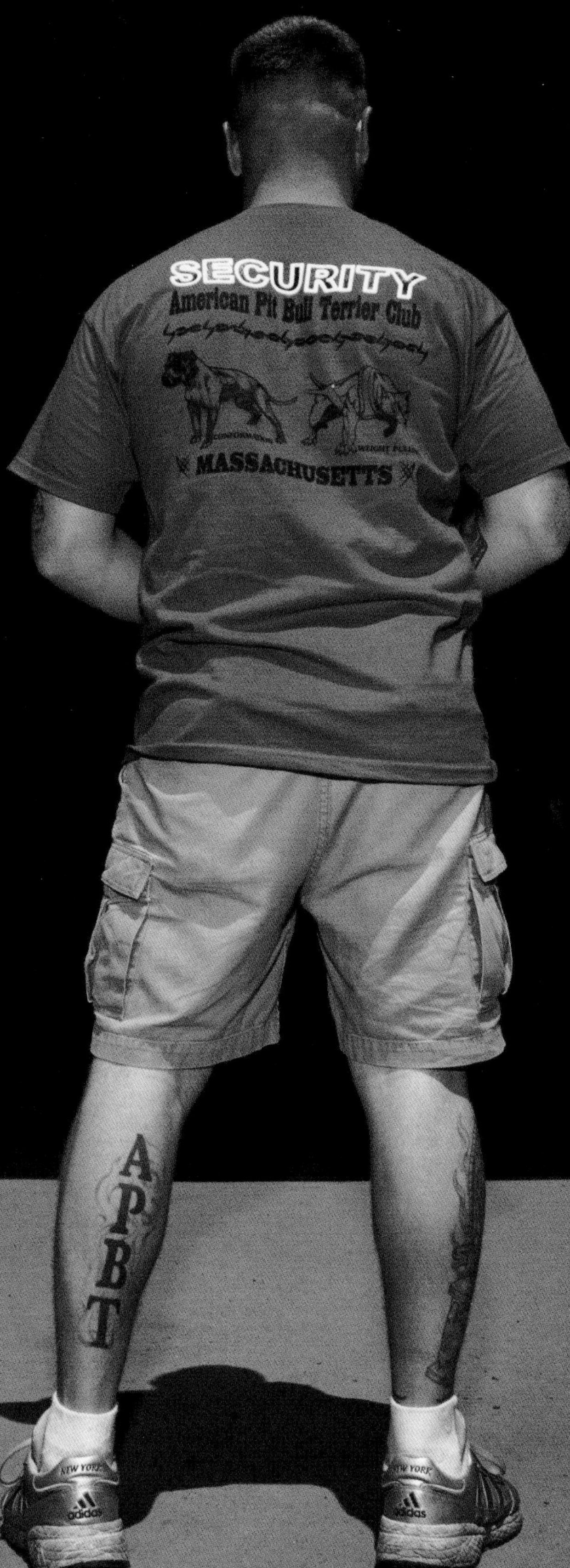
SECURITY
American Pit Bull Terrier Club
MASSACHUSETTS
APBT
NEW YORK
adidas

FRONT END: 20 POINTS

Rib Cage

Deep and elliptical. From side view should be even with the elbow
Well sprung at top, tapering to bottom

Shoulders

Wider than rib cage at the eighth rib, well laid back
Broad enough to support adequate musculature

Scapula

Forty-five-degree angle to the ground
Broad and flat

Humerus

Forty-five-degree angle
Elbow comes below bottom of rib cage
Elbows lie flat

Forearms

Slightly longer than humerus and solid
Two X thickness of metatarsal at hock

Feet

Small and tight
Set high on pasterns

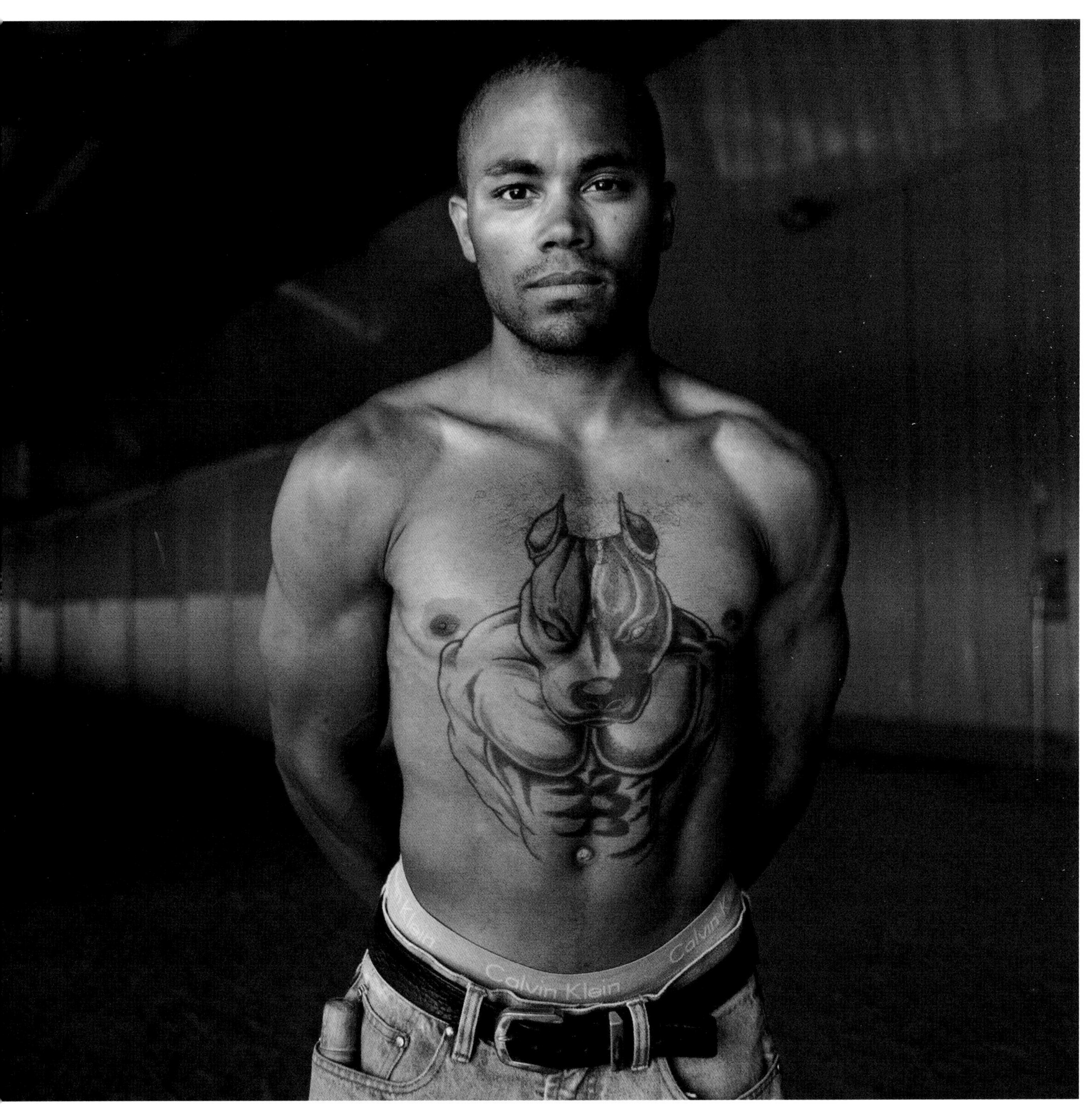
Calvin Klein

HEAD AND NECK: 15 POINTS

Balanced in relationship to rest of body.

Two/three width of shoulders
Cheeks twenty-five percent wider than neck at base of skull
Nose to stop—stop to back of head
Bridge well developed—wider than head at base of ears
Depth of head
Straight box like–muzzle
Lips tight
Teeth—wide at base, top cutters fit behind bottom cutters
Eyes—small and deep set

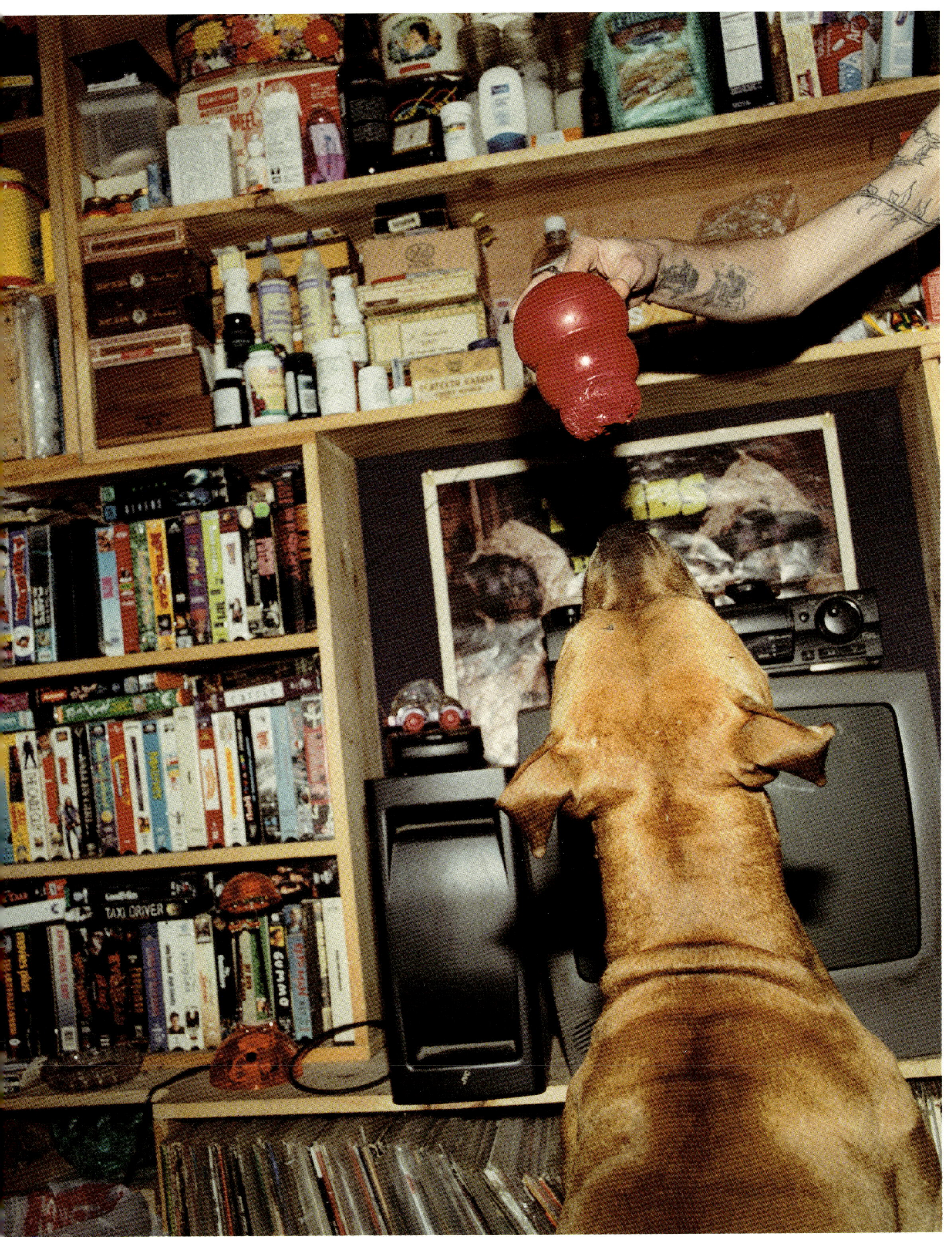
TAXI DRIVER
GUMMO

TAIL AND COAT: 5 POINTS

Skin thick and loose around neck, tight over rest of body
Vertical folds around neck and chest
Short and bristled—glossy
Tail length—just about point of hock
Shape—held down like a pump handle
Color—any color or combination of colors

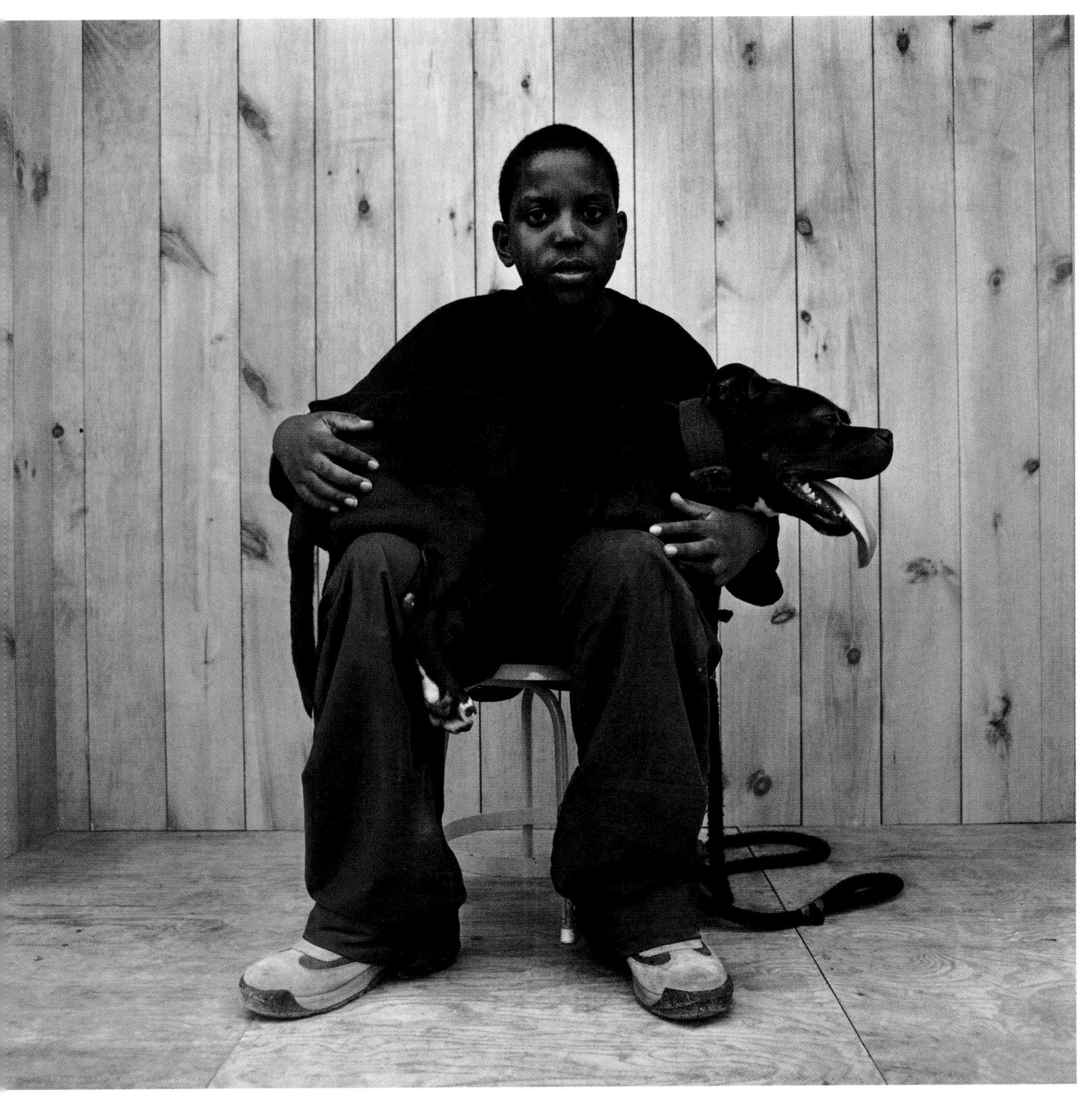

DISQUALIFICATIONS

Bitches in heat cannot be shown
Monorchid or cryptorchid
Spayed or neutered dogs

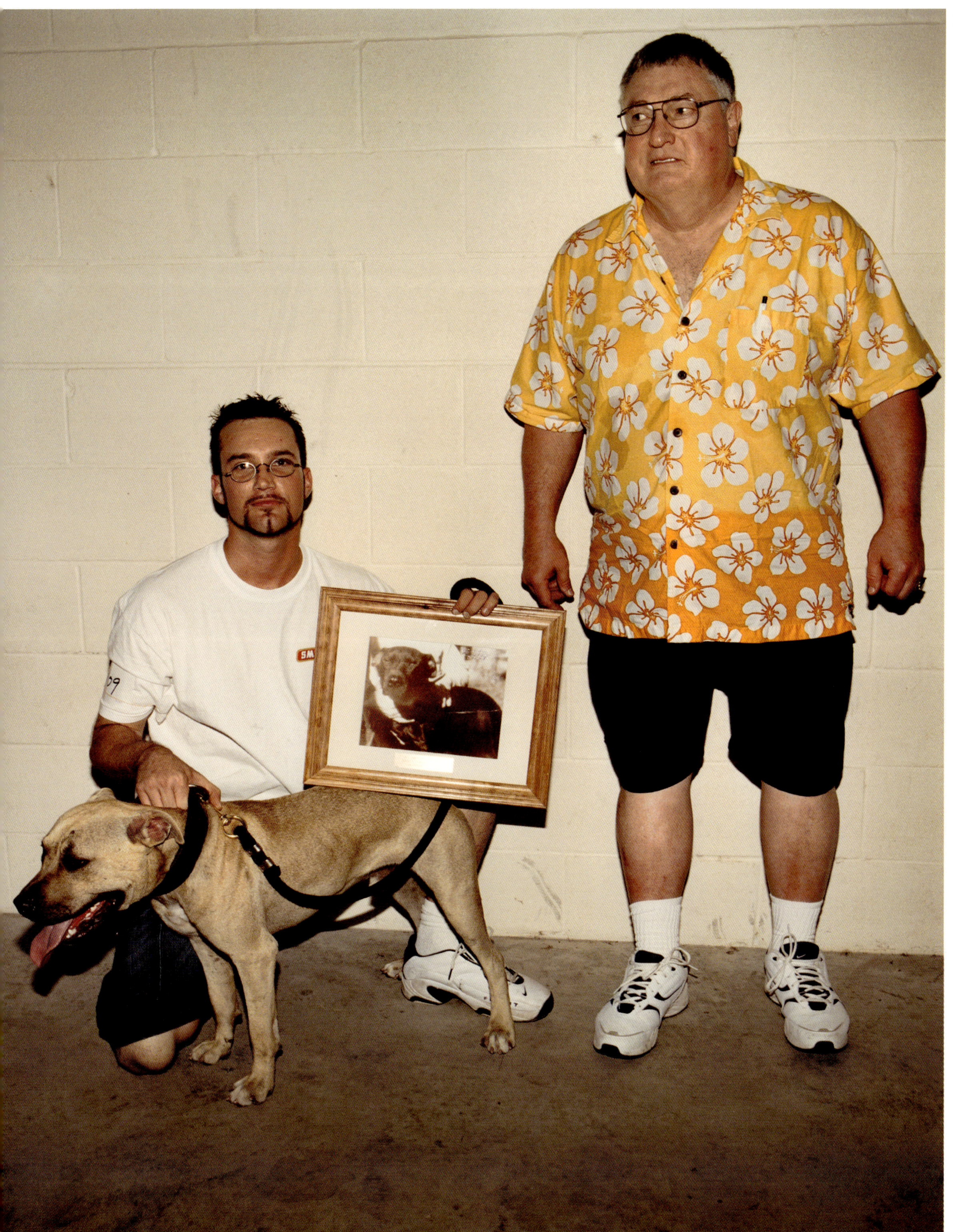

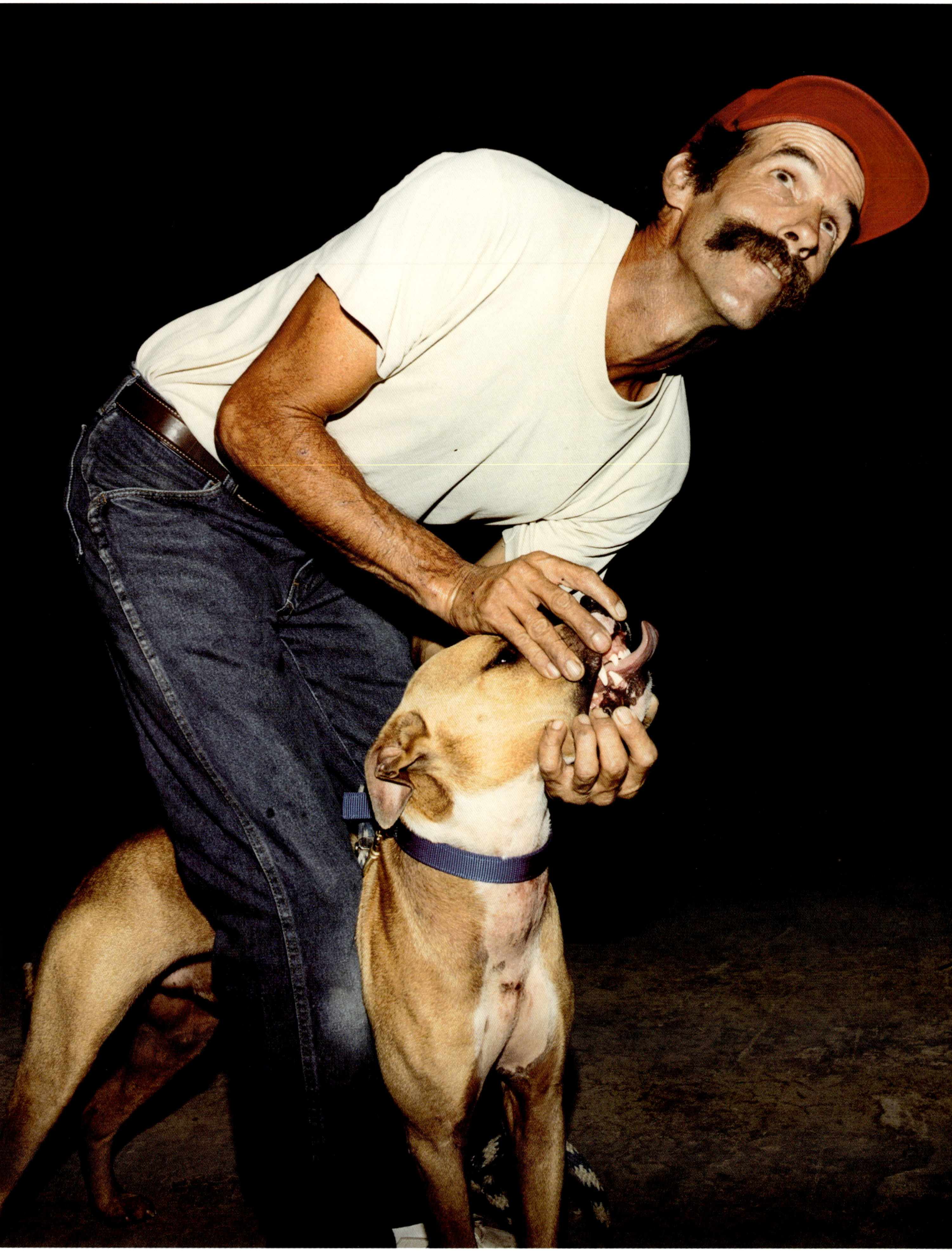

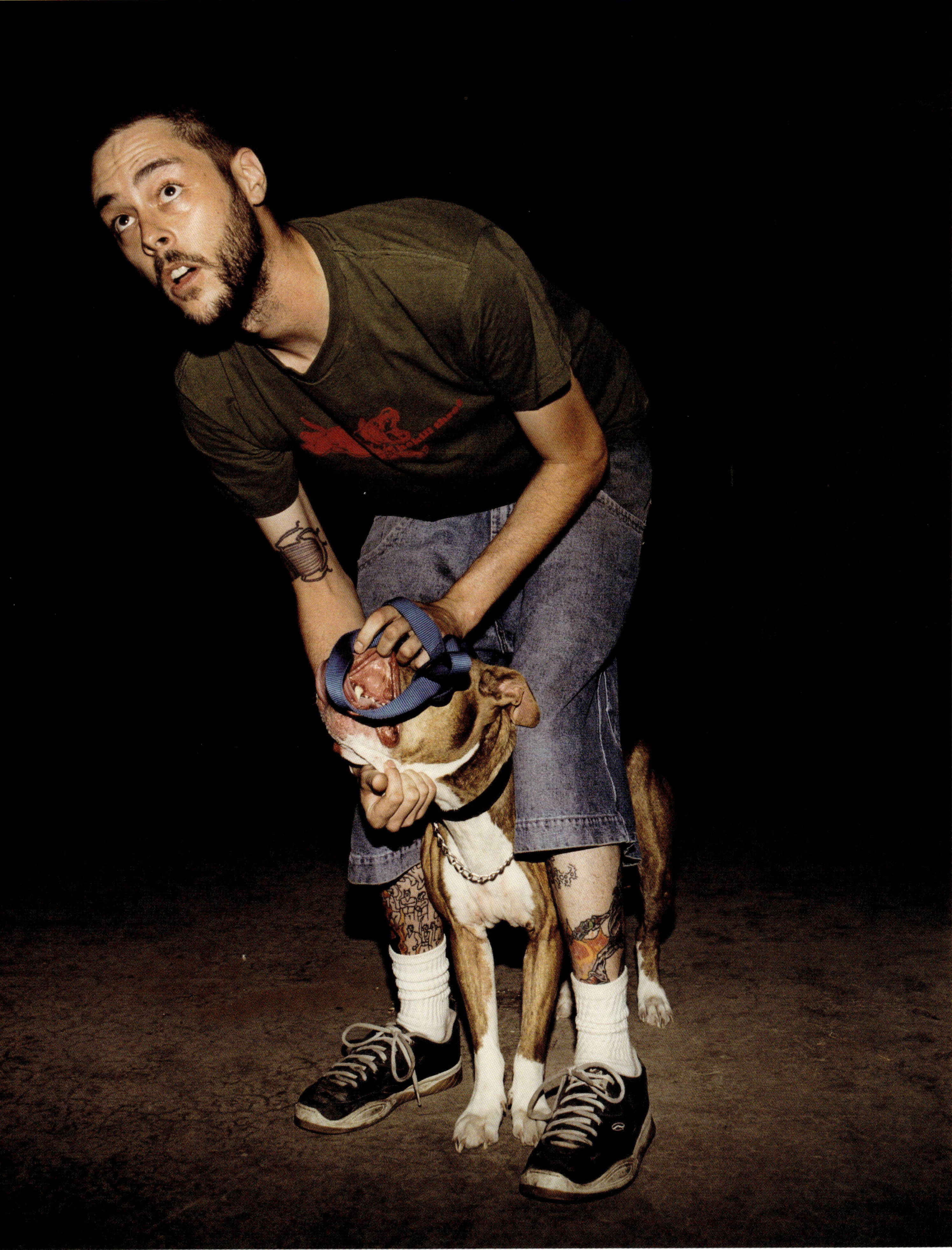

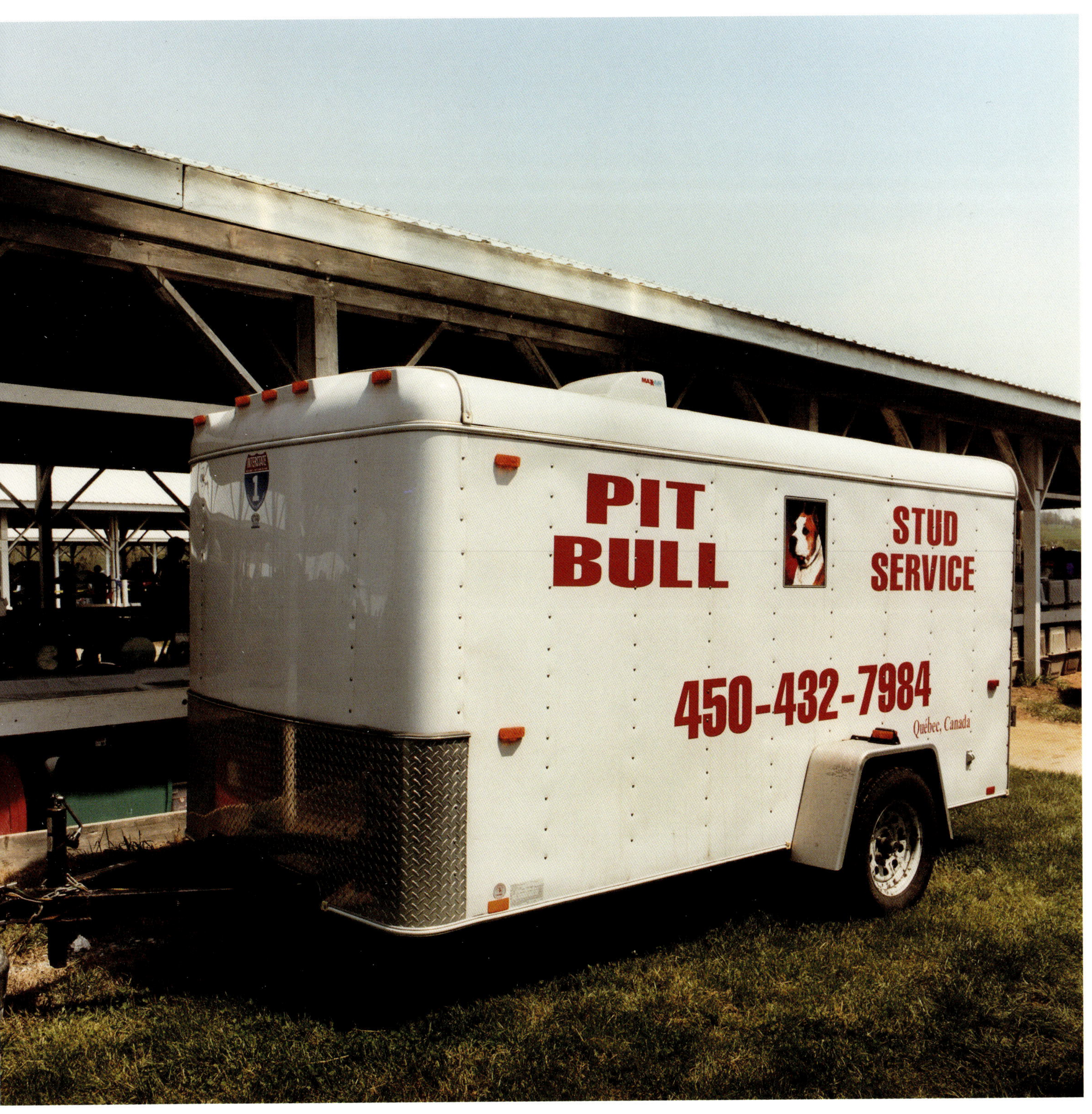
PIT
BULL
STUD
SERVICE
450-432-7984
Québec, Canada

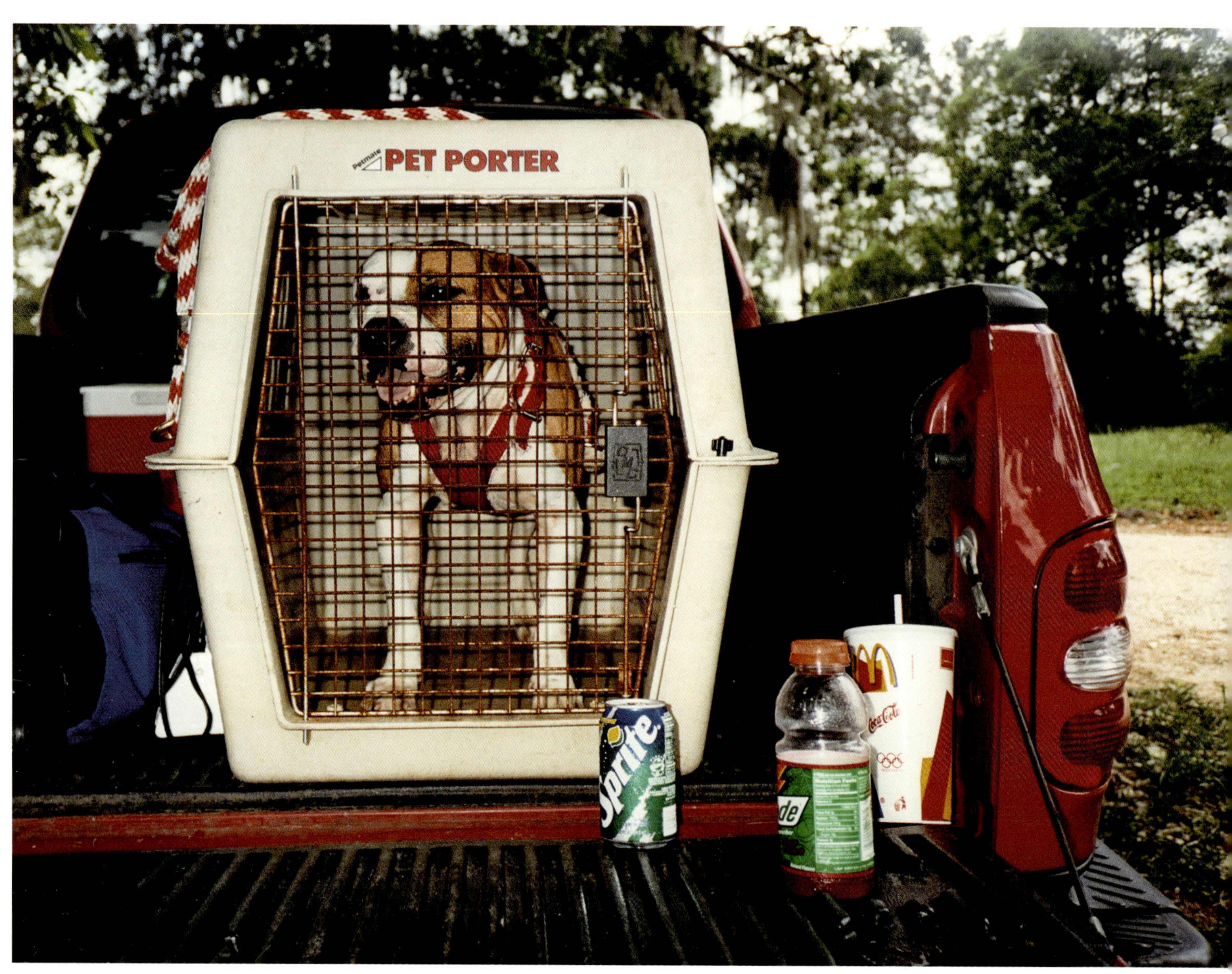
PET PORTER
Sprite

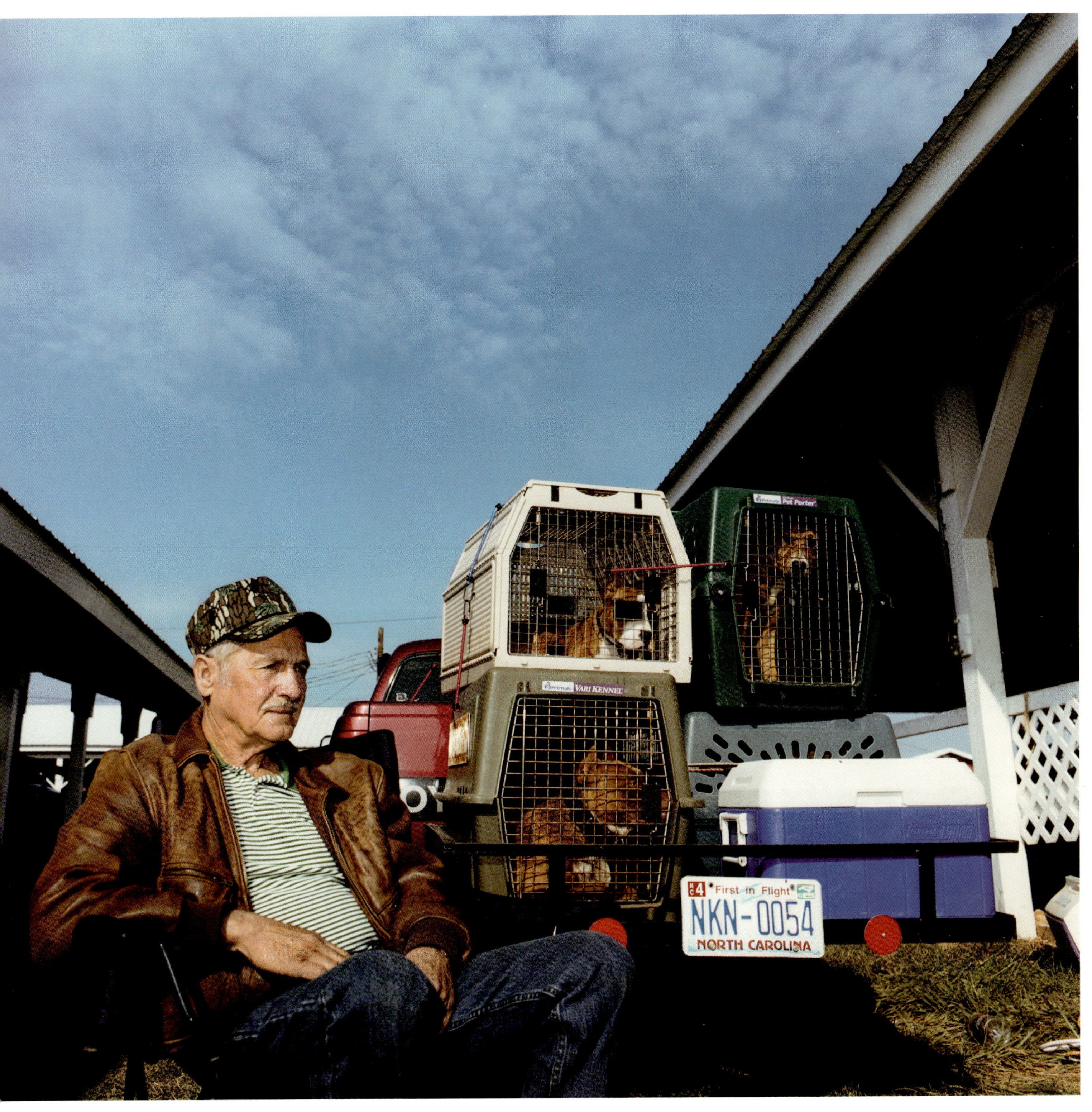
VARI KENNEL
Pet Porter
First in Flight
NKN-0054
NORTH CAROLINA

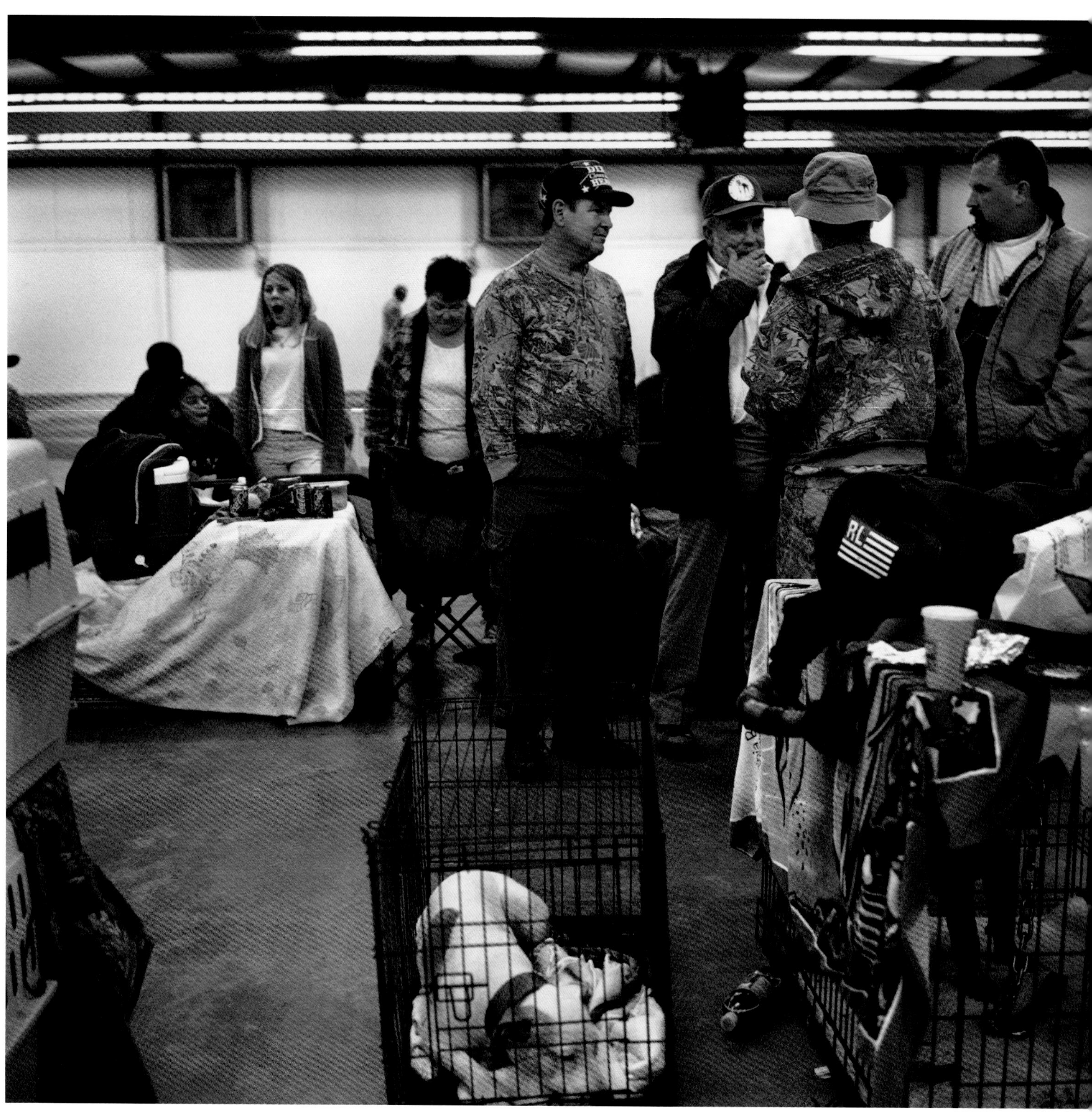
RL

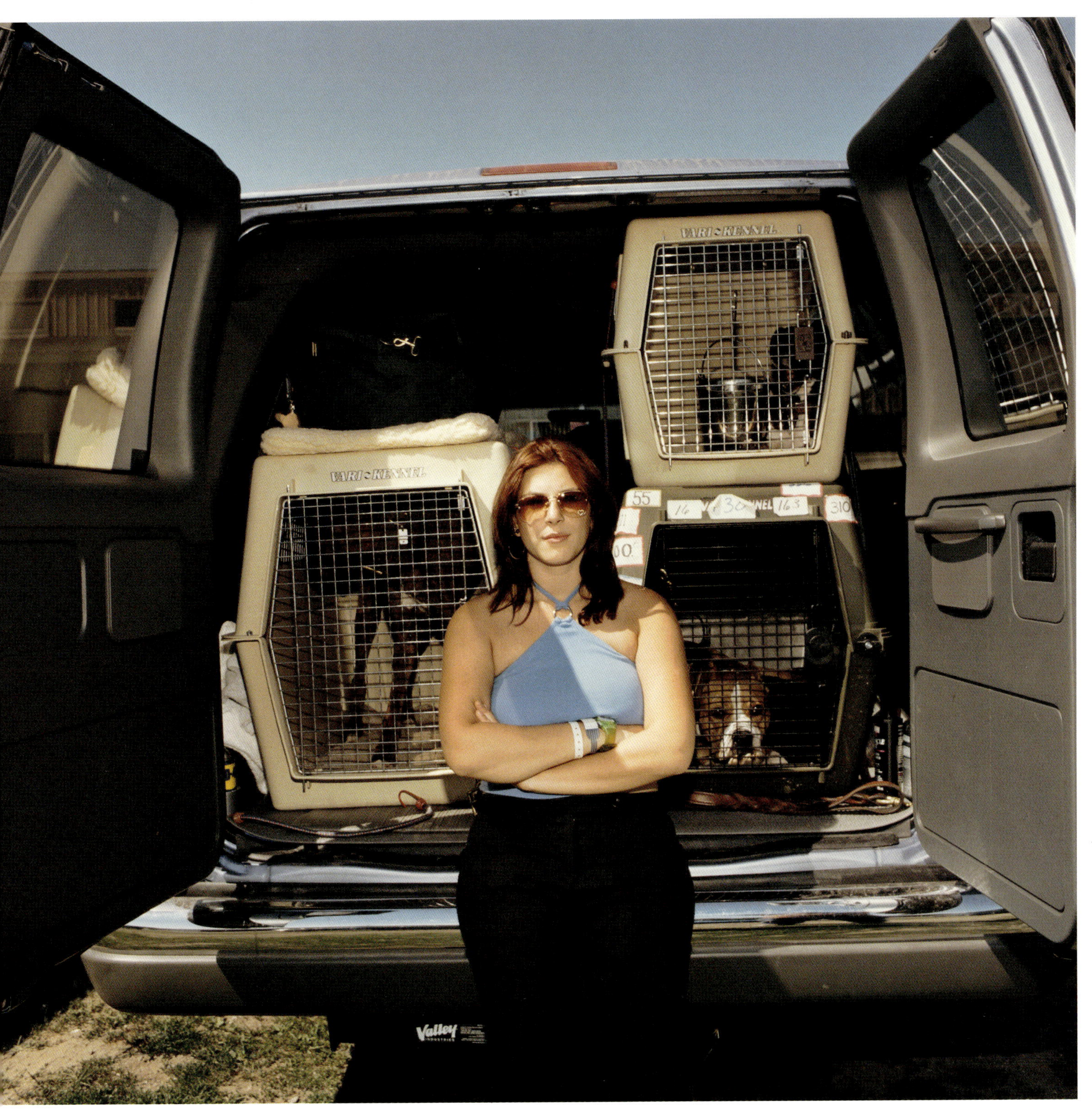
VARI-KENNEL
VARI-KENNEL
Valley

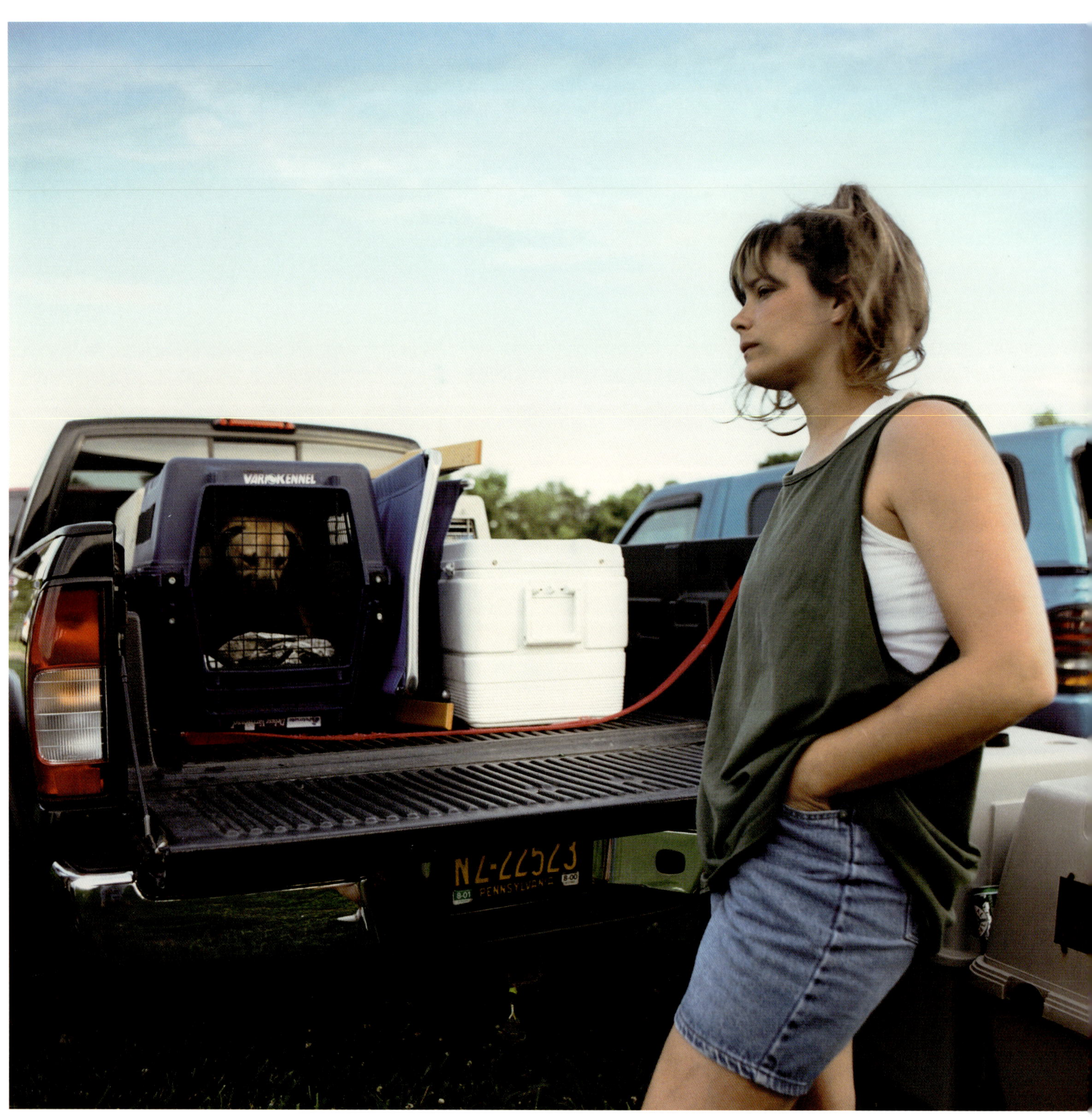
VARI KENNEL
PENNSYLVANIA

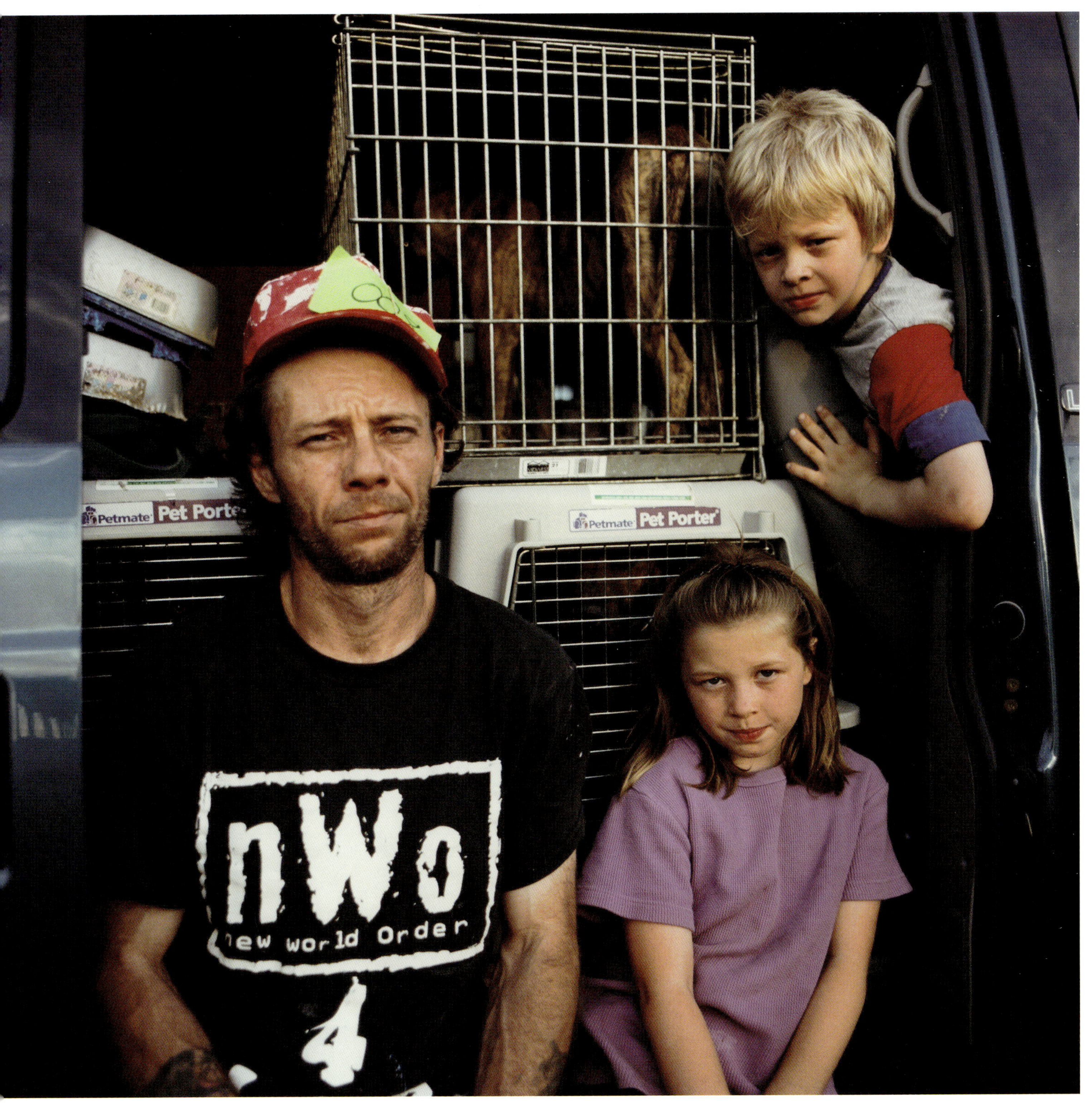
Petmate Pet Porter
Petmate Pet Porter
nWo
new world Order
4

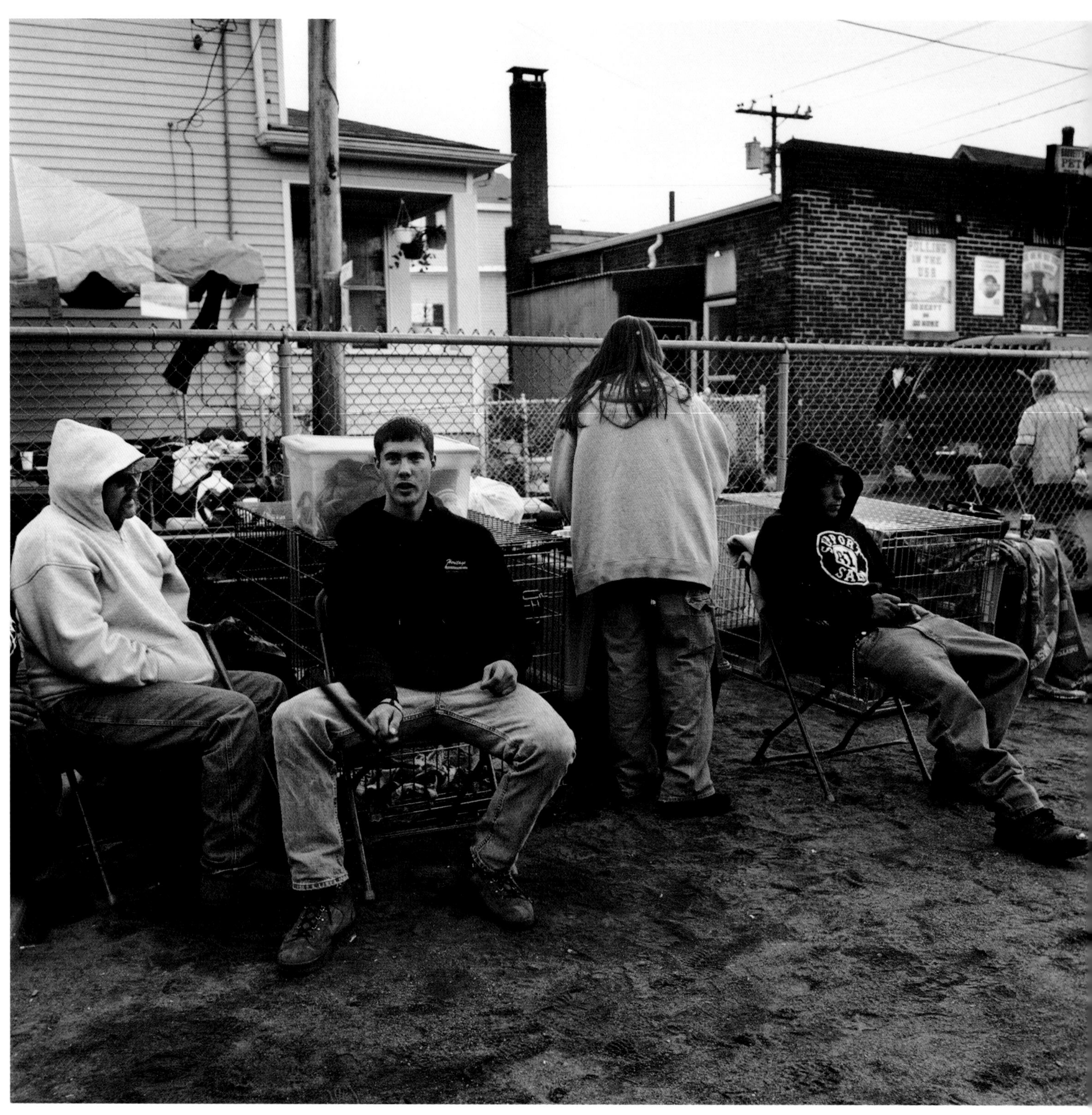

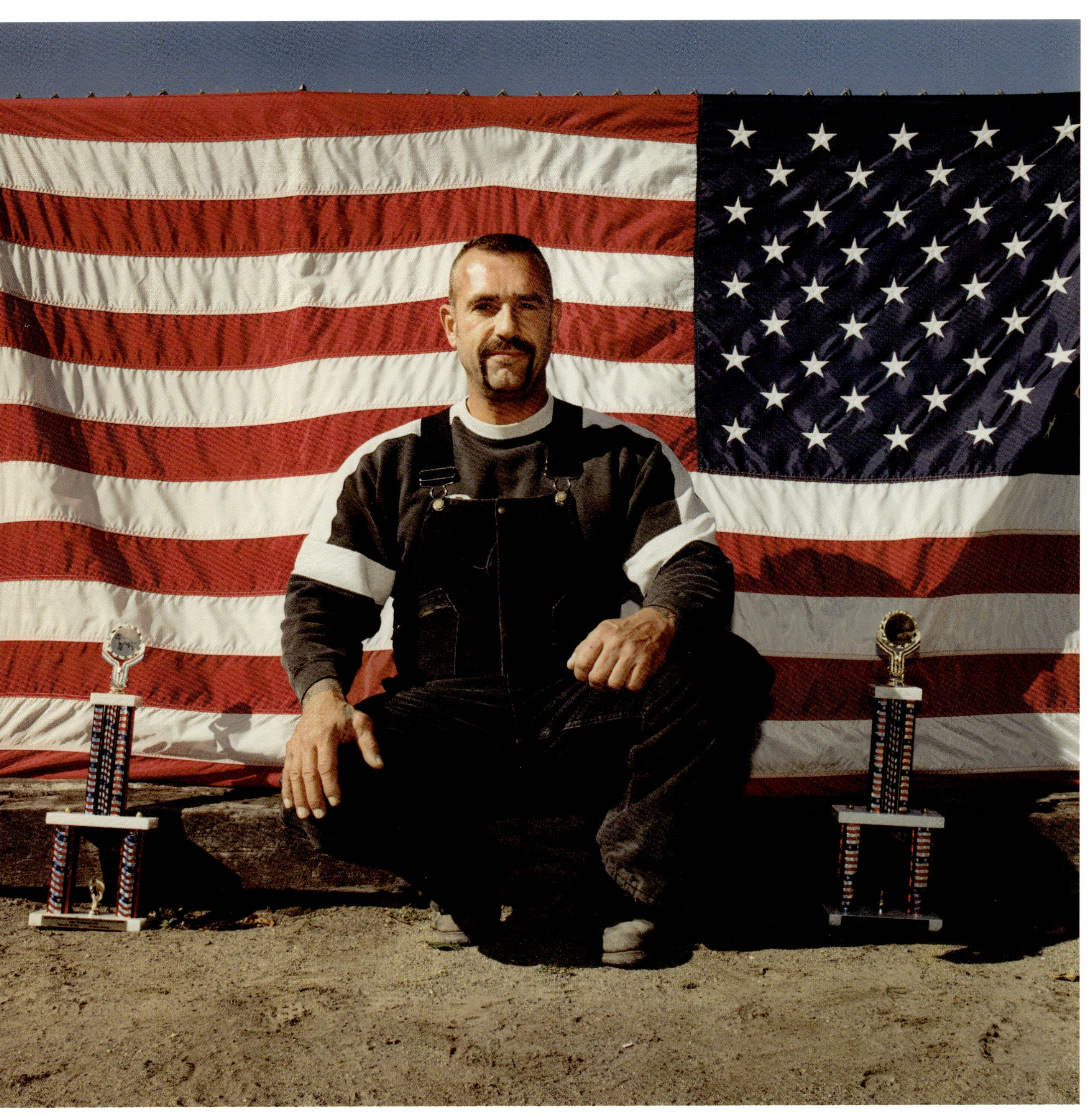

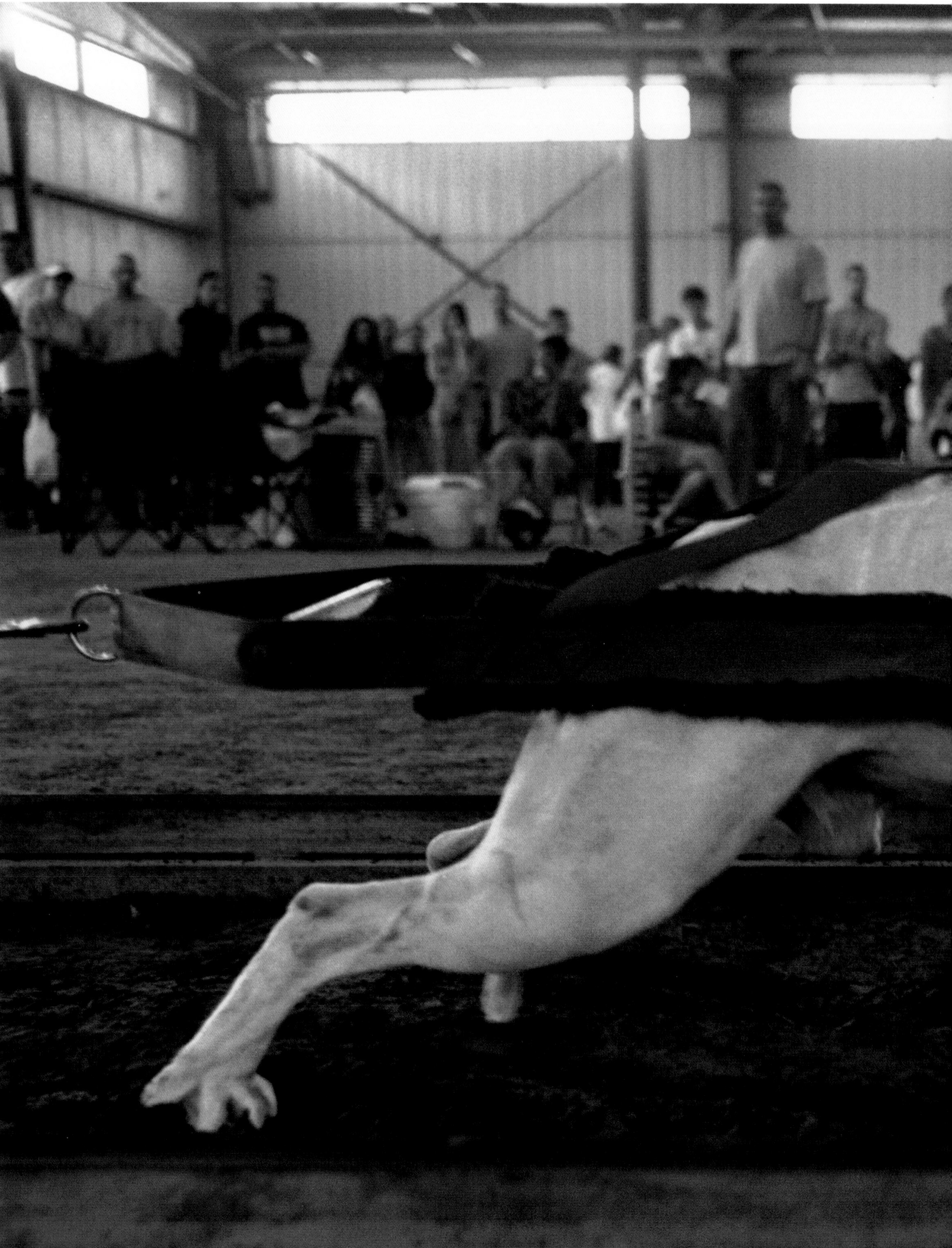

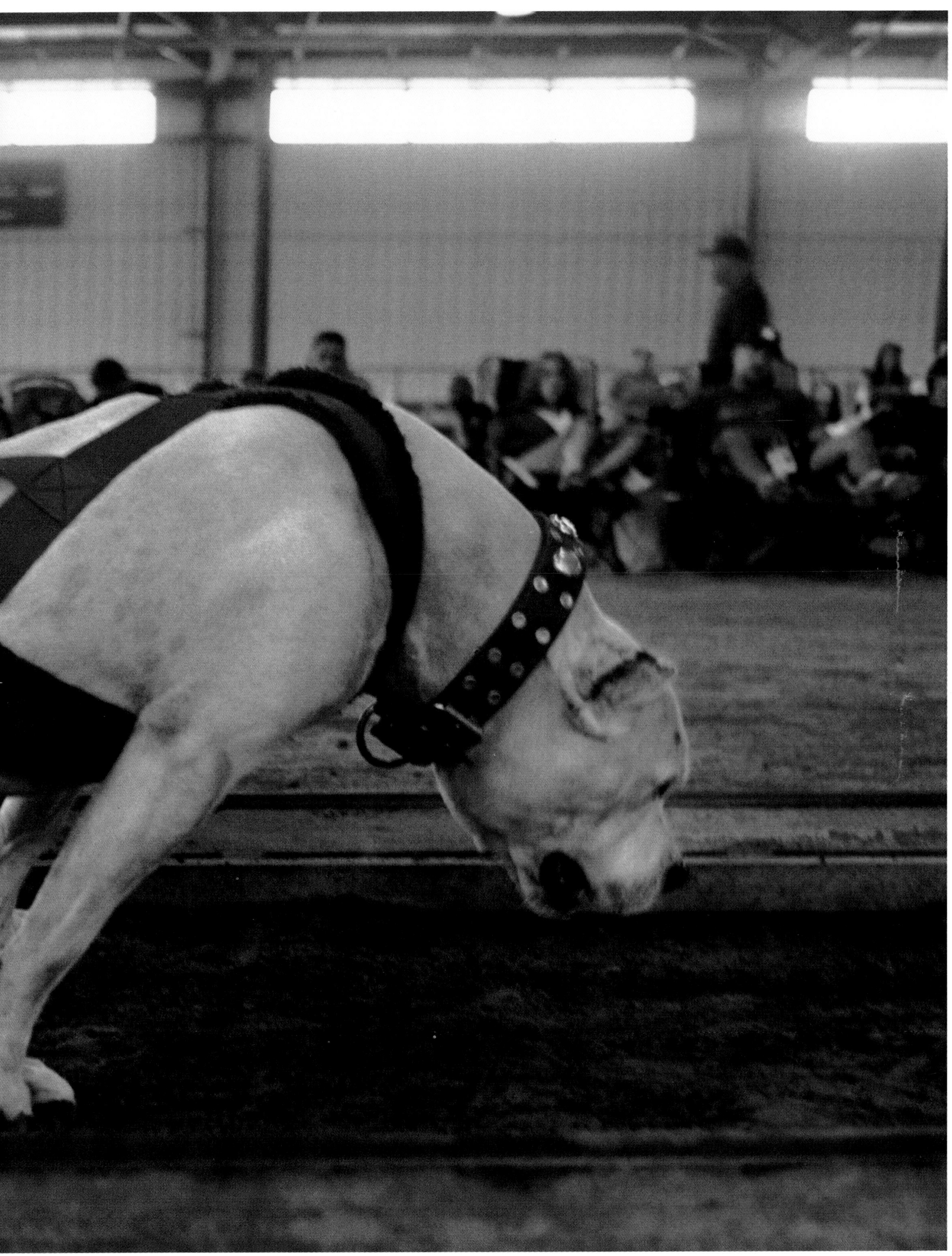

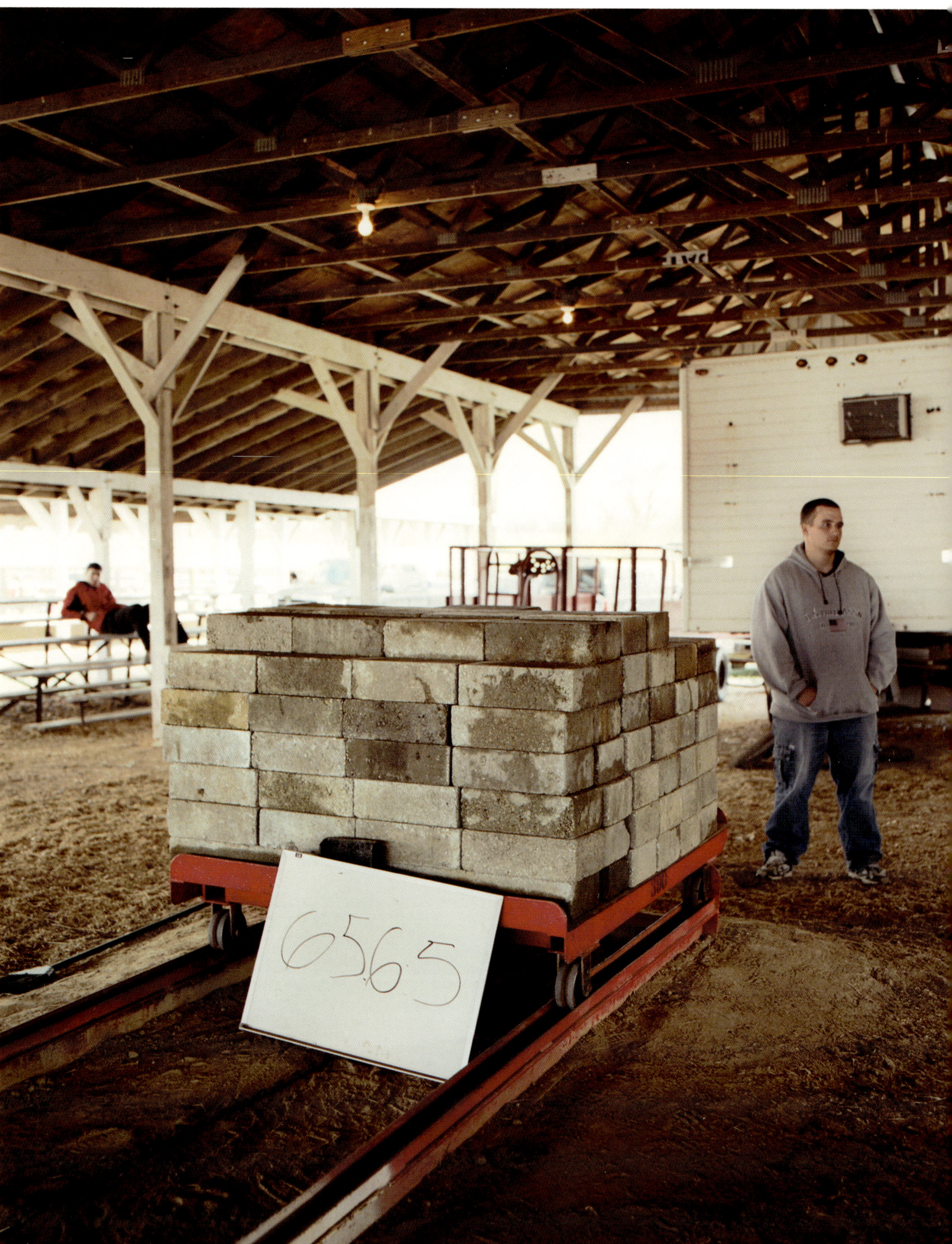
6565

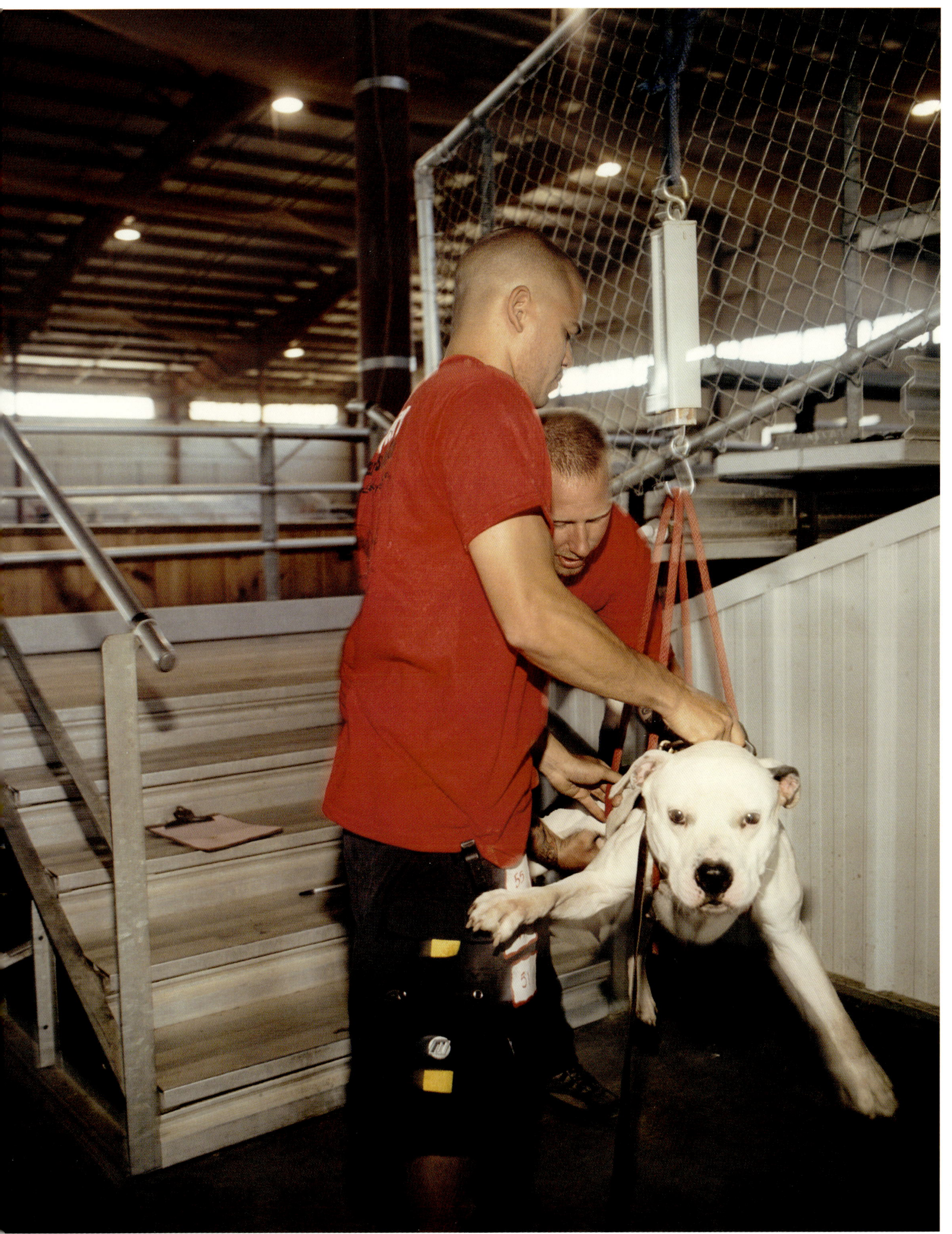

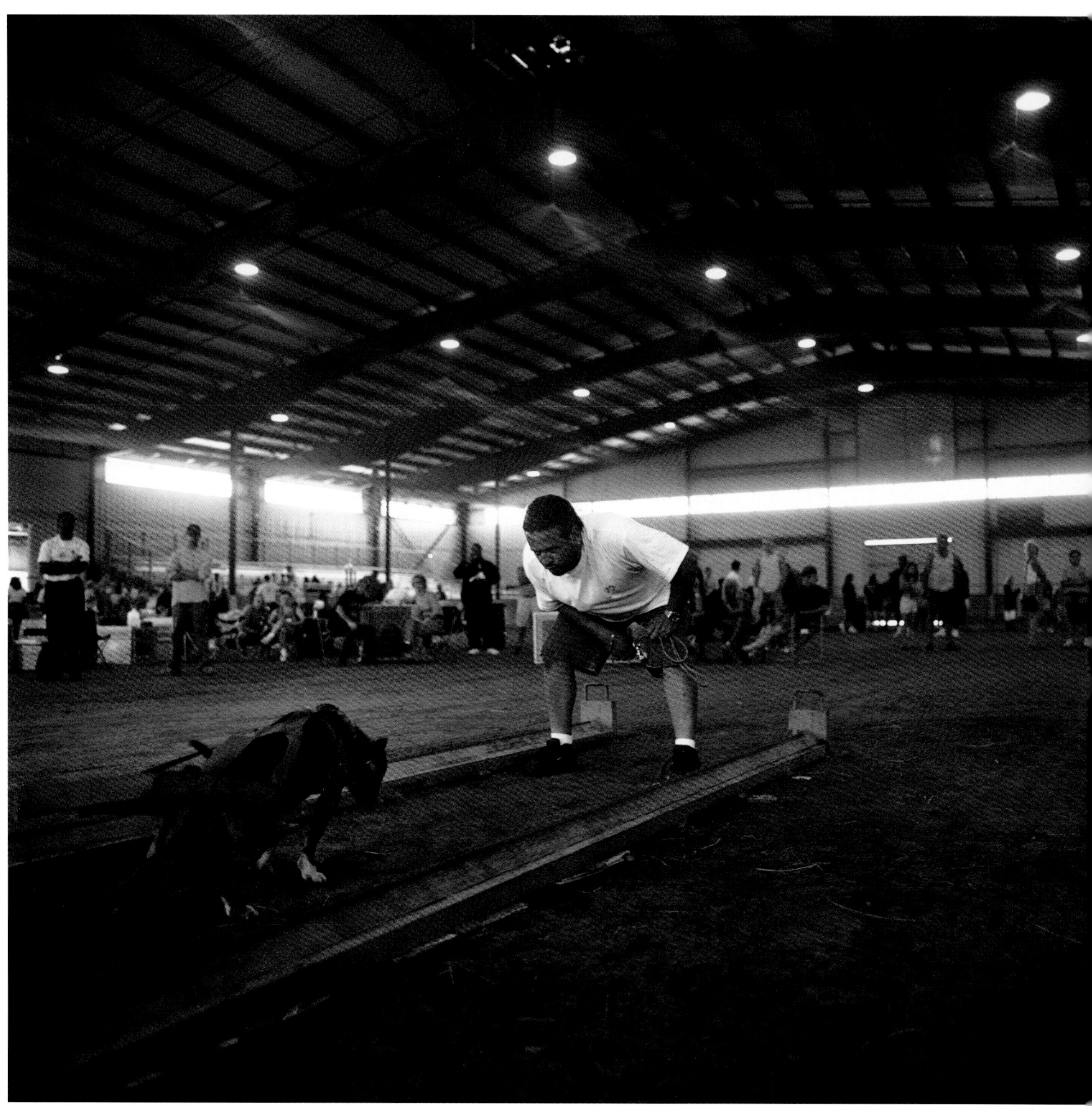

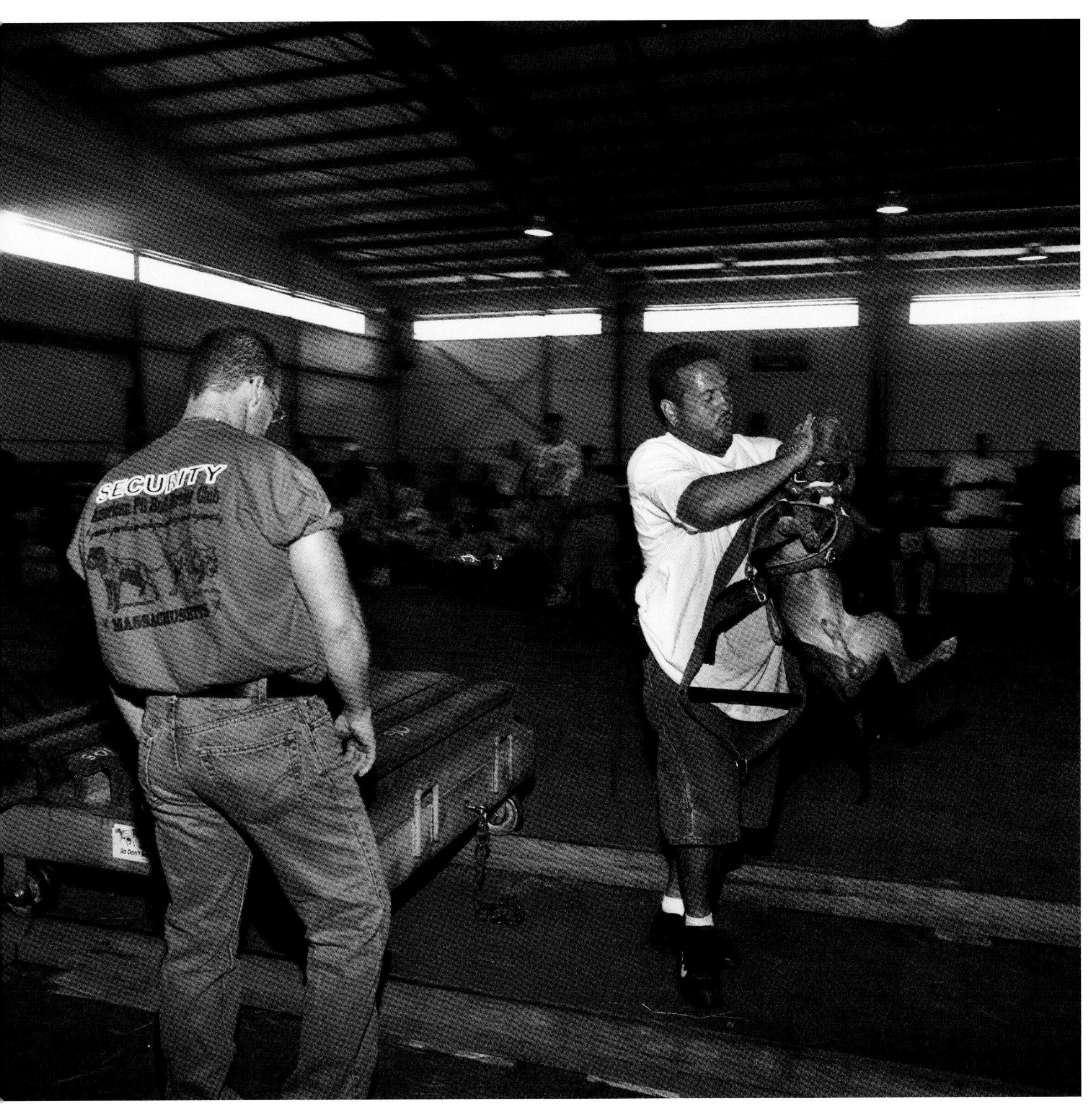
SECURITY
MASSACHUSETTS

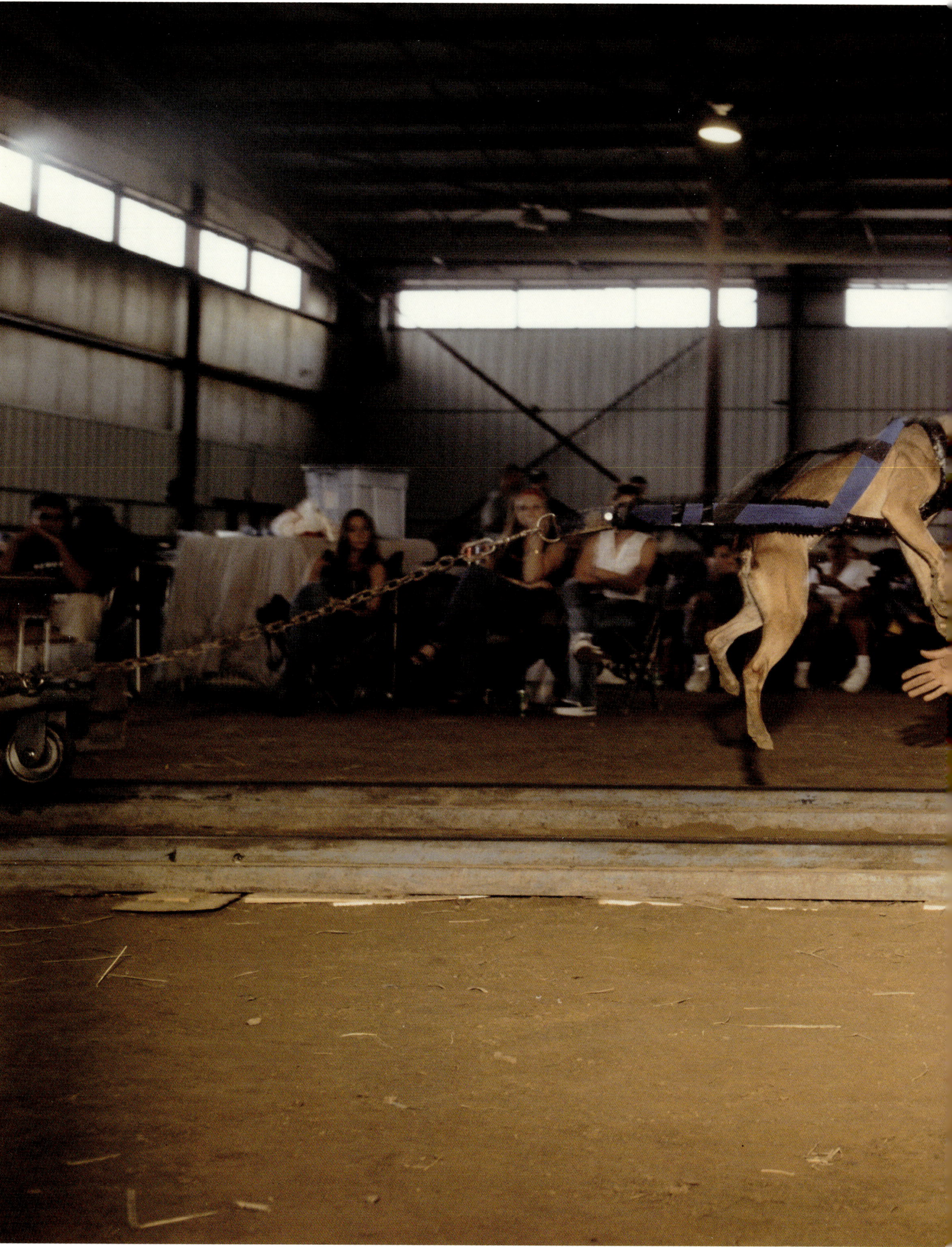

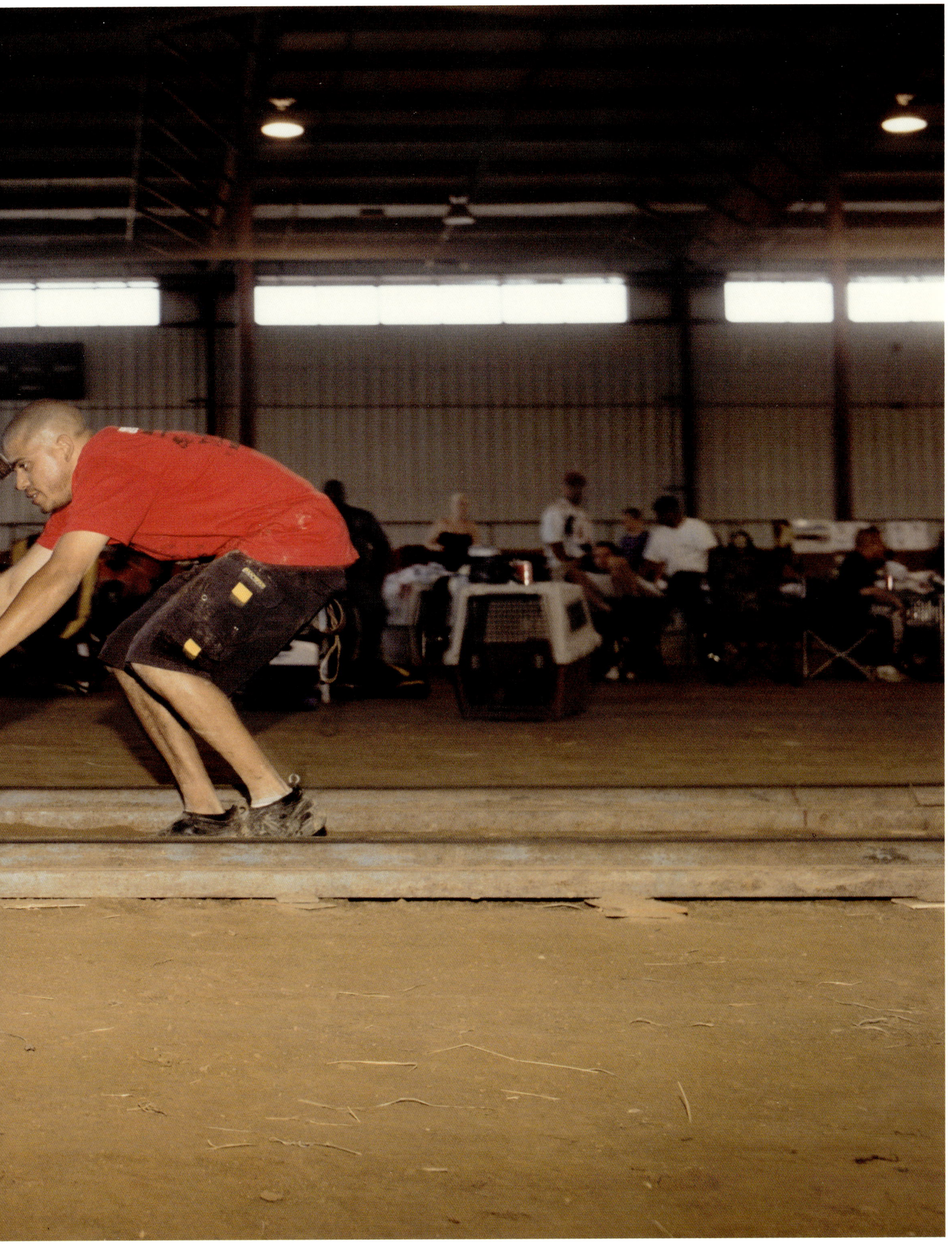

Nino Bussa came to American from Palermo, Sicily, in 1971. Since then he has lived in Brooklyn, New York, where he has owned more than one hundred American Pit Bull Terriers—and just as many carrier pigeons.

• I like to condition my dogs for the weight pulls. You got to start training the dogs when they're very young. They get about twenty seconds to pull the weight, maybe two or three thousand pounds, down twenty feet of track. It's really beautiful to see what a dog can do. About nine years ago, I saw a female pull about six-thousand pounds. And she only weighed about thirty-five pounds! A little dog like that—oh my God, I was crying when I saw what she could do.
• I like to buy my dogs inbred: father/daughter breeding. That way the dog is beautiful, it's mellow. It's nice—it won't do nothing to nobody. When you breed within the family, you keep the beauty of the dog. With people you can't do that. But the more you inbreed an animal, the better it is.
• My animals don't bother my neighbors because I don't live in a nice neighborhood. Plus, people know me. I've lived there thirty years, and I've had animals the whole time.
• I guess you've got to be a little bit strong with these dogs. This is not a regular dog. Sometimes they'll go after another animal because the bloodline has been bred like this for so many years. I don't believe the Pit Bull breed belongs loose on the streets of New York —you've got to keep them on a leash. But you know, I don't believe *any* dog belongs off the leash.
• Now, a Rottweiller can cost three-hundred dollars, so you don't see a lot of them getting abandoned in the streets. But Pit Bulls, people give away. That's why so many get abandoned. You get a free dog, you forget to feed him, you forget to take him to the doctor. But pay two-thousand dollars for a dog and you won't forget to feed him.
• One time the cops came to my house and talked to me because one of my dogs had scars. But let me tell you, if you have more than one Pit Bull, they're gonna get a scar sooner or later! If they get loose, they fight. And when you got six, seven, eight dogs, like I do, things happen sometimes.

NINO BUSSA Brooklyn, New York

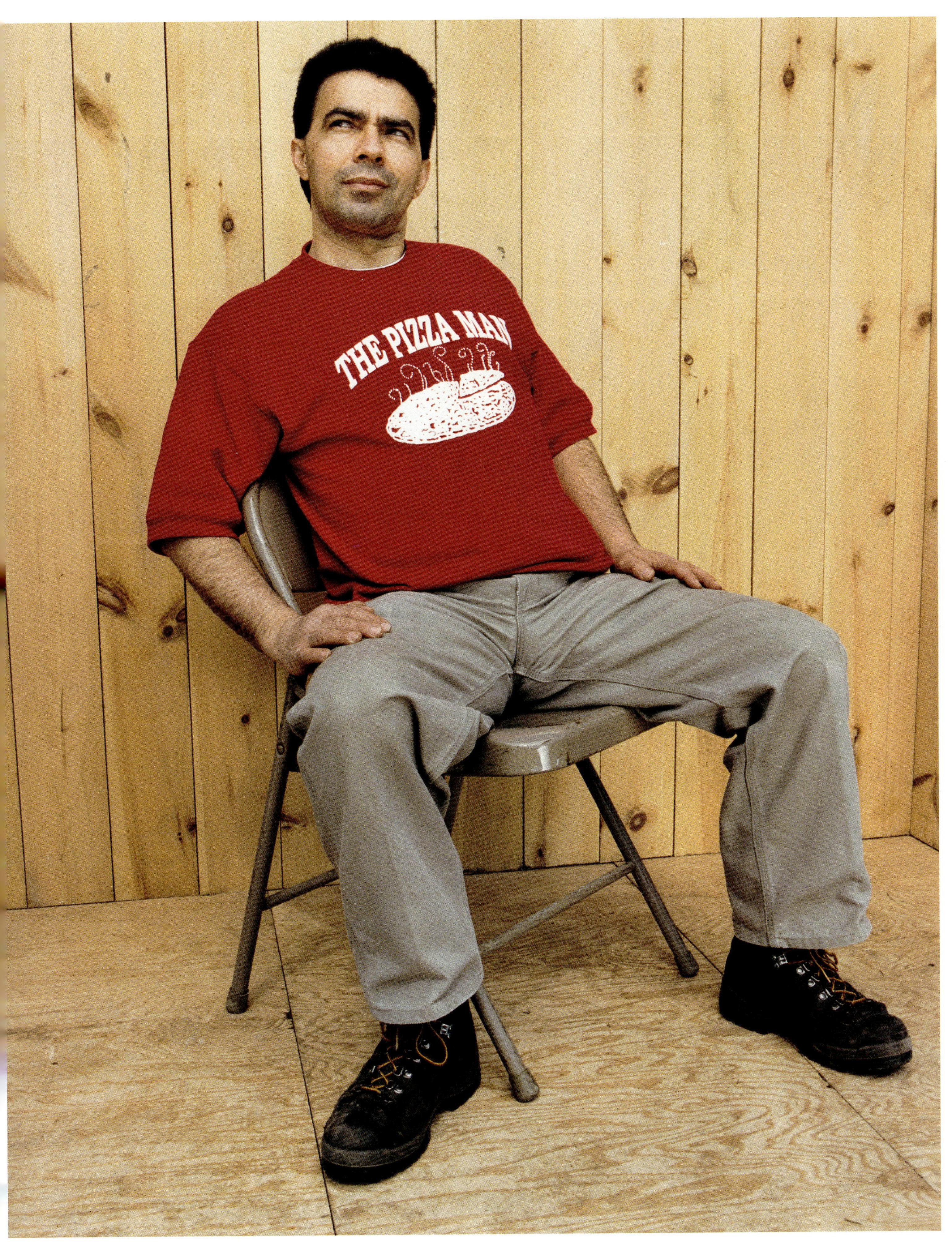
THE PIZZA MAN

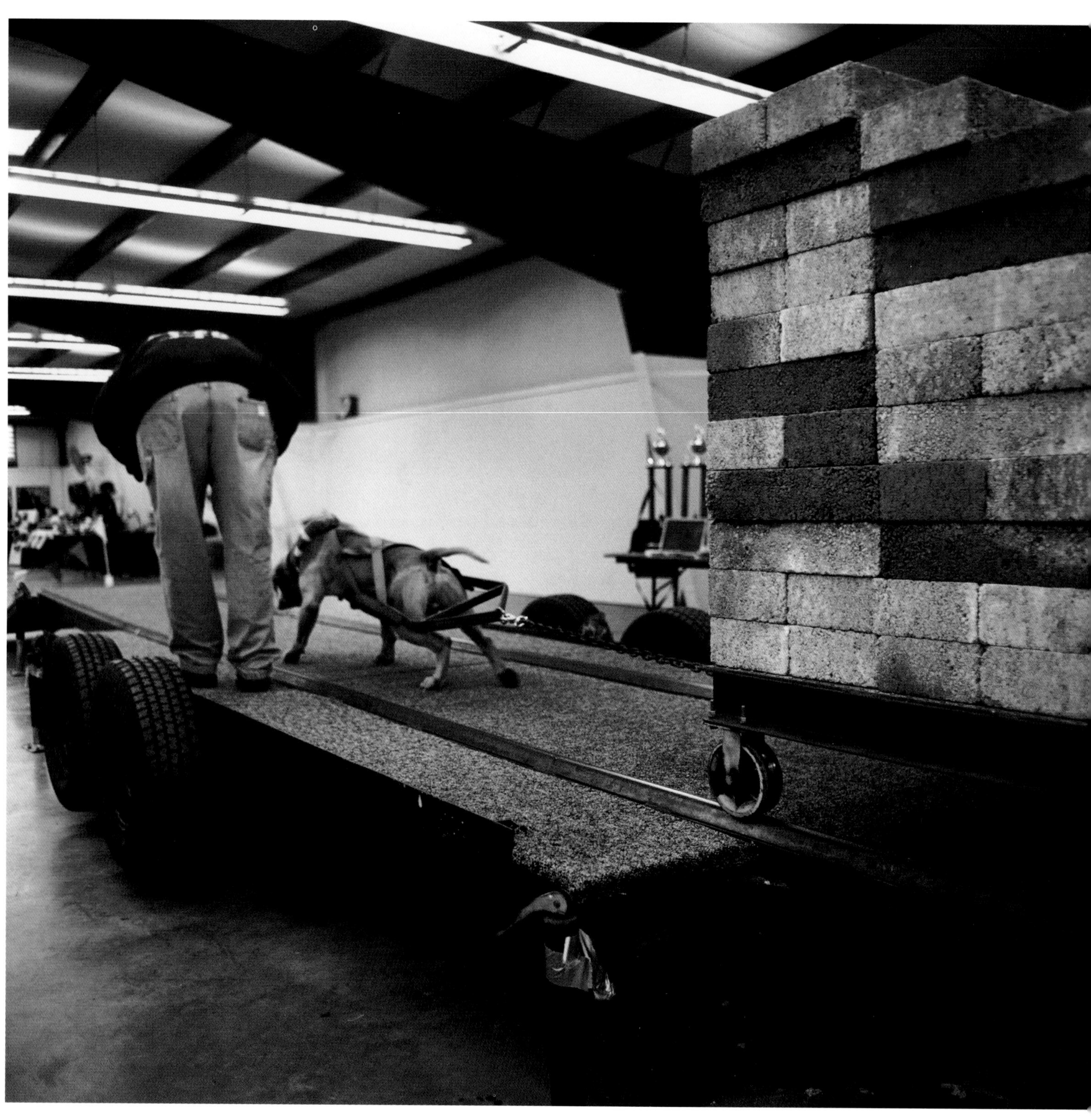

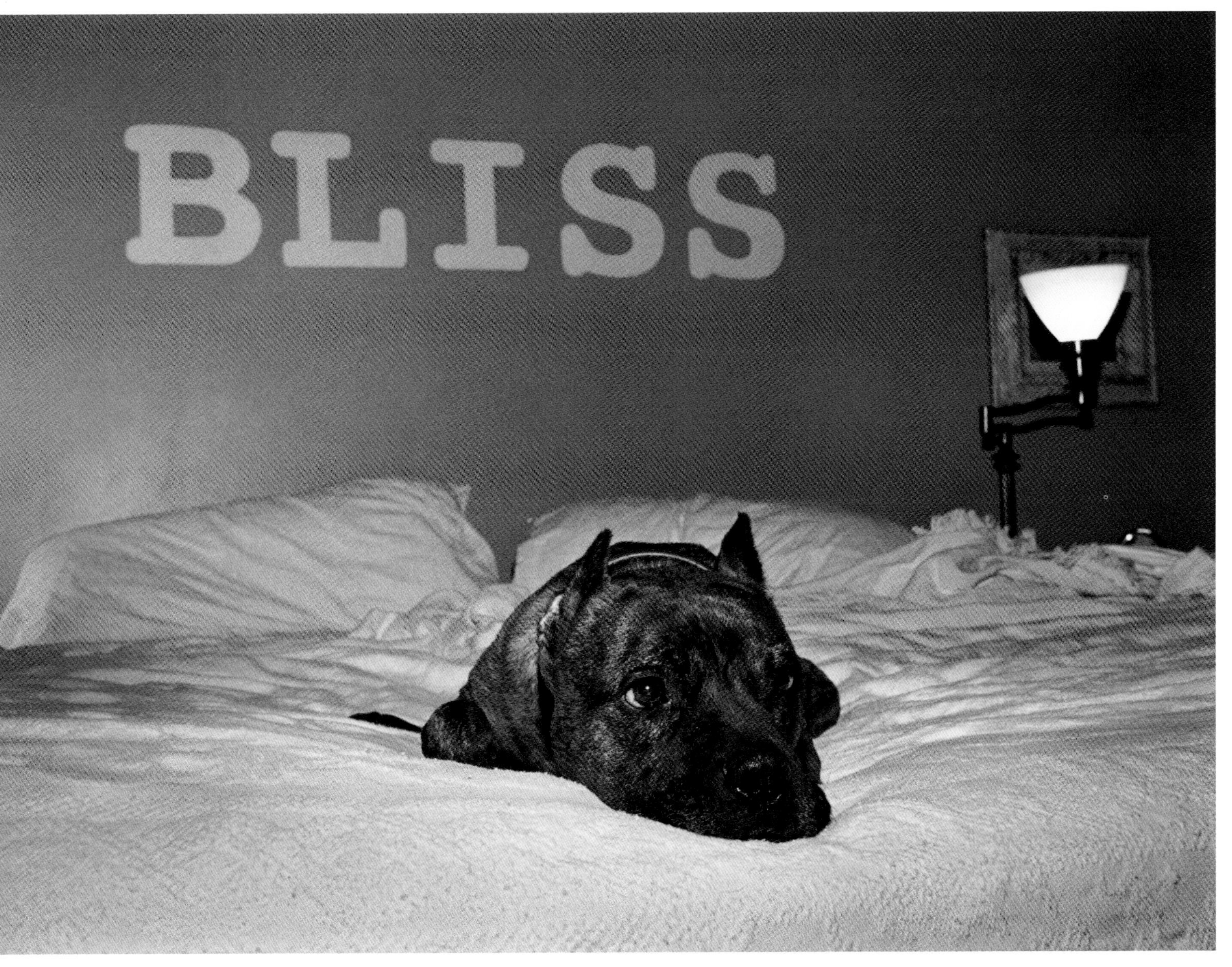
BLISS

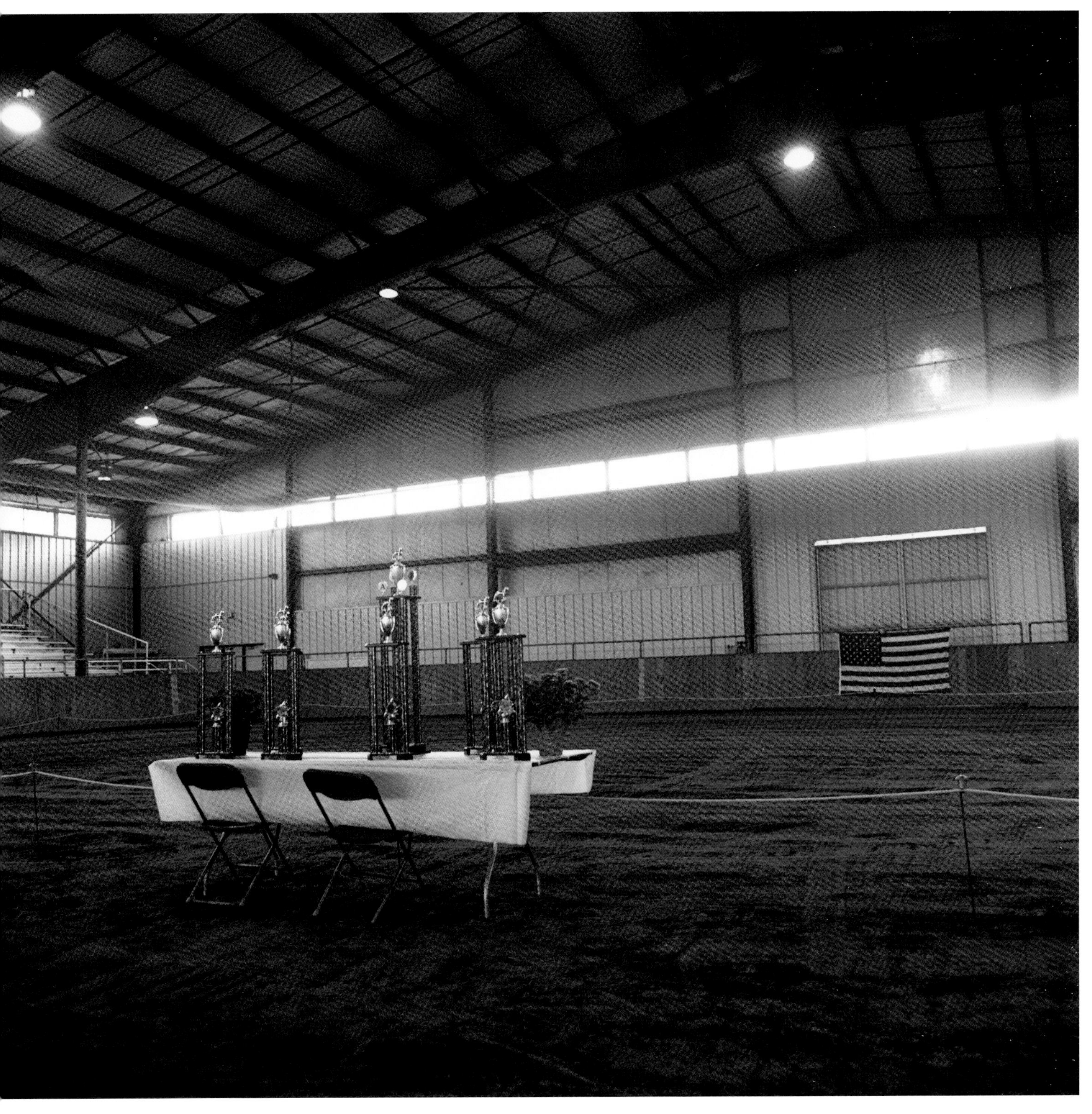

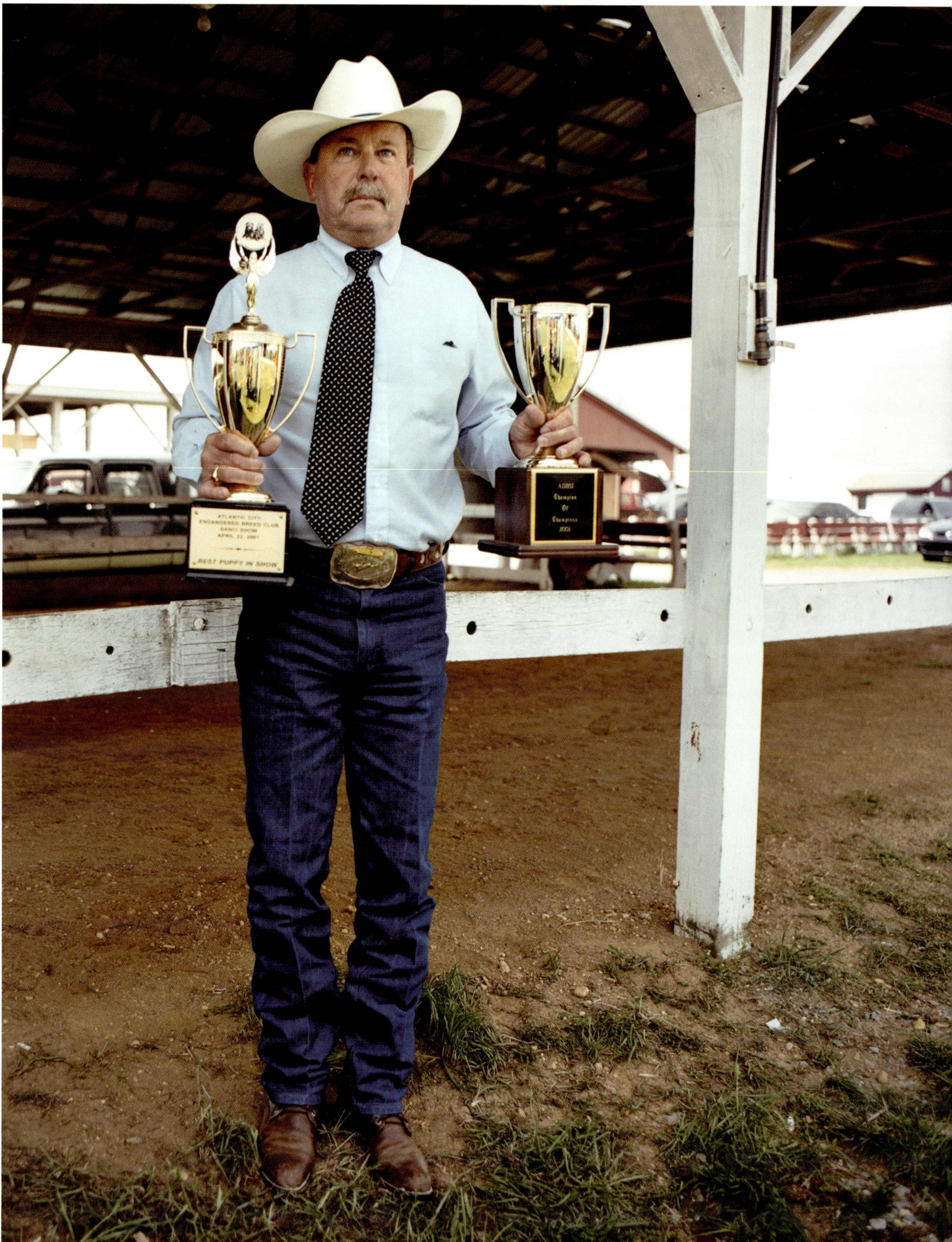
ATLANTIC CITY
ENDANGERED BREED CLUB
BEST PUPPY IN SHOW
ADBSI
Champion
Of
Champions
2001

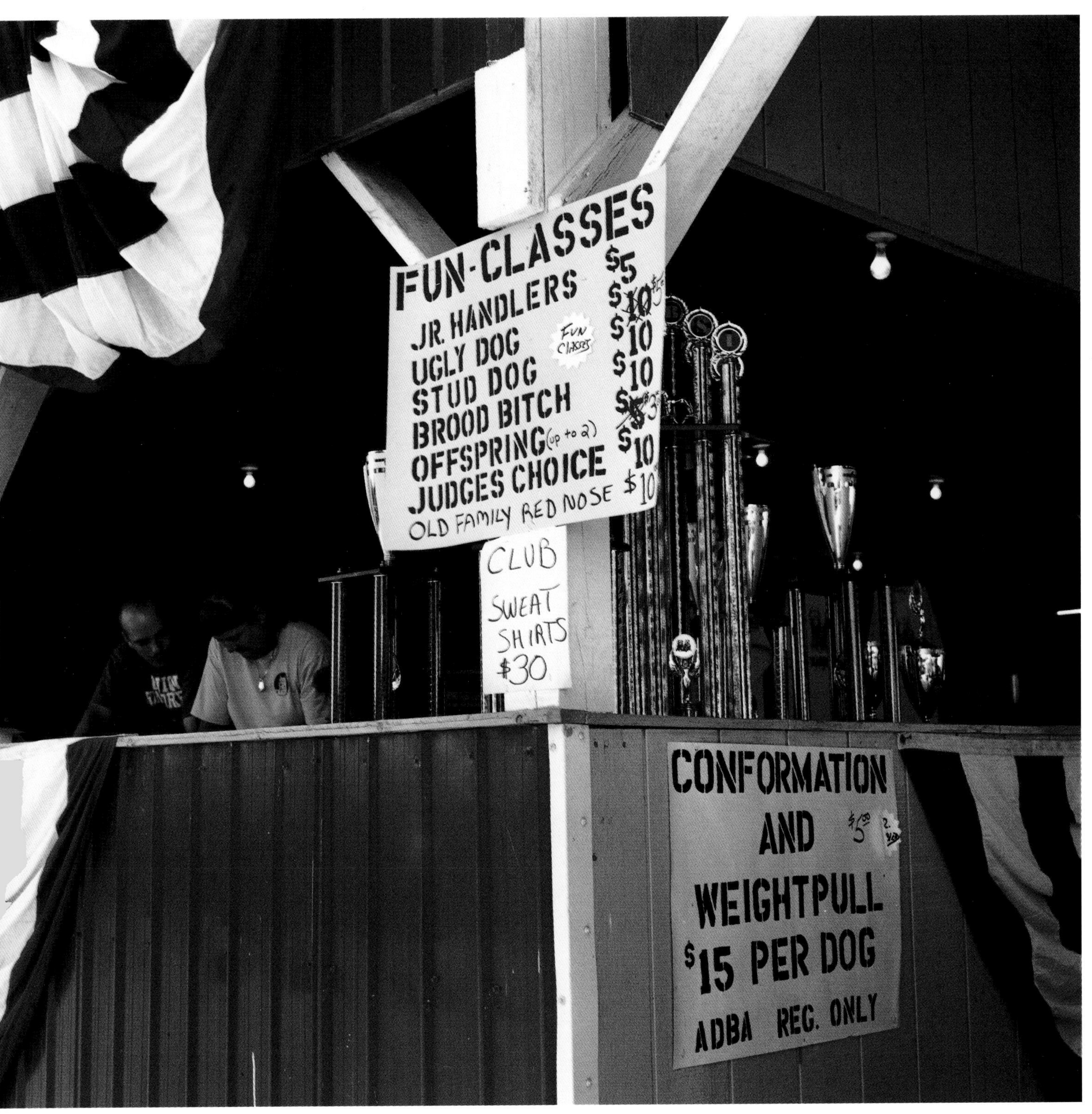
FUN-CLASSES
JR. HANDLERS $5
UGLY DOG $10
STUD DOG $10
BROOD BITCH $10
OFFSPRING (up to 2) $5
JUDGES CHOICE $10
OLD FAMILY RED NOSE $10
FUN CLASSES
CLUB
SWEAT
SHIRTS
$30
CONFORMATION
AND
WEIGHTPULL
$15 PER DOG
ADBA REG. ONLY

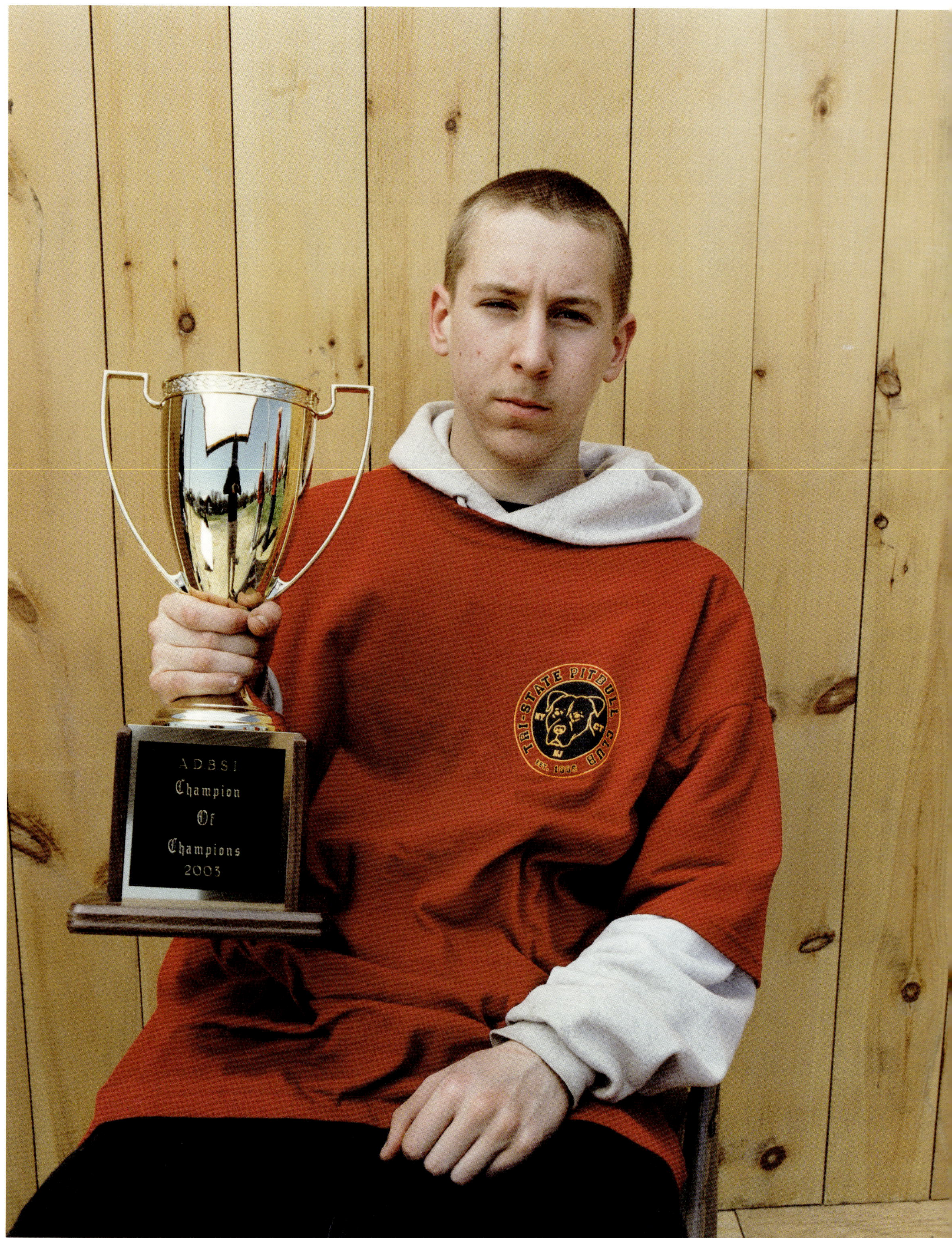
ADBSI
Champion
Of
Champions
2003
TRI-STATE PITBULL CLUB
NY
CT
NJ

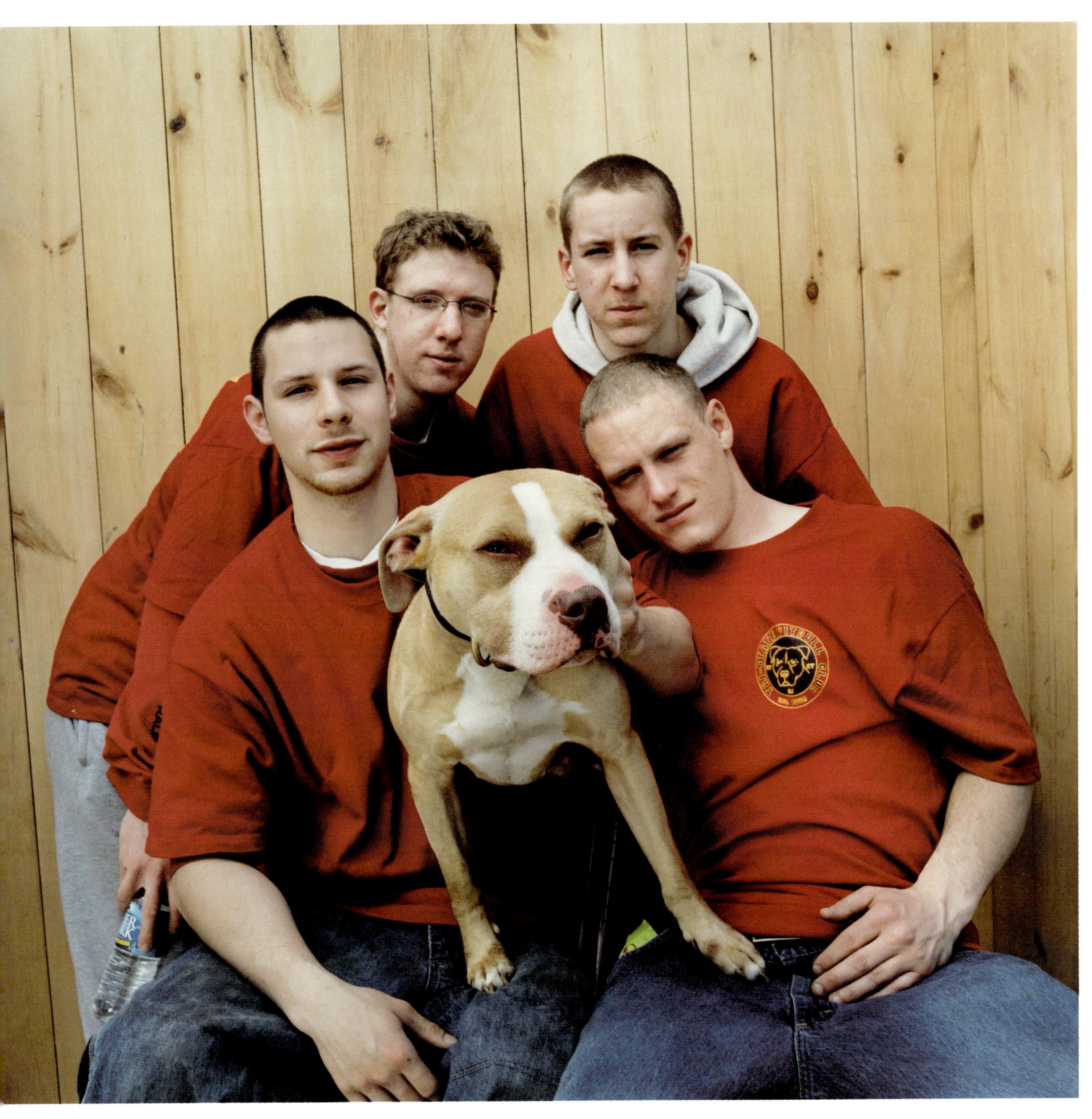

Frank Rocca is a writer and a full-time college student who has owned, bred, and trained American Pit Bull Terriers for thirty years. As well-known and admired as he is knowledgeable in matters of the breed and its history, he is a highly sought-after judge at sanctioned Pit Bull shows across the United States and internationally.

• Despite their portrayal in the media, American Bull Terriers are very much family dogs, and the dog shows are real family events. A lot of the people who own these dogs don't have the kind of money to go to the Bahamas or go gambling on the weekends. So they do these little mini-vacations at the dog shows.
• This breed, according to the ADBA [American Dog Breeders Association], is called "The American Pit Bull Terrier." But the word "pit" could be dropped at any time, and hopefully it will be. I prefer the name American Bull Terrier, which is what the breed used to be called when it was first brought to this country from Ireland and England. I don't like the word "pit" because it has negative connotations. As soon as you hear the word, you think of brutality and gambling—and that's not what this dog is about. The only way a dog is a "pit" dog is if it's in a pit. And any breed of dog can be a fighting dog. Akitas and Sharpeis were both bred to fight—but they're not banned.
• People don't want to read good news. They want to read horror stories, they love to hear about bombings and killings. That's why they go to the Indy 500. They're hoping to see a 300 mile-per-hour collision, fireballs, everything smashed up. So the average citizen watches the news and gets force-fed the media hype... and they just buy it. Consequently, hard-working citizens who just own a dog as a pet, who have never committed any crimes, are forced to get dog insurance that they can't even find. They have to keep their dogs muzzled even when it's out in the yard; they have to keep their yards padlocked.
• I know for a fact that if Jesse Jackson and Al Sharpton owned Bulldogs our problems would be over, because the prejudice against this breed is discrimination and nothing else. American Bull Terriers are not the biters or the killers. They're the victims.
• In the early 1900s dog fighting was still prevalent and accepted in this country. It was sanctioned by the police and reported in their magazine, the *Police Gazette*. In fact, the *Gazette* used to send referees out to judge matches. Anyway, during any given match a dog would be handled by a number of people, some of whom would be perfect strangers. For example, a dog would be handled and conditioned by one person, maybe handled in the pit by another. Once the contest started, the dog would be in a traumatic situation with his own handler, the other dog's handler, and a referee [present]. Afterwards, the dog would have to be doctored by a veterinarian. All of these people would have to know that they could be hands-on with a dog, and that it would not get panicky. You couldn't breed the type that would bite and freak out under pressure. This dog has been bred for centuries to be in traumatic situations around people and not to be human aggressive. And as a rule, they're just not.

FRANK ROCCA Cuyahoga County, Ohio

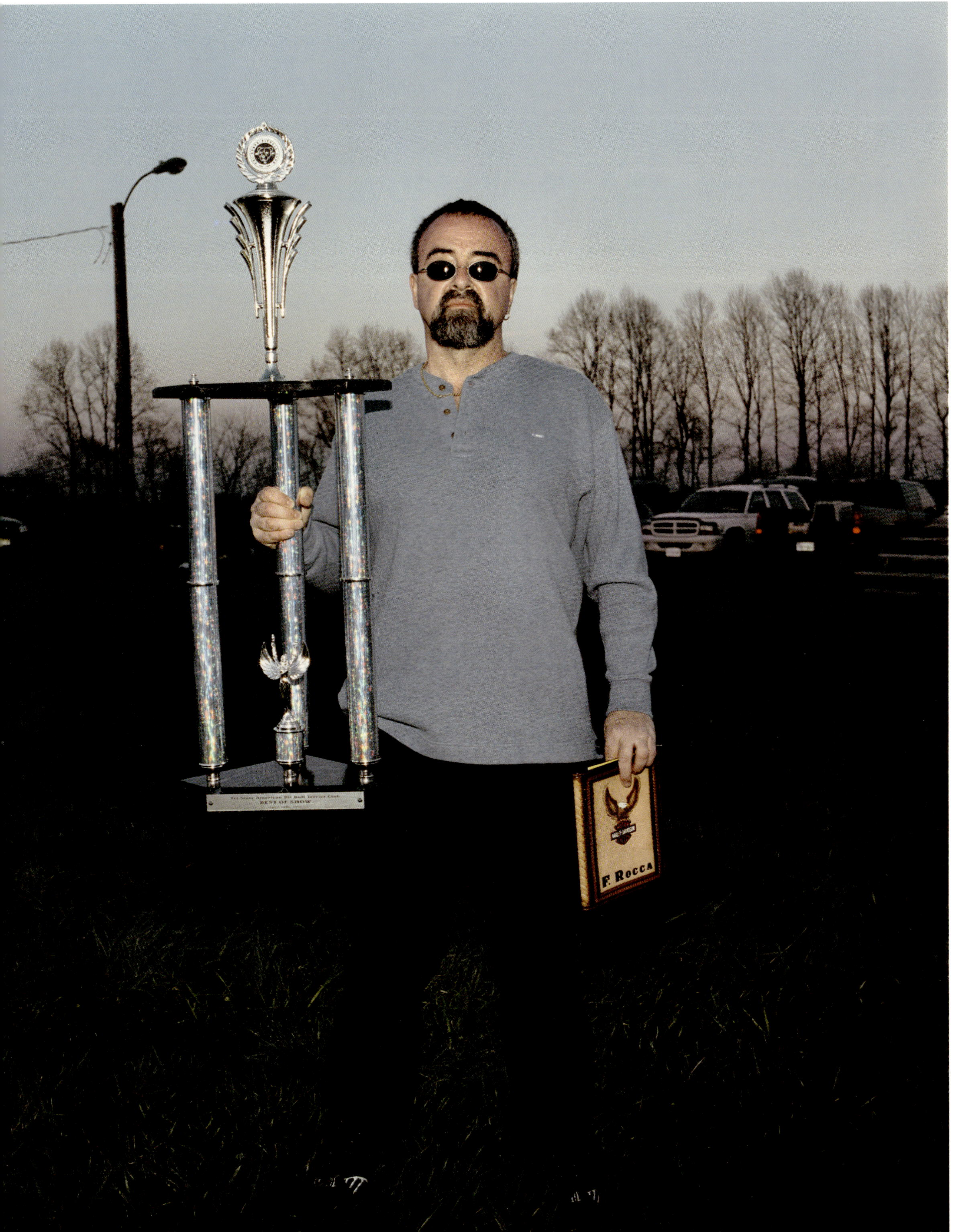
Tri-State American Pit Bull Terrier Club
BEST OF SHOW
F. Rocca

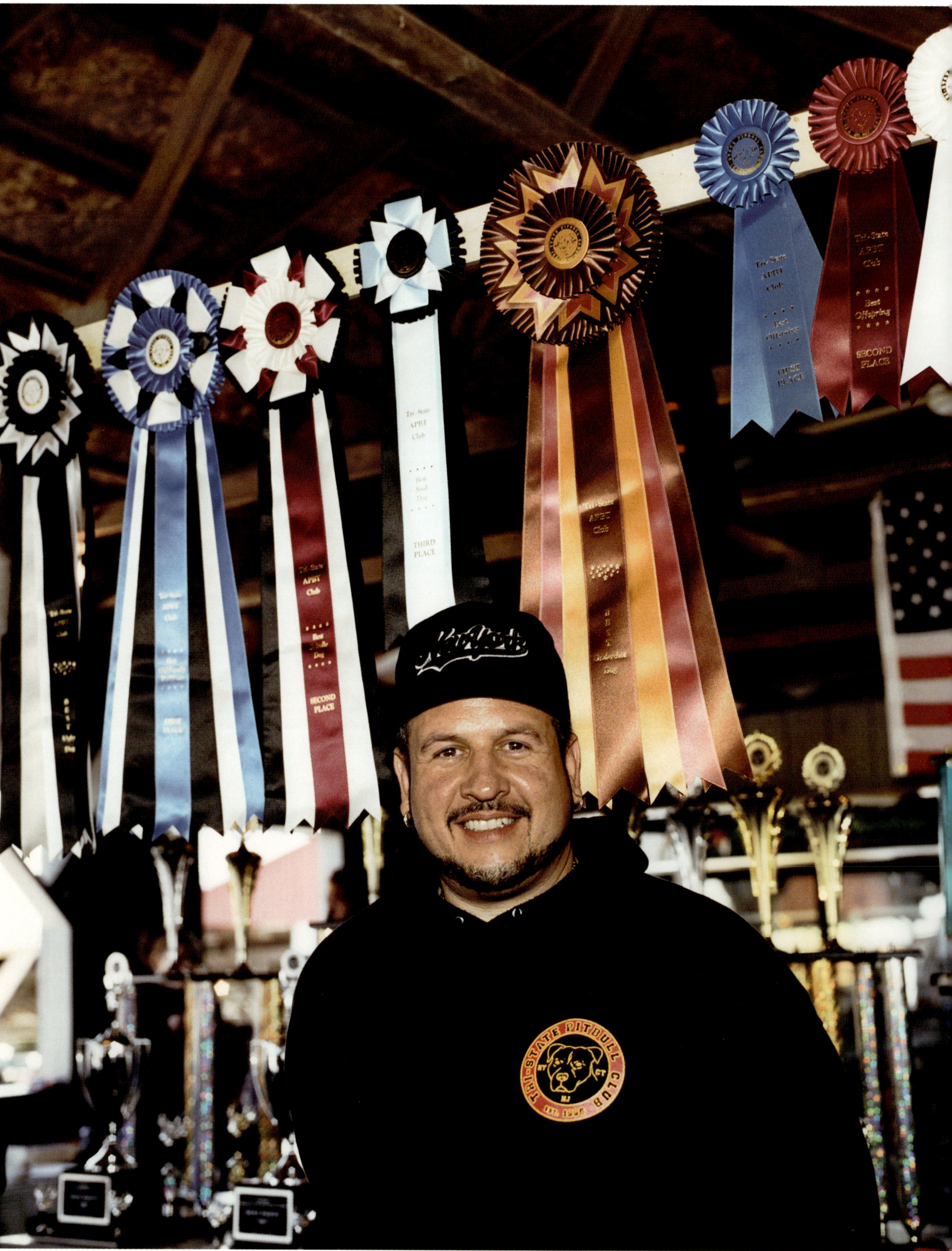
Tri-State APBT Club
Best Stud Dog
THIRD PLACE
Tri-State APBT Club
SECOND PLACE
Tri-State APBT Club
Best Offspring
FIRST PLACE
Tri-State APBT Club
Best Offspring
SECOND PLACE
TRI-STATE PITBULL CLUB

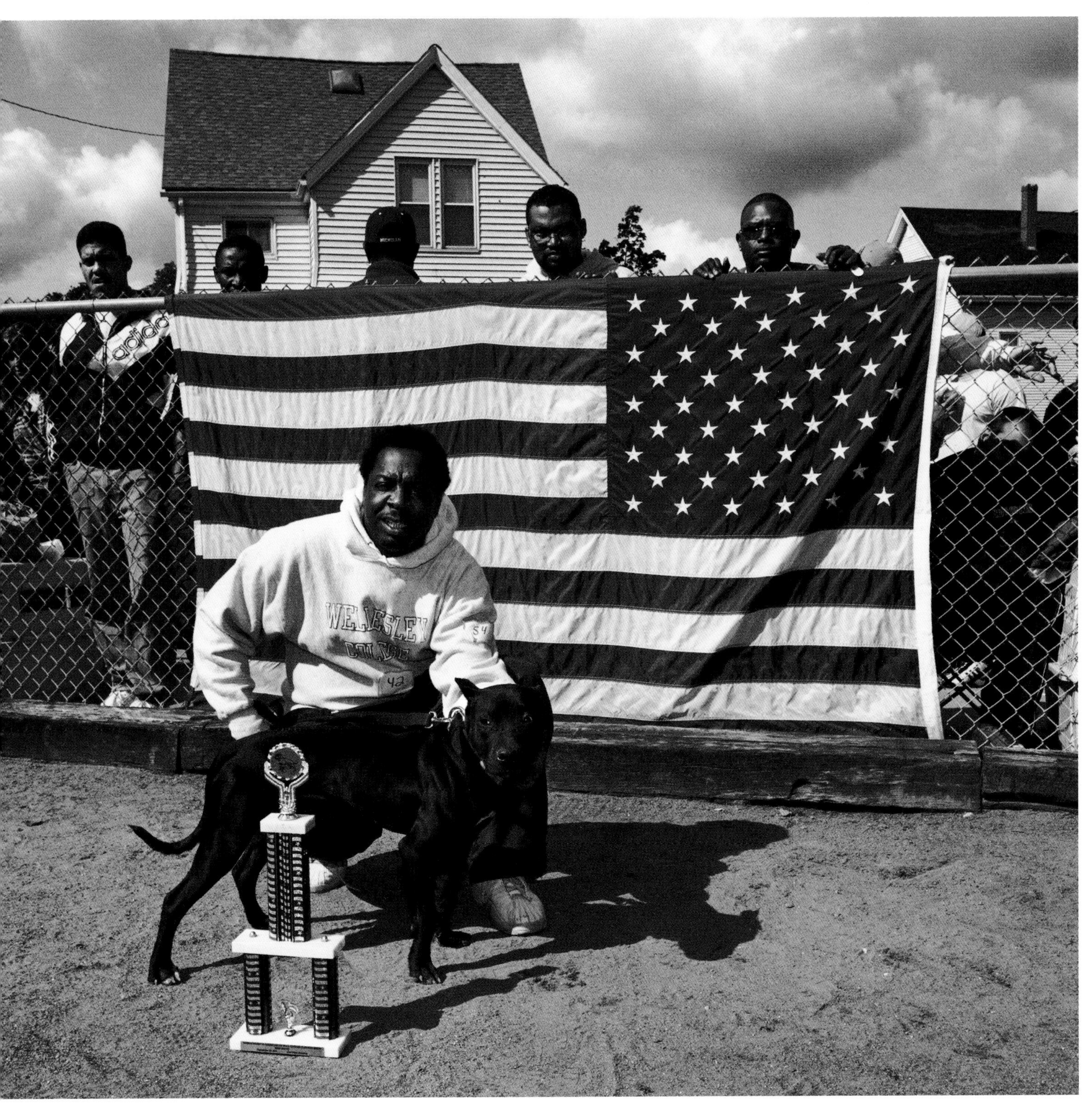
WELLESLEY
42

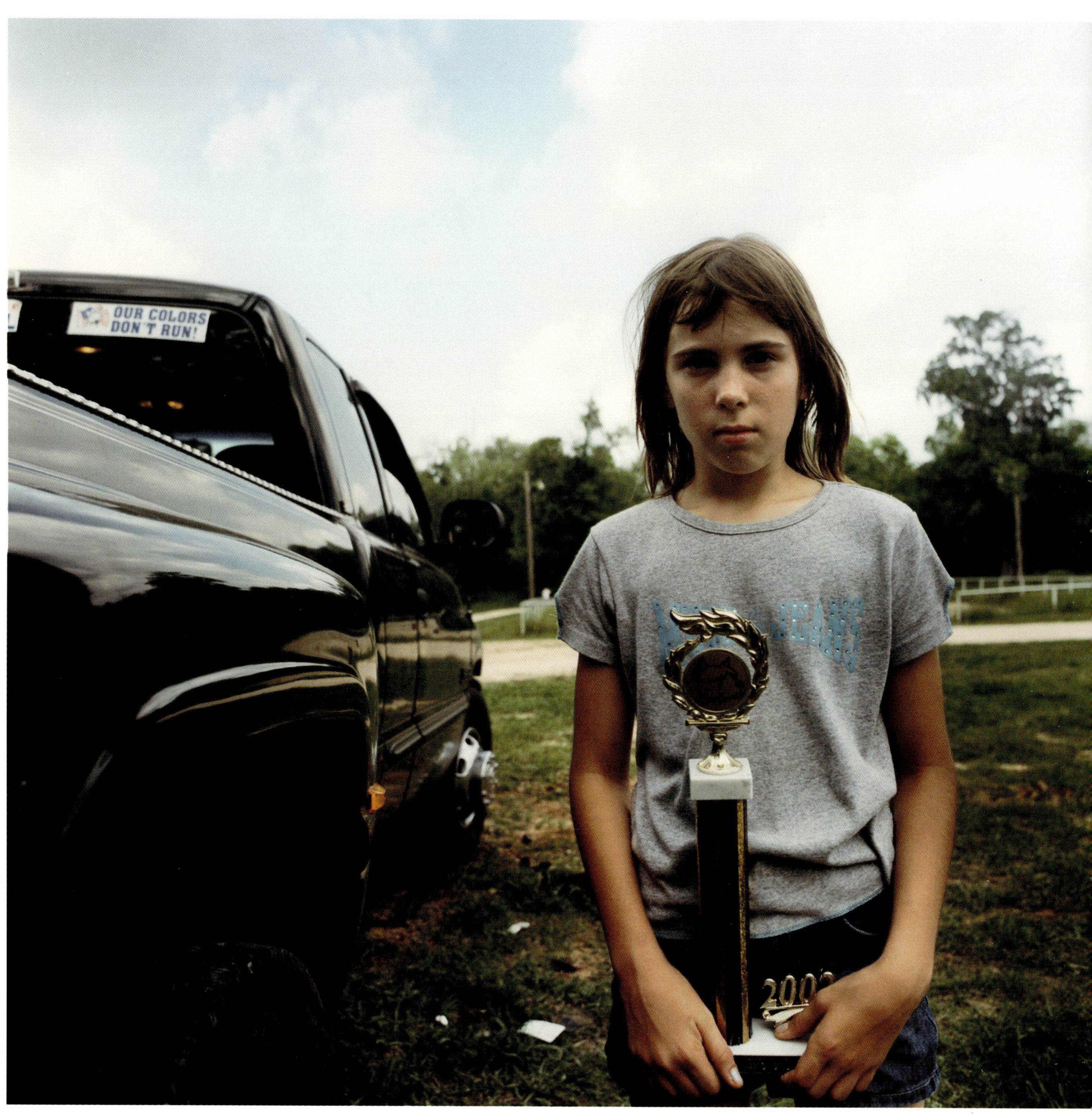
OUR COLORS
DON'T RUN!

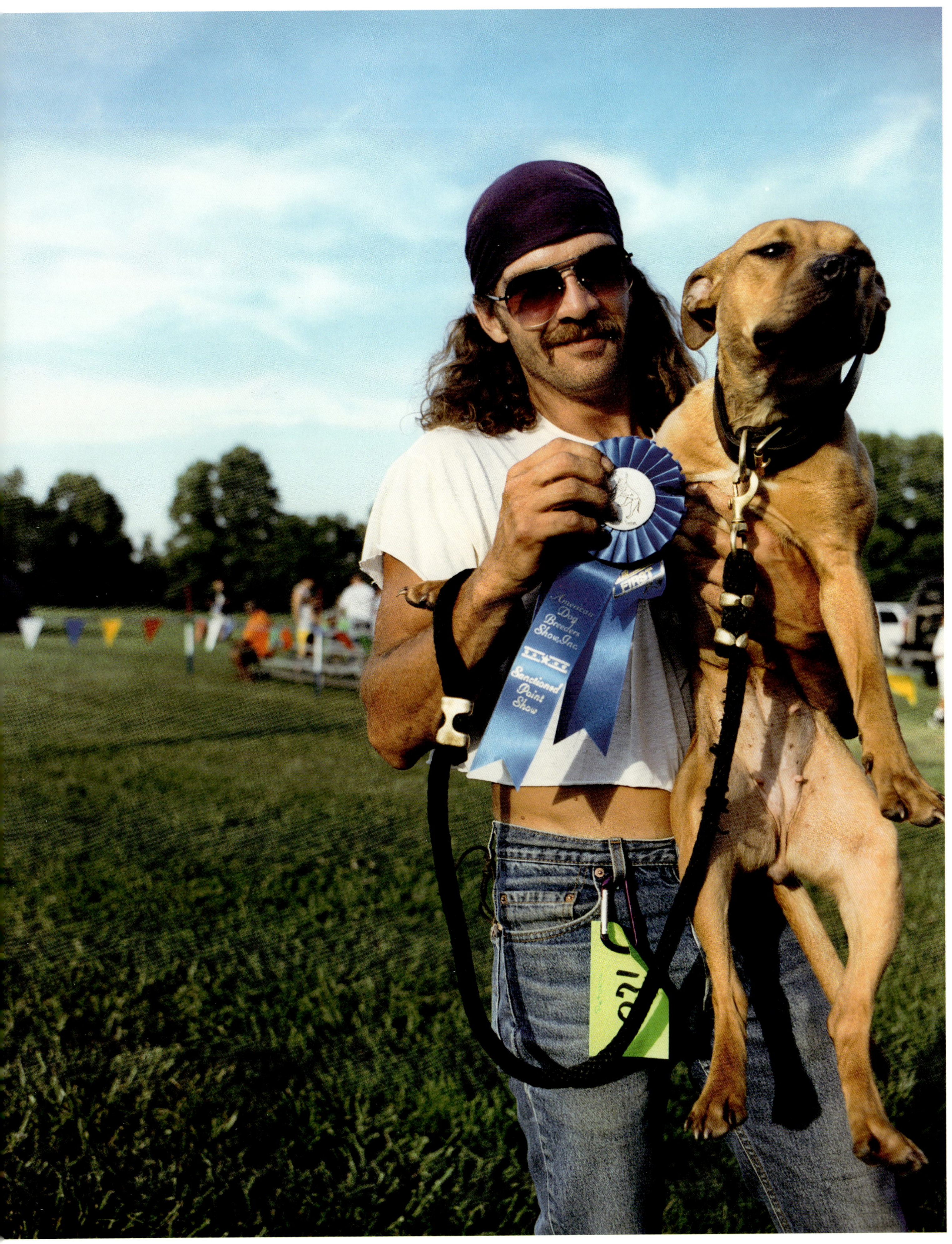
American Dog Breeders Show, Inc.
Sanctioned Point Show
FIRST

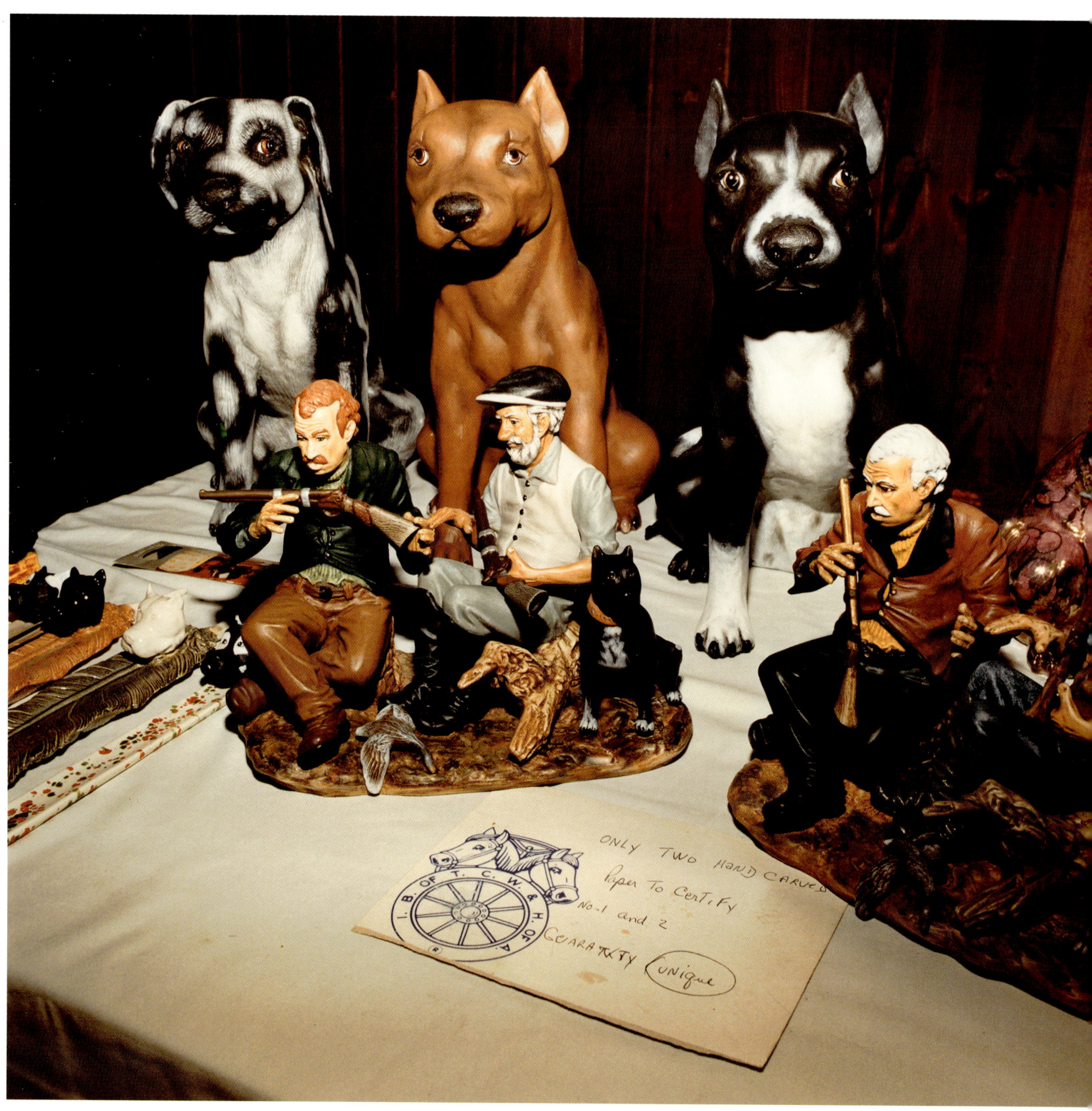
I. B. OF T. C. W. & H. OF A.
ONLY TWO HAND CARVED
Paper To CerTiFy
No-1 and 2
GUARANTY
unique

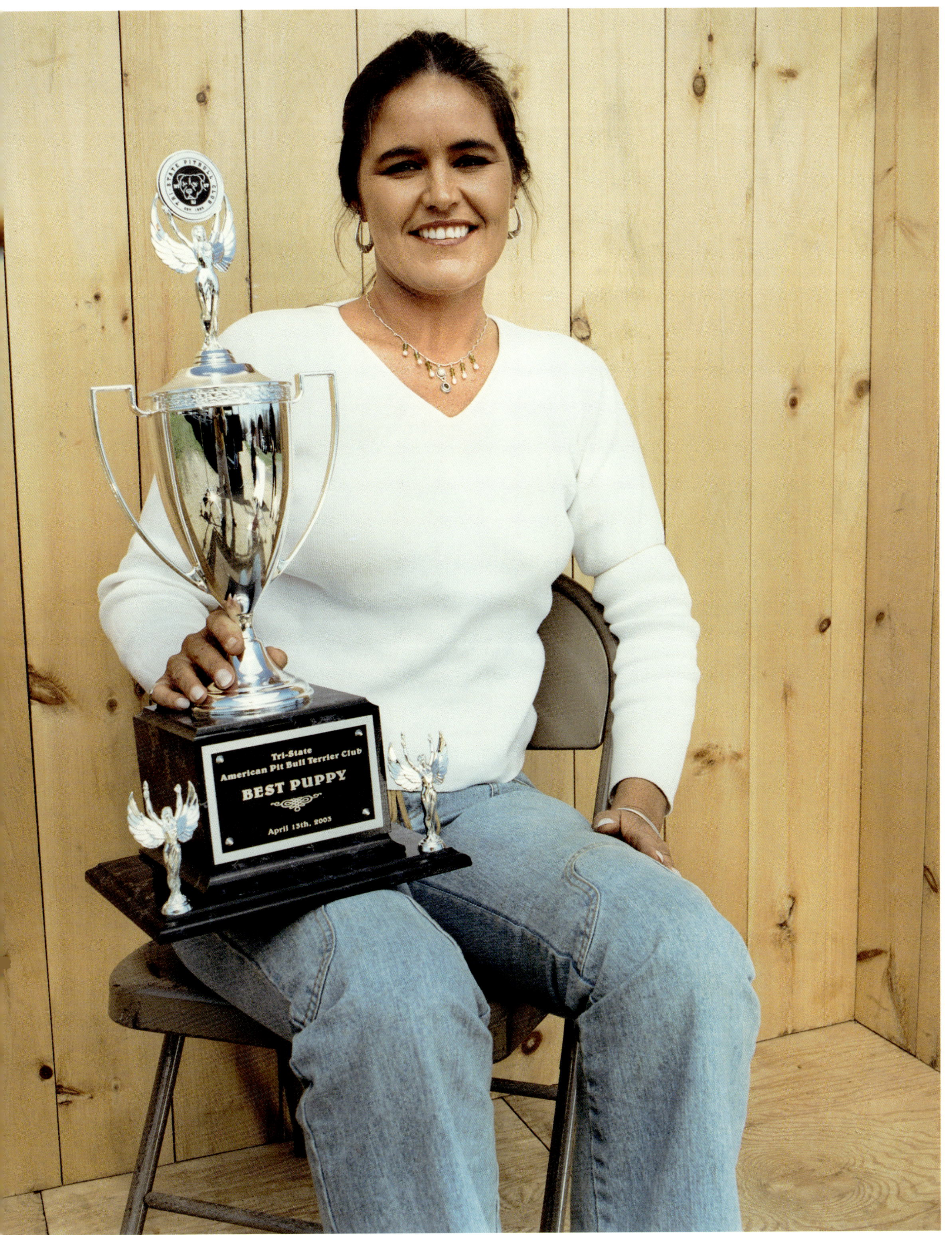
Tri-State
American Pit Bull Terrier Club
BEST PUPPY
April 13th, 2003

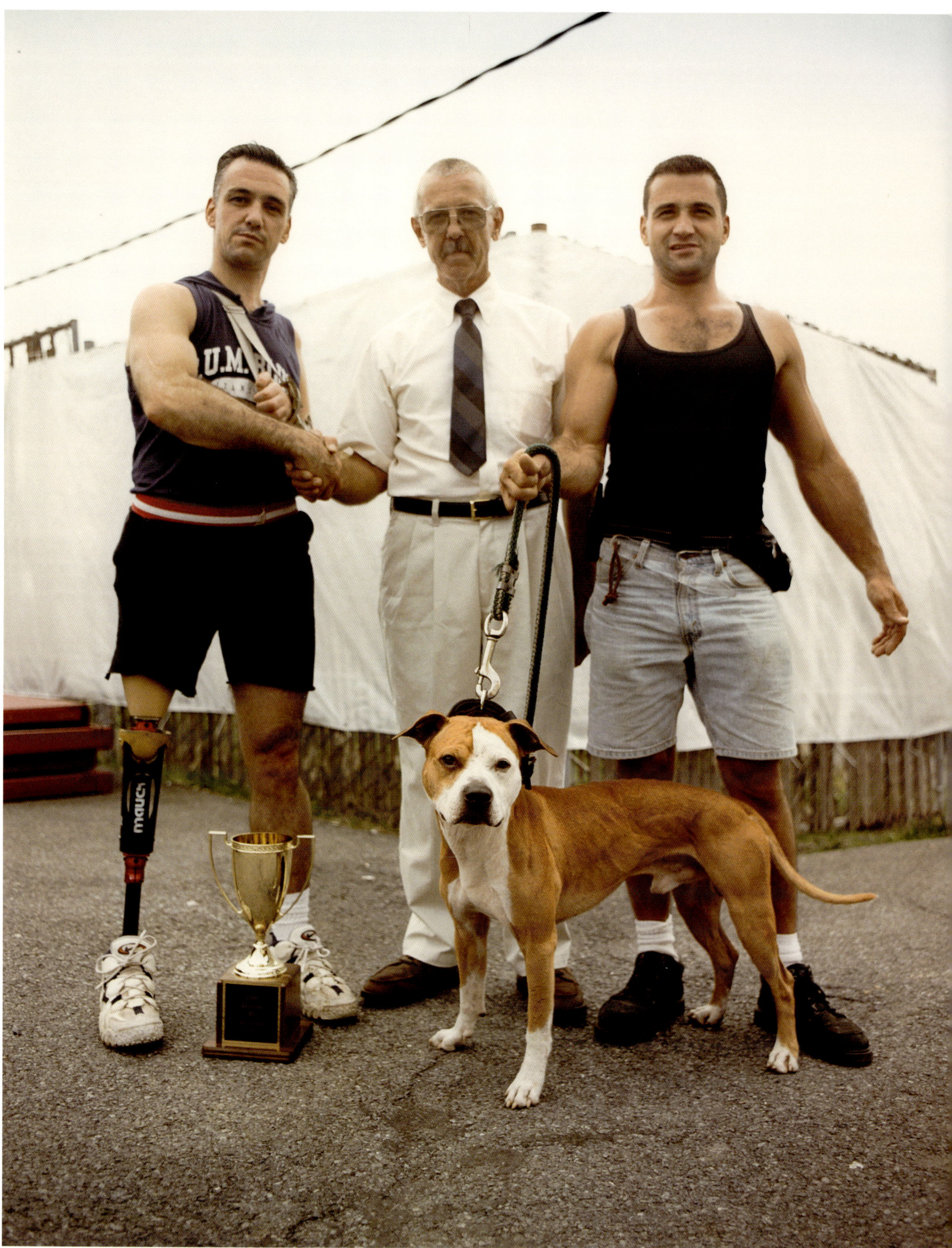
mauch

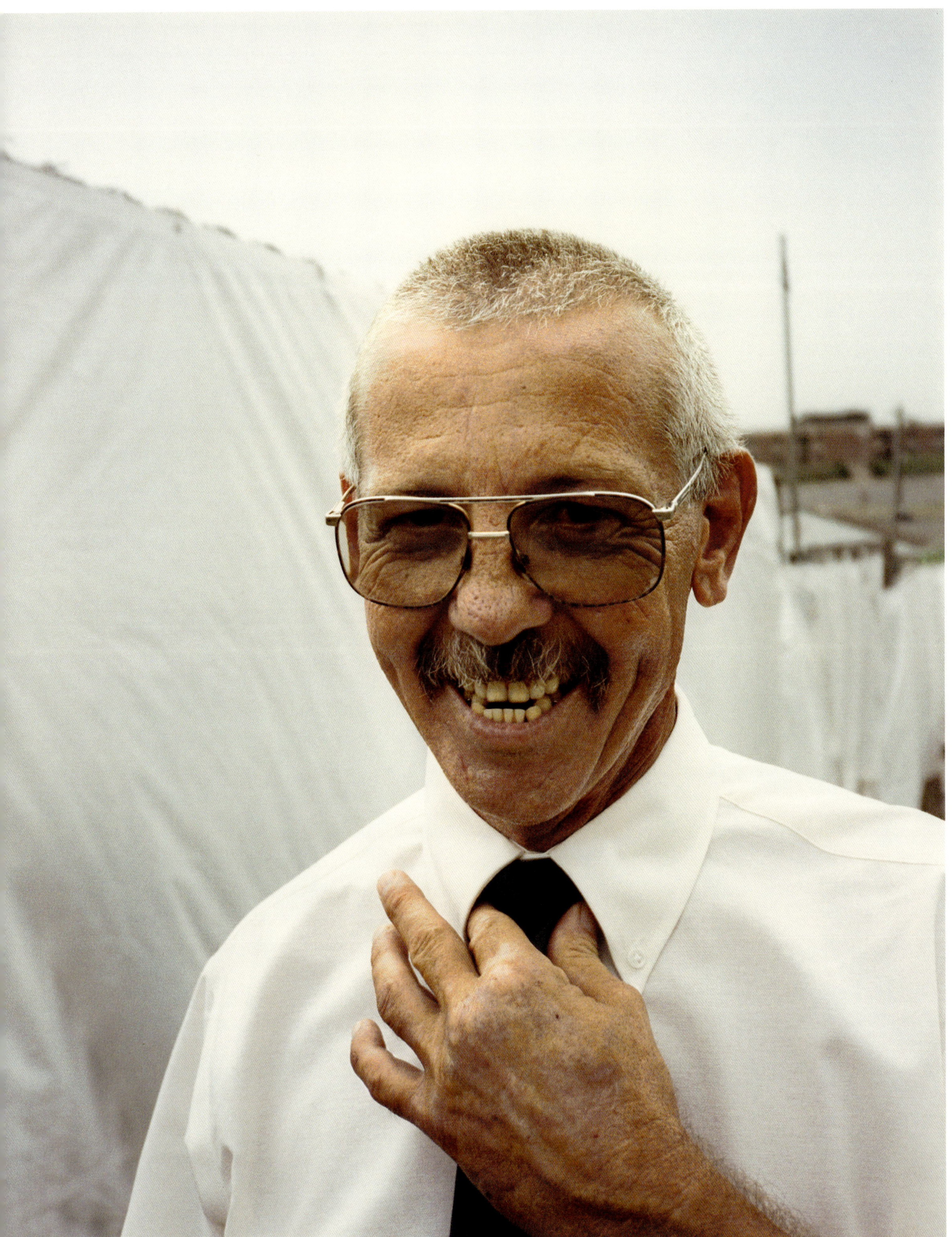

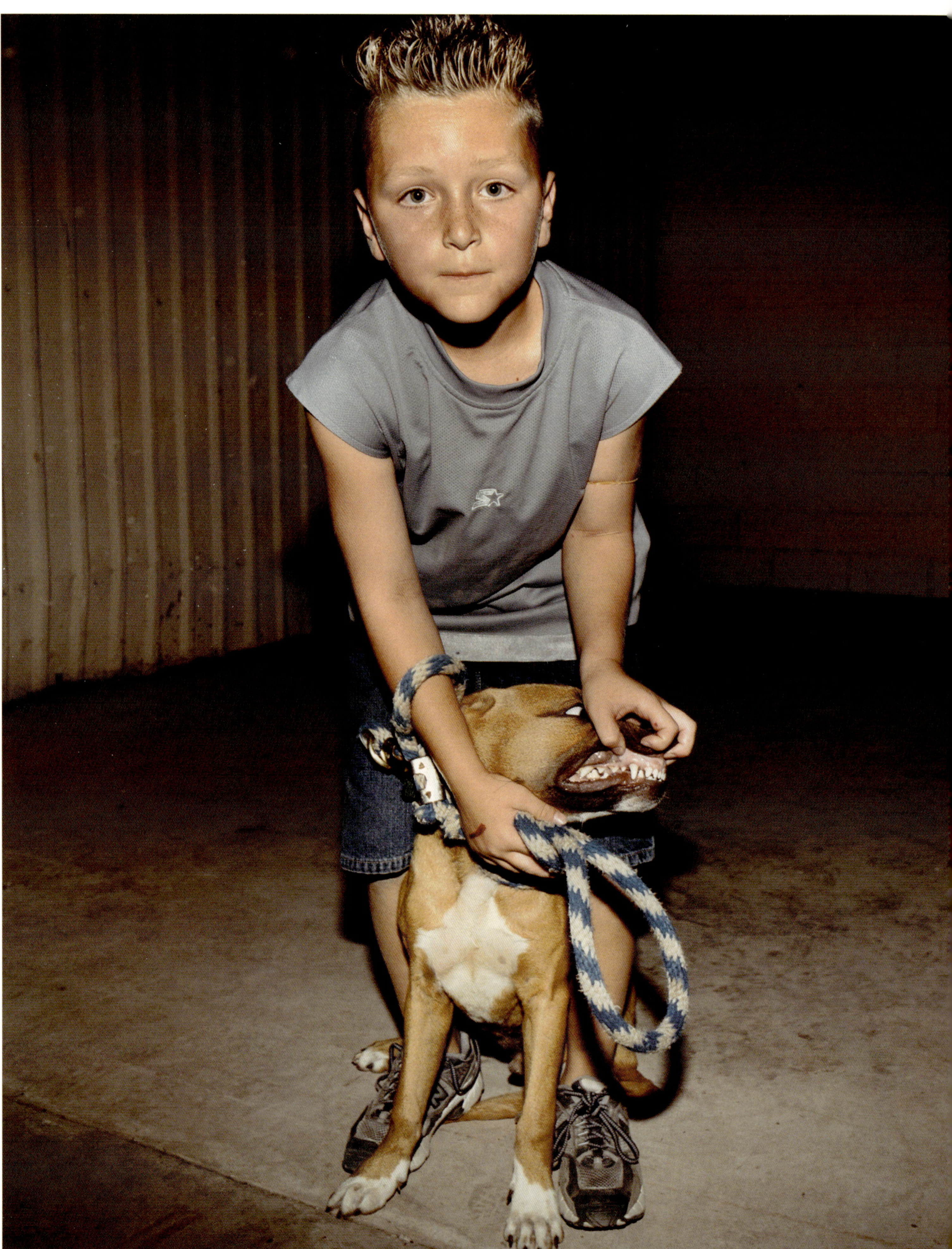

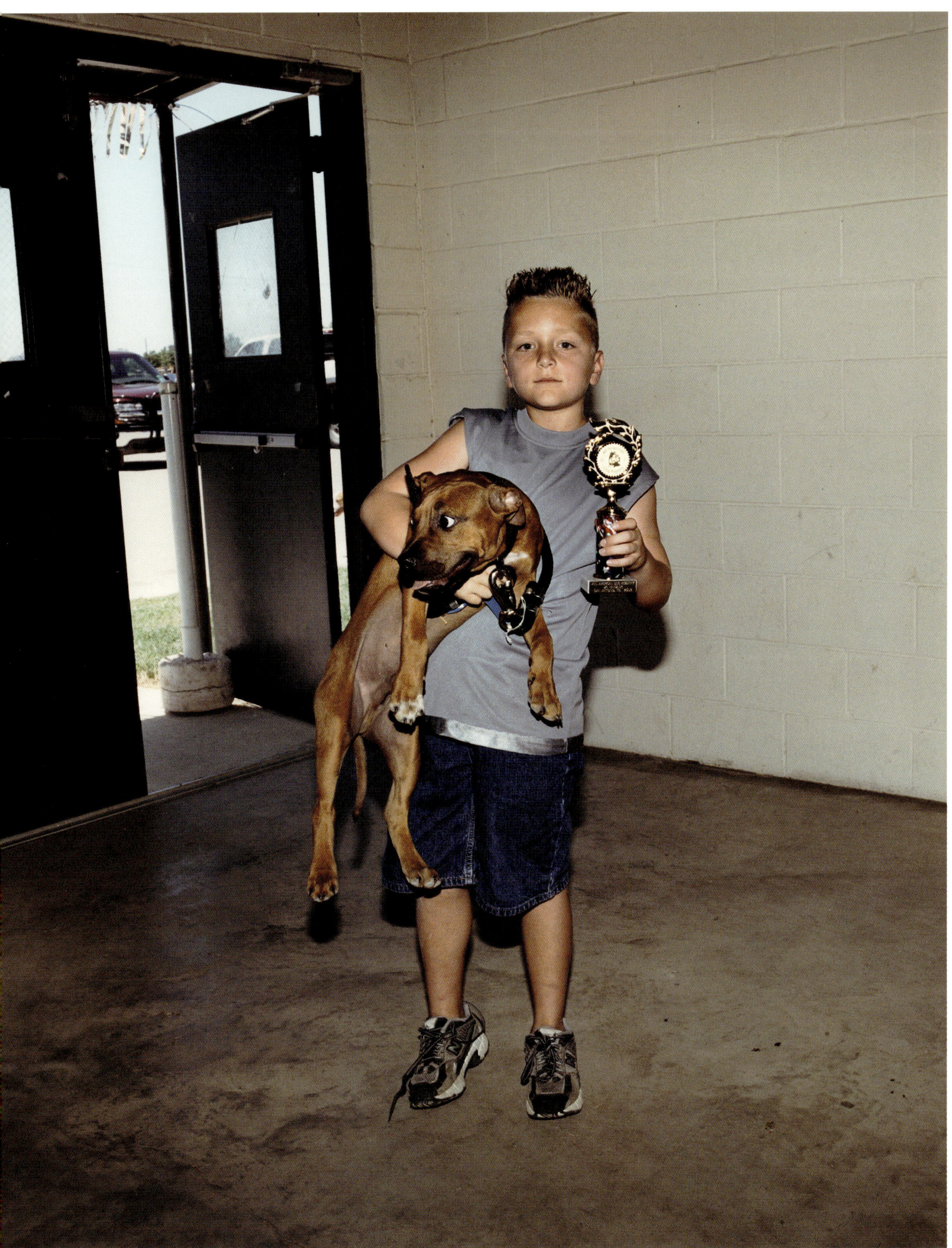

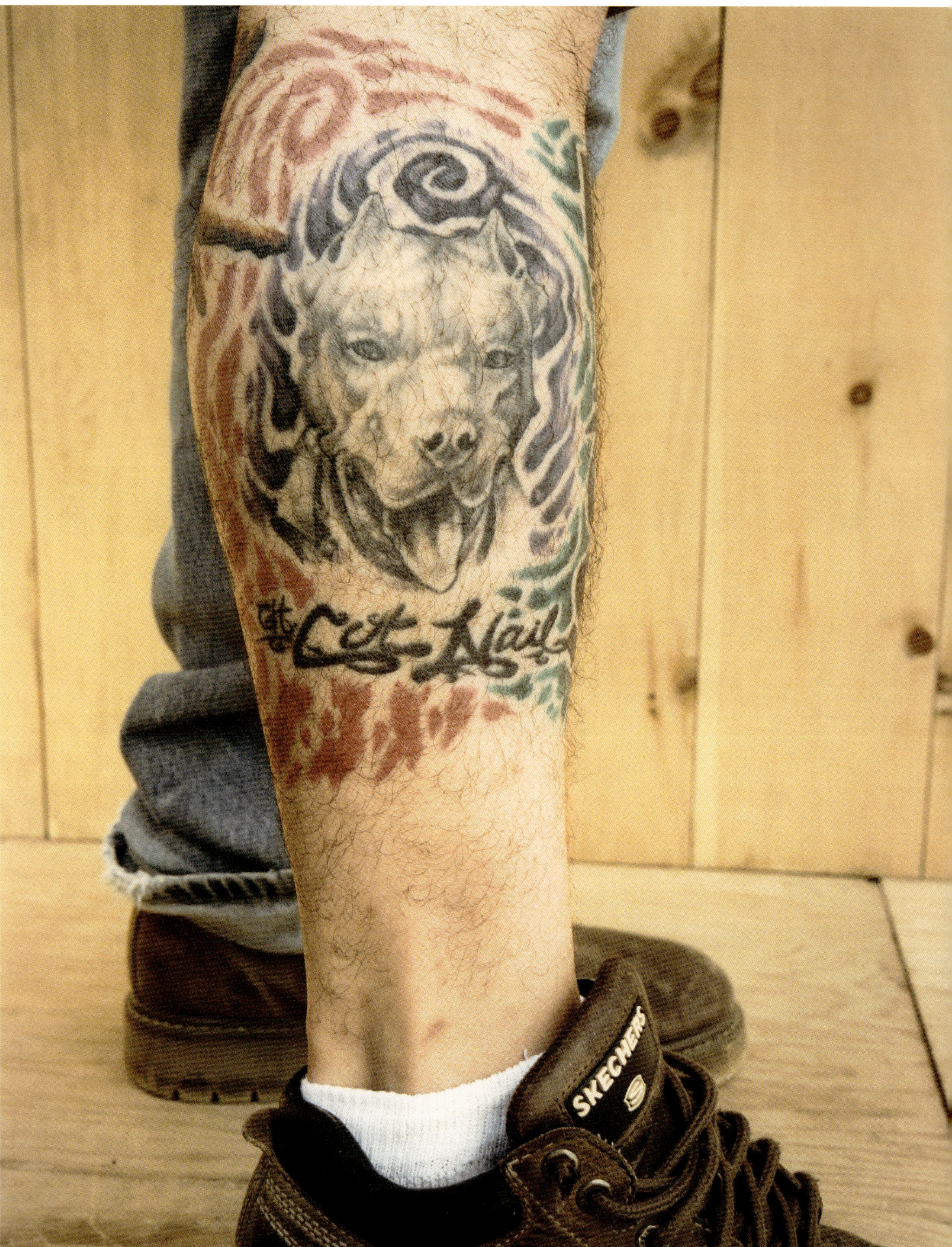
Cut Nail
SKECHERS

48 PITBULLS

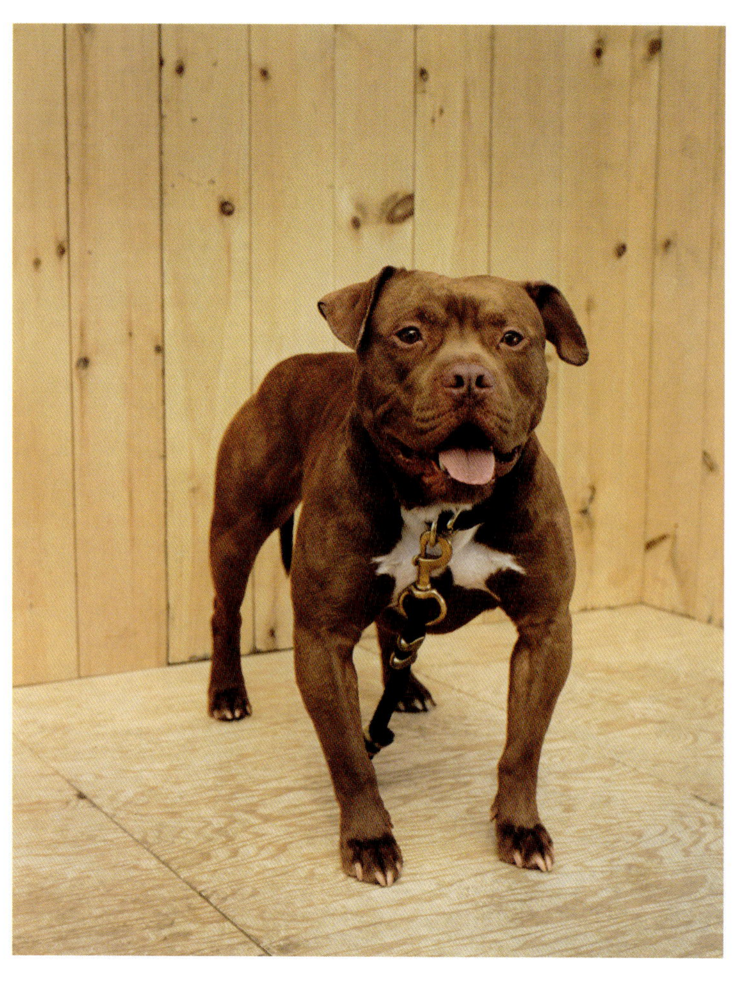
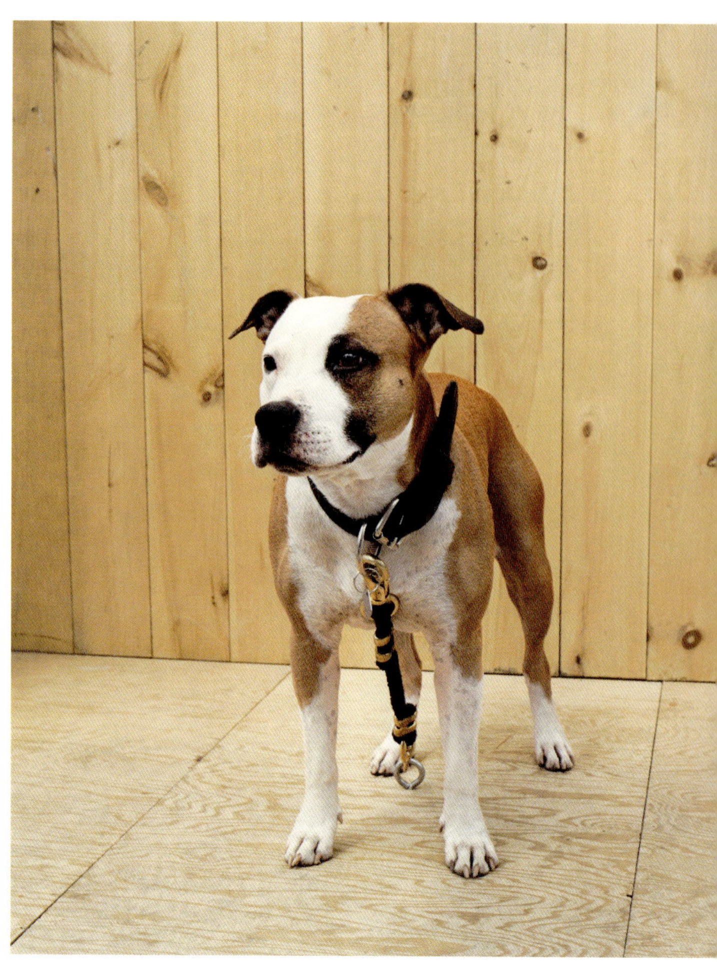
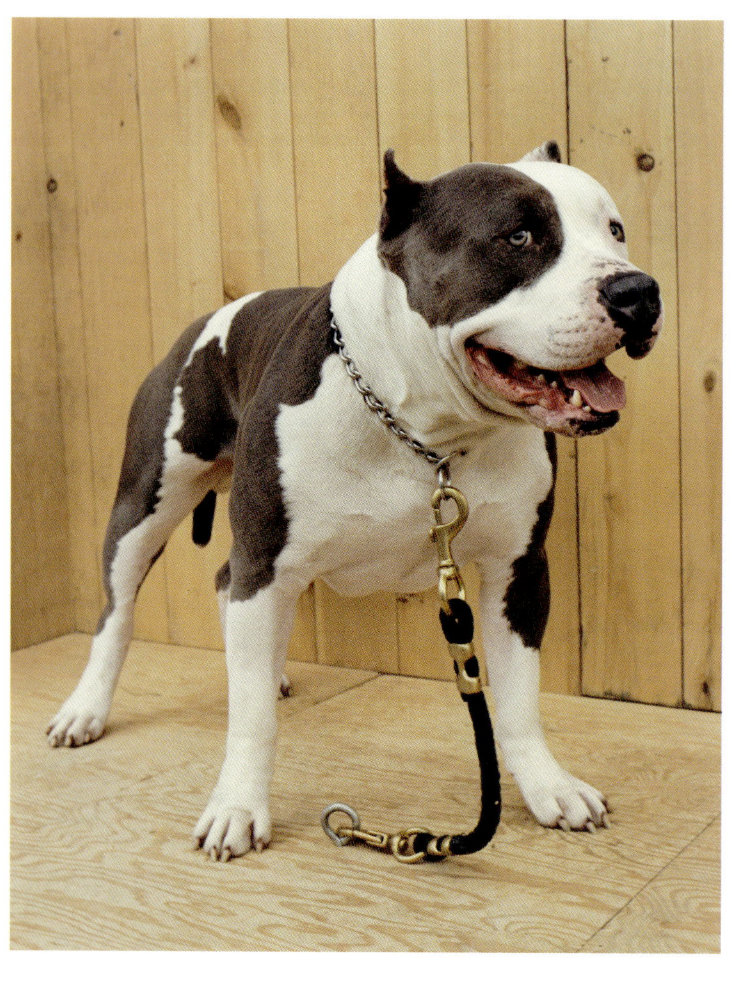
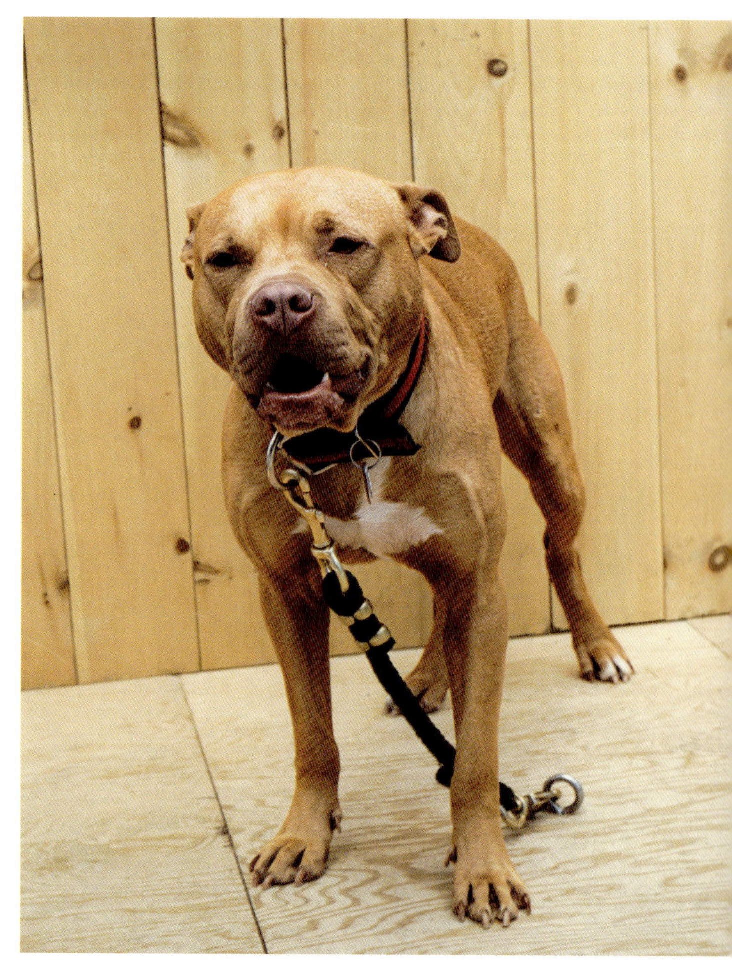

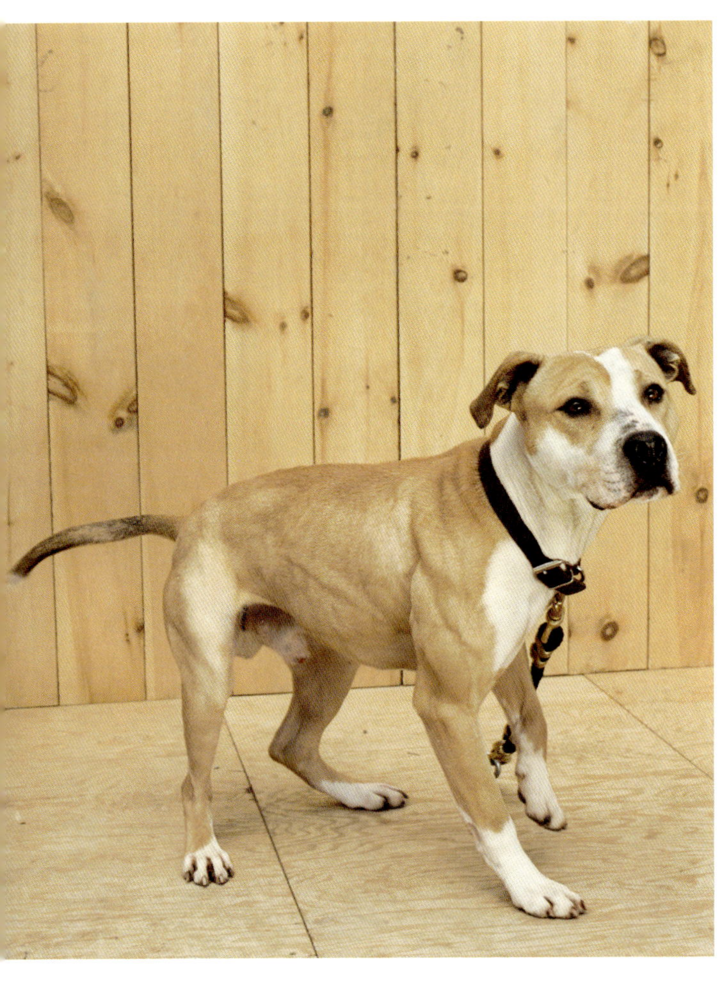
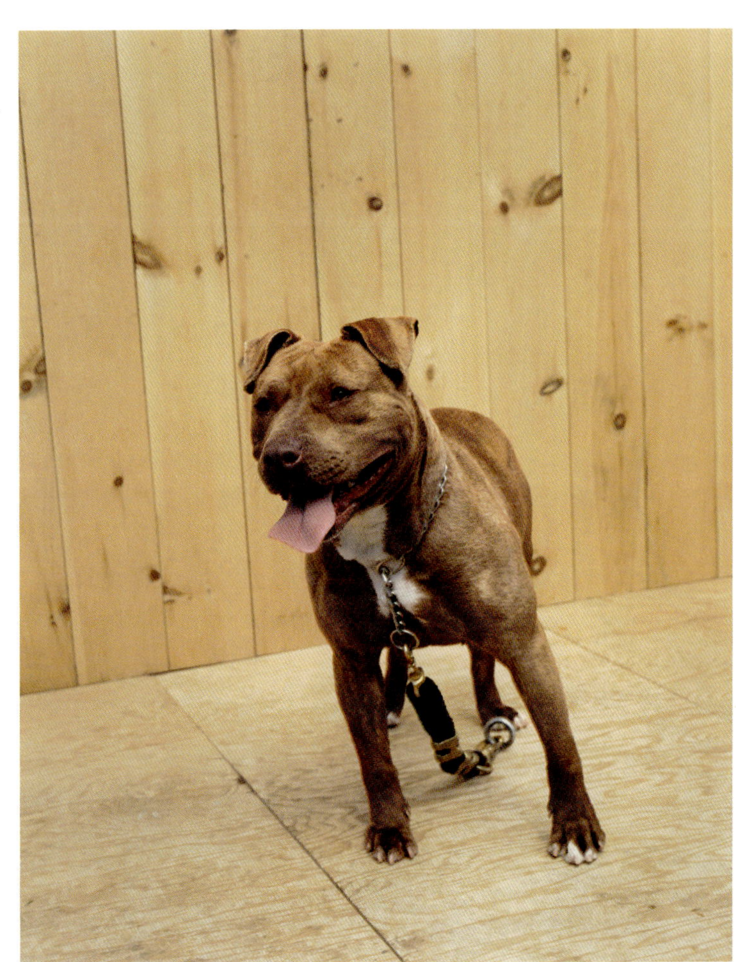
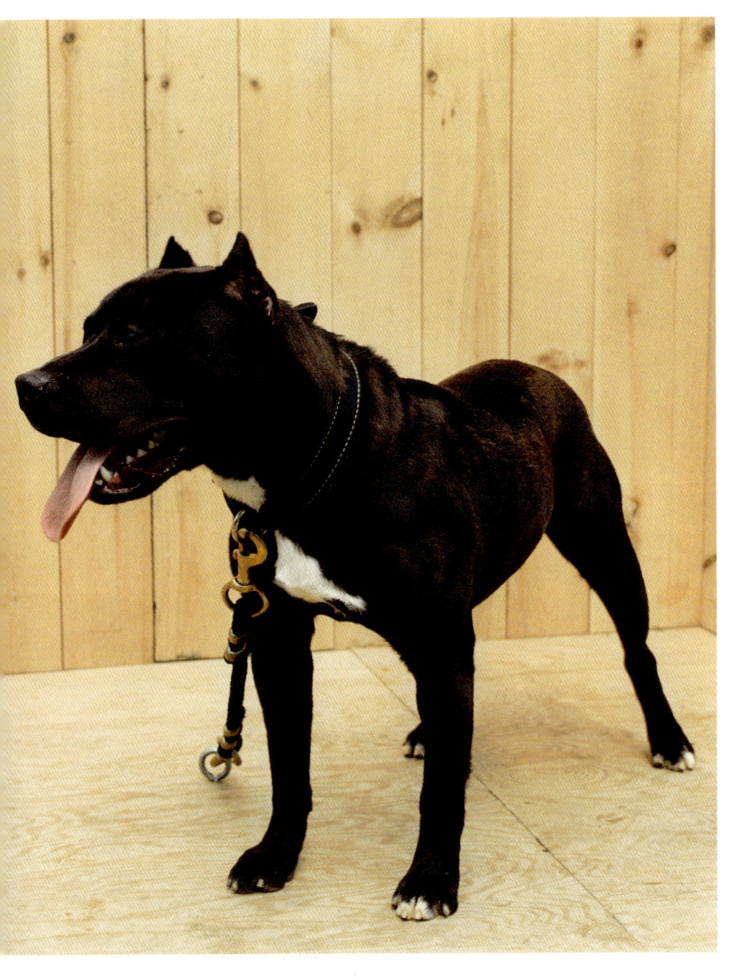
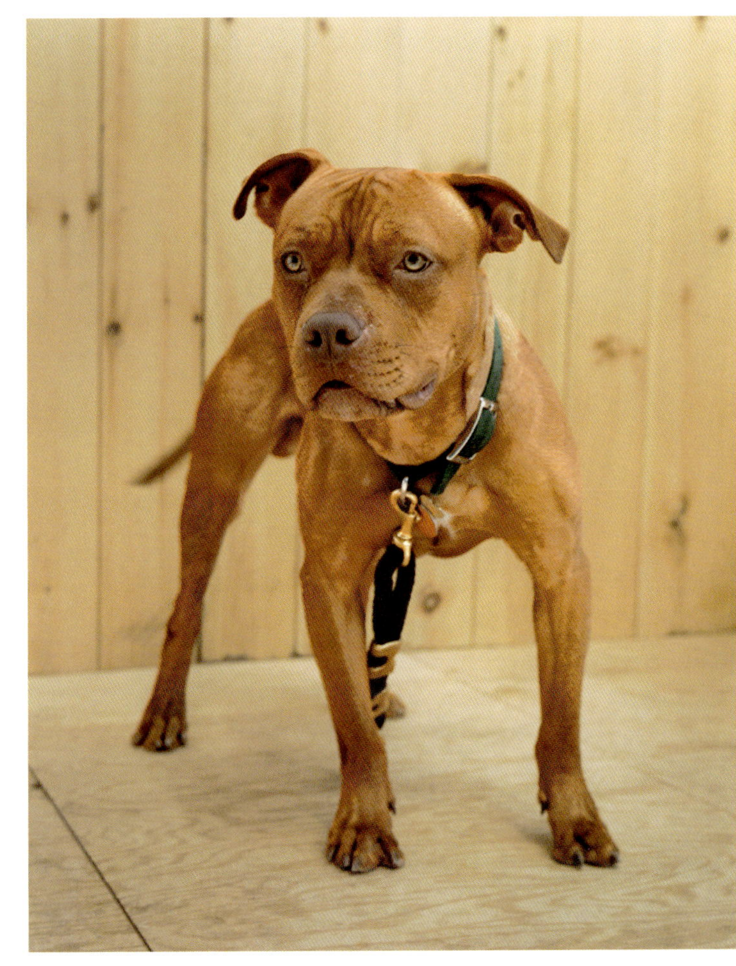

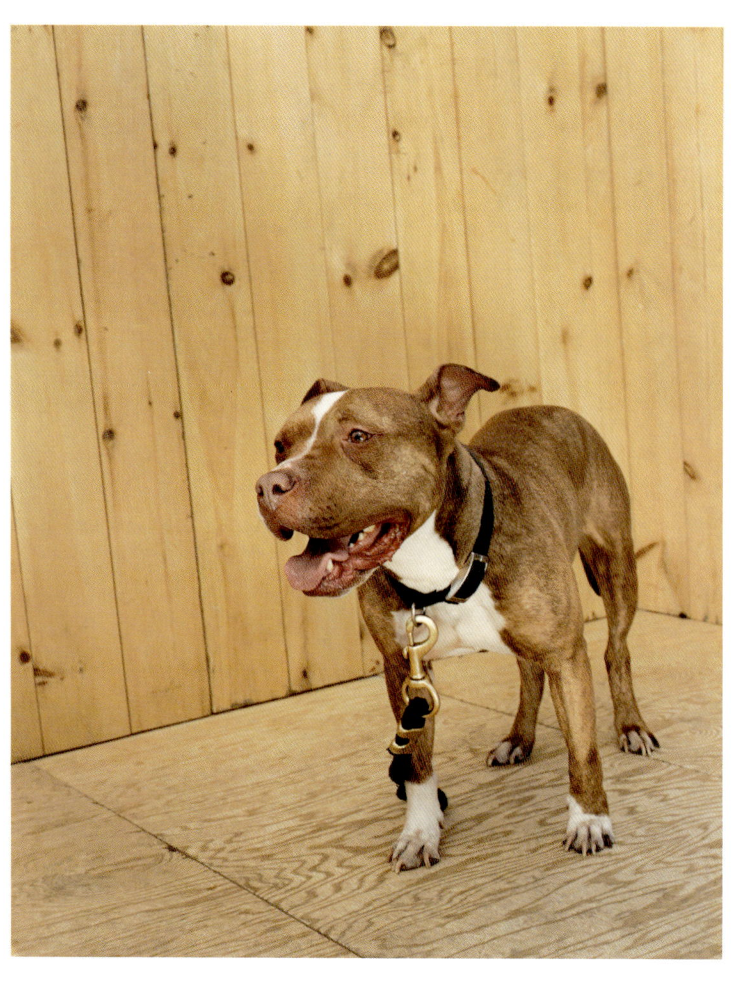
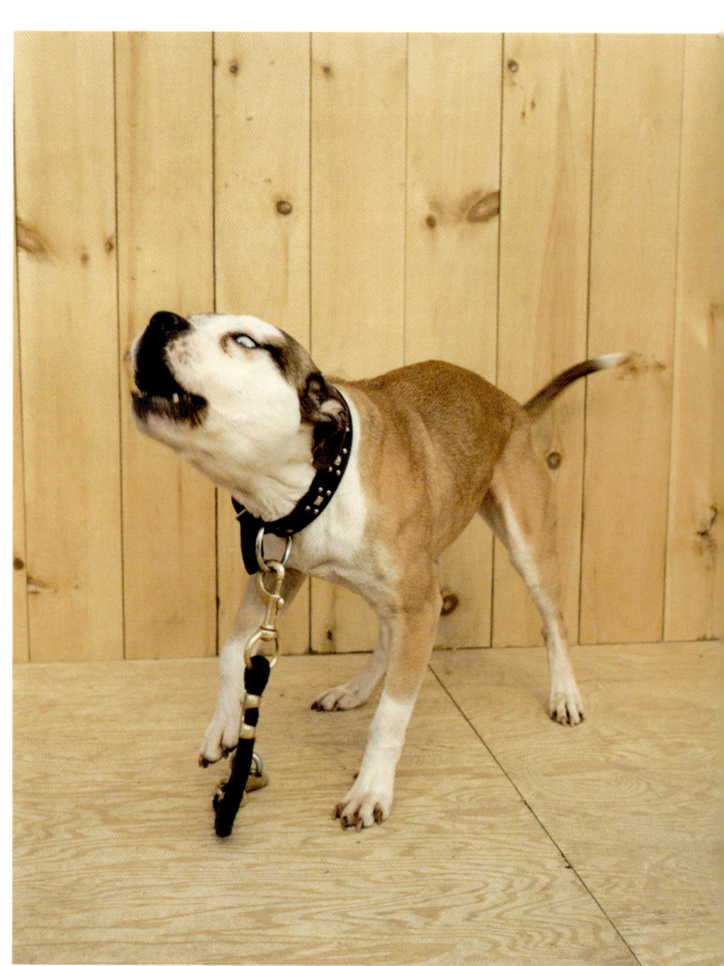
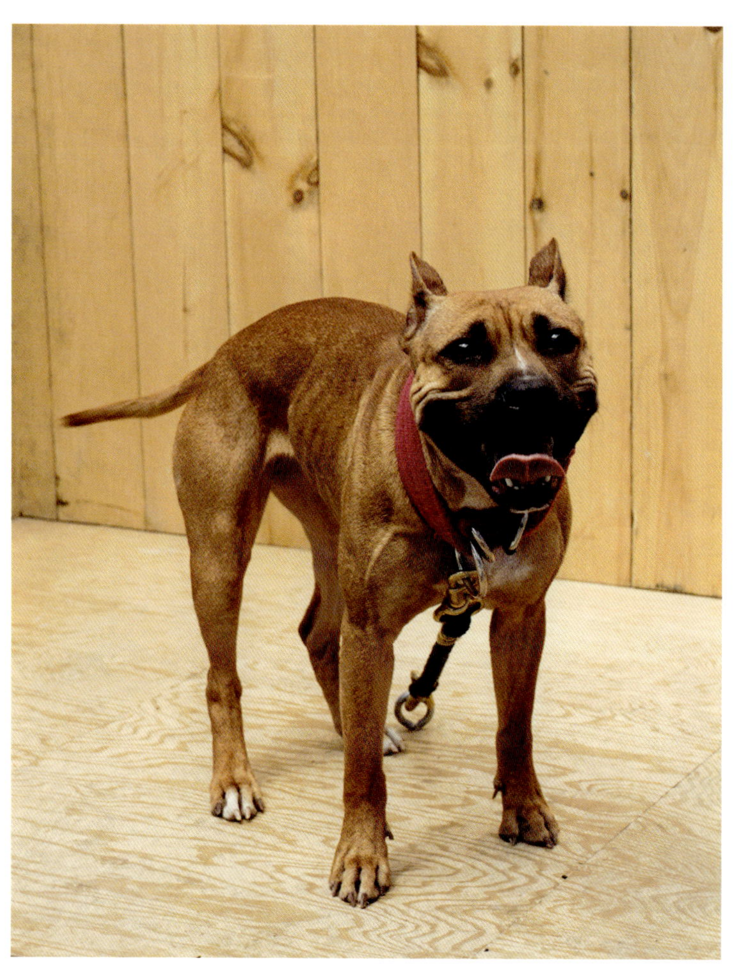
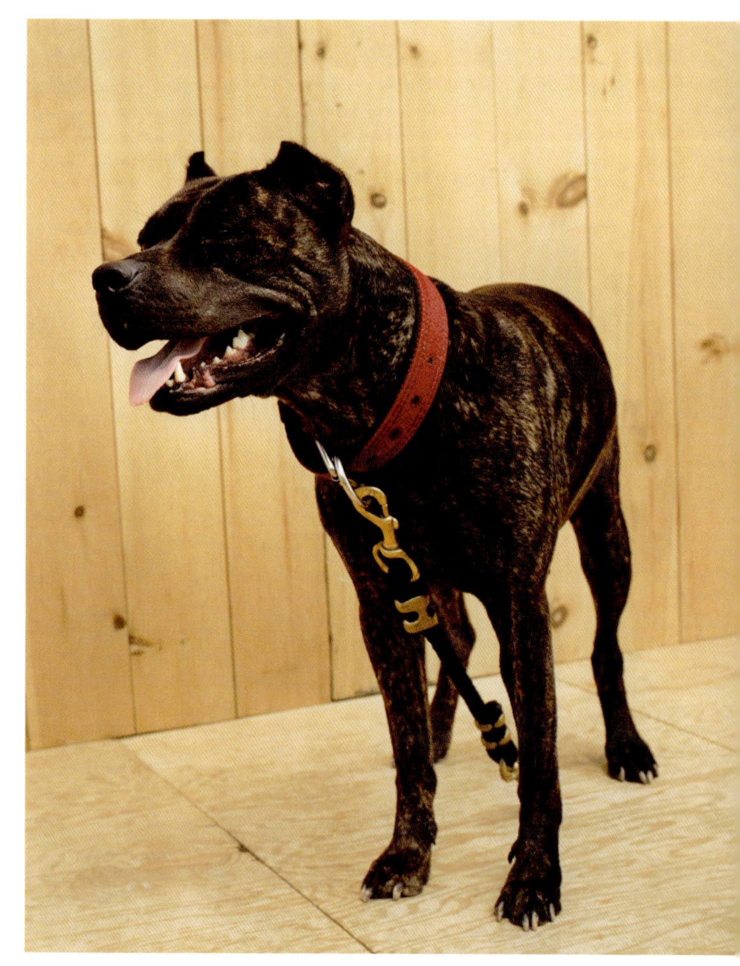

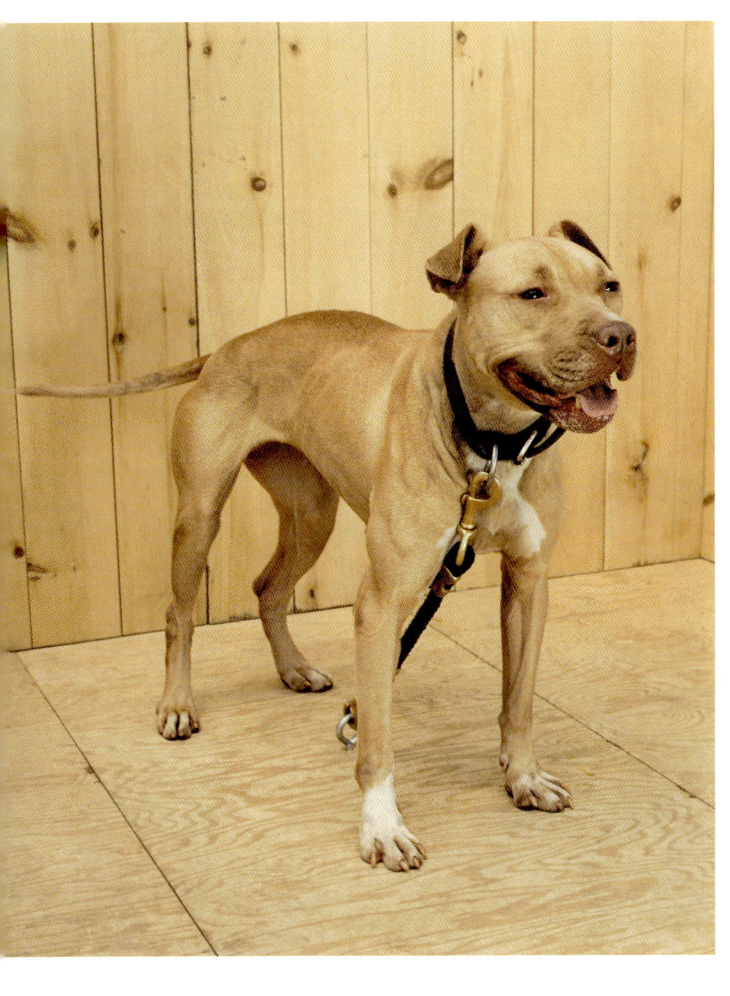

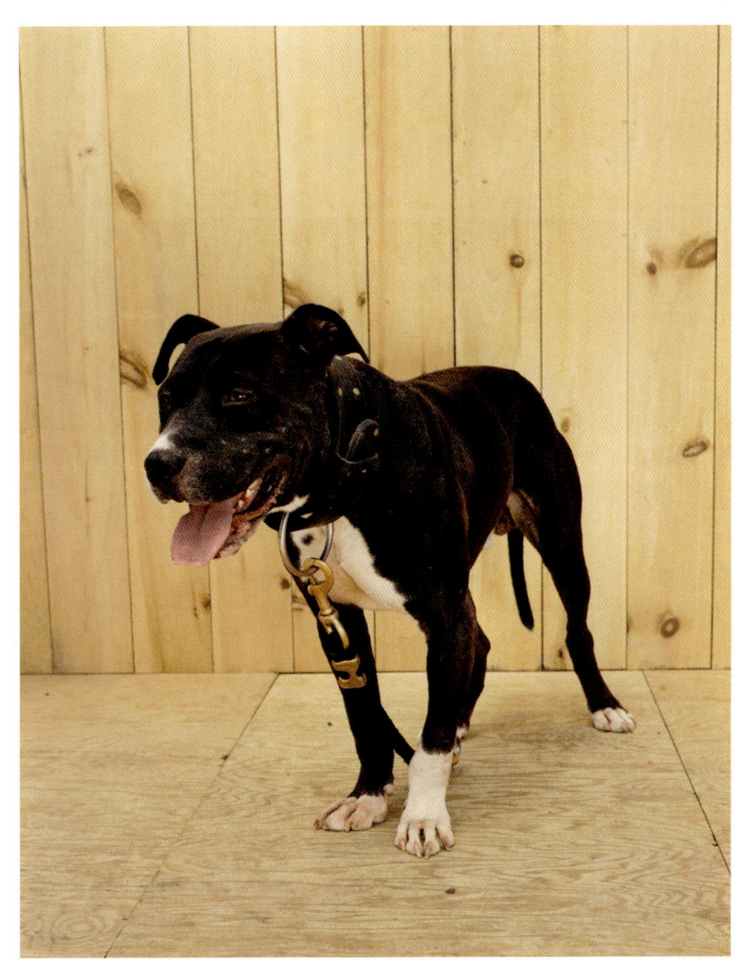

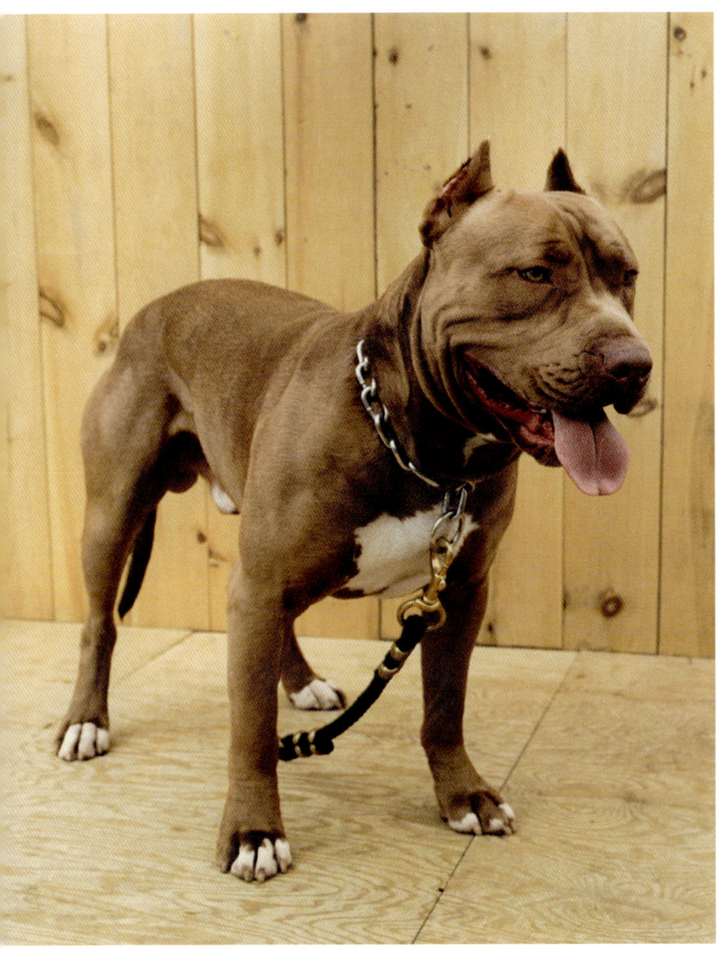

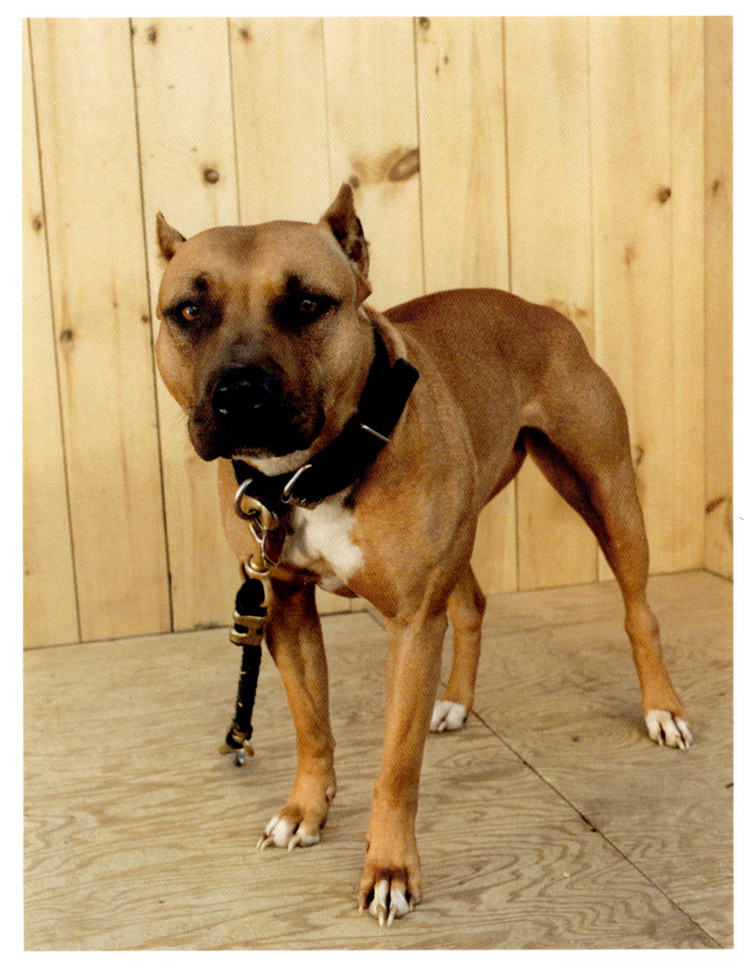

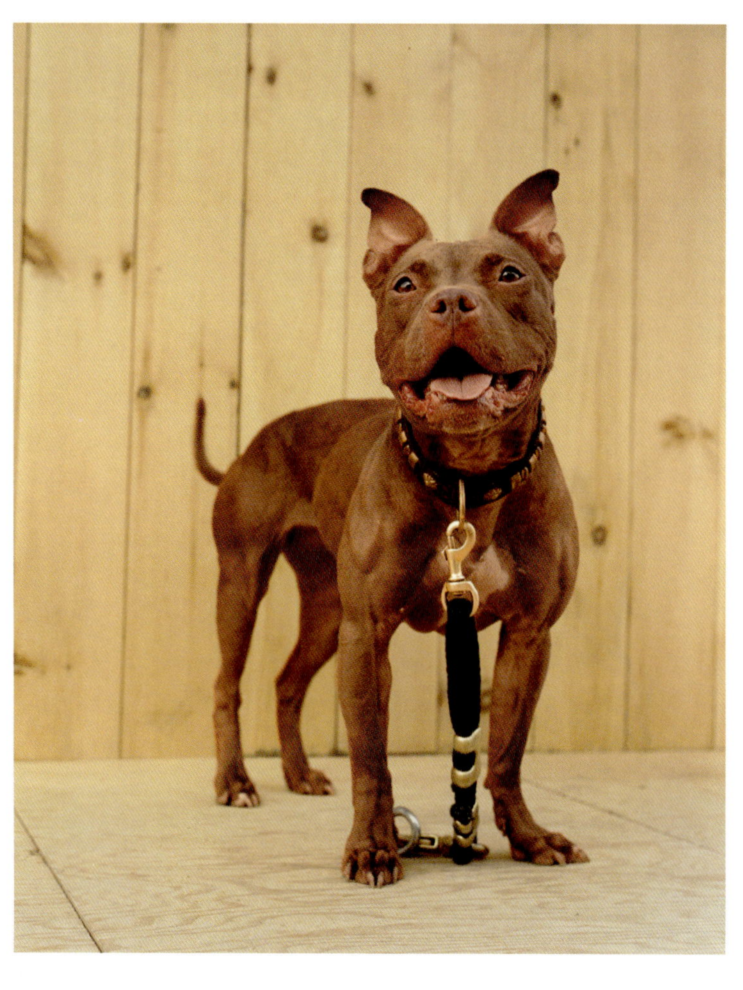
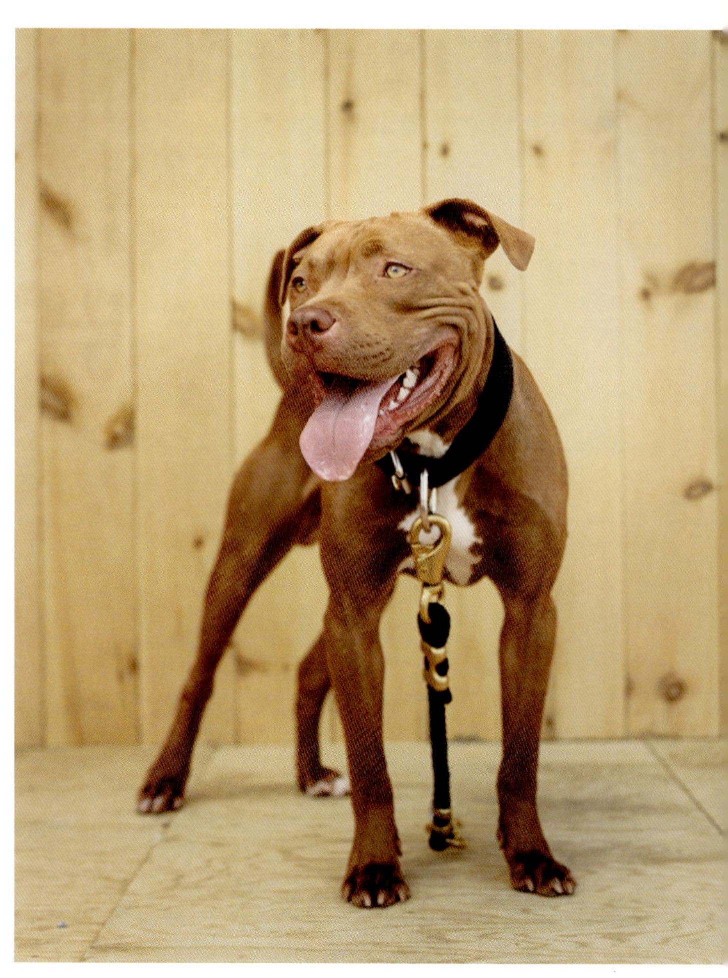
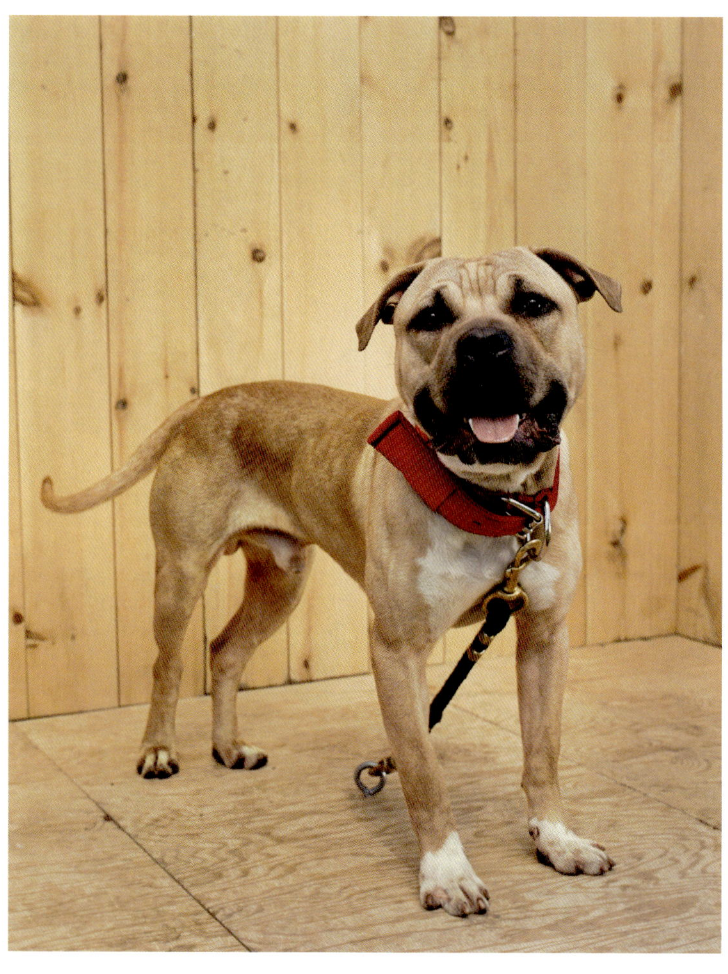
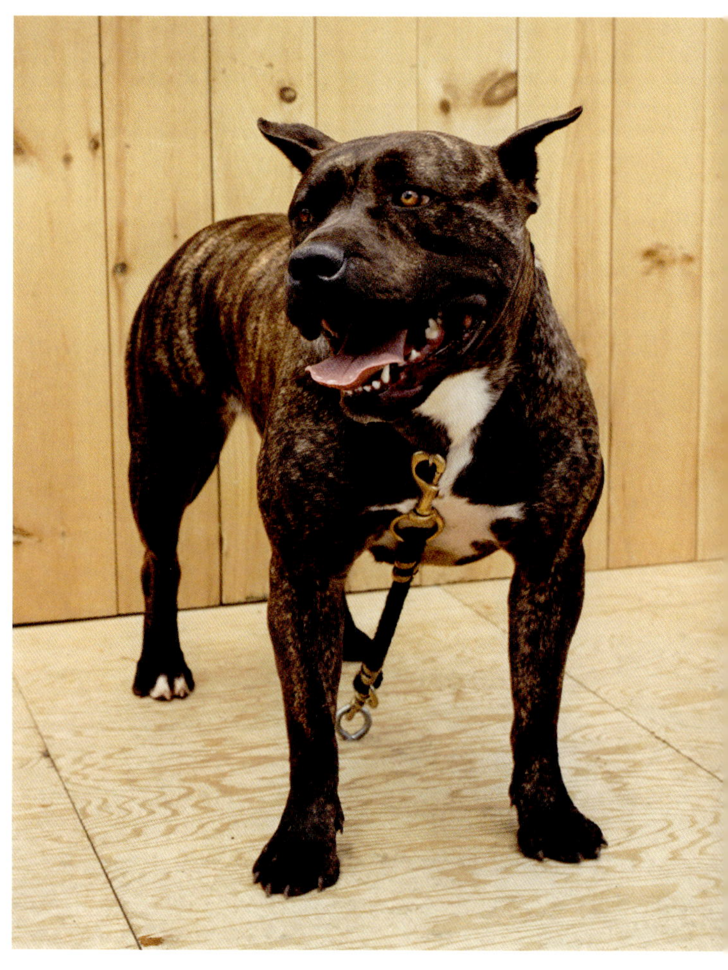

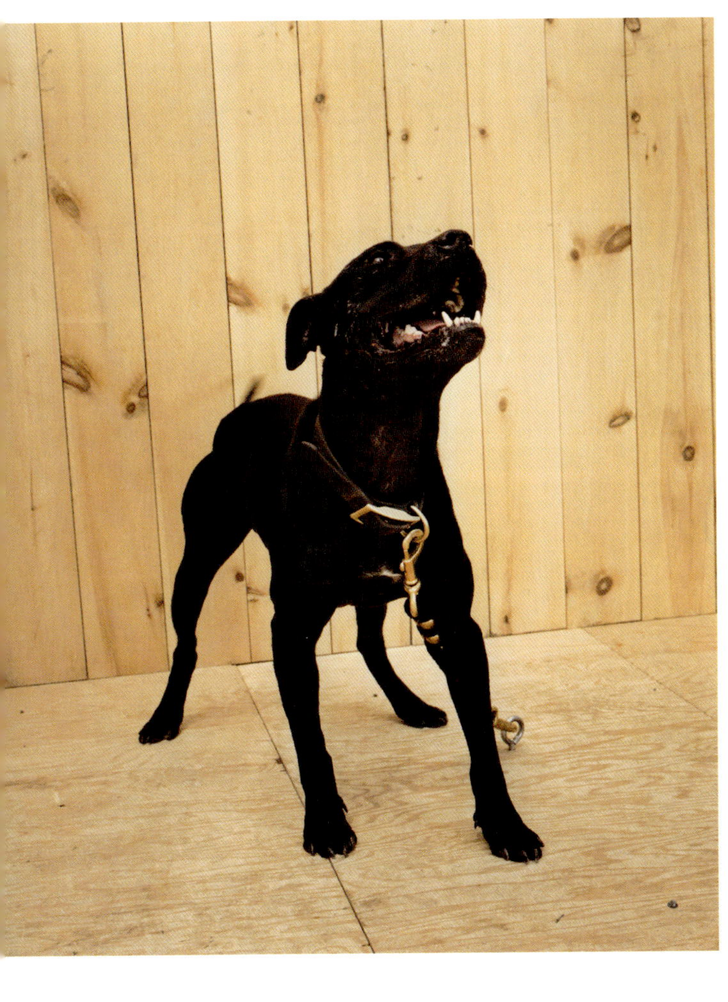
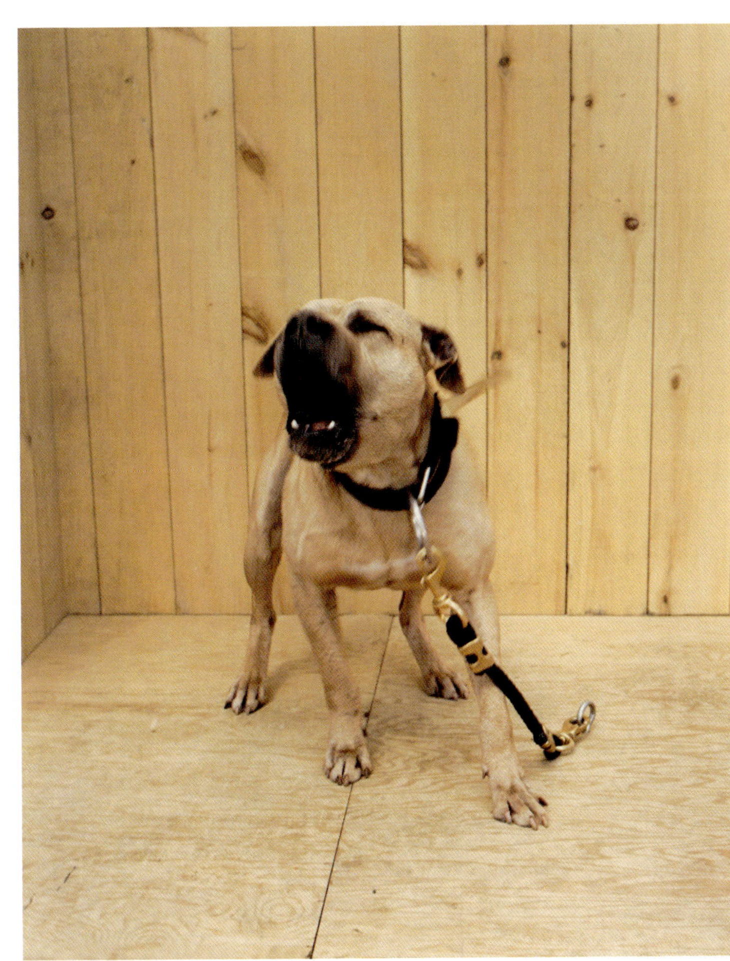
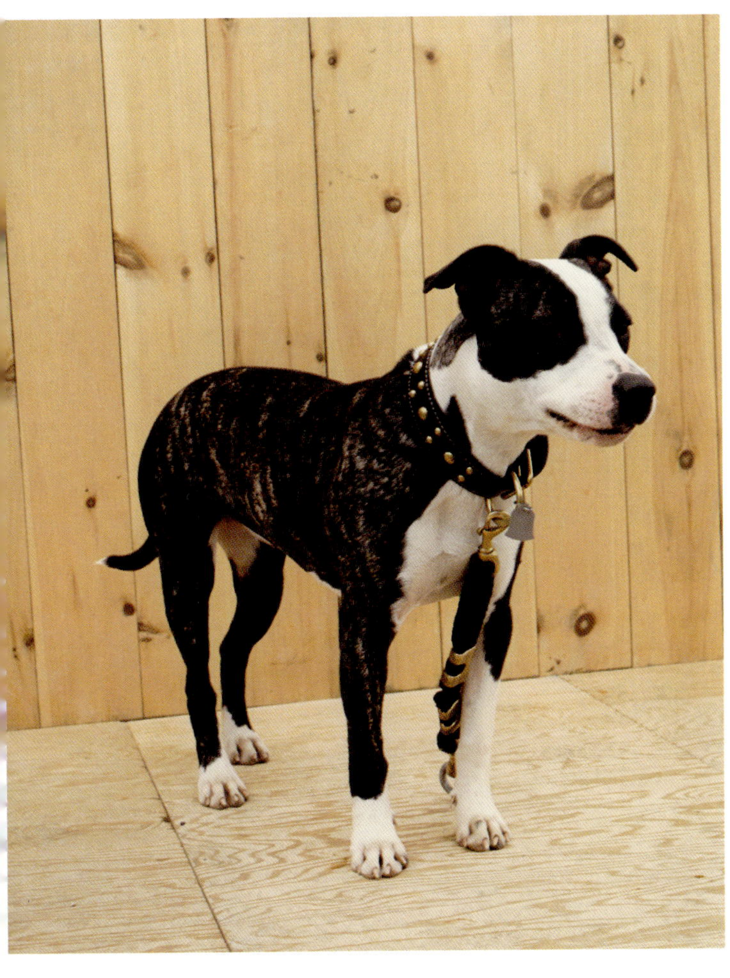
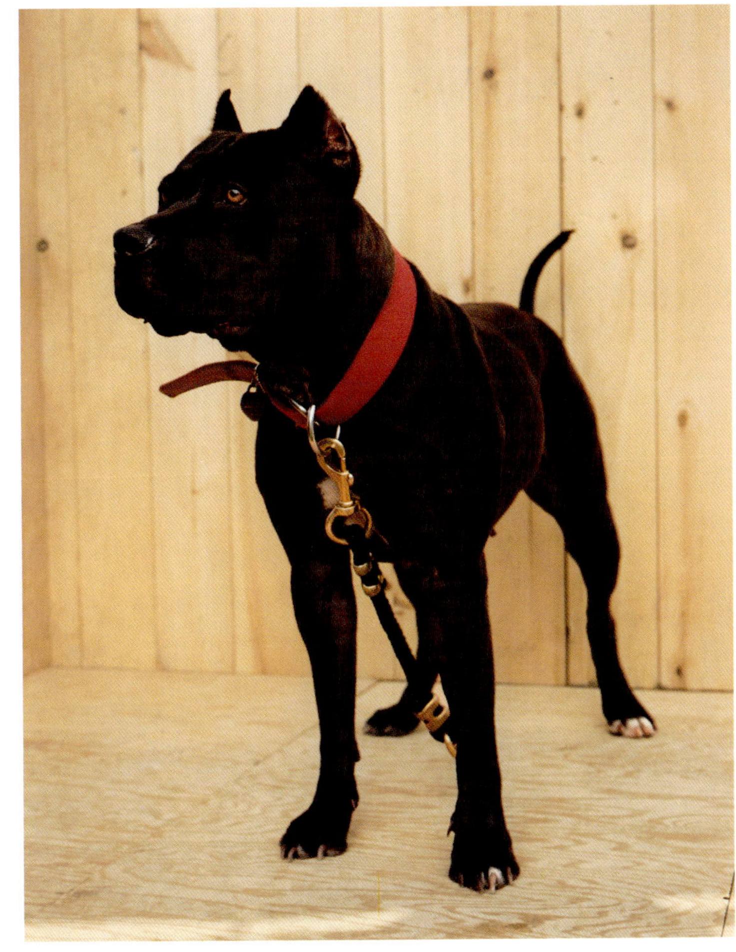

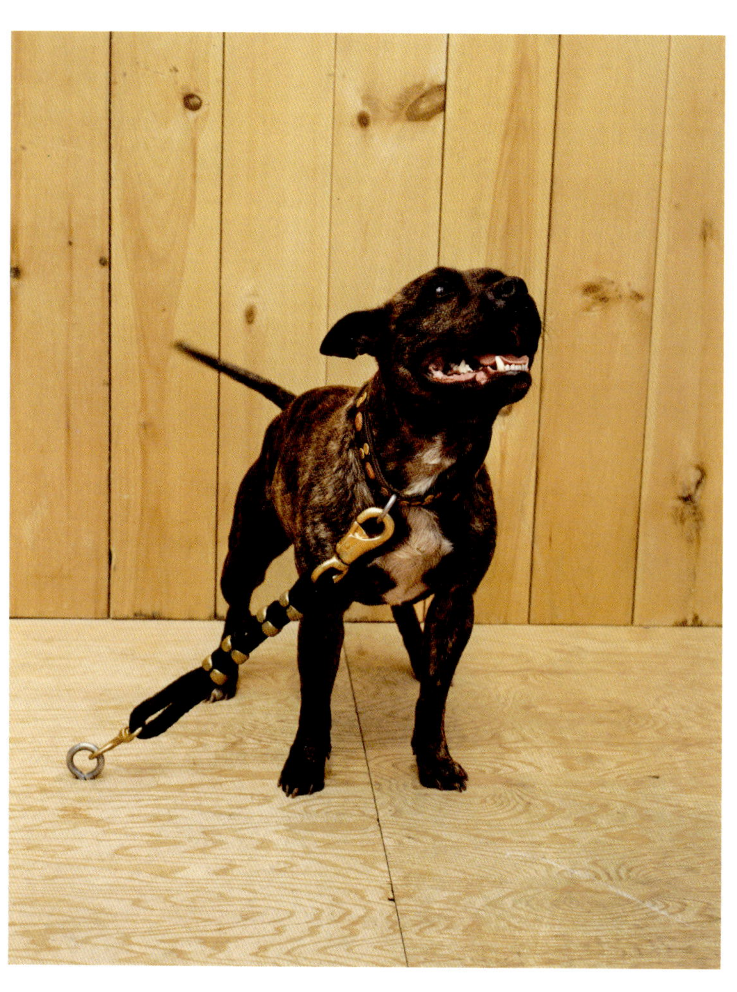
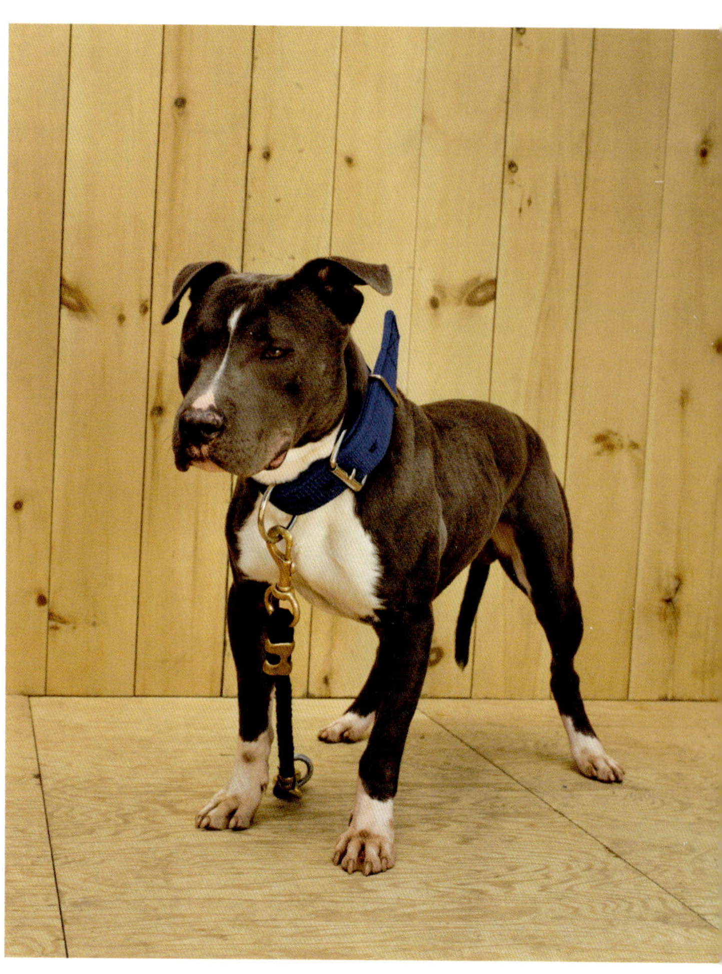
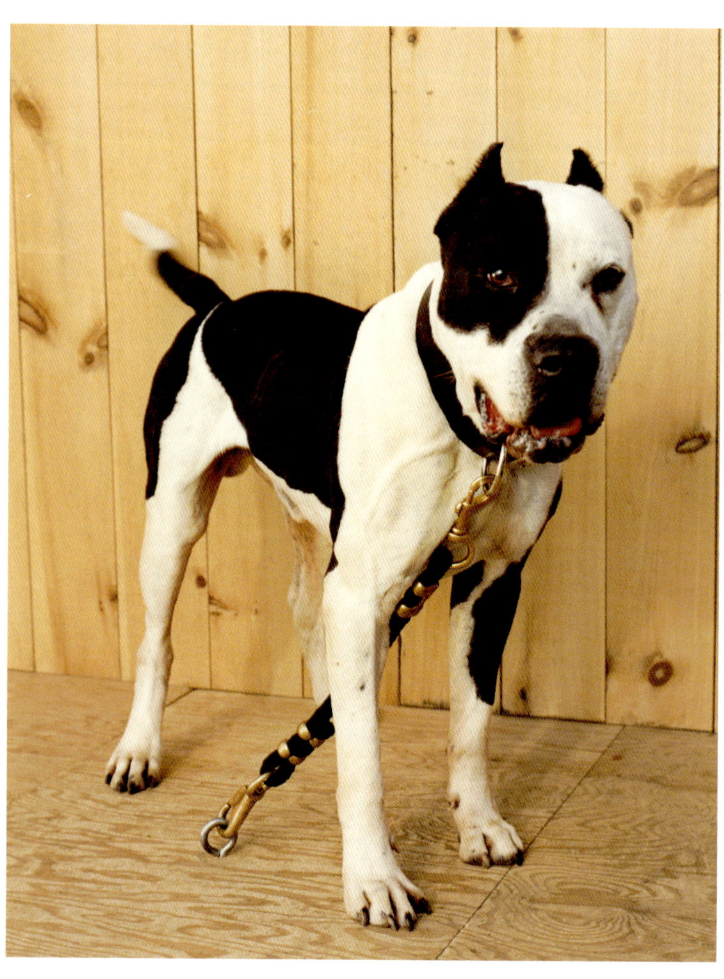
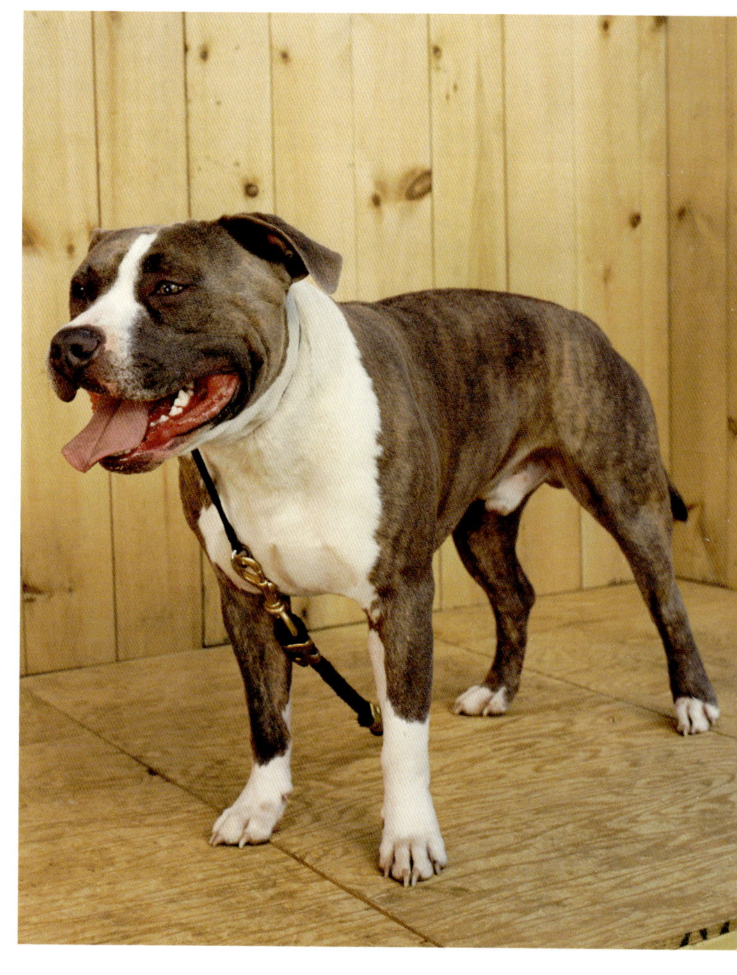

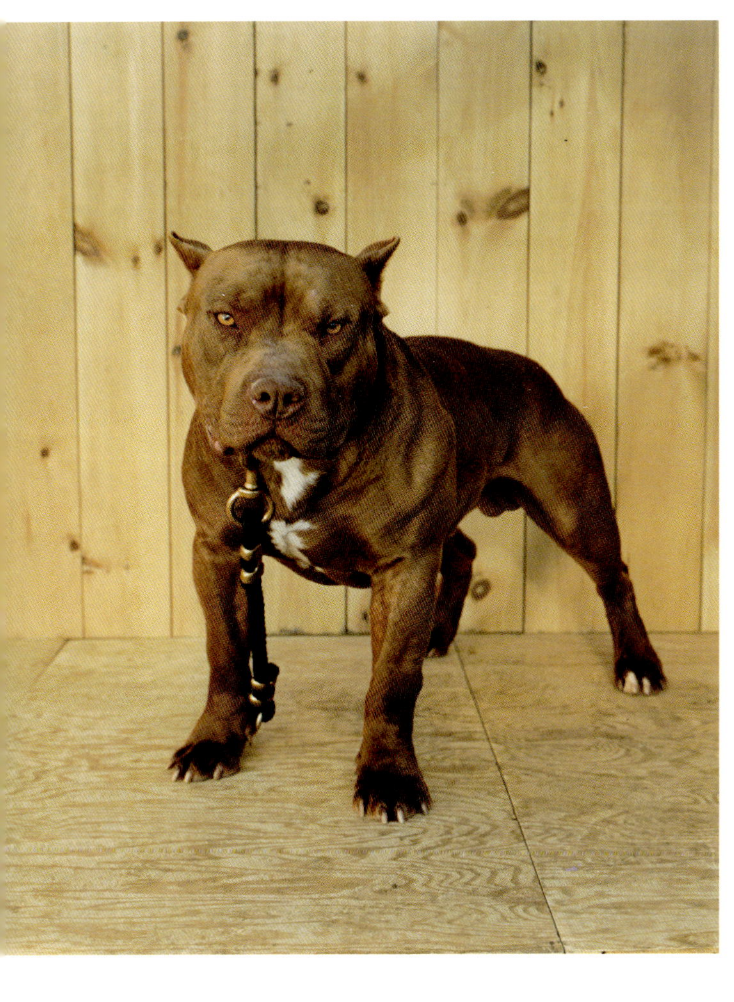
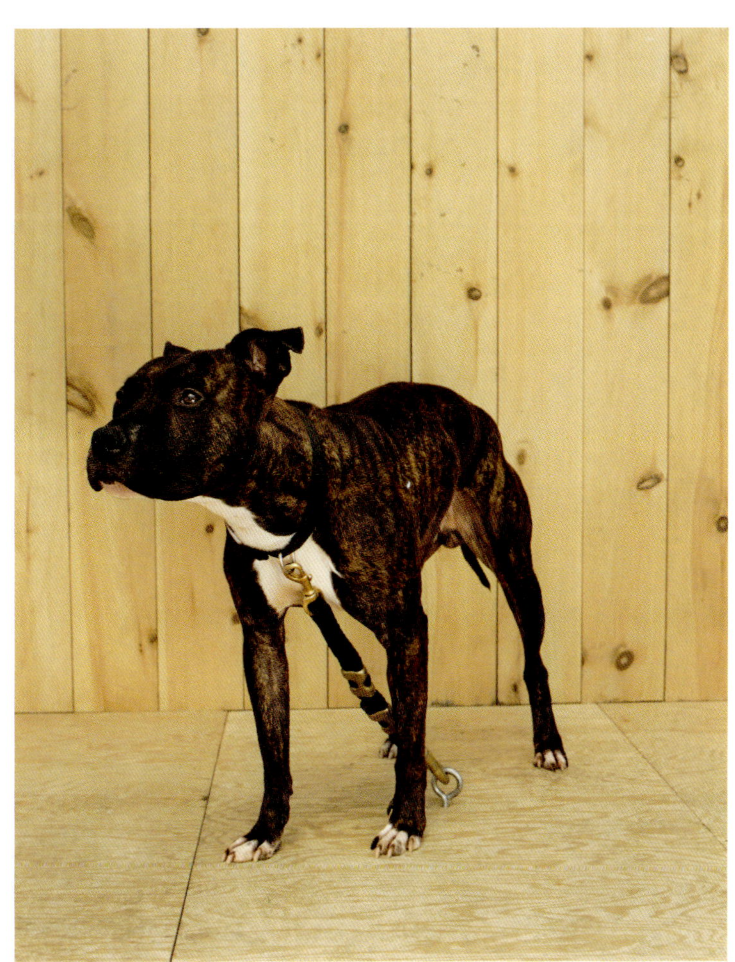
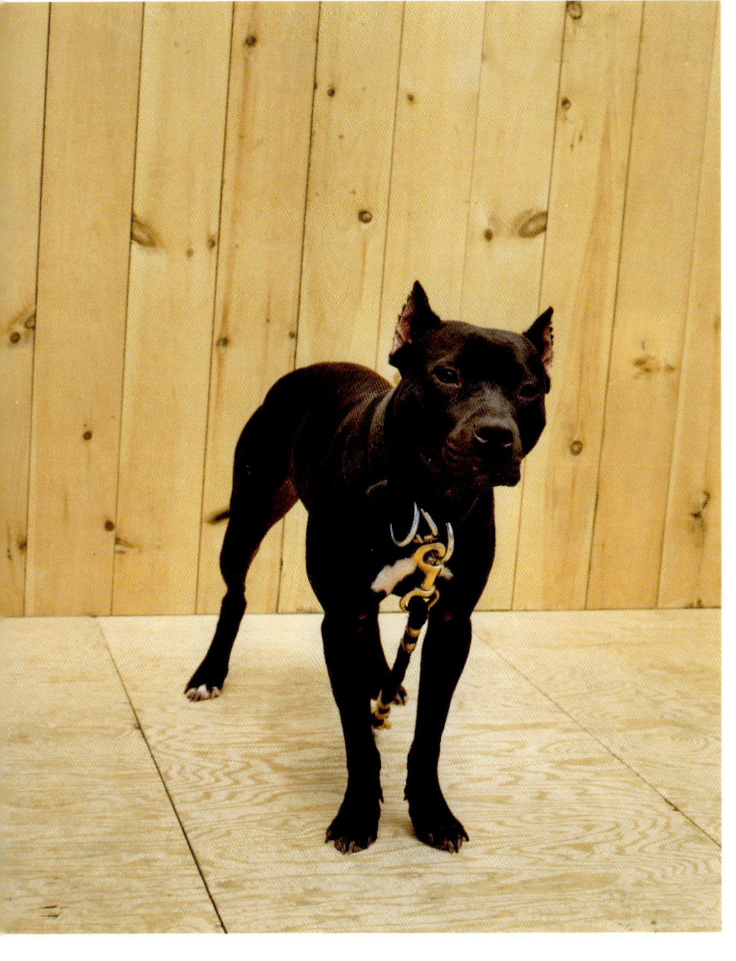
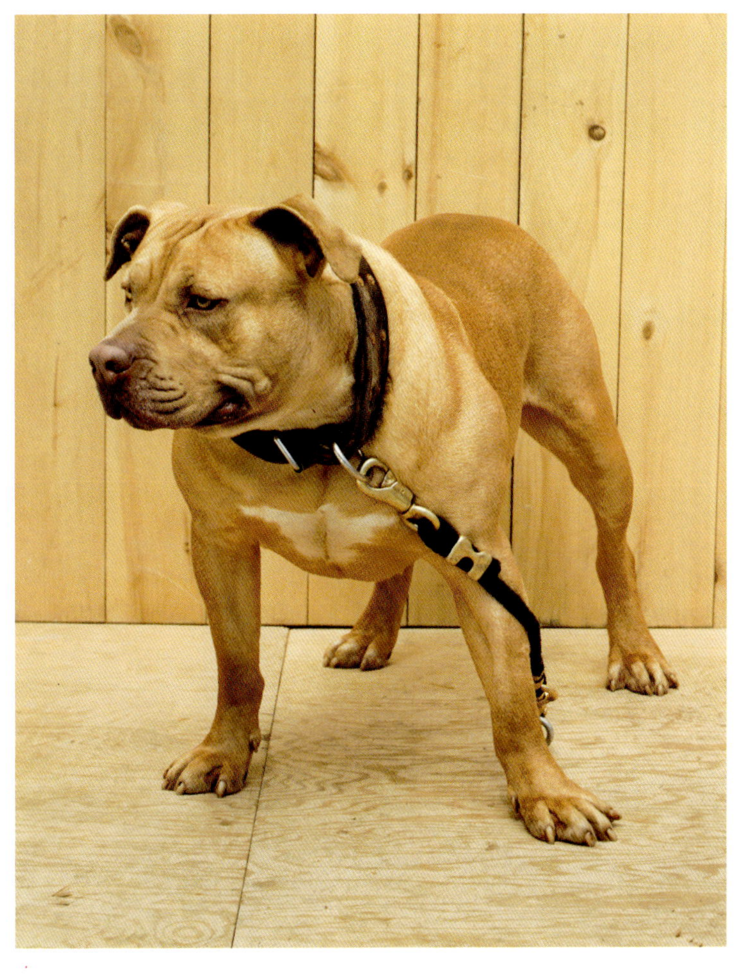

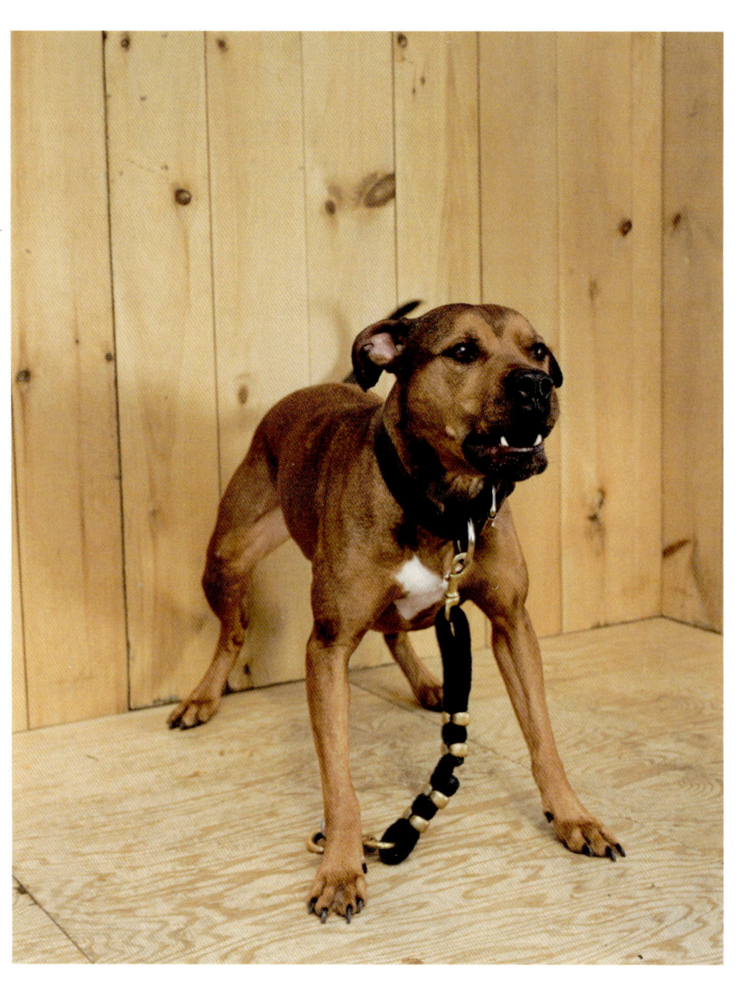
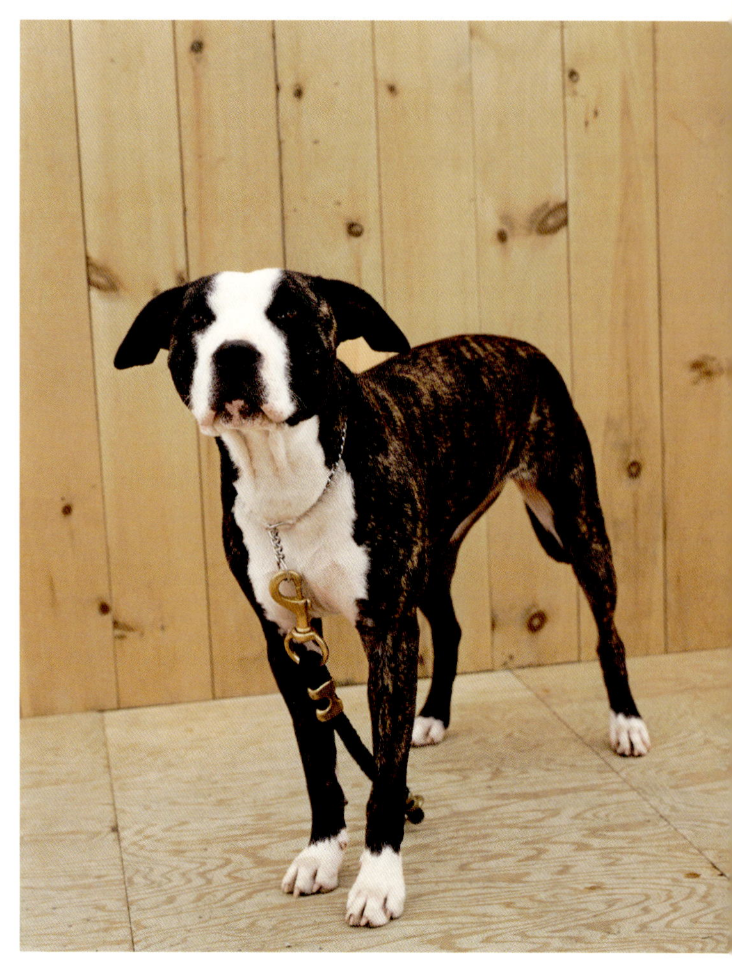
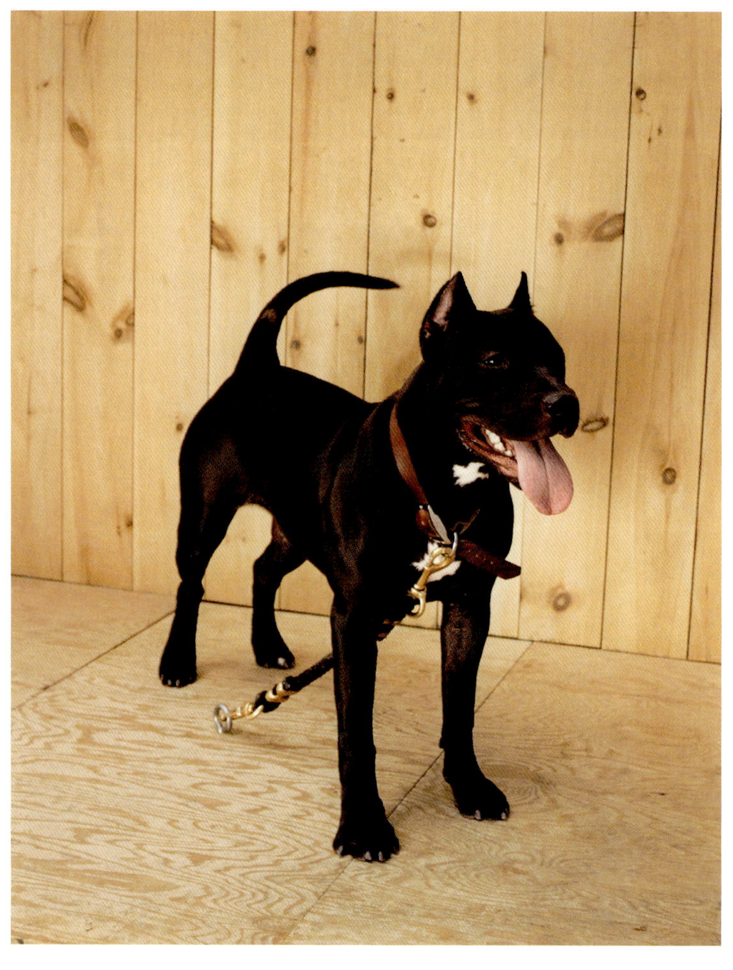
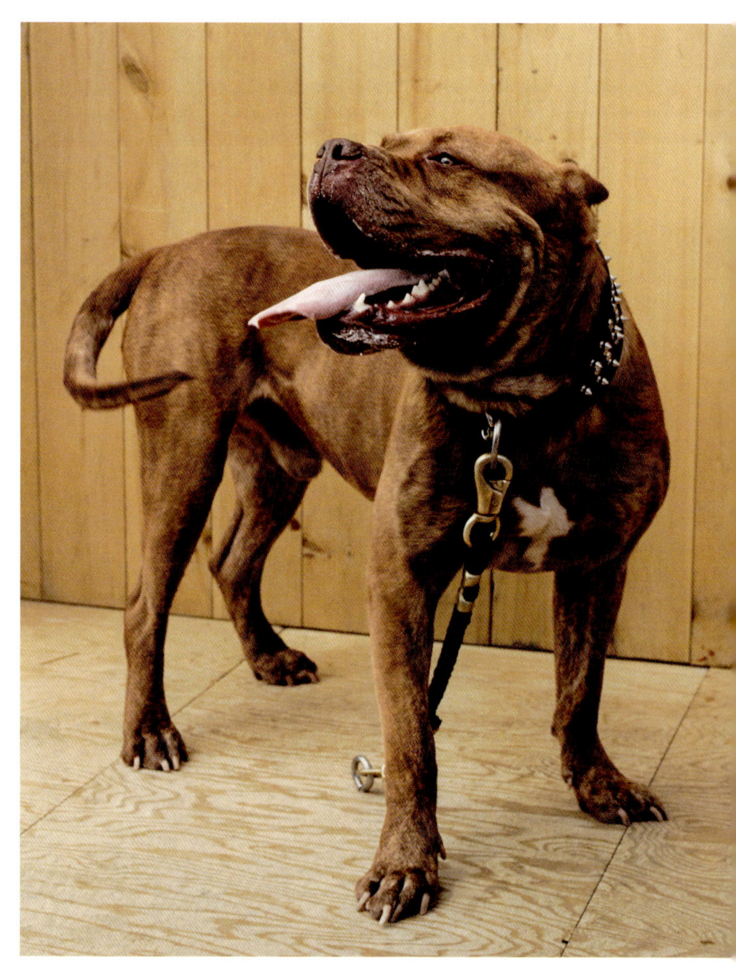

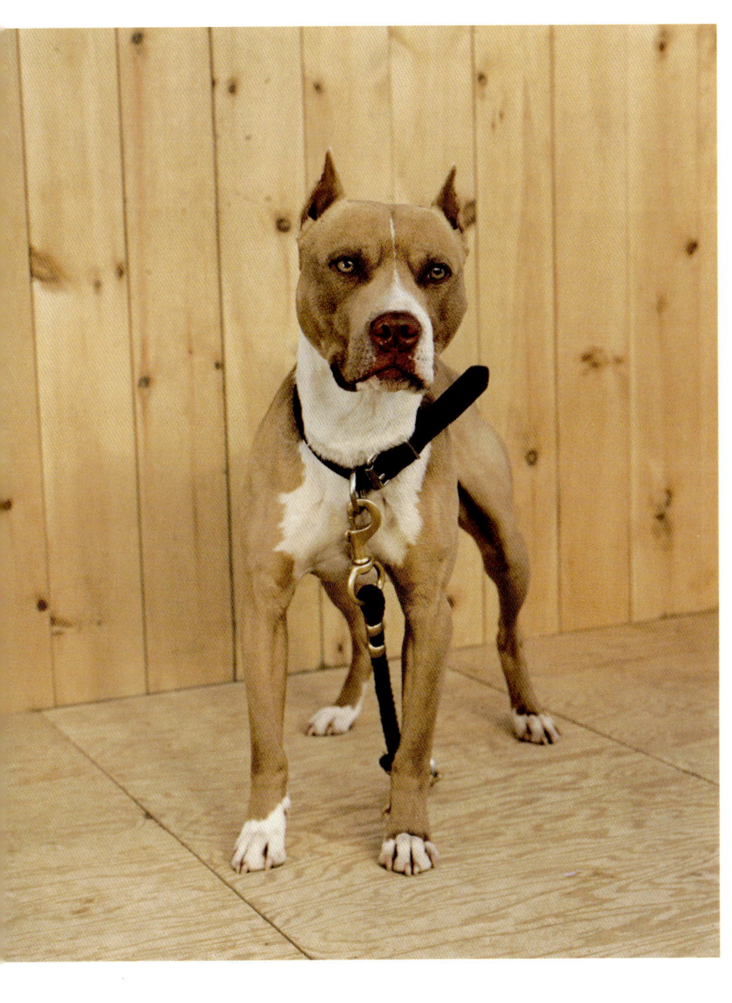
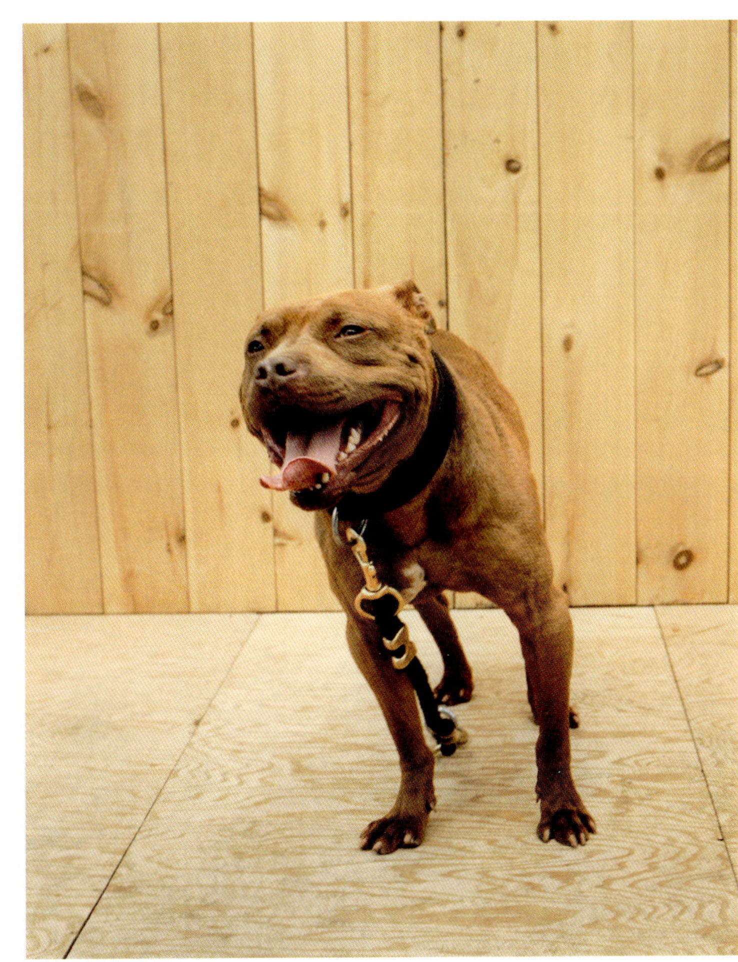
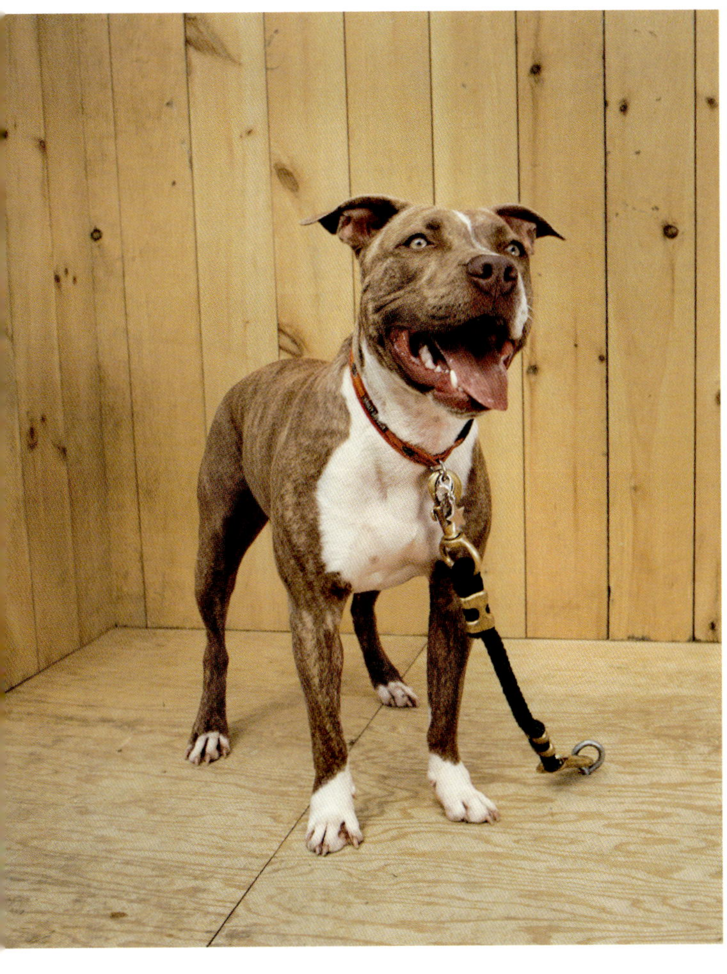
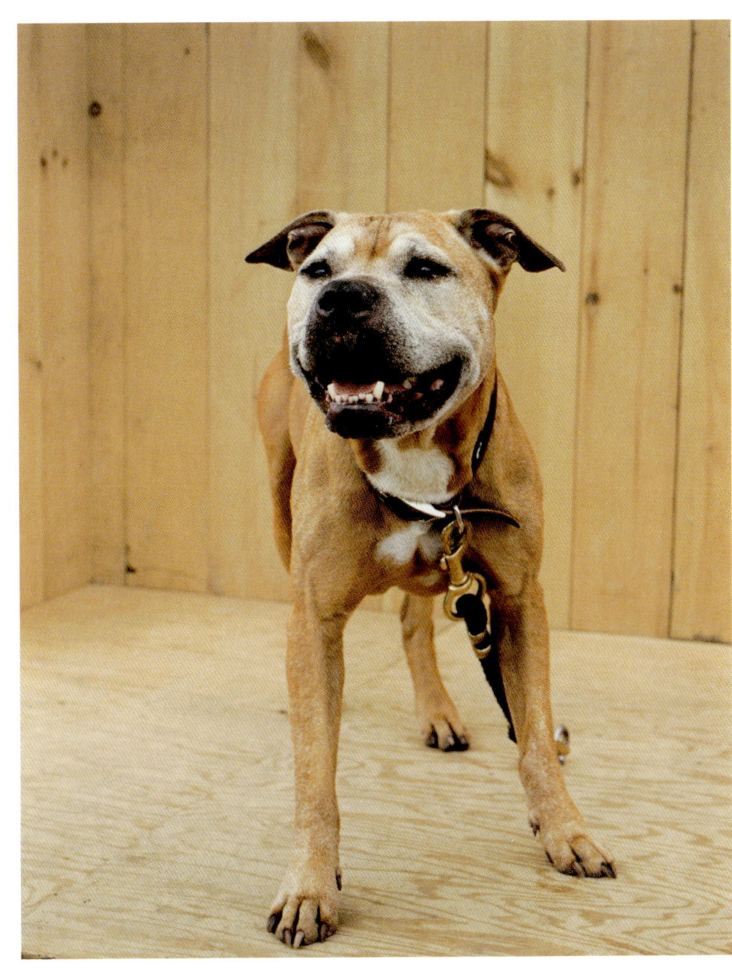

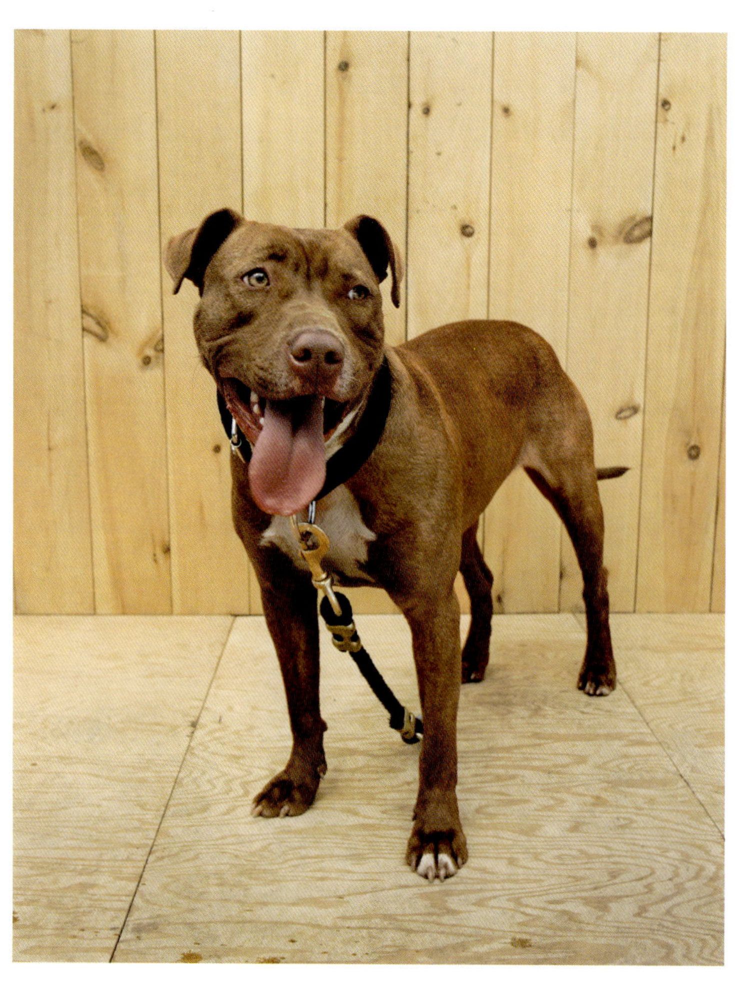
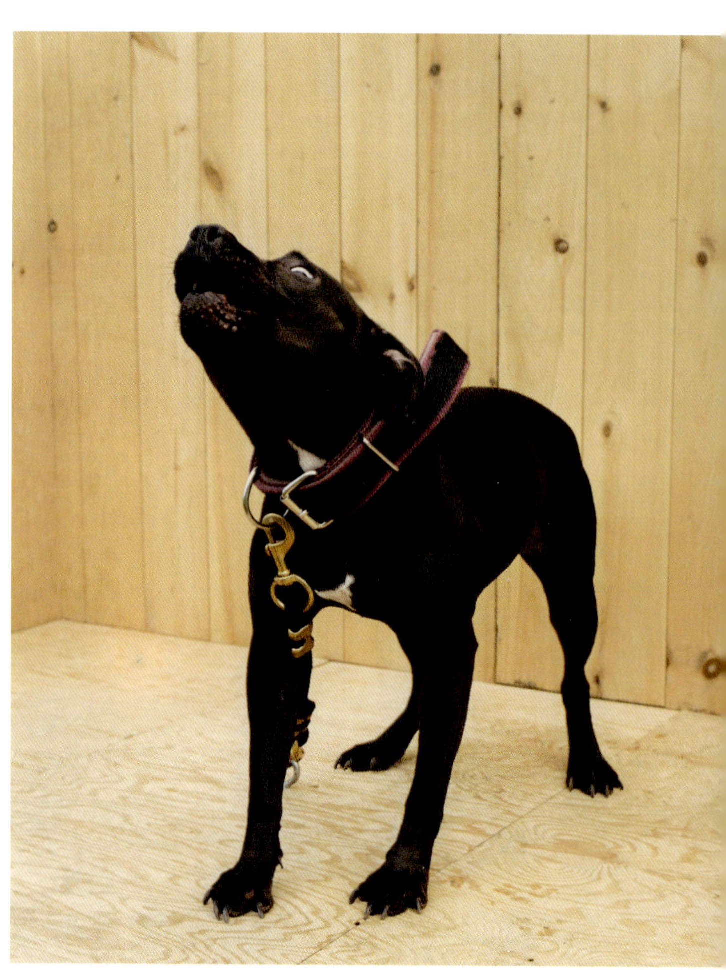
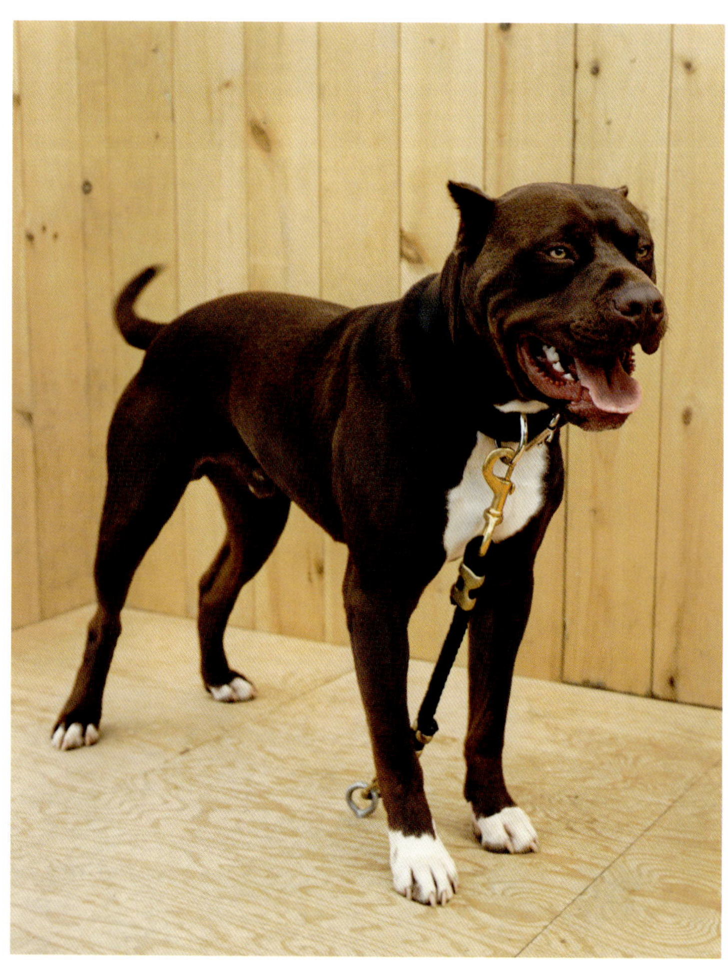
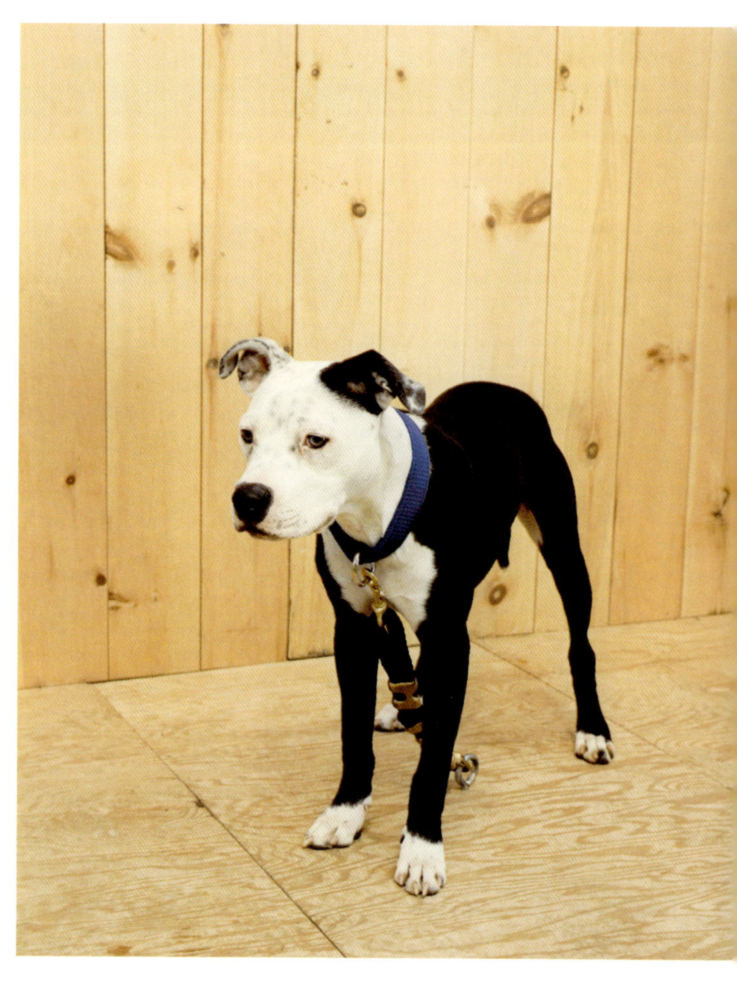

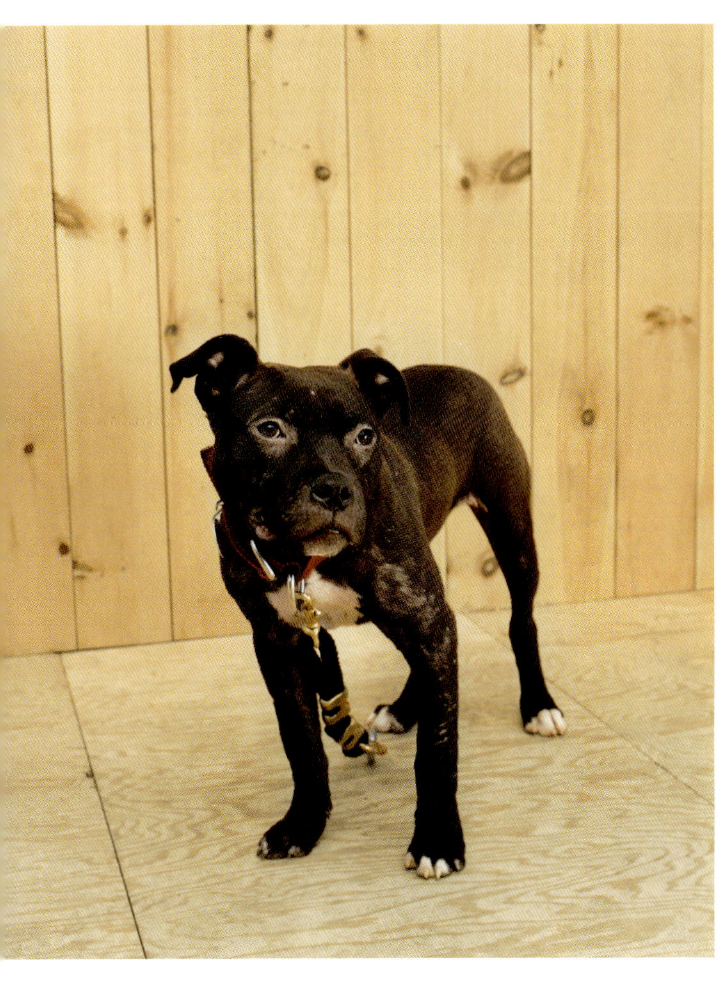
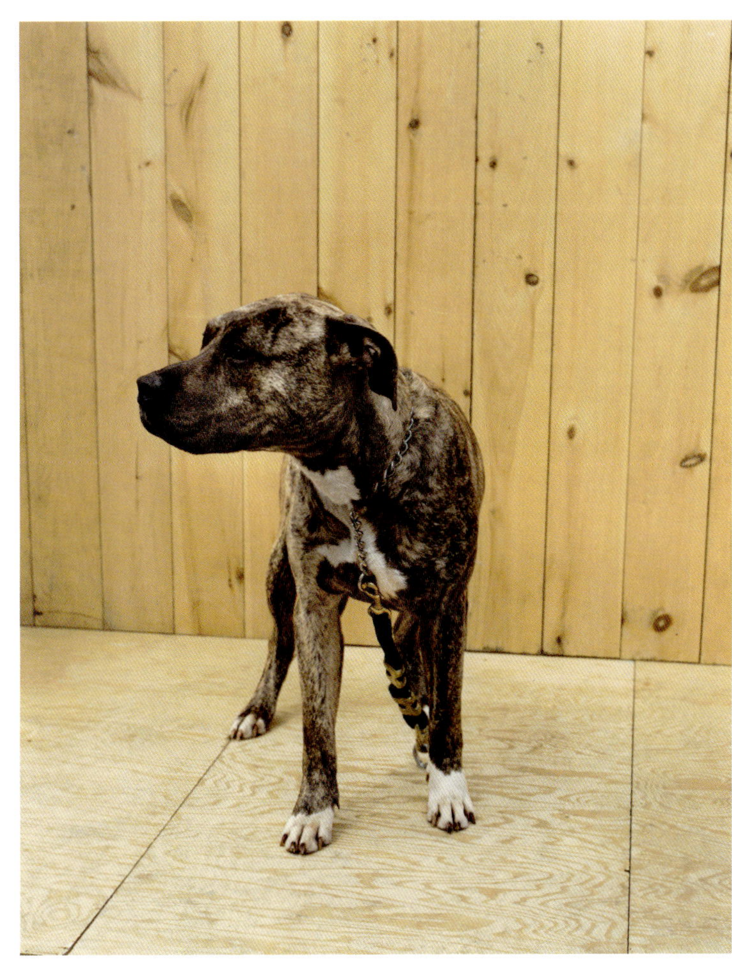
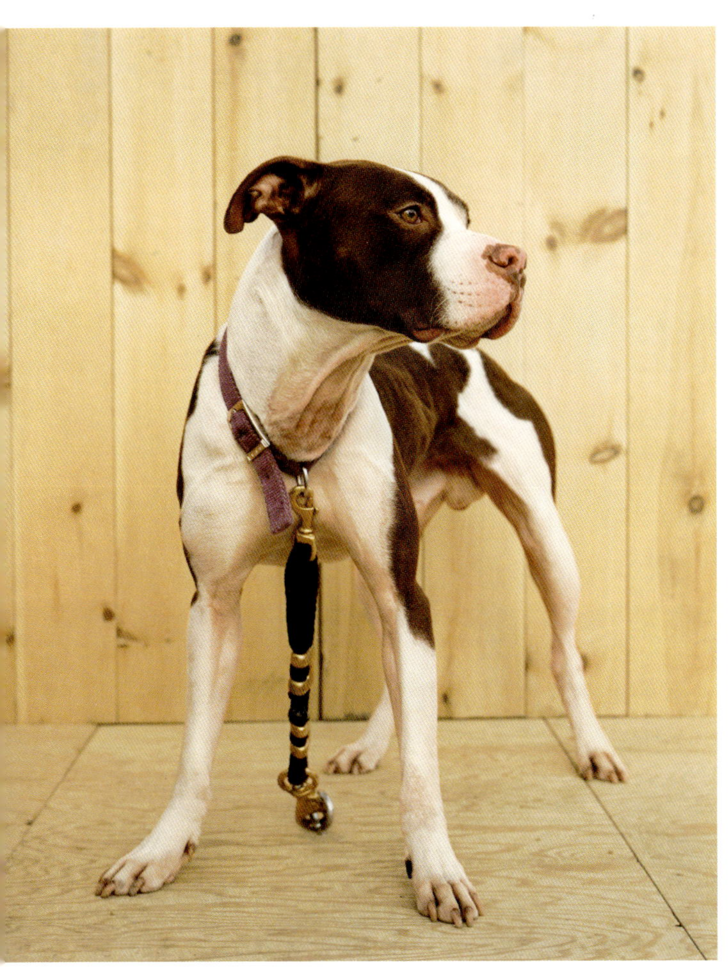
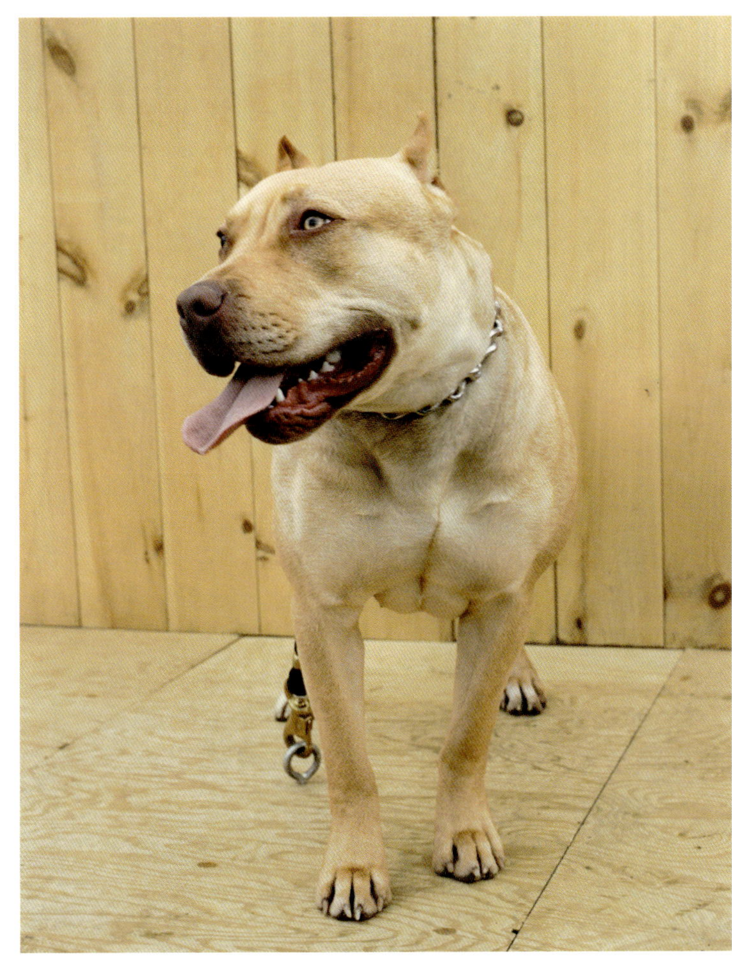

American Pitbull.

Two words.

American Pitbull.

Two simple words.

American Pitbull.

How do they make you feel?

American Pitbull.

Do you smile or do you cringe?

Do you respect or do you fear?

Do you love or do you hate?

American Pitbull.

There is no middle ground.

You either smile or cringe, respect or fear, love or hate.

American Pitbull.

You feel something.

American Pitbull.

You feel something.

There is no middle ground.

AMERICAN PITBULL

pit bull *noun* a short, broad chested breed of dog with large, powerful jaws, a short, smooth coat, and great strength and tenacity, developed to combine the traits of Terriers and Bulldogs; also **pit bull terrier**, **American Pit Bull Terrier**

by James Frey

The history of the American Pit Bulldog, a breed type of several specific breeds including the American Pit Bull Terrier, the American Staffordshire Terrier and the Staffordshire Bull Terrier, is roughly correspondent to the history of the United States as a nation. The first mentions of dogs resembling Pit Bulldogs came in the latter parts of the 18th century. The United States, having successfully rebelled against the reign of King George, began rapidly expanding westward into the vast forests of the American continent. The forests were packed with game and the colonists needed the game to survive. Sometimes, as with bears, they needed to defend themselves against the game. The weapons used at the time were muskets, single shot rifles that fired balls of lead. The muskets were strong enough to bring down men, but not the bears or other large animals, and often, after being wounded, the animals would fight back and sometimes kill colonists. The colonists' solution to the problem was to use dogs to go after wounded animals and bring them down. They tried using Mastiffs, Shepherds and English Bulldogs, which at the time were still used to bait bulls. None of the dogs were able to accomplish what was needed. Mastiffs were too slow, the Shepherds did not have the courage, and the English Bulldogs were not obedient enough. The colonist's solution was to start breeding their own type of dog. They sought the characteristics of strength, courage, speed, stamina and obedience. The goal was to create a dog that was the strongest, fastest, most agile, most animal aggressive, most intelligent and well-mannered dog on earth. They cross-bred Mastiffs for strength, English Bulldogs for courage, smaller terriers for aggressiveness, traditional hunting dogs such as Spaniels and Retrievers for intelligence and obedience. Over time a breed began to emerge. A truly and uniquely American breed. A breed capable of bringing down a full-grown bear.

As this new and, at the time, nameless breed of dog began living and working throughout the colonies, the United States continued to grow. Immigrants by the thousands, the tens of thousands, the hundreds of thousands began arriving on American shores. Throughout most of the 19th century, the bulk of those immigrants came from England, from Wales, from Scotland, from Ireland. Crossing the Atlantic was a perilous journey, and was often made on over-crowded cargo ships. There was little or no room on the ships.

The immigrants brought a minimum of belongings with them: a bag of clothes, a bag of tools, if they could, a prized possession. For many families, the prized possession was a dog. Many of those dogs were fighting dogs.

For as long as there has been a recorded history of the British Isles, fighting dogs have been part of that history. When the Romans conquered Briton, as it was then called, in the year 50 AD, they reported encountering broad-mouthed fighting dogs called *pugnaces*, which were used for hunting and contests in amphitheaters. When Norman kings conquered the Saxons in 1066, they returned home with Saxon fighting dogs described as having large, thick heads and short muzzles. Sometime around 1406, Edmond De Langley, the Duke of York, wrote a treatise called *The Master of the Game and of Hawks*, in which he described hunting with dogs that had remarkable courage, that attached themselves to other animals and refused to let go of them. There are numerous accounts of dogs fighting for sport during the reigns of Queen Mary and Queen Elizabeth, and King James and King Charles. In 1700, there was an account of dog fighting written by a man named Burnette, who describes fighting dogs as small, fierce, indomitable animals that may well be the most courageous creatures on Earth.

These were the dogs that came with the immigrants. Small, fierce, indomitable, the most courageous creatures on earth. They had wide heads, strong jaws and heavily muscled bodies. They weighed between twenty and thirty pounds. They had thick skin, which resisted tearing, and they were bred to have a high threshold for pain and superior blood-clotting ability. Because the arenas that they fought in were small, the dogs were agile and quick. They had a heightened sense of aggression towards other dogs. Once engaged, they would fight until their bodies no longer let them fight. Because their handlers needed to be able to control them, they were bred to be extremely obedient to humans. If a dog ever turned on, attacked or showed aggression towards a human it was killed. This led the fighting dogs to become extremely affectionate.

As the dogs came, the culture of fighting them came as well. Despite its brutality, dog fighting became popular in immigrant communities throughout the country. Practitioners of it began breeding fighting dogs on American soil, and they quickly discovered the hunting breed earlier colonists had developed using the war dog, fighting dog, hunting dog and terrier stock. They began breeding those dogs with the smaller British fighting dogs. The goal was to create a breed of gladiator dogs. Dogs that would be, pound for pound, the strongest, fastest, most agile, most animal aggressive, most intelligent, most obedient dogs on the face of the earth. The trait most specifically sought after was *gameness*. Gameness, simply defined, is a willingness to see a job through to its end, regardless of what the job might be, regardless of the conditions. If the job were pulling a sled, a game dog would pull the sled until its heart burst. If the job were chasing down an animal, a game dog would run until it dropped. If the job were fighting another a dog, a game dog would fight to the death. Over time, the new breed was refined. Bred on American soil, its primary activity fighting in a pit, its blood most heavily infused with that of the bulldog and the terrier, the breed became known as the American Pit Bull Terrier. Pound for pound, the strongest, fastest, most agile, most animal aggressive, most intelligent, most obedient dogs on the face of the earth. The ultimate canine gladiators.

As the post-Civil War population of the United States exploded, the new breed flourished, and its population exploded as well. Because of the diversity of its origin, scores of bloodlines were developed. With the intent of establishing the concept of the "total dog," based equally upon performance and aesthetics, Mr. C. Z. Bennett, a well-known Pit Bulldog breeder and fancier, founded the United Kennel Club, the first registry to officially recognize the American Pit Bull Terrier (now the second largest all-breed canine registration service in the United States). In 1898, he assigned his own Pit Bulldog, Bennett's Ring, the first U.K.C. registration number: 1.

In the early 1900s the Pit Bulldog was one of the most popular breeds in America. Tige, Buster Brown's companion in the comic strip, was a Pit Bulldog, as was the dog we still see today on R.C.A. products, which was Thomas A. Edison's beloved Pit Bull. Theodore Roosevelt kept two Pit Bulls in the White House as his family's pets, Helen Keller traveled with her Pit Bull, and the United States Navy named the Pit Bulldog America's watchdog, producing posters with a Pit Bull wearing a Navy cap which read, "We're not looking for trouble, but we're ready for it."

In 1909, believing that the Pit Bulldog's role as a sporting dog was in danger, and believing that gameness was a trait being selectively bred out as Pit Bulls became more popular, the American Dog Breeder's Association was founded. Having evolved into the largest exclusive registry of the breed, the ADBA's purpose—continuing today—is to preserve the original standard and heritage of the American Pit Bull Terrier. In 1936, bowing to public pressure brought on by the popularity of Petey, the Pit Bull companion of the children in the *Our Gang* series, the American Kennel Club began registering Pit Bulldogs as American Staffordshire Terriers.

The population of the Pit Bull continued to grow as the population of the United States grew. As more blood mixed, and as the gene pool was broadened, both populations became more diverse. America became white, black, red, yellow and brown, accepted immigrants from every country on the globe and assimilated them. Pit Bulldogs began appearing in white, black, red, yellow, brown, tan, blue, brindle, and every combination thereof. Certain lines were bred to be large, certain lines to be small, some with big heads, some with small heads, some to be more game, some less. Four distinct cultures within the Pit Bull community began to emerge: the game dog culture, the show dog culture, the weight pull culture (where competing dogs pull a cart of weight down a track) and the pet culture.

Today there are over a million American Pit Bull Terriers in the United States and many more throughout the rest of the world. Despite bad and often unwarranted publicity, as well as breed specific legislation (resulting in breed bans, both in the United States and abroad), the breed type continues to thrive. As with the United States itself, this breed of dog, born out of violence and a will to prevail, born out of multiple cultures and mixed blood, has established itself and has proliferated within the greater world. Pit Bulls have demonstrated power and displayed grace: the ultimate canine gladiators. Pound for pound, they are the strongest, fastest, most agile, most animal aggressive, most intelligent, most obedient dogs on the face of the earth. They are also devoted friends, loyal companions, courageous defenders, and intelligent, gentle, courteous, even-tempered pets.

PIT BULL MYTHS:

1. Pit Bulls are naturally aggressive towards human beings.
2. Pit Bulls bite more than other dog breeds.
3. Pit Bulls have the strongest jaws in the animal world.
4. Pit Bulls have locking jaws.

PIT BULL FACTS:

1. Properly bred and raised Pit Bulldogs are naturally passive towards human beings. Select other breeds used for personal protection and security work (often used in the service of law enforcement and the military), may favor human aggressiveness and/or develop this trait. The American Pit Bull Terrier is not, by its nature, a human-aggressive breed of dog.
2. According to statistics kept by the United States Center for Disease Control, American Pit Bull Terriers and mixed breeds who are predominantly Pit Bulls account for 0.89% of all recorded dog bites in the United States. The American Pit Bull Terrier does not rank among the top 15 breeds of dog who bite humans with the greatest frequency.
3. American Pit Bull Terriers have very strong jaws. They are bred to have very strong jaws. There is no way, however, to actually test an animal's jaw strength, so there are no accurate statistics. It is generally believed that most large predators have stronger jaws than Pit Bulls.
4. American Pit Bull Terriers do not have locking jaws. They do not have a special mechanism that allows them to lock their jaws. They have the same basic jaw structure as every other breed of dog.

I live with an American Pit Bull Terrier. I have lived with at least one American Pit Bull Terrier for the last decade. I don't say I own my Pit Bull because I respect her too much to say that I own her. I live with her. She is a great friend. A wonderful pet. A joyous presence in my home. I am lucky to have her in my life. I don't own her, just live with her. I am a lucky man.

Ten years ago, I was living in Los Angeles and I wanted a dog. I was trying to decide what kind of dog when I met a Pit Bull named Grace 2000. Grace 2000 lived with a friend of mine. She was short and heavily muscled, white with brown patches, and had deep brown sparkling eyes. She was very excitable, ran in circles around my friend's house and loved to play catch. Sometimes she hung from a spring attached to the branch of a tree and bounced bounced bounced. Sometimes she chased her tail. She never barked and she loved to give kisses and if given a chance, she would climb into my lap. She was a fifty-pound ball of energy and love.

After meeting Grace, I decided that I wanted a Pit Bull. I bought a paper, looked in the classifieds, saw ad after ad after ad, Pitbull Pitbull Pitbull. One of the ads said Sons of Cholo. I didn't know what Cholo meant or who Cholo was, but I liked the sound of it. I called the number and got an address. I got in my car and I started driving.

The address was in East Los Angeles. A working-class Hispanic neighborhood. I parked, walked towards the house. There were two men sitting on the front porch. They were drinking beer and smoking cigarettes, their arms were covered with tattoos. I stopped in front of them, they stared at me. I said hello, they nodded. I asked if they were selling the dogs, they said no habla Ingles. I don't speak Spanish. I held up the paper, said Sons of Cholo. They smiled, nodded, one of them stood up and motioned for me to follow him.

We walked around the house. In the backyard there was a small fenced area. Inside the fence was a small doghouse. The man whistled and a giant Pit Bull stormed out of the doghouse and started barking.

I had never seen a dog like him in my life. He was short and gigantic. He had layers and layers of rippling muscle. His coat was the color of milk chocolate and he had bright green eyes. His head was huge and thick, as if it was carved from stone, and it was covered with scars. He stood at the fence and snarled at me. His teeth were huge and a perfect white. I stared at him. He barked and snarled. He looked like he wanted to eat me. I was scared to death.

The man tapped me on the shoulder and pointed at the dog. He smiled and he said Cholo, undefeated a *campeon*. He motioned for me to follow him.

We walked to a garage. He lifted the door and puppies began streaming out. They were adorable little chocolate puppies. Small versions of Cholo, minus the scars, minus the snarling. They were yipping and tumbling over each other, jumping on my feet, biting at the bottom of my pants. The man pointed to the puppies and said Sons of Cholo.

I smiled. I sat down on the concrete. The puppies all ran into my lap, started jumping on my chest, licking my face. A hierarchy had been established among them, and the larger puppies started muscling the smaller puppies away. The smallest of them fell off my lap and immediately started climbing back. He was pushed off again, and started climbing again. All he wanted was to get close enough to lick my face. He'd fall off, climb on, fall off, climb on. He was the smallest of them. He had a big heart. All he wanted was to lick my face.

I stood up, the puppies started nipping at my feet again. I looked at the man and pointed to the smallest puppy, the man nodded and held up three fingers. The price had been listed in the advertisement. I had brought cash with me. I took it out of my pocket and handed it to him. He picked up the puppy and handed him to me. We shook hands, he said gracias, I said gracias.

I walked towards my car. The puppy started whining. The further we got from the garage, the louder the whining. When I opened the driver's door, the puppy started crying, looking towards the garage, where the other Sons of Cholo were still running around, and crying. I sat down in the driver's seat. I had brought some puppy toys and puppy treats with me. I held the puppy in my lap and tried to get him interested in them. He just looked towards the garage and cried. I gave up trying to make him stop and I started the car. I drove away.

He sat in my lap on the ride back to my house. He cried and he started shaking. He peed on my lap. So much for the myth of the big bad Pit Bull. When we got home he stopped crying, but he wouldn't let me out of his sight. Everywhere I went, he went with me, even the bathroom. When I went to sleep, he crawled under my covers and snuggled against my legs. If I moved, he would move so that he was always touching me.

Despite his cries and his need, there was something regal about him, something noble. I decided to name him Cassius, after the Roman Emperor. It took him two or three days to recognize his name, it took a week to house train him, within a month he could sit, stay, heel, shake, roll over. As he learned he grew. The day I had brought him home, he was twelve weeks old and weighed fourteen pounds. Eight weeks later he weighed thirty-four pounds. At eight months he weighed fifty-five pounds. At ten months, seventy pounds. When he turned one, he weighed ninety pounds.

We went everywhere together. I took him to stores, to work, I took him running, took him to the park. When he came with me to visit friends, he would play with their dogs and their children. When I went out to eat, I tried to go to restaurants with outdoor seating and he would lie under the table and sleep. People always reacted to him. He was too big and too handsome and too imposing not to react in some way. People either stared at him in fear and scampered away, or came up and asked to pet him and were quickly overwhelmed by his willingness to give kisses. He loved giving kisses. Cassius, Son of Cholo, was a softie.

I saw his genetics come out. I saw his game face emerge, I saw him protect himself and protect me. We were hiking on a trail in the hills above Los Angeles. We came around a corner, and we were met by two adult male Chows and an adult male Labrador. None of the dogs were on leashes. They saw Cassuis and snarled and immediately charged us. I let go of his leash so that he could defend himself. Thirty seconds later all three of the other dogs were running away, tails between their legs, with Cassius chasing them. Two of them were bleeding. I chased after Cassius and caught him 200 yards up the trail. The dog's owner had appeared and started screaming. I got Cassius off of one of the Chows and waited for her to calm down. I told her to keep her dogs on leashes, told her that aggressive male dogs had no place on the trail. She apologized, said it wouldn't happen again. Cassius and I walked away. Three full-grown male dogs had charged him. I let him defend himself. All three full-grown male dogs ran away.

Two months later we were at the vet. Cassius was having a check-up. I had been thinking about getting another dog, and I asked the vet if she had any advice for me. She said she thought having two dogs was better for the animals, that she thought it would be good for Cassius. She asked if I wanted another Pit Bull. I told her yes, and she excused herself, said she would be back in a minute. When she came back, she came back with a dog. A twenty-pound, five-month-old female Pit Bull. Cassius started wagging his tail, ran up to her. They sniffed each other, circled each other, started kissing each other. I started asking questions.

The little girl's name was Bella. Someone had left her in a box on the front stoop of the vet's office two months earlier. She was in good health, she was good with people, children and other dogs. I could take her home immediately. I glanced down, Bella and Cassius were still kissing. They looked like they had been friends for years. When I left the office, they both came with me.

Cassius and Bella became inseparable. If I tried to separate them, they would cry until they were reunited. They ate together, played together, went walking together, had to sleep touching each other. Occasionally, they would sneak out of my house late at night. We lived in the Hollywood Hills, which are filled with small animals. Cassius and Bella would hunt the animals, and once or twice a month I would wake up to find a dead raccoon, a dead possum or a dead fox lying at the foot of my bed. The first time it happened, I called my vet and asked her if I should be worried. She said no, the dogs were bringing me gifts, were trying to please me. She said don't worry, they're just hunting together.

We had three wonderful years together. We had three years in which we were rarely apart. Cassius and Bella moved with me, traveled across the country with me, watched me laugh and cry, stayed with me through good times and bad times. They were my best friends. My closest confidantes. They filled my life with joy and happiness. They were my children. My kids. I took care of them and, in their own way, they took care of me. Shortly before his fourth birthday, Cassius got sick. My vet told me that there was no way he was going to get better. She recommended that I put him down. I cried like a baby. Cried and cried and cried. He didn't know that there was anything wrong with him. He didn't know why I was crying. He sat with me and tried to make me feel better. He snuggled against me and gave me kisses. He followed me around and tried to make me play with him. He was my little boy. My best buddy. My Mister Big Man. He wasn't going to get better. I took him to the vet. I cried and cried and cried. When I came home without him, Bella cried and cried and cried. We cried together. Our best friend was gone. We still miss him.

Bella is still with me. Bella my little Pit Bull. Bella who loves everyone she meets. Bella who thinks she's a lap dog. Bella who likes to sit with little children and give them kisses. Bella who has never started a fight in her life. My Little Bella. The American Pit Bull Terrier. There is no middle ground with her. She makes people smile. They respect her. She shows them love and she receives love from them. There is no middle ground. American Pitbull.

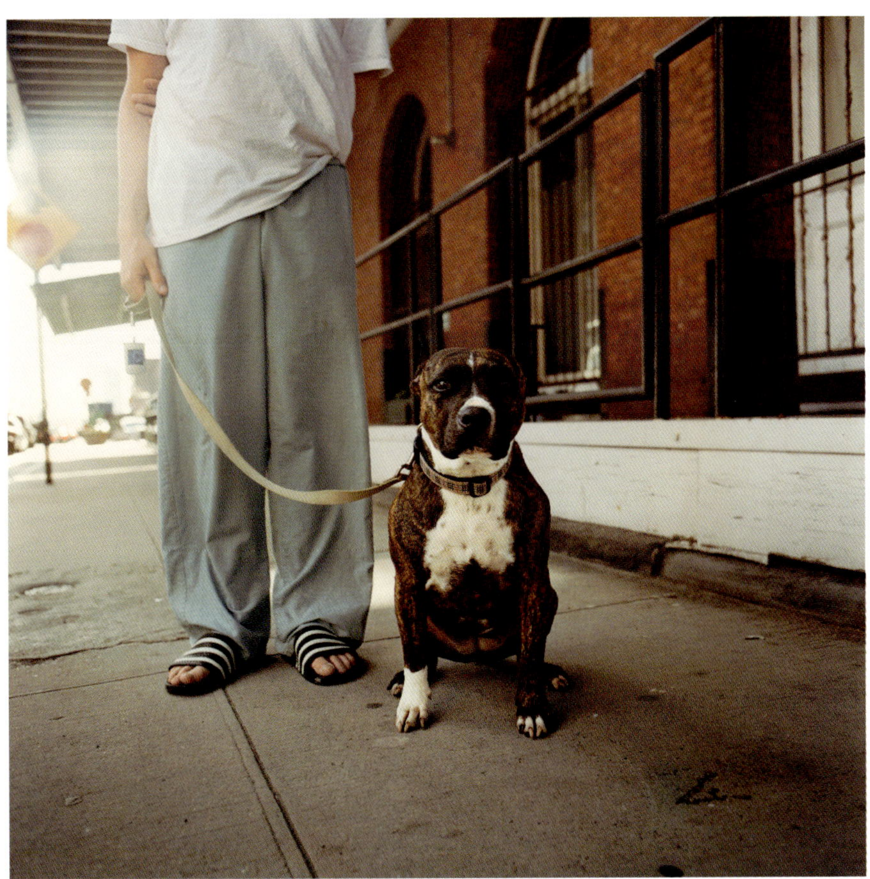

JAMES FREY and BELLA New York City, June 2003

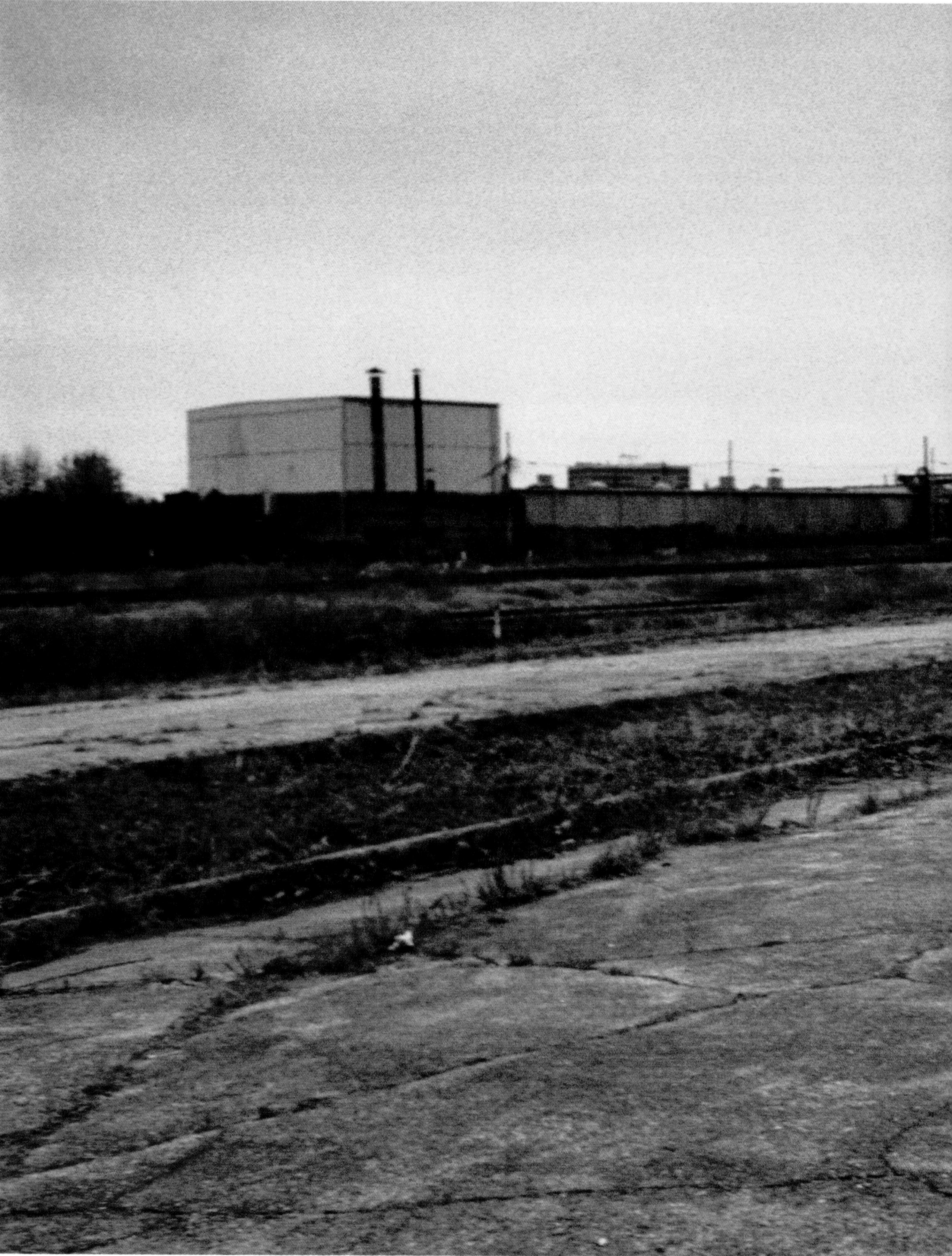

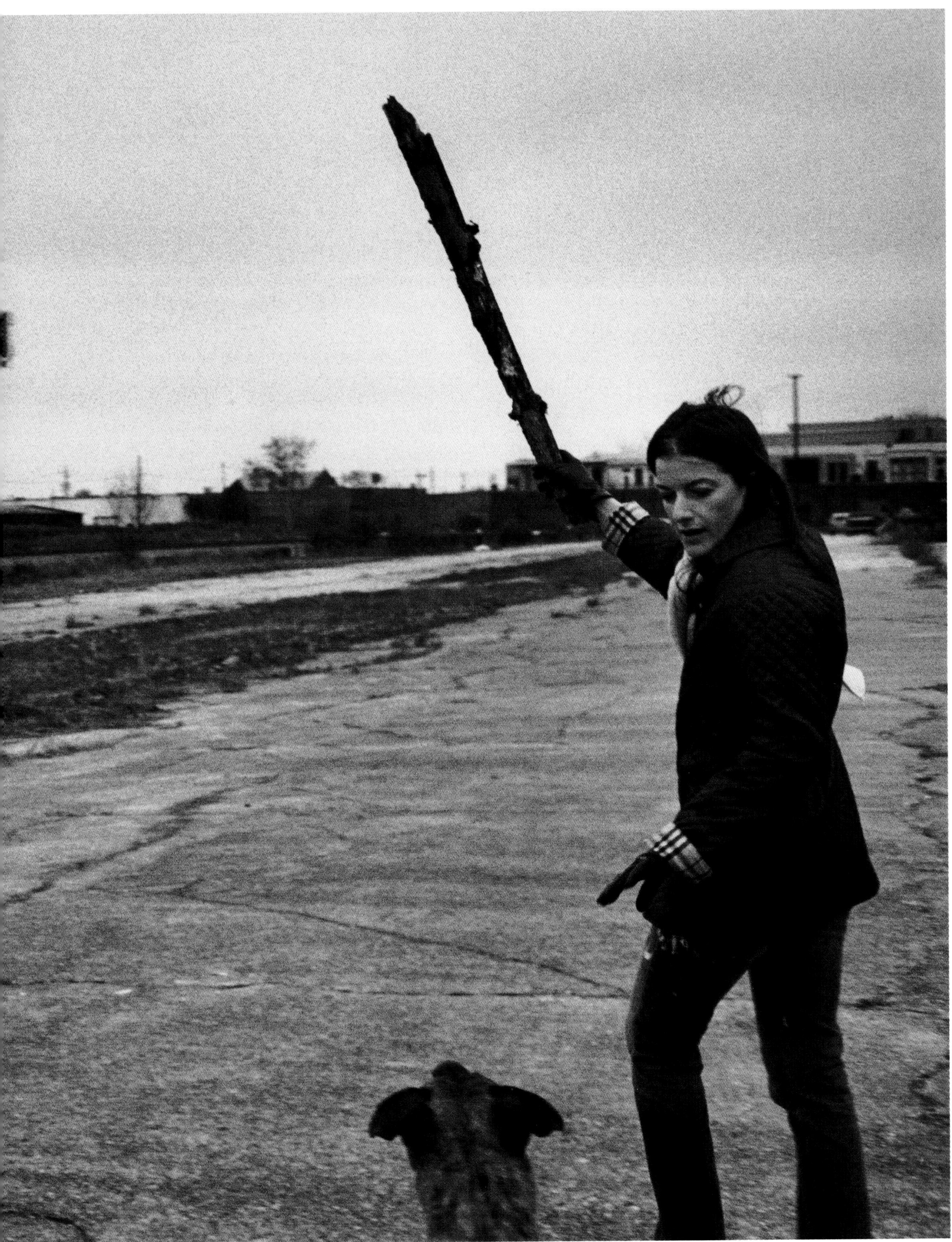

Together with his younger brother Markus, breeder James Patton operates Pitfall Kennels on twenty sprawling acres in Fairburn, Georgia. Patton's stocky, photogenic blue Pit Bulls are often featured in music videos and photo shoots, along with their celebrity owners—including James' older brother Big Boi of the hip-hop group, Outkast.

• At Pitfall Kennels, we mostly sell to entertainers, especially athletes and rappers. They love the Blue Dog. We work with Roy Jones, Jr., the boxer. He's bought about twelve dogs from me. Serena Williams, she got a dog from me. A couple of football players—one was in the Super Bowl this last year. Jermaine Dupris, 8-ball... See, a dog is part of the image, part of the status, of a person. If you walk around with a Pit Bull you have high status. Nobody's going to mess with you, 'cause they know the dog represents what you are.

• The guy who really started all this, the guy who set the foundation for the Blue Dog, his name was Frame, and he had Main Frame Kennels right here in Atlanta. Frame's locked up now, he's incarcerated, but he'll be getting out real soon. He don't have dogs no more, but I talked to him about a year ago and he congratulated me on what I'd done with the dogs. Because even though a lot of people own this *type* of dog now, they don't have nothing like what we have.

• Anyway, my friend started the line off with a dog called Bratt, who is now deceased. She was one of the best dogs we ever had. From there, we began to ship dogs in from everywhere—Texas, California, New York. We like to work with champion bloodlines—Gaff Kennels, Hot Shots, we got some Chaos dogs. That's how we started the Pitfall line. Nowadays, I'd say we have about fifty dogs out here. We have a big indoor/outdoor kennel, and we have four large running fields where the dogs can get their exercise. Also we have a nice big whelping facility for the puppies in the back. But I don't really do much business in Atlanta. I mostly ship my dogs out, because I like to have the blood spread out so no one in town will have access to the same stuff that I'm producing.

• My dogs all have a wide chest and a wide head. That's what I breed for. I love short muzzles. I love real fat chests, extremely muscular. I don't breed that little skinny-head, skinny-body dog. I hate that look. We represent the Blue Dog to the fullest.

JAMES PATTON pitfallkennels.com, Fairburn, Georgia

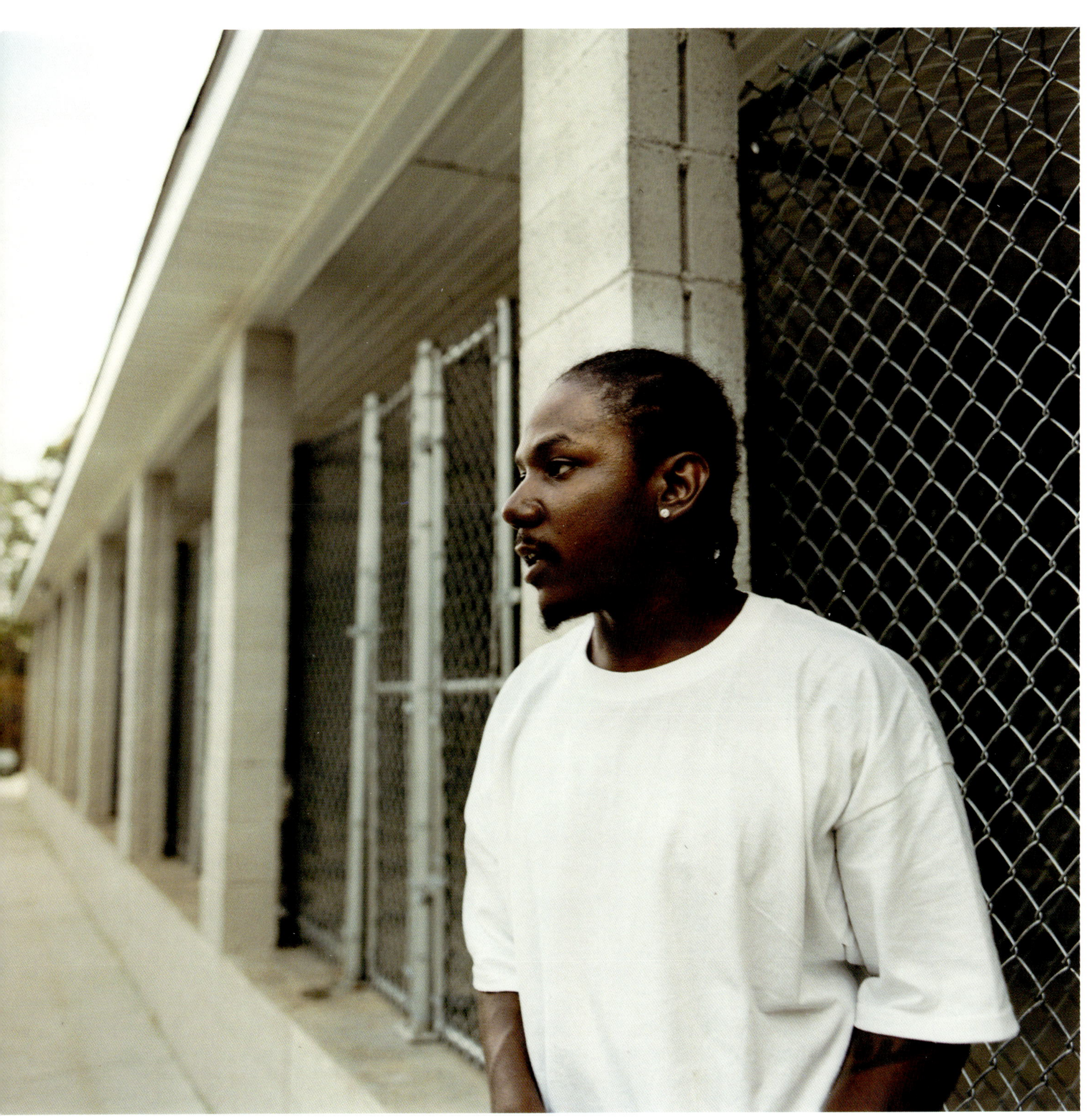

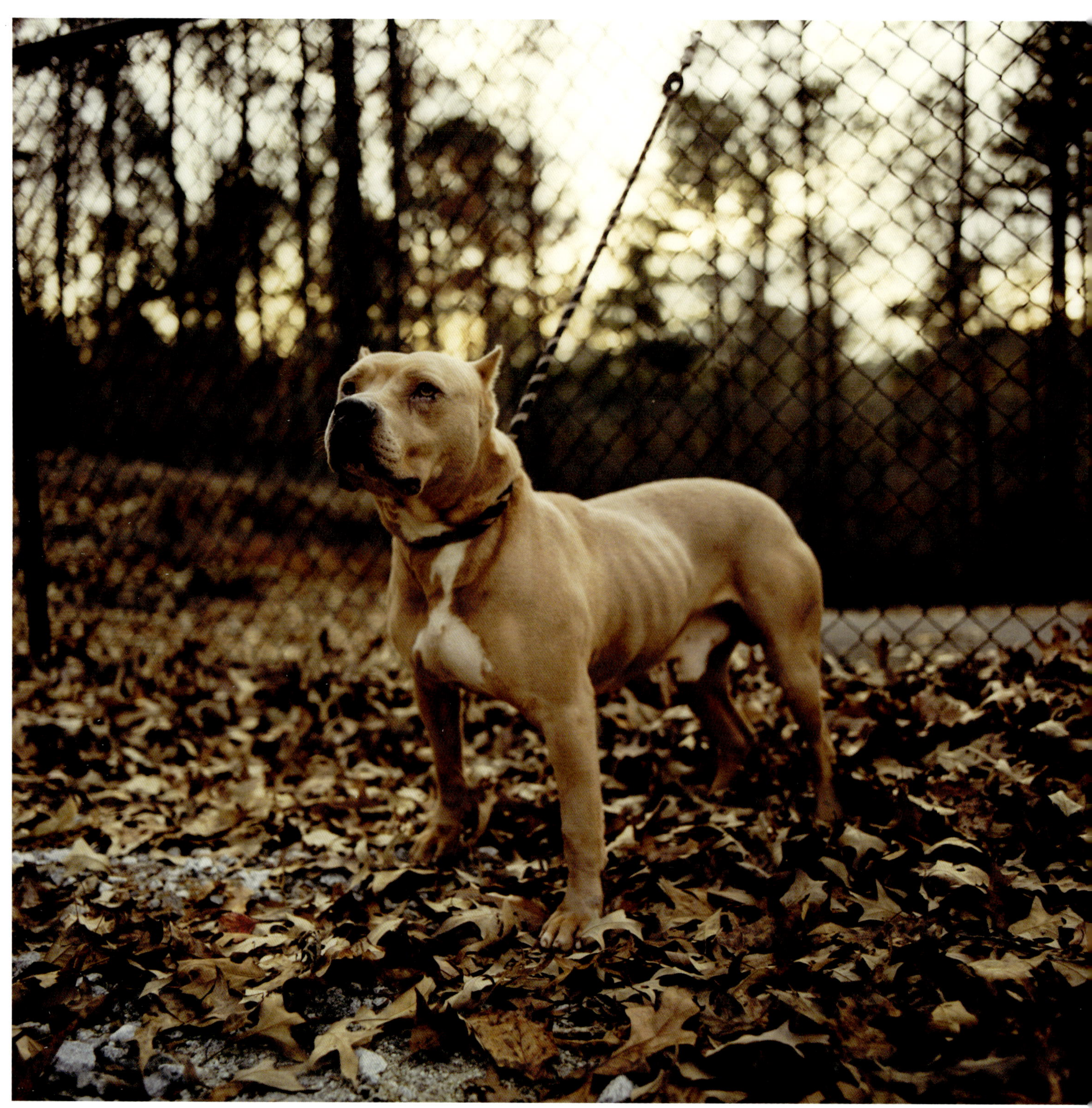

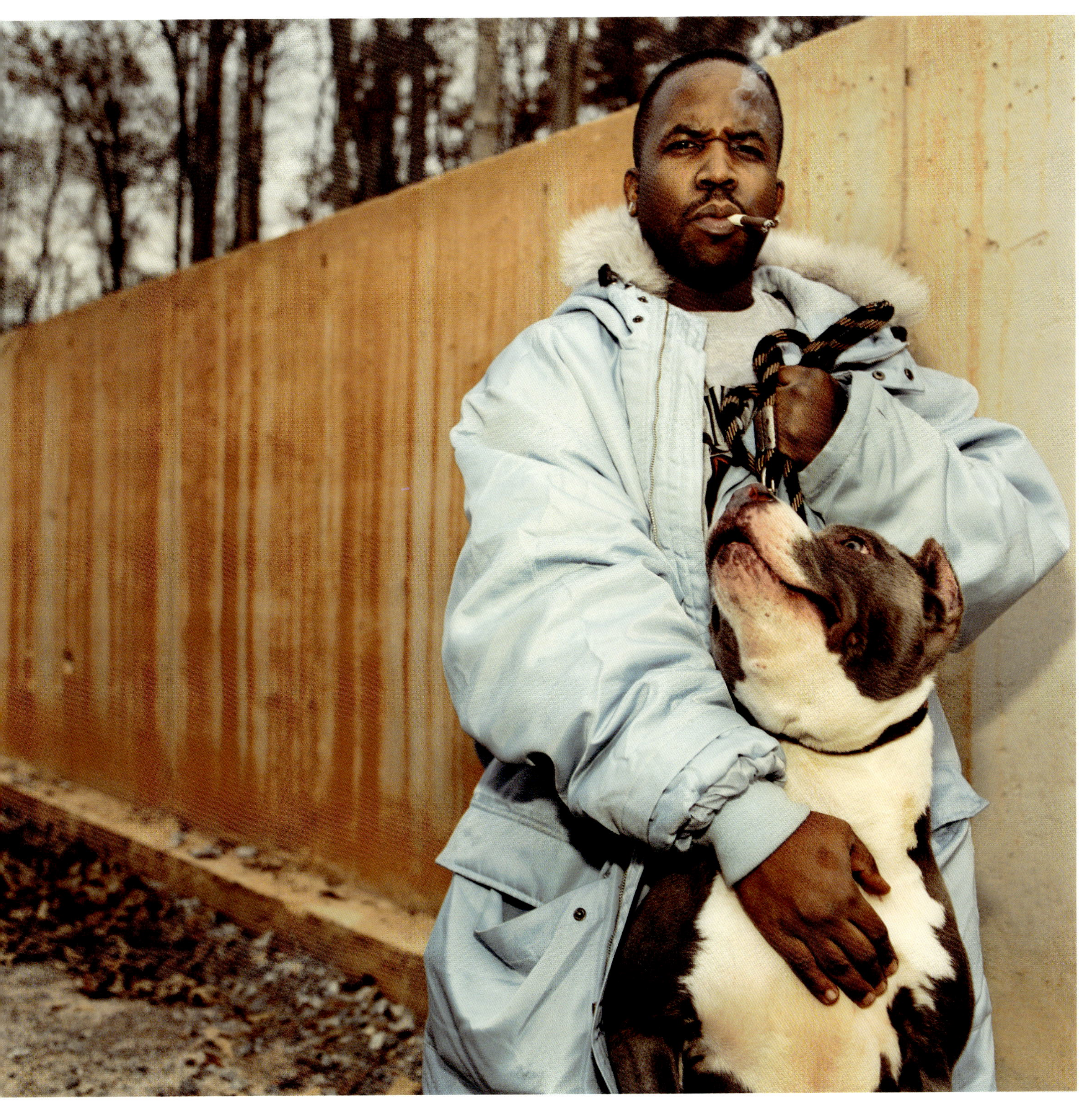

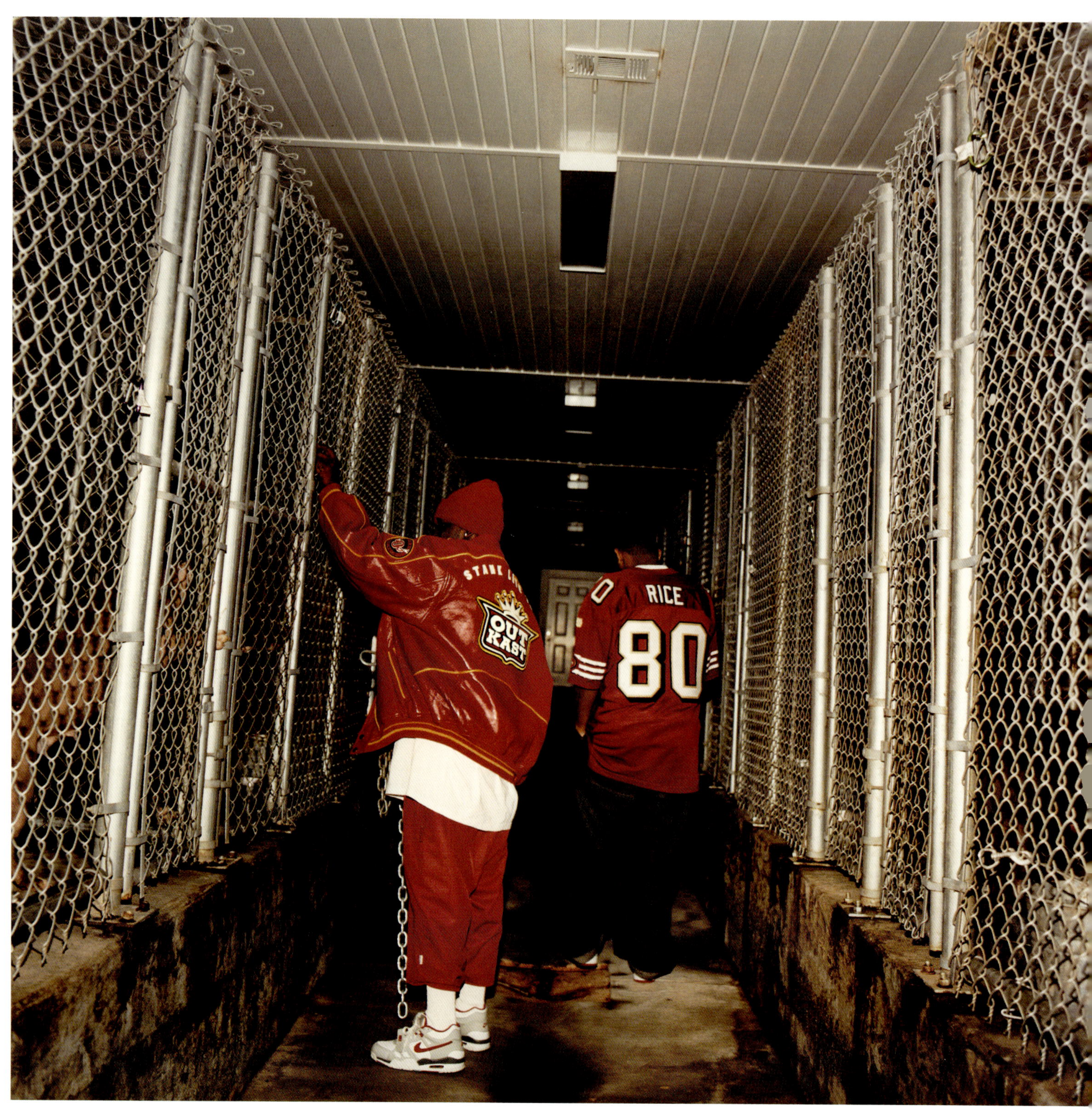
OUT KAST
RICE
80

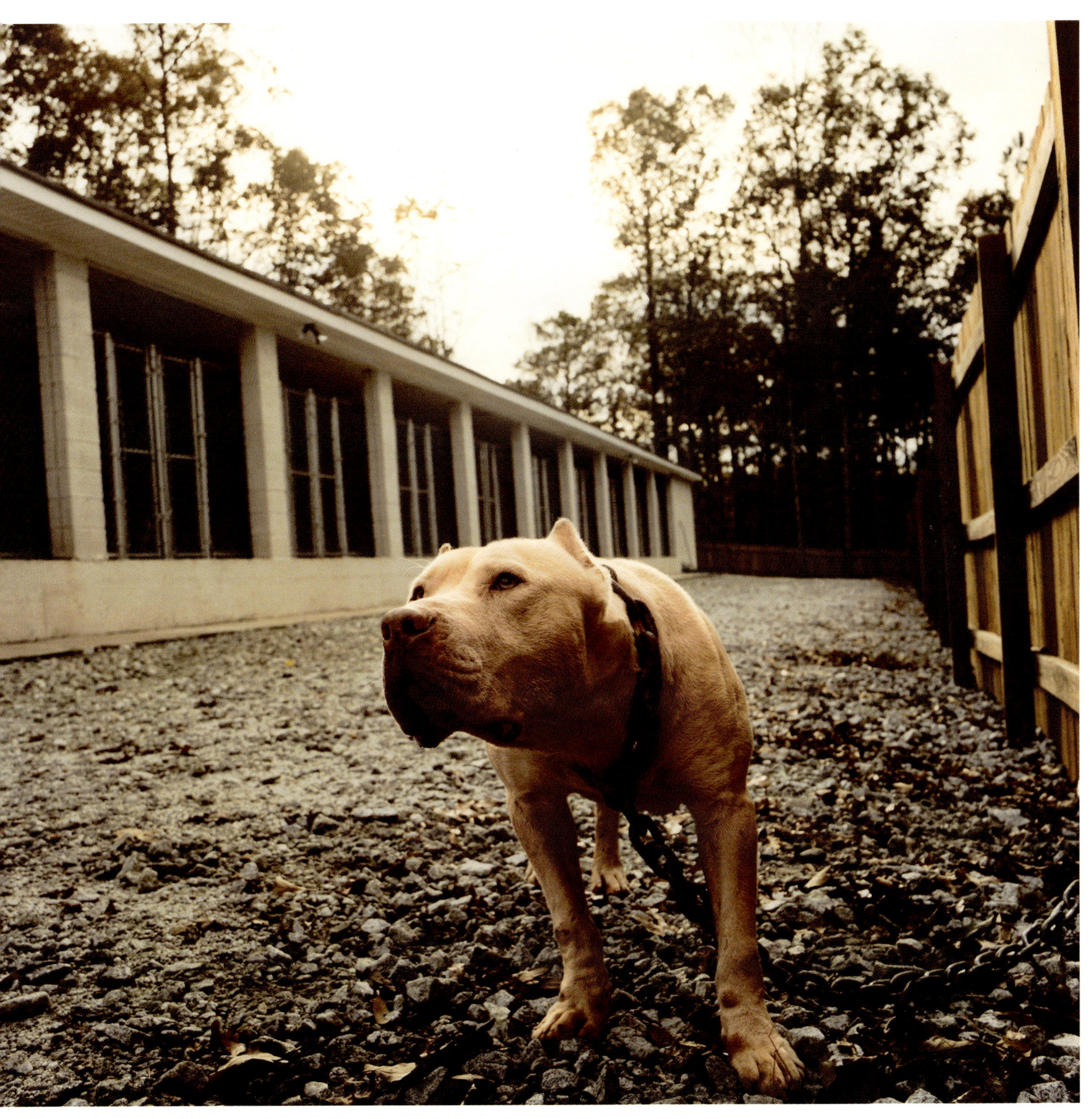

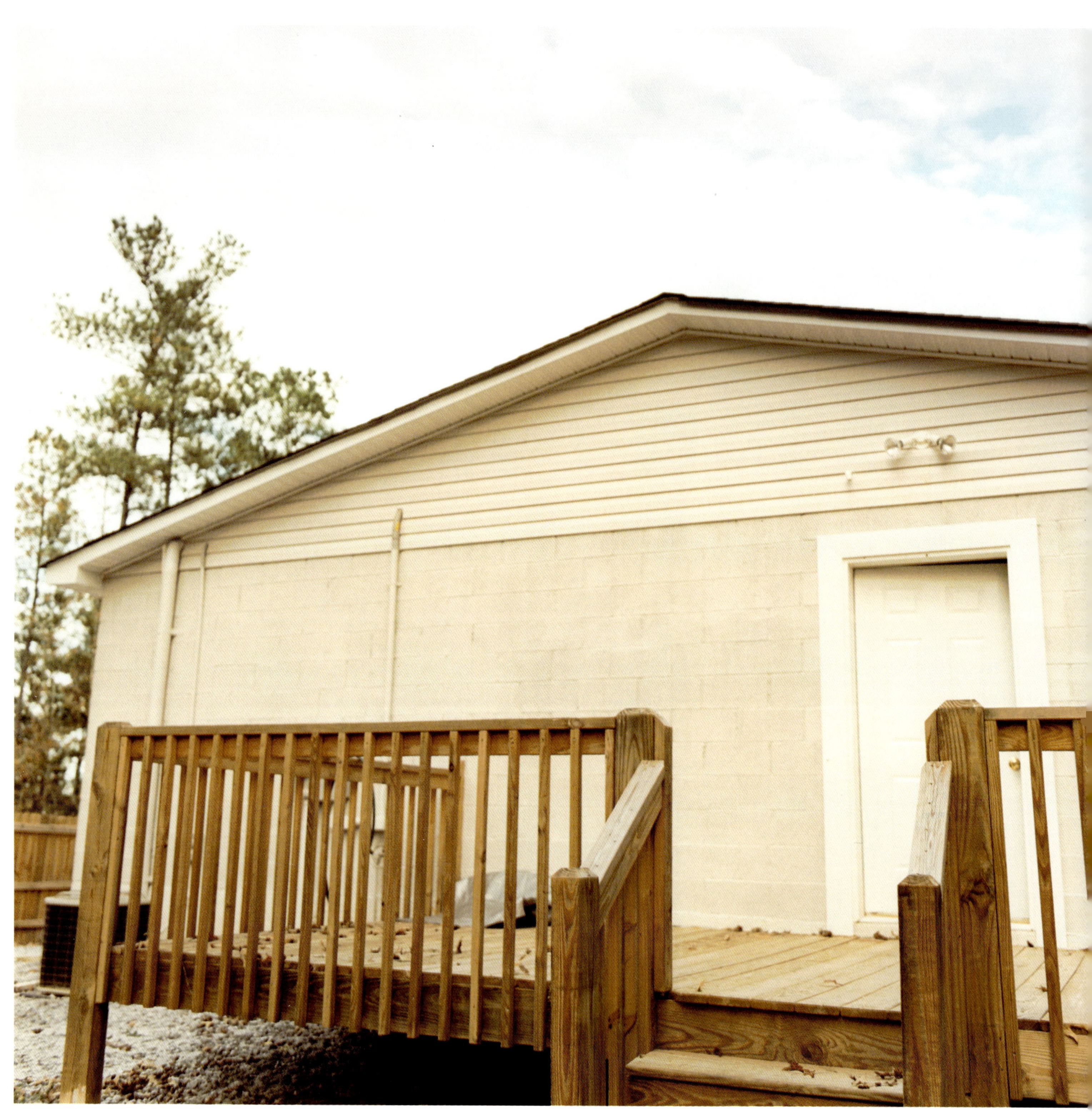

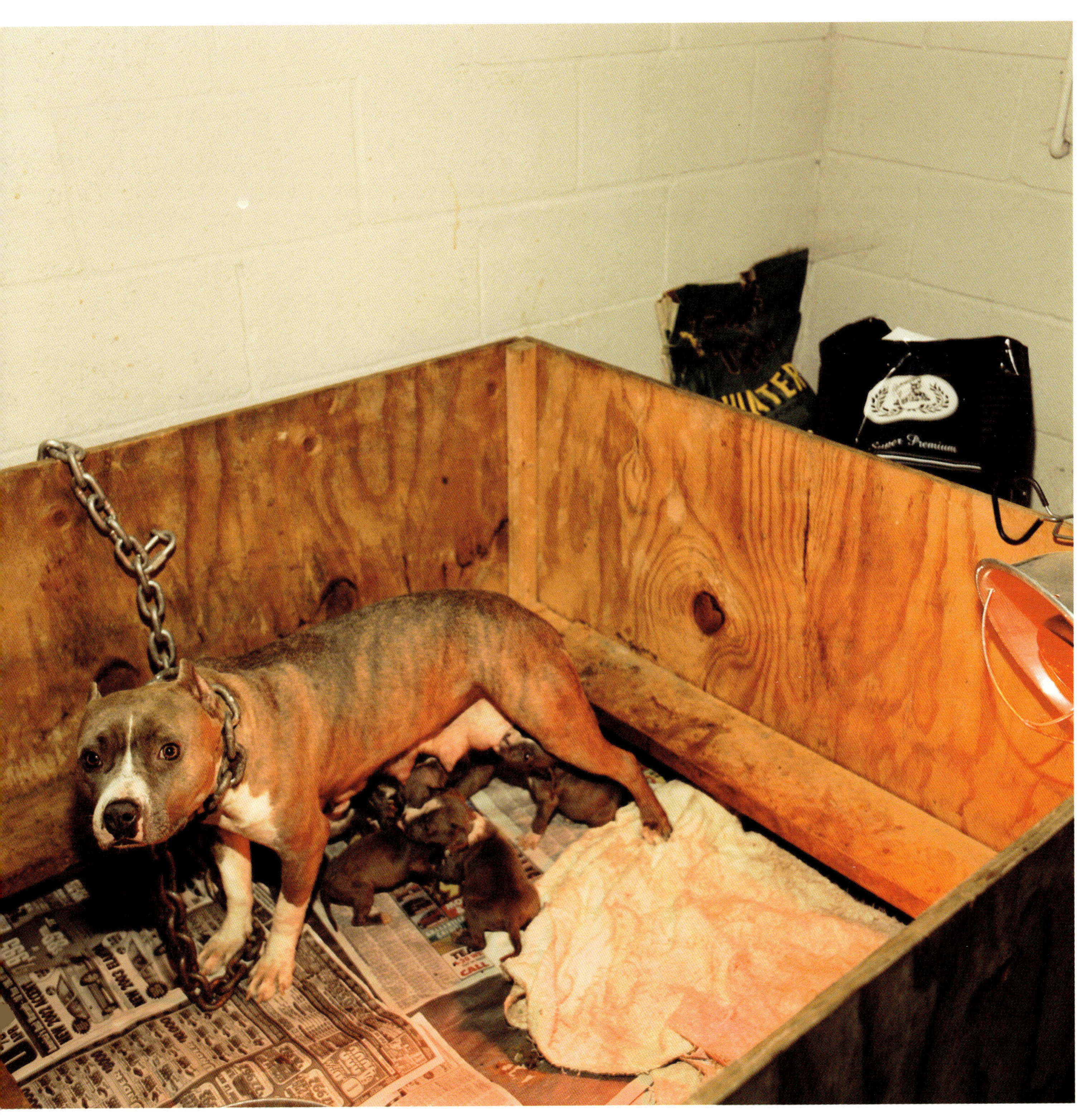
Super Premium

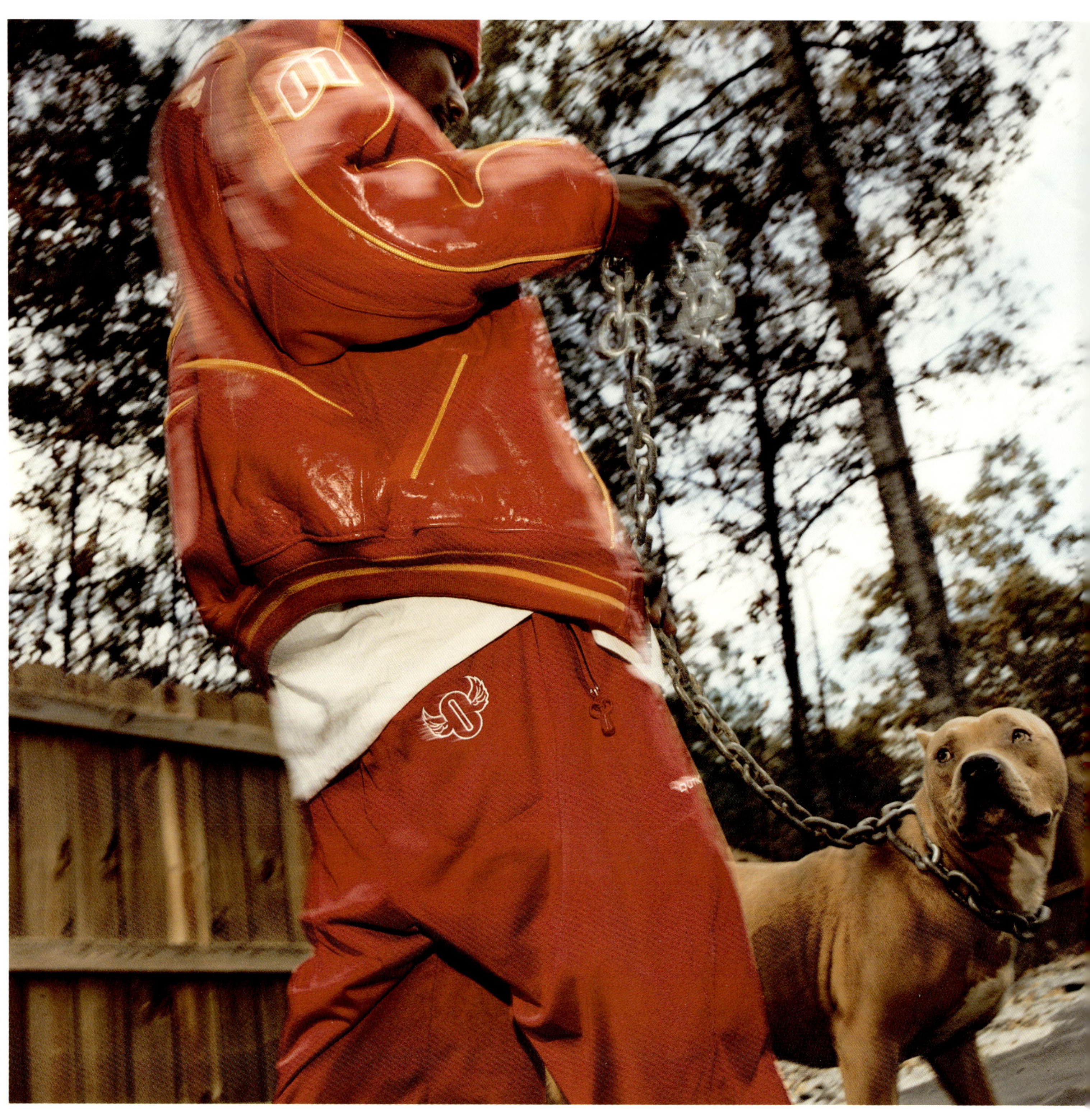

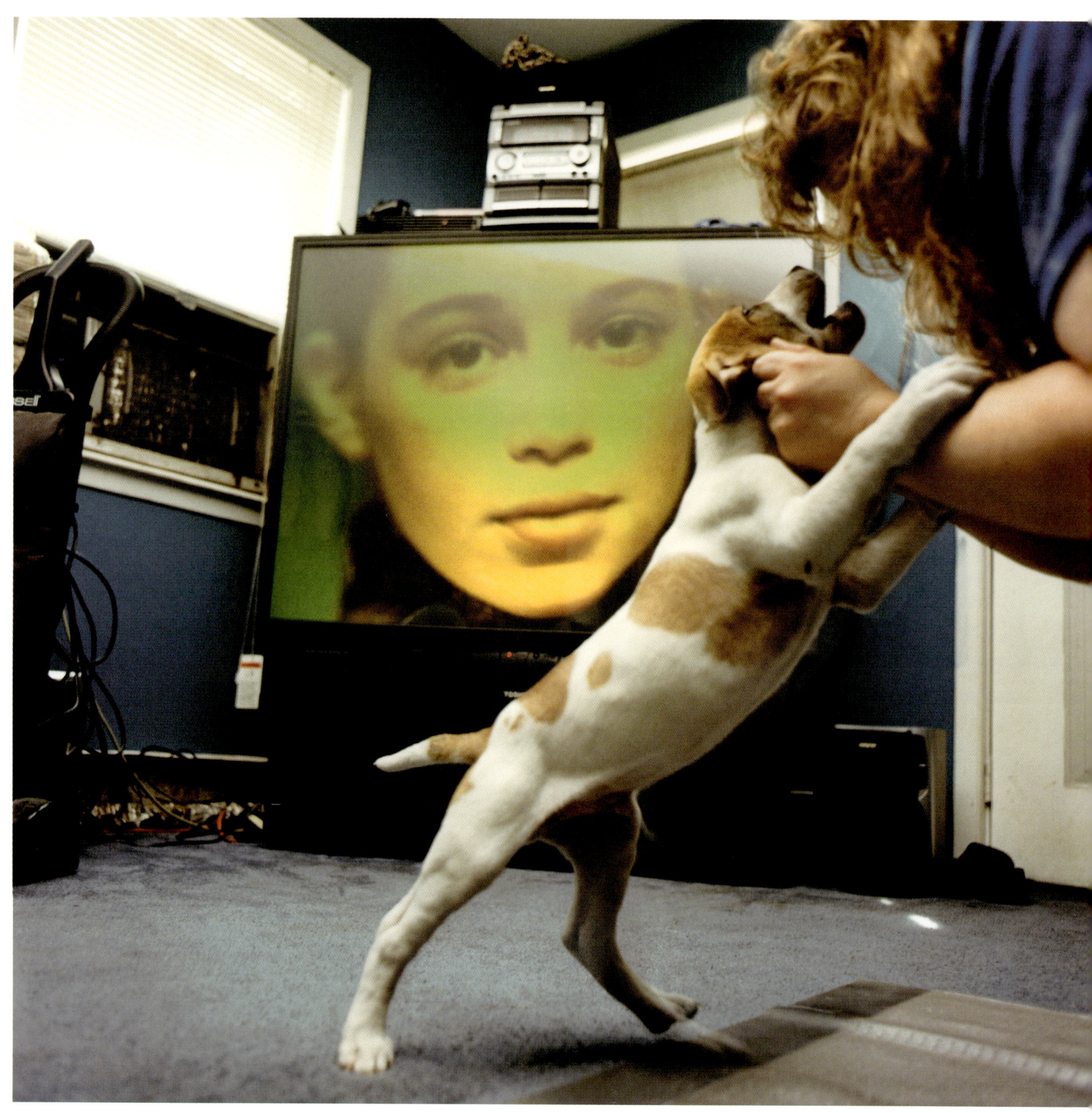

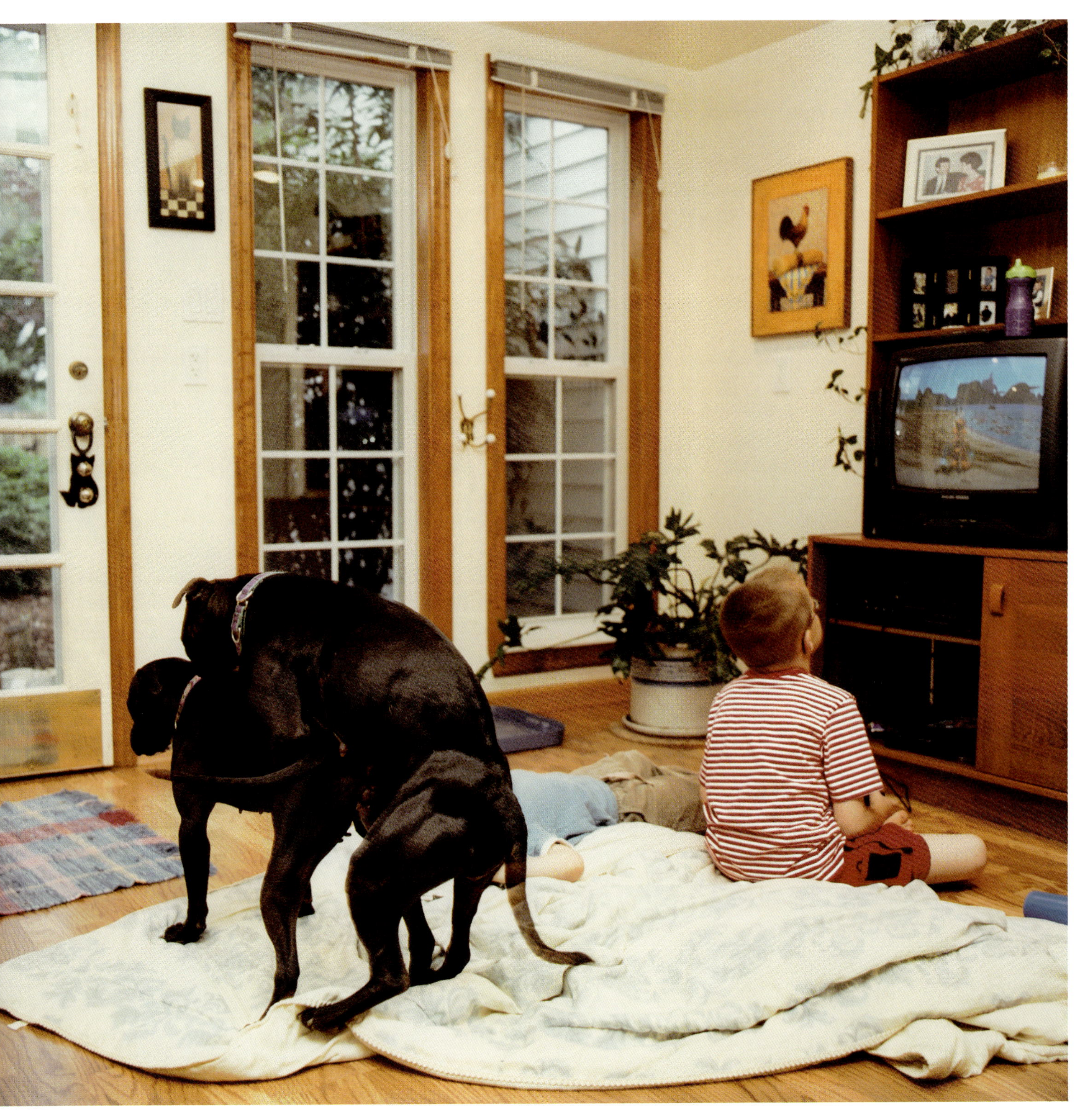

Paula Thomas is a veterinary technician and an obedience instructor. Her husband Cuyler Thomas is a chef. They have two young sons Paul and Adam, several horses and goats, and seven Pit Bulls.

PAULA The breed is so easy to handle in the veterinary setting. The vast majority of dogs are really difficult to handle. Pit Bulls are almost never human aggressive—they'll let you do anything to them. Other breeds don't tolerate restraint, they don't like strangers touching them, and they don't handle pain well either, so something as simple as an injection will cause a lot of dogs to scream or bite. With Pit Bulls, you don't have to deal with that.

When we have playgroup in my obedience class, the likelihood of another breed biting a human is fairly high—whereas a Pit Bull just does not do that. On the other hand, a Pit Bull *will* occasionally fight with another dog. If that happens, you can just grab a pit bull by the back of the neck or scoop it from under the chest. You can put your hands right up against the face because they've been bred for so long not to bite humans. Back when there was pit fighting, one dog would grab a hold of another one and keep the hold. If you wanted to break up the fight, there was something called a parting stick, or a breaking stick. That's still the best way to break up a dogfight if one accidentally happens. You gently insert it...

CUYLER ...in the back of the jaw, where the molars are. You don't pry it, you just stick it all the way through, and that breaks the hold, opens the mouth. If you twist the stick it can break a tooth, so you have to be careful. But it's the only reasonable way to break them up. We got our dog Exit right around the time that all those hysterical news reports started coming out about attacking and mauling.

PAULA Yeah, that's how we lost our first two dogs. Our neighbors petitioned the county and claimed we owned dangerous dogs, and they didn't want them in the area. This was because of what they were hearing about the *breed*, not because there was anything suspicious about our individual dogs. The neighbors actually made up lies about them.

CUYLER I was living in New York at the time, studying to be a chef at the CIA, the Culinary Institute. One day a guy called me *at school* to say that if Paula and I didn't get rid of the dogs, he was going to poison them. This was an affluent guy, a businessman.

PAULA I was still in high school at the time. Another neighbor claimed that one of our dogs had gotten loose and chased a kid down the street and into his house—and that the dog was snarling at the front door. Well, our dogs were kept in an outdoor pen with a padlock! Sure enough, when I got home that day the dogs were still in the pen with the lock on. When Animal Control got involved I remember asking, "So it's their word against ours?" They just said, "Basically." That was absolutely devastating. We got in a lot of trouble—the court battle lasted about three months—and we had to find new homes for the dogs. We were so young. It's still hard to talk about.

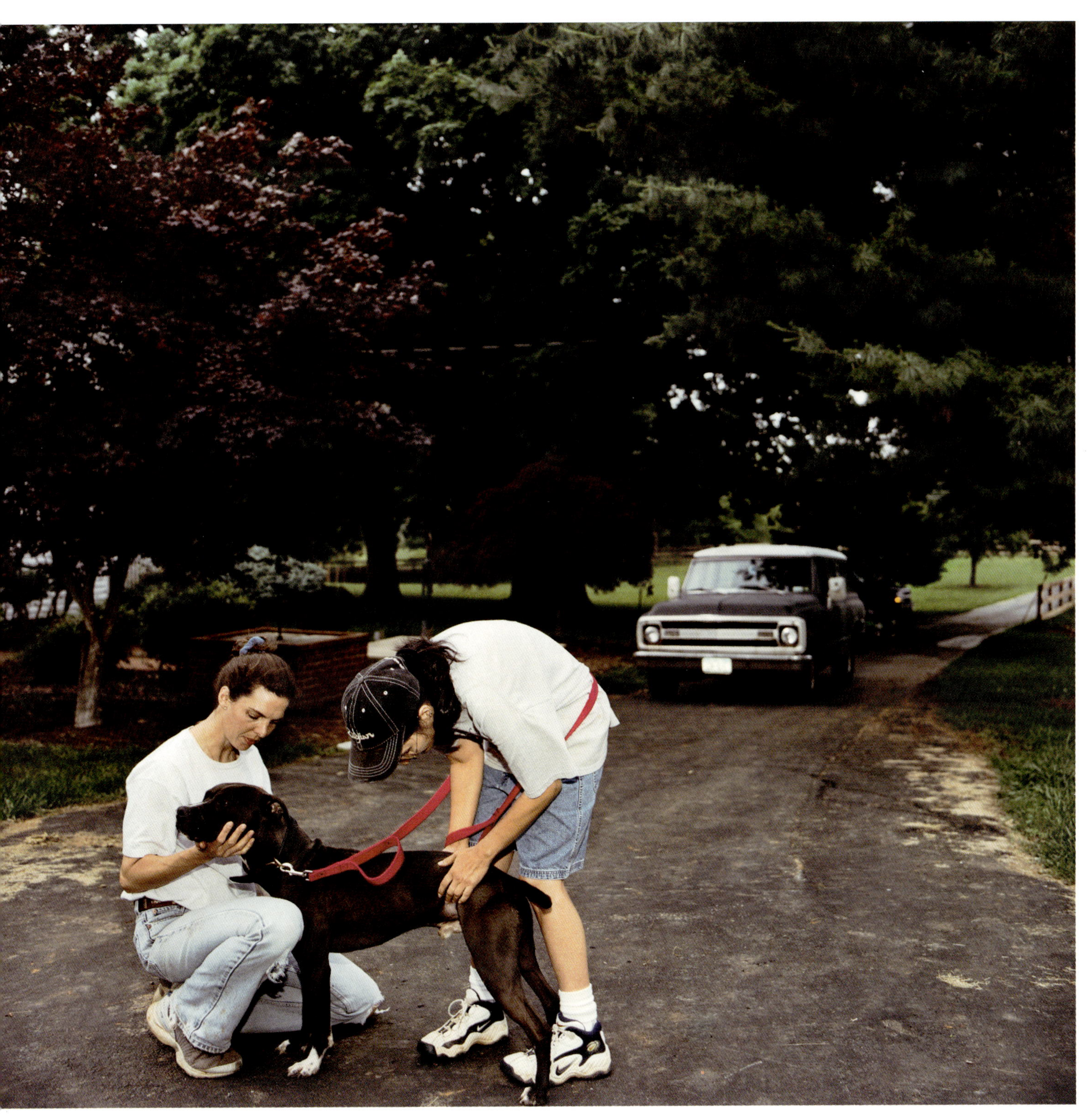

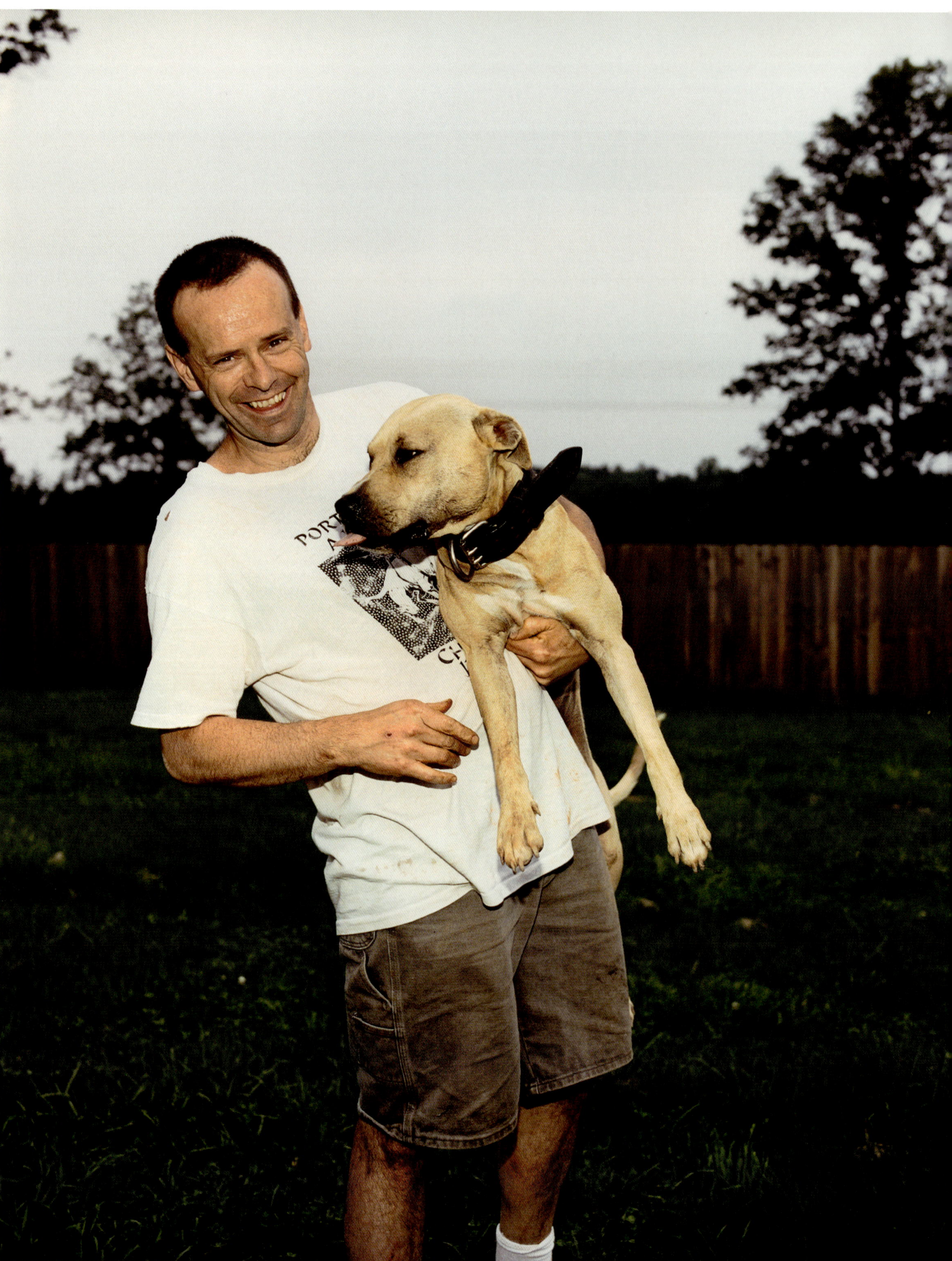

CUYLER A spring pole is great for exercise and upper body strength. You tie a rope to a tree and attach it to a big spring—something like you'd see on a garage door. Then you use another rope to tie a piece of cowhide to the other end of the spring. You want the hide just high enough to be reachable when the dog's rear feet are still on the ground so that they can really tug on it.

PAULA The spring pole is a super mental outlet. Pit Bulls need so badly to tug. They thrive on it, just like retrievers love to chase that tennis ball.

CUYLER If I went to a dog park and saw a Pit Bull running around off the leash... I would not let my dog go to that park.

PAULA We used to go to the park all the time—we didn't know any better. Then one of our females started going after the other dogs. I couldn't believe that I couldn't train her not to be dog-aggressive, that I couldn't fix this. I was wrong of course.

CUYLER You always have to remember what they were bred for. It wasn't to go to the dog park.

PAULA Now I have really strong feelings about this. There are some really good, responsible people out there who think they can bring their pet Pit Bulls to the park and let them run around with the other dogs. They say, "Oh, my dog's so friendly." But as far as I'm concerned, being "responsible" means understanding that any day could be the day. People always think they'll be able to see a change in temperament coming on. That frustrates me because it indicates that they don't really understand the breed. Cuyler and I have had so many dogs, and there have been quite a few who went to sleep nice one day and woke up and attacked the dog they were playing with the next day. It's almost like someone flips a switch. And this is not to say that Pit Bulls are ever aggressive towards people, because as a rule they're not. This sudden aggression really only happens with other animals. But anything can trigger it, from a unique sound, to the way something moves, to a change in the maturity level of a certain dog. And then, boom. So many people do not know what they're holding in their hands.

PAULA and CUYLER THOMAS Fredericksburg, Virginia

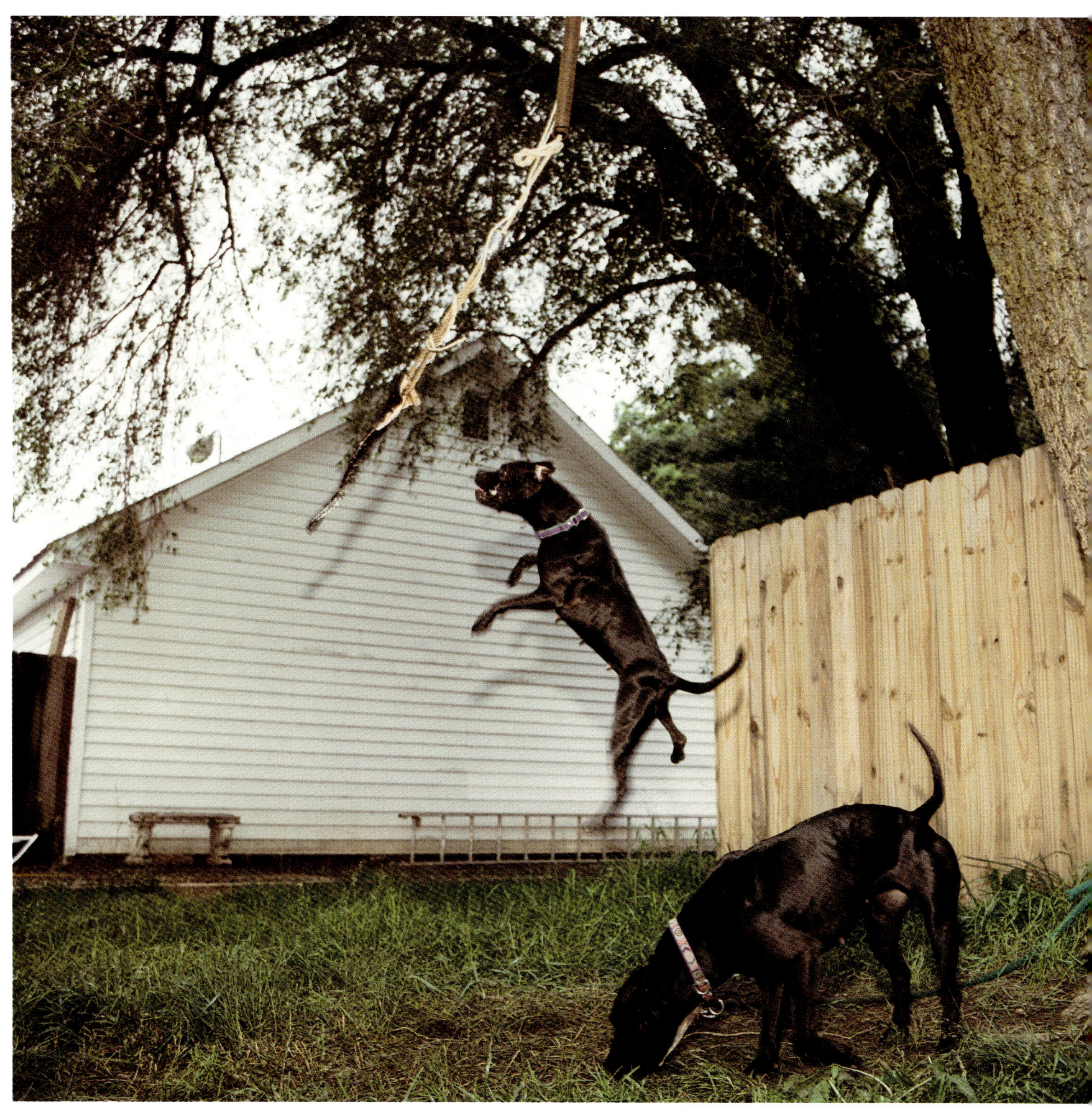

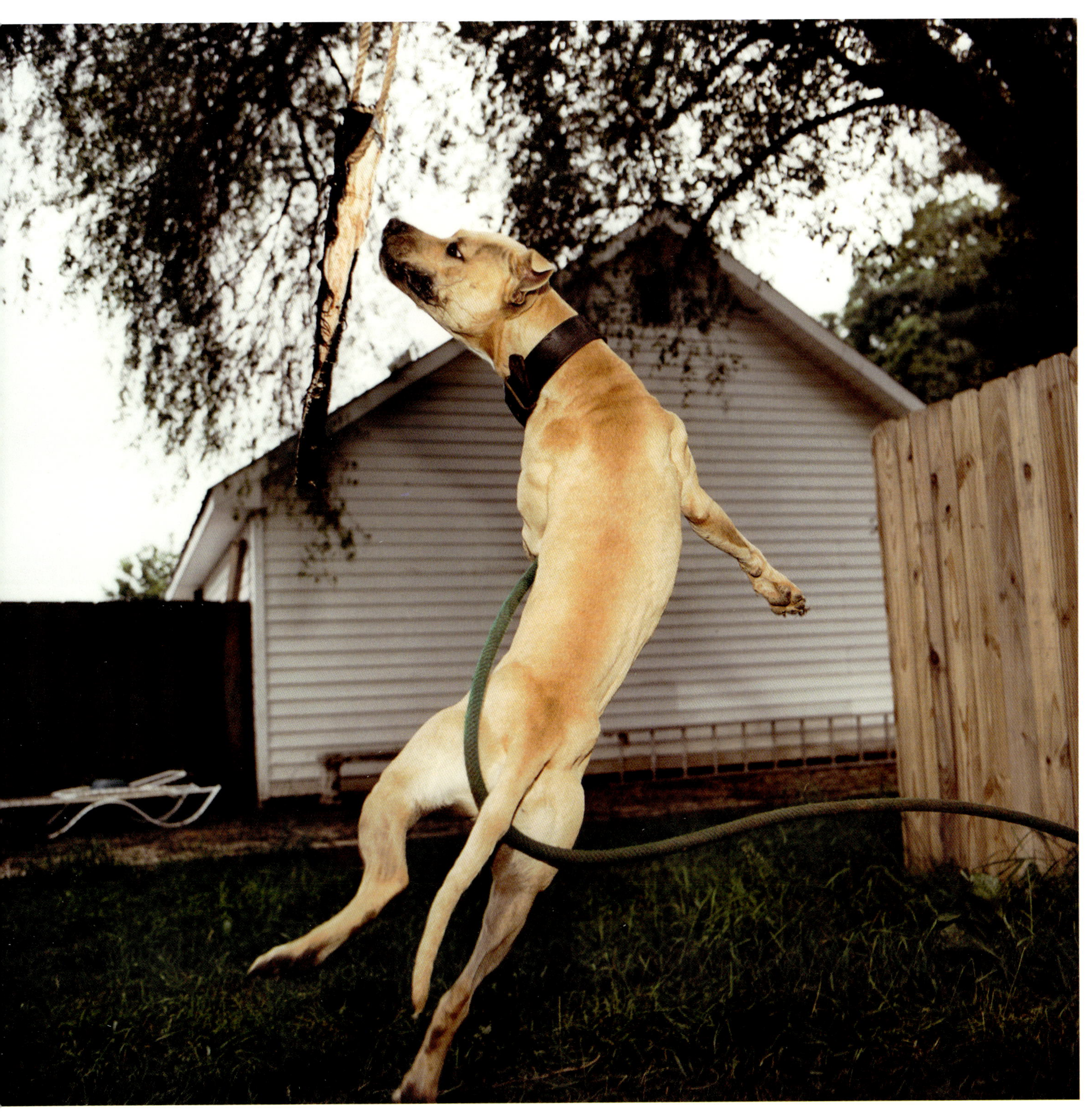

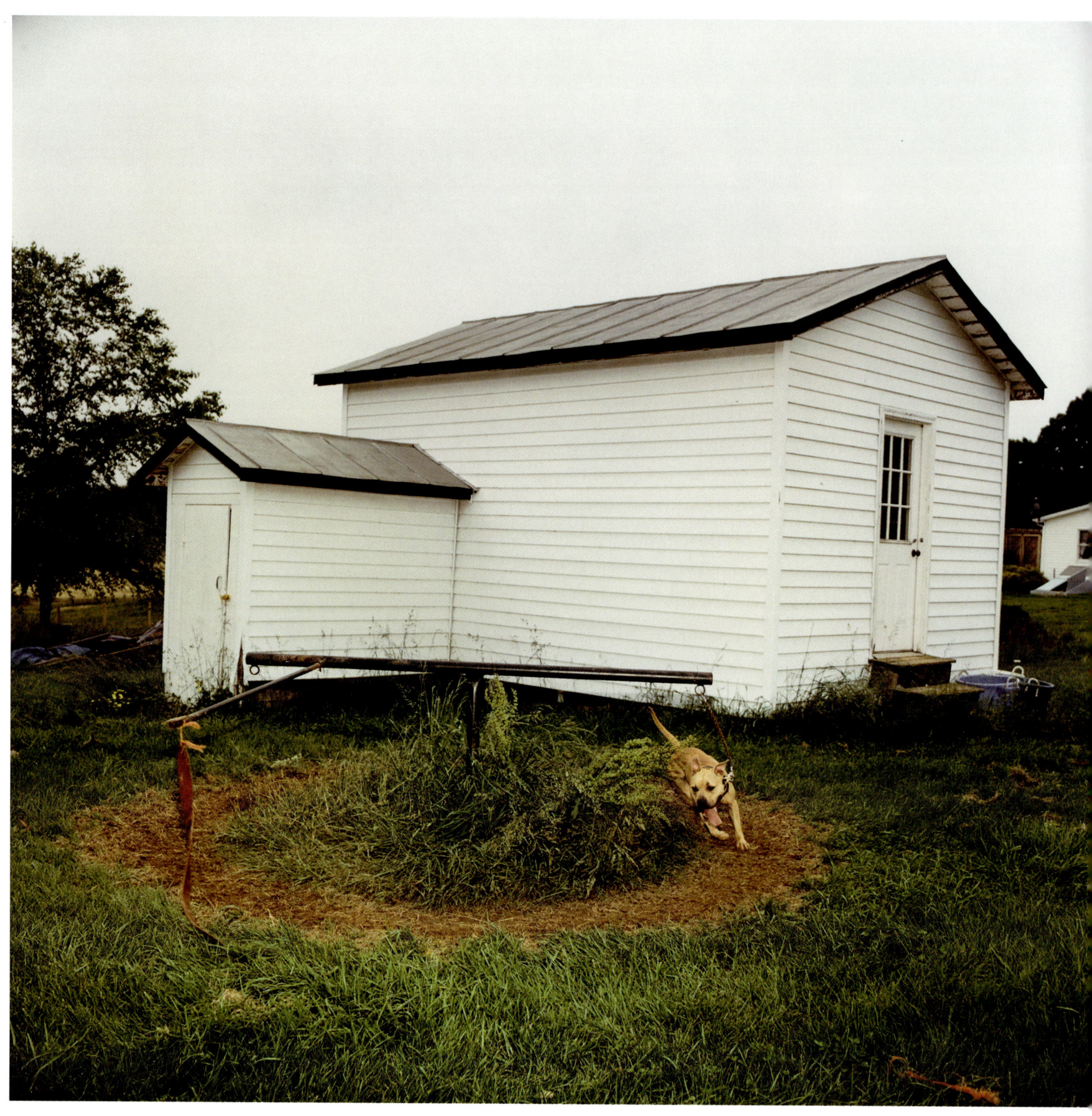

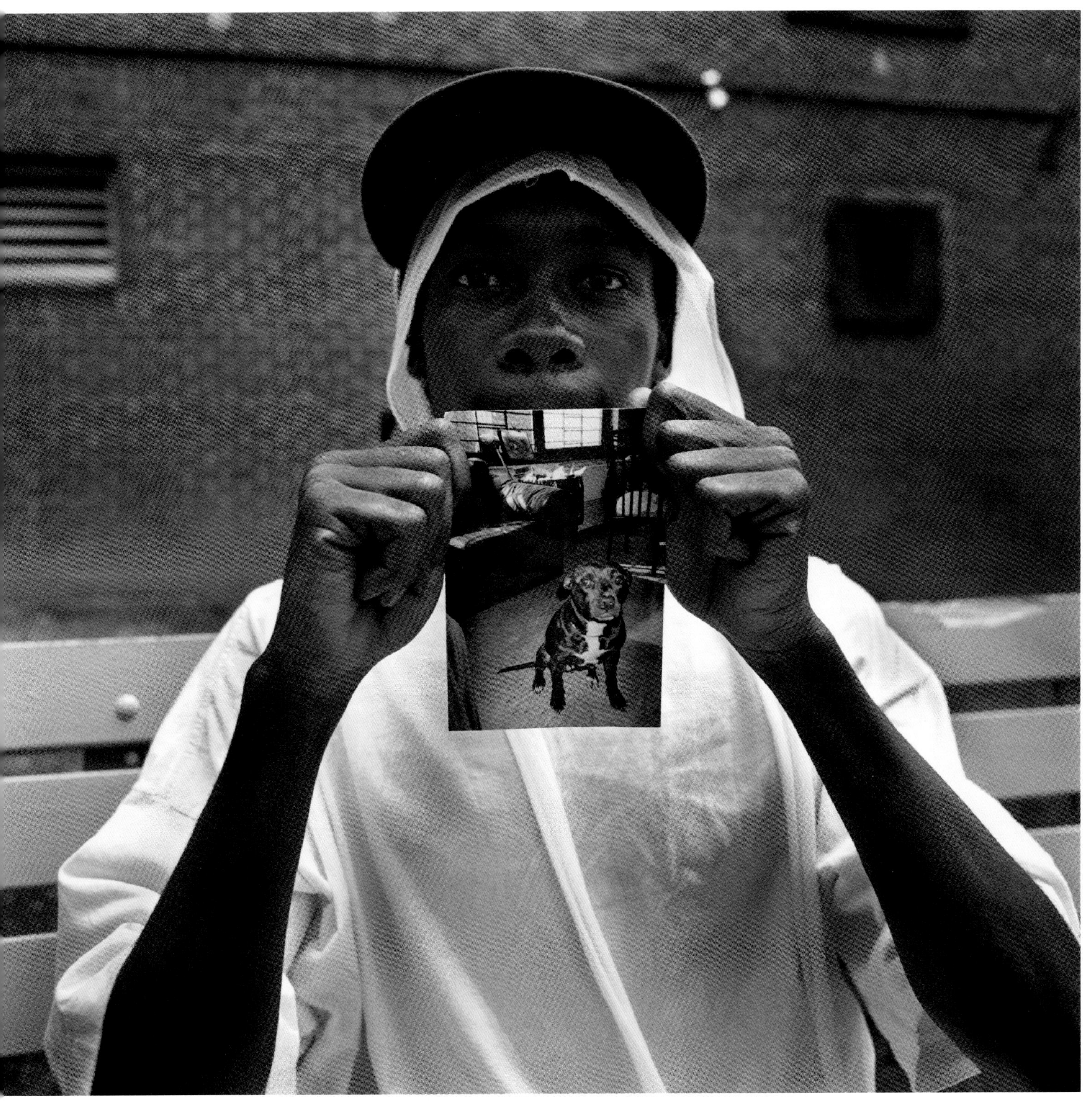

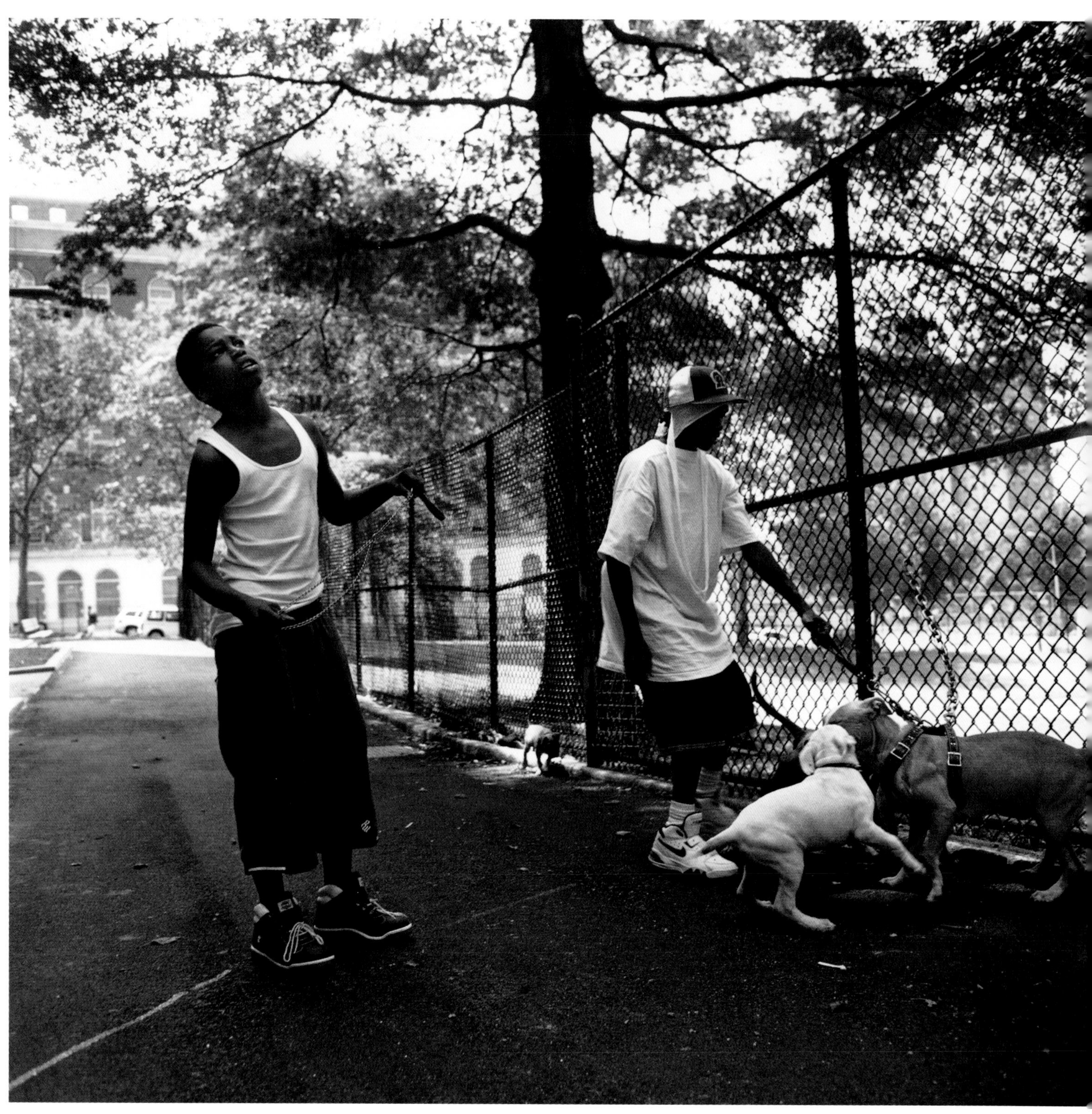

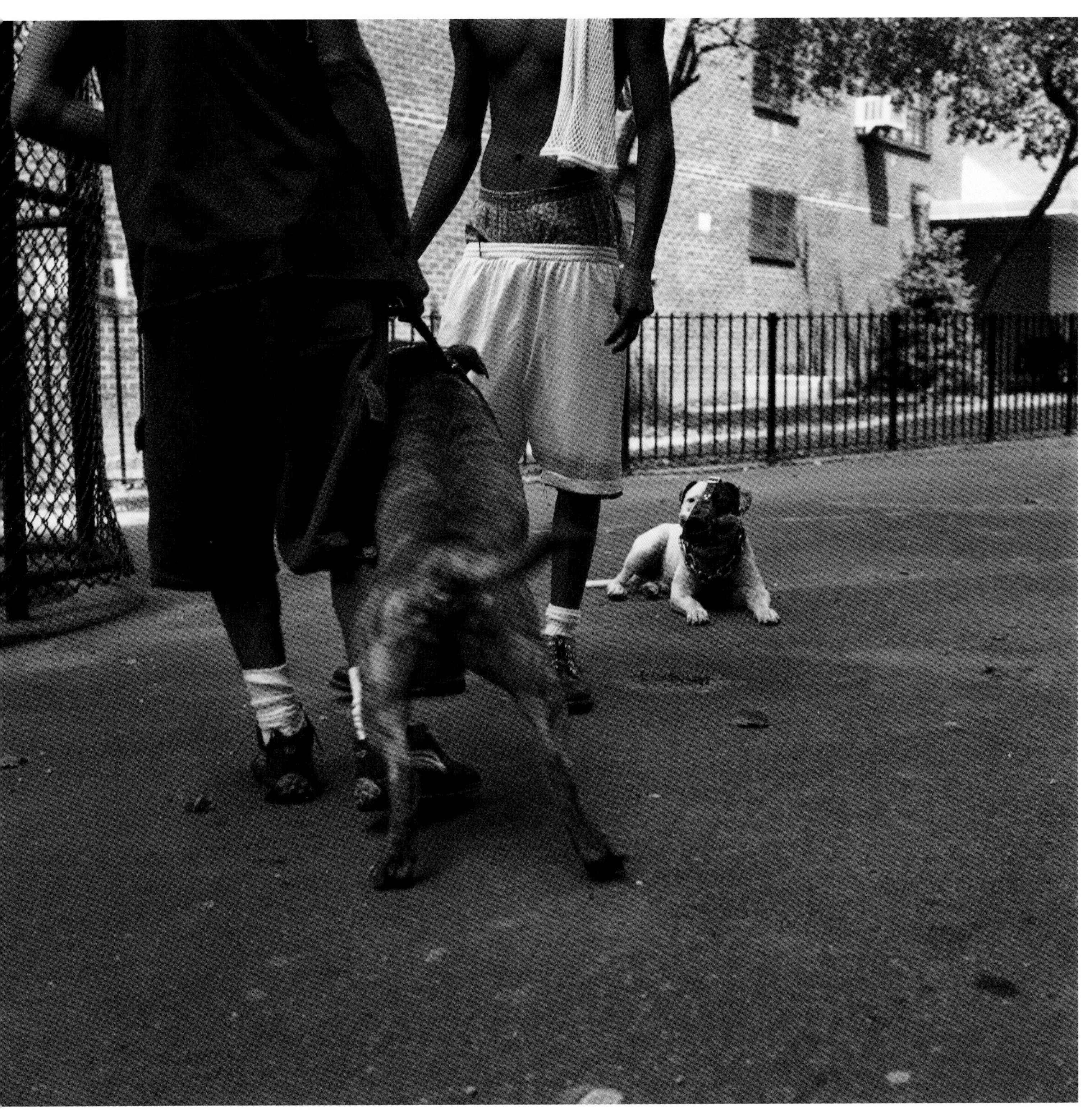

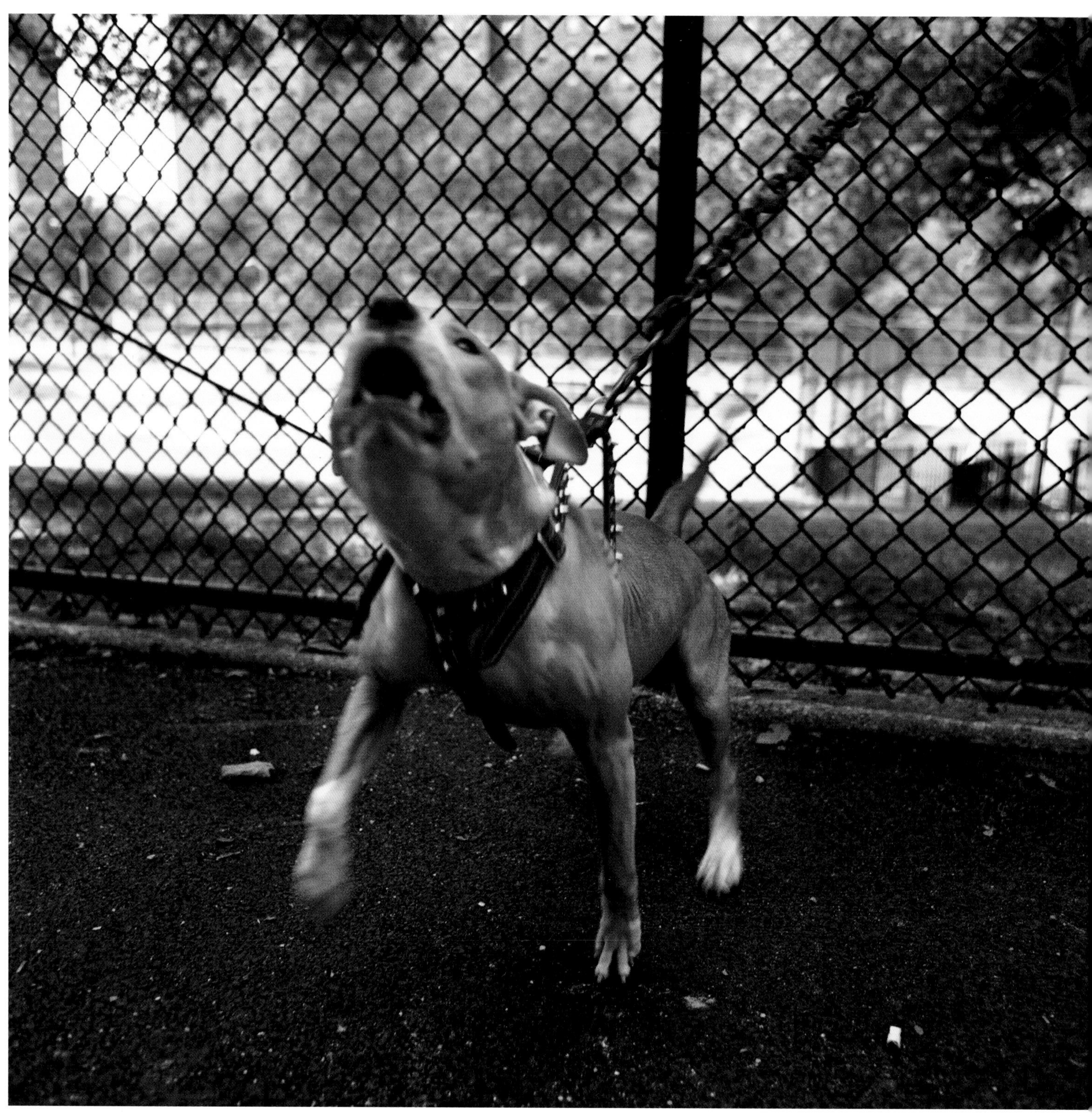

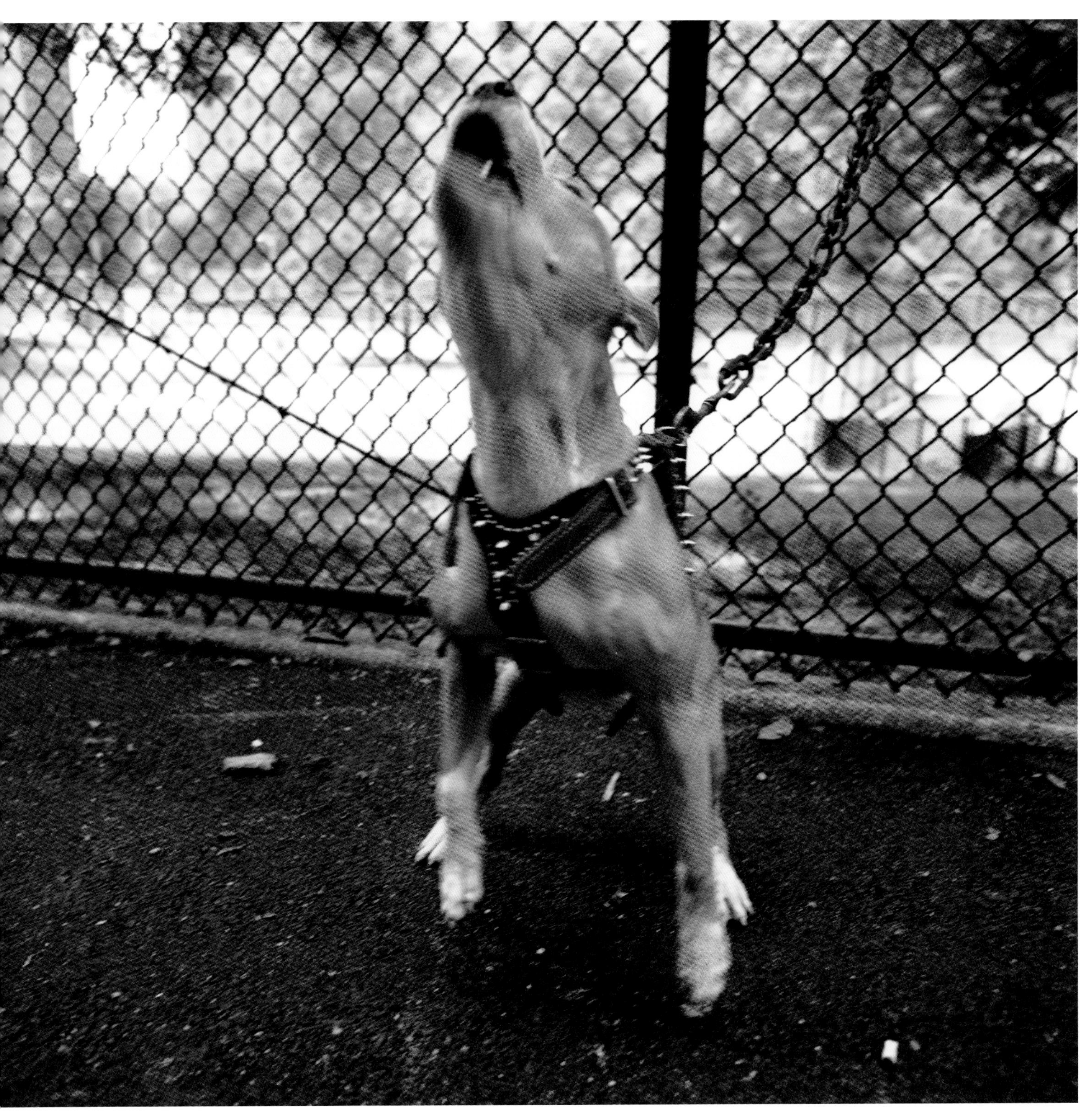

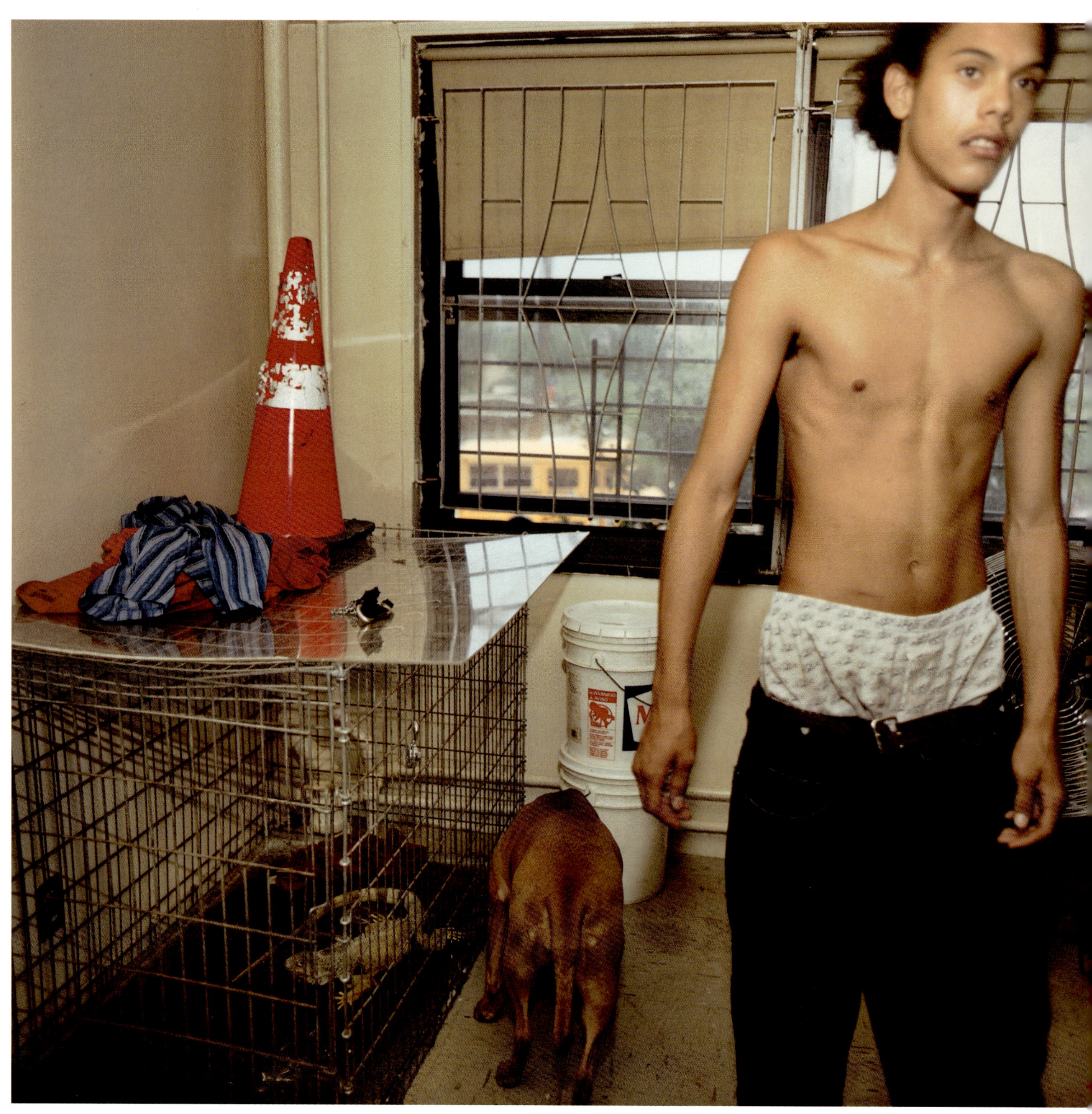

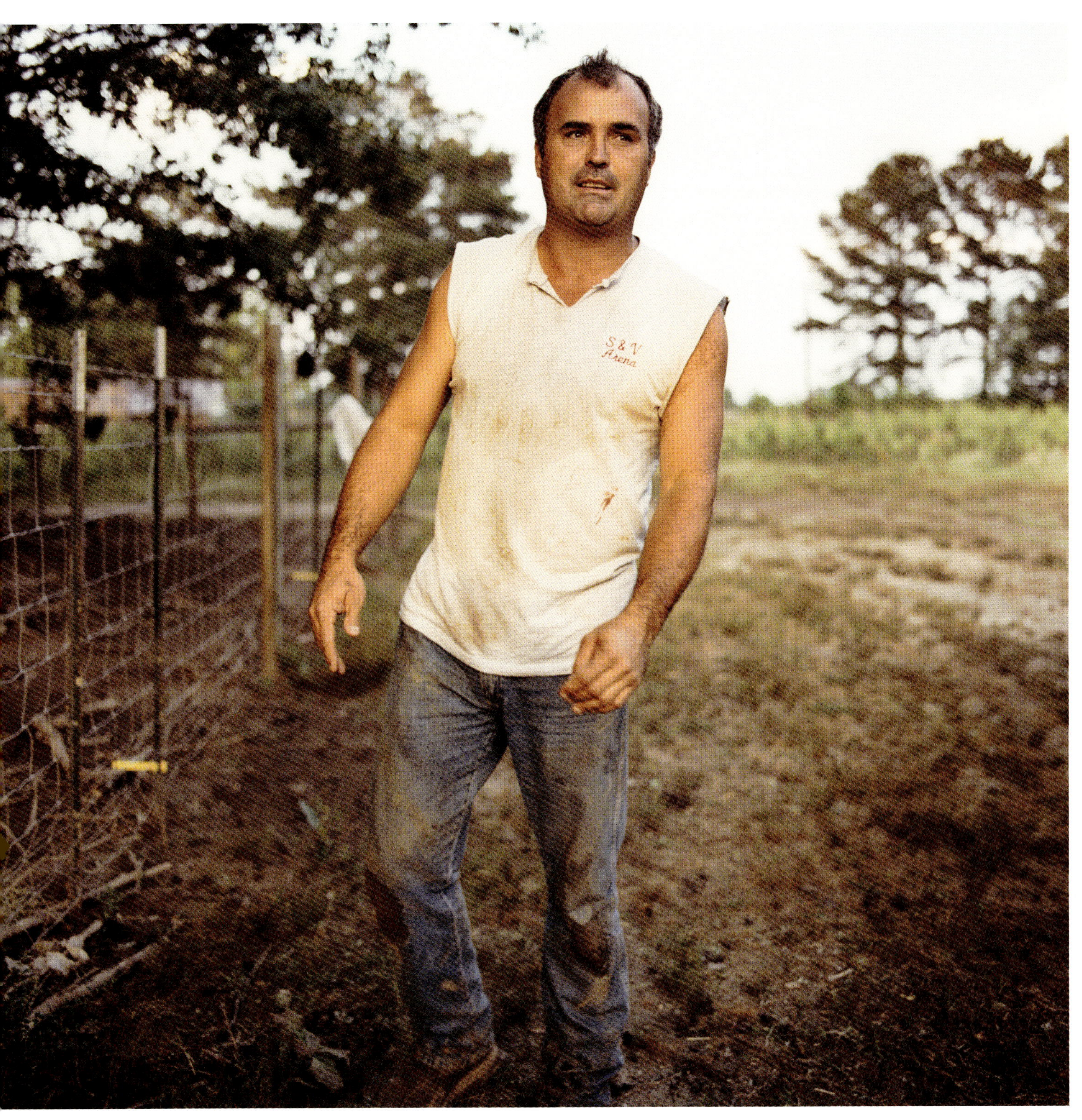
S & V
Arena

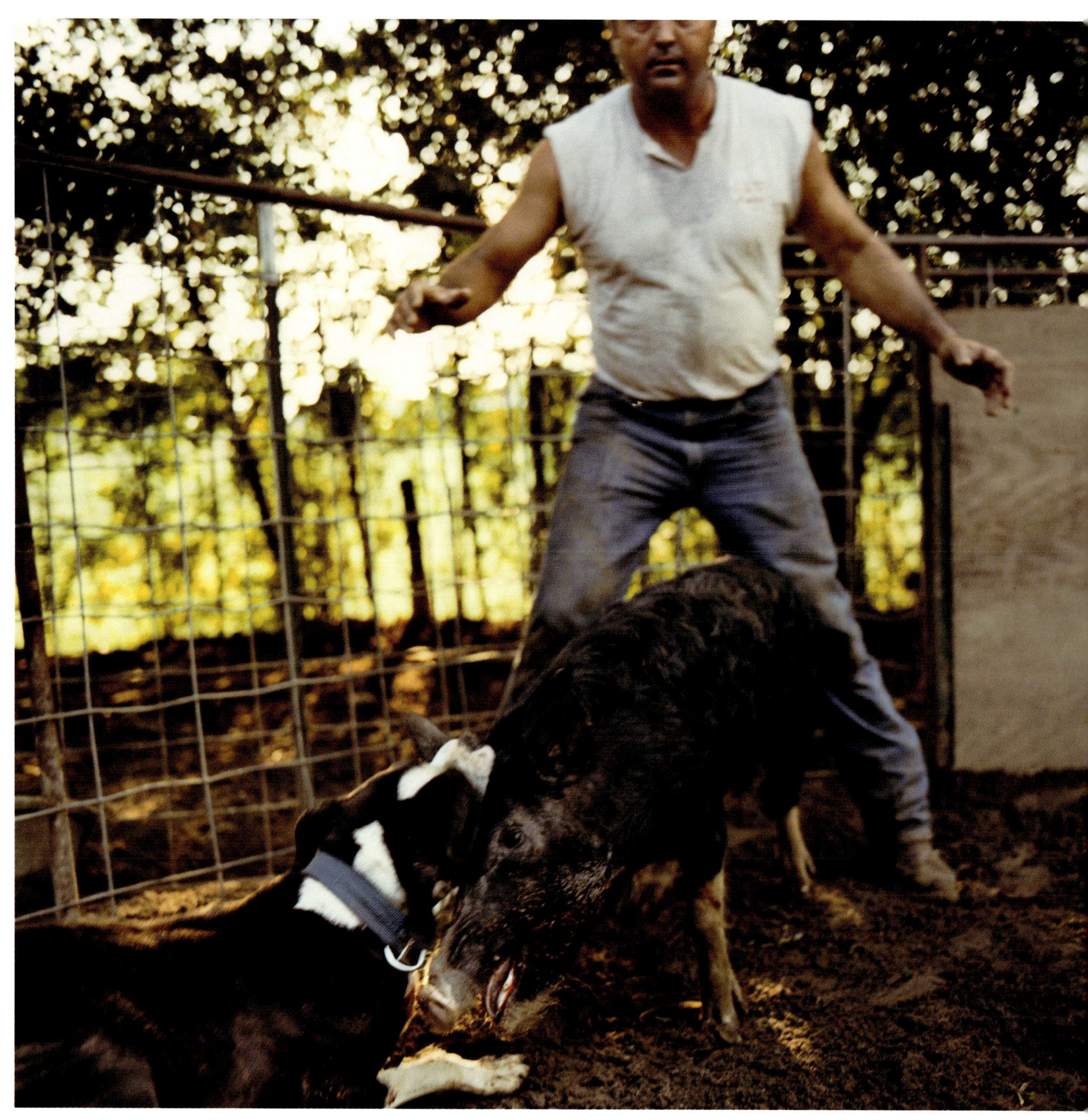

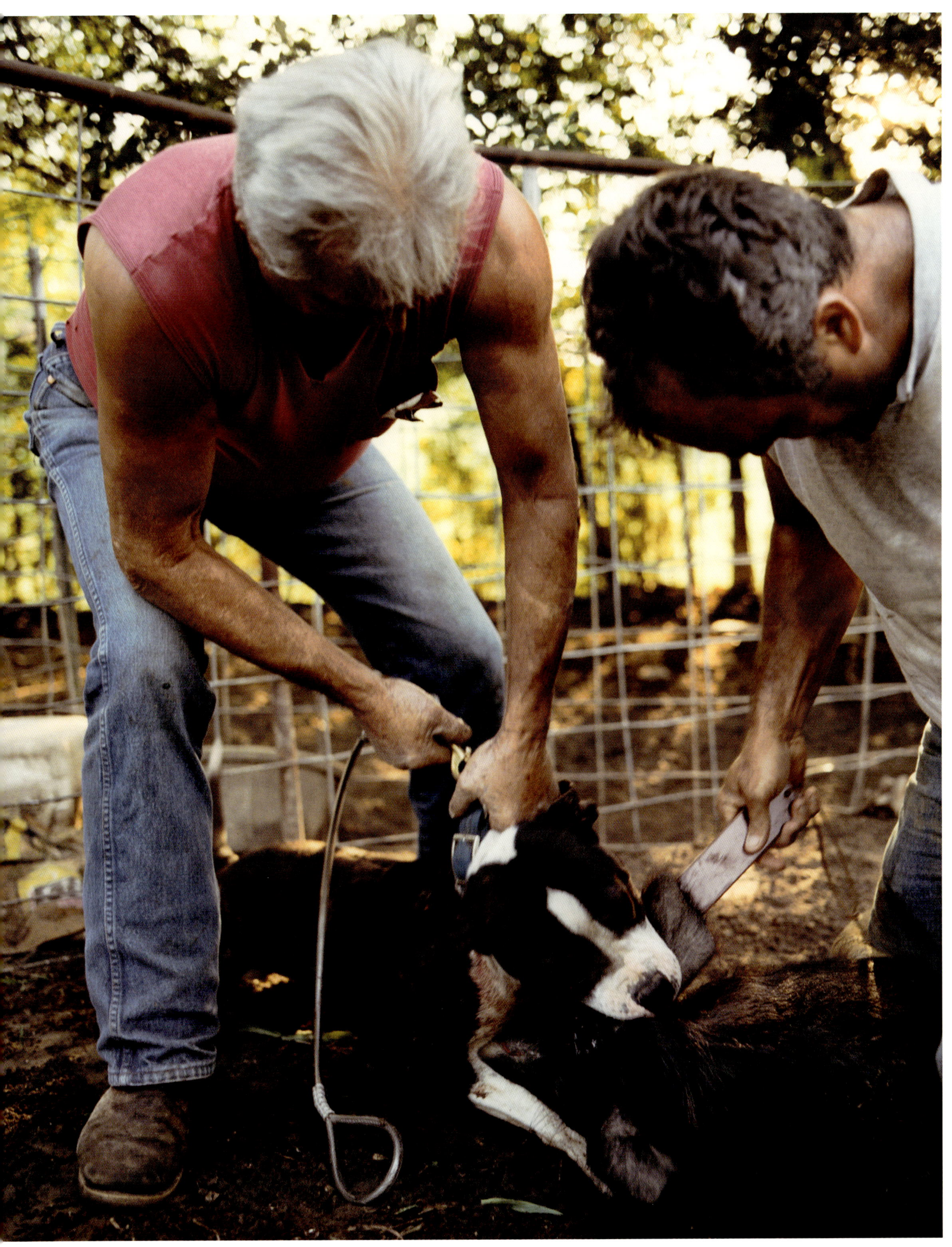

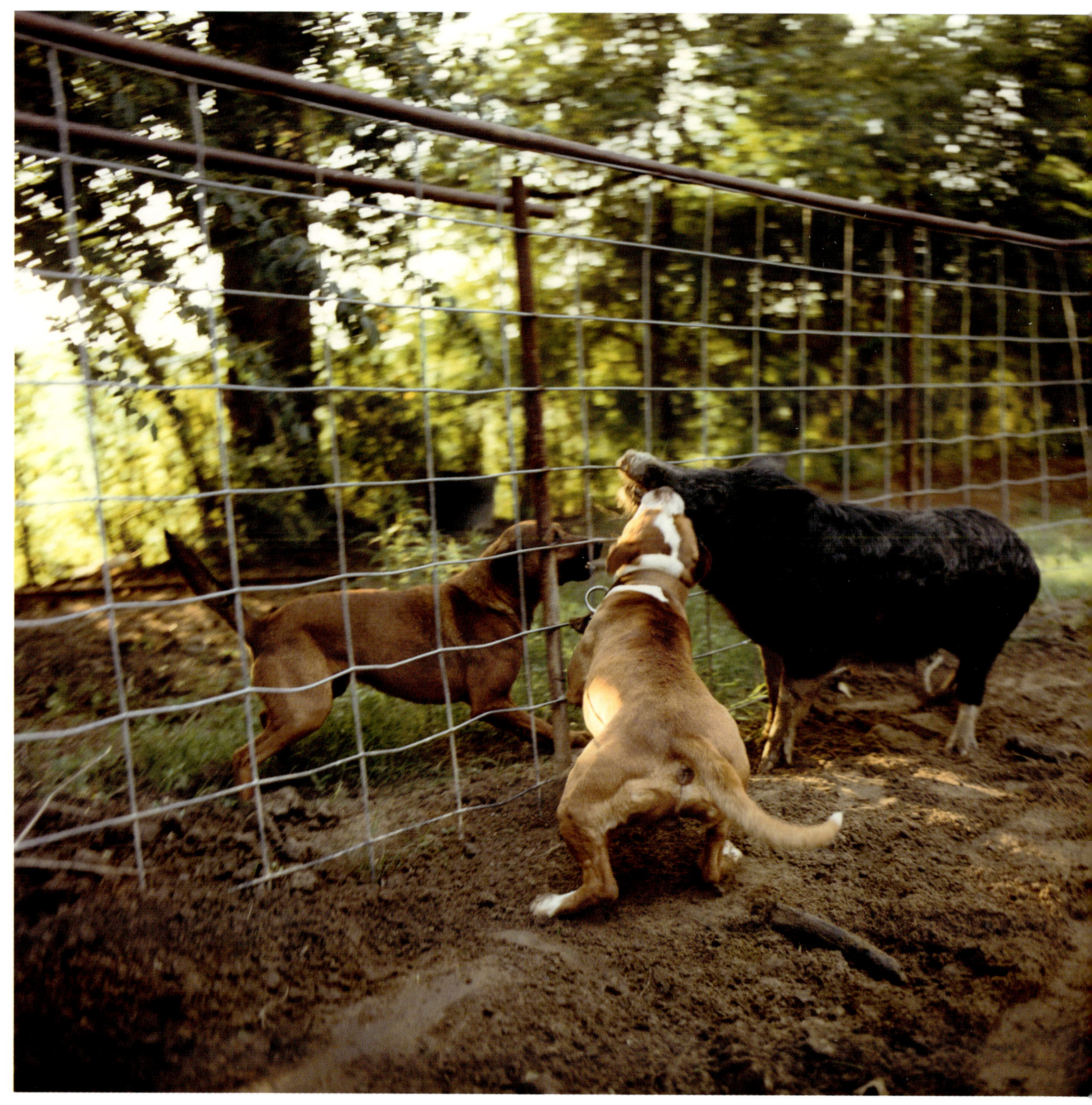

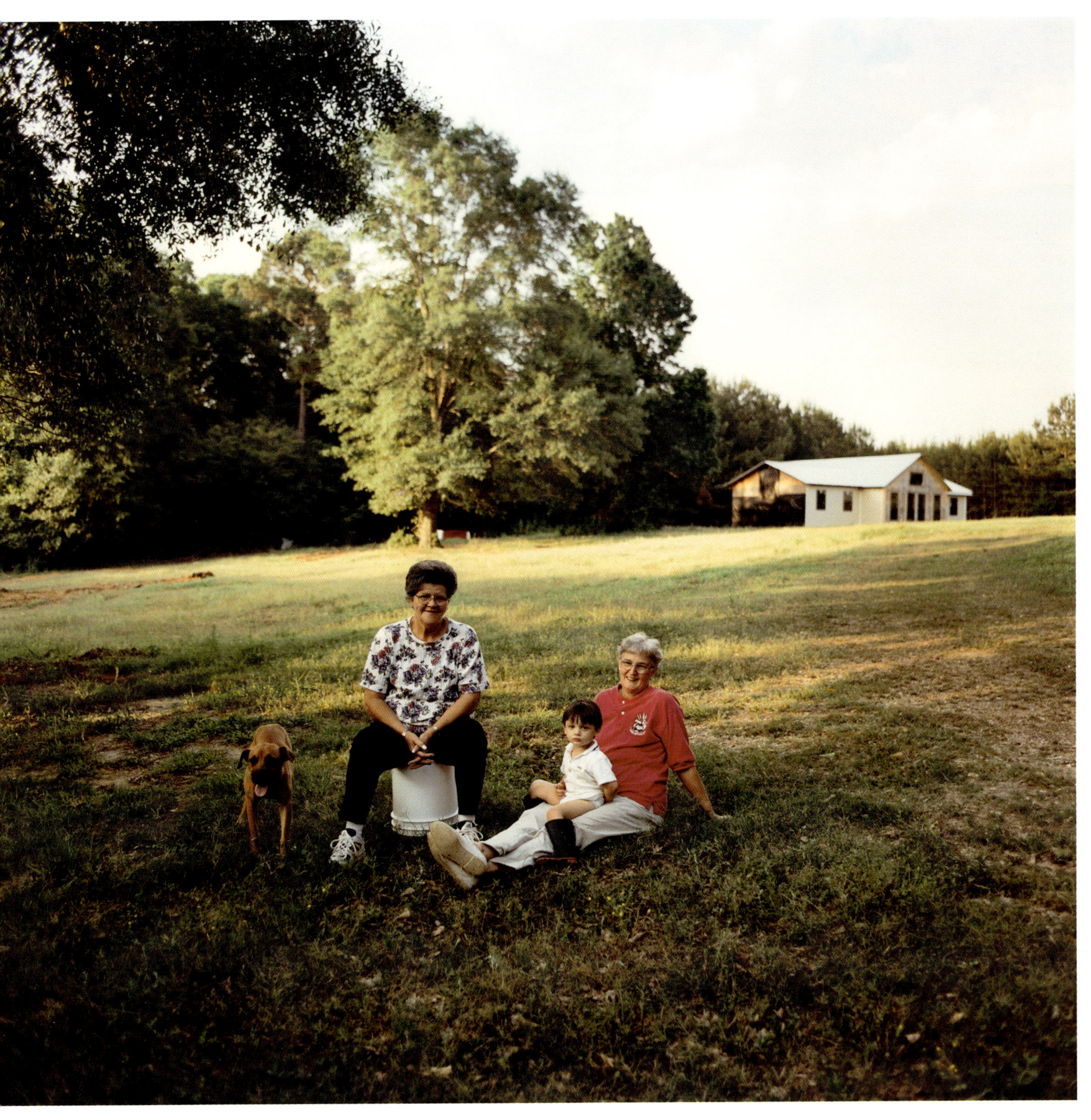

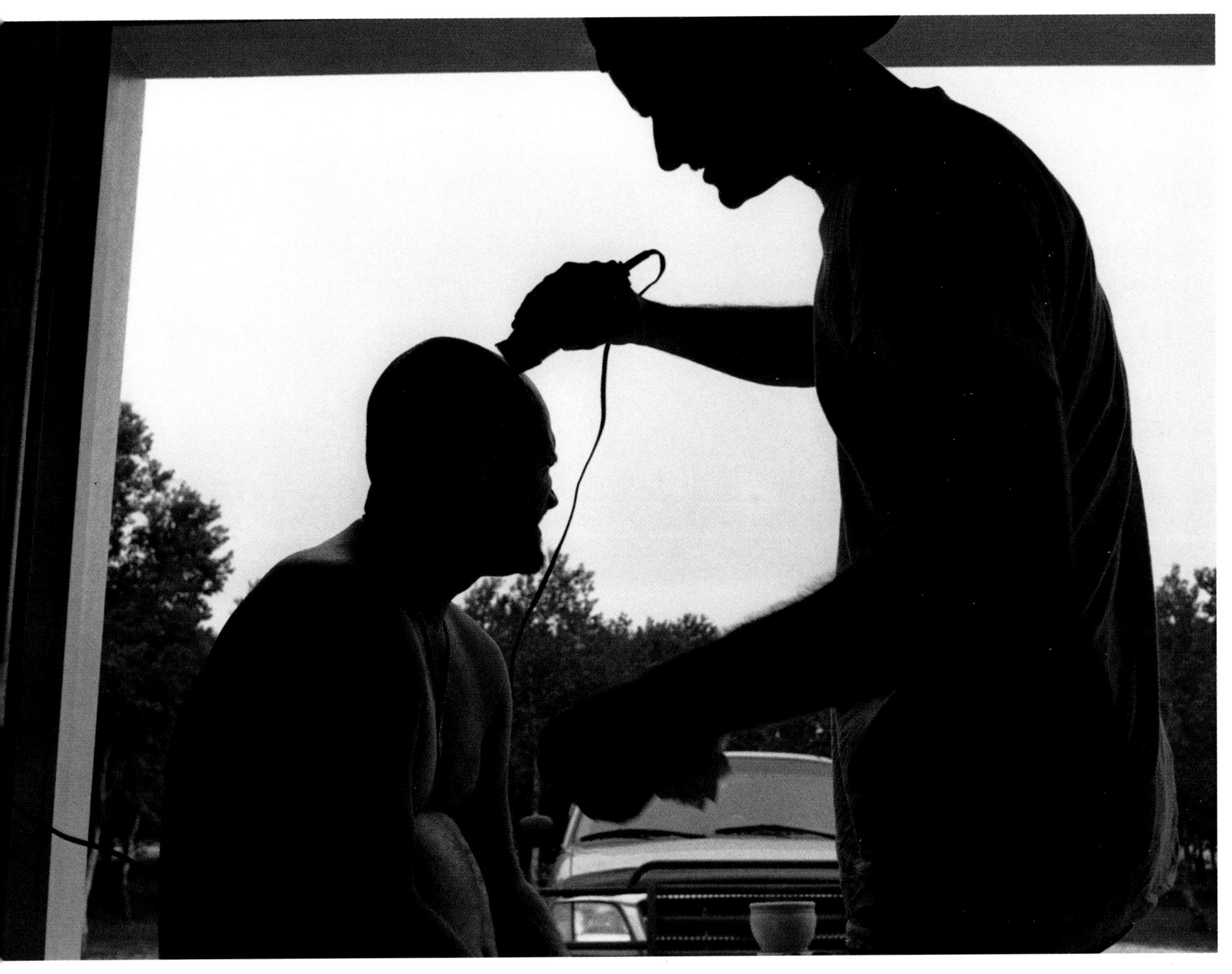

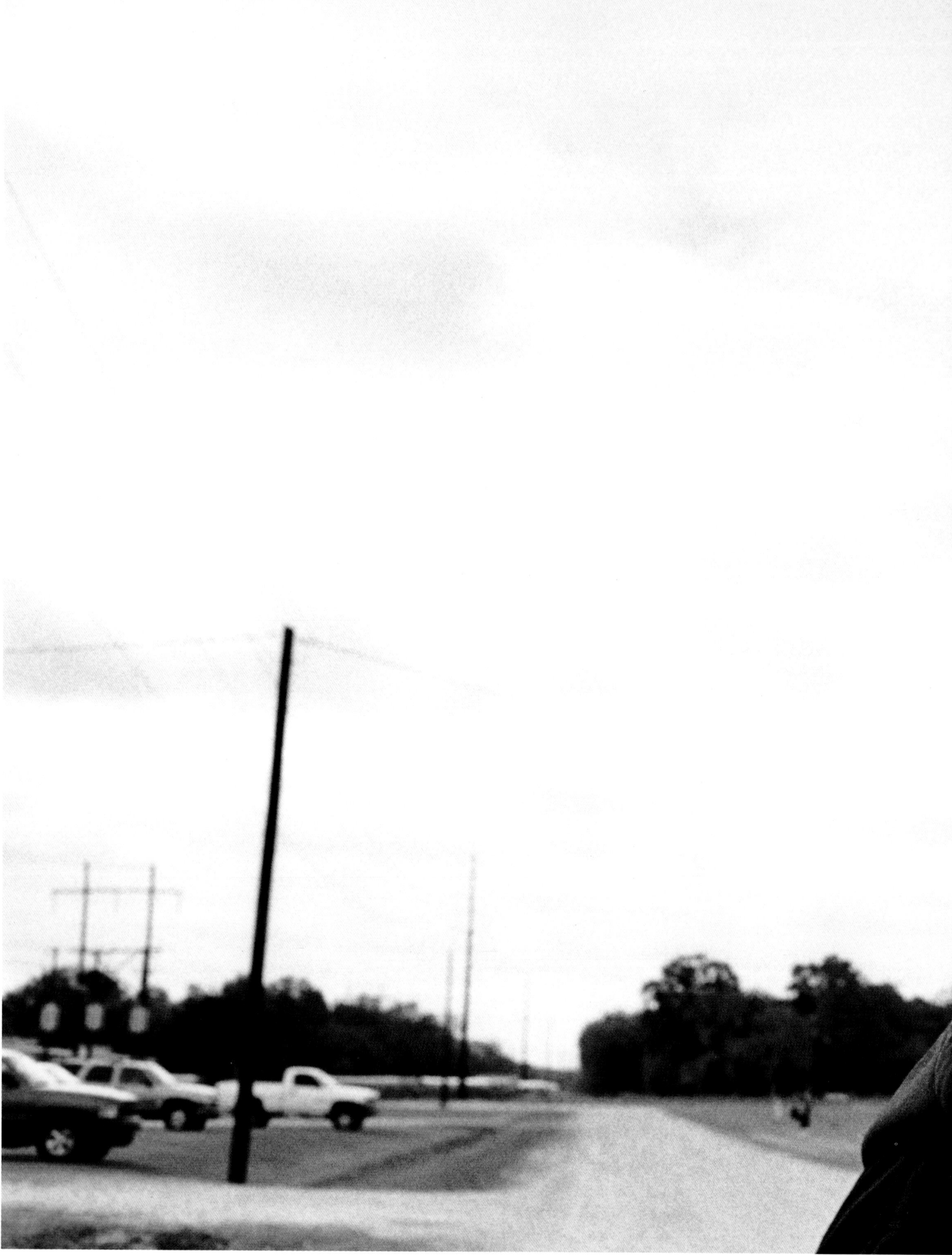

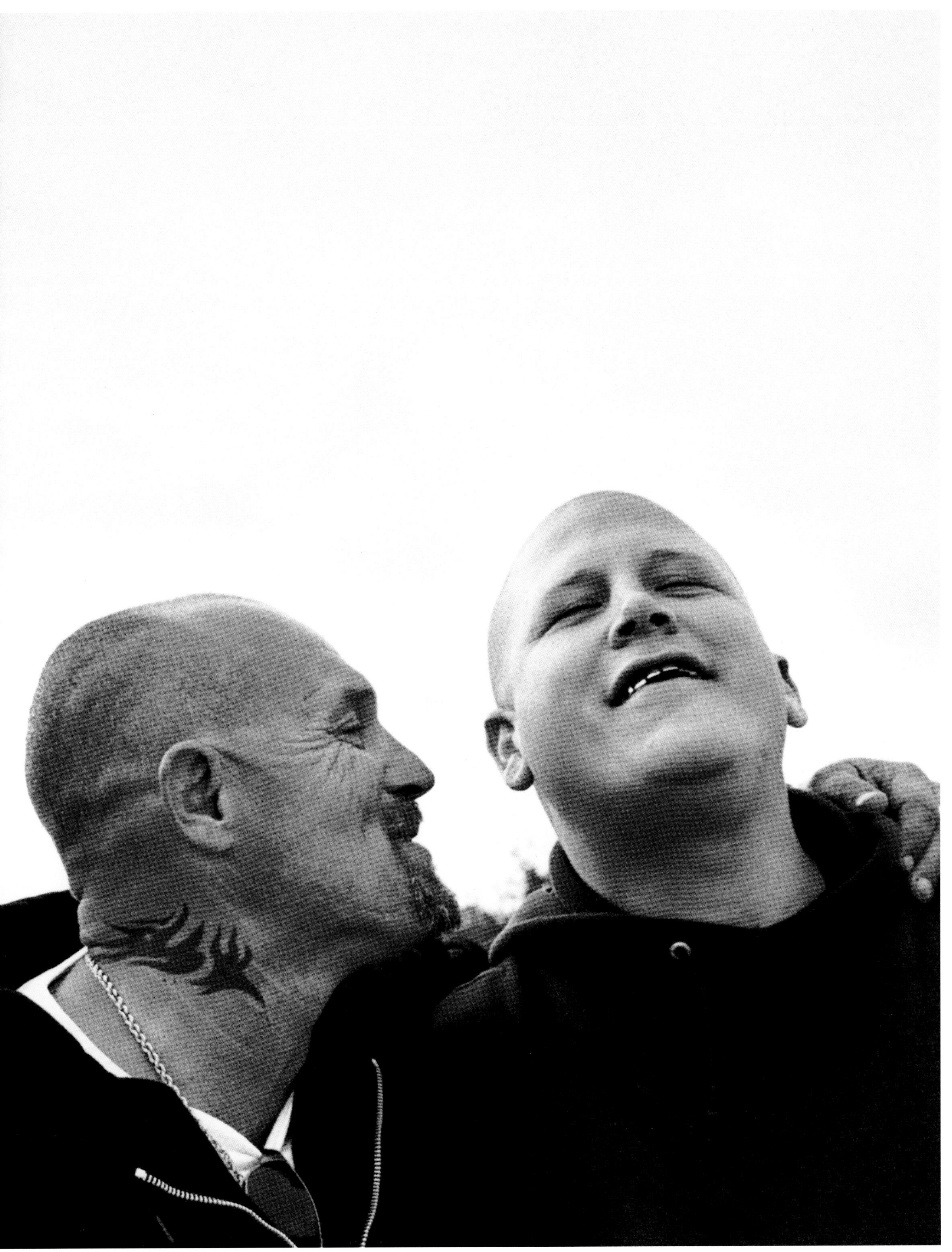

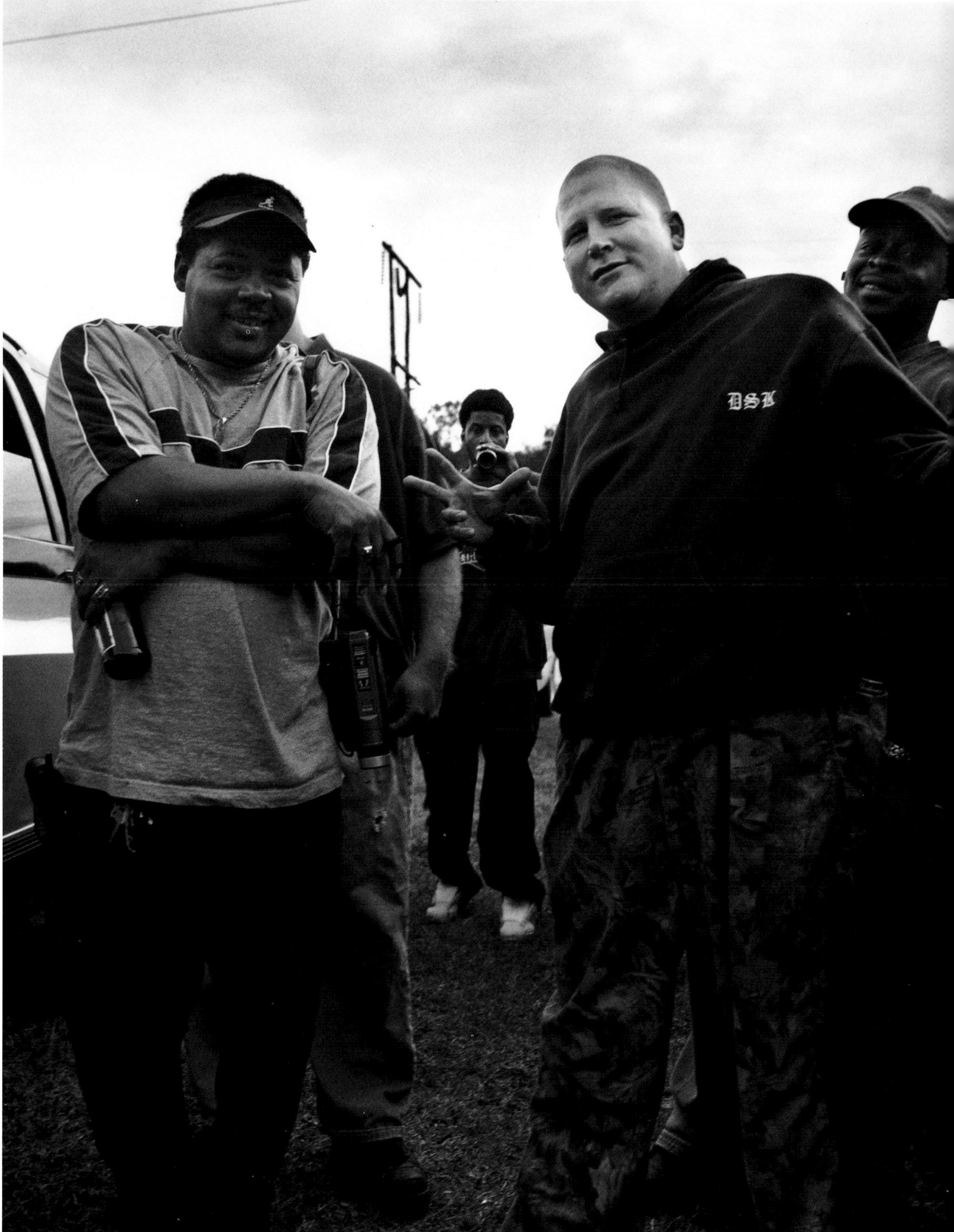
DSK

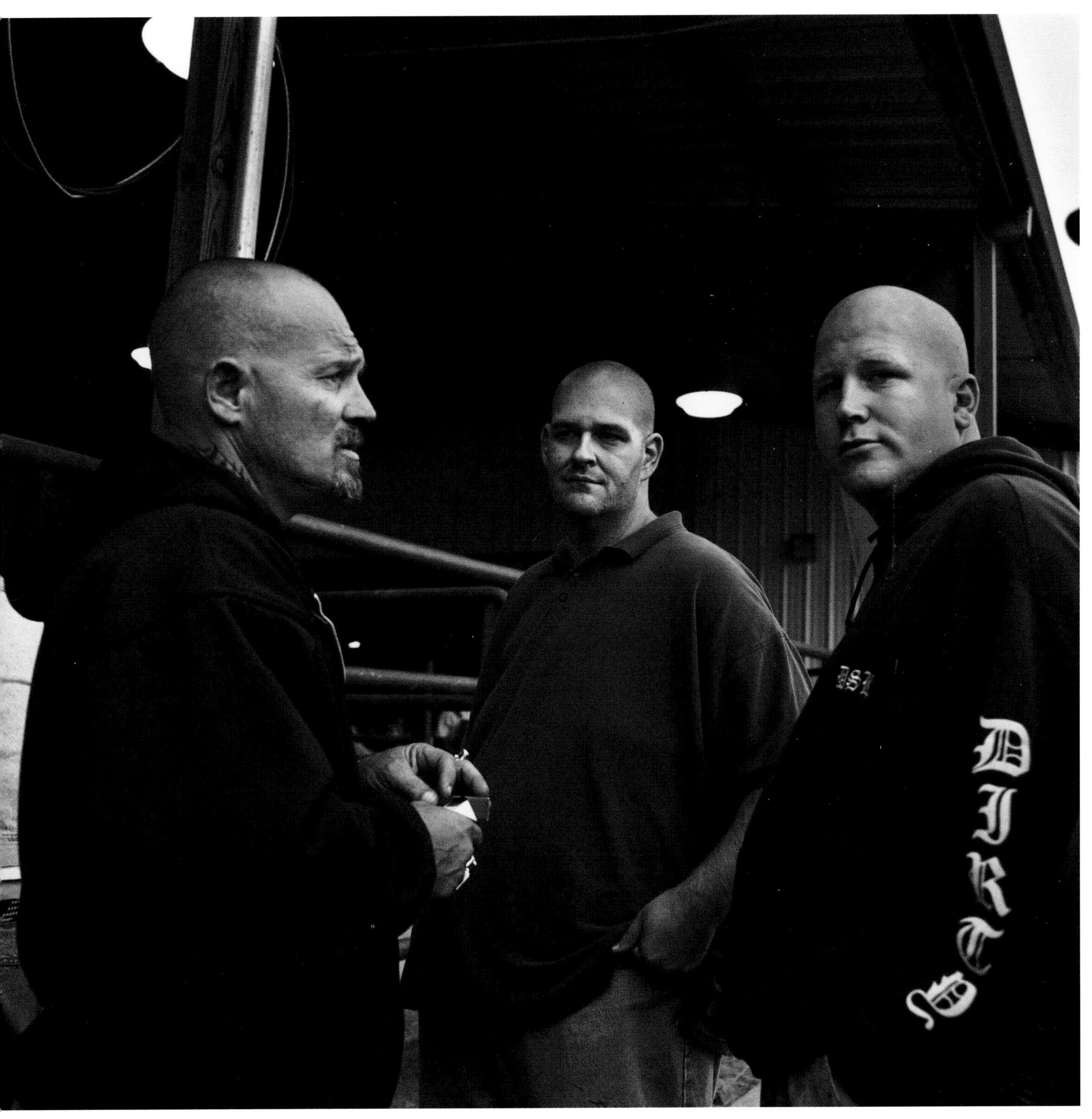
DIRT

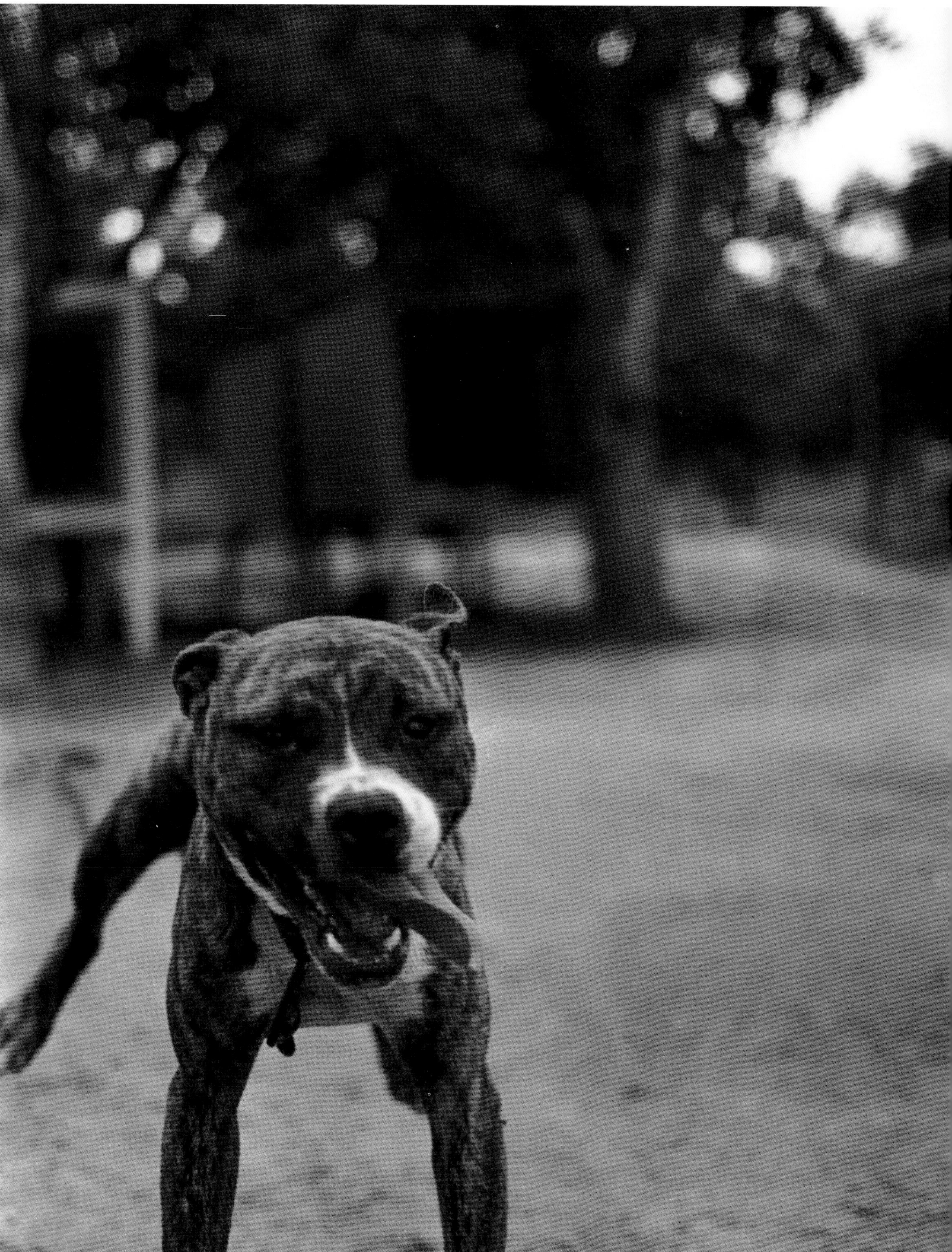

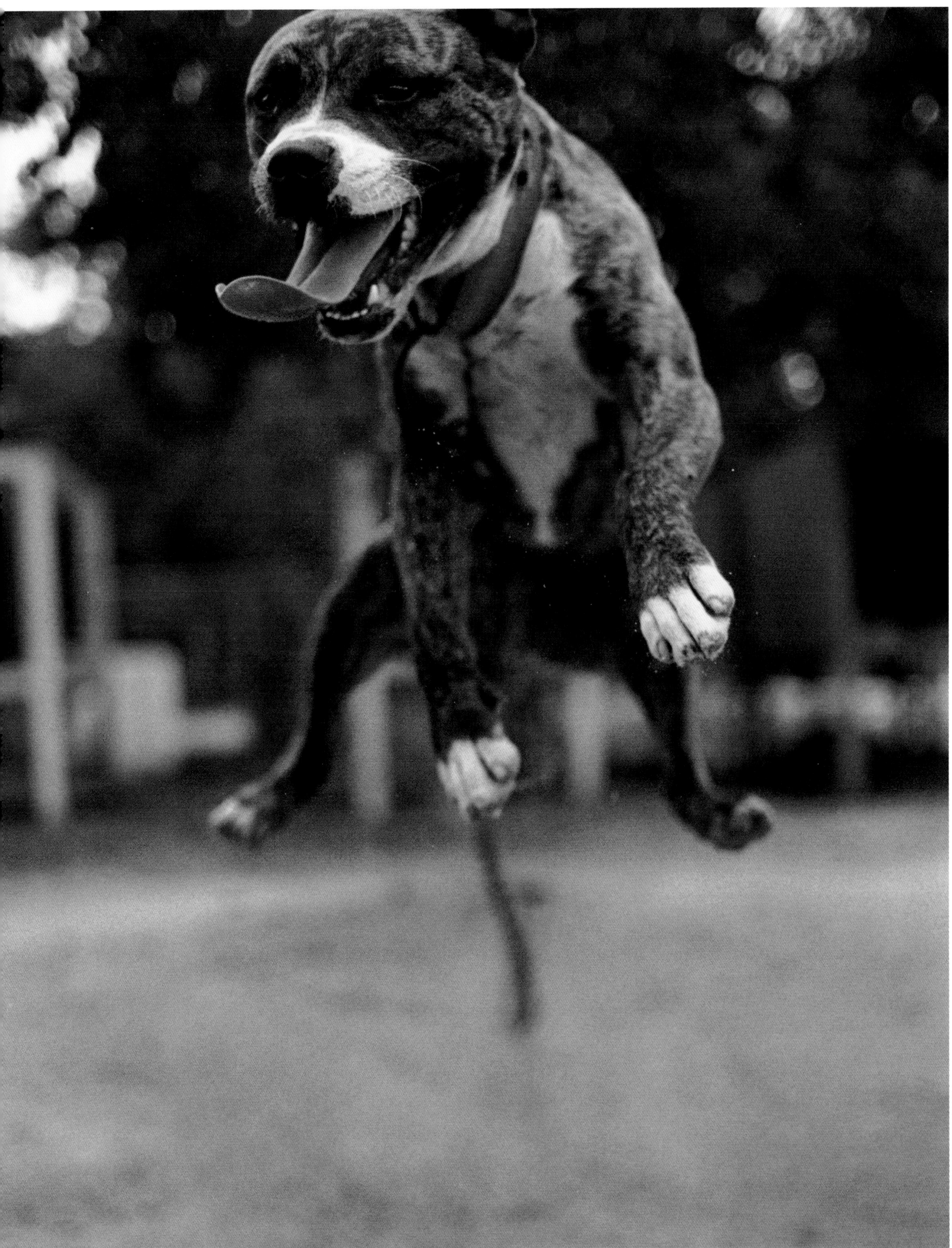

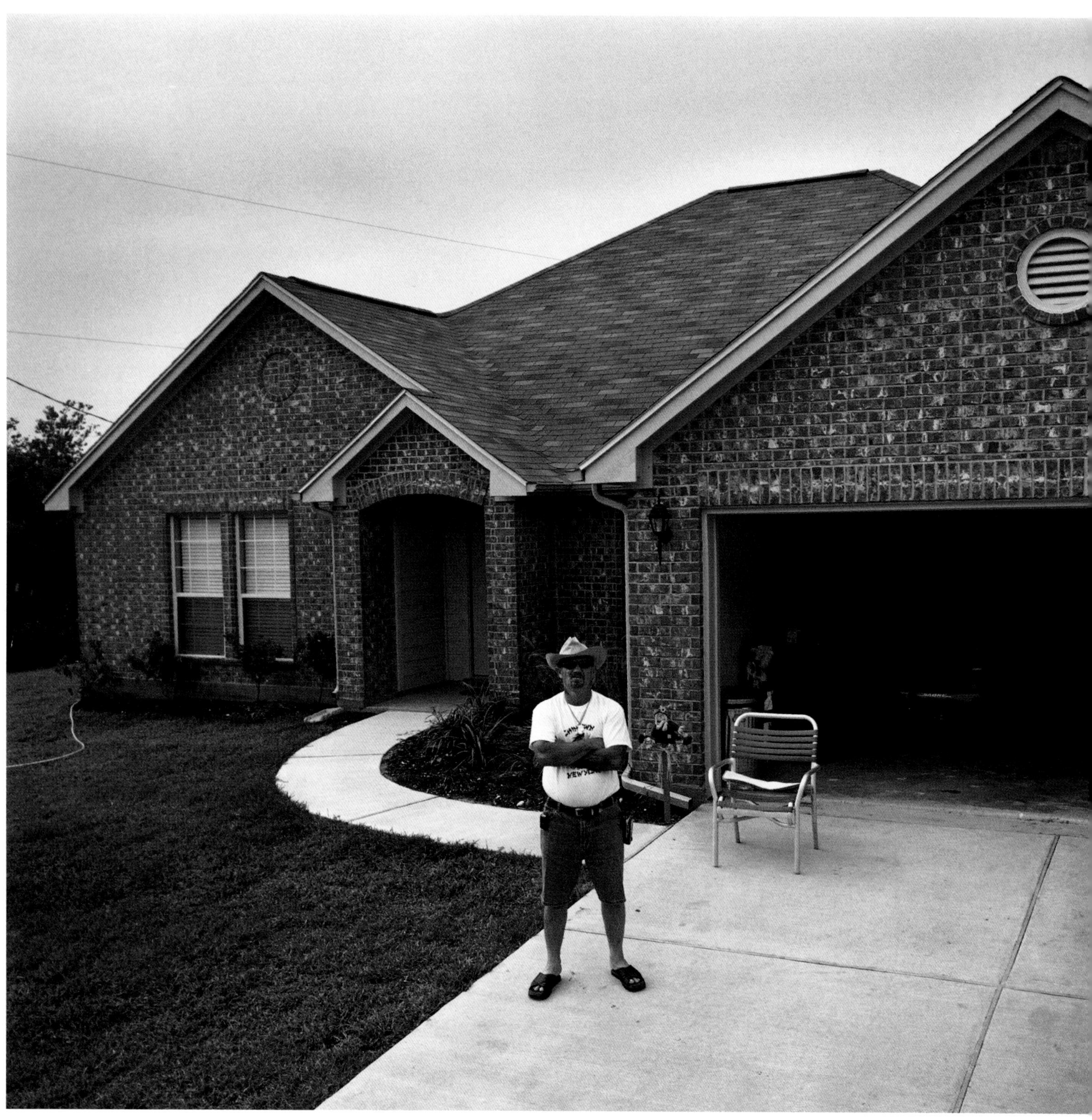

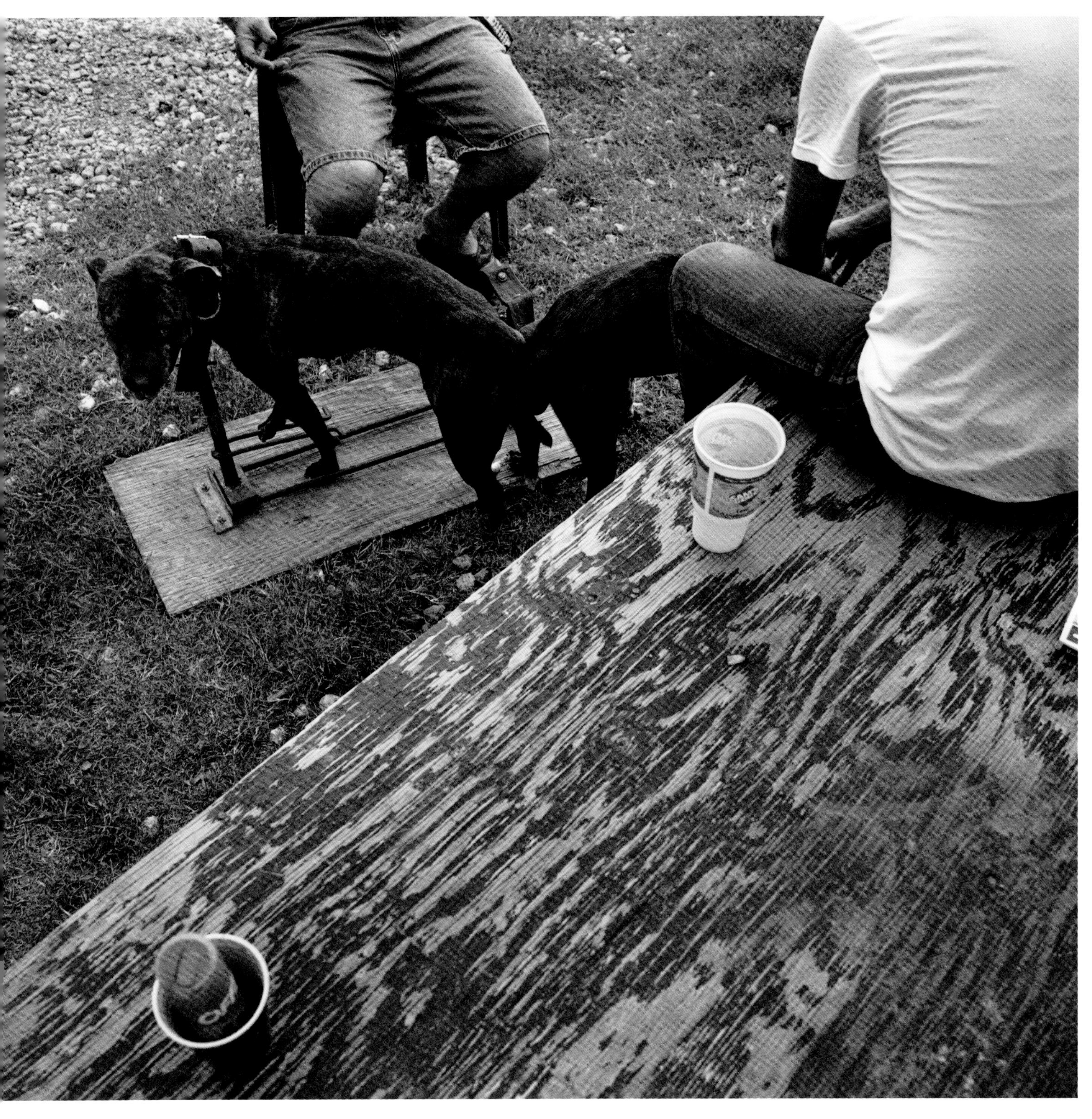

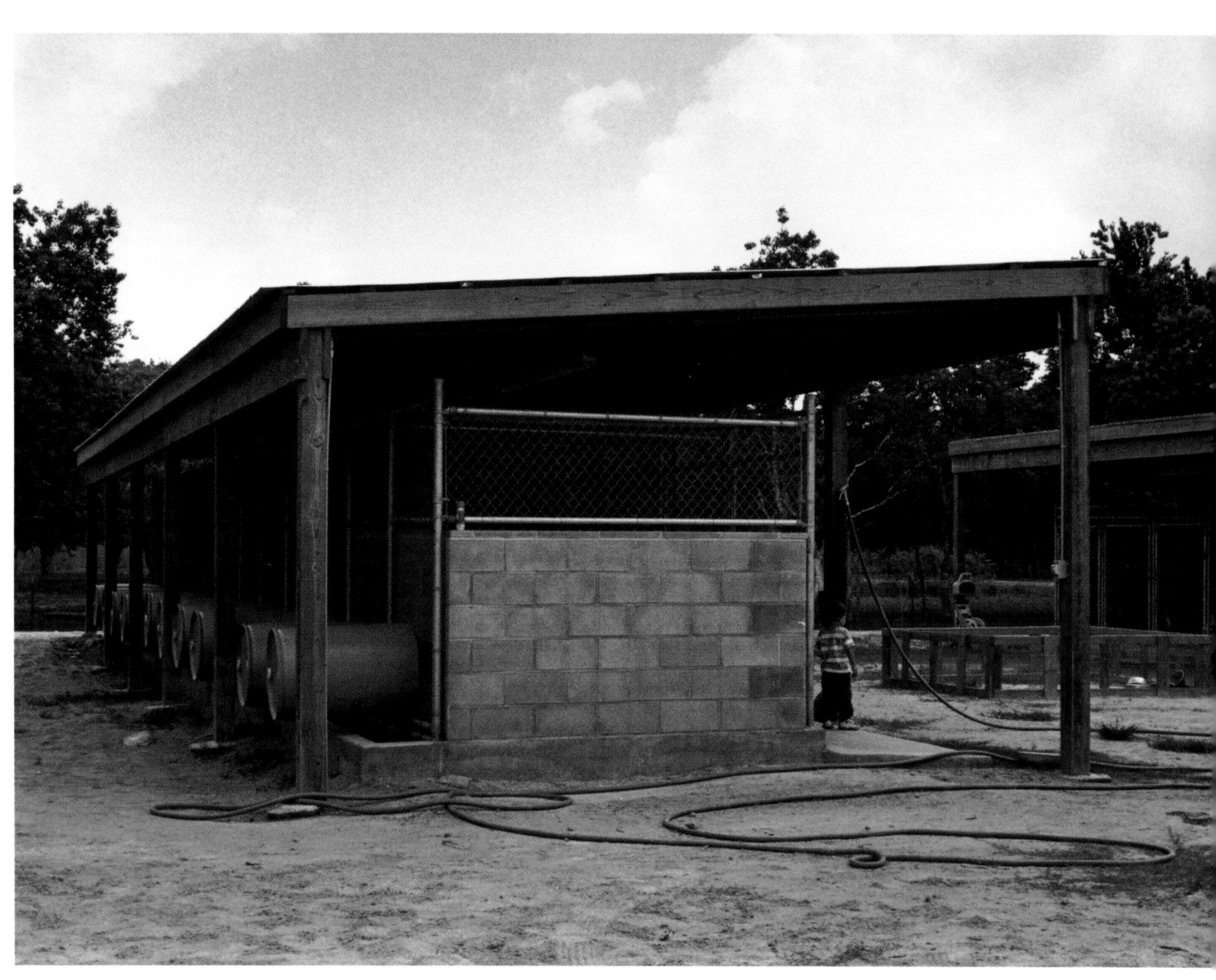

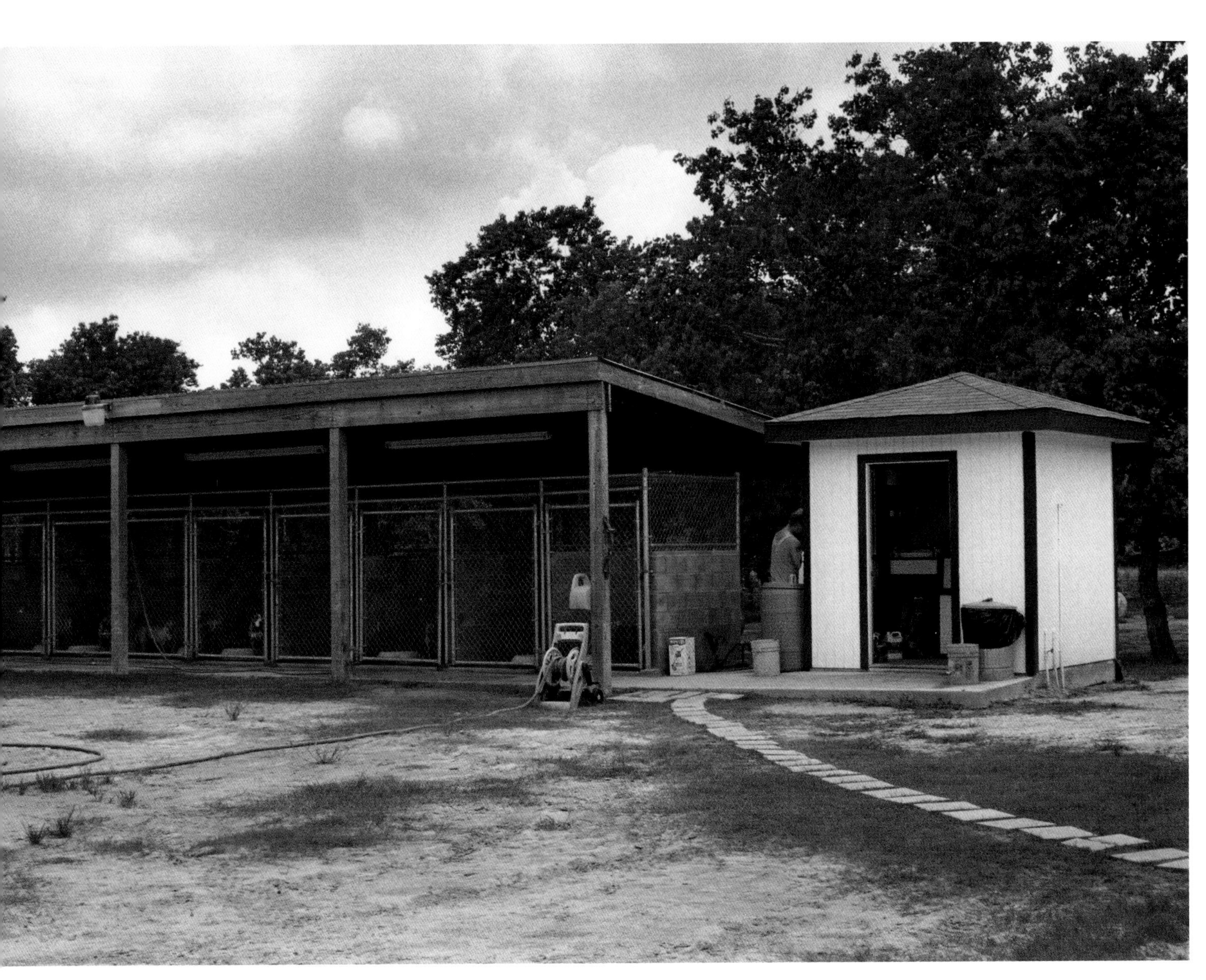

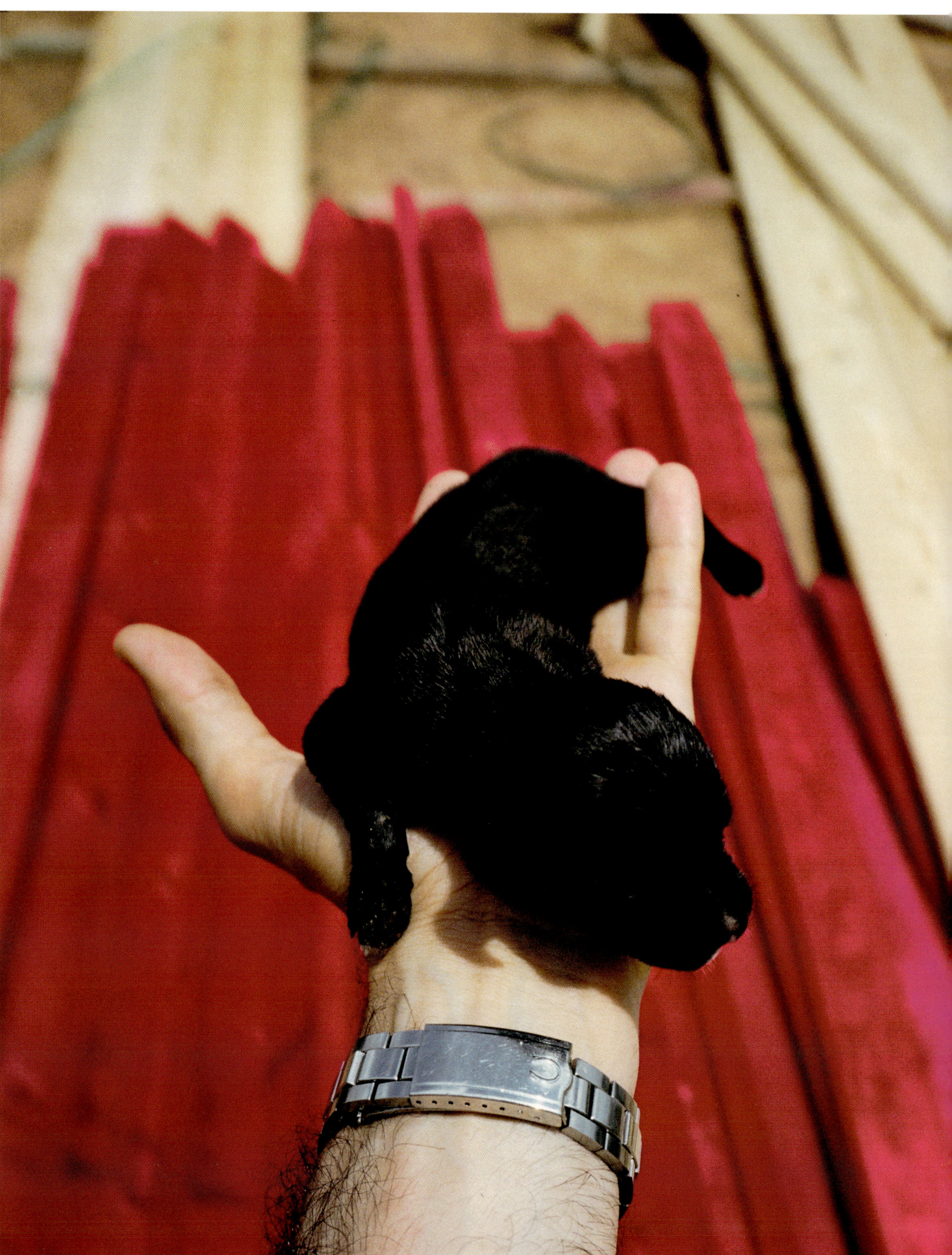

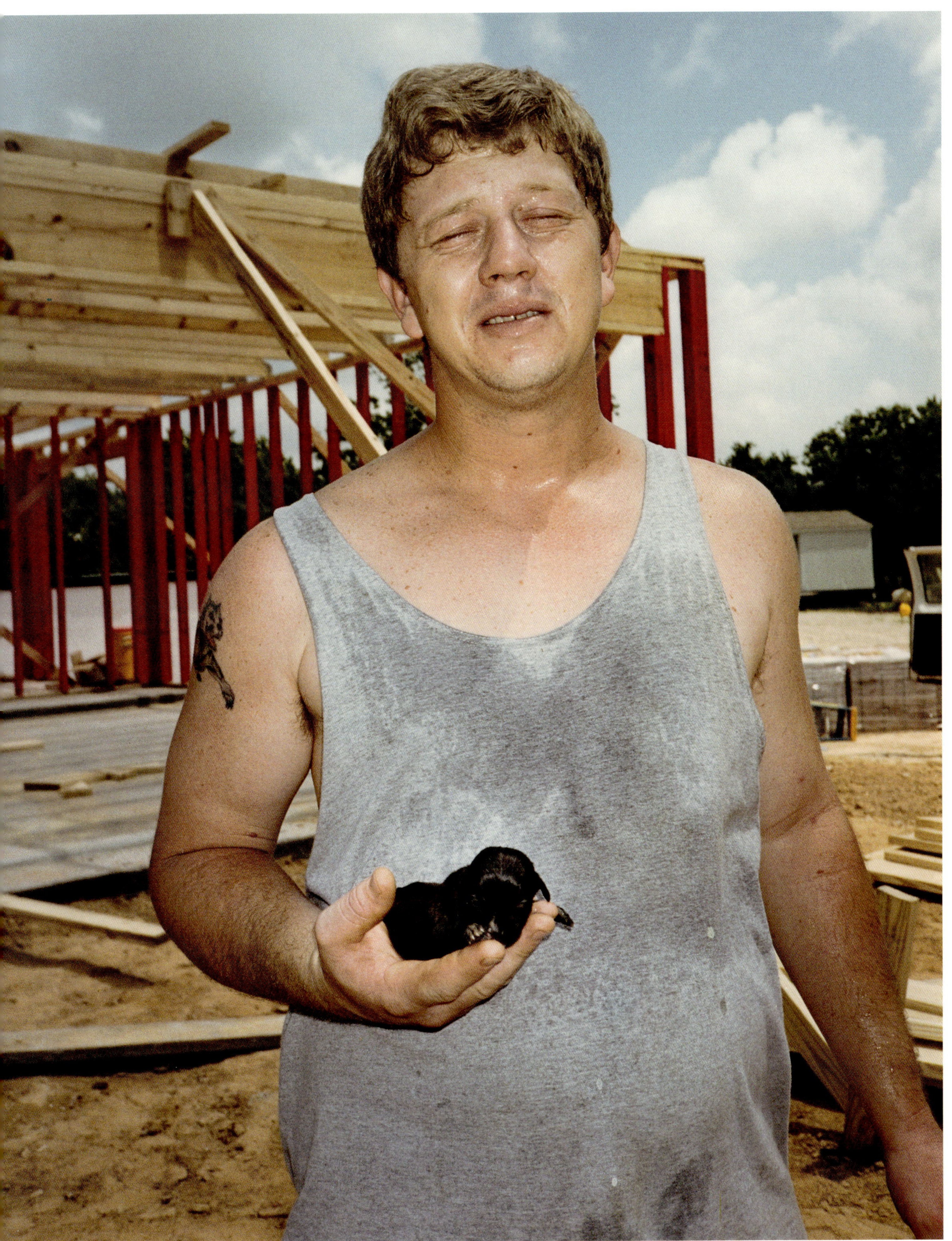

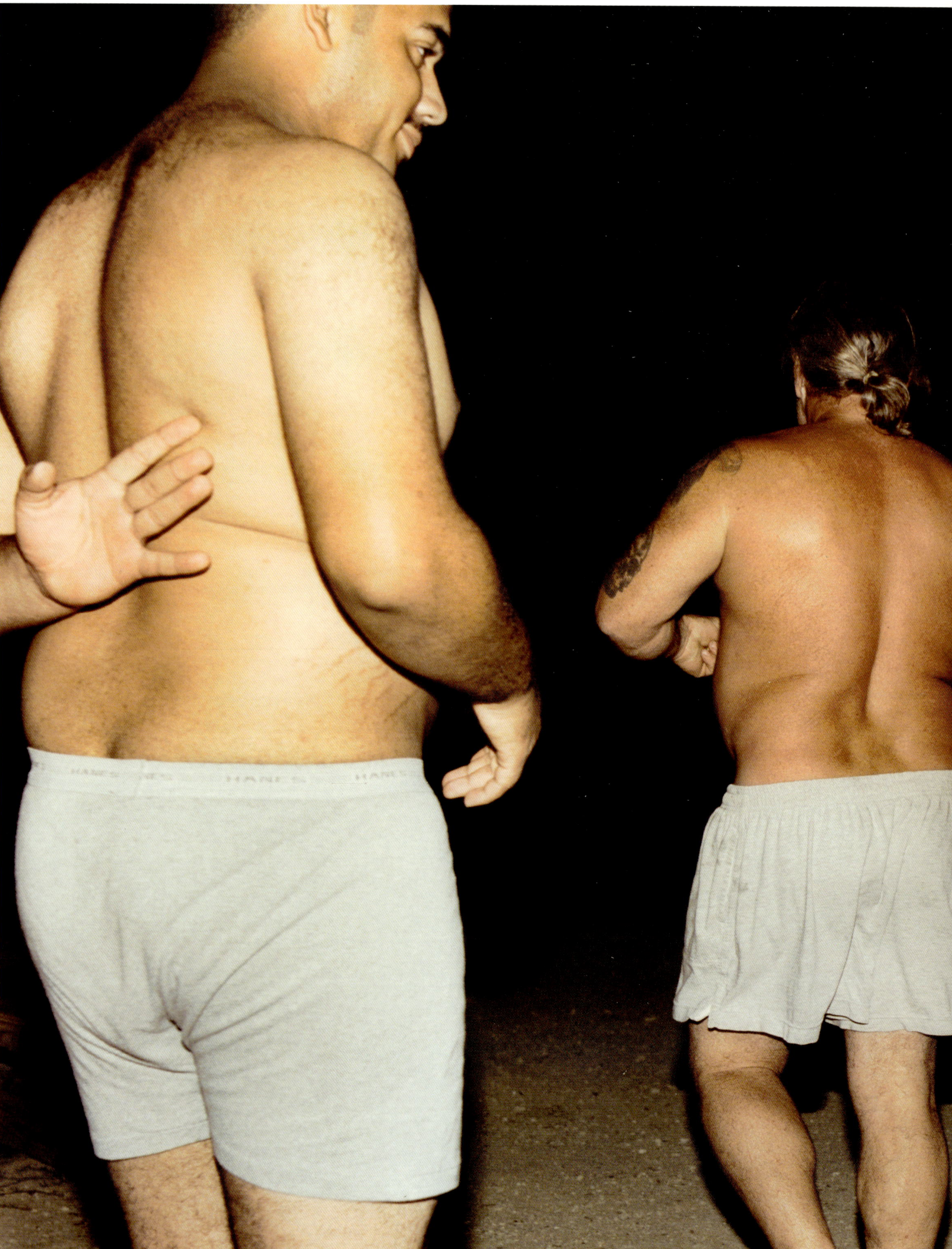
HANES

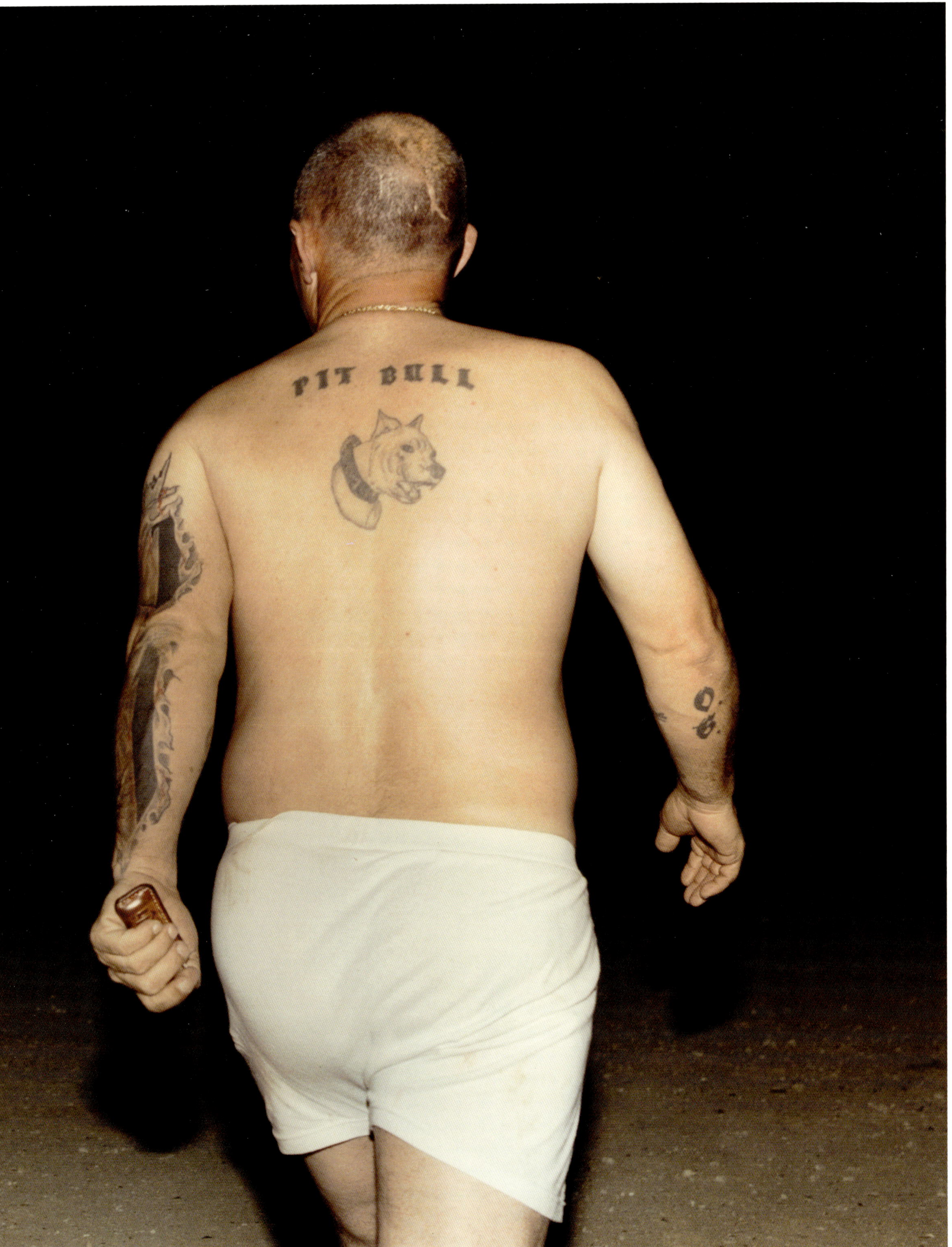
PIT BULL

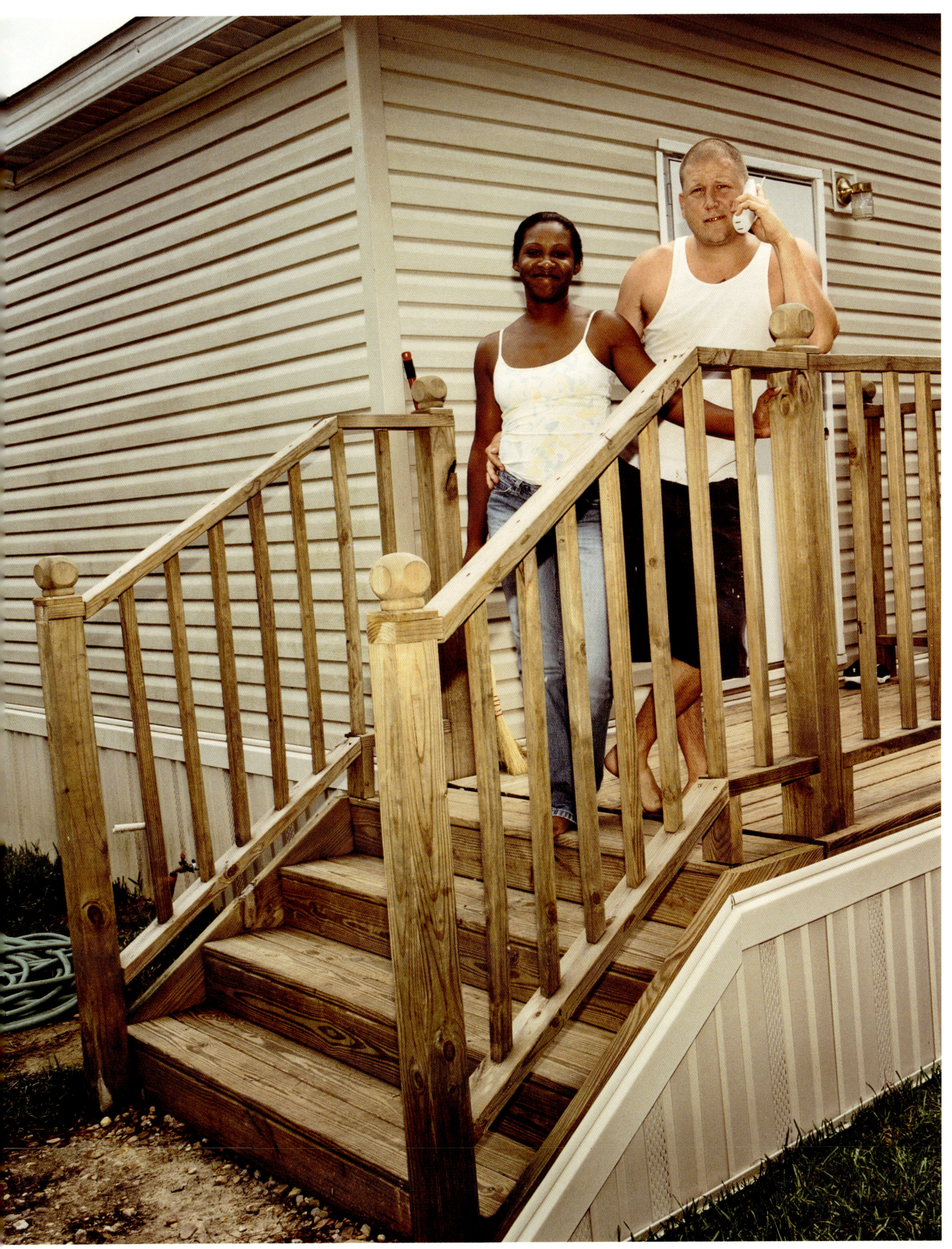

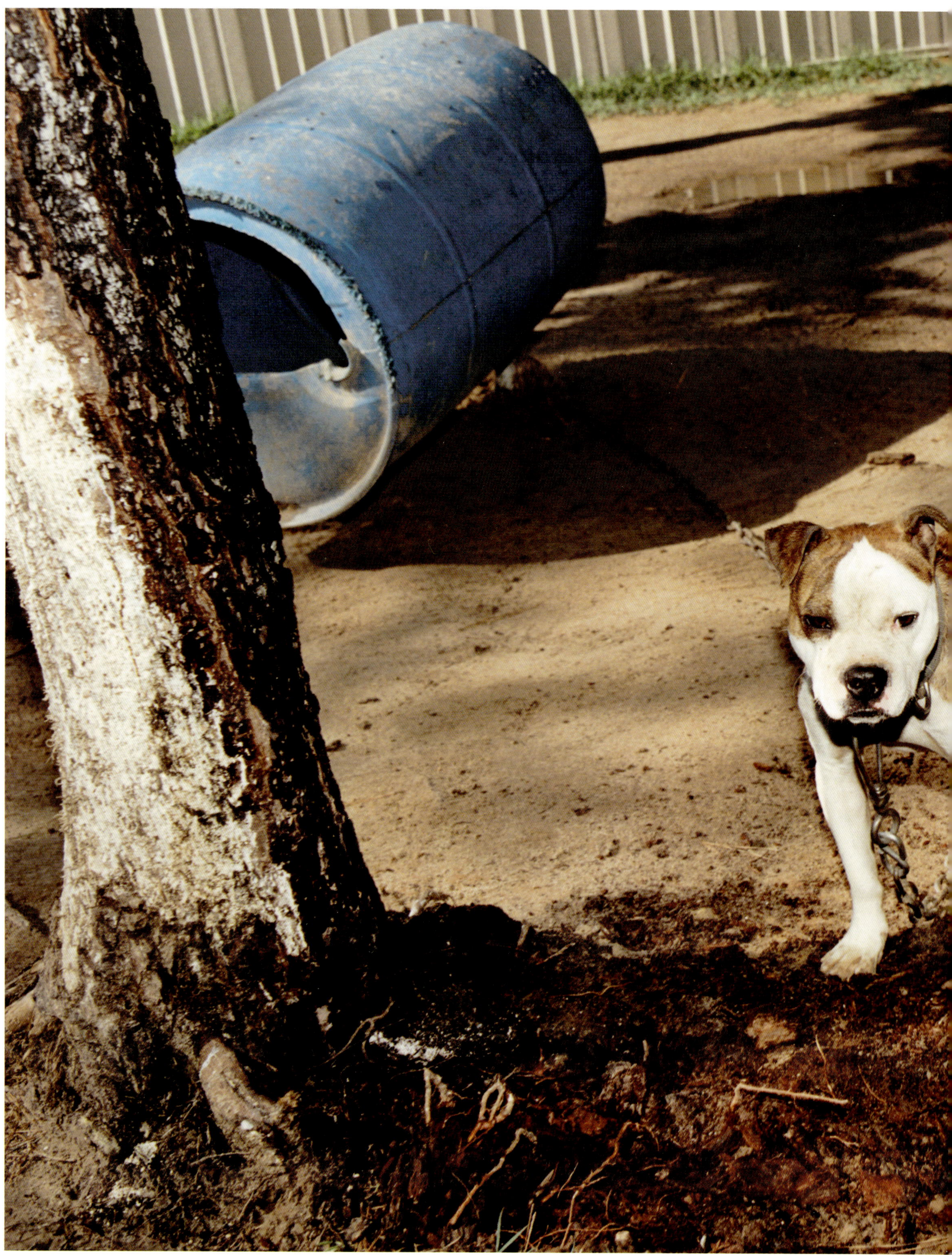

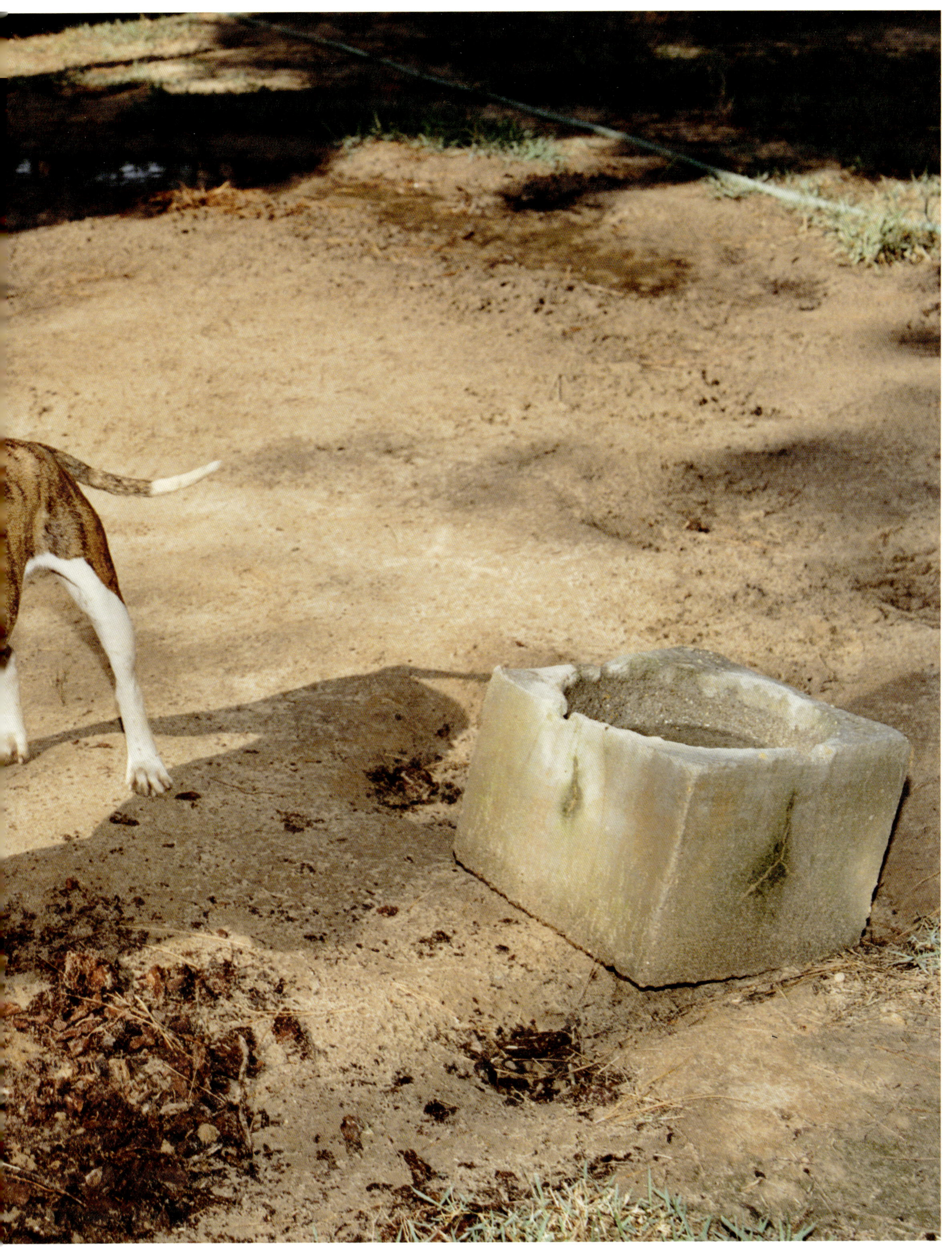

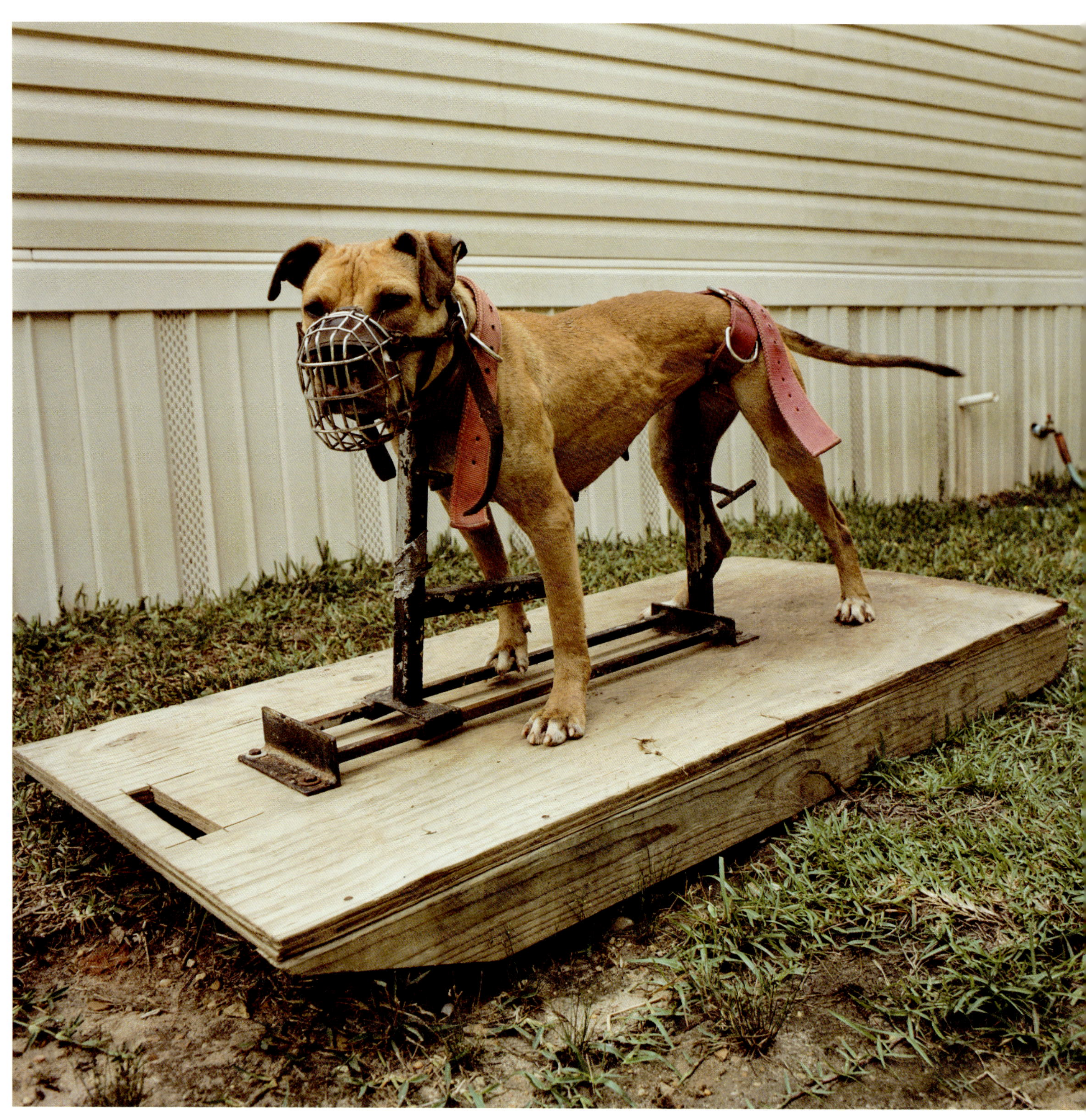

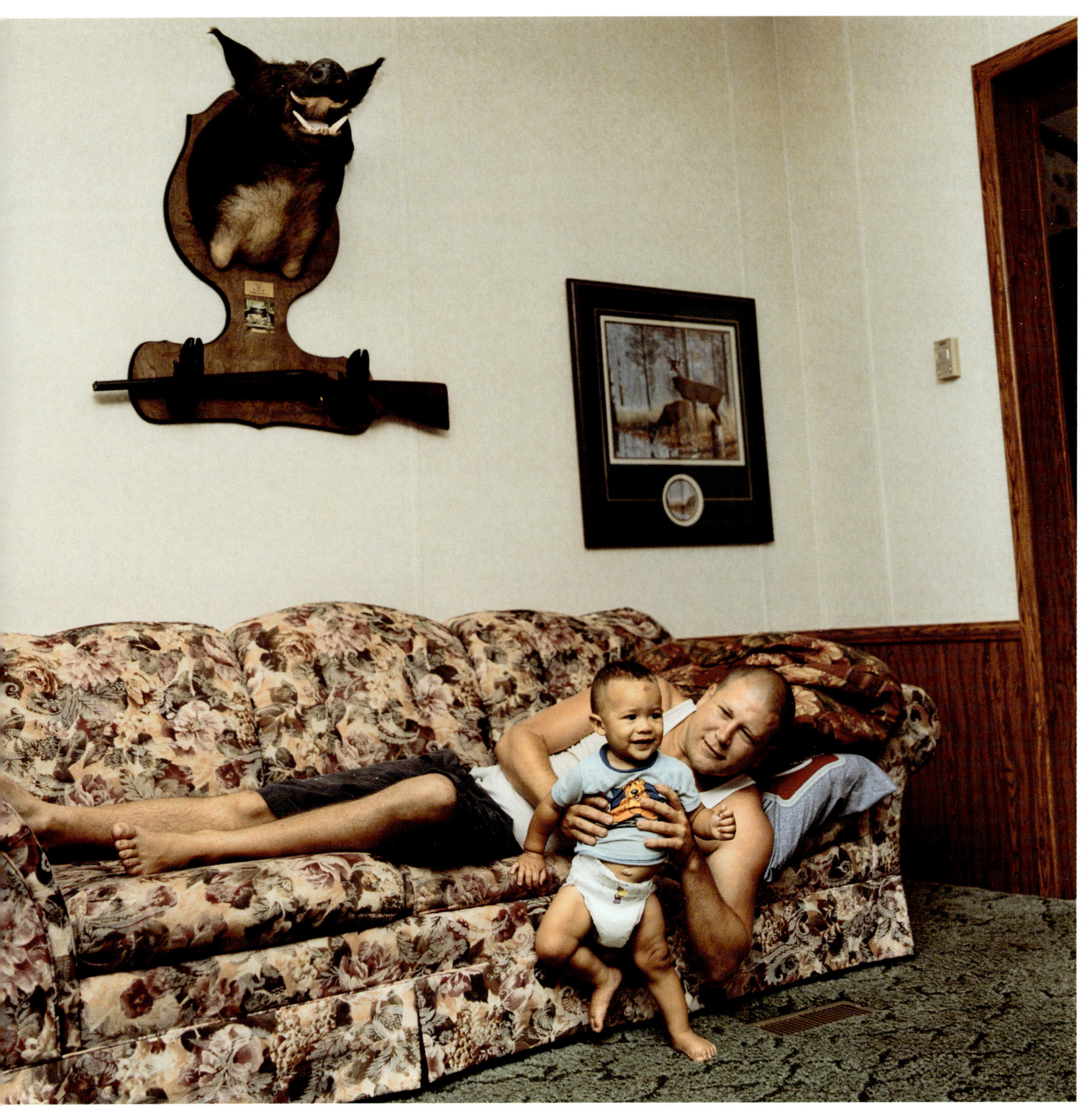

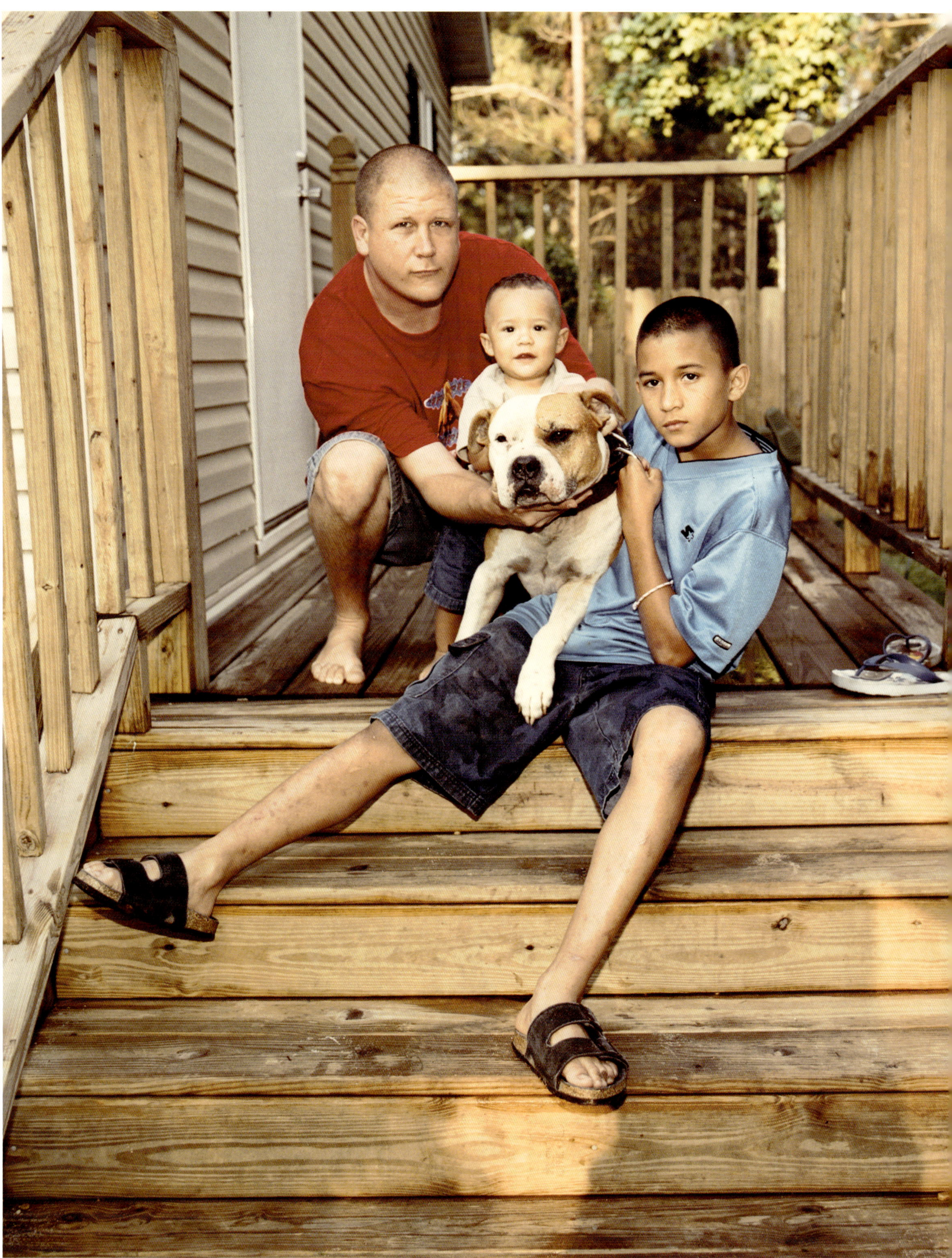

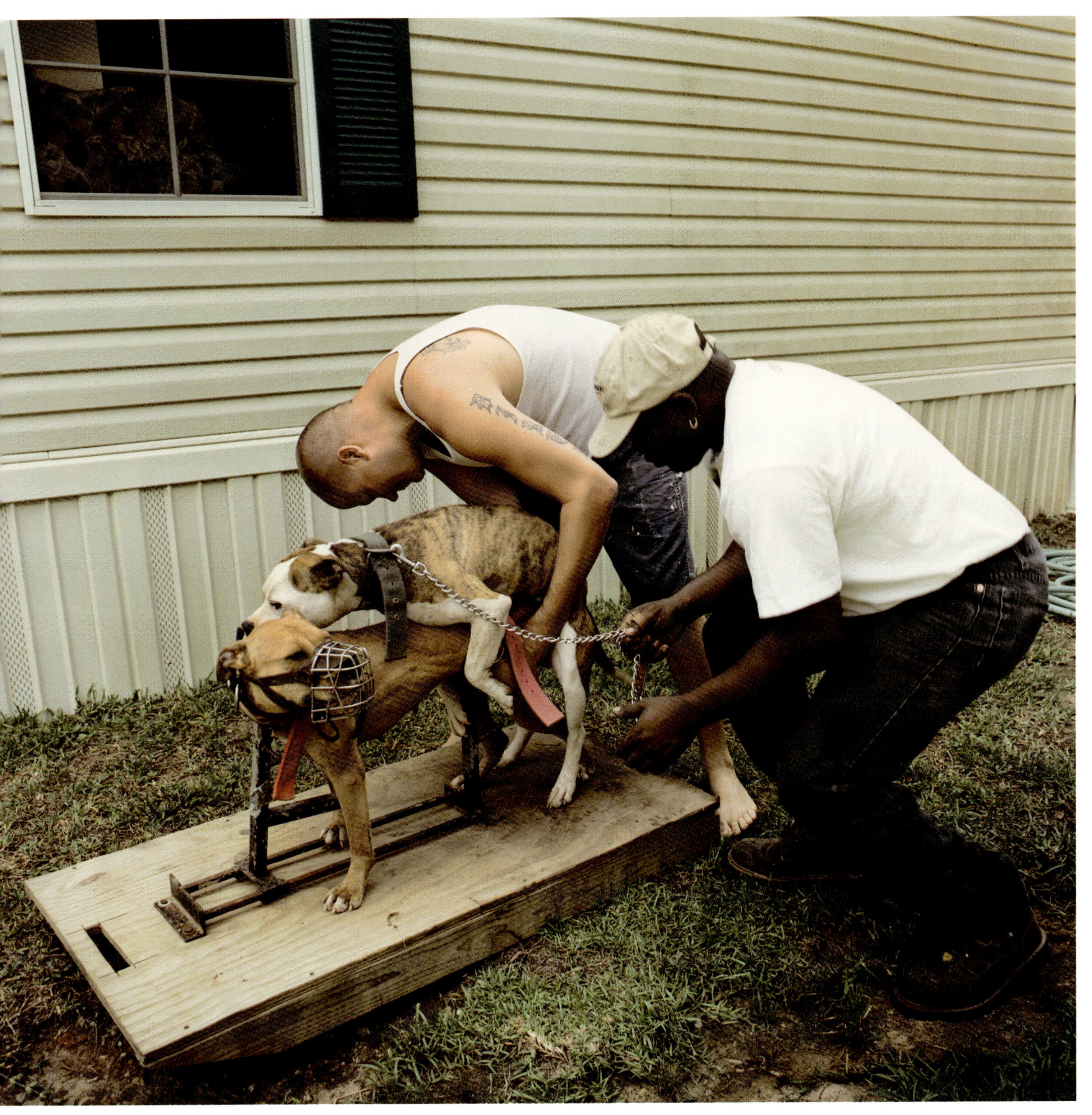

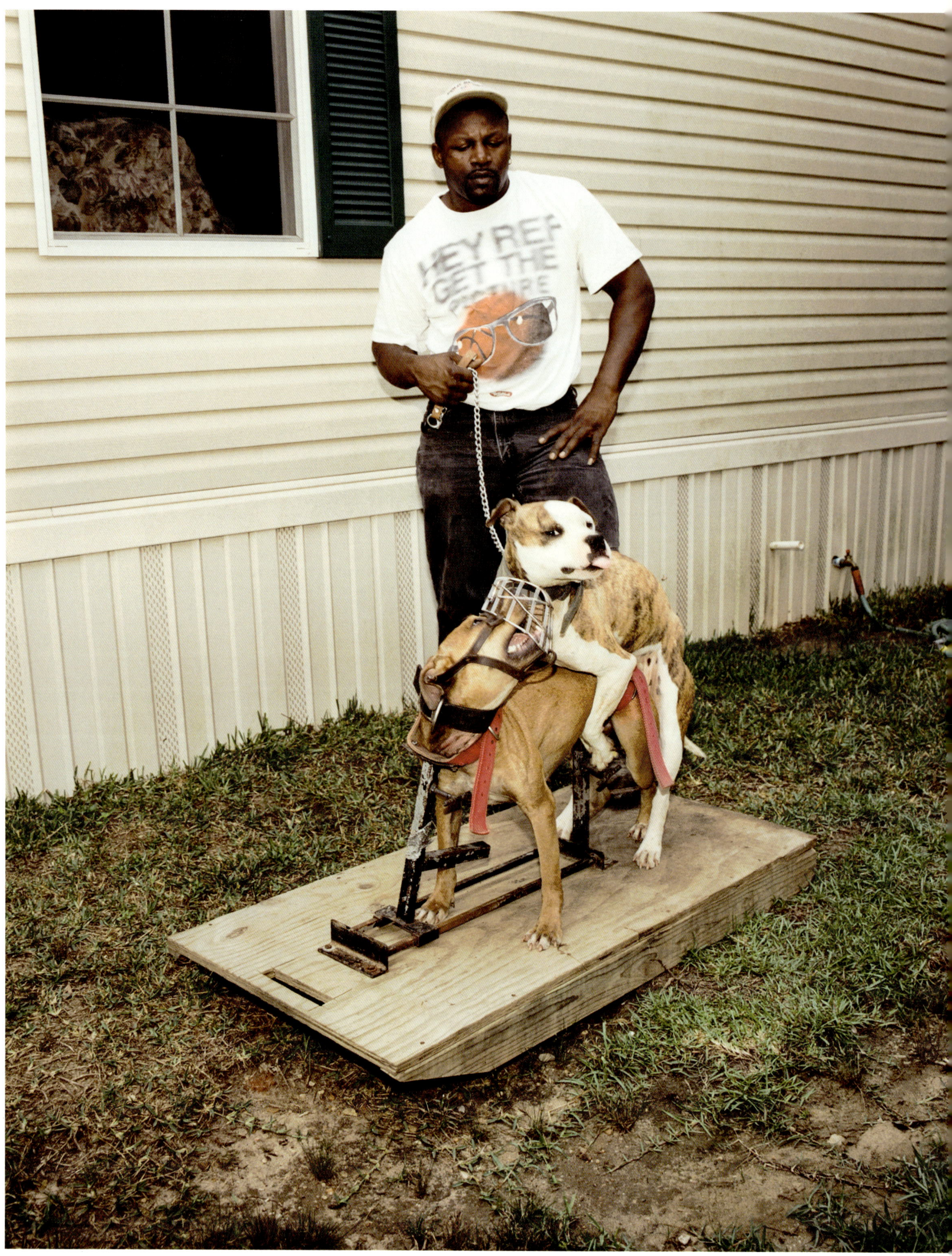
HEY REF
GET THE

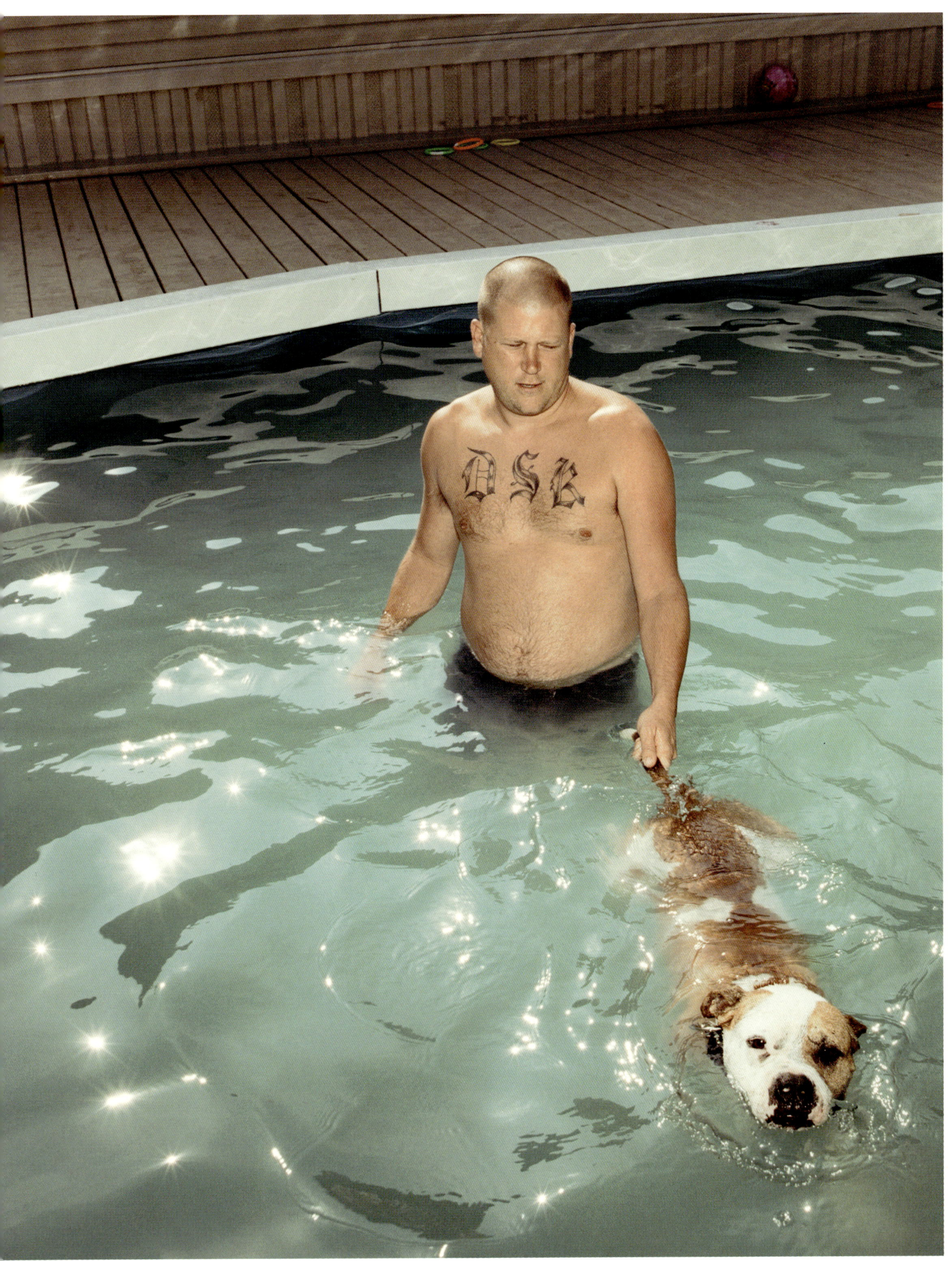
DSK

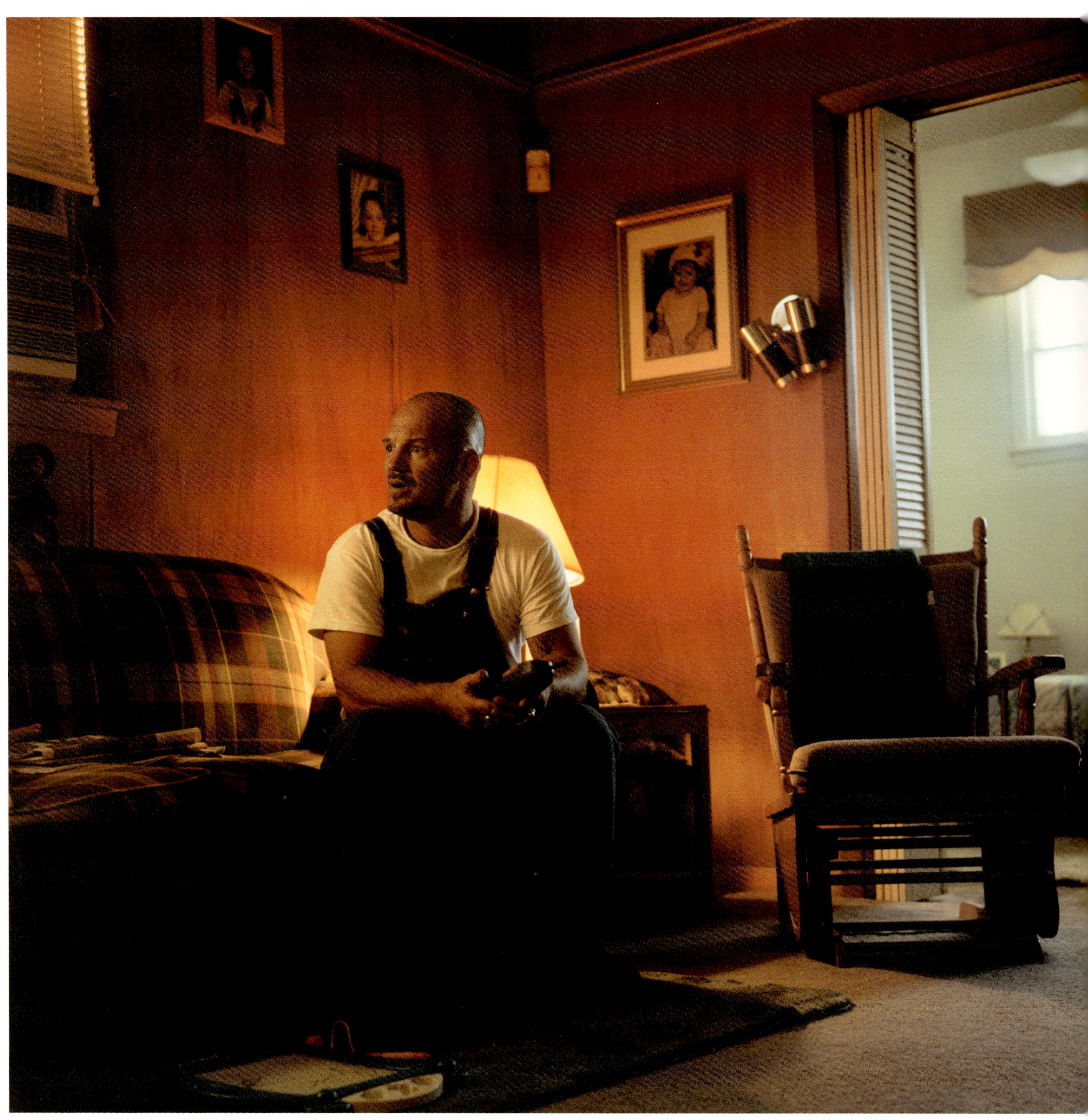

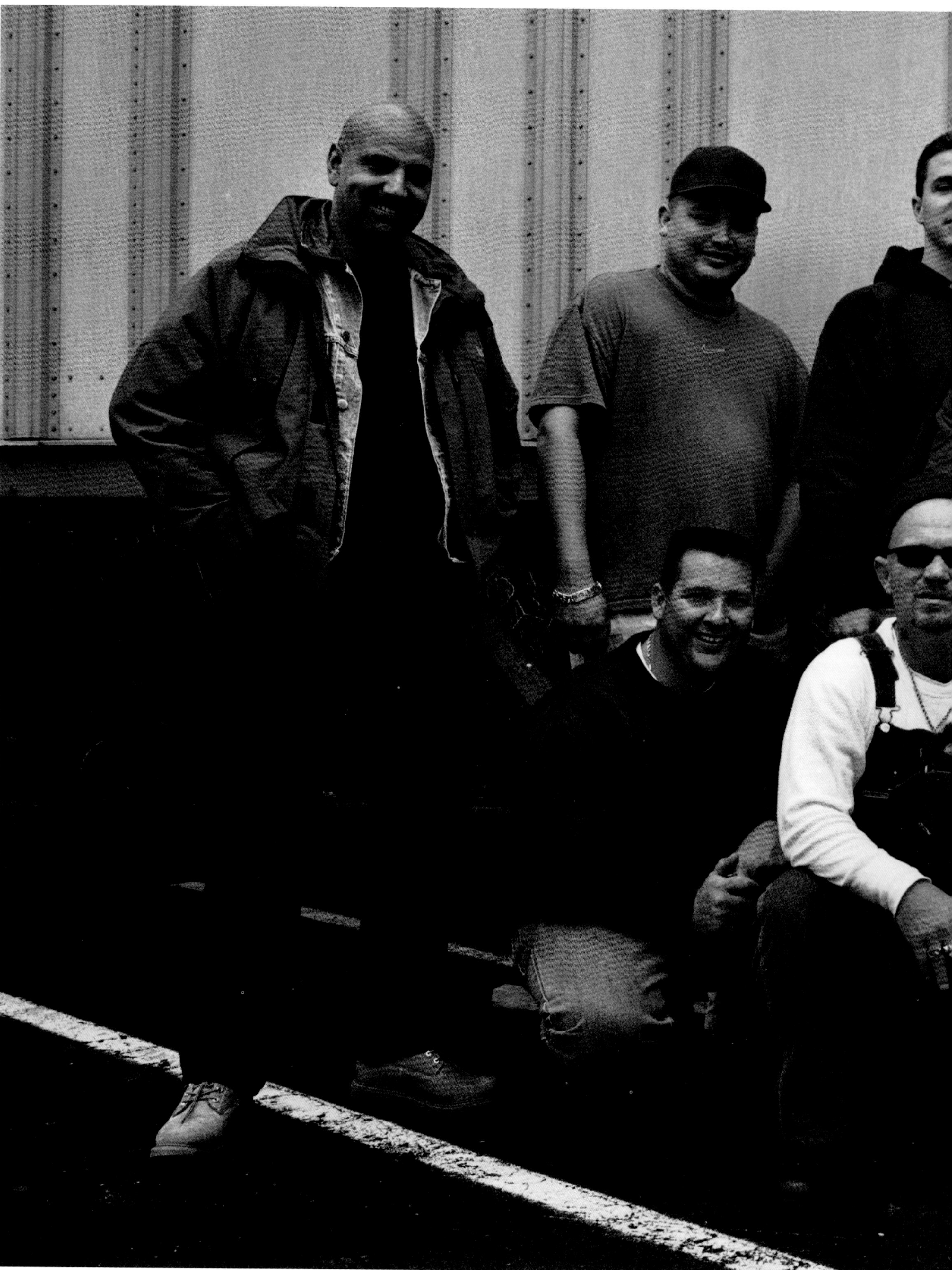

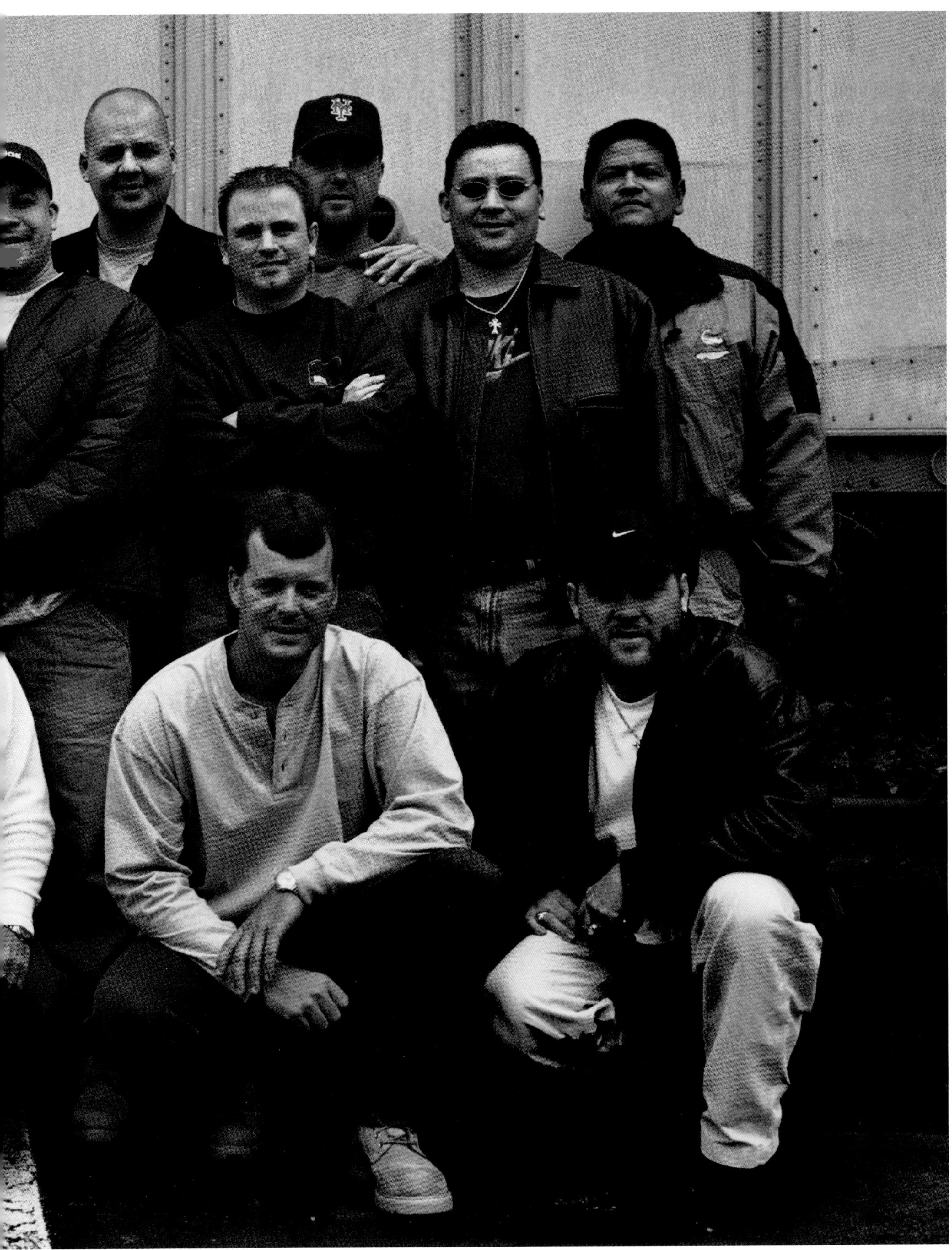

Joaquin Dean is the brilliant and restless mind behind the Ruff Ryder music empire. Since founding the company in 1988, he has led the label to meteoric success with hip-hop recording artists such as Eve, DMX, and others—most of whom share his passion for American Pit Bull Terriers.

• It started with some stray dogs that I found in the back of the woods behind my building when I was seven years old. I tied them up with some string right next to the flower pots. I used to live on the third floor, on top of Cool Herc, who was one of the guys who started hip-hop with Grandmaster Flash back in the day. Cool Herc used to play a lot of loud music, and our room was over his. His brother and I used to feed the dogs from his window. This was in the Bronx, back when hip-hop and break dancing were just starting up.

• ...and then I thought, "I better get loose. I'll get two more, three more..." Then I got into the Pits. I got my first ones from a bum off the street—he had puppies—and they were some of the best Pits I ever had. "Lady" and "Man." I was only about fourteen or fifteen. At the time, I was working with my pops in his warehouse, and I used to hide the dogs on the third floor. See, my father had his own business; he distributed fish to different stores within the five boroughs of New York. He was an entrepreneur, and I grew up in that spirit. You know, we aren't too good at working for nobody—we don't do that too well. So anyway, my father didn't know the dogs were up there. I only brought them out at night. Then one day they got loose and he couldn't get into the warehouse to open up his business in the morning. The dogs were growling. He didn't really like that.

• After we got the Pits out of there, I started living at his house. Fortunately or unfortunately, I brought two more dogs in his house. I told him, "The dogs are part of Ruff Ryder. It's what we represent... You gotta respect that." My father said, "I don't gotta respect nothing. You gonna get these dogs out of here!" Everything I would do, he would knock it. I'd be like, "I'm doing this rap thing." He'd say, "You're doing this rap thing! You're cursing, you got the dogs in here, you're breaking down my house. You have my wife mad at me... Good for nothing!... You're really taking this too far." I told him not to worry about it, that I'd make it up to him. It took a while, but he's convinced now. He's even into hip-hop. I was kind of shocked to see him crossing over into the field, you know?

• I got a team of guys who work with the breed. Blue Pits, all-black Pits, different blood lines. We're formulating our celebrity dog crew right now. X is a dog lover like me—DMX. We got pretty much the same blood. We give dogs away to some people, and we sell some off of the web... When it's all over, you'll probably catch me out on the farm. My fiancé, she's not too good with all this. I tore her mom's house up with all the dogs—every room had a dog in it. You've got to really have the love for them. If you've got love for the dogs, you've got love for me. If you can't take the dogs, you can't take me. It's a blessing to be with them. People who really have love for animals have instant love for life.

• I'm real busy right now, but the dogs fit in my program every day. They live in my house on all levels. So when I come in, the first thing I smell is dogs. All I can say is, Pit Bulls are real good dogs. I'd die before I'd get rid of any of my dogs. They do their time on earth and when it's time to leave I bury them. Or, the last crew I buried. The next crew, I'm gonna stuff 'em.

JOAQUIN DEAN President and CEO, Ruff Ryder Records, Rockland County, New York

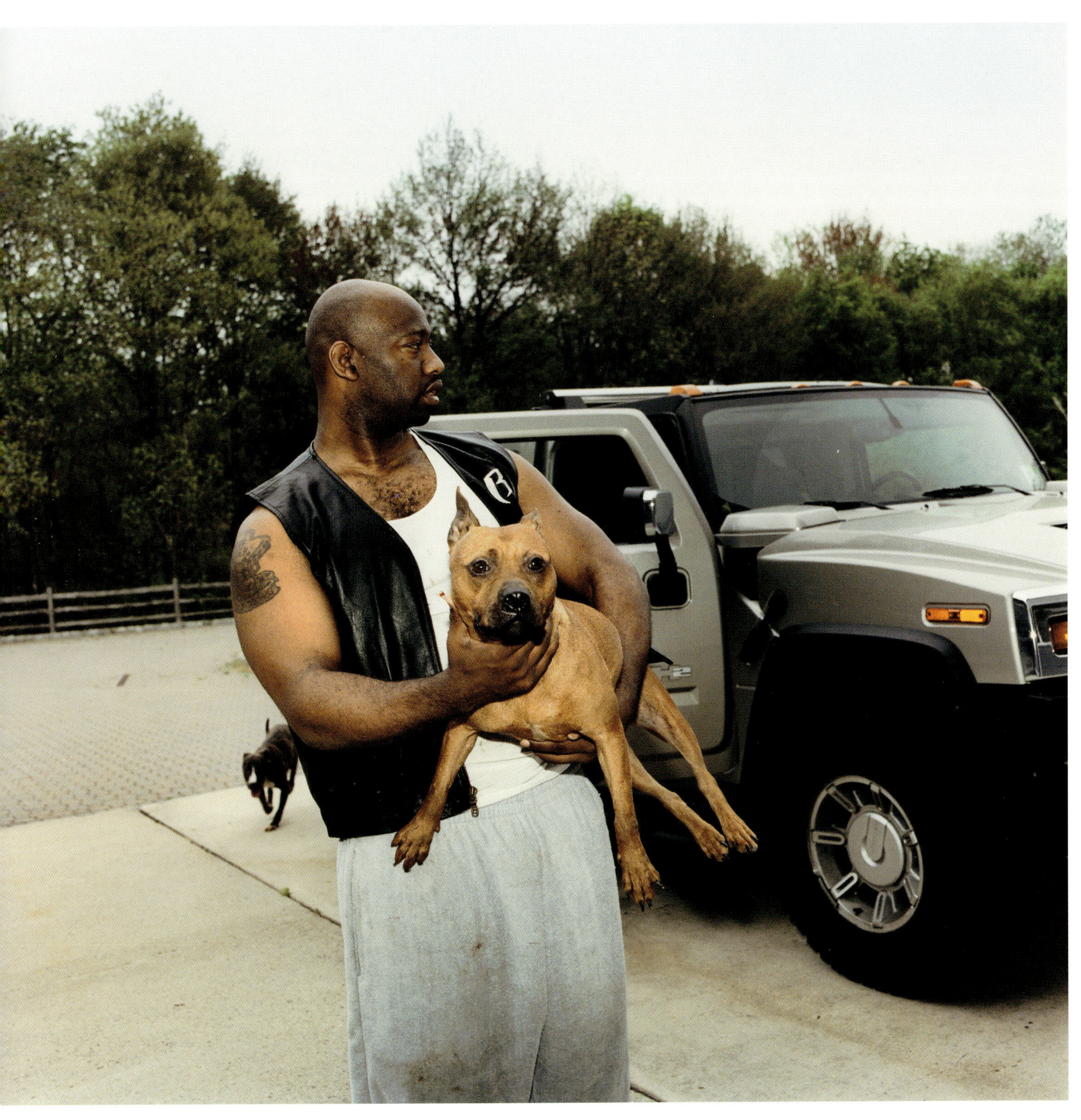

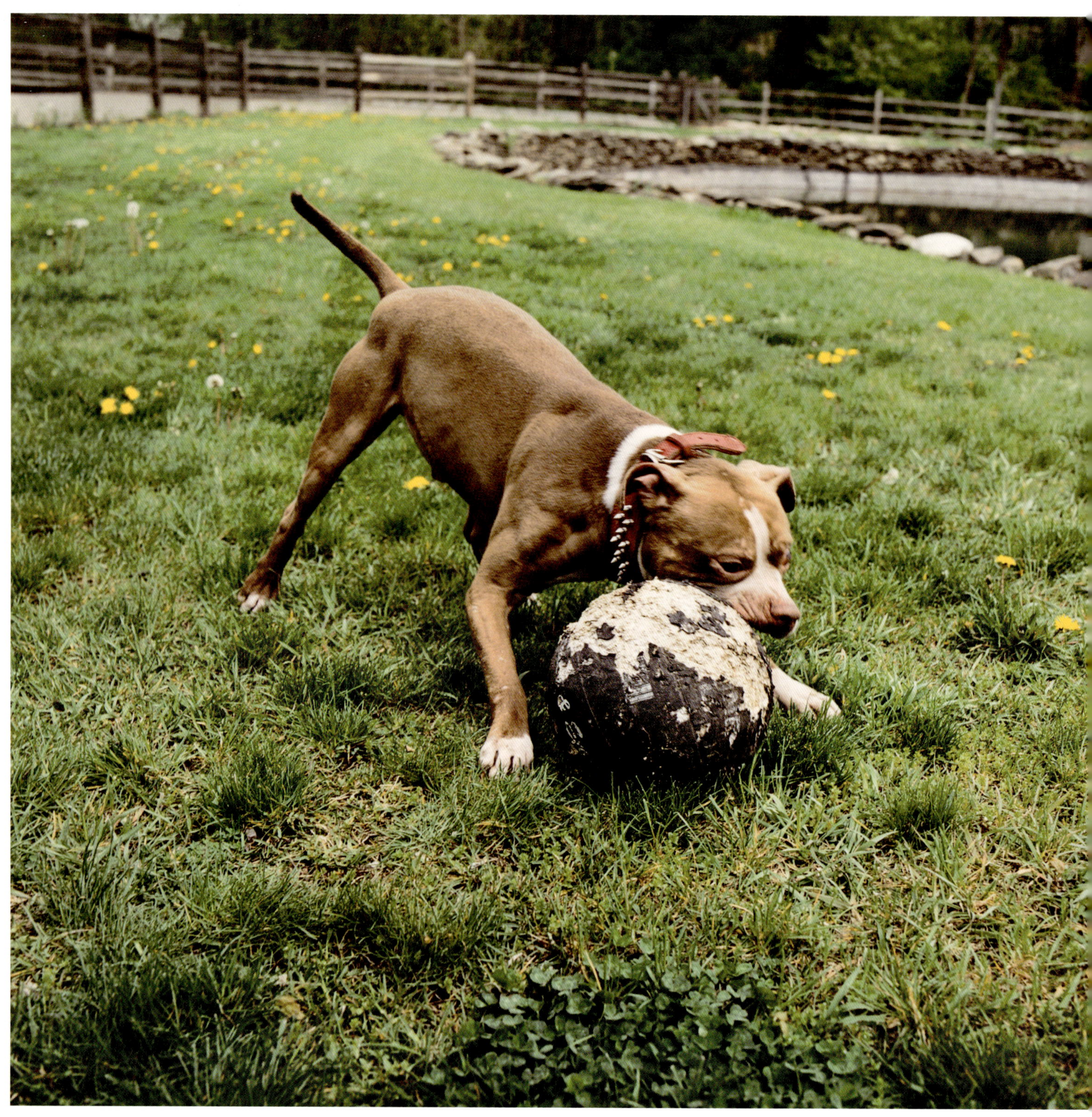

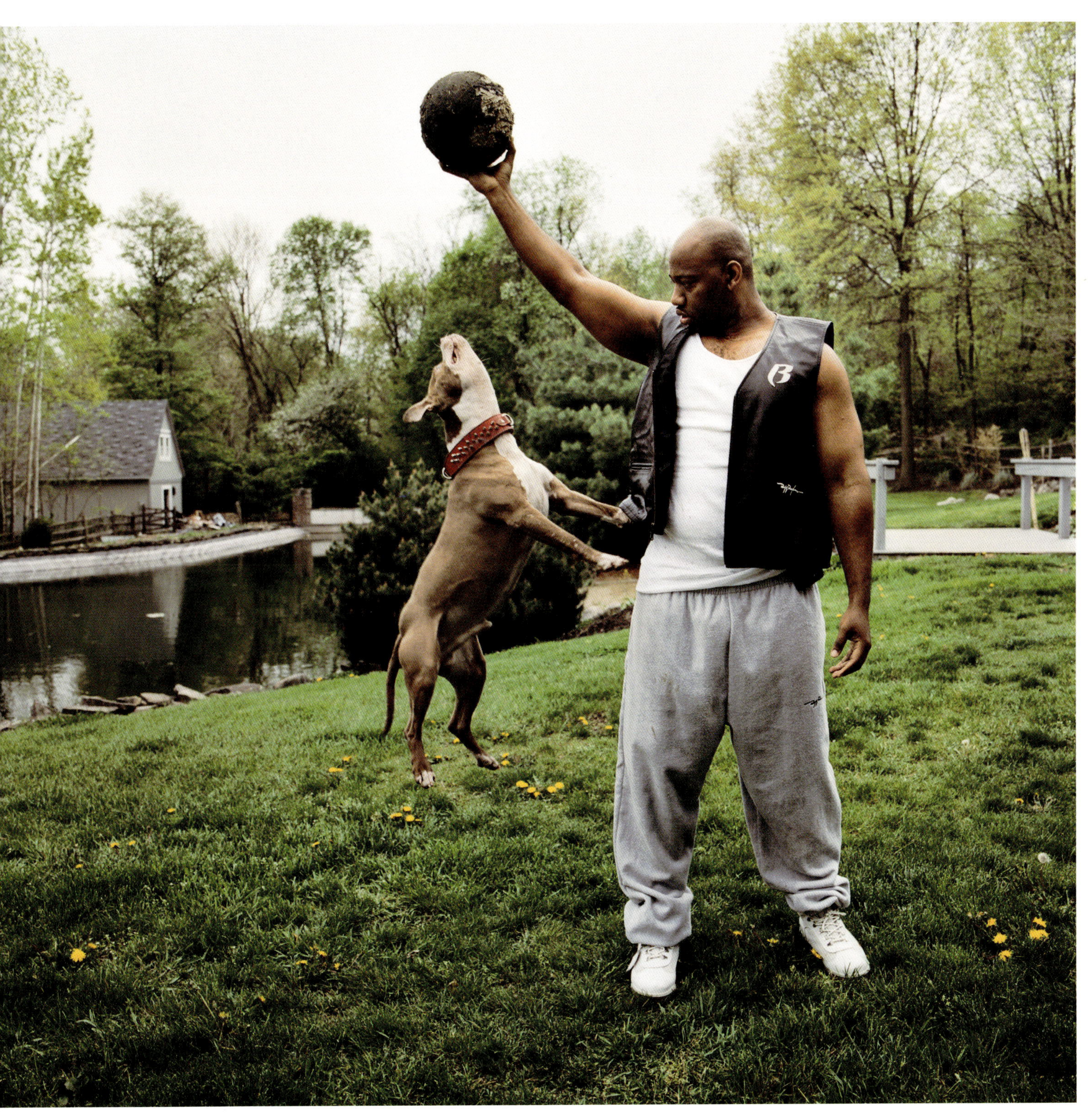

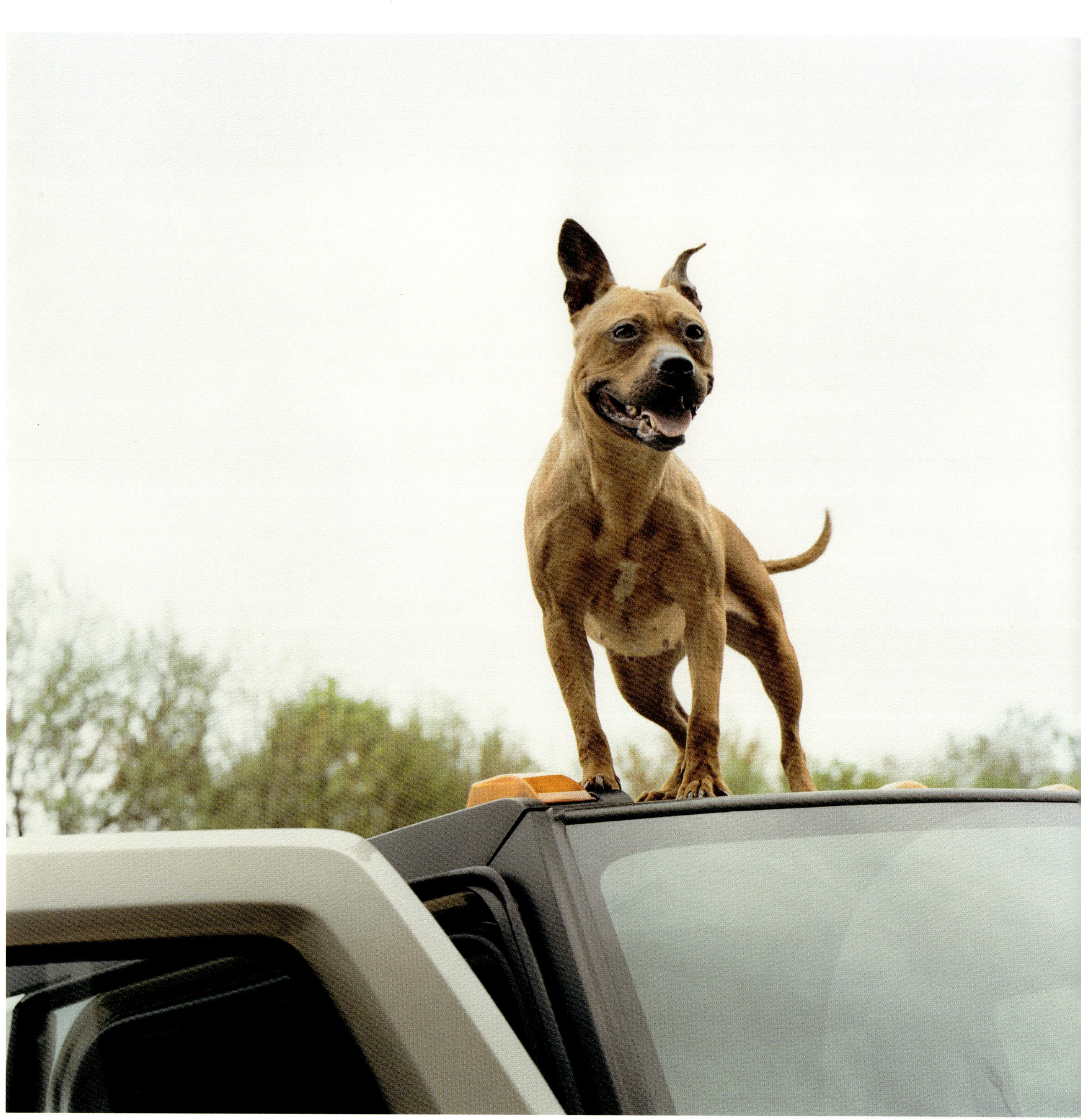

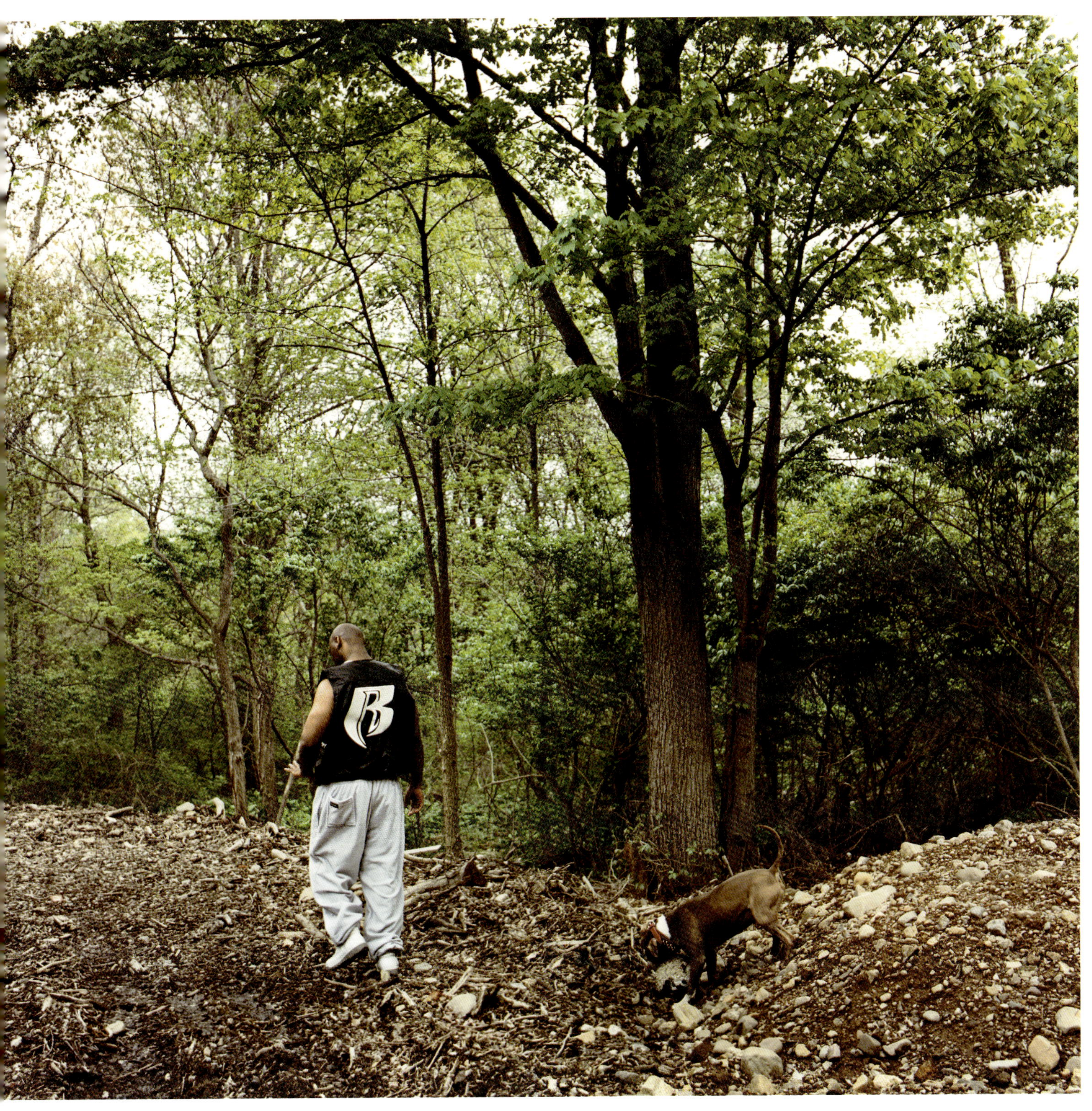

Jacqueline Wakefield-Jones is the proprietor of Forbidden Forest Kennels and the President of the Pennsylvania Bull and Terrier Association. A certified professional veterinary technologist, she has been breeding and showing Pit Bull Terriers for almost twenty years.

• I'm a vet tech. I used to work for a veterinarian who raised English Bulldogs. One day somebody traded this vet his pickup truck cab for a little red-and-white Pit Bull. So he started to come in every day with this little puppy on a string, and I used to think, "Boy, this dog is pretty." Then one day he came in and said, "Well, I'm going to have to find a home for her or I'm going to have to put her down." I asked why, and he said, "She's not starting any fights at the house—the English Bulldogs are—but she's sure finishing them. And I get $1500 for a pet-grade puppy, so I can't have this Pit Bull beating up on my Bulldogs." So I said, "I think I'd like to have one." That's seventeen or eighteen years ago. Right now I have more than twenty!

• The dog shows have always been family friendly. I don't want to lump people together, but a lot of Pit Bull people are middle or working class and don't have a ton of money. So when there's a show, everybody in the family goes, and so do all the dogs, including the housedogs! I used to show Rottweilers before I got into Pit Bulls, but I didn't like the political red tape that went along with the American Kennel Club. You've got to have your pleated skirt and your blazer—it was too much for me. So when I got my first Pit Bull and found out about the shows, I got bit by the bug, big time.

• We keep the dogs in kennels and chain spaces—because we have enough space for that. Dogs on chains actually make out better than kennel dogs because they get twenty feet in either direction, whereas our kennels are about eight feet by twelve feet. Of course, it all depends on the dog—we have a couple that just will not take to being on the chain. Either way, we go through *serious* straw. I mean, my compost pile is the size of a barn! This is a short-coated dog, so when it's cold out you have to really pack the doghouses so that there's very little space for the dog. They curl up in there and make a nest and heat the space around them. A dog's body temperature is higher than ours and they can take the cold better than we can. But still, they track the hay down and chafe it. So you gotta take the chafed, wet, and muddy straw and you gotta replace it regularly. It's a real production.

• The people who want to use these dogs as protection for their homes are misinformed. They're just not protection dogs. I mean, you could walk up to just about any dog in my yard and say, "Come on, let's go for a ride," and it would jump in the car and go with you. In fact, I have an American Bull Dog in my house because my Pit Bulls stink as watchdogs! They'll bark, but they're just not human aggressive.

• However, they are animal aggressive. And not everybody is prepared to have the sixth sense, or the third eye. For example, if you take this breed on a walk through the woods, you've still got to have him on lead. And even when you have him on lead, you still have to be extremely vigilant because it's the Golden Retriever that *isn't* on lead that runs up and gets you in trouble. It's not your fault if your dog snaps at another dog that's running loose, but ... you have to be very responsible since you'll always be perceived as the bad guy because you have the Pit Bull.

JACQUELINE WAKEFIELD-JONES Berks County, Pennsylvania

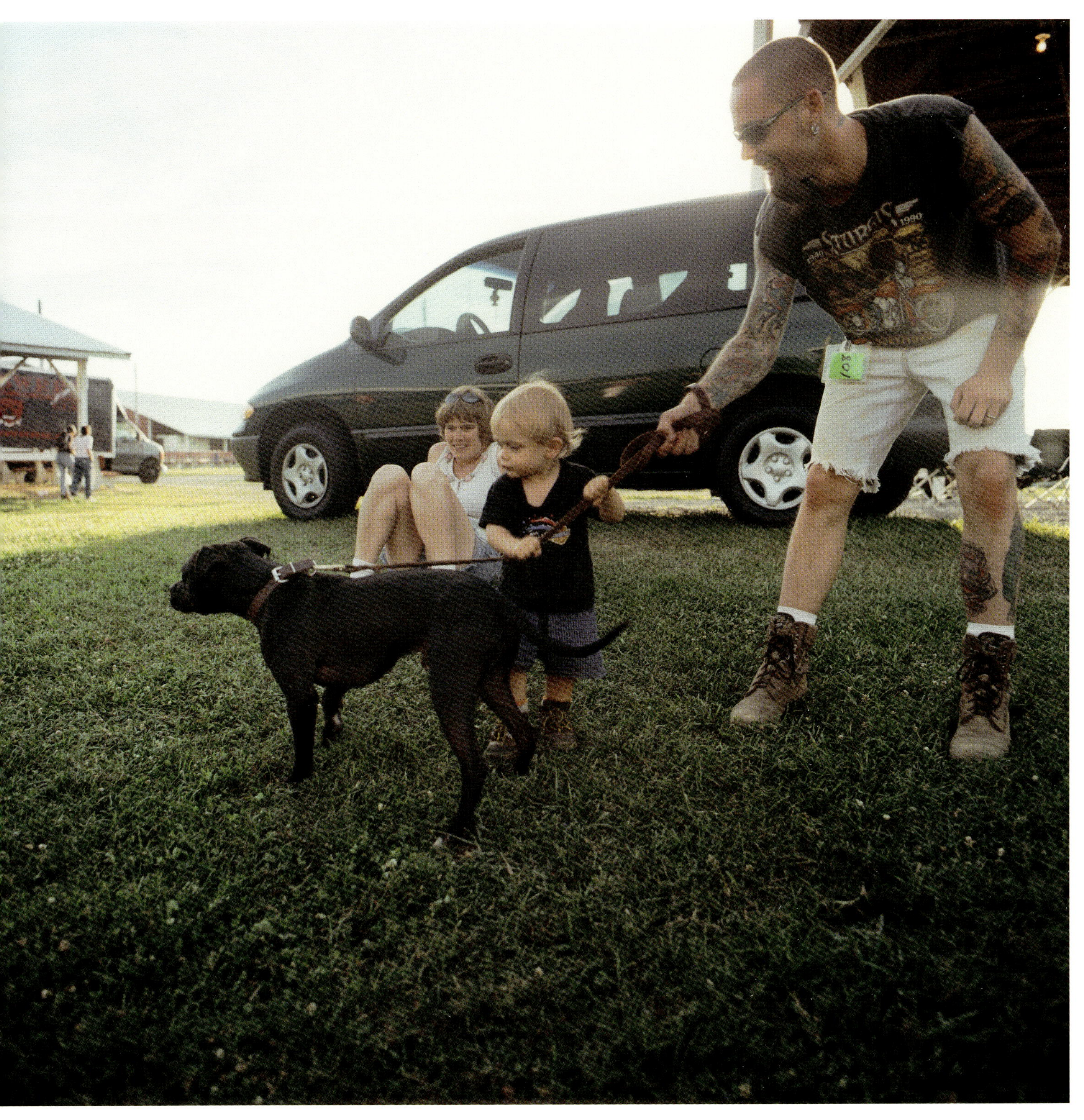
1940
Sturgis
1990

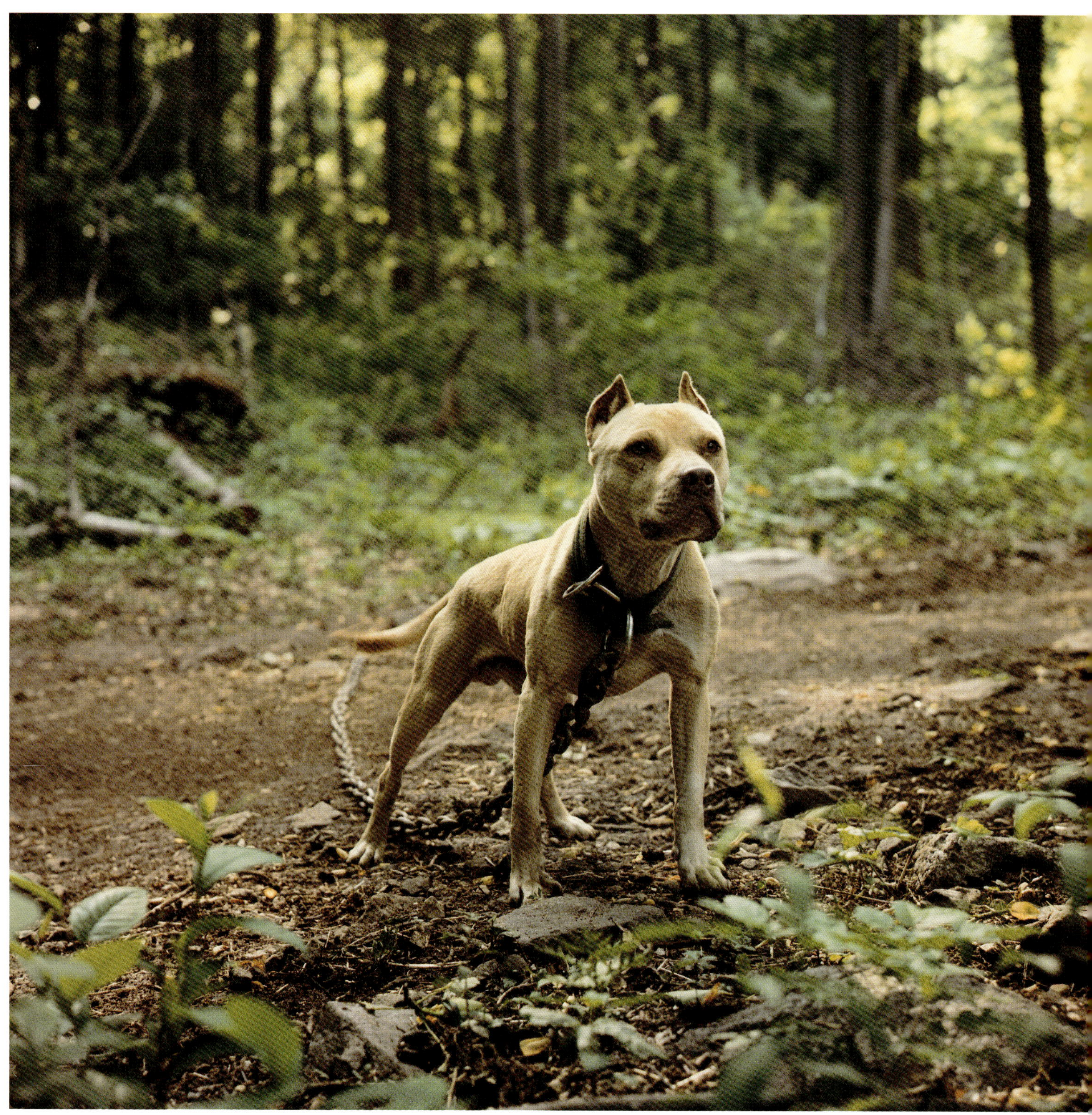

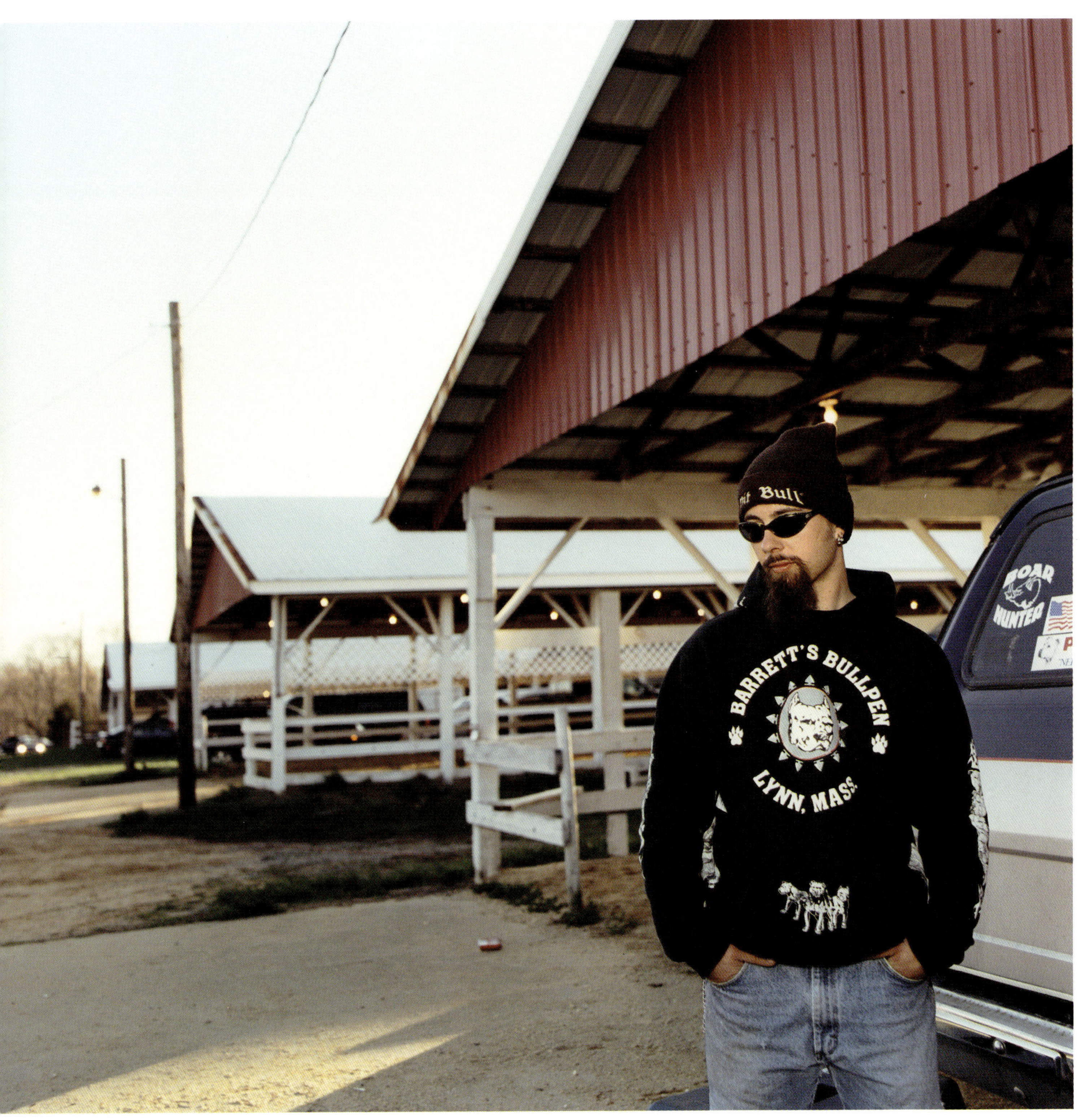
BARRETT'S BULLPEN
LYNN, MASS.
BOAR HUNTER

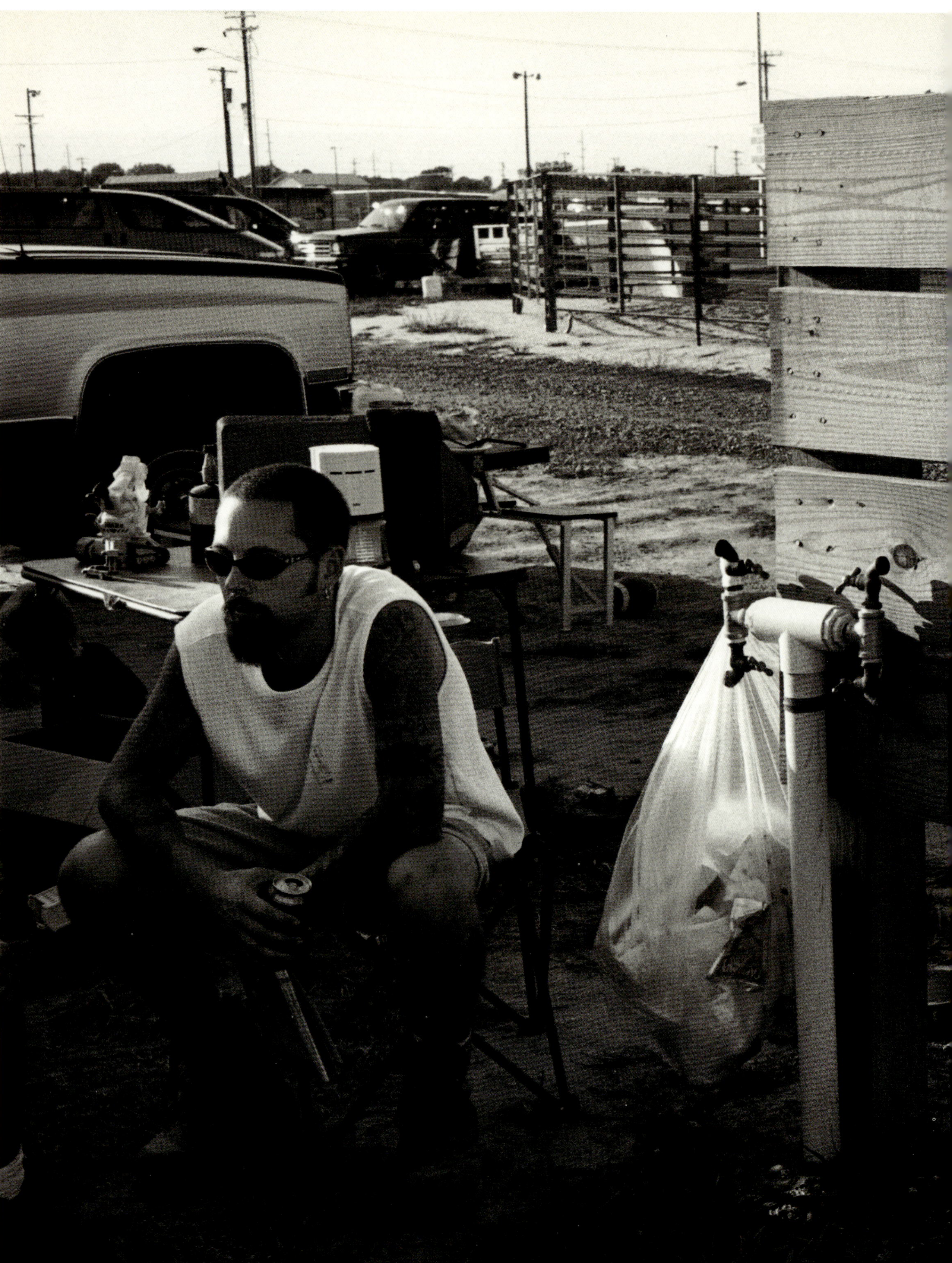

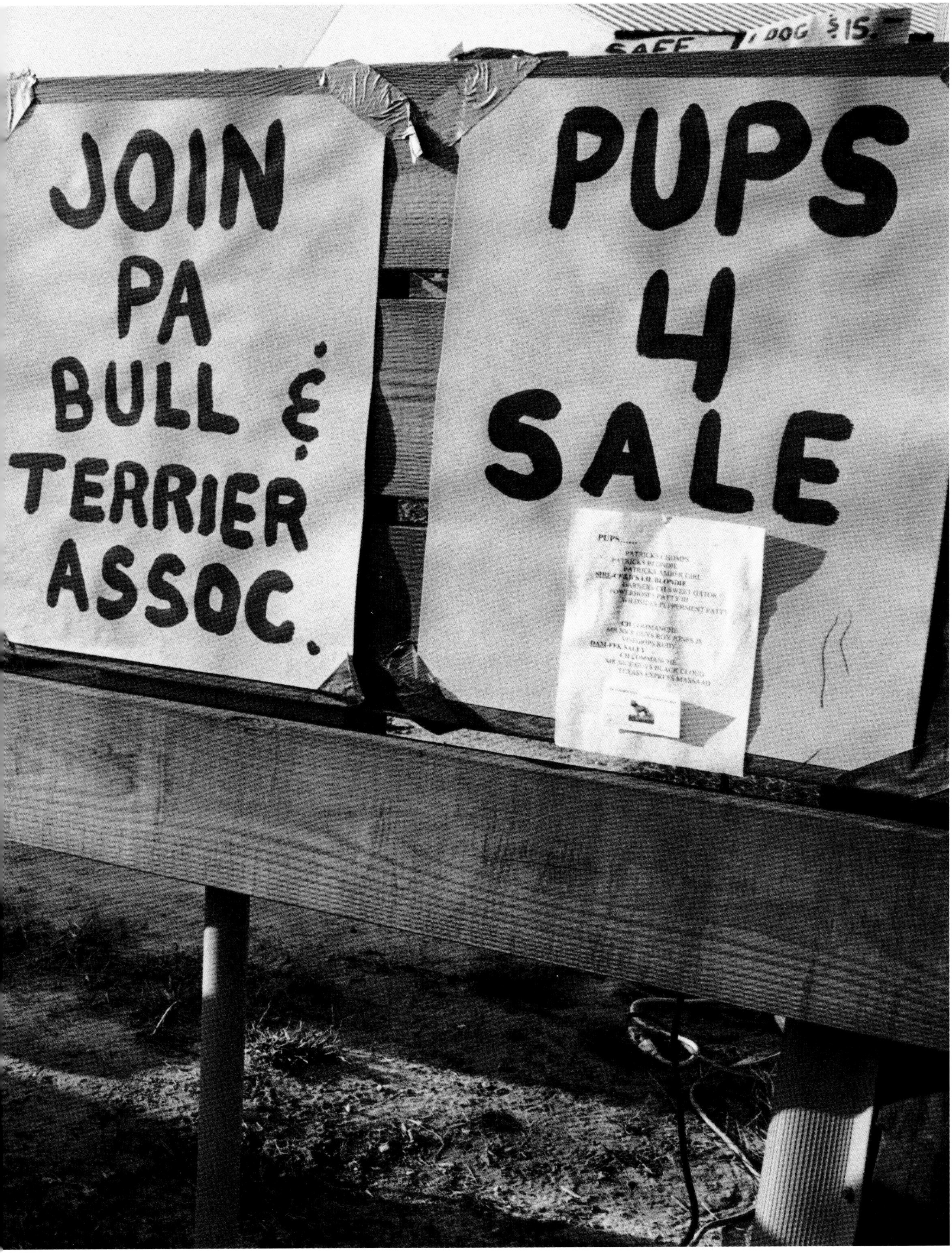

JOIN
PA
BULL &
TERRIER
ASSOC.
PUPS
4
SALE

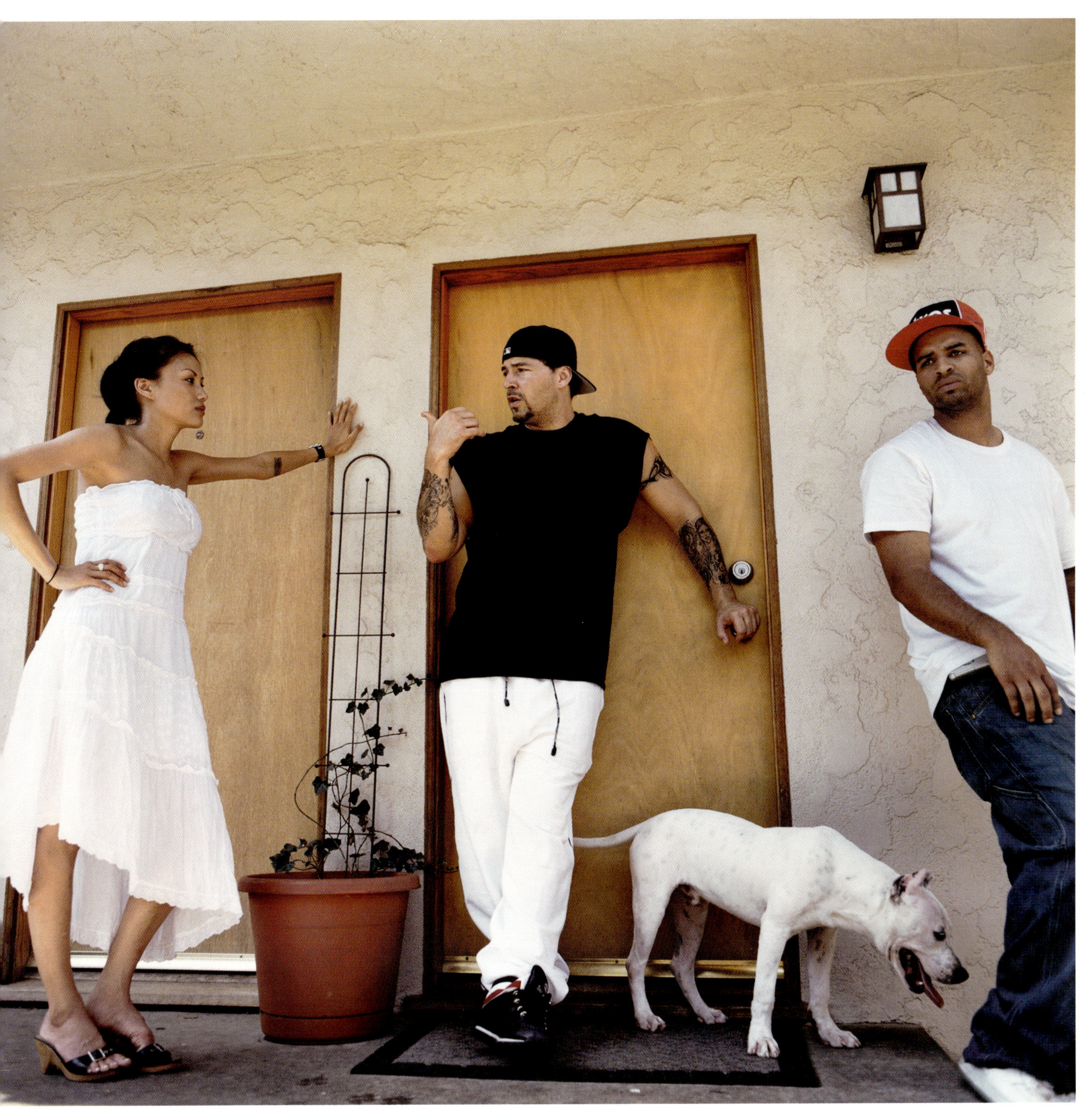

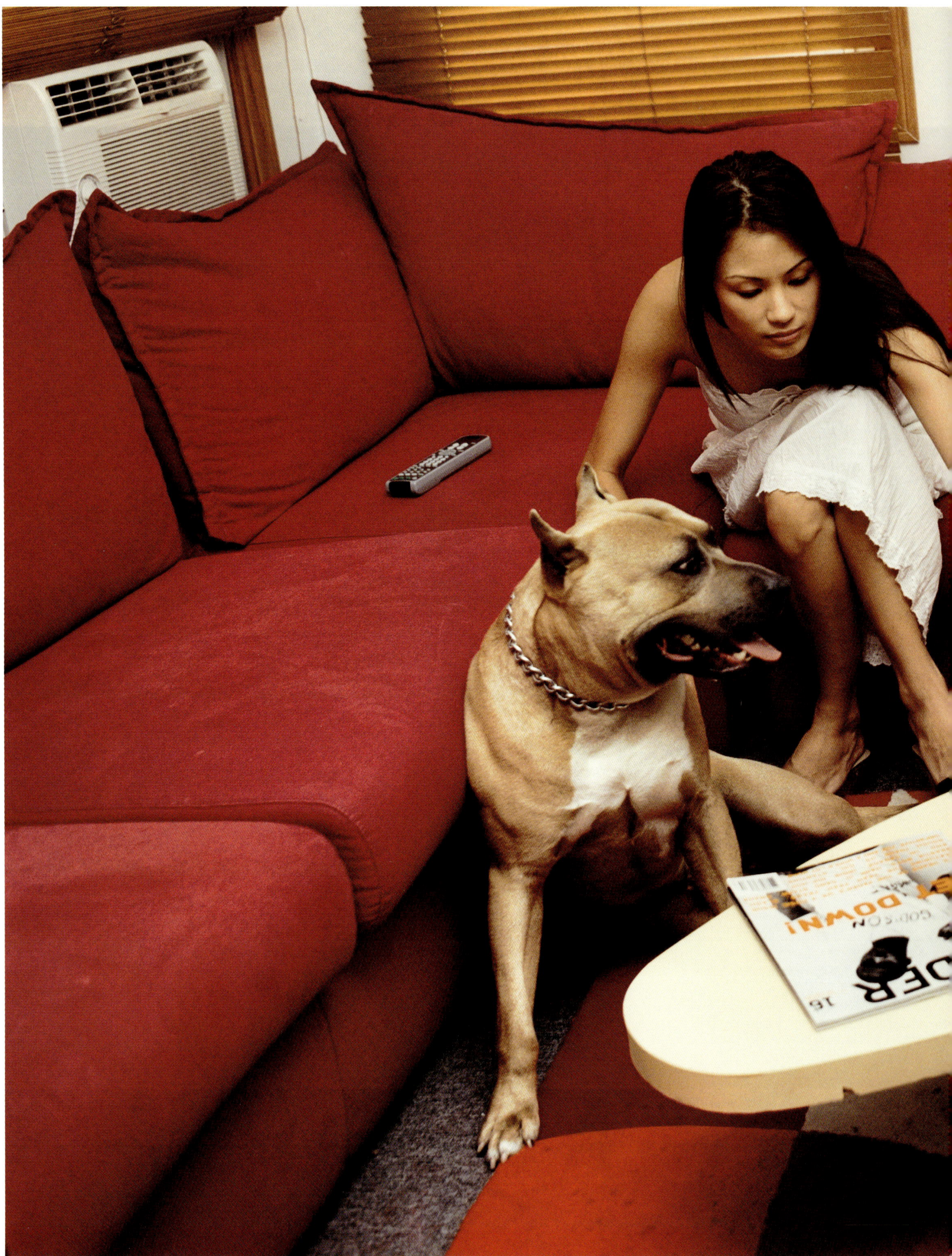

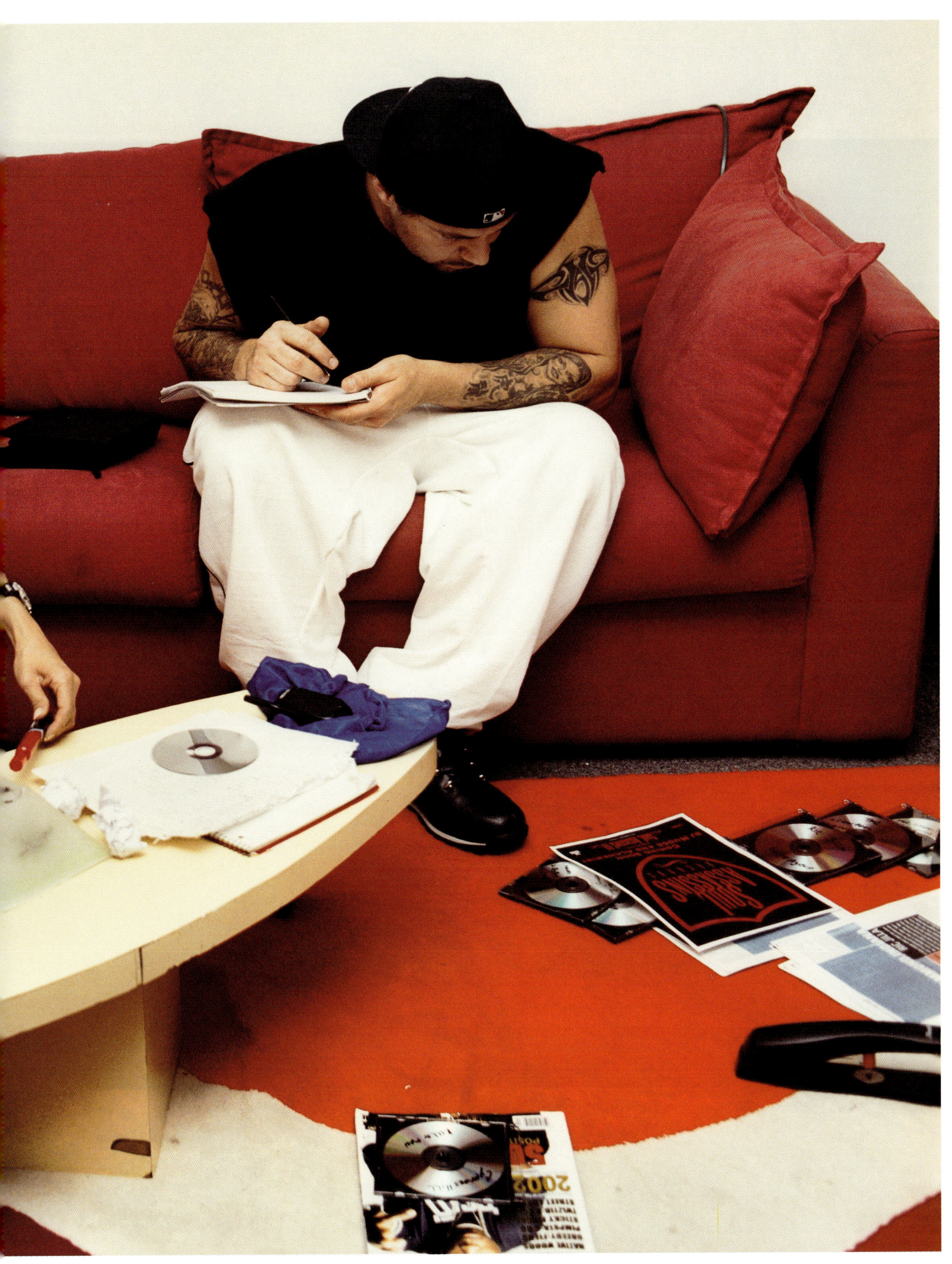

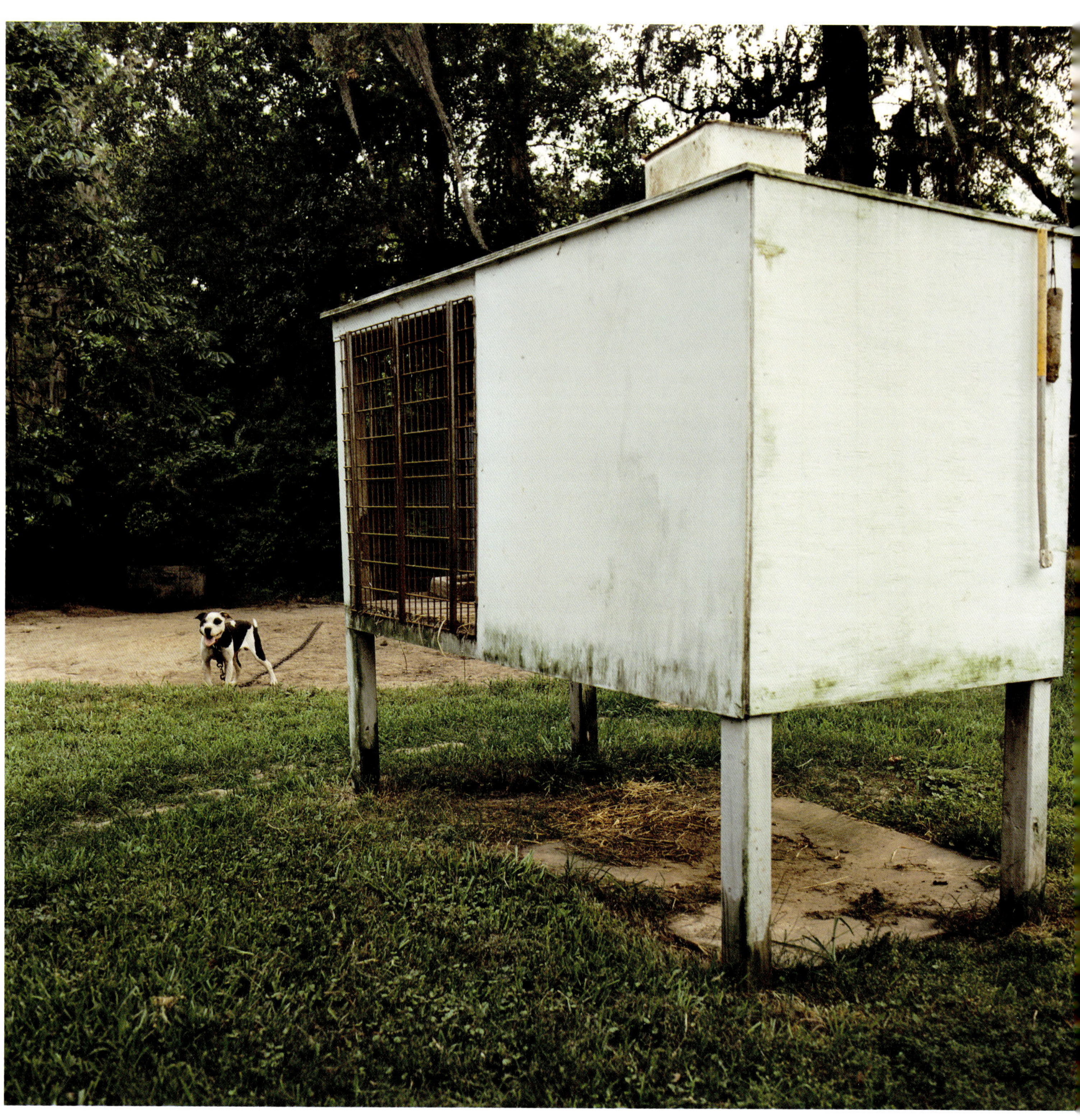

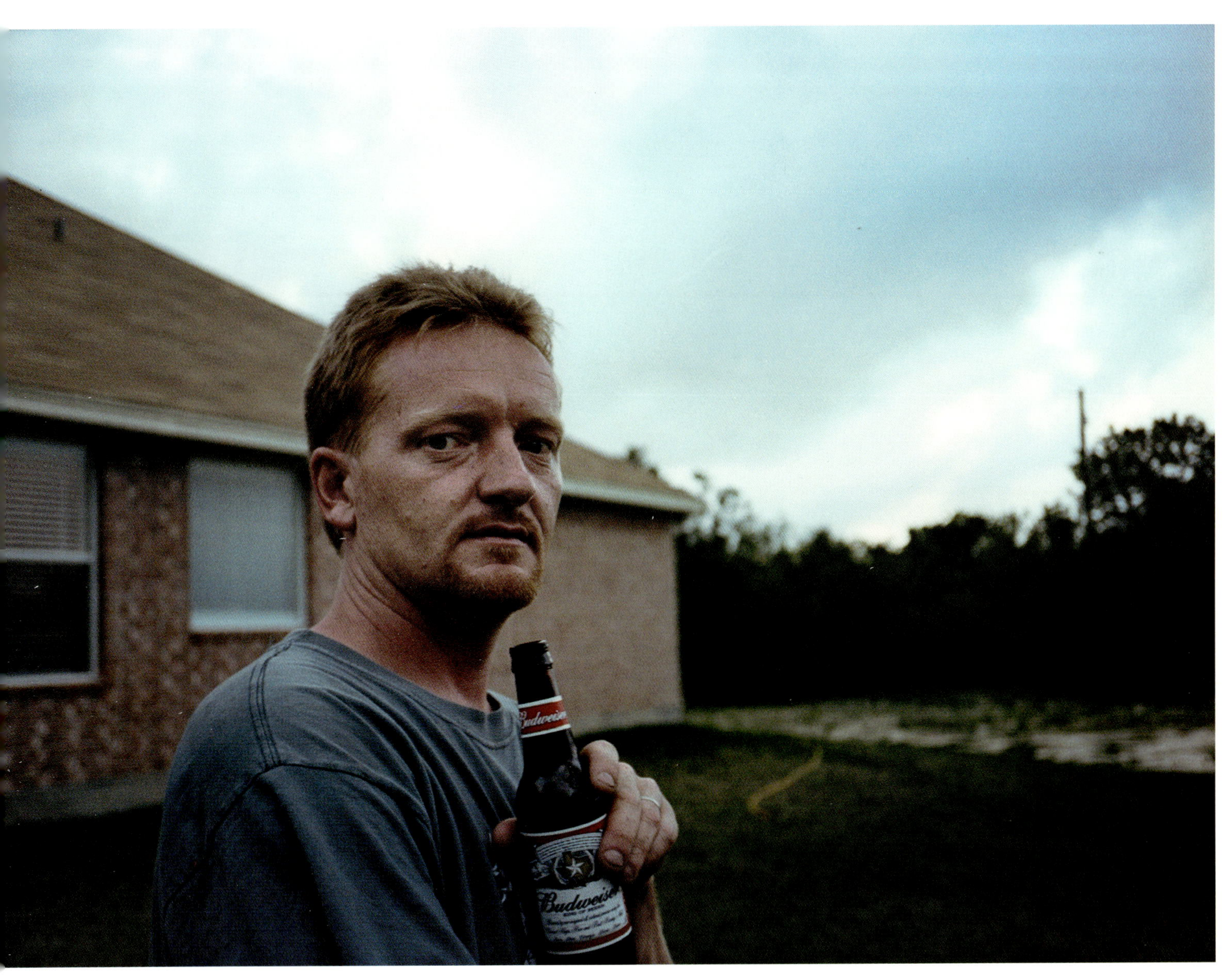
Budweiser

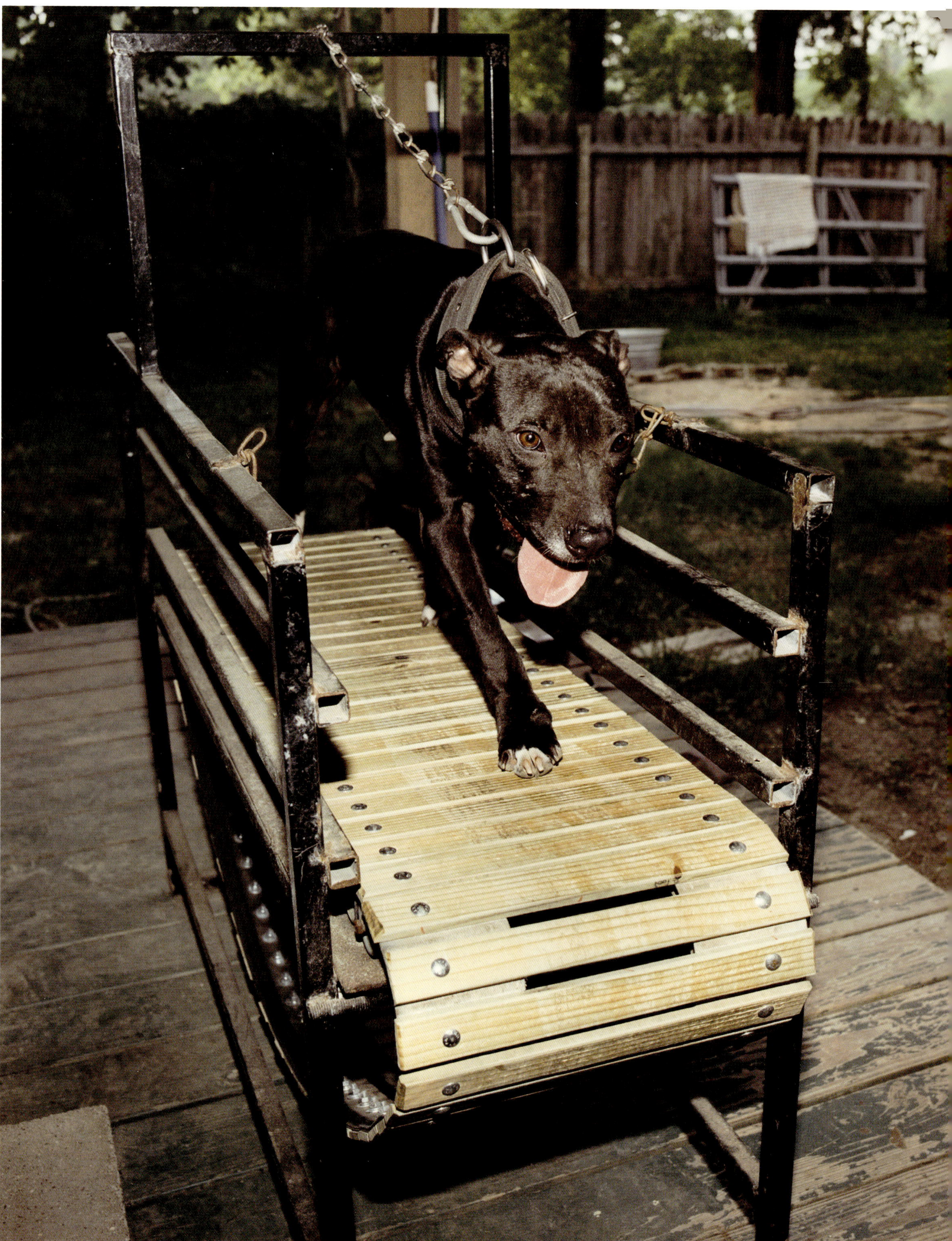

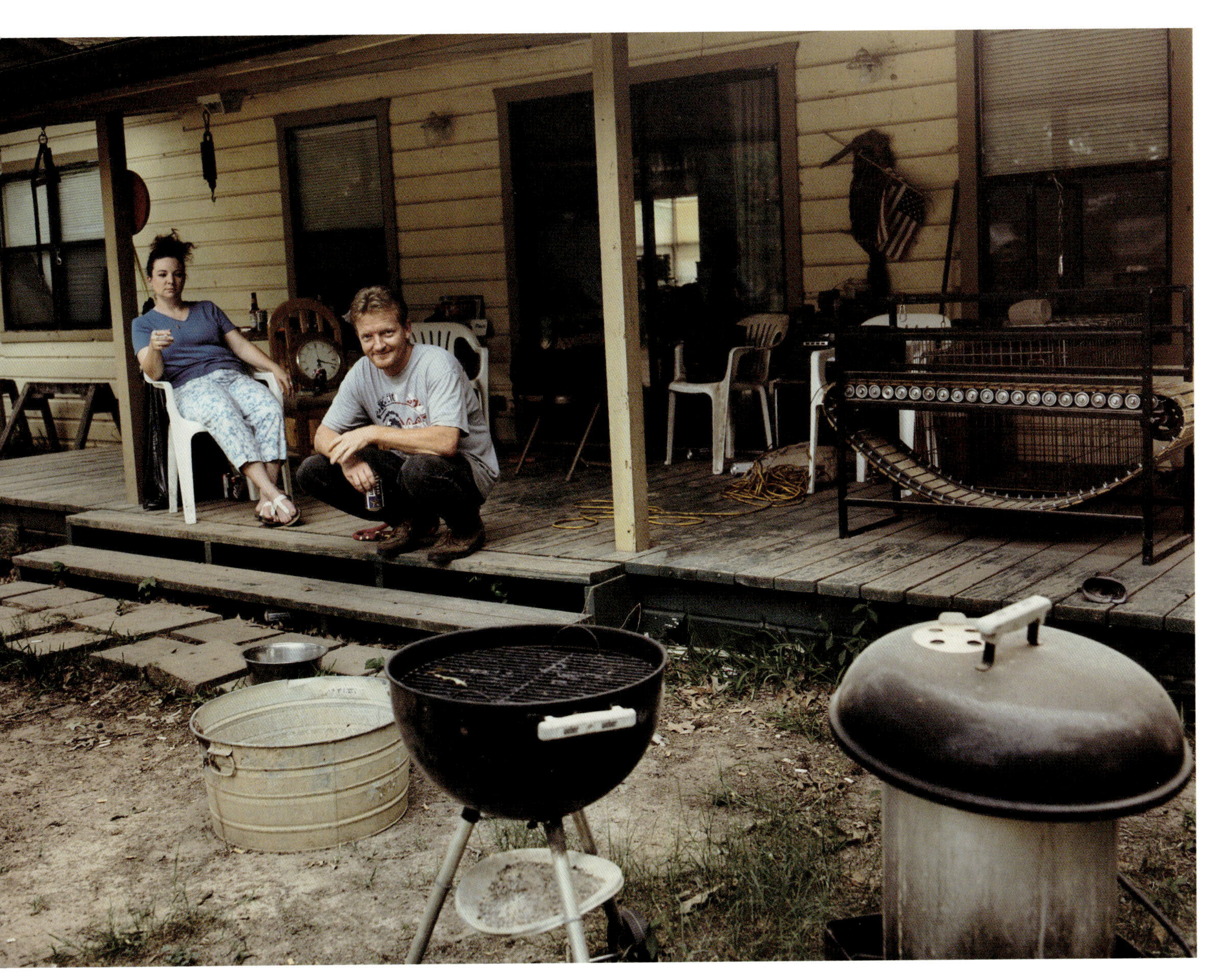

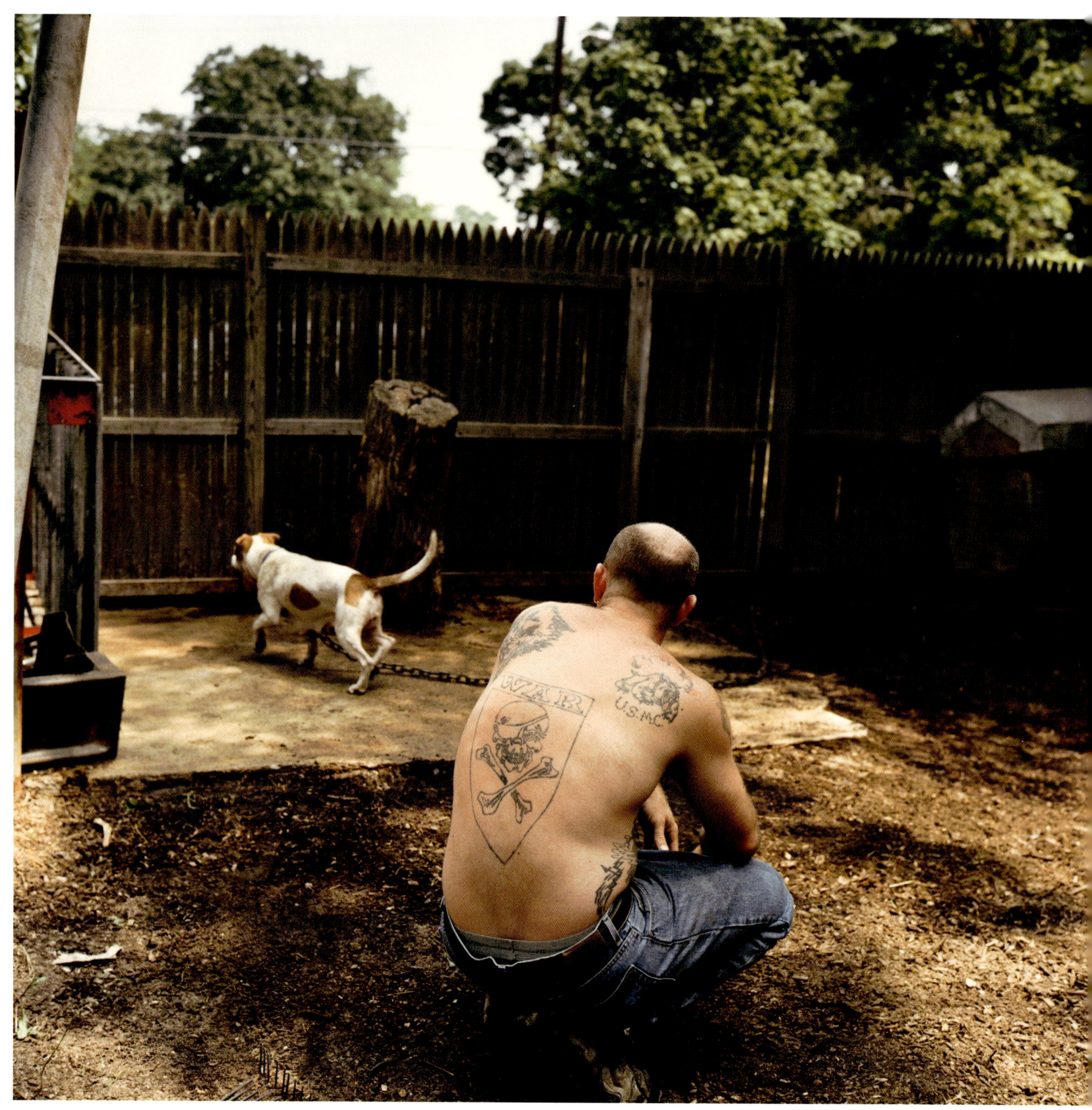
WAR
U.S.M.C.

Joe and Lucretia Ashcraft live with their dogs on lush forest land in the heart of east Texas. Their yard includes homespun puppy pens, dog houses, and a cabin they are constructing by themselves, entirely of trees felled and skinned on their property.

• Joe and I were born and raised in southeast Texas, where we live now. We got our first Bulldog in 1986, when we were living out in California. Her name was Sugar, and she was just a great dog; her temperament was great, her loyalty. At the time we were living in an equipment yard where Joe worked. He's a heavy equipment operator, and he kind of oversaw the yard both during the day, and the nighttime. And this guy, one of the operators, had left Sugardog on the yard where we lived, underneath a trailer. And she was not cared for. So Joe and I started feeding her and taking care of her, and eventually she just moved in with us. She was a registered hog dog. See, a lot of people use these dogs for hog hunting. They use the baying dogs to find the hogs and they use the Pit Bulls to catch them behind the ear and the neck. The Pit Bulls hold the hogs till the hunters get there.
• So anyway, we moved back to Texas in 1990 and Sugardog came with us. She was getting old, so we also bought a little old unregistered dog and we started breeding him with a female that some friends of ours had. We just got into it step by step from there, and by now I guess I've raised hundreds in the house from puppies. We've had lots of litters, which we raise in specially-made birthing pens. In the beginning, most of the puppies were unregistered. Now they're all registered. We used to sell them to the public, but due to the kind of untrustworthy people who would sometimes come to the house, the riff-raff, we put a stop to that. Now we pretty much stay within the dog world and trade with our friends. I'm the Vice President of our local Pit Bull Club.
• The dogs are our passion. Joe's been home for a while because the union jobs are real slack right now, construction work-wise. If he goes to work, it's been local—two or three week jobs. So he's been here taking care of dogs and doing what needs to be done around the property. I take care of the medicines, the shots, any illnesses the dogs get. If it's out of my control, I do go to a vet. But I'm the midwife for all the girls who have puppies. I make sure the deliveries go okay. In the last ten years, I've assisted in almost every one of them 'ere, around fifty. And a lot of these first-time girls go into trouble. If Joe and I hadn't been here, lots of them would've died—the mothers and the puppies. Because some puppies come out breech, or some the head's too big, or the mama just can't push out. Sometimes we rush them to the vet for an emergency C-section. It's upsetting, but it's wonderful too. We do get attached to them all. We have quite a few on the property right now, including puppies.
• Joe and I were both born and raised pretty much country folks. We're getting older, and we don't like all the hustle and the bustle, and the fast moving, and the people. We like being back here by ourselves in more quiet surroundings. In fact, we're building a log house. That's how we choose to live. Other than the dogs, I've got a rabbit. I've got a chicken. We used to have horses. We had a peacock. I even had a boa constrictor for 14 years, which I raised from a baby. I used to keep her in the house in a big aquarium, and some of the dogs were pretty used to her. They'd let her lay right across their backs! But we got rid of a lot of the other animals because the finance part of it just got to be too great, along with all the dogs. We used to have a real menagerie.

LUCRETIA ASHCRAFT In the Piney Woods of East Texas

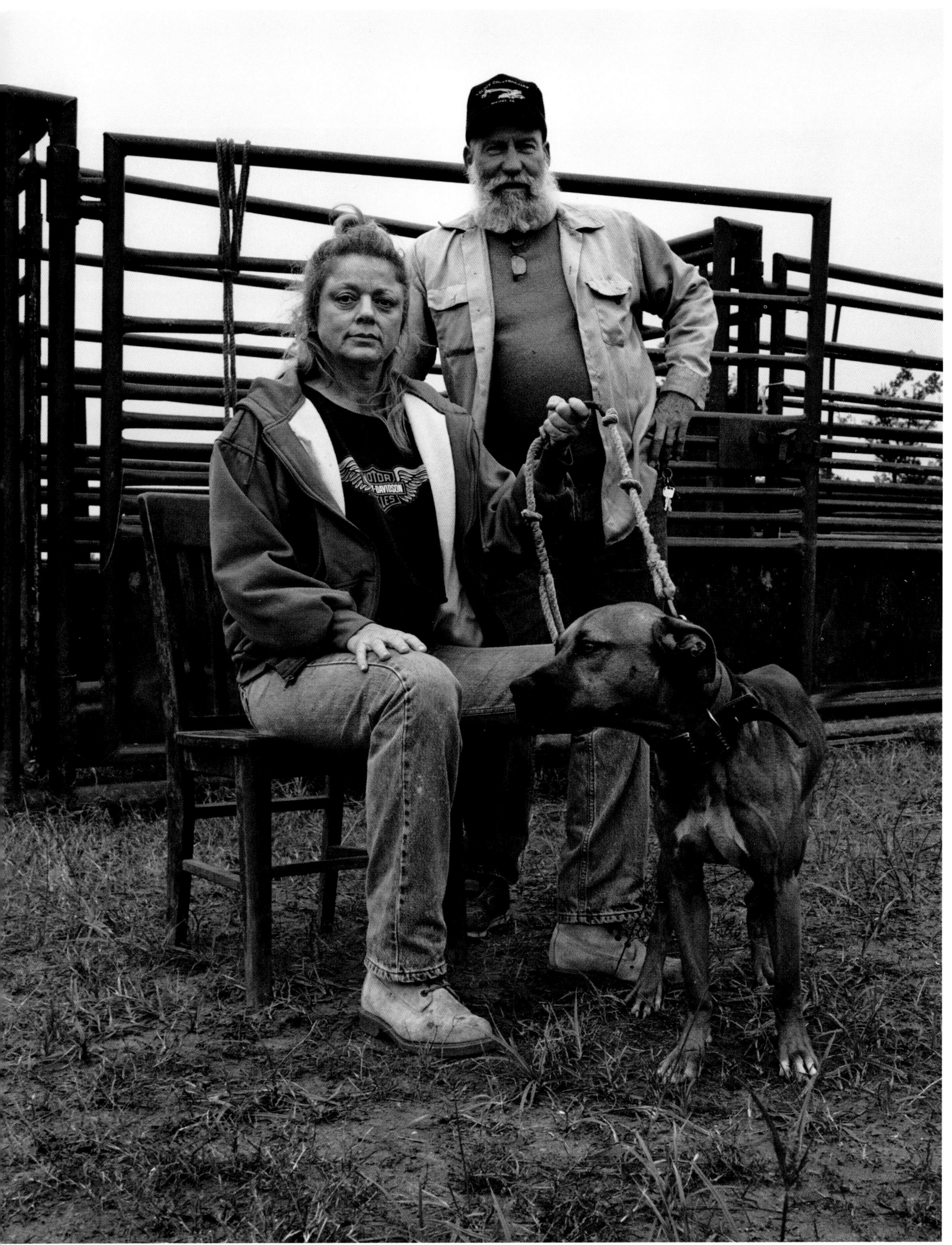

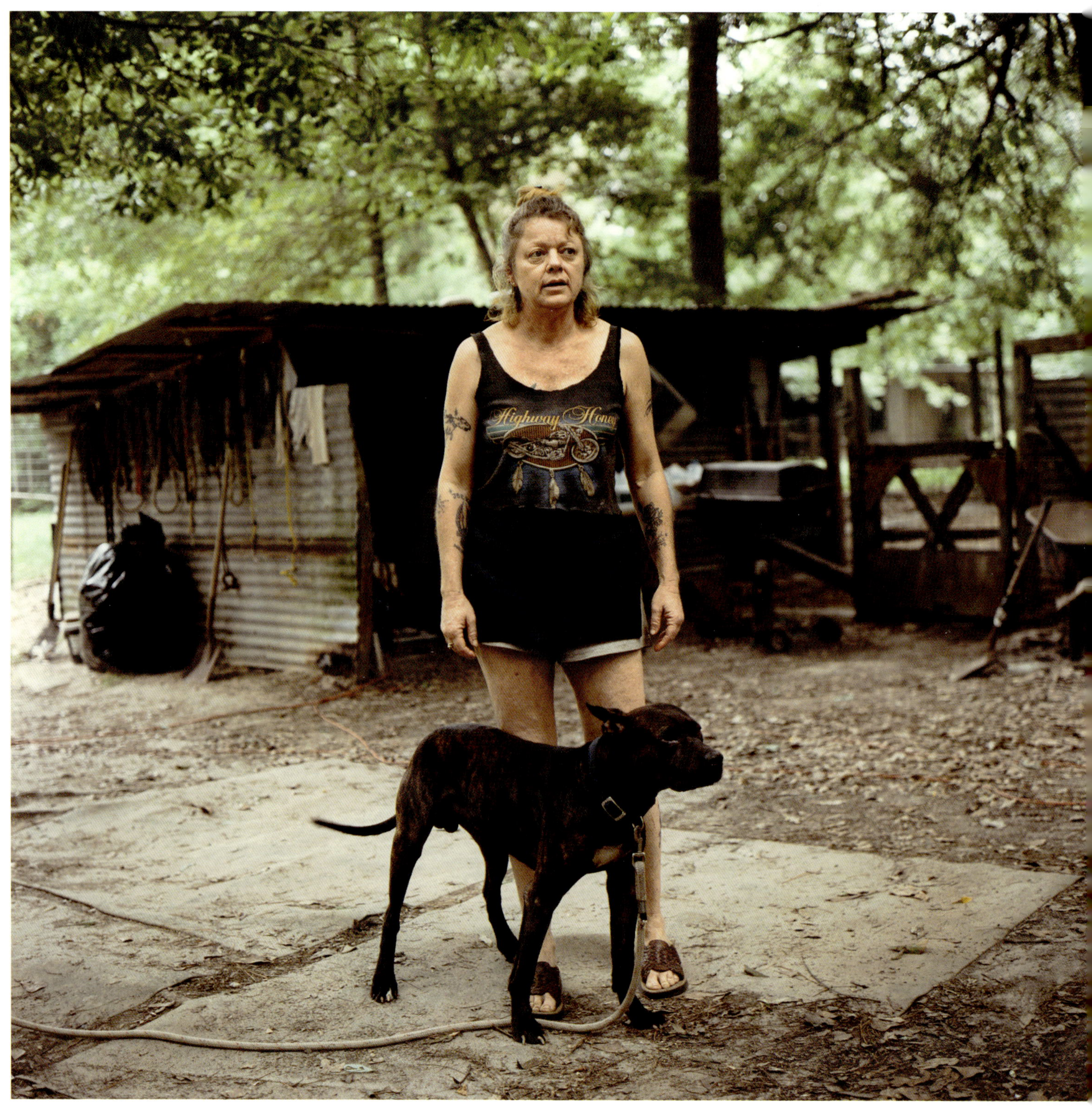

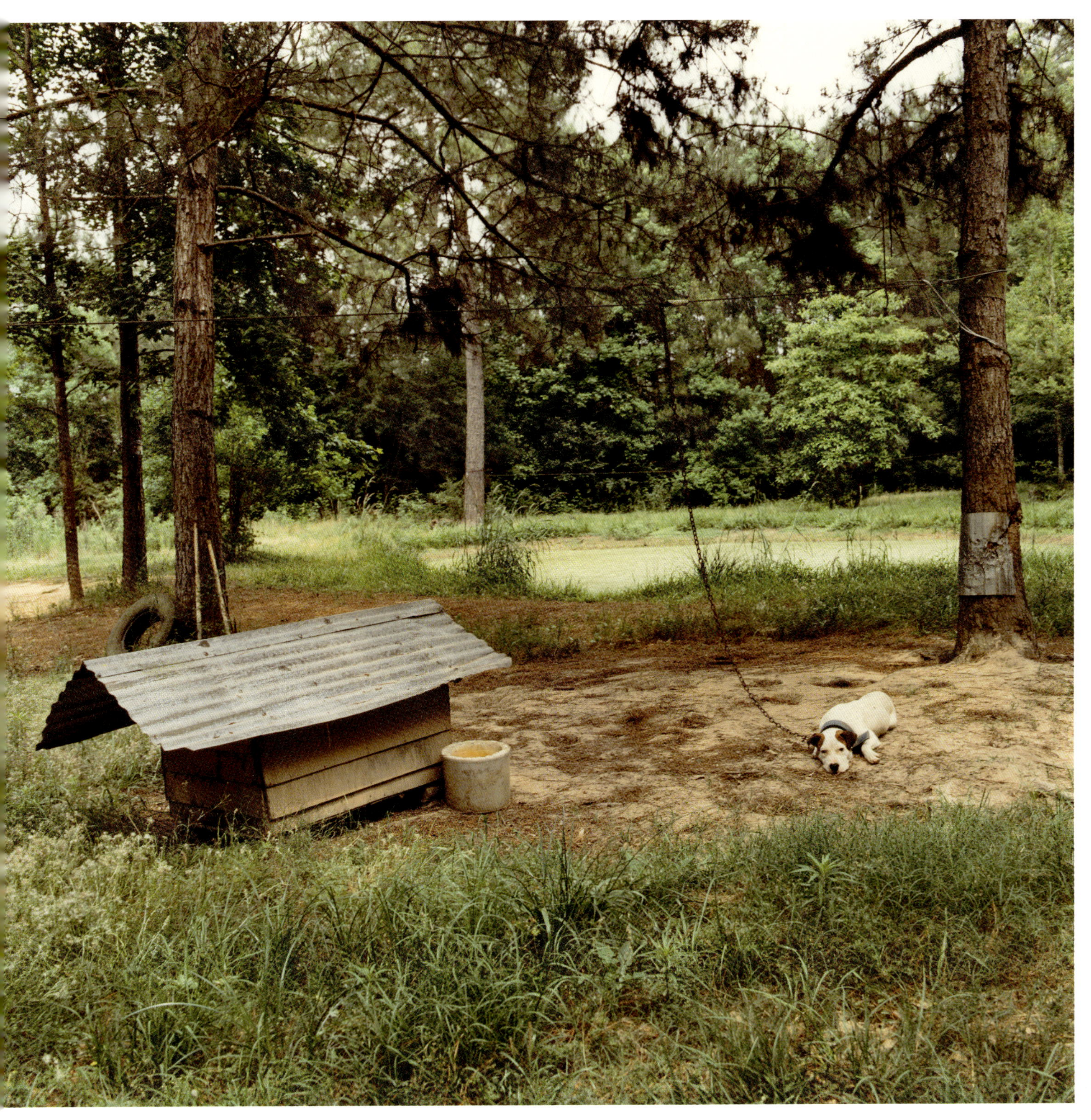

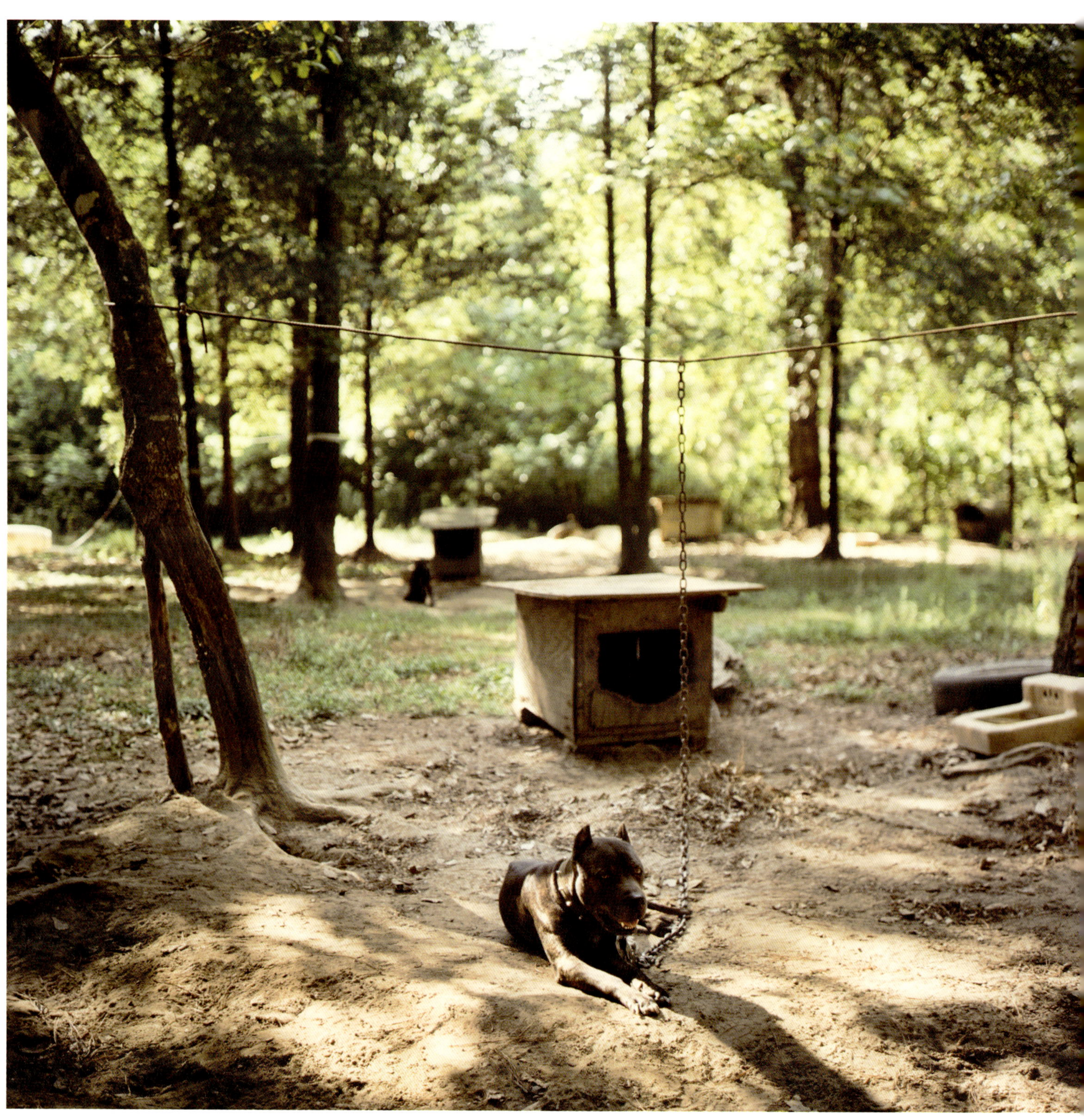

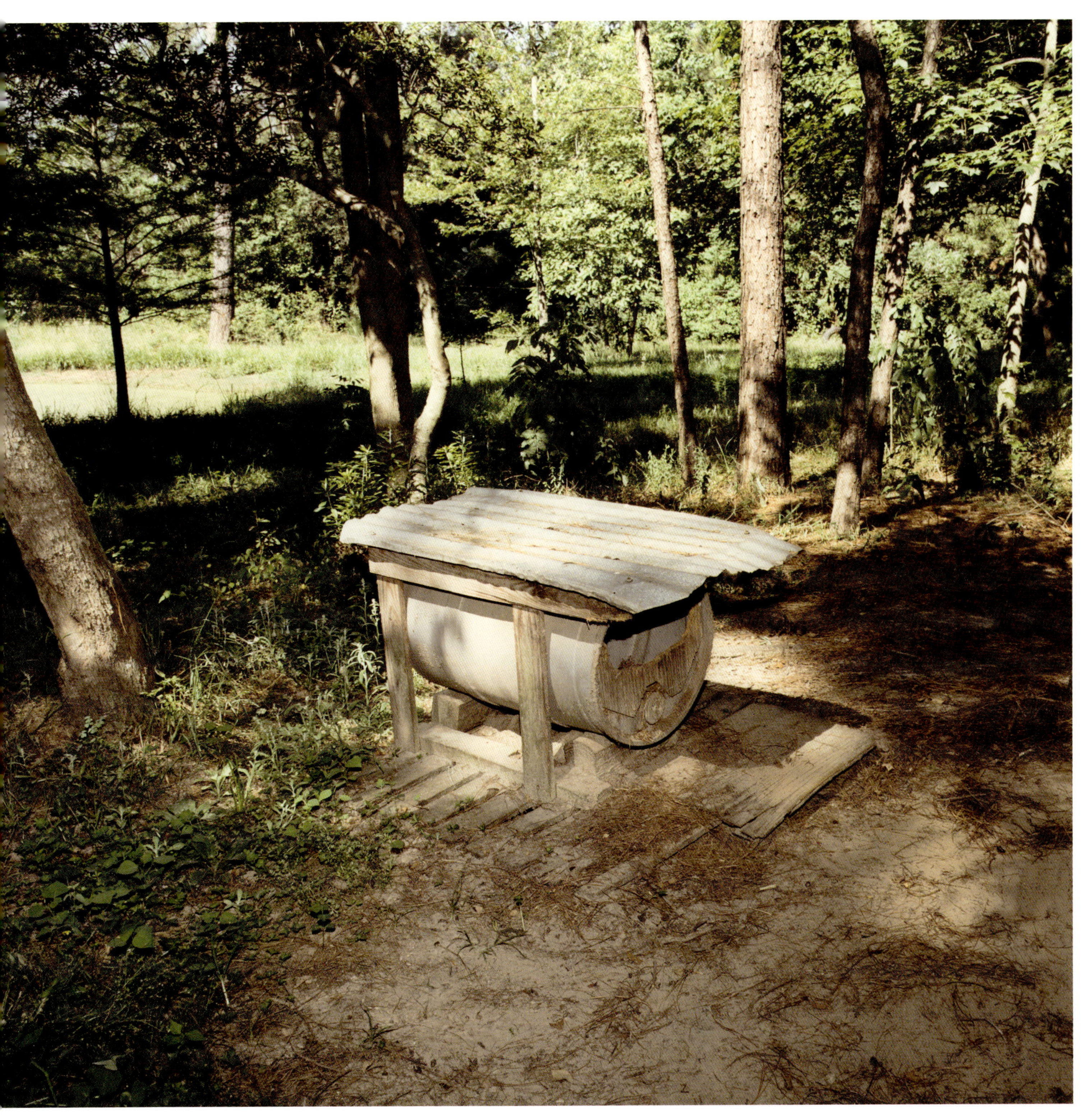

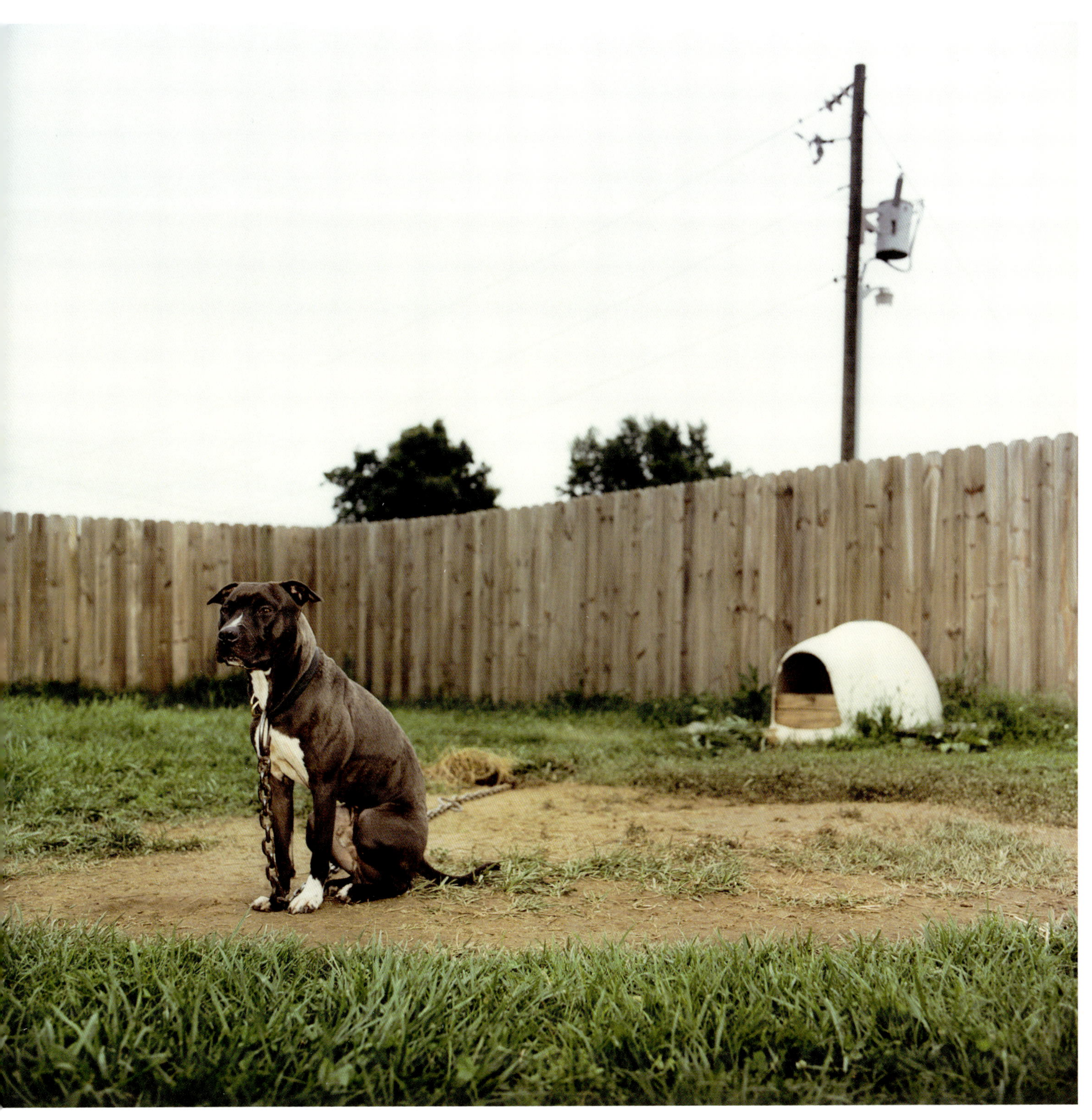

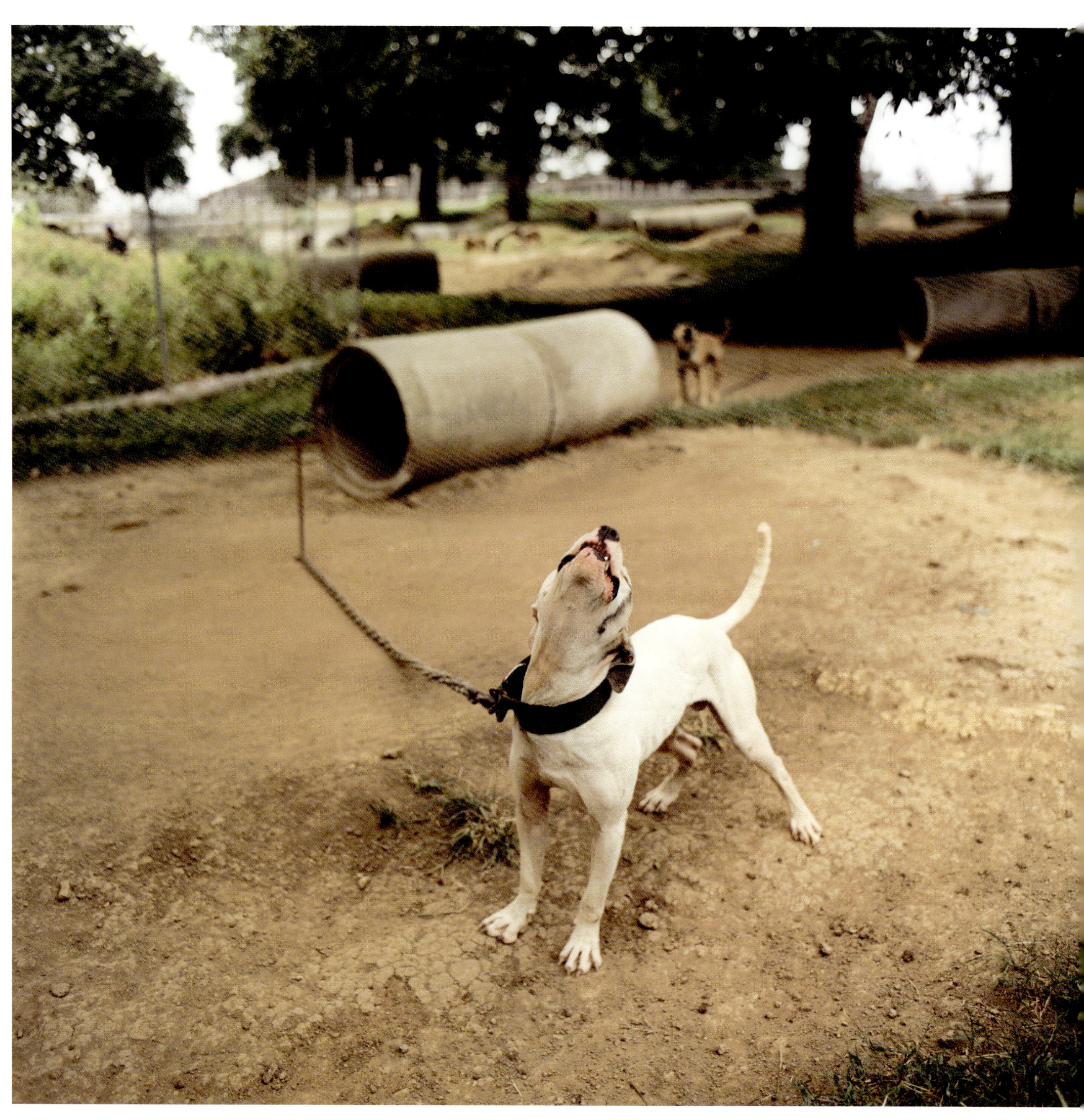

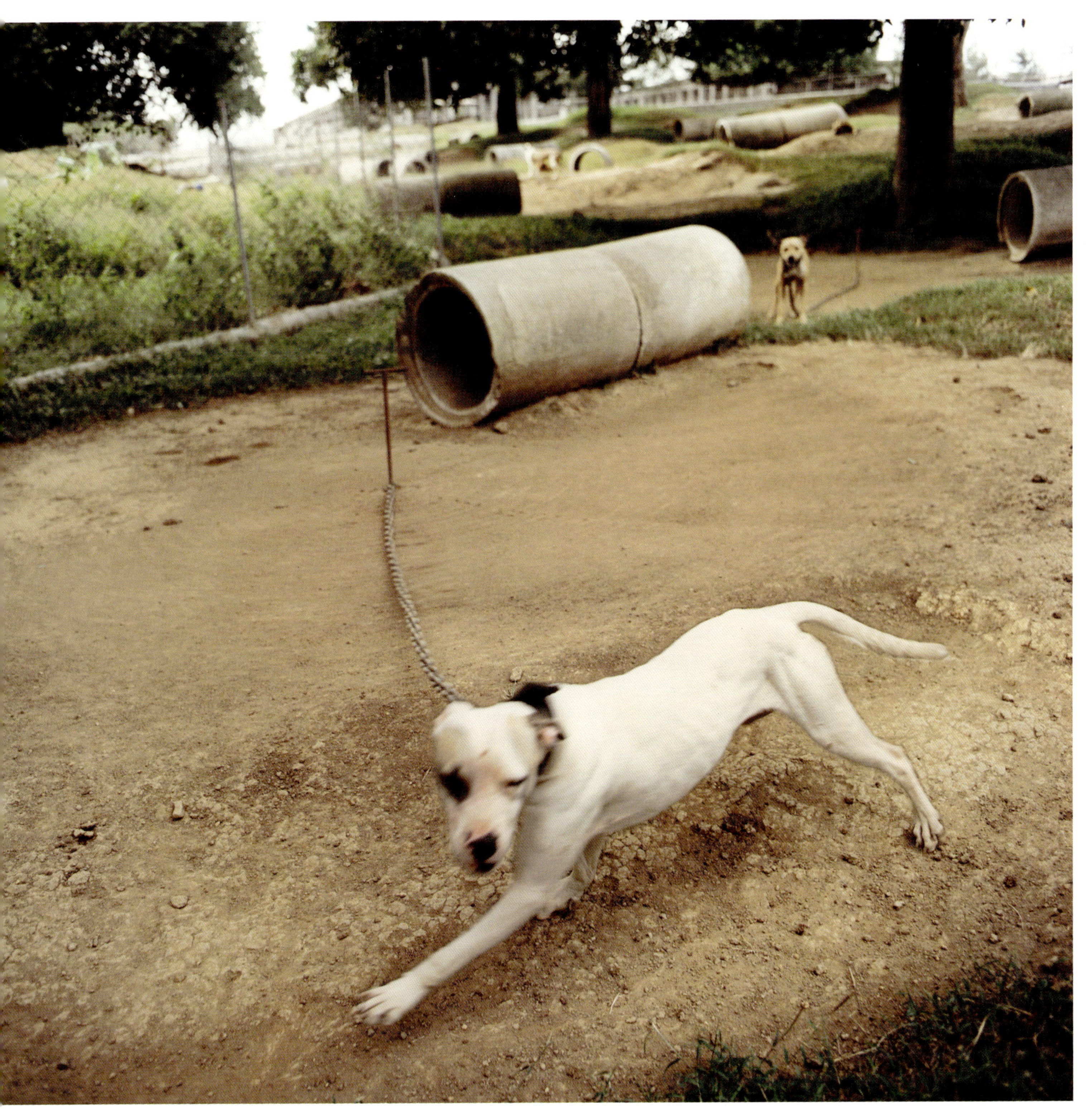

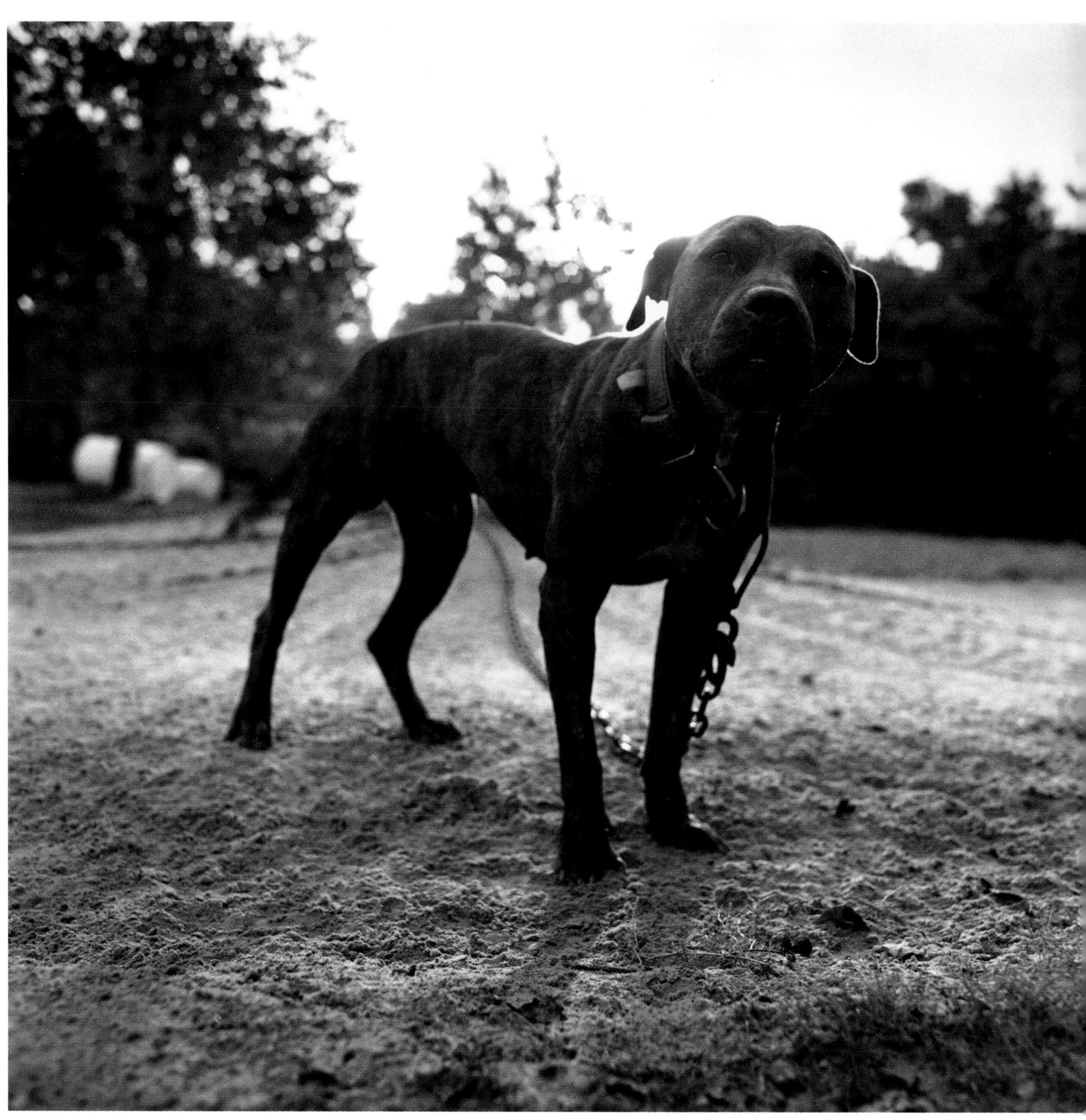

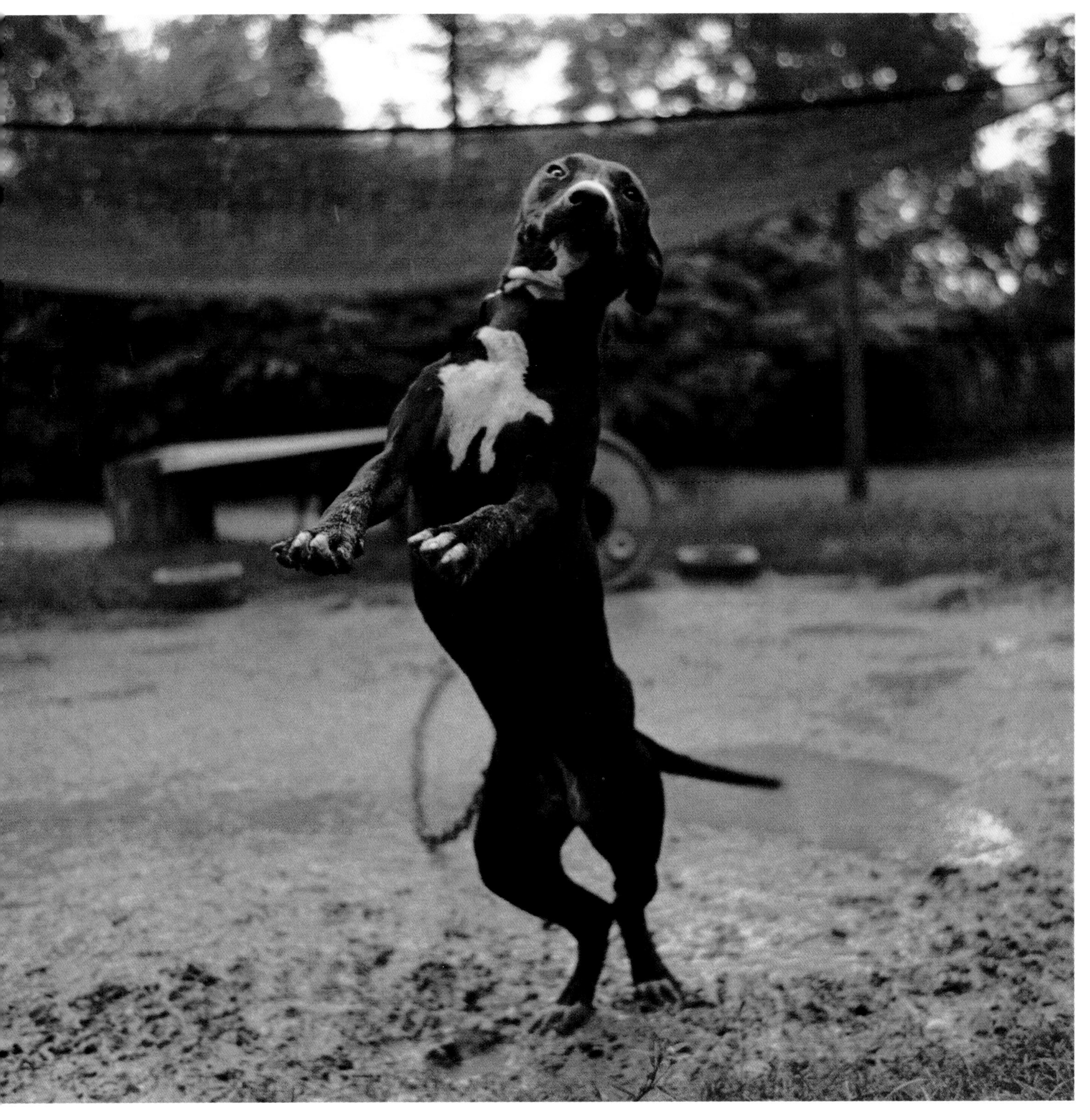

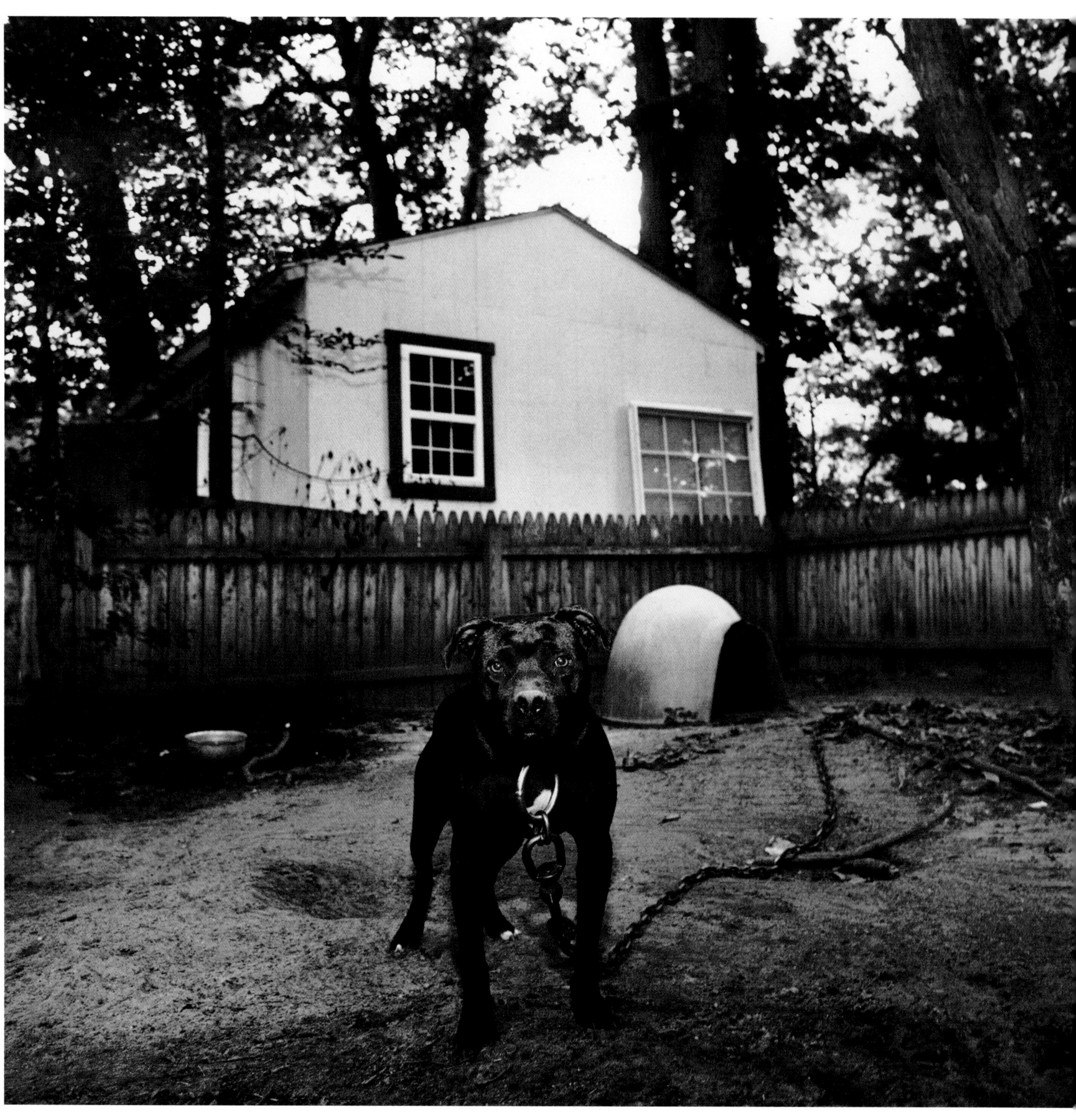

INDEX

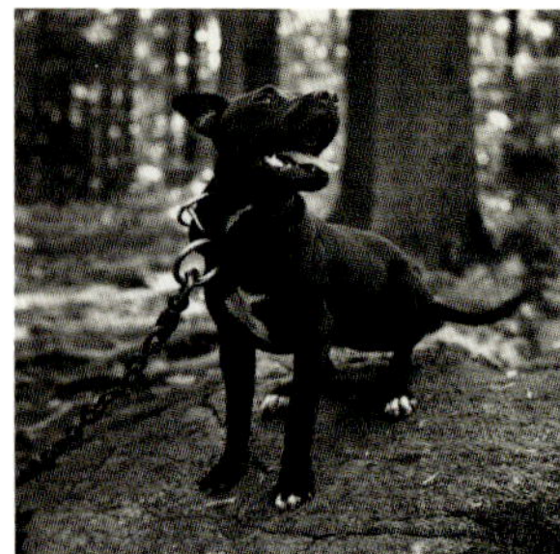
Onx page 2
Berks County, Pennsylvania
May 2001

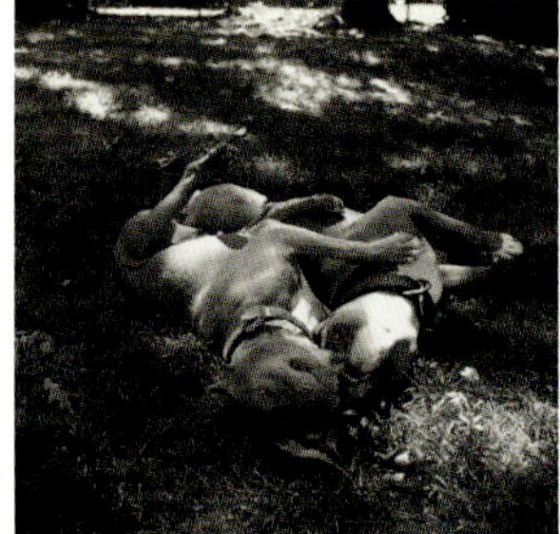
Flame and Friend page 4
Brentwood, New York
July 2001

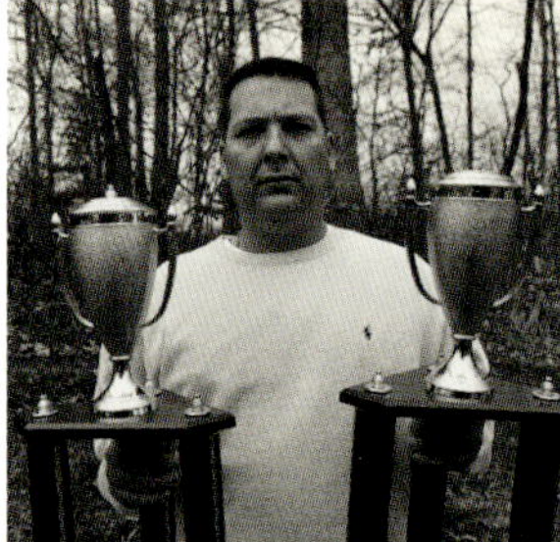
John John page 6
Delaware
April 2001

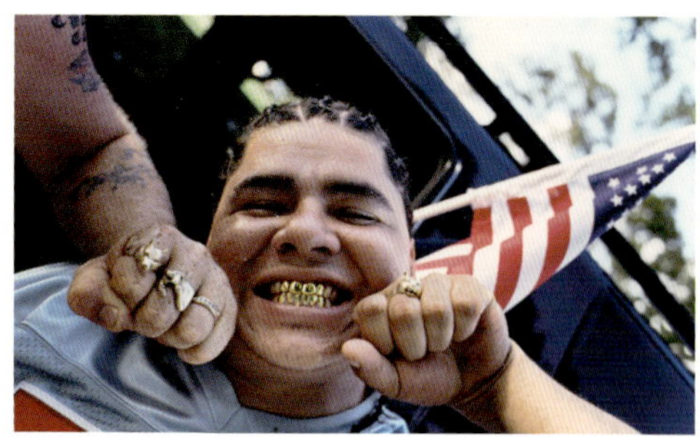
Juan pages 8/9
Liberty, Texas
April 2002

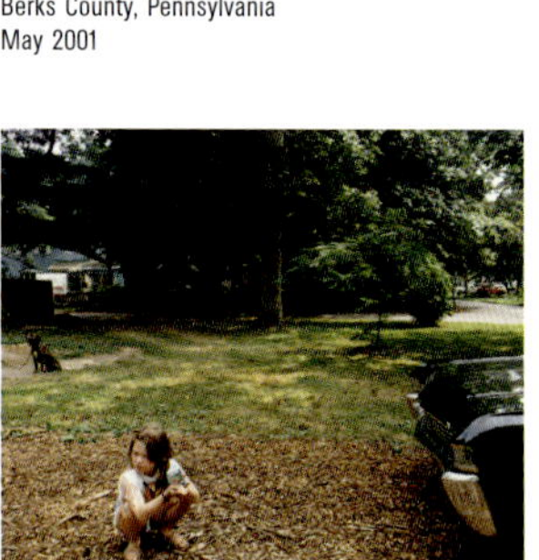
Flood's Daughter page 10
Long Island, New York
August 2001

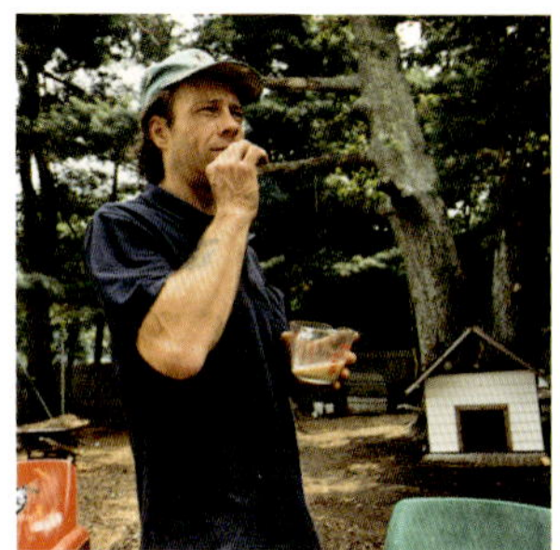
Mr. Mike Flood page 12
Long Island, New York
August 2001

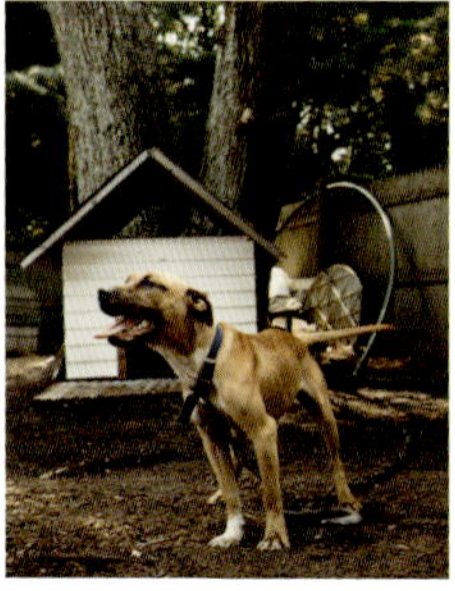
Mike's Dog Speedy page 13
(Looks Like Hasso)
Long Island, New York
August 2001

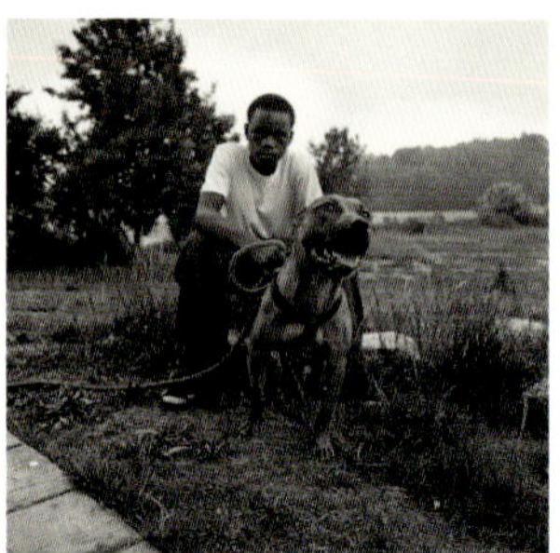
Ernie's Nephew, with Billy page 14
Delaware
June 2001

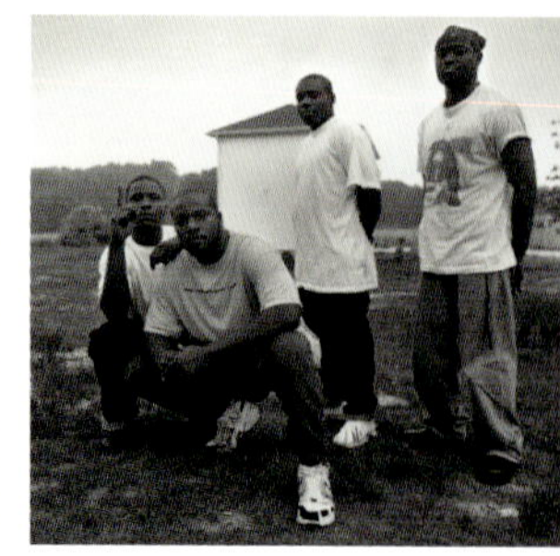
Untitled (Portrait) page 15
Delaware
June 2001

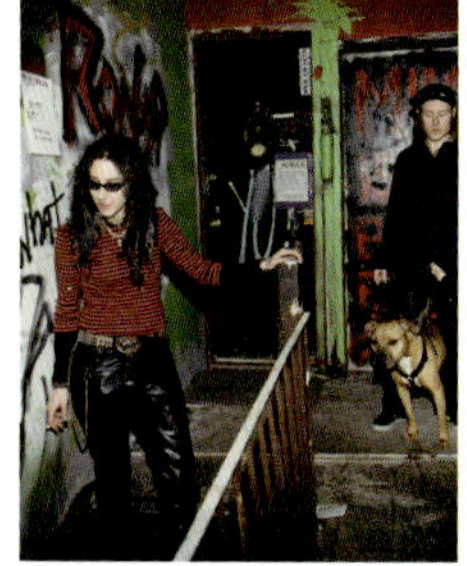
Stacey, Tony, and Cerveza page 16
(Avenue C)
New York, New York
April 2003

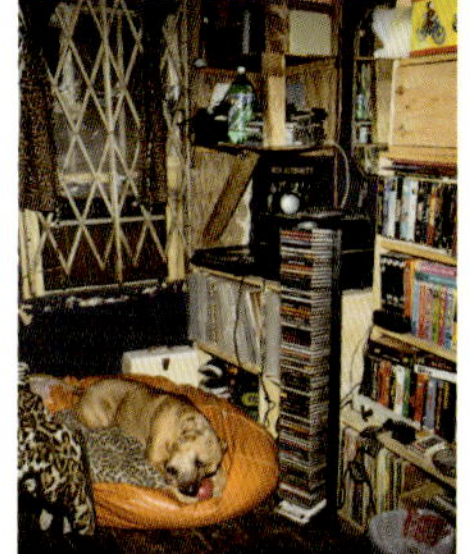
Cerveza page 17
(Avenue C)
New York, New York
April 2003

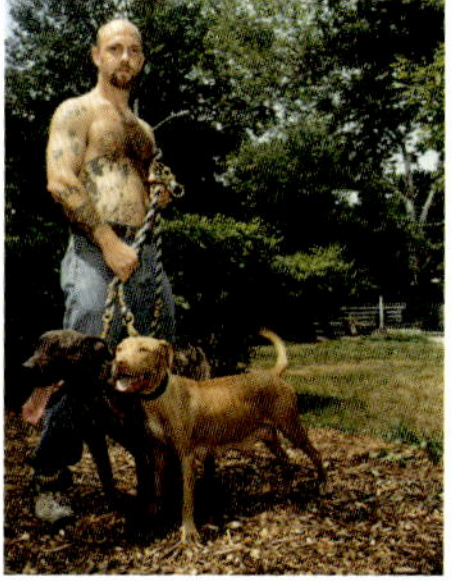
Andrew page 18
Long Island, New York
August 2001

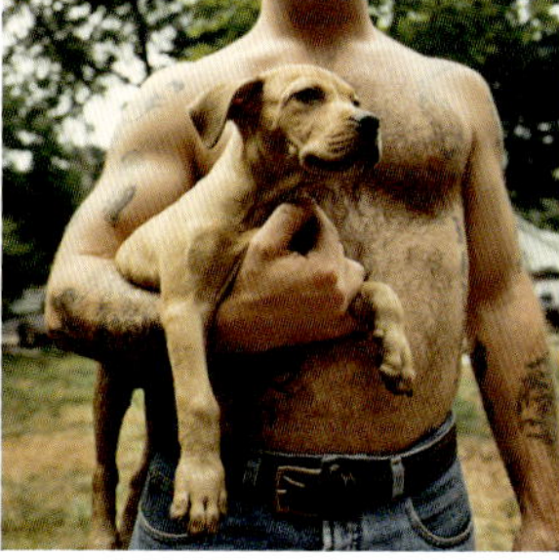
Andrew, with a Buckskin Pup page 19
Long Island, New York
August 2001

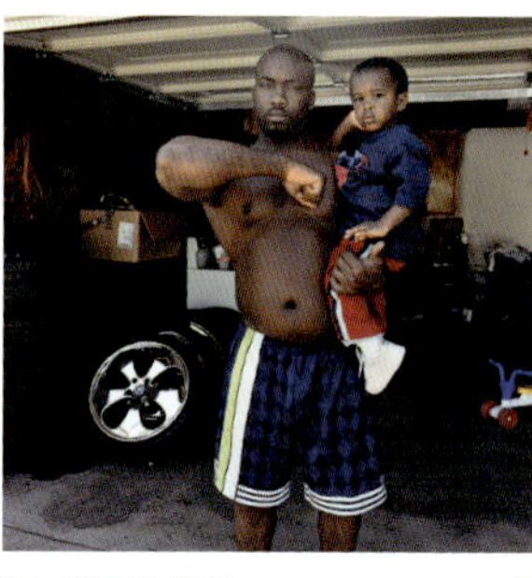
Bone and Little Beeze page 20
Compton, California
May 2003

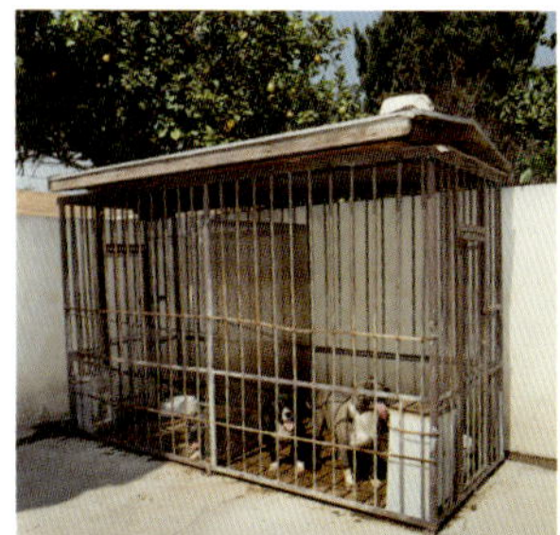
Untitled (Dog Pen) page 21
Compton, California
May 2003

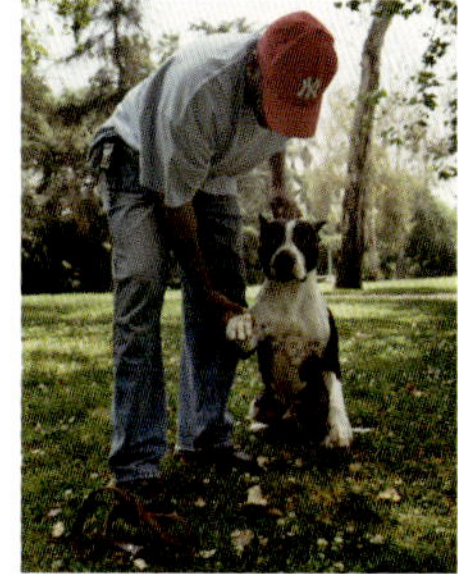
Daryll Young and Trevor page 22
Los Angeles, California
May 2003

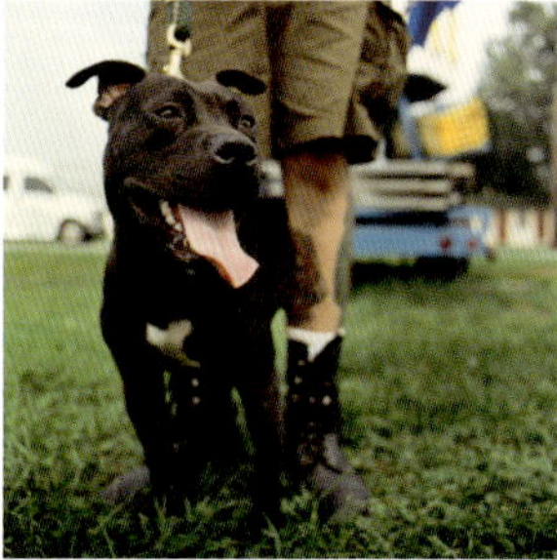
Bo and Coolito page 23
Berks County, Pennsylvania
September 2001

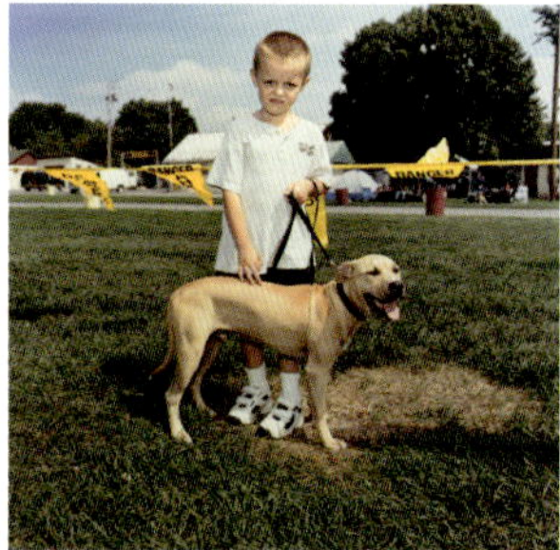
Adam Thomas and Leader page 25
Berks County, Pennsylvania
September 2001

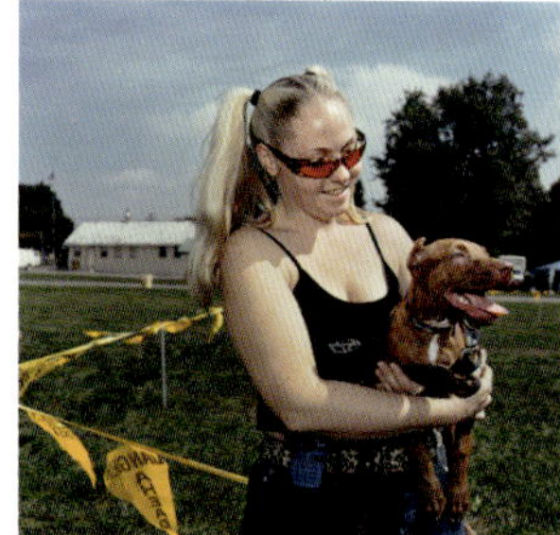
Sue and her Dog page 26
Berks County, Pennsylvania
September 2001

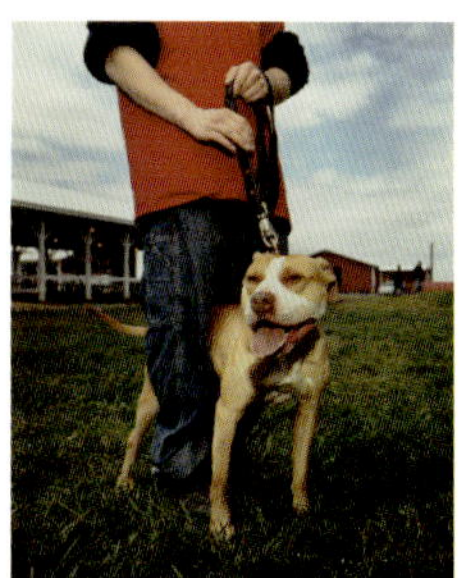
Boo page 27
Salem County, New Jersey
April 2003

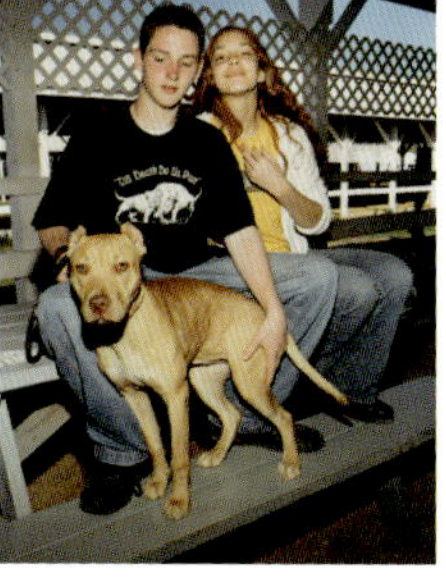
Michael and Christa, with Dog page 28
(Till Death Do Us Part)
Salem County, New Jersey
April 2003

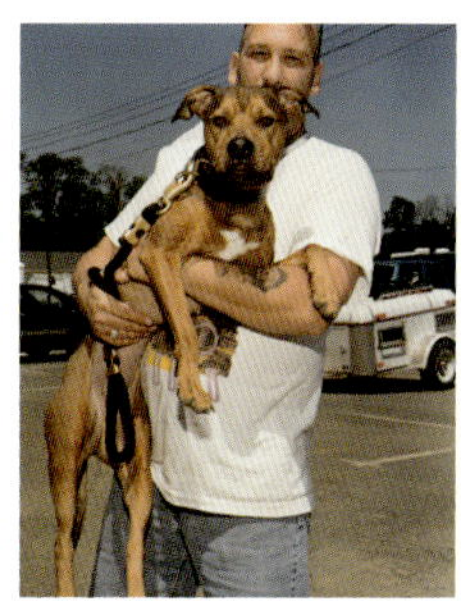
Rob and Moody Bitch page 29
Essex County, Massachusetts
July 2001

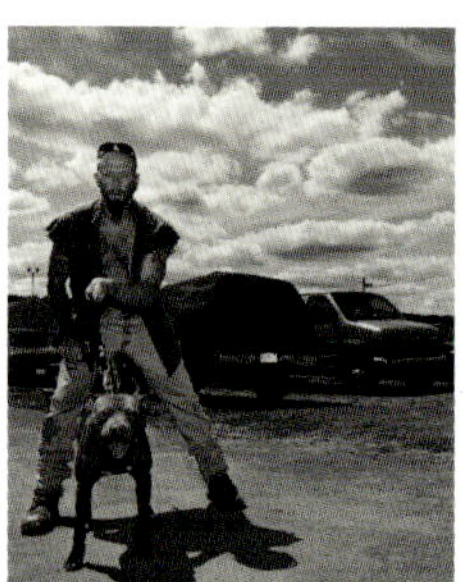
Brian and Cain page 30
Essex County, Massachusetts
July 2001

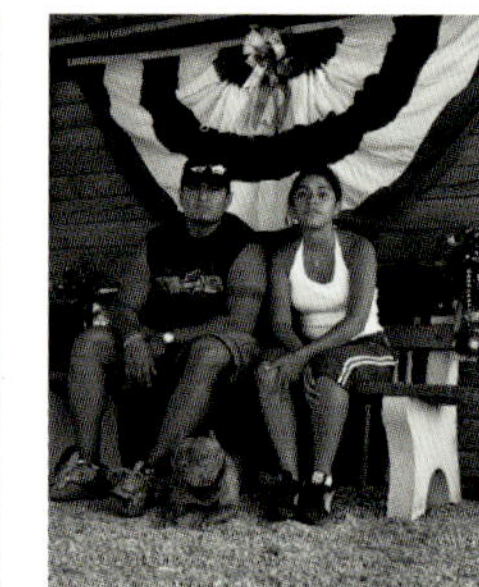
Untitled (Portrait) page 31
Salem County, New Jersey
April 2001

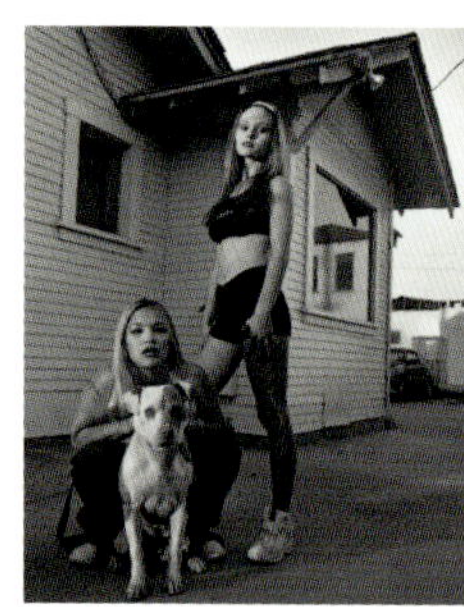
Angel, Ronnie, and Cypress page 32
(Southside) Whittier, California
December 2000

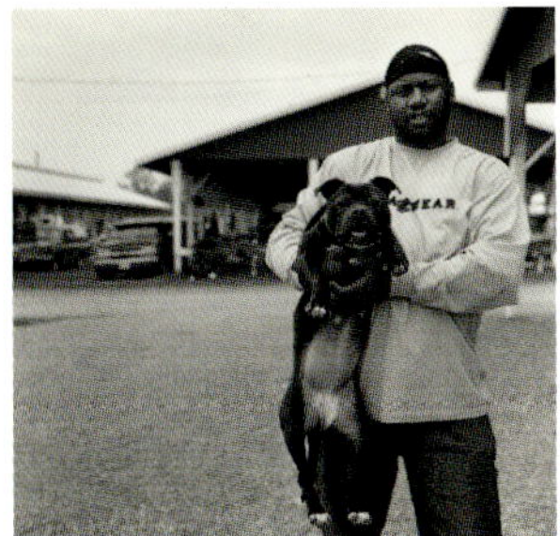
Shabazz and Candy page 33
Salem County, New Jersey
April 2001

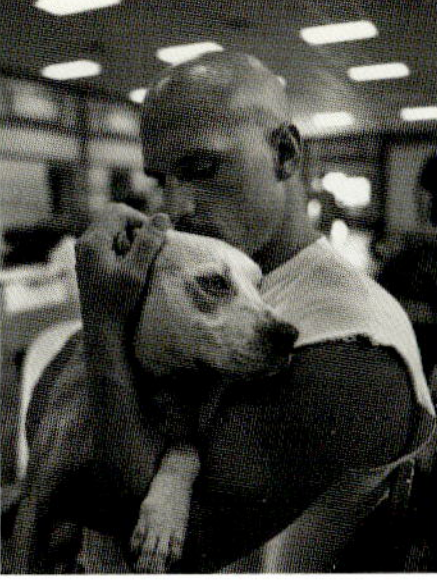
Richard and Rosie page 34
Berks County, Pennsylvania
September 2000

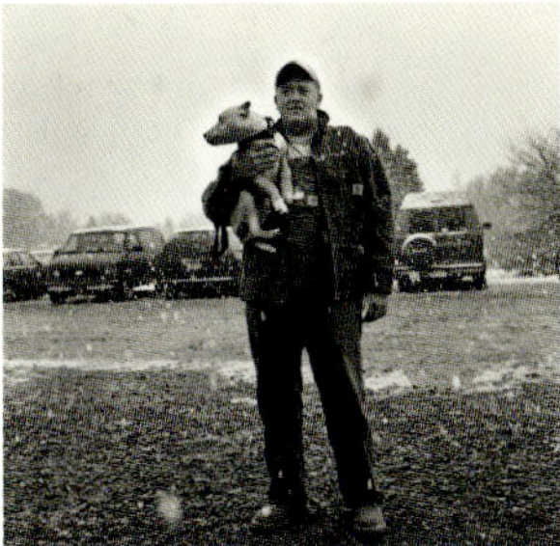
Untitled (Portrait) page 35
Charlotte, North Carolina
November 2001

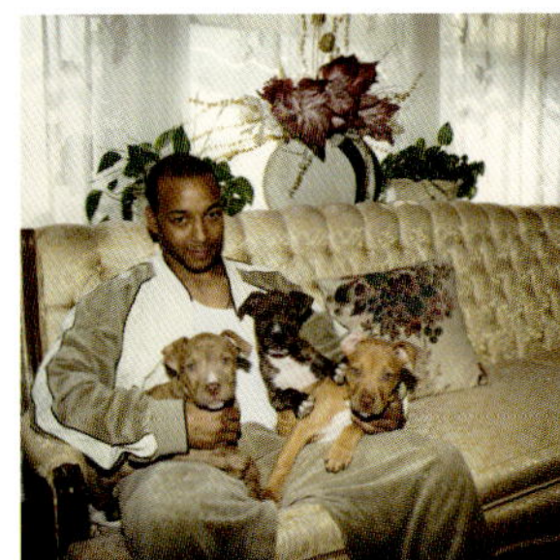
Glenn Wilson, with Pups page 36
Newark, New Jersey
April 2003

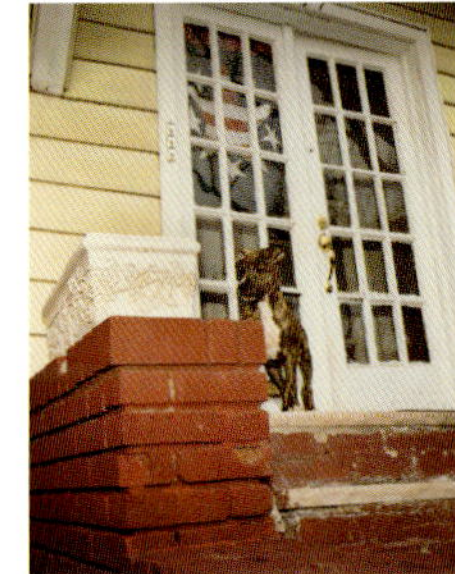
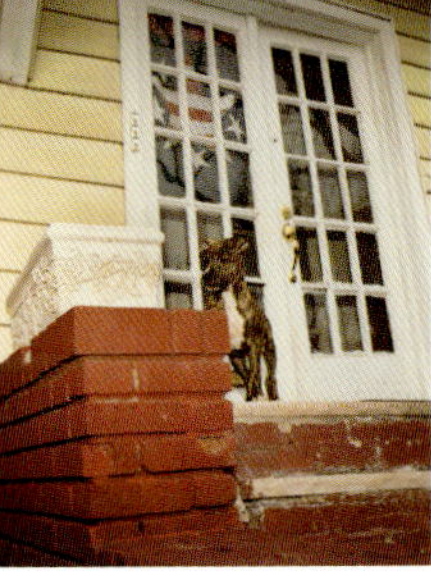
Glenn's Brindle Pup page 37
Newark, New Jersey
April 2003

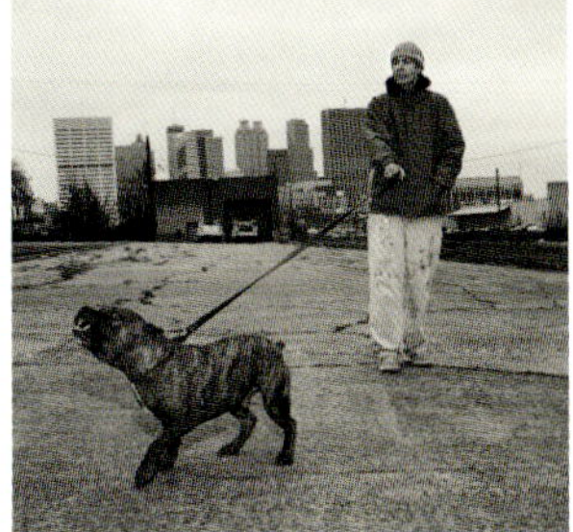
Michael Gibson and South page 38
Atlanta, Georgia
November 2002

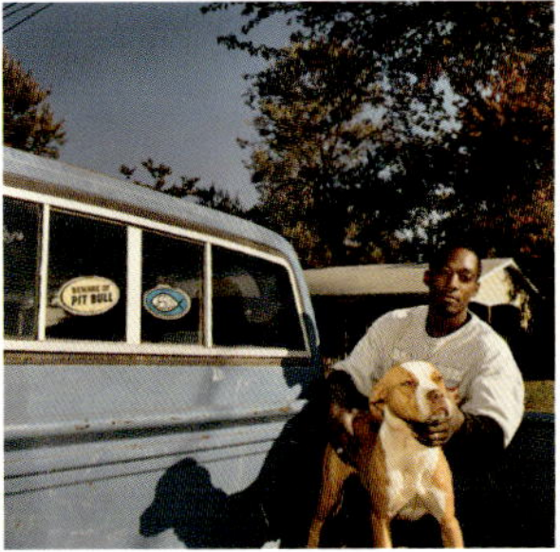
Alonso, and his Dog page 39
Woodbridge, Virginia
November 2002

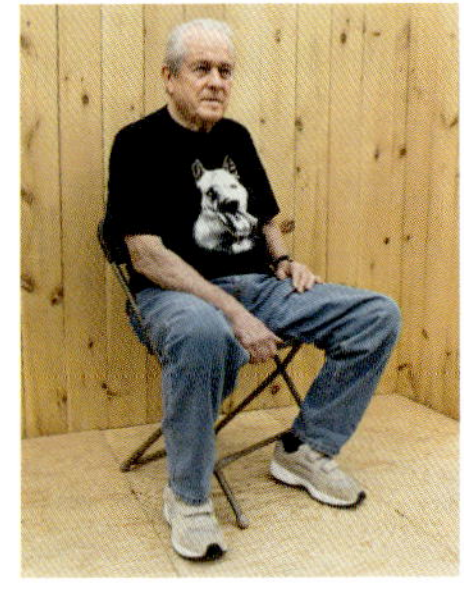
Mr. Louis B. Colby page 41
Essex County, Massachusetts
June 2003

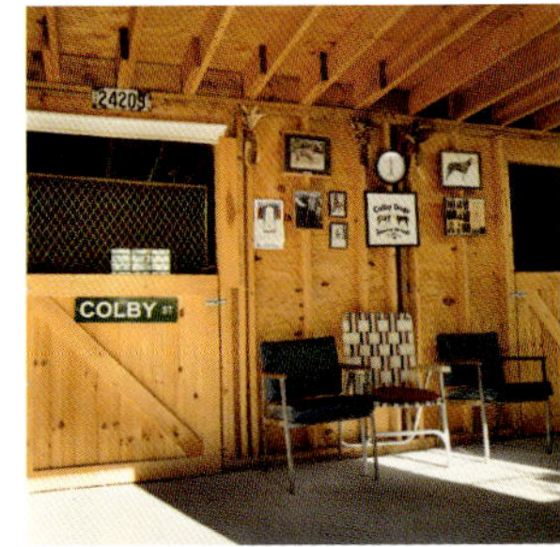

Colby Barn / Kennel page 42
Newburyport, Massachusetts
June 2003

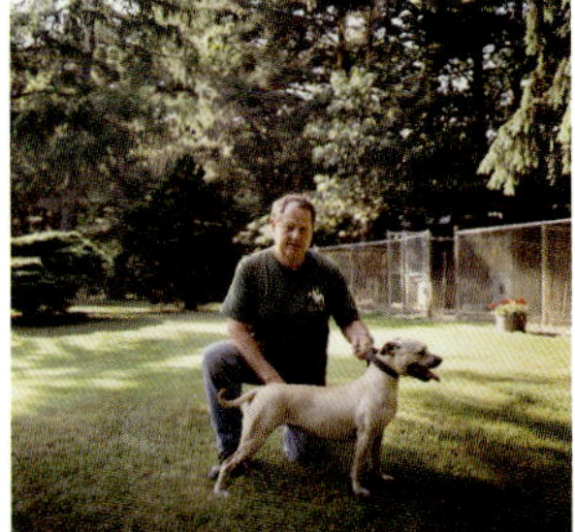
Mr. Scott Colby and Miss Kitty page 43
Newburyport, Massachusetts
June 2003

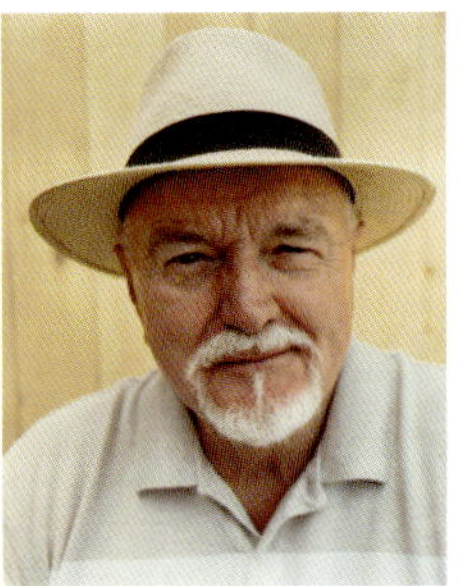
Mr. Jack Kelly page 45
Salem County, New Jersey
July 2002

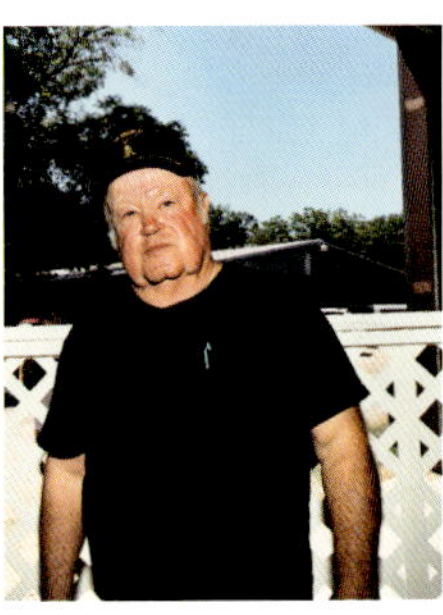
Mr. Bobby Corn page 45
Seguin, Texas
May 2003

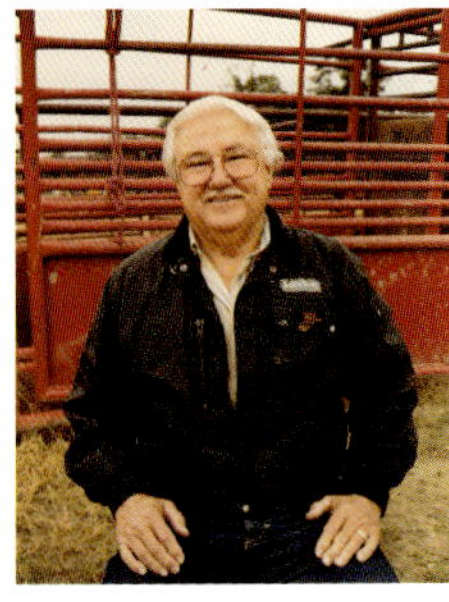
Mr. Bobby "Bullyson" Hall page 45
Sorrento, Louisiana
October 2001

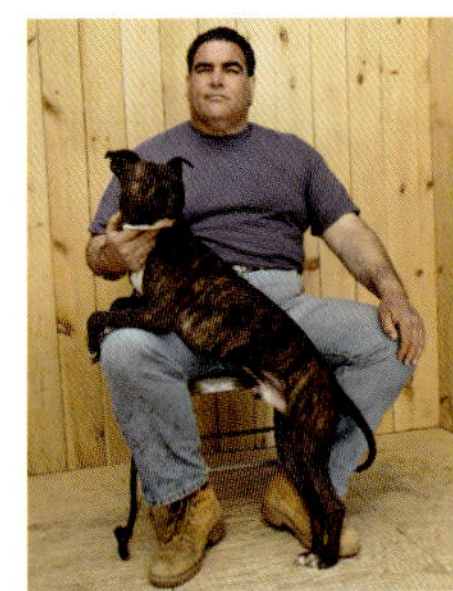
Mr. Peter Carnavale page 45
Salem County, New Jersey
April 2003

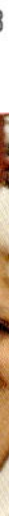
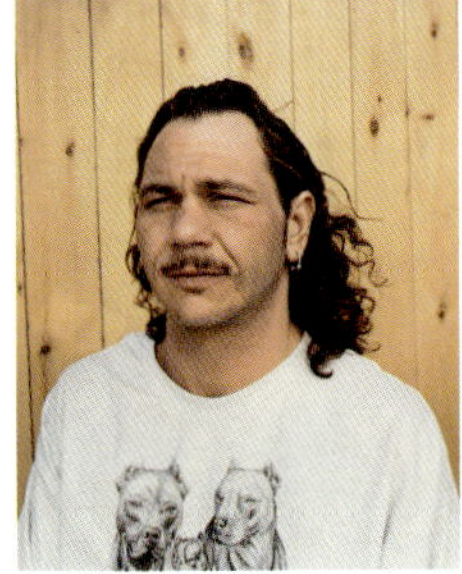
Mr. T.L. Williams page 46
Seguin, Texas
May 2003

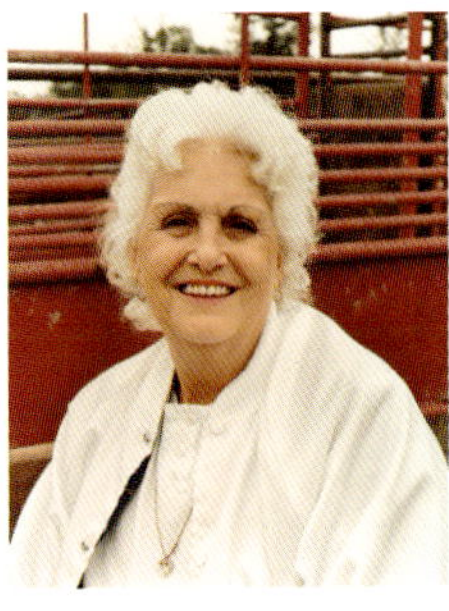
Mr. Rich Issell page 46
Salem County, New Jersey
April 2003

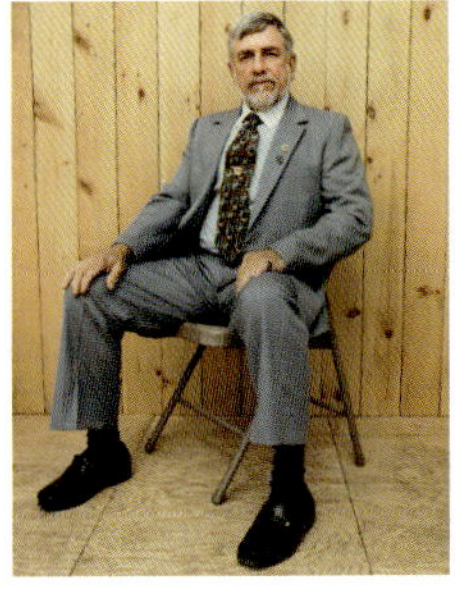
Mrs. Jo Ann Le Blanc page 46
(2002 Dog Man of the Year)
Sorrento, Louisiana
October 2001

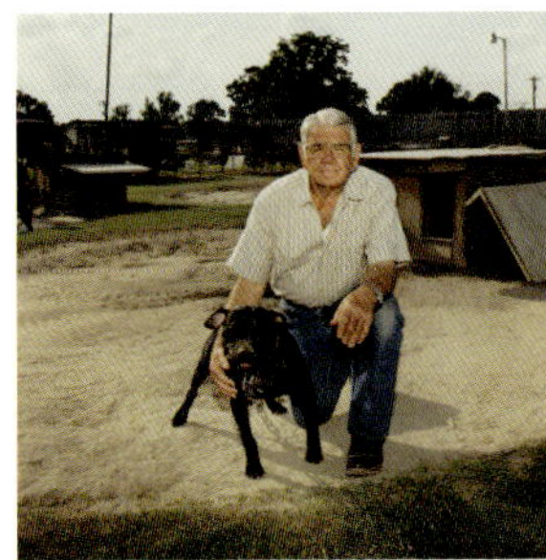
Mr. "Irish" Jerry Holcomb page 46
Salem County, New Jersey
April 2003

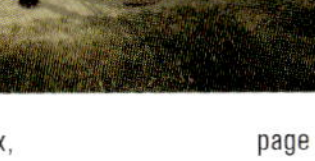
Mr. Floyd Boudreaux, page 49
and One of his Dogs
Lafayette, Louisianna
May 2003

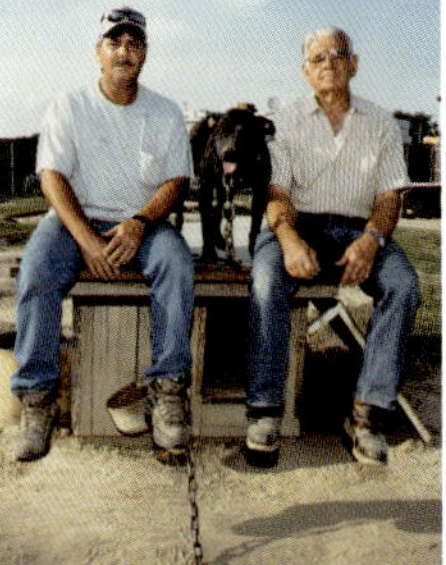
Guy and Floyd Boudreaux, page 50
with a Boudreaux Dog
Lafayette, Louisiana
May 2003

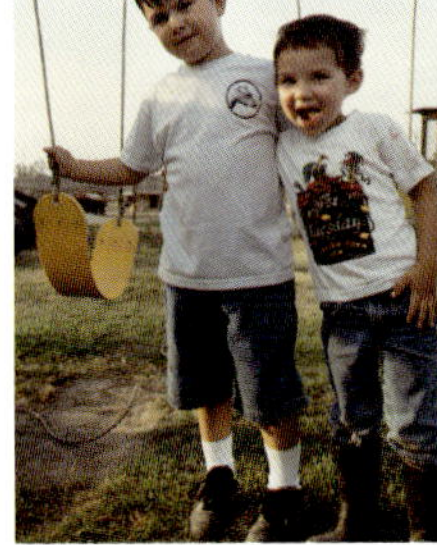
Colin and Lane, page 51
Mr. Floyd's Grandsons
Lafayette, Louisianna
May 2003

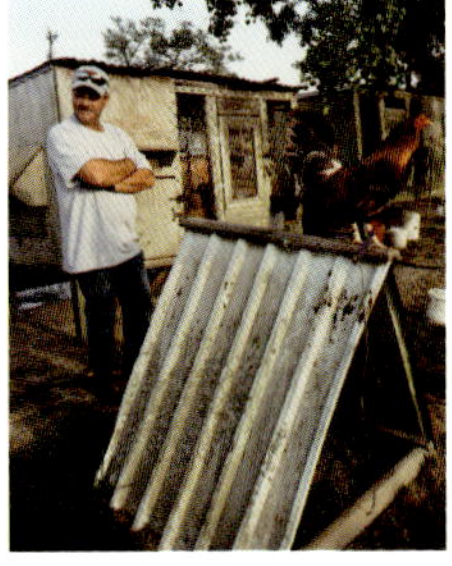
Guy Boudreaux, page 52
with a Game Cock
Lafayette, Louisianna
May 2003

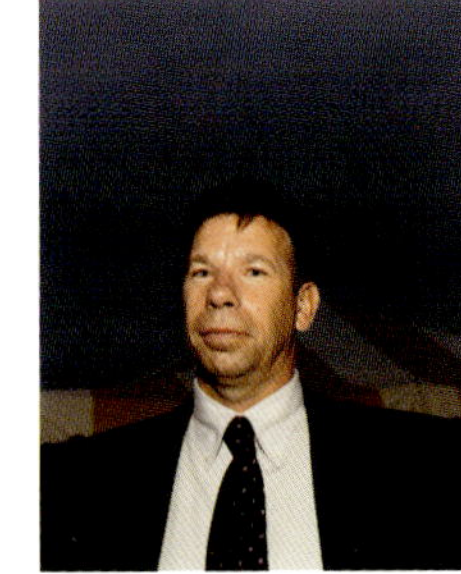
Mr. Hank Greenwood page 54
Sorrento, Louisiana
October 2001

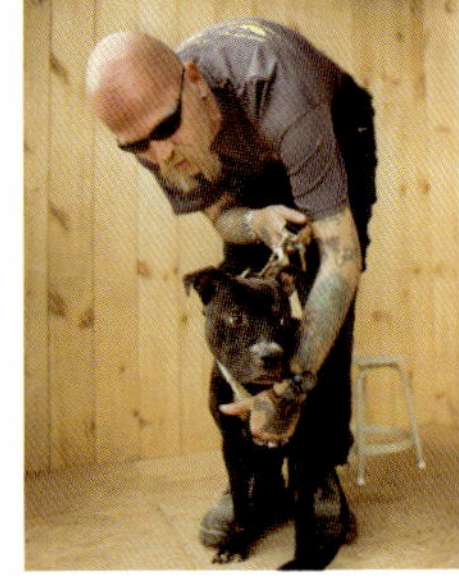
Untitled page 57
(Overall Appeal)
Salem County, New Jersey
April 2001

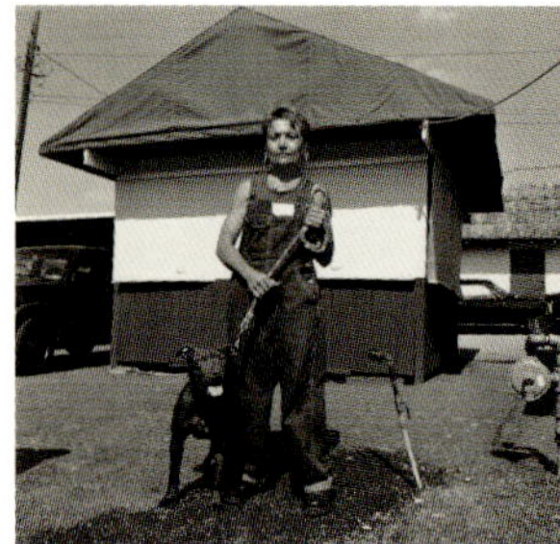

Brenda Clayton and Boy
(Attitude)
Berks County, Pennsylvania
September 2001
page 59

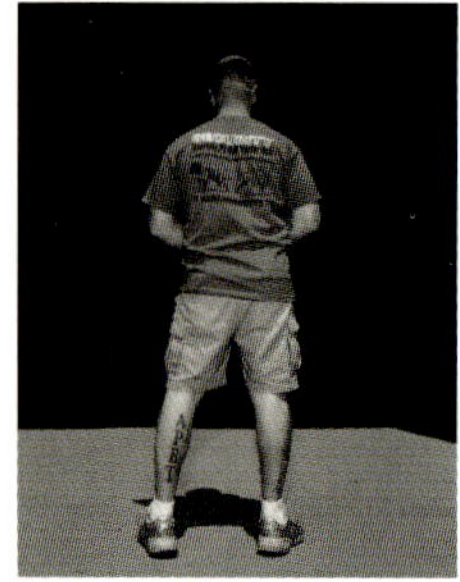

Security
Essex County, Massachusetts
July 2001
page 61

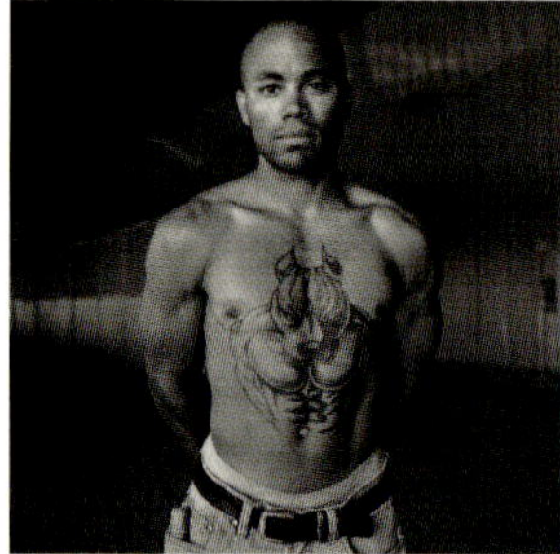

Joseph
Essex County, Massachusetts
July 2001
page 63

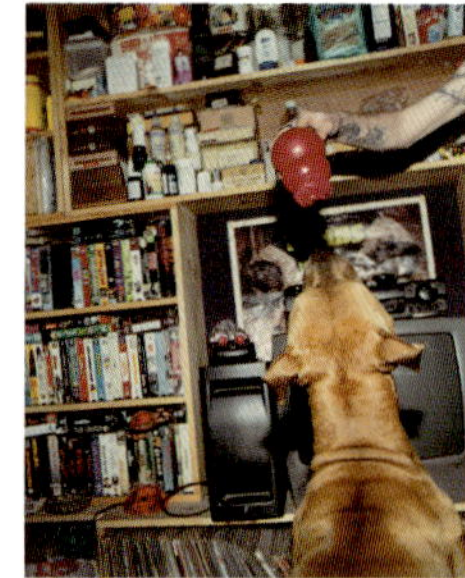

Cerveza
(Head and Neck)
New York, New York
April 2003
page 65

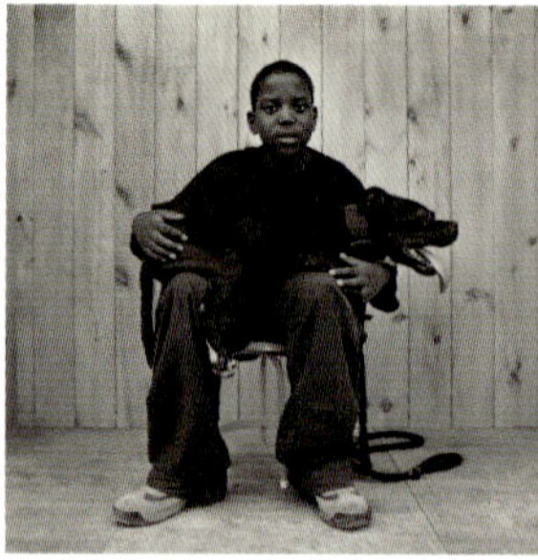

Chris Moore and Candy
Salem County, New Jersey
April 2001
page 67

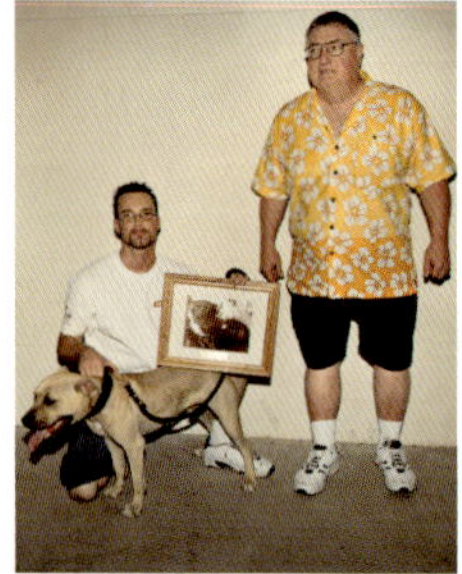

Untitled (Dog Show)
Seguin, Texas
May 2003
page 69

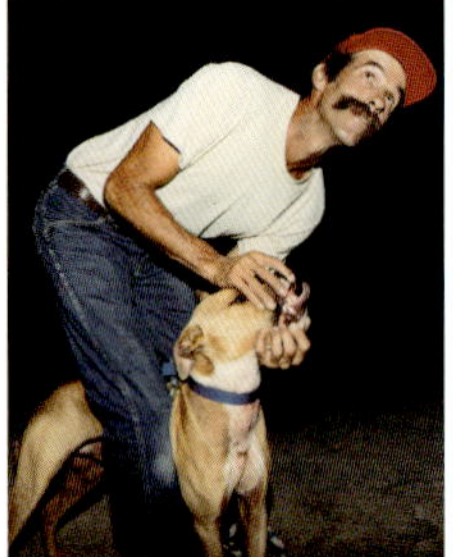

Untitled (Entrant #1)
Seguin, Texas
May 2003
page 70

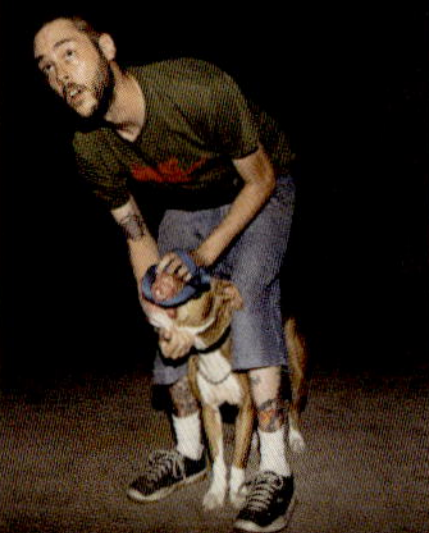

Untitled (Entrant #2)
Seguin, Texas
May 2003
page 71

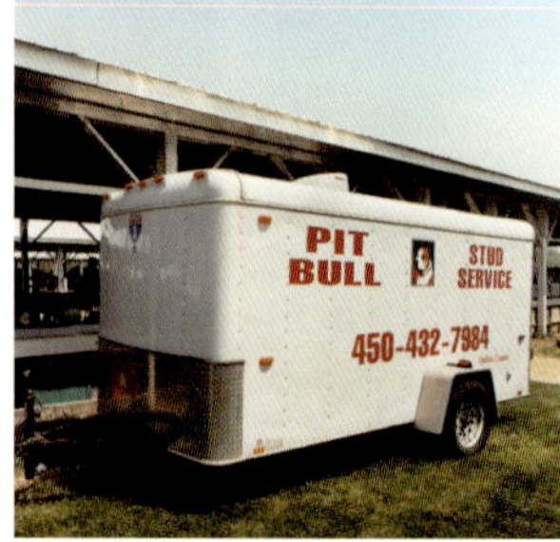

Stud Service
Salem County, New Jersey
April 2001
page 73

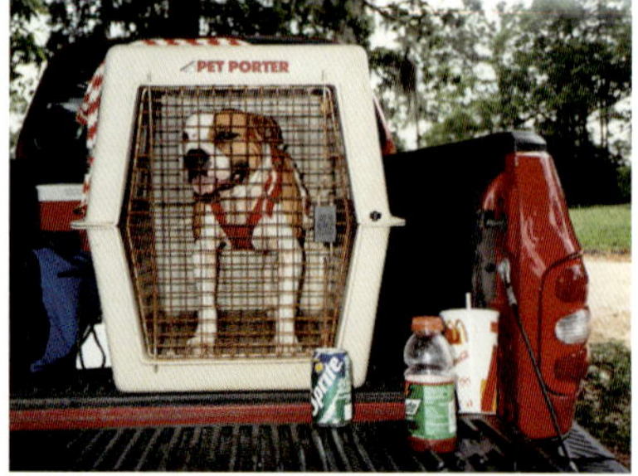

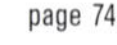

Coachise
Liberty, Texas
April 2002
page 74

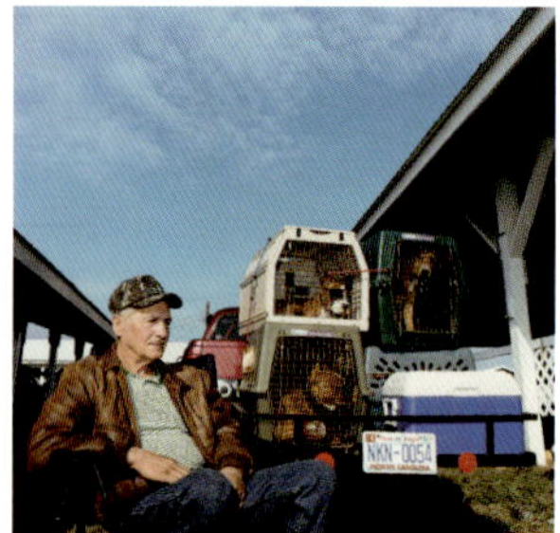

(The Guy From) Rude Dawg Kennels
Salem County, New Jersey
October 2002
page 75

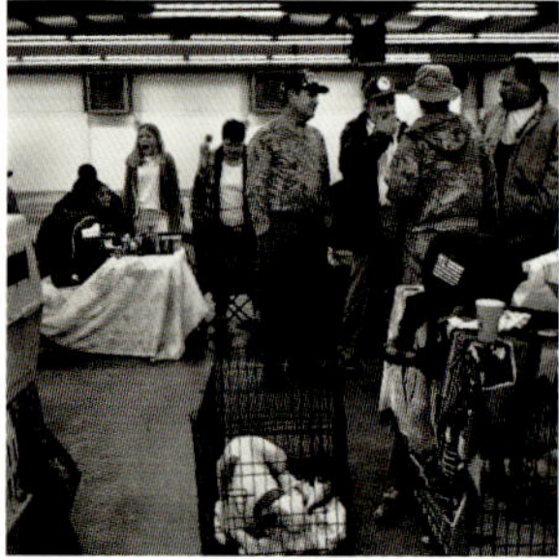

Ernie Swain, Irish Jerry, and Others
Charlotte, North Carolina
November 2000
page 76

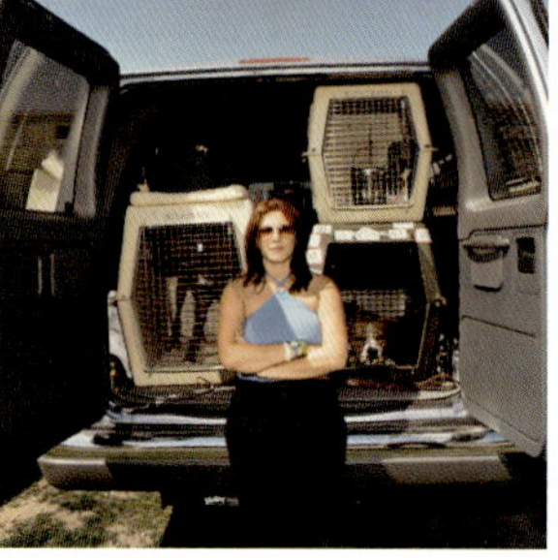

Andrea
Essex County, Massachusetts
July 2001
page 77

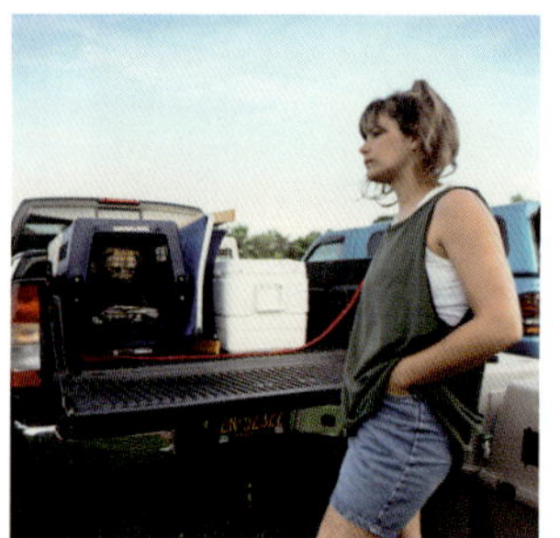

Untitled
(Woman at Truck)
Salem County, New Jersey
July 2002
page 78

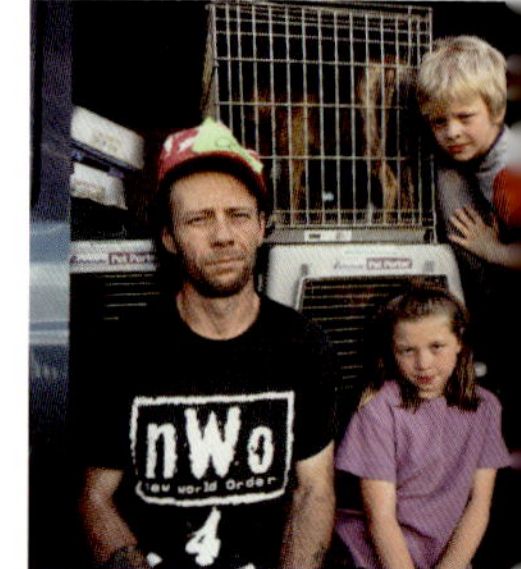

Mike and his Kids
Salem County, New Jersey
July 2002

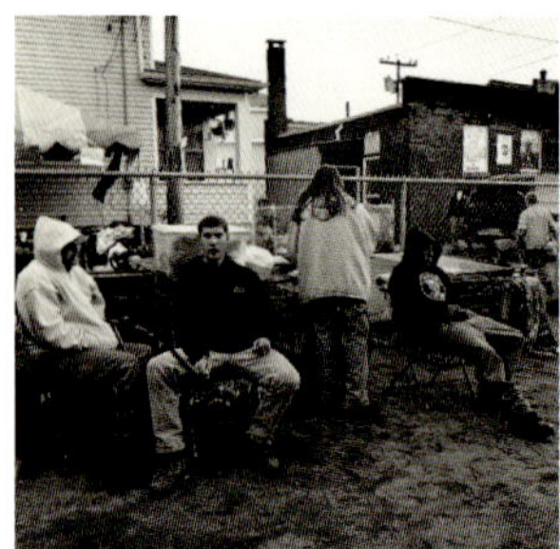

Joe's Dad, Joe, and Jesse
Lynn, Massachusetts
September 2001
page 80

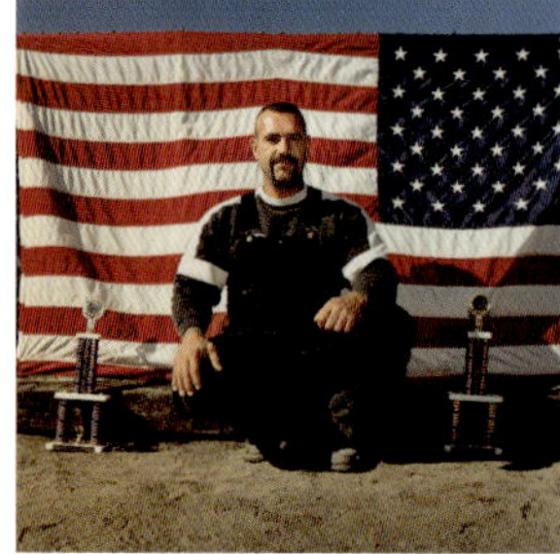
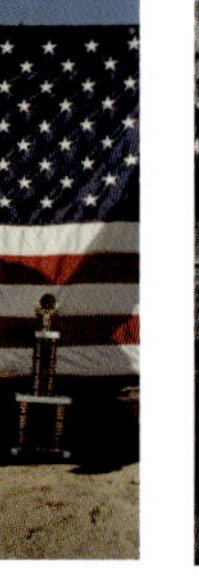

Mr. Lee Barrett
Lynn, Massachusetts
September 2001
page 81

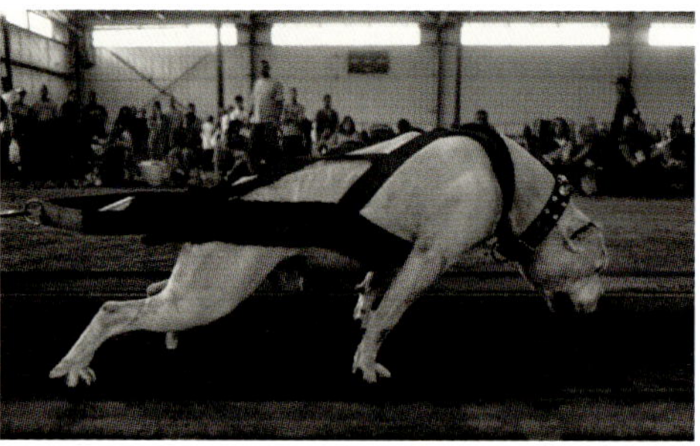

Work!
Essex County, Massachusetts
July 2001
pages 82/83

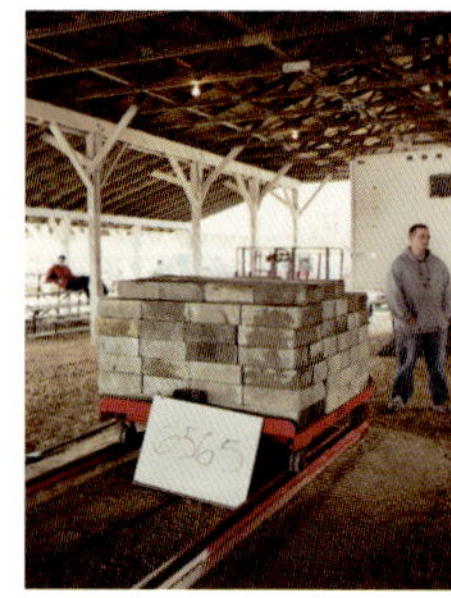

The Weight
Salem County, New Jersey
April 2003
page 84

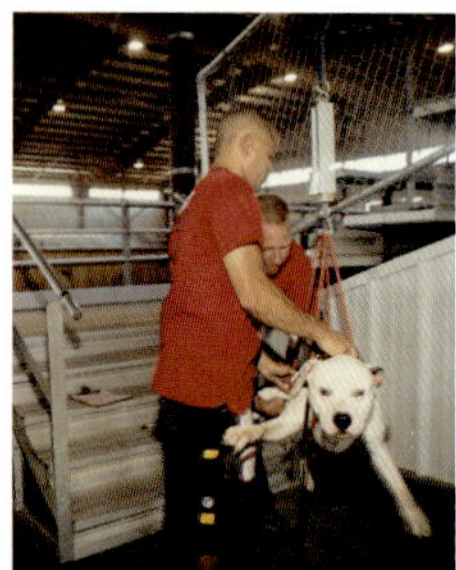

Herbie and Rich
(Weigh-in)
Essex County, Massachusetts
July 2001
page 85

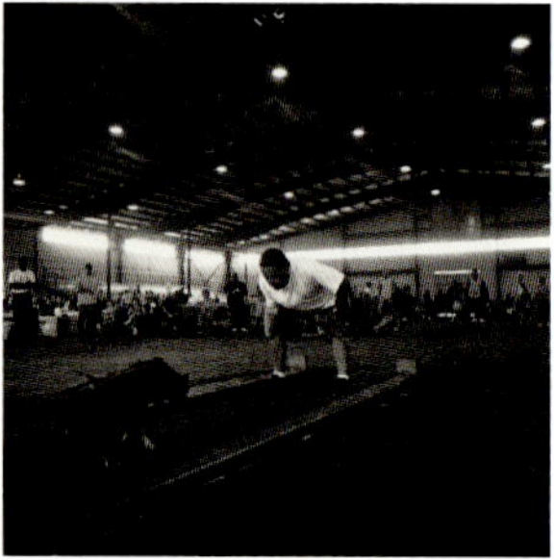

Frank #1
Essex County, Massachusetts
July 2001
page 86

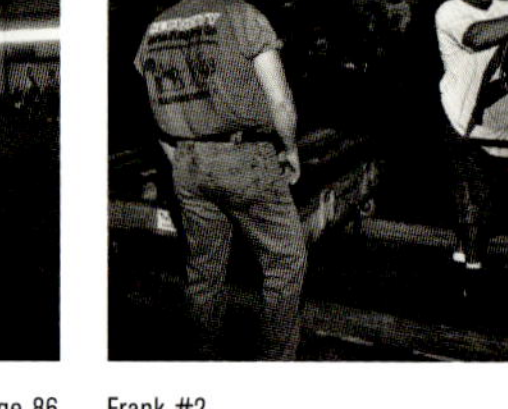
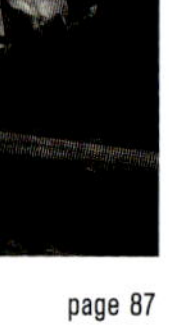

Frank #2
Essex County, Massachusetts
July 2001
page 87

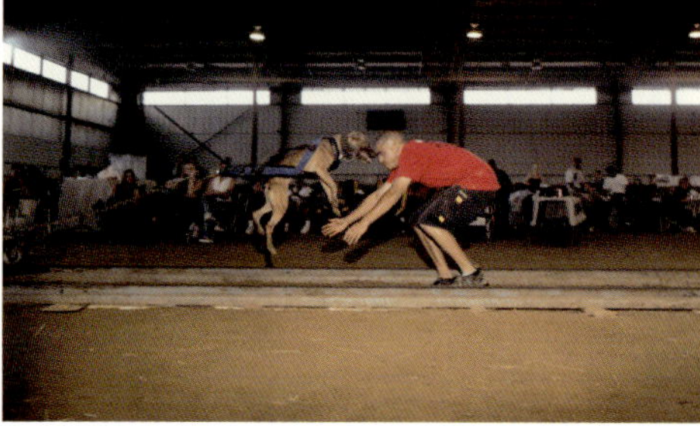

Rich, with Spics-n-Pits' China
Essex County, Massachusetts
July 2001
pages 88/89

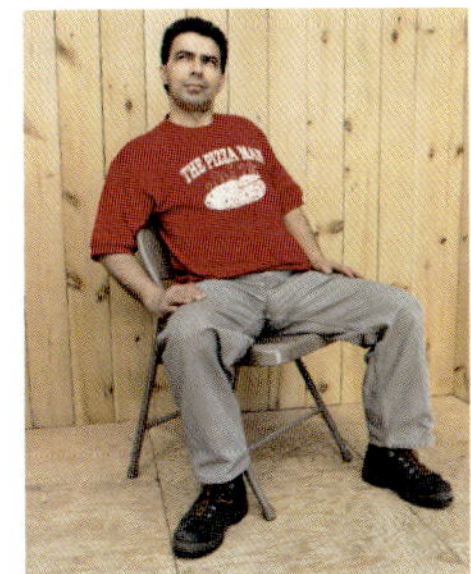

Mr. Nino Bussa page 91
Salem County, New Jersey
April 2003

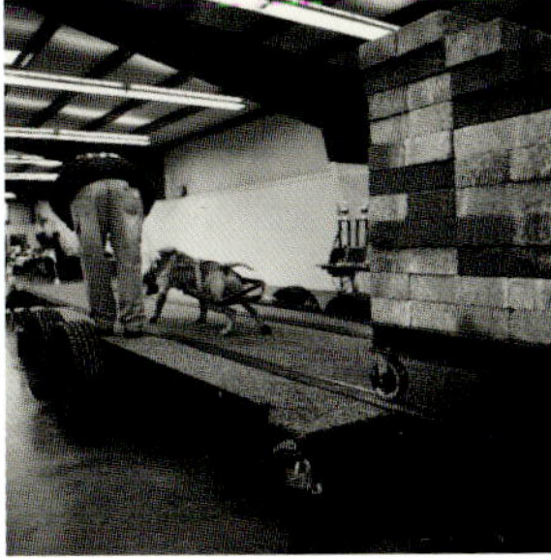

Weight Pull page 92
Charlotte, North Carolina
November 2000

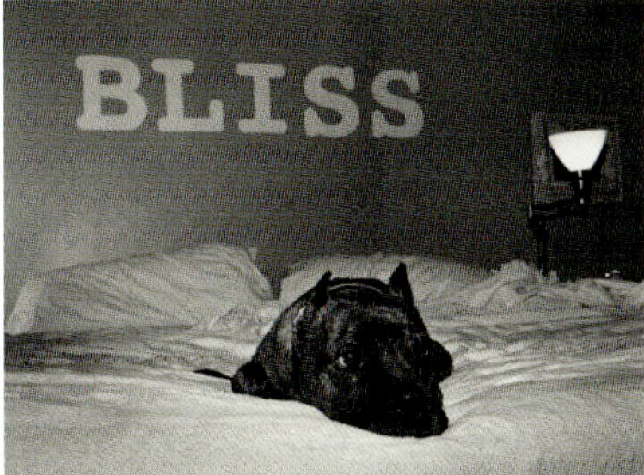

South (D. June 2003) page 93
Atlanta, Georgia
November 2002

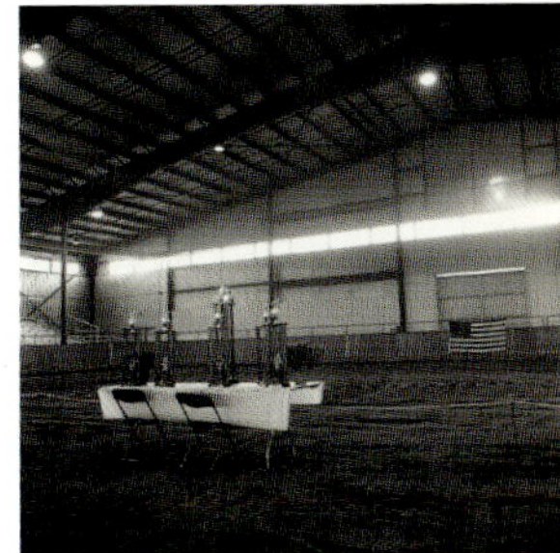

Show Ring page 95
Essex County, Massachusetts
July 2001

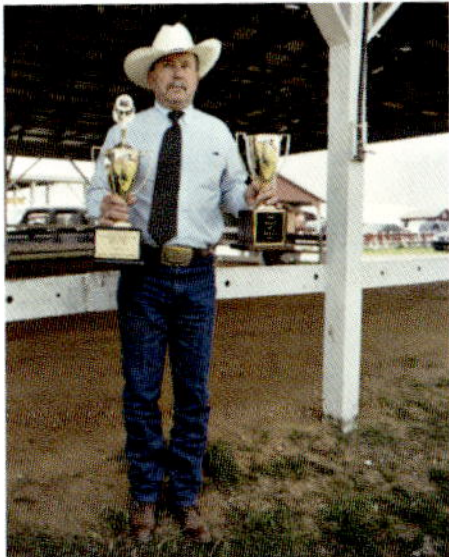

Mr. Ronnie Ewing page 96
Salem County, New Jersey
April 2001

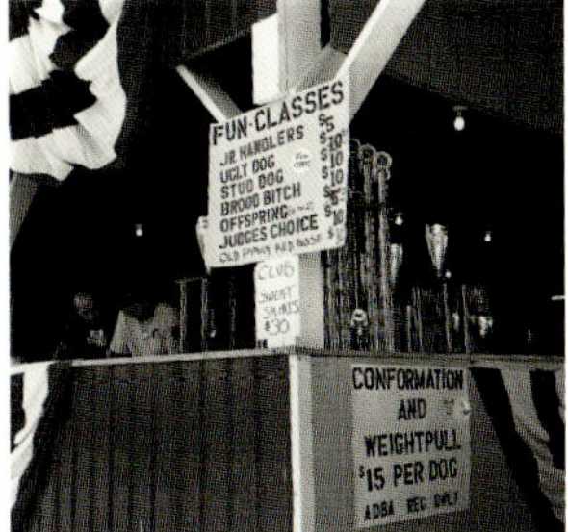

Fun Classes page 97
Salem County, New Jersey
April 2001

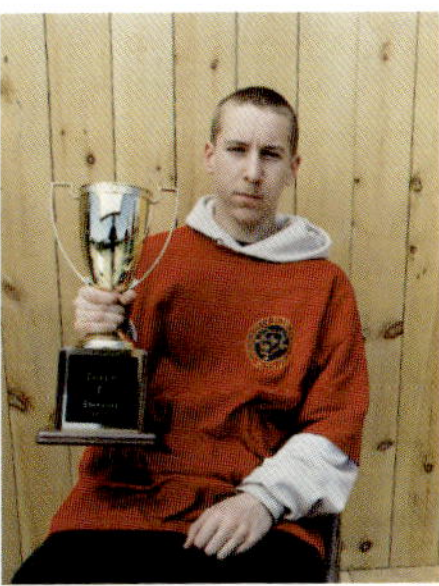

Mark page 98
(Champion of Champions)
Salem County, New Jersey
April 2003

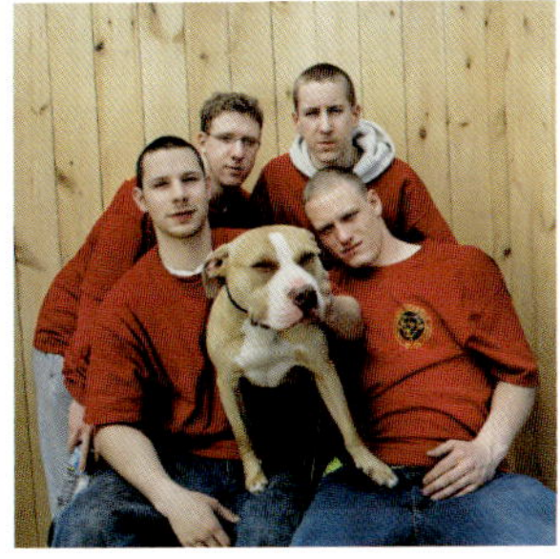

Boo's Crew page 99
Salem County, New Jersey
April 2003

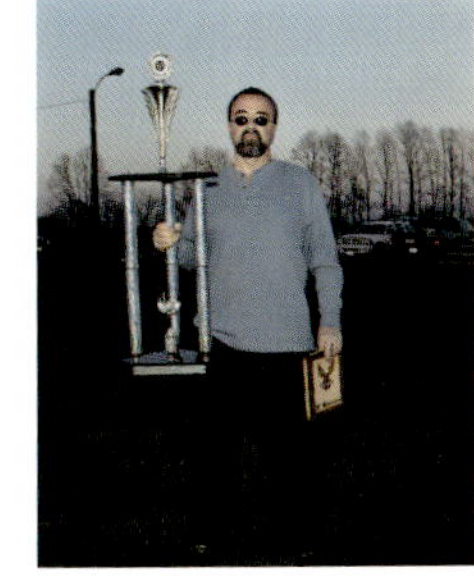

Mr. Frank Rocca page 101
Salem County, New Jersey
April 2003

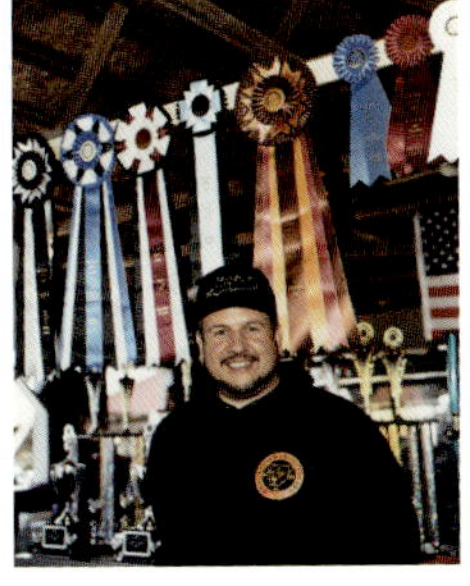

Mr. Frank Perez page 102
Salem County, New Jersey
April 2003

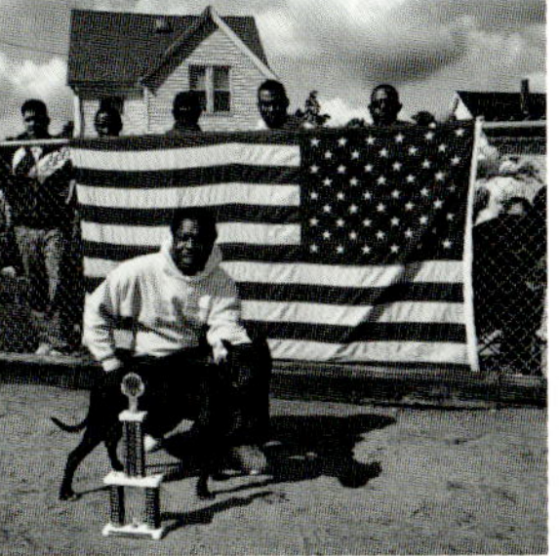

Spider G page 103
Lynn, Massachusetts
September, 2001

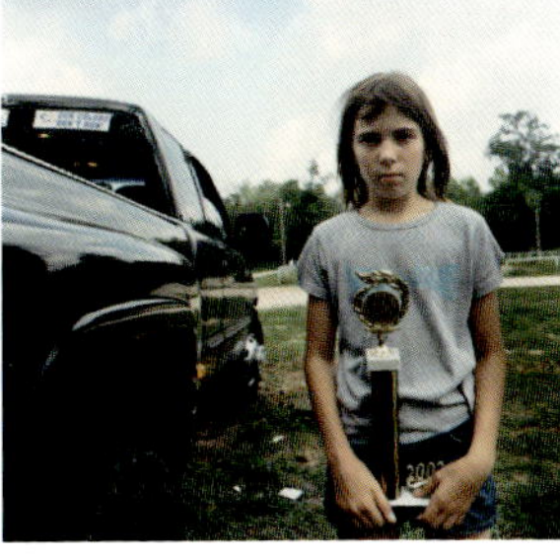

Farron's Daughter page 104
Liberty, Texas
April 2002

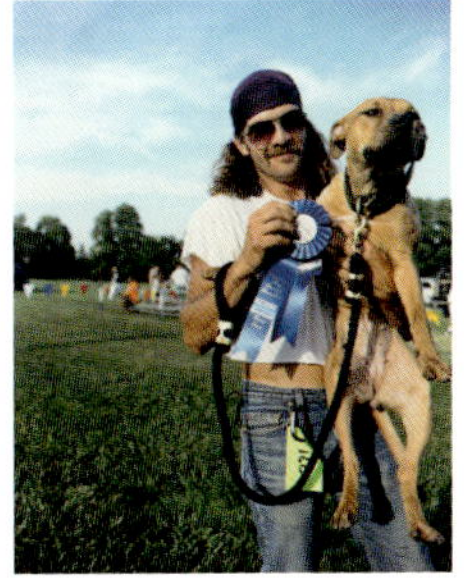

First page 105
Salem County, New Jersey
July 2001

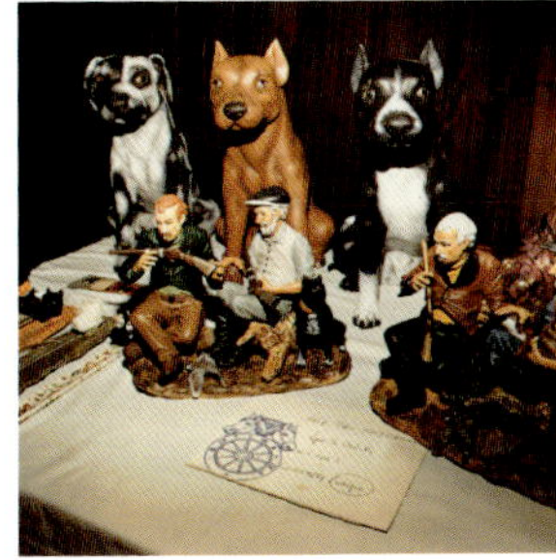

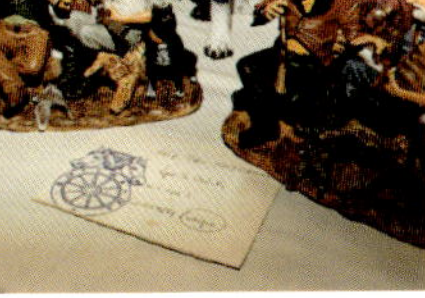

Untitled (Statues) page 106
Essex County, Massachusetts
June 2003

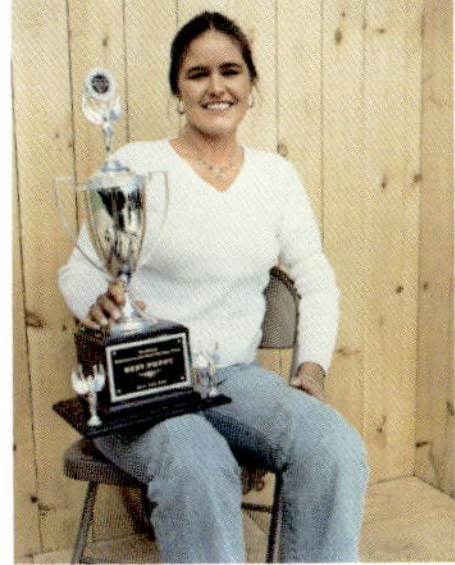

Shawn Gibbs page 107
(Best Puppy)
Salem County, New Jersey
April 2003

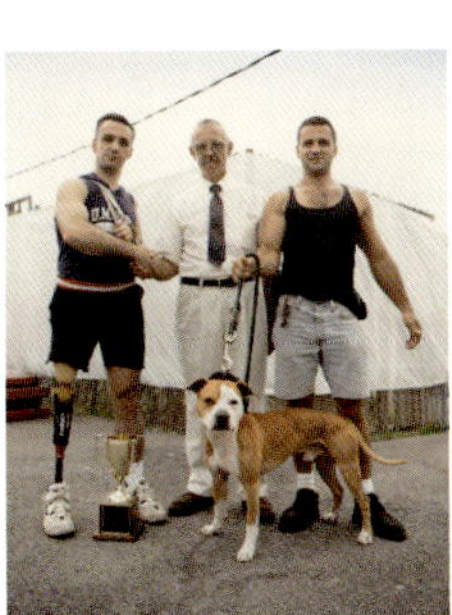

Lonnie and the page 108
Li Butti Brothers
Berks County, Pennsylvania
September 2000

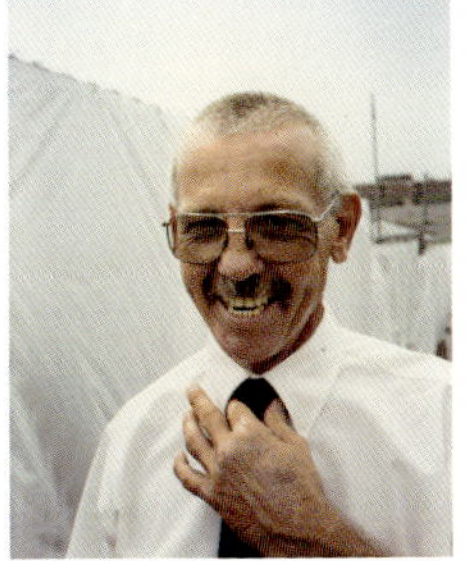

Mr. Lonnie Boruff page 109
Berks County, Pennsylvania
September 2000

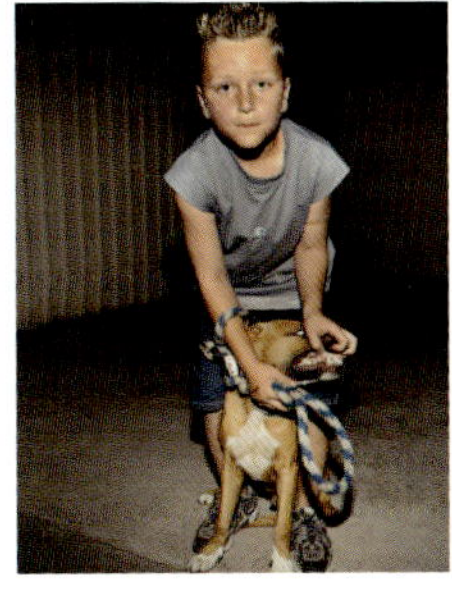

Junior Handler page 110
Seguin, Texas
May 2003

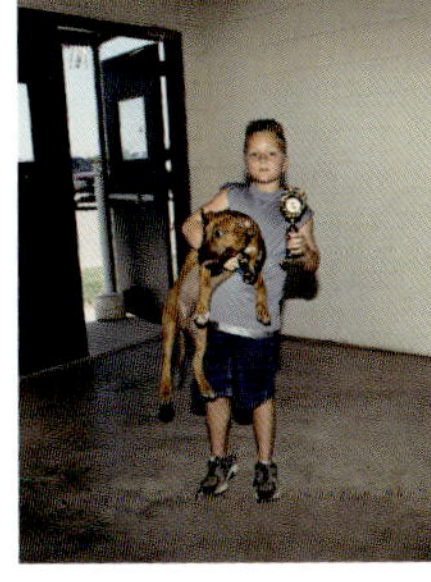

Junior Handler (Winner) page 111
Seguin, Texas
May 2003

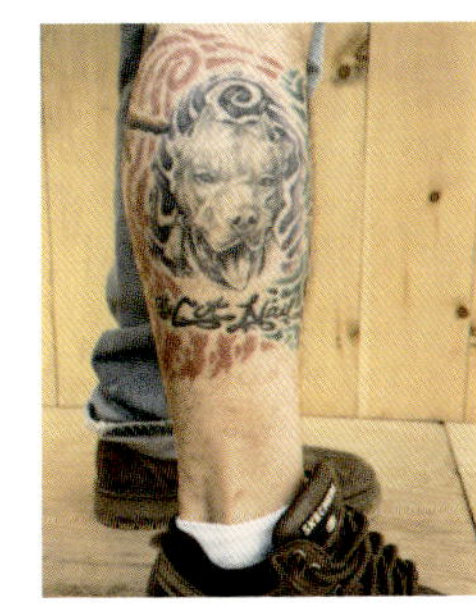

Cut Nail (Rich's Tattoo) page 112
Salem County, New Jersey
July 2002

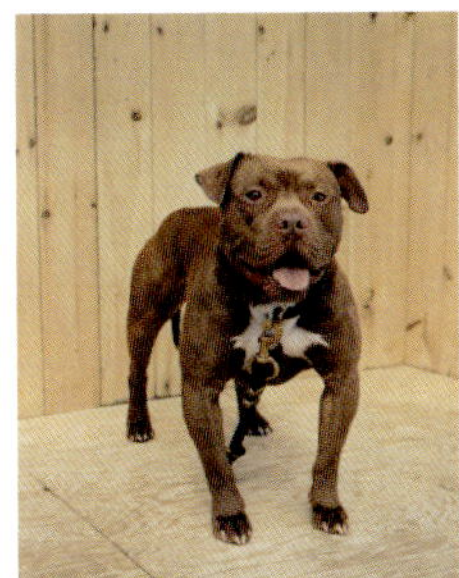

Hunk page 114

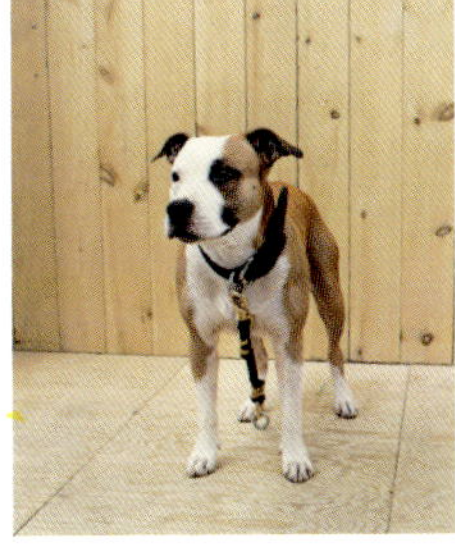

Brandy page 114

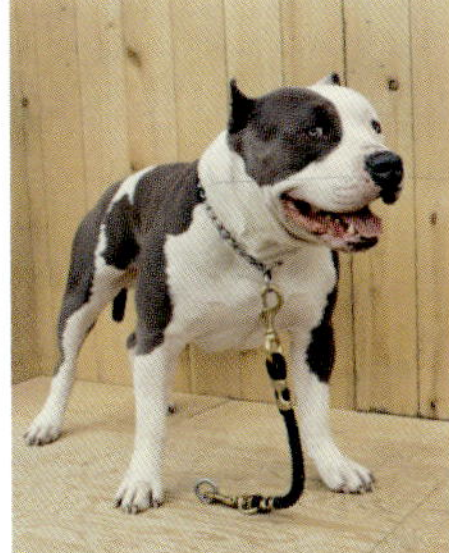

Boomslang page 114

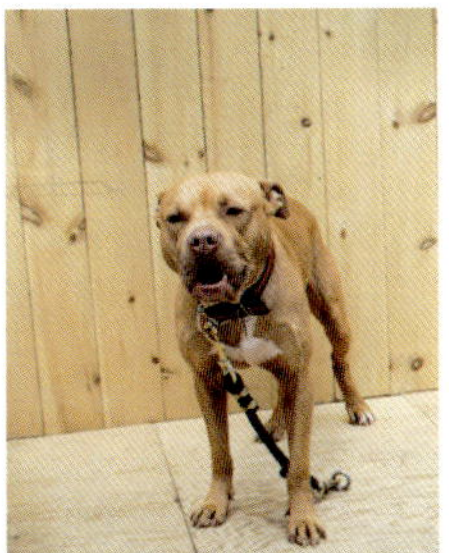

Red Boy page 114

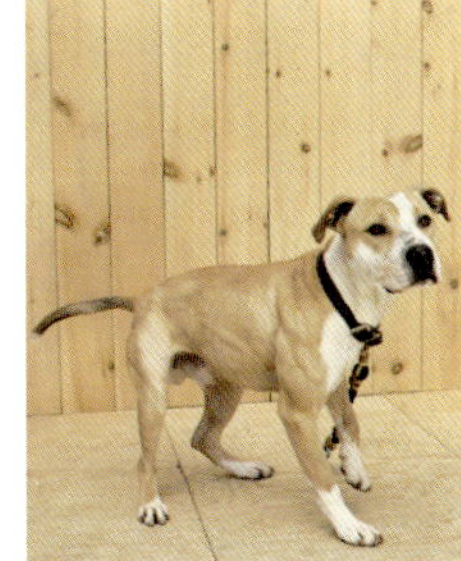

Magnum page 115

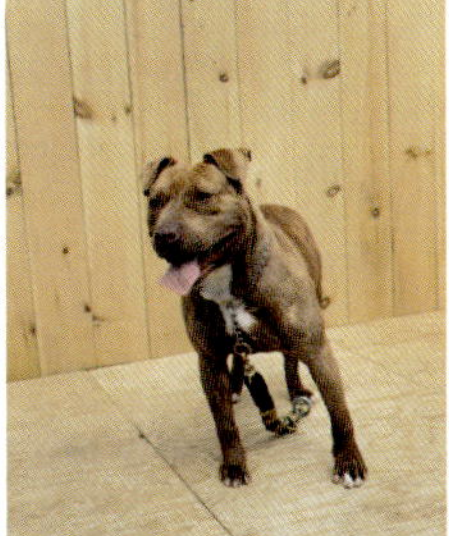

Justice page 115

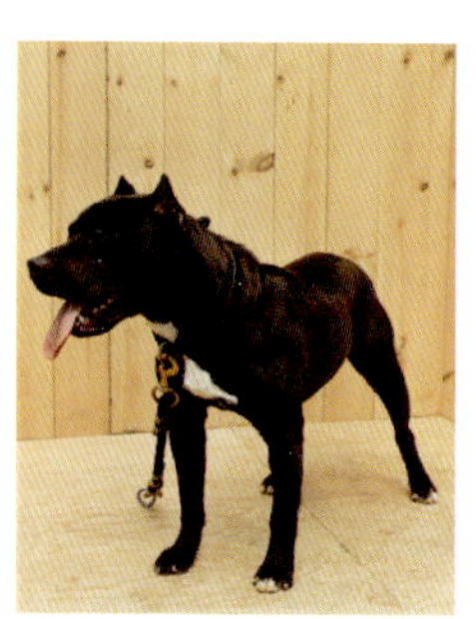

Bingi-Stout page 115

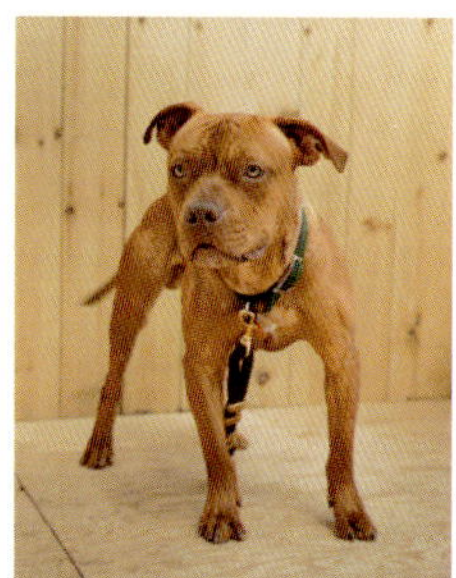
TJ page 115

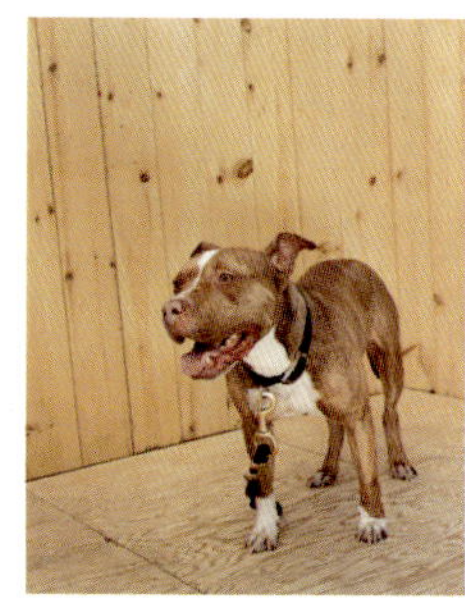
Tracy page 116

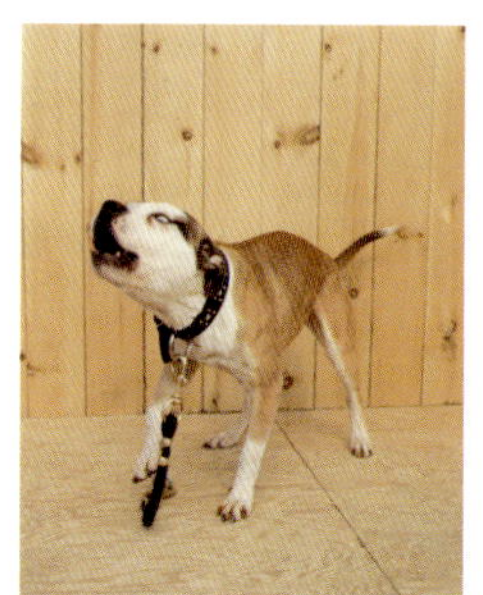
Luna page 116

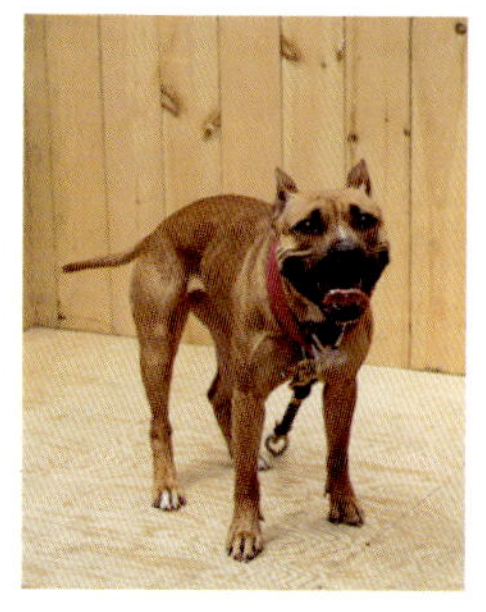
Drama page 116

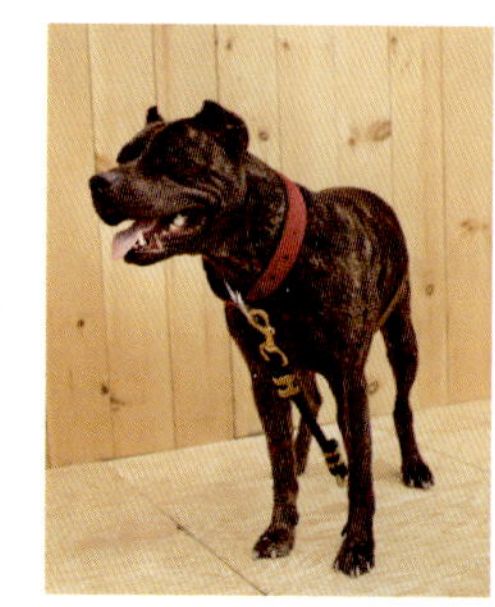
Stacia page 116

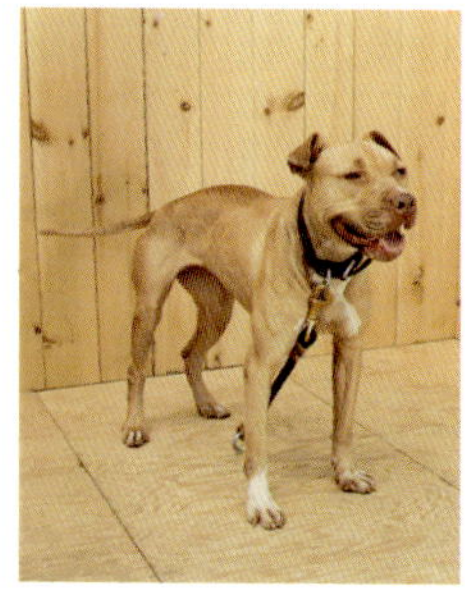
Boo-Boo page 117

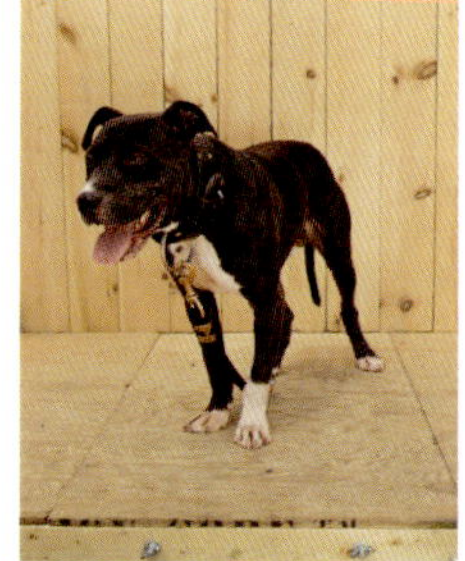
Combiachi page 117

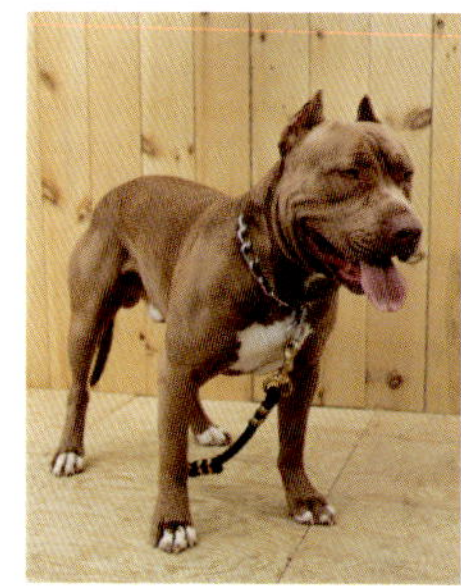
Gucci page 117

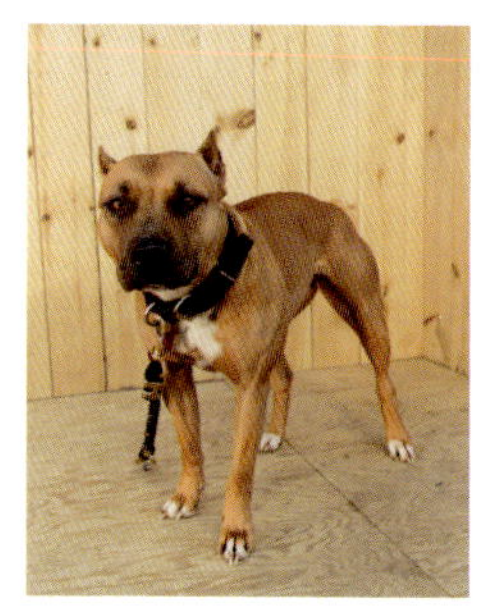
Angel page 117

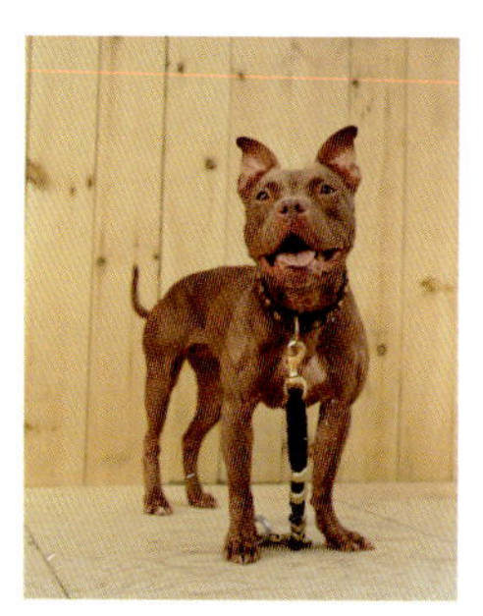
Try-N-Stopper page 118

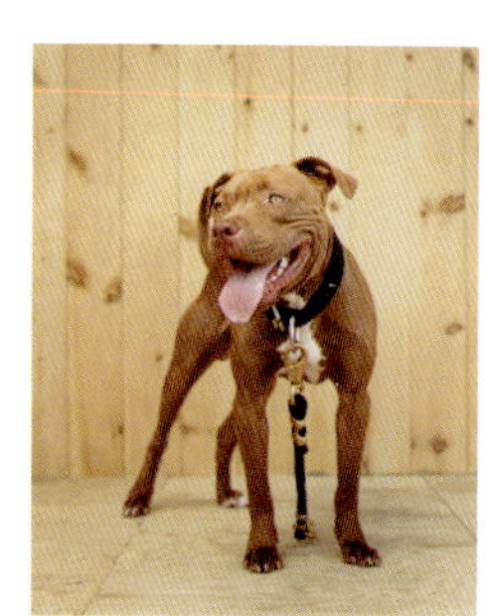
Taz page 118

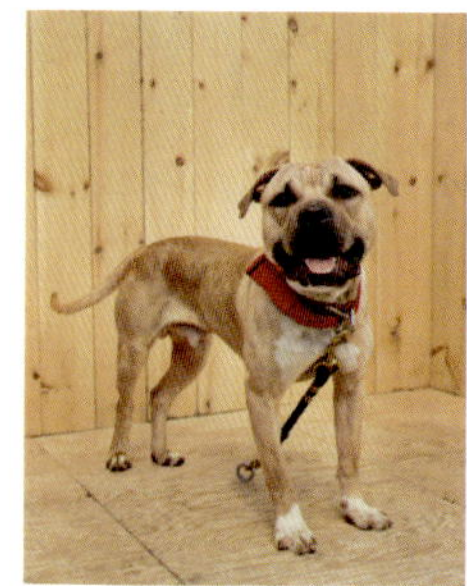
Charlie page 118

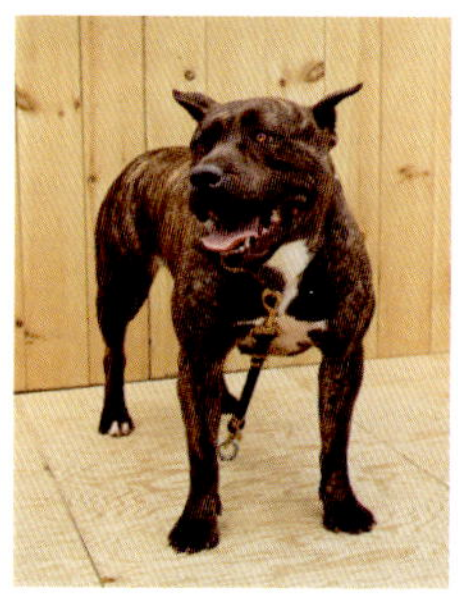
Clea page 118

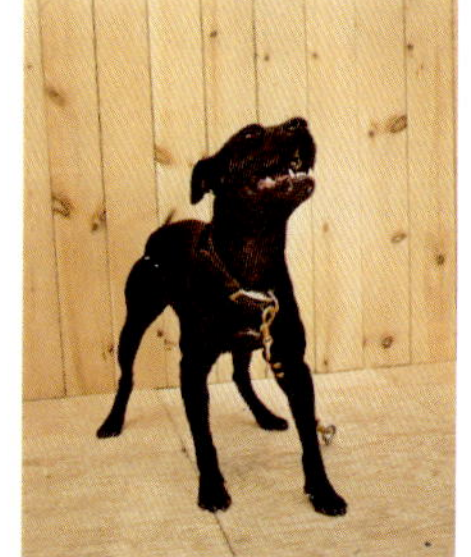
Warren page 119

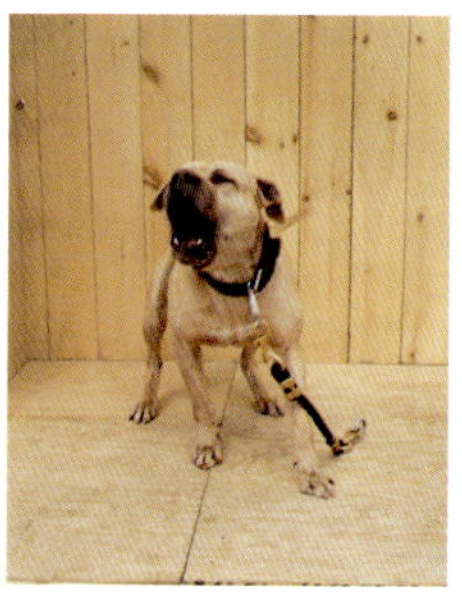
Sammy page 119

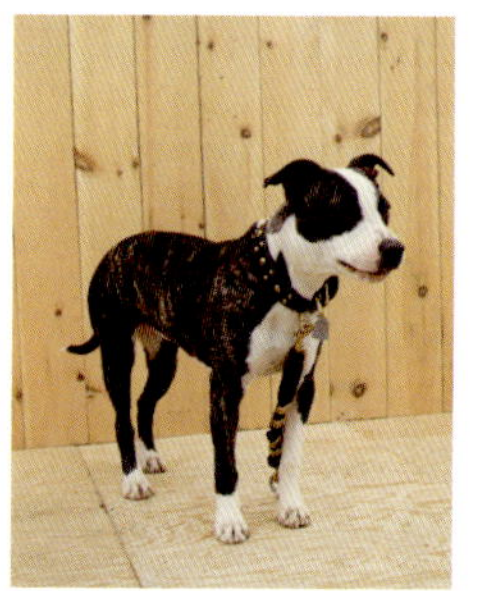
Jane page 119

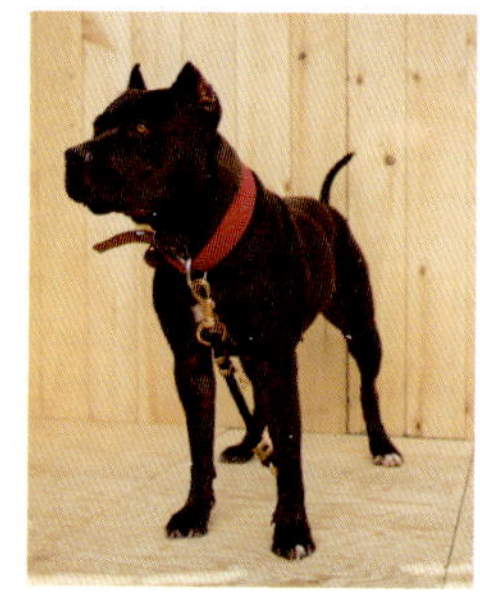
Felony page 119

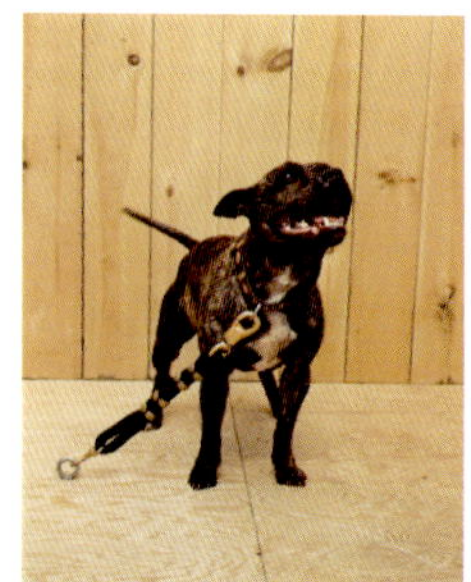
Mugsy page 120

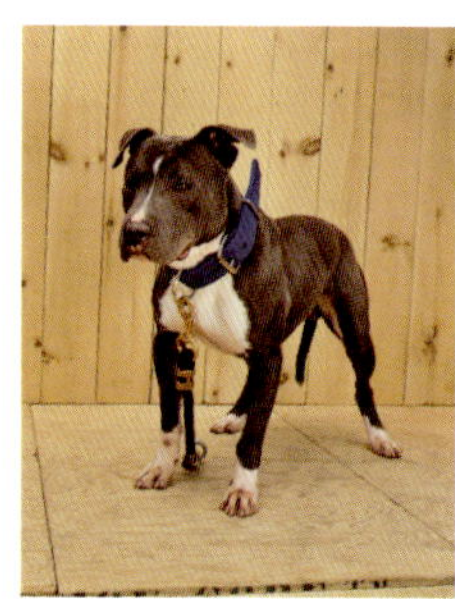
Caesar page 120

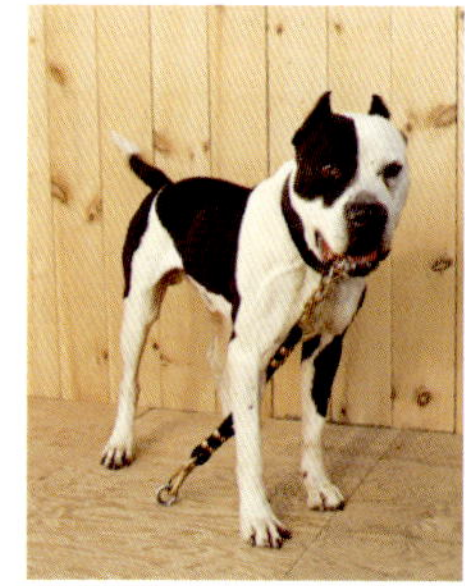
Mac page 120

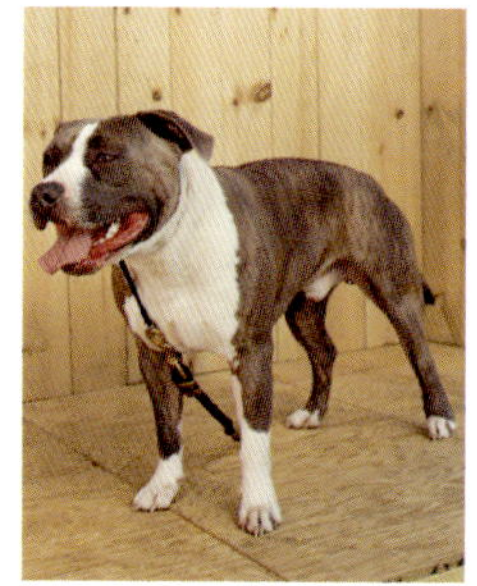
Onyx page 120

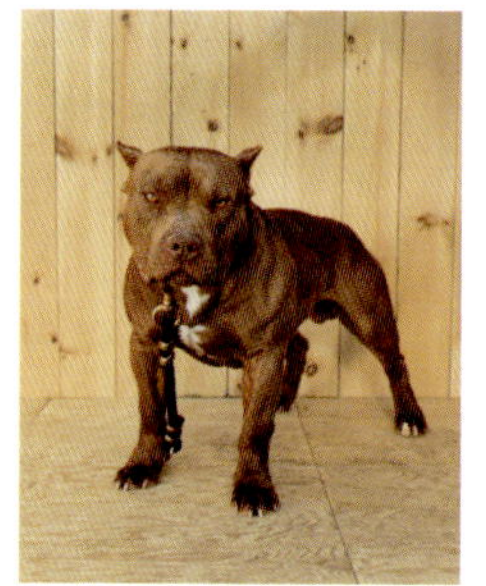
Reno page 121

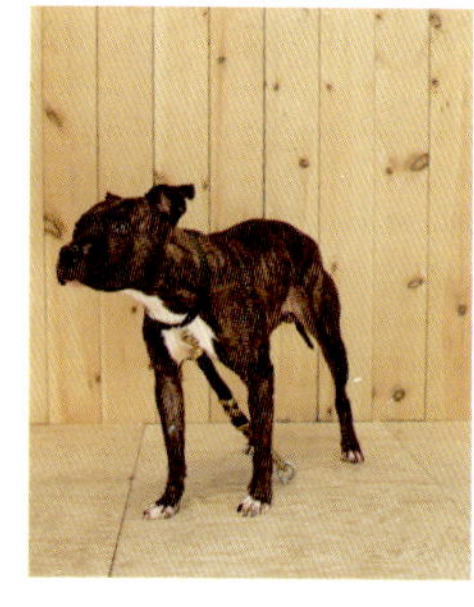
Tonghy-Boy page 121

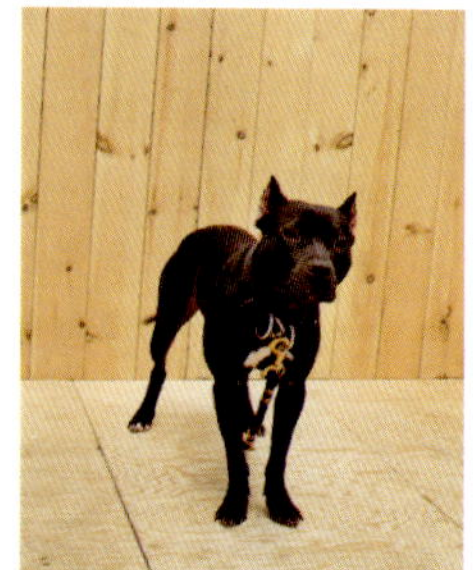
Maxine page 121

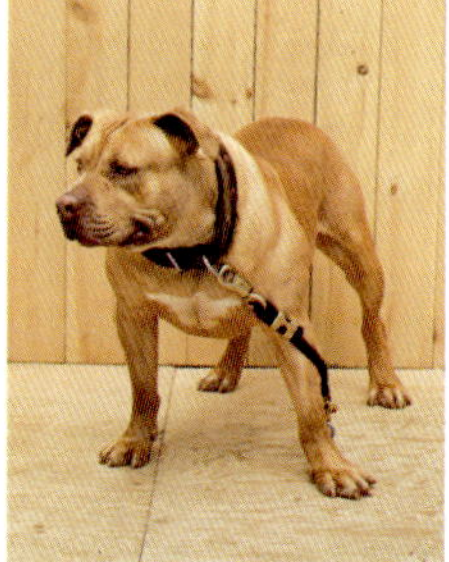
Calvin page 121

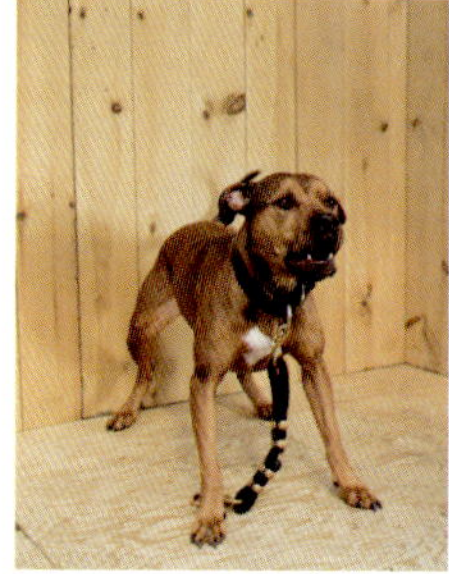
Moody Bitch page 122

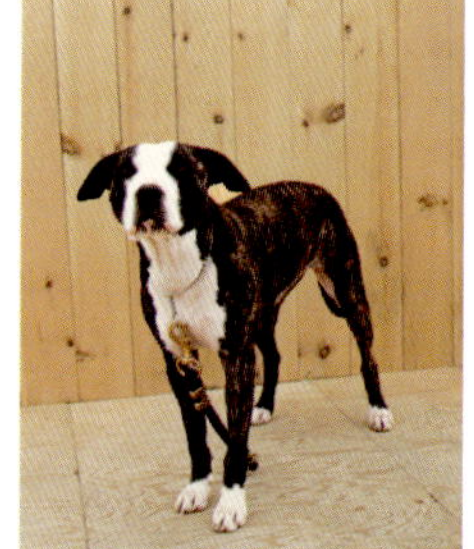
Neha page 122

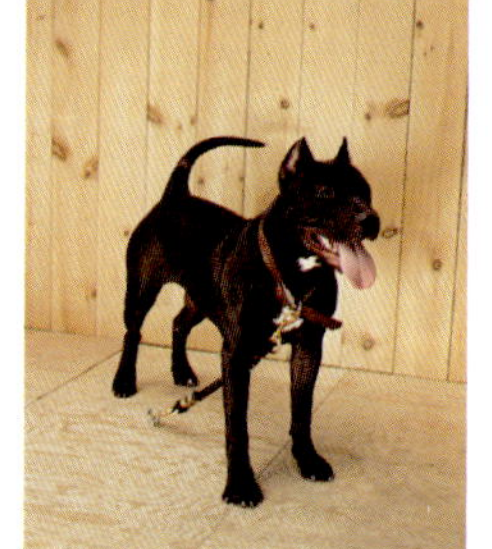
Kalia page 122

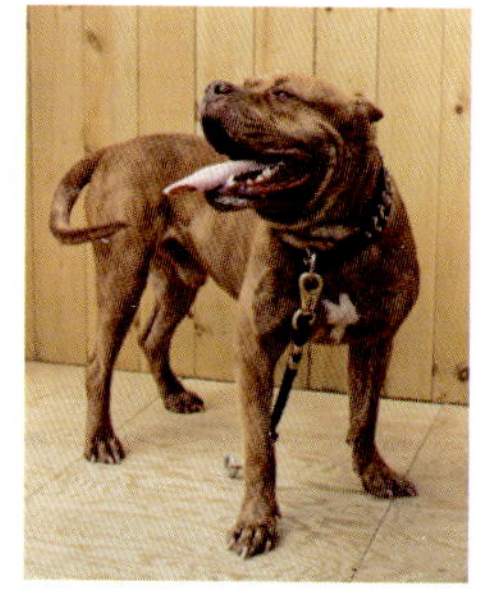
Savage page 122

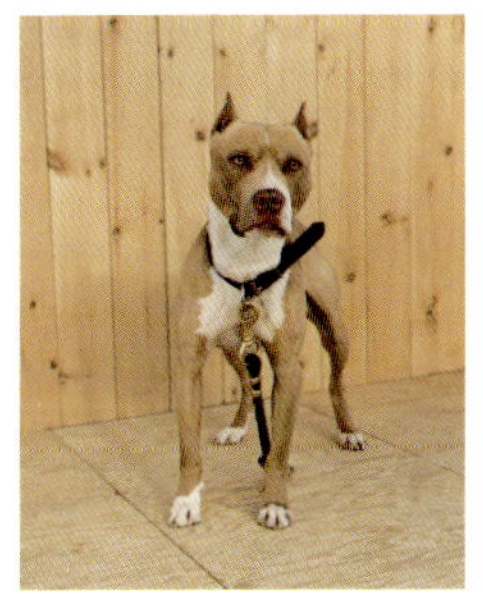
Thinner page 123

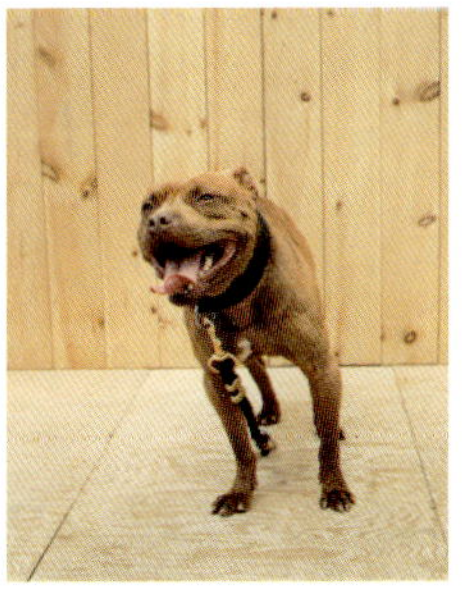
Cosmo page 123

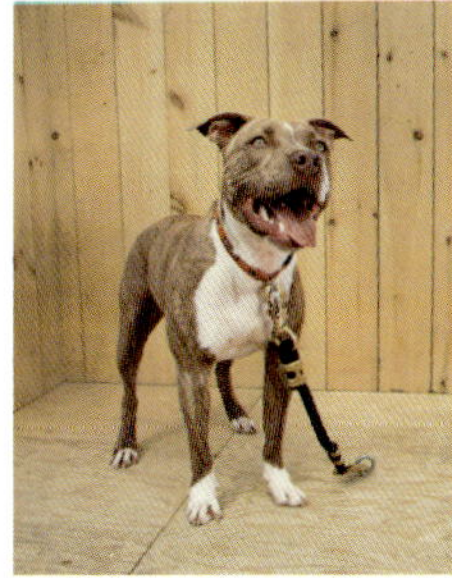
Thor page 123

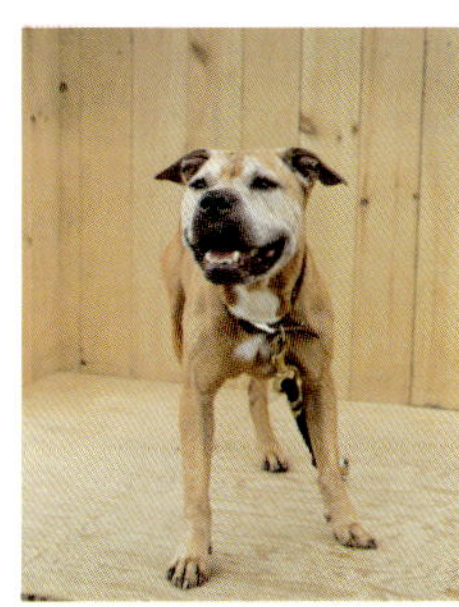
Nicky page 123

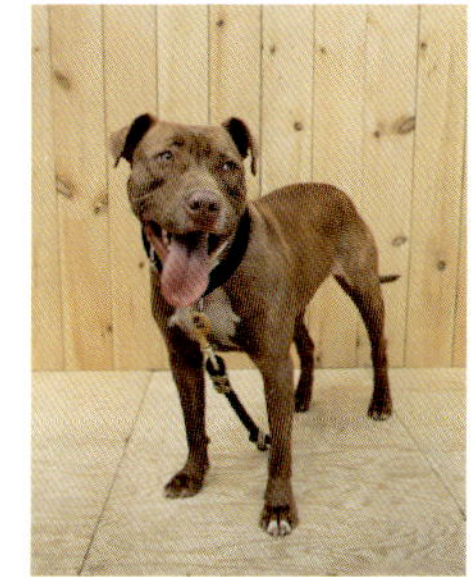
Bella page 124

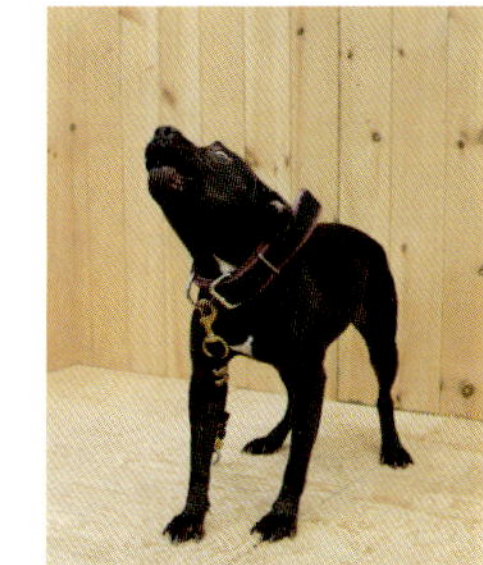
Prada page 124

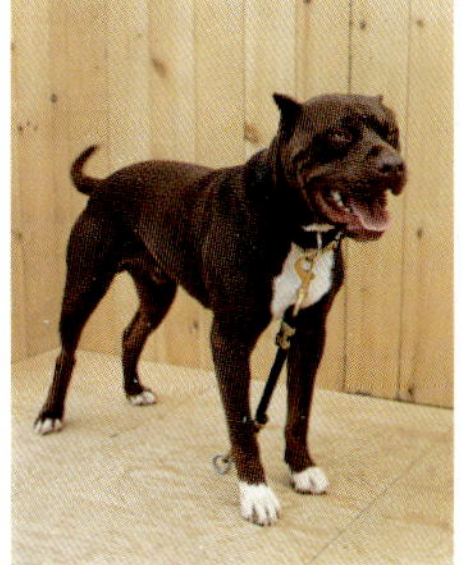
Ox page 124

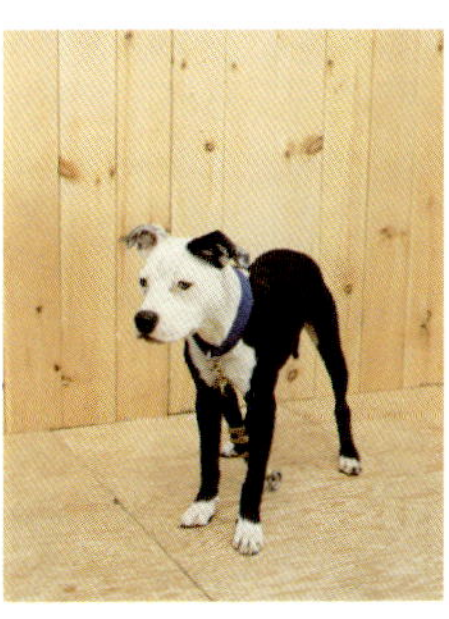
J.J. page 124

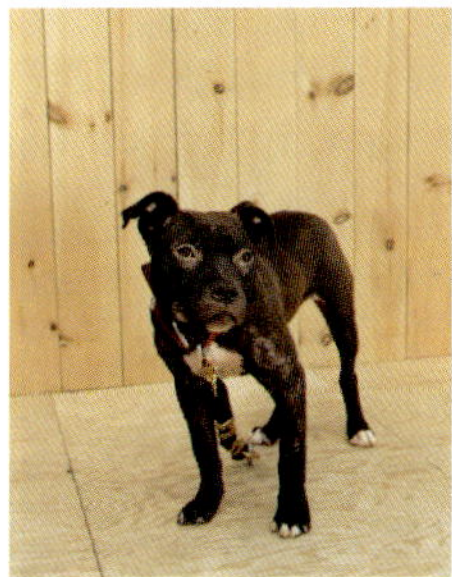
Cane page 125

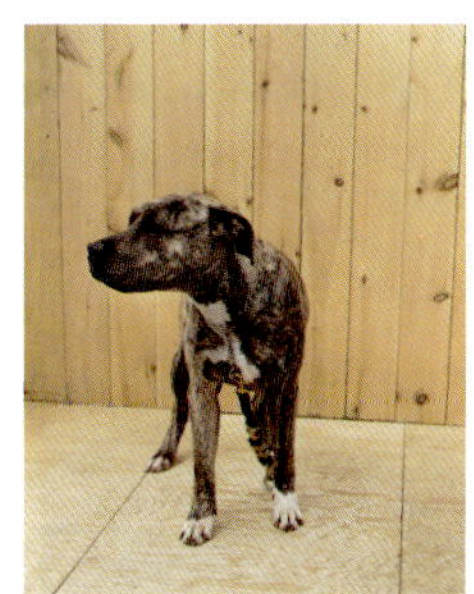
Rock page 125

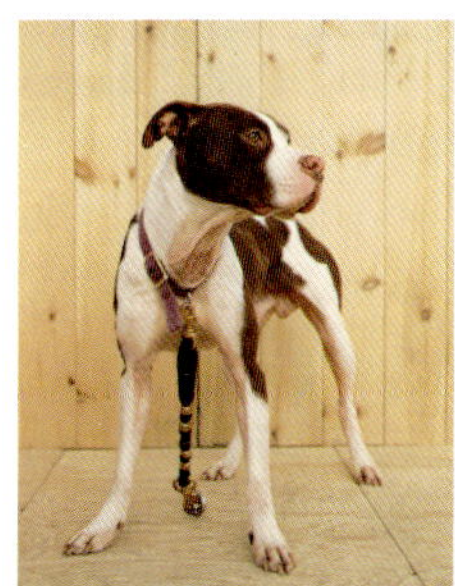
Dewey page 125

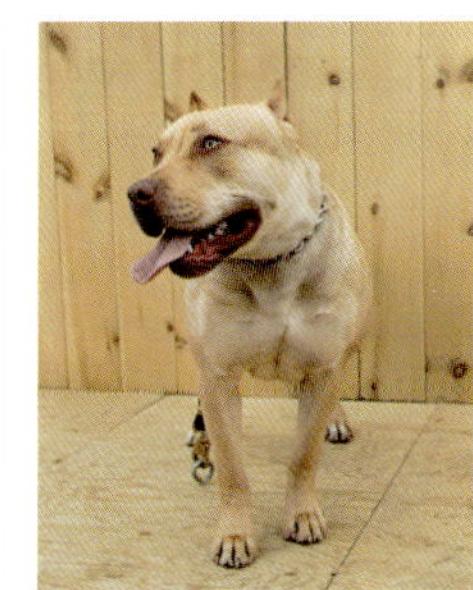
Envy page 125

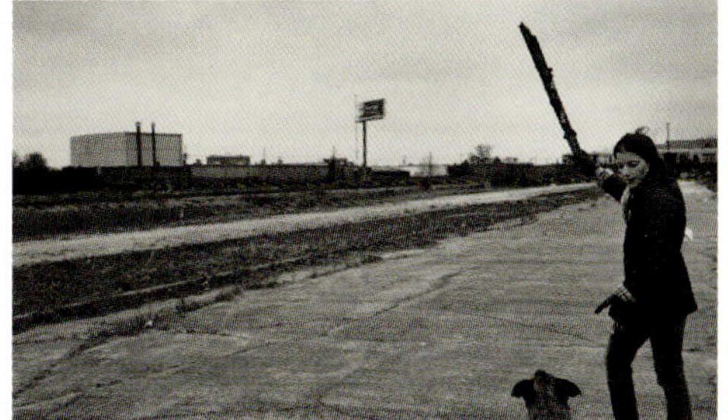
Carolyn Carr and Lillian pages 134/135
Atlanta, Georgia
November 2002

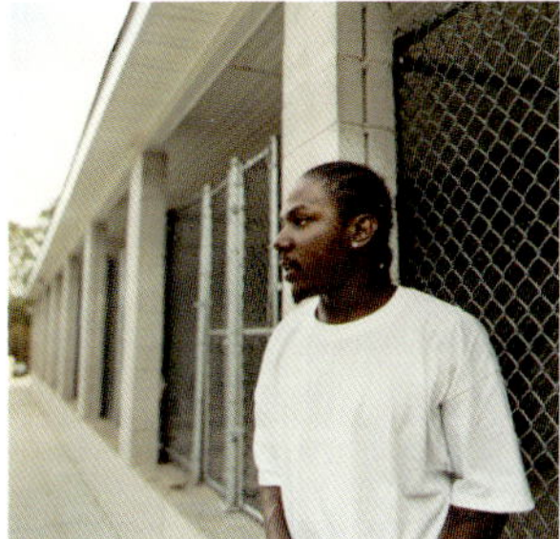
Mr. James Patton page 137
(pitfallkennels.com)
Fairburn, Georgia
November 2002

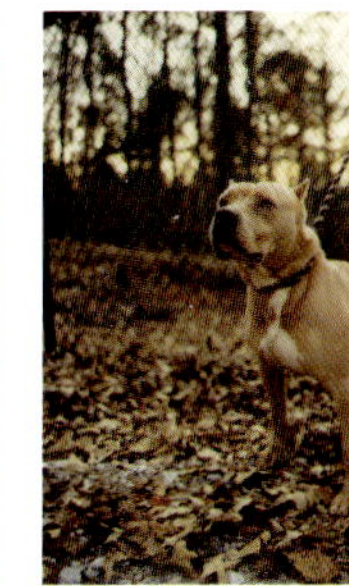
Fawn Dog page 138
(pitfallkennels.com)
Fairburn, Georgia
November 2002

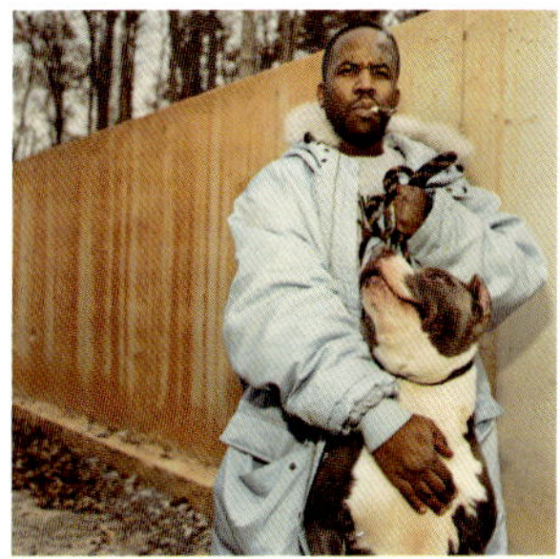
Big Boi from Outkast, with Blue Dog page 139
(pitfallkennels.com)
Fairburn, Georgia
November 2002

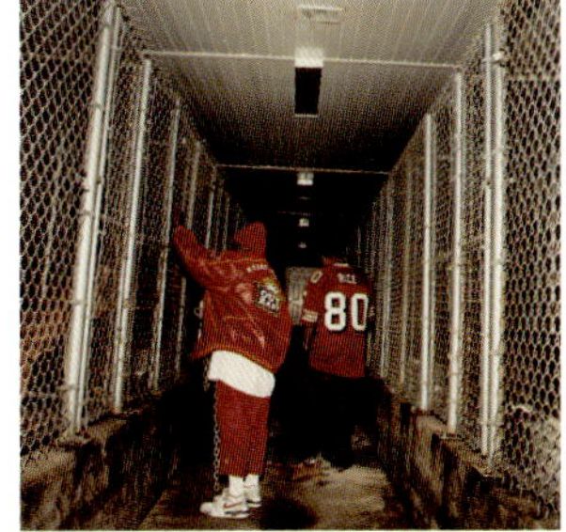
Indoor / Outdoor Kennel page 140
(pitfallkennels.com)
Fairburn, Georgia
November 2002

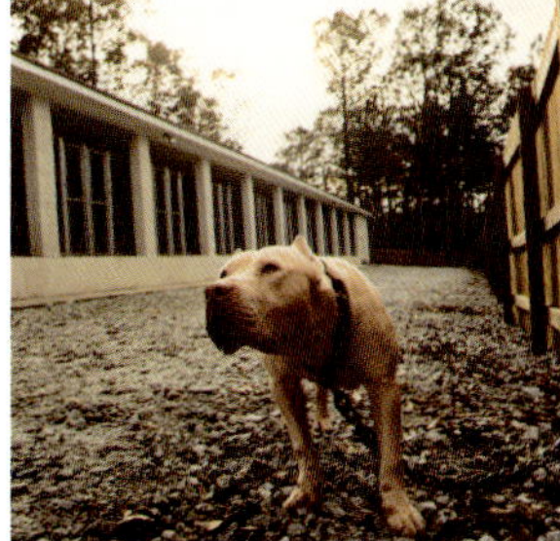
Light Fawn Dog and Kennel page 141
(pitfallkennels.com)
Fairburn, Georgia
November 2002

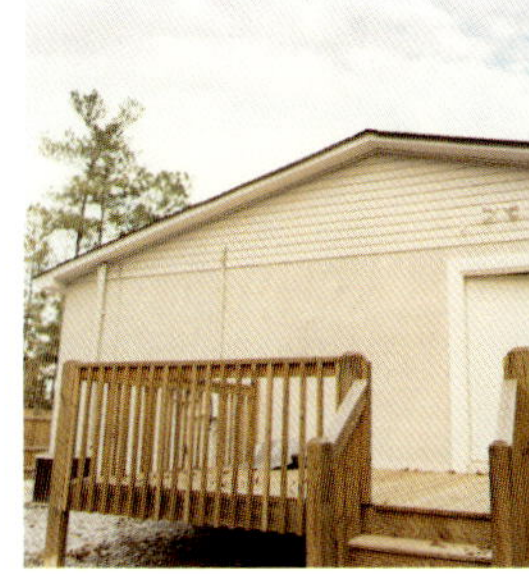
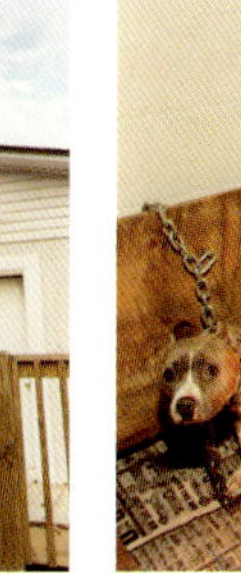
Kennel House page 142
Fairburn, Georgia
November 2002

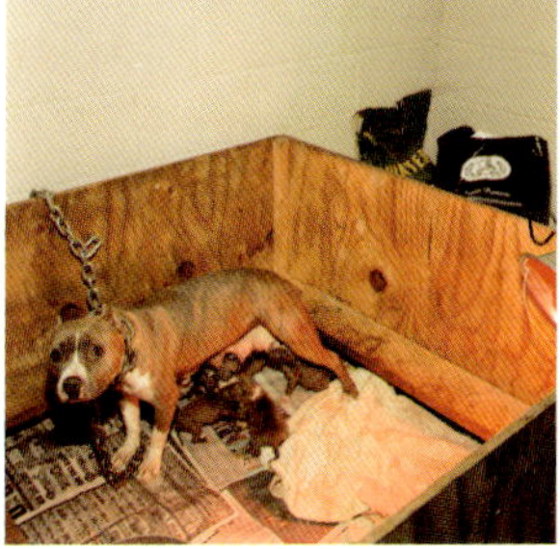
Mother and Pups page 143
Fairburn, Georgia
November 2002

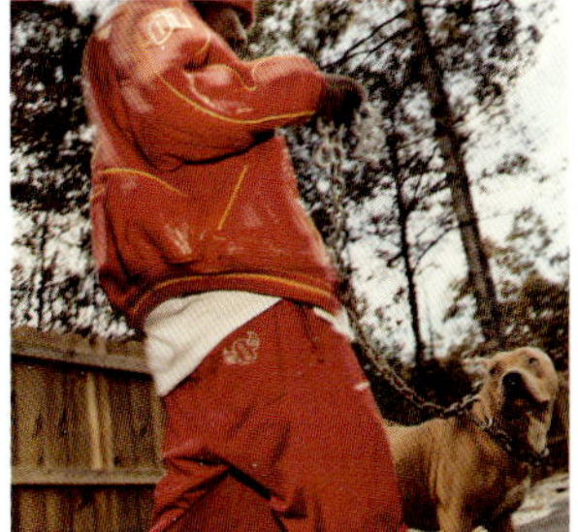
James, with Dog page 144
(pitfallkennels.com)
Fairburn, Georgia
November 2002

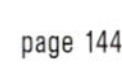
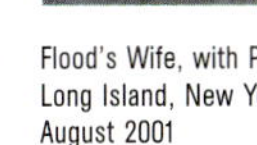
Flood's Wife, with Pup page 146
Long Island, New York
August 2001

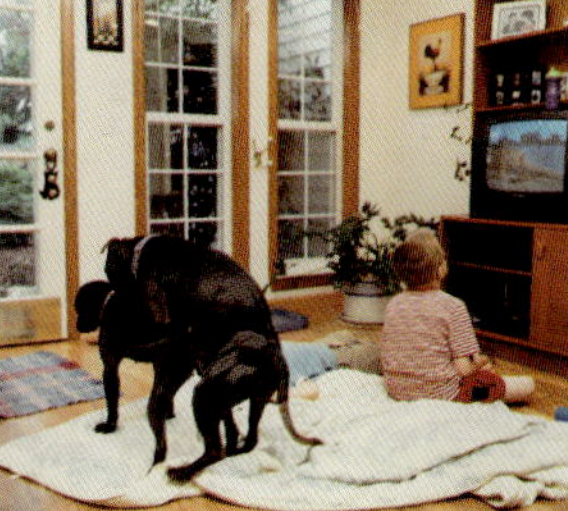
Tarly and Nipper, page 147
Adam, and Paul (Napping)
Fredericksburg, Virginia
June 2003

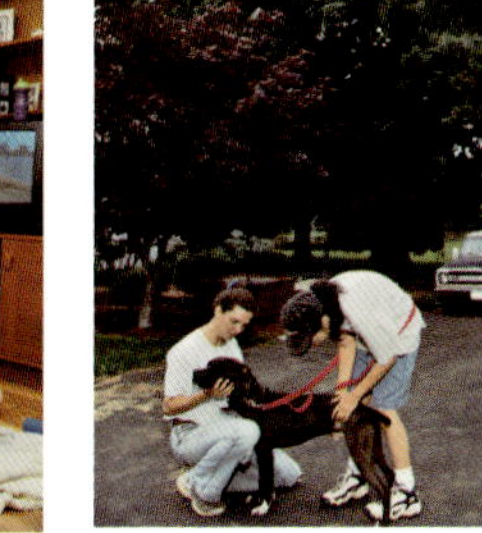
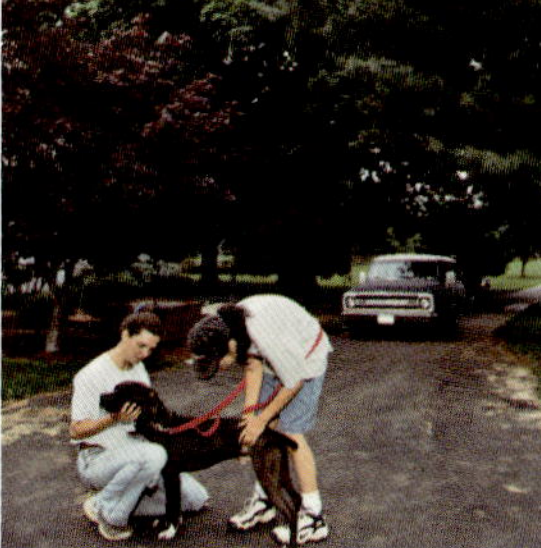
Paula and Chris, with Skillet page 149
Fredericksburg, Virginia
June 2003

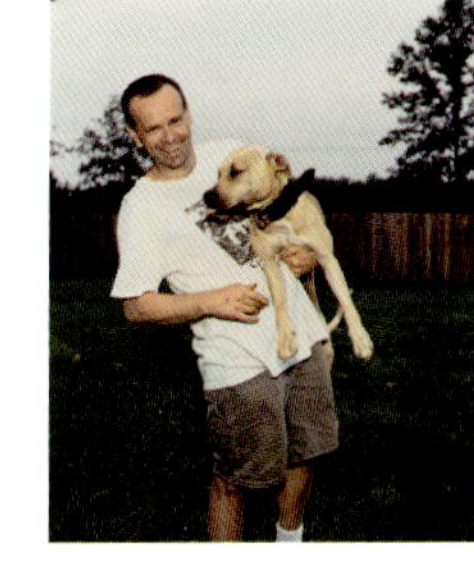
Cuyler and Leader page 150
Fredericksburg, Virginia
June 2003

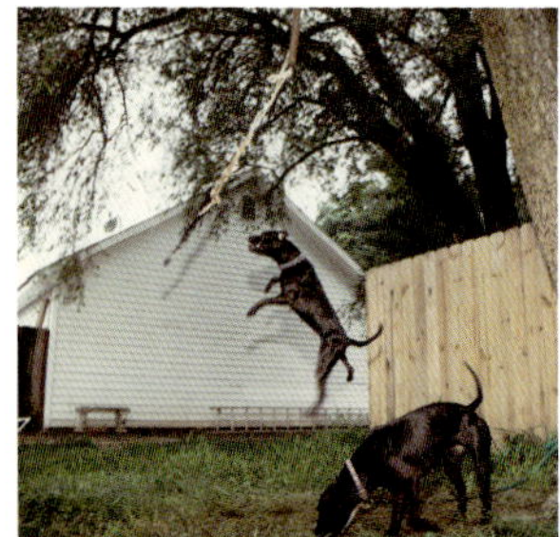

Tarly and Nipper, page 152
on the Springpole
Fredericksburg, Virginia
June 2003

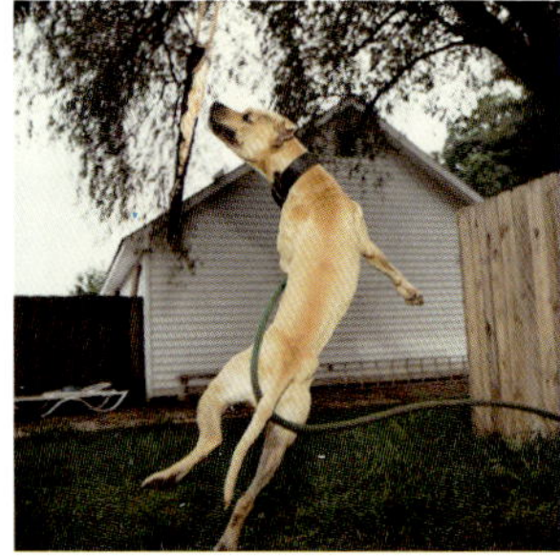

Leader, on the Springpole page 153
Fredericksburg, Virginia
June 2003

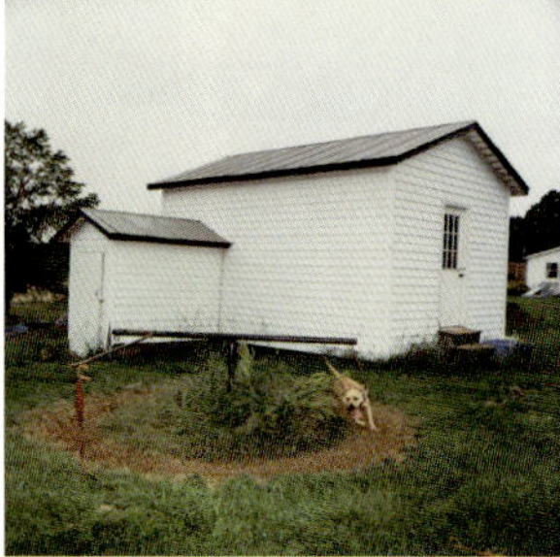

Taffy page 154
Fredericksburg, Virginia
June 2003

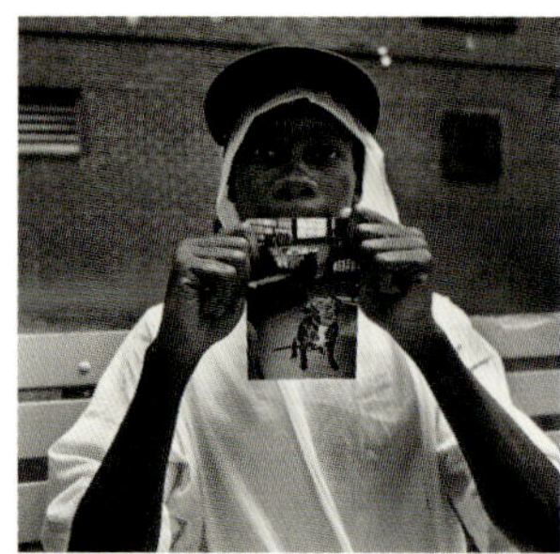

Untitled #1 (Portrait) page 157
Bronx, New York
August 2002

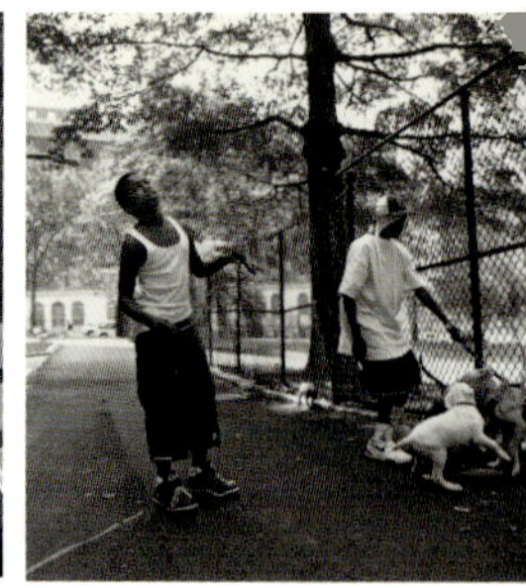

Untitled #2 (Kids and Dogs) pag
Bronx, New York
August 2002

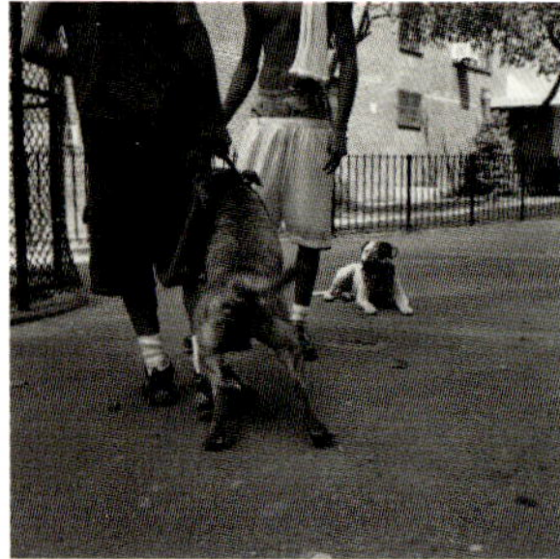

Untitled #3 page 159
Bronx, New York
August 2002

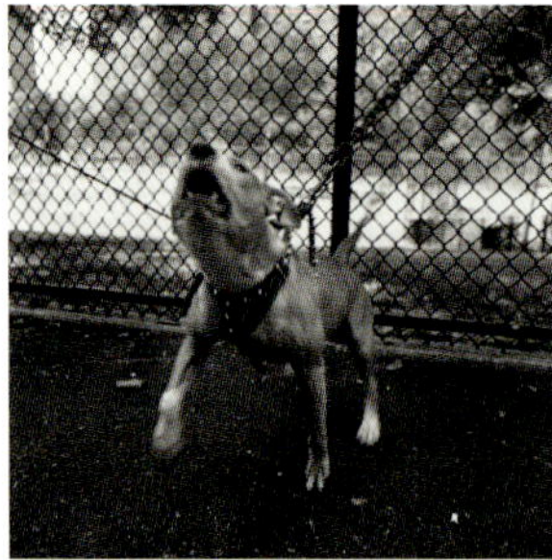

Untitled #4 (Dog) page 160
Bronx, New York
August 2002

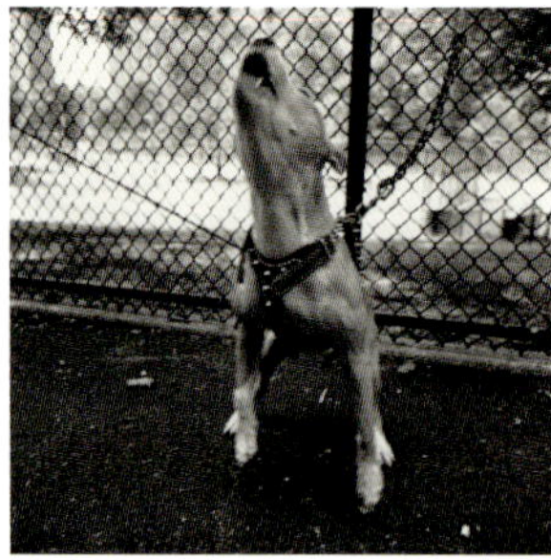

Untitled #5 (Dog) page 161
Bronx, New York
August 2002

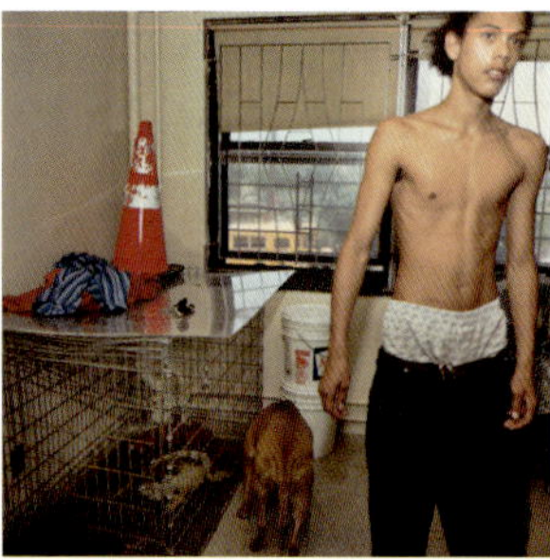

Untitled #6 (Interior / Iguana) page 162
Bronx, New York
August 2002

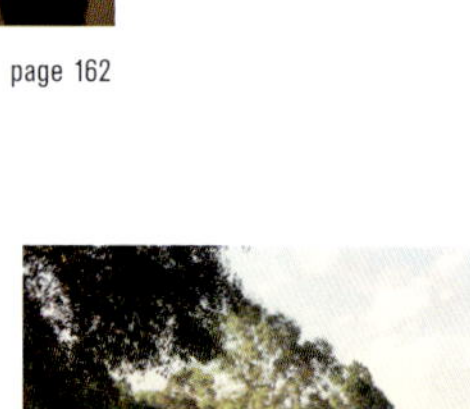

Mike Howell page 165
Louisiana
May 2003

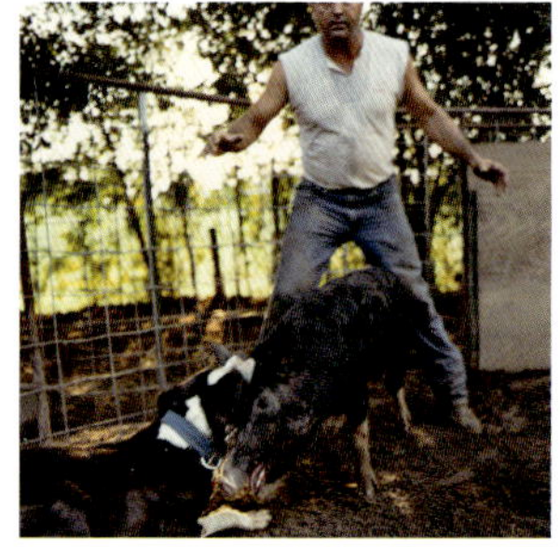

Untitled (Catchdog, Hog, and Mike) page 166
Louisiana
May 2003

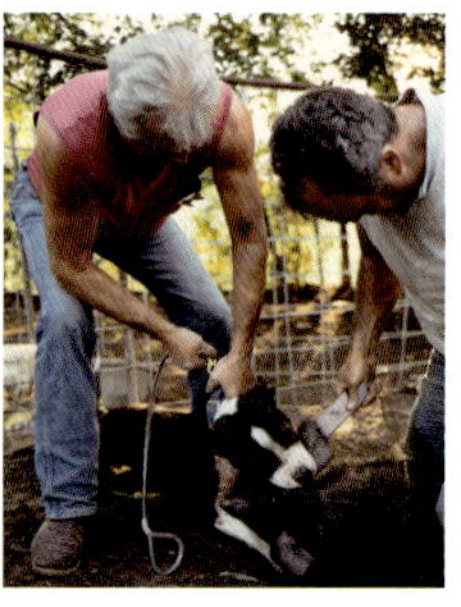

Mike's Dad and Mike page 167
Break a Dog Off a Hog
Louisiana
May 2003

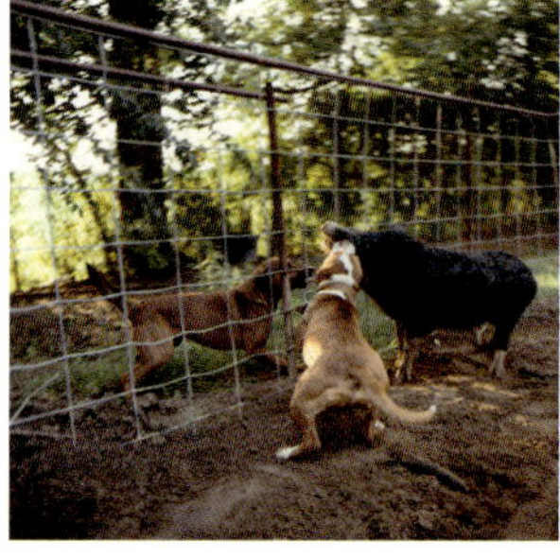

Untitled (Bay Dog, page 168
Catch Dog, and Hog)
Louisiana
May 2003

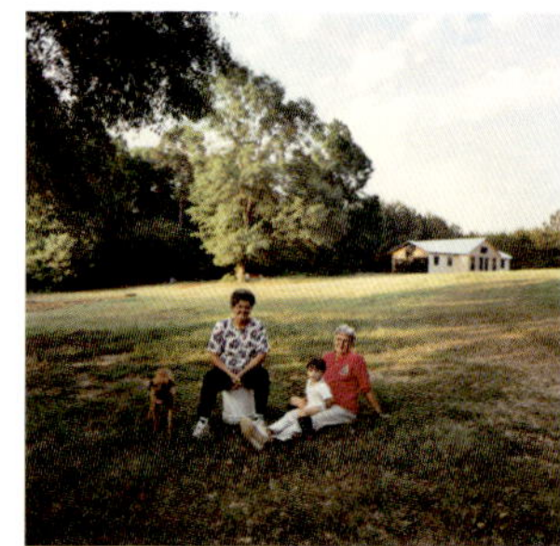

The Howells page 169
Louisiana
May 2003

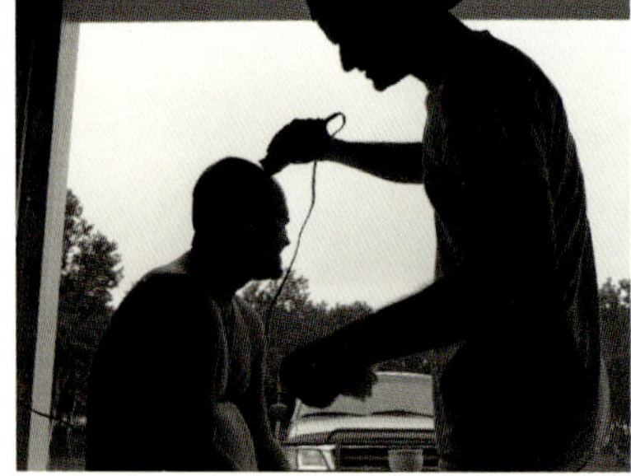

Untitled (Grooming) page 171
East Texas
October 2001

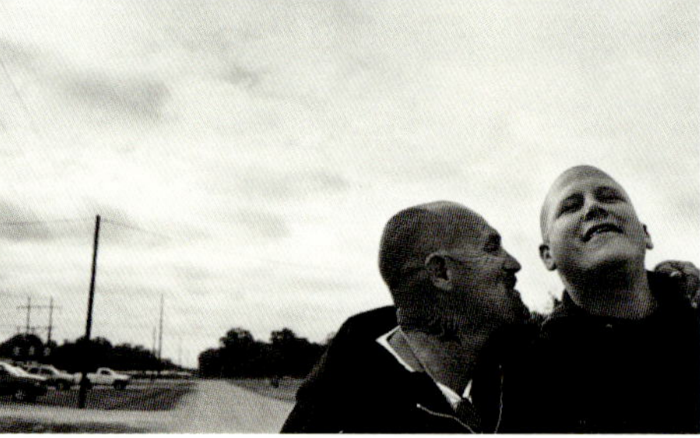

Jerry and Darren pages 172/173
Sorrento, Louisiana
October 2001

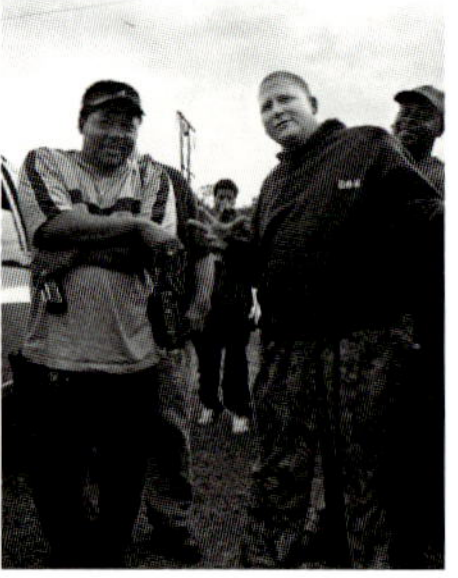

Darren and Friends page 174
Sorrento, Louisiana
October 2001

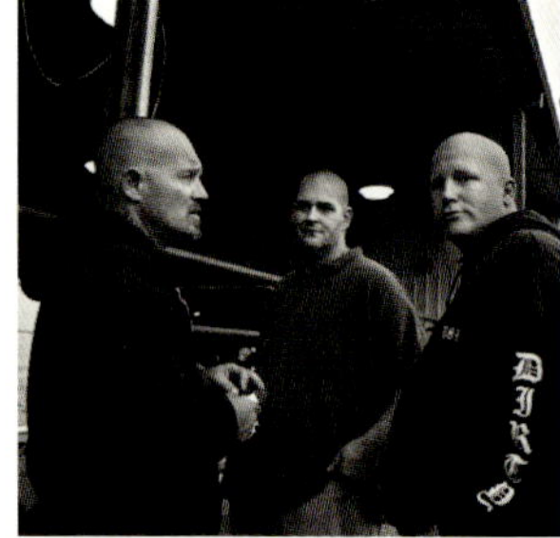

Untitled page 175
Sorrento, Louisiana
October 2001

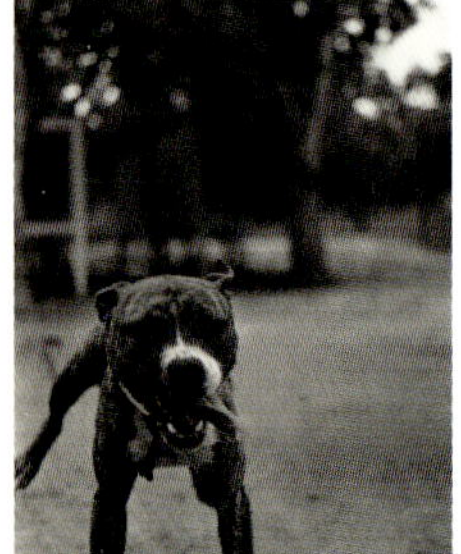

Johnny Holmes #1 page 176
East Texas
June 2001

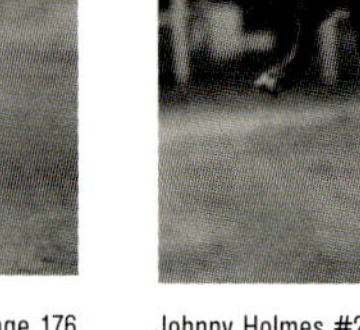

Johnny Holmes #2 page 177
East Texas
June 2001

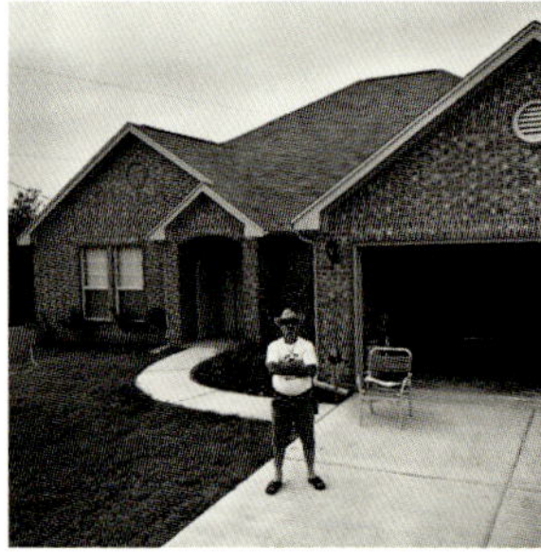

Mr. Jerry Gilbert Wylie page 178
(at his New Place)
East Texas
October 2001

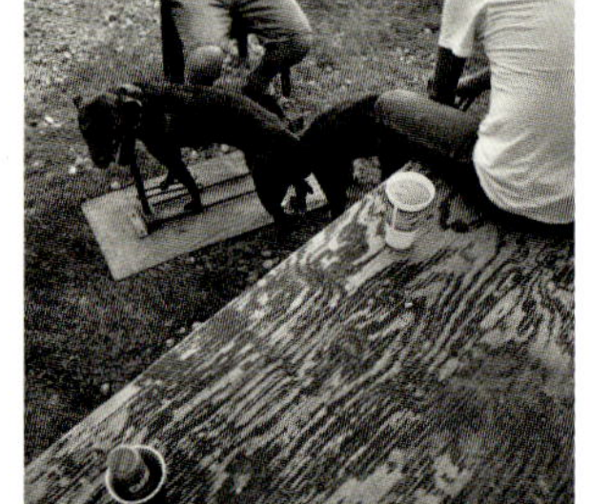

Untitled (Breeding) page 179
East Texas
October 2001

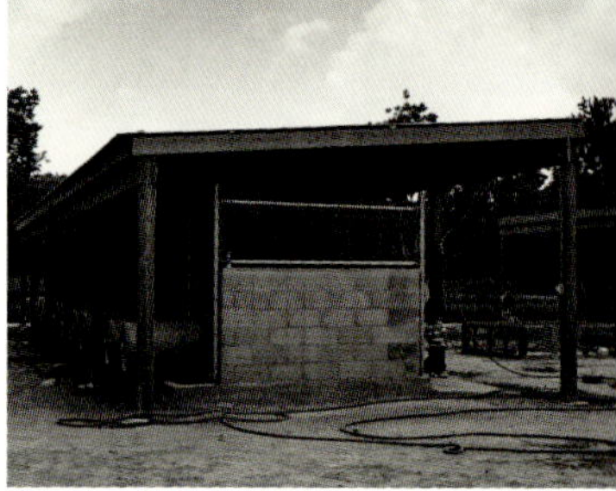

Kennel Facilities (A) page
East Texas
June 2001

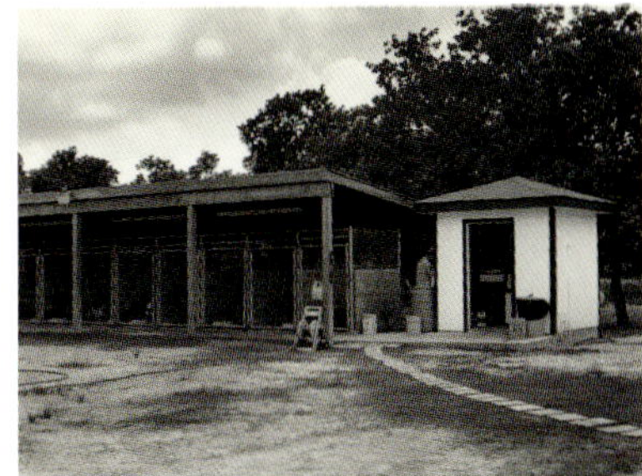

Kennel Facilities (B) page 181
East Texas
June 2001

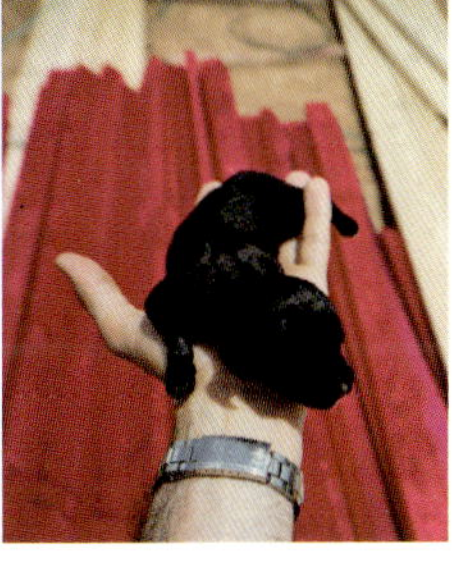

Black Puppy page 182
East Texas
June 2001

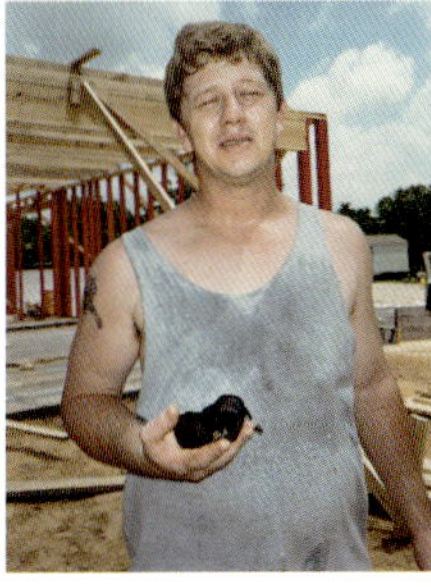
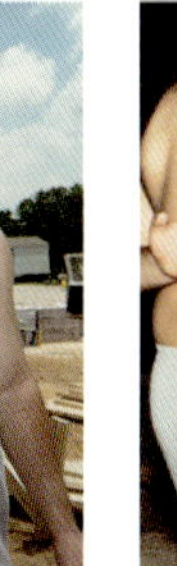

Damian, with Black Pup page 183
East Texas
June 2001

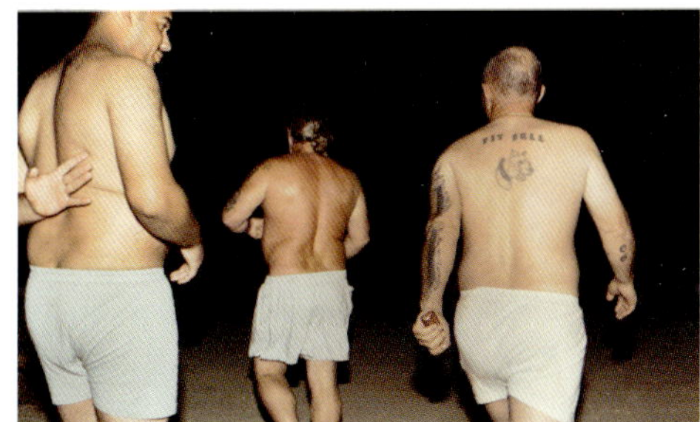
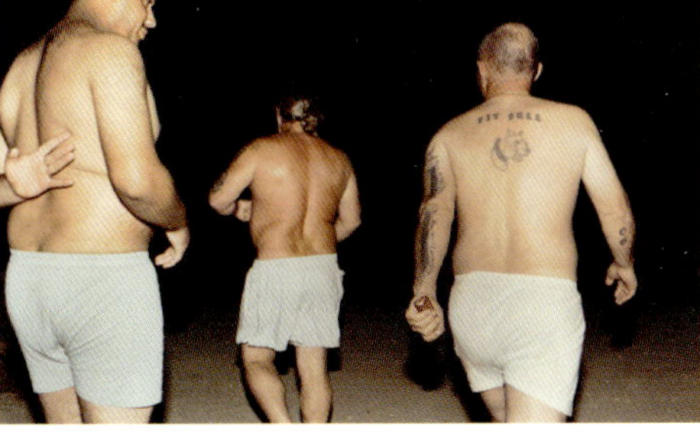

Pit Bull pages 184/185
East Texas
May 2003

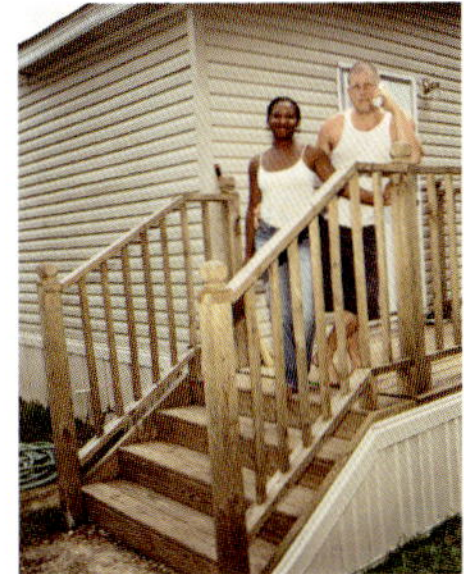

Darren and Tamika page 187
Louisiana
May 2003

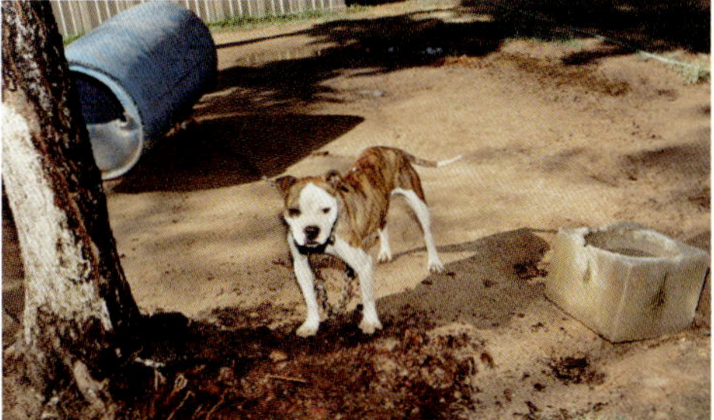

Rudy Junior pages 188/189
Louisiana
May 2003

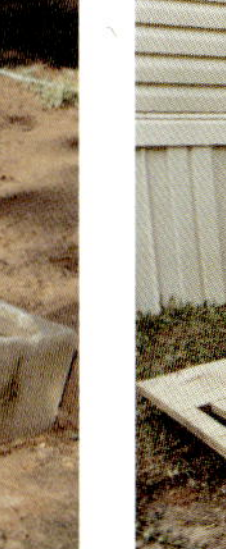
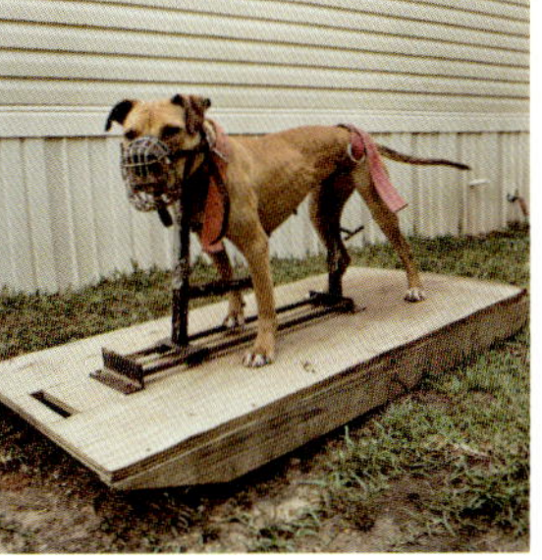

Miss Tom page 190
Louisiana
May 2003

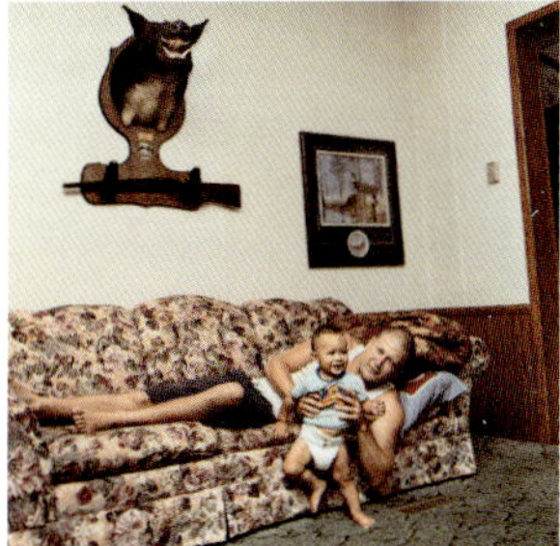

Darren and Little Darren page 191
Louisiana
May 2003

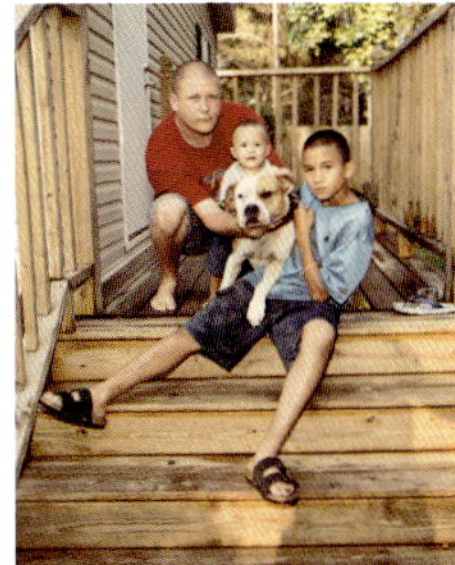

Darren, Little Darren, page 192
Darius, and Coachise
Louisiana
May 2003

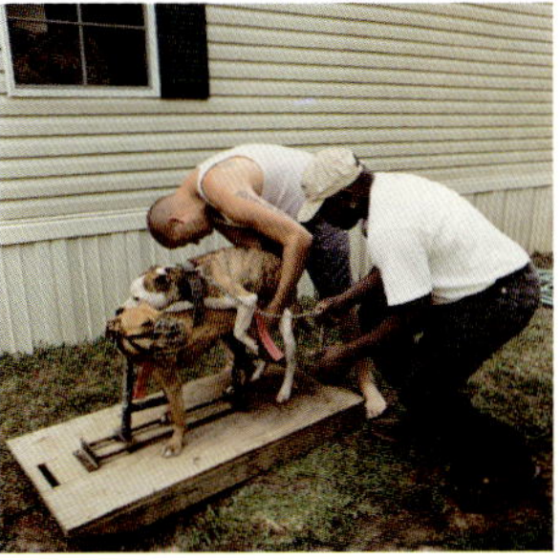

Darren and Bo Leggs, Breeding page 193
Rudy Junior to Miss Tom
Louisiana
May 2003

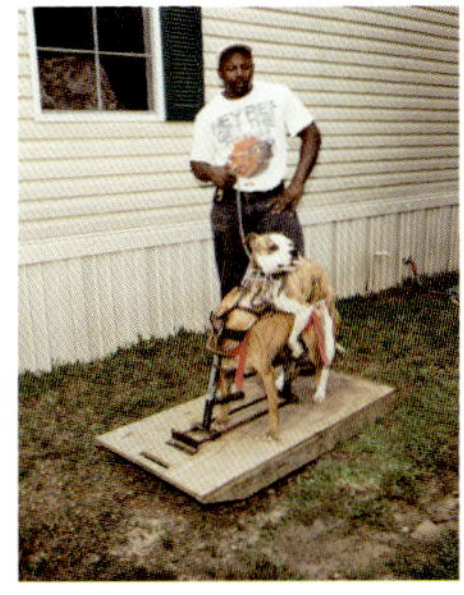
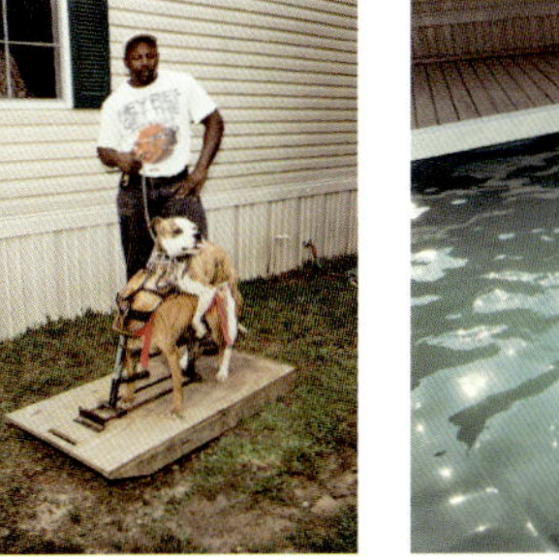

Bo Leggs, Rudy Junior, page 194
and Miss Tom
Louisiana
May 2003

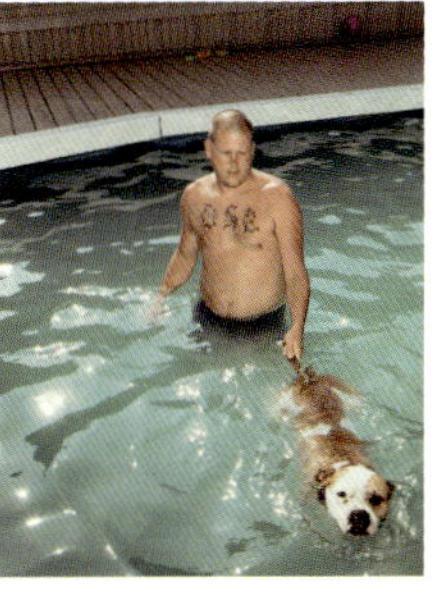

Darren and Coachise page 195
Louisiana
May 2003

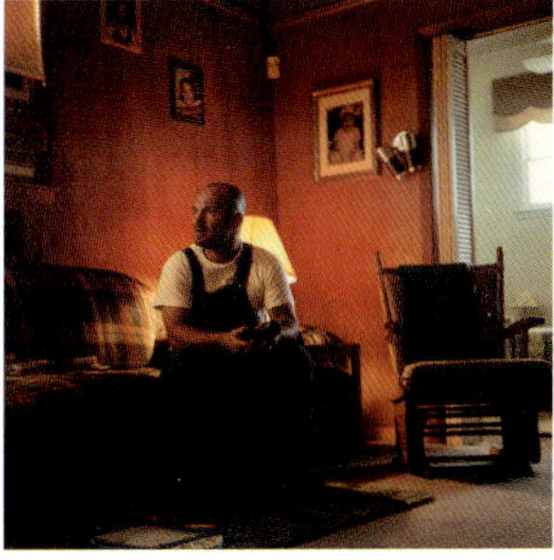

Jerry, at the Old Place page 196
Galveston, Texas
June 2001

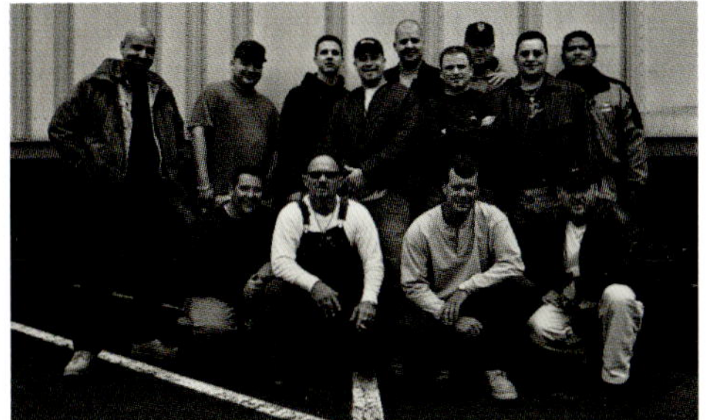

Untitled (Group Portrait) pages 198/199
Delaware
April 2001

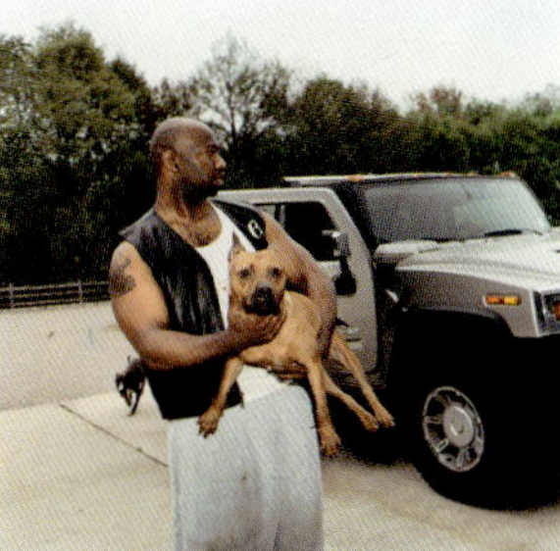
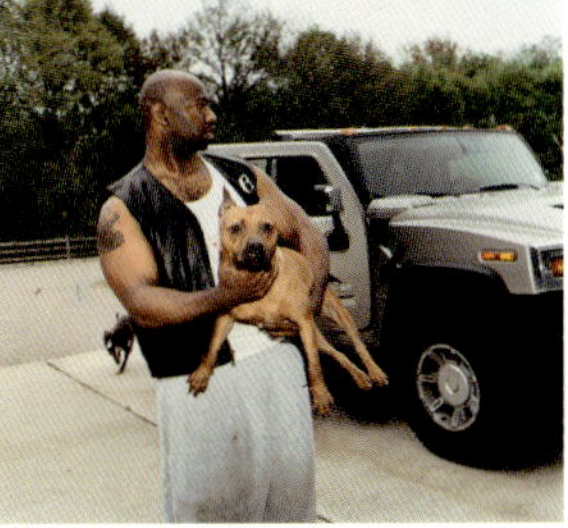

Joaquin Dean page 201
Rockland County, New York
May 2003

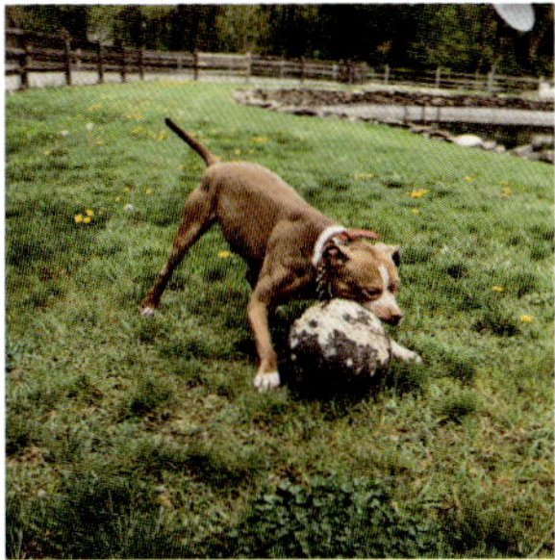

A Ruff Ryder Dog page 202
Rockland County, New York
May 2003

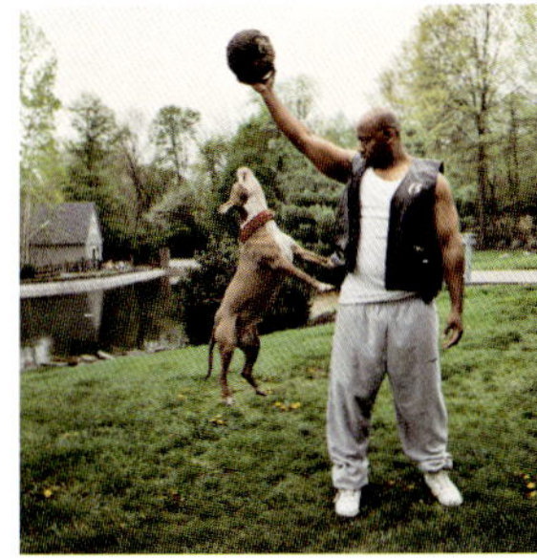
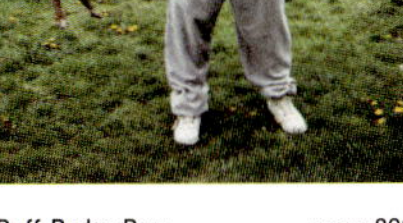

Joaquin, and Ruff Ryder Dog page 203
Rockland County, New York
May 2003

A Ruff Ryder Dog, On Top page 204
Rockland County, New York
May 2003

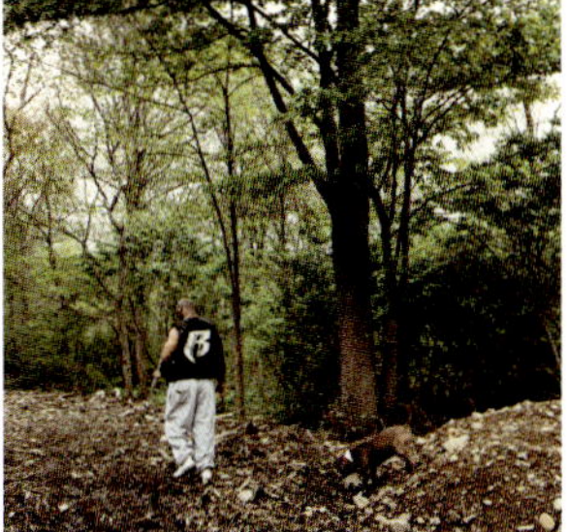
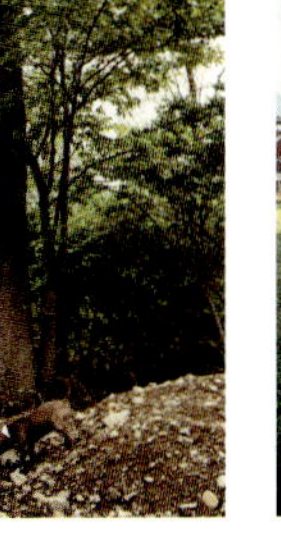

Joaquin, in His Woods page 205
Rockland County, New York
May 2003

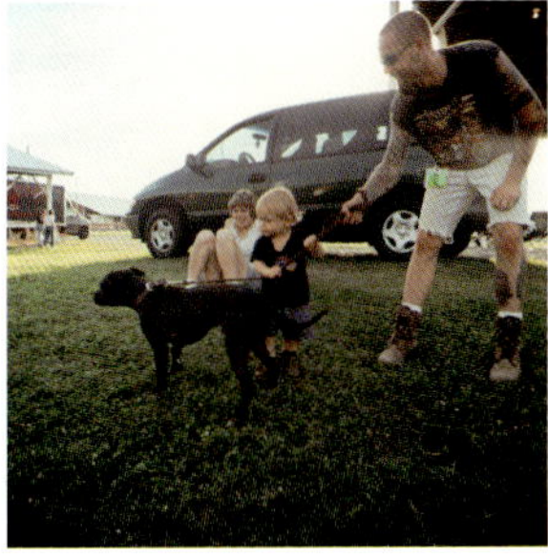

The Jones page 207
(Jackie, Hunter, Bo, and Onyx)
Salem County, New Jersey
July 2001

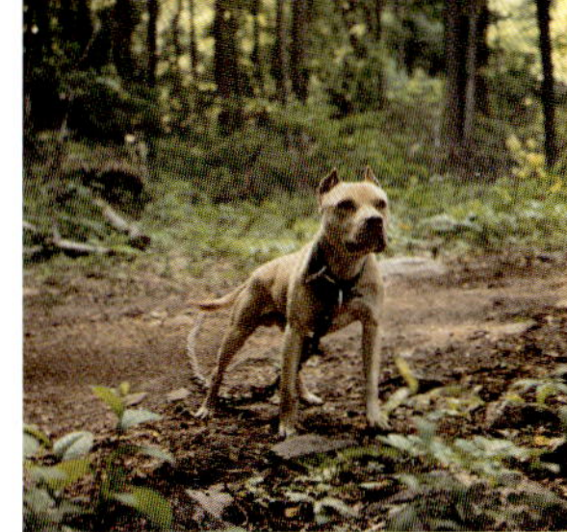

Ch. Sabotage AKA Ch. Ruger page 208
(Bo's Dog)
Berks County, Pennsylvania
May 2001

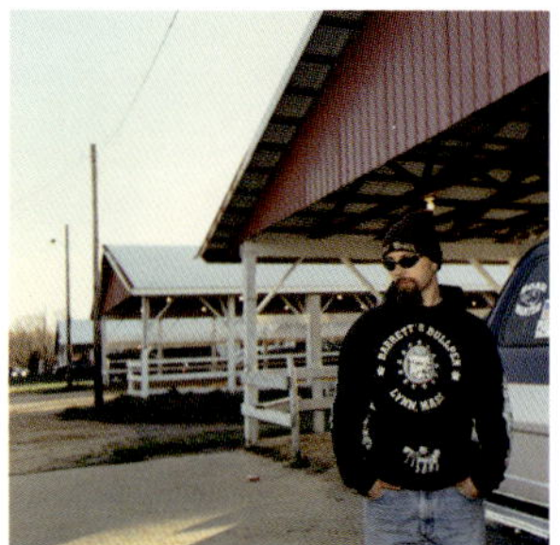

Bo Jones page 209
Salem County, New Jersey
April 2003

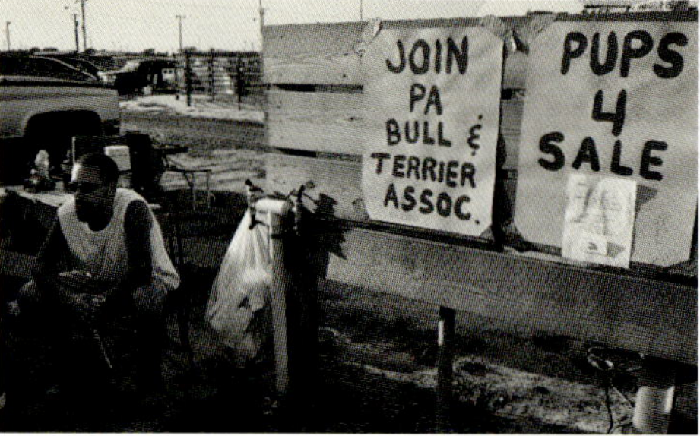

Bo (Pups 4 Sale) pages 210/211
Harrington, Delaware
November 2002

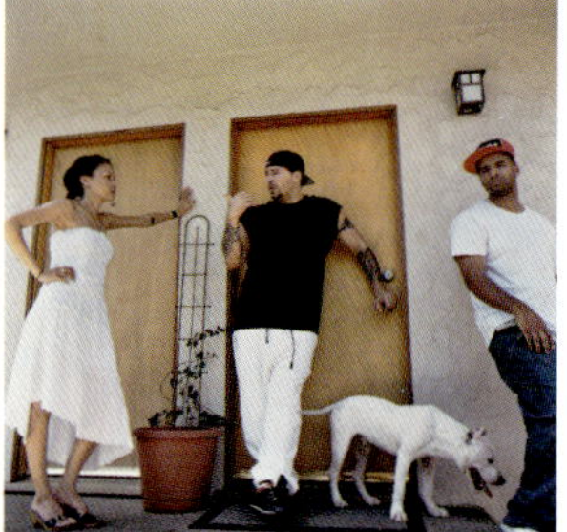

Stephanie, Muggs, page 213
D-Trick, and Caine
Burbank, California
May 2003

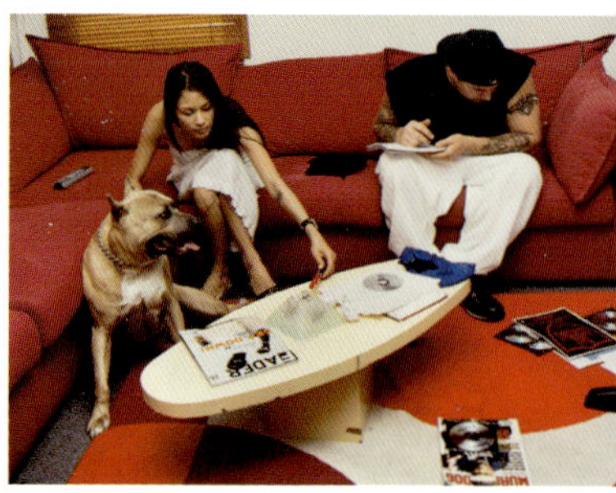
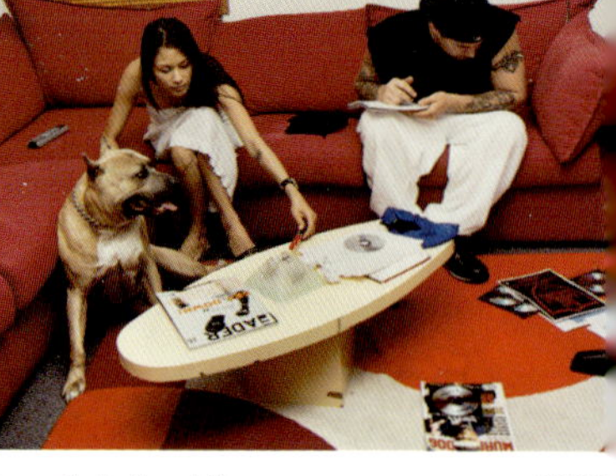

Muggs, Stephanie, and Blue pages 214/215
Burbank, California
May 2003

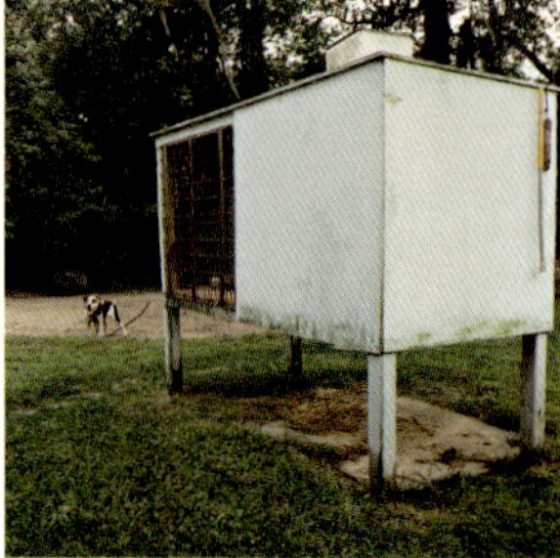

Lachlan / Puppy Pen page 216
East Texas
May 2003

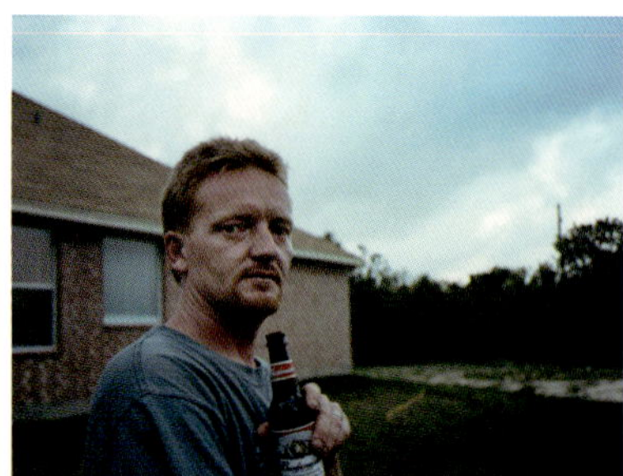

Redd page 217
East Texas
April 2002

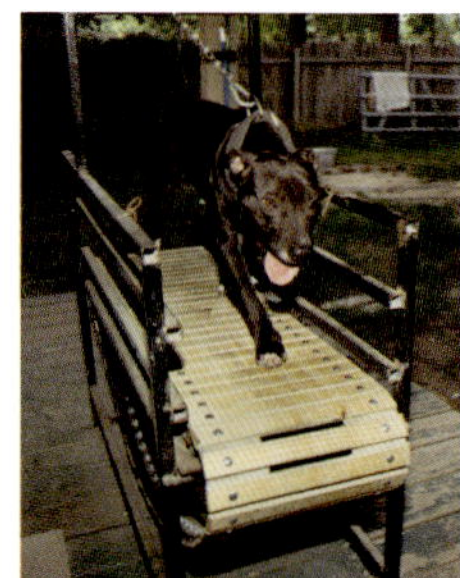

Treadmill page 218
East Texas
May 2003

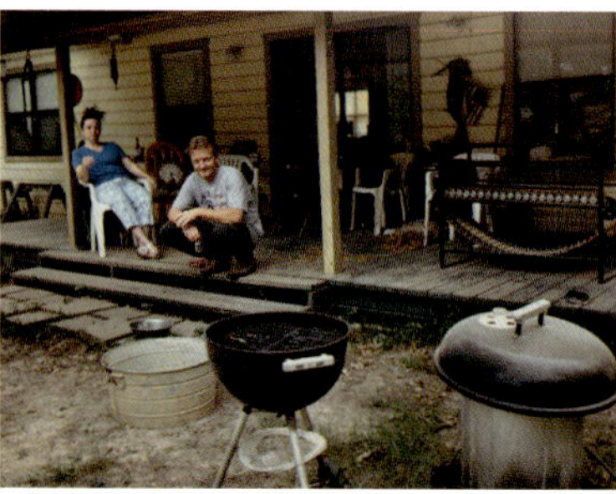

Liz and Redd page 219
East Texas
May 2003

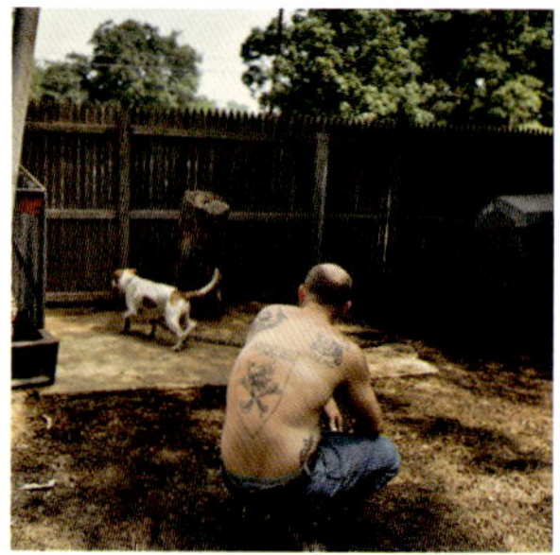

Flood's Yard page 220
Long Island, New York
August 2001

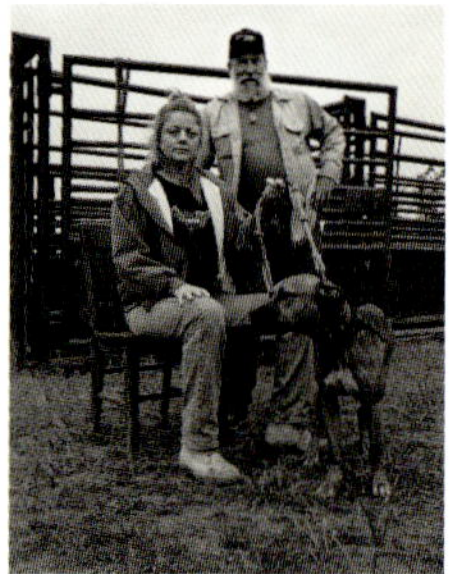

Lucretia, Joe, and Gunnar page 223
Sorrento, Louisiana
October 2001

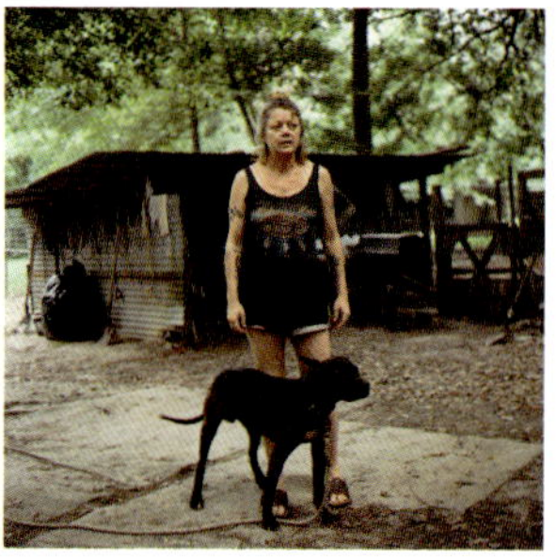

Lucretia and Coal Dust page 224
In The Piney Woods of East Texas
May 2003

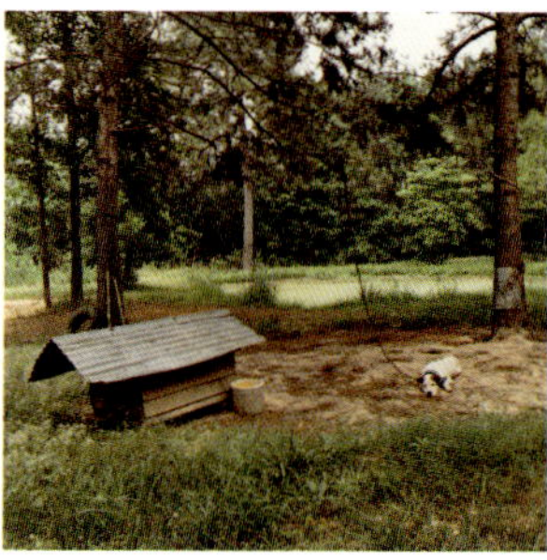

One of Joe and Lu's Dogs page 225
In The Piney Woods of East Texas
May 2003

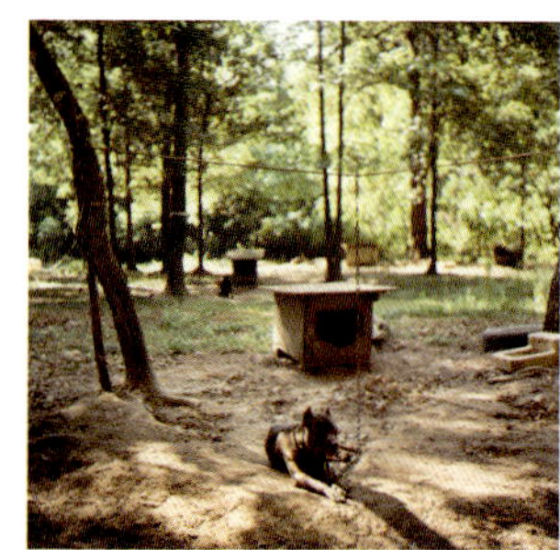

Cajun page 226
In The Piney Woods of East Texas
May 2003

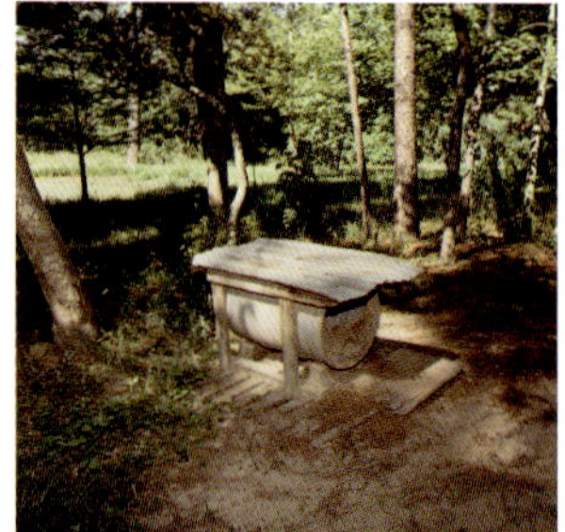

Dog House page 227
In The Piney Woods of East Texas
May 2003

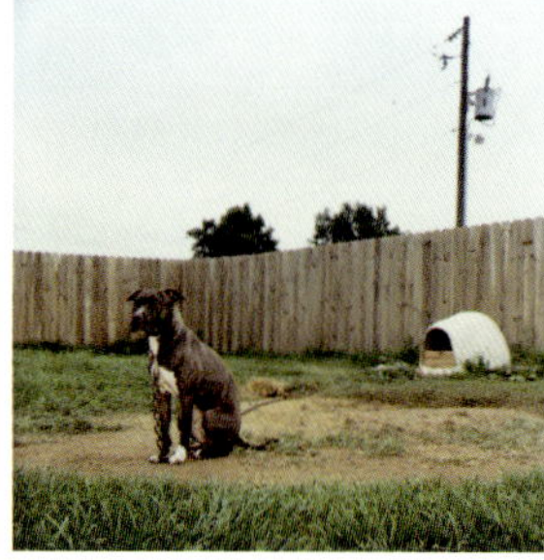

Skillet page 229
Fredericksburg, Virginia
June 2003

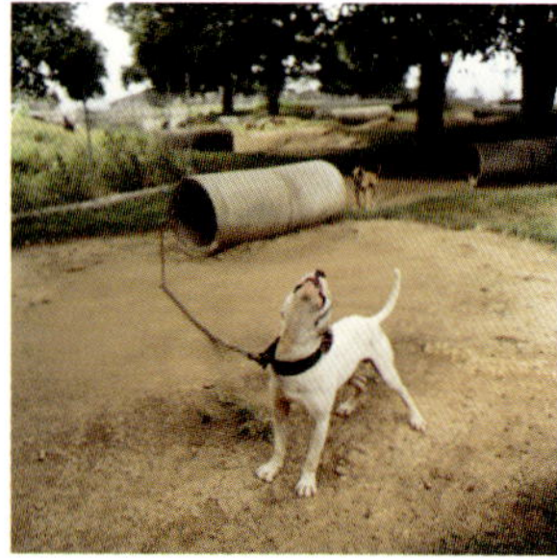

Untitled (White Dog- A) page 230
Ayala Alaisang, Philipines
December 2002

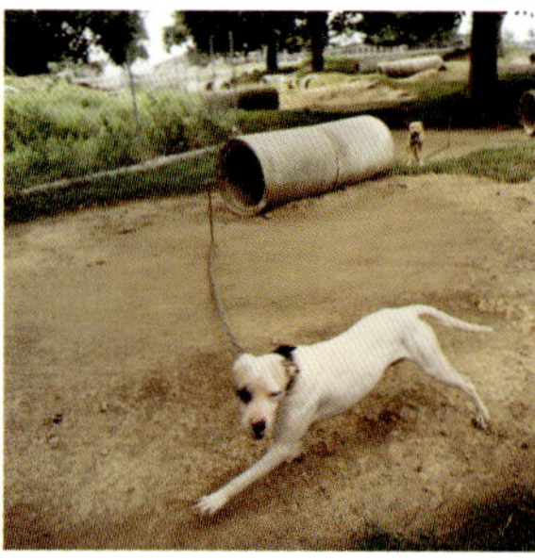
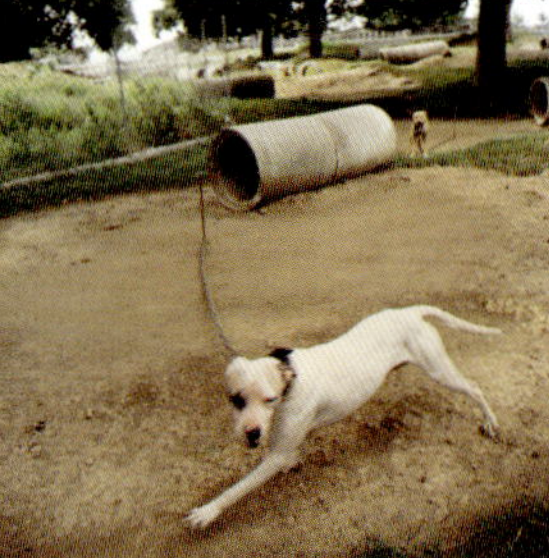

Untitled (White Dog- B) page 231
Ayala Alaisang, Philipines
December 2002

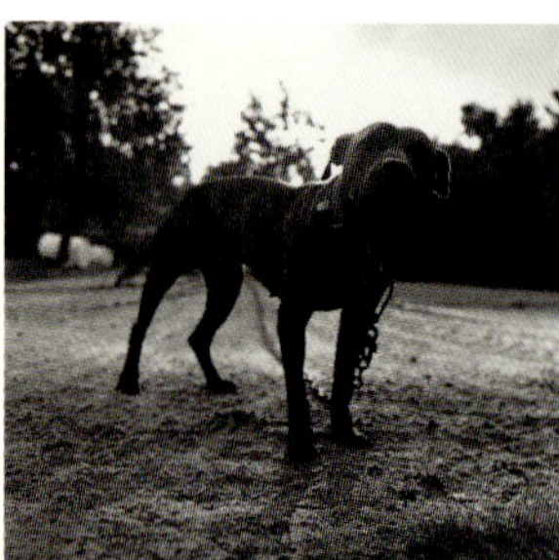

Latino Boy page 232
East Texas
October 2001

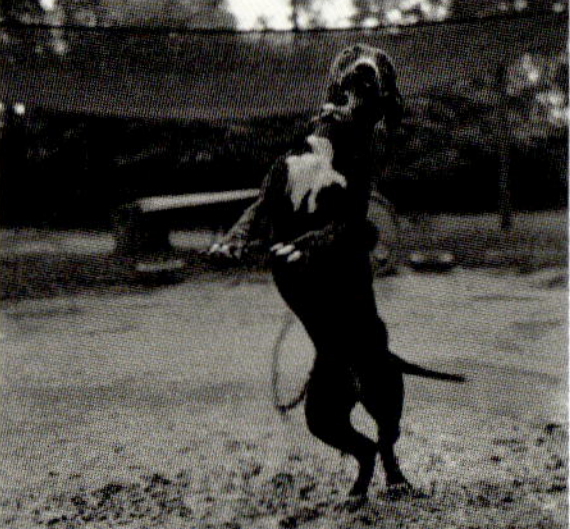

Bridget page 233
East Texas
October 2001

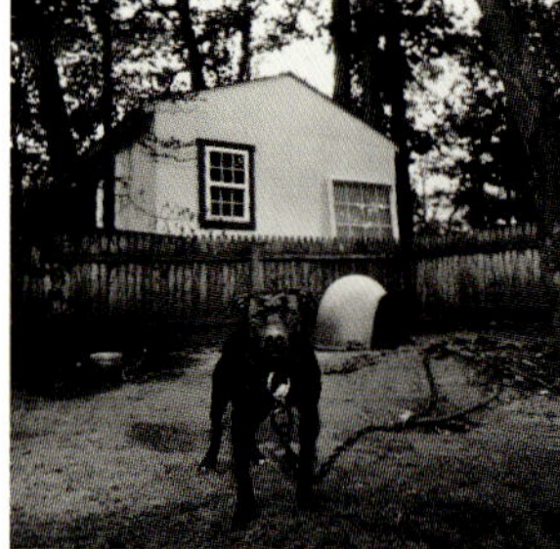
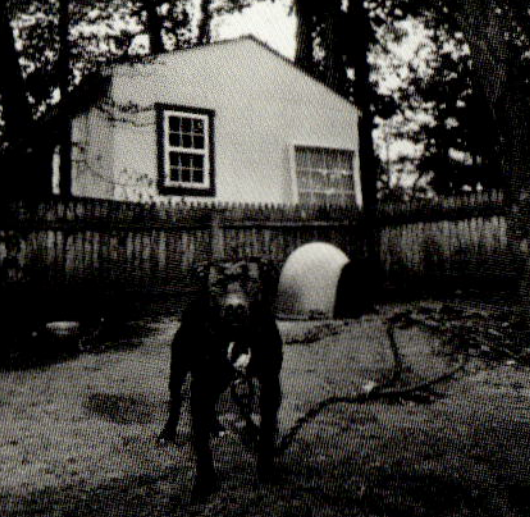

Black Dog (at Rich's) page 234
South New Jersey
July 2001

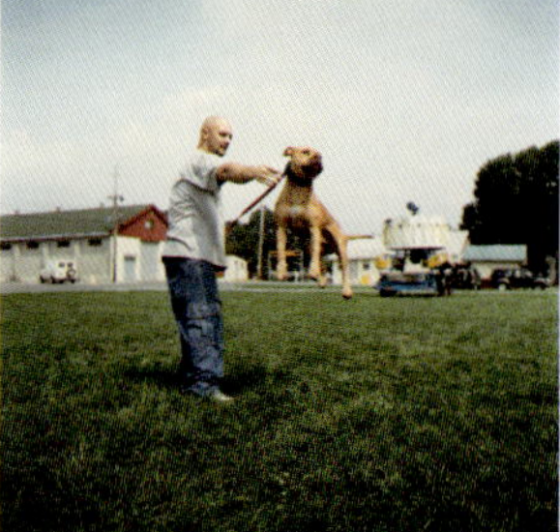

Stefan Kichta and Bullet page 246
Berks County, Pennsylvania
September 2000

FOR MORE INFORMATION ON THE AMERICAN PIT BULL TERRIER:

www.adba.cc

www.colbypitbull.com

www.workingpitbull.com

FOR INFORMATION ON PIT BULL RESCUE ORGANIZATIONS:

(see "links" pages for information in your area)

www.outofthepits.org

www.pbrc.net

www.badrap.org

www.animalfarmfoundation.org

www.thelastresortrescue.tripod.com

www.vrcpitbull.com

www.forpitssake.org

www.spindletoppitbullrefuge.org

SUPPORT RESPONSIBLE OWNERSHIP–FIGHT BREED SPECIFIC LEGISLATION:

Endangered Breeds Association (USA)
PO Box 1148
Albany, LA 70711
www.angelfire.com/la/breeds

American Dog Owners Association (USA)
www.adoa.org

Endangered Dogs Defense and Rescue Ltd. (UK)
www.endangereddogs.com

Domino Dogs (UK)
www.dominodogs.org

Dogwatch
www.dogwatch.net

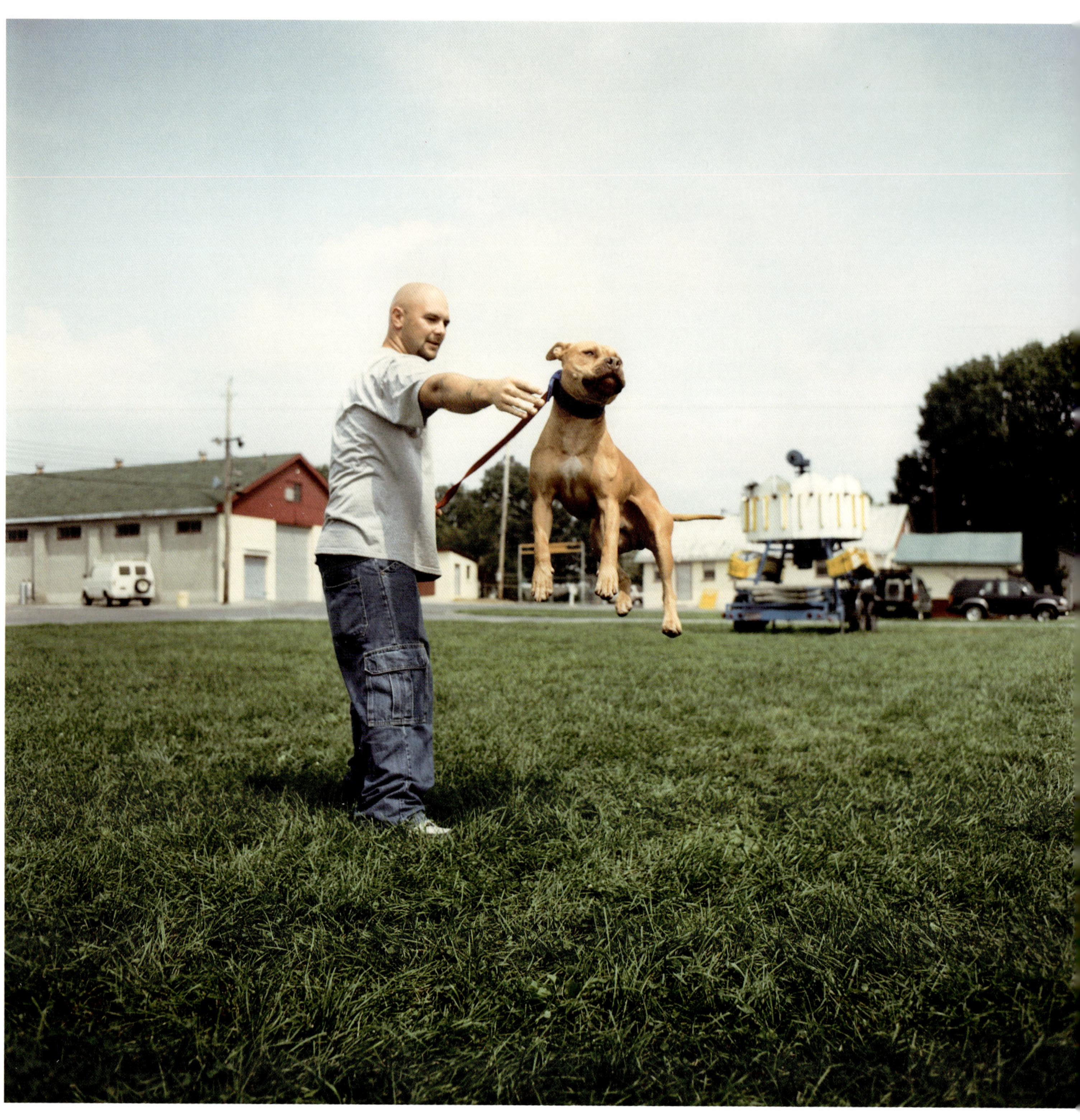

ACKNOWLEDGEMENTS

Thank you Gerhard Steidl, my Publisher.
James Frey, thank you for Writing.
Carol LeFlufy, thank you for seeing it.
Cory Reynolds and Jeremy Sigler, thank you.
Nick Tosches, thank you.
Joel Sternfeld, thank you.
Bobby and Lauren Turner, thank you.
Vivian Goldstein, thank you.

For your tireless enthusiasm and brotherhood, thank you Joshua McHugh.

Thank you Amy Guip and Rick Patrick, Frances Pennington and Curt Smith, Phillip Odom, Jacqueline Schnabel, Jeffrey Kane and Kim Martin, Dr. Michael J. Paley, Paul Coppe, George Skelcher, Dan Rosner, Carla Serrano and Phillip Toledano, Kevin Bray, James Brett, John Falls, Michelle Chant, Gina Harrell, Isabel Snyder, Sophie Toulouse, Laurent Suchel and Dovie Mamikunian, Azzedine Alaïa, Diane and John Hollier, William Frawley, the Bialas Family, Mark Shapiro, Patrick Hoelck, Hillary Easton, Ouattara Watts (Bakari), Joanna Yas from *Open City*, Holly and Isa, Michael Gibson and Carolyn Carr, Anne and Conrad Sanderson, Randy and Christine Hoffman, Gary Hustwit, Edy Ferguson, David Kreiger, Maggie Sumner, Lisa and Andy Fiewel, Sandra Zane, Karyn Hansen, Jimo Toyin Salako from *Next Level*, Caroline Metcalfe from *Conde Nast Traveler*, and Kassie Evashevski at *Brillstein-Grey*.

Thank you to all at Steidl, Göttingen: Bernard Fischer, Claas Möller, Jonas Wettre, Julia Braun, Katja Töpfer, Judith Lange, Ines Schumann, Reiner Motz, Stefan Hartmann, Detlef Otten, Jan Strümpel and Claudia Glenewinkel.

Thank you very much, D.A.P: Sharon Helgason Gallagher and Skùta Helgason, Avery Lozada, Yvonne Puffer, Jane Brown, Todd Bradway, Donna Wingate, Alexander Galan, Sabrina Mansouri, Lori Waxman, Tamae Ouchi, and Elisa Leshowitz. Very special thanks to Kenny Cummings.

Thank you Julie Pochron and everyone at Pochron Studios: Marietta Davis, Don Felix Cervantes, Nicole Lloyd, Lety Vesasquez, Meredith Arena, Jack Pulliam, Emmett, and Goose; Jacob Dresdner, George Hertz, Boris Miller, and Irving Landau at Adorama; Shazi Hussain, Timina Faraz, and Sunny Kumar at Print Zone; Keith Samnath at Midtown Color; Kevin Amer.

Thank you Jinda Phommavongsa, Stewart Isbell, Frederick Skogkvist, Franck Mura, Rich Micelli, Ben Mistak, Ilya Popenko, Greg Colebourne, Andreea Radulescu, and Sharon Margeotes—for having my back, with *American Pitbull* and other work.

Thank you Mitch Epstein, Paul Graham, and Michael Mack, for camaraderie and fine guidance in the home stretch.

Thank you Mr. Jerry Gilbert Wylie, Mr. Darren Williams and Tamika Williams, John John, Polly, Cindy, PoPo, Johnny (Amigo), Daryll, Trash, Mr. and Mrs. Joe and Lucretia Ashcraft, Mr. Bo Jones and Mrs. Jacqueline Wakefield-Jones, Mr. Lee Barrett, Herbie and the entire Mass. Club, Joe, Jesse and Joe's Dad, Mr. Louis B. Colby, Mr. Scott Colby, Holly Strychalski, Mr. Floyd Boudreaux, Mr. Guy Boudreaux, Big Boi from Outkast, James from Konkrete, Pitfall Kennels, Janice Faison at Outkast Inc., Soul Assasins Estevan Oriol, Mr. Cartoon and DJ Muggs, Stephanie, D-Trick, Mr. Daryll "Dogman" Young, Mr. Joaquin Dean at Ruff Ryder Records, As Four, Mr. Edwin Oquendo, Liz and Redd Cowan, Mr. Mike Flood, Mr. Rich Issel Sr., Mr. Rich Issel Jr. and the AC and Del-Val Clubs, Noel and Manny over in Cavite, Mr. and Mrs. Cuyler and Paula Thomas, Mr. Frank Rocca, Mrs. Jo Ann Le Blanc, Mr. Frank Perez and the Tri-State Club, Mr. T.L. Williams, Mr. Bobby "Bullyson" Hall, Mr. "Irish Jerry" Holcomb, Mr. Bobby Corn, Mr. Lonnie Boruff, the Howell Familiy, Rob from Pitstar (up in the Bronx), Mr. Nino Bussa, Mr. Peter Carnivale and Spider G, Tony and Stacey from Avenue C, Rene, Kate, Amy, Hank, the entire Greenwood Family, and the ADBA. My heartfelt gratitude goes to all of these people, their families, and the many others who allowed me to photograph them and their beloved Bulldogs.

Thank you, my beautiful family—Dad, Mom and Howard, Steve, Alice and Tom, Tommy, Jackson, and Michael—with love.

AUTHOR'S NOTES

The title of this book is *American Pitbull*. The name of the breed is the American Pit Bull Terrier. This difference is intentional; the title is intended to represent the dogs and their people.
Every effort was made to record the names of the people and/or dogs photographed. If your picture is here, and your name or your dog's name is missing or is incorrect, please forgive the error.

Marc Joseph / American Pitbull

Second Edition 2005

Essay: James Frey
Interviews: Cory Reynolds

Editor (Pictures): Carol LeFlufy
Editor (Writing): Lori Waxman

Book Design: Gerhard Steidl, Marc Joseph, and Claas Möller
Production: Bernard Fischer, Julia Braun
Maquette: Jonas Wettre
Scans: Steidl's Digital Darkroom, Göttingen
Printing and Production: Steidl, Göttingen

Color printing: Julie Pochron / Pochron Studio, Brooklyn, New York
Black and White Printing: Kevin Amer Darkroom, New York

Color processing: Shazi Hussein / Print Zone, New York
Black and White processing: Jeffrey Kane / Lexington B+W, New York

Frontispiece: "Rudy" (1991-2000) Painting by Nina Roberts

Thank You to the Hasselblad, Rollei, and Contax Cameras,
the Apple Computers, and the Epson Scanners and Printers.

Steidl Publishers
Düstere Strasse 4
D-37073 Göttingen
Phone: +49.551.49.60.60
Telefax: +49.551.49.60.649
E-mail: mail@steidl.de

Orders can be placed directly at our publishing house or via the internet
www.steidl.de

Distributed in North America by D.A.P./Distributed Art Publishers, Inc.
www.artbook.com

Distributed throughout Europe, Asia, and Africa by Thames and Hudson
www.thamesandhudson.com

ISBN 3-86521-094-5

Printed and bound in Germany

www.pitbullbook.com